Prayers, Mantras and Gayatris

A Collection for Insights, Protection, Spiritual Growth, and Many Other Blessings

By Stephen Knapp

Dedicated to
all who wish to raise their consciousness
by invoking the higher energies,
chanting the sacred vibrations,
and meditating on the spiritual insights
that are indicated and described
in the Vedic Sanskrit prayers and mantras.

Copyright © 2011, by Stephen Knapp

Cover Print: Arjuna on the chariot just before the battle of Kurukshetra offering prayers to Lord Krishna who is revealing His unlimited universal form. This was while Arjuna was being advised by Lord Krishna with the instructions that became the *Bhagavad-gita*.

ISBN 13: 978-1456545901
ISBN 10: 1456545906

Other books by the author:

You can find out more about
Stephen Knapp
and his books, free ebooks, research,
and numerous articles and photos,
along with many other spiritual resources at:
http://www.Stephen-Knapp.com

CONTENTS

Sri Nandanandana), *The Krishna Arati*, and the *Krishna Chalisa*. Also has two other prayers on the sacredness of the Lord's holy names, the *Sri-Harer Namastakam* and the *Man Radhe Krishna*.

Angry, My Dear Lord Nitai! Please be Merciful to Me, and The Lotus
Feet of Lord Nityananda, Prayers to Nitai.

INTRODUCTION

The main purpose of this book is to provide the essential instructions on chanting mantras, which is covered in Chapters One, Two and Three, and to supply an assortment of prayers, mantras, gayatris, and what are called *stotras* that would serve all the needs that a person may have in their basic request to progress in life, both materially and spiritually, the latter being the ultimate and final goal.

This is what I would call an "efficient" collection because, although there are thousands of Sanskrit mantras and *stotras* or prayers for particular purposes, and a second volume could easily be assembled with little effort, you will be able to find in this collection much of what you need for almost any purpose that you will have.

Most of the mantras in this volume can also be found and downloaded from my website, but to print them all from the website would require a fair amount of paper. And there have been numerous requests for the full book. The problem was that there was no book until now to allow you to succinctly have in hand most of those mantras and *stotras*.

One point of consideration is that this book and the mantras within it are especially written in a way for those who do not know Sanskrit. Thus, the English transliterations are written primarily as they would be pronounced when reading basic English. This, hopefully, will provide the reader with the best ways to accurately pronounce the mantras. However, there also have been an increase in websites that offer recordings of mantras and *stotras* so a person can hear how to accurately pronounce them. So things have progressed in this manner quite a bit. Plus, other books are available to provide further instructions on how to chant Sanskrit mantras, which may also be helpful.

The mantras within this volume offer such things as the knowledge and insights for spiritual progress, including higher perceptions and understandings of the Absolute or God, and the means for blessings of all kinds, both material and spiritual. They also offer the sound vibrations for uplifting our consciousness, aim of life, attitude, and outlook. They can provide the means for requesting protection on our spiritual path, or from enemies, ghosts, demons, or for receiving the means of overcoming obstacles, health problems, or acquiring wealth and other benefits. Some of them are important for daily practice, while others are especially effective for use on important holidays or festival celebrations. There is something here for every need.

CHAPTER ONE

Mantra-Yoga:
A Necessity for this Age

Using mantras or prayers is a means of doing a number of things, depending on our purpose. First of all, it is a method to raise our consciousness and prepare ourselves for perceiving higher states of being. It can also help us enter into the spiritual dimension, or to invoke the blessings of the Divine. It is also a means to call on the positive energies to help us overcome obstacles, enemies, or to assist in healing our minds and bodies from disease or negativity. And this book has an assortment of mantras or prayers to do any of these.

There are two basic kinds of mantras, those for spiritual and inner progress, and those for outer or more material needs. You can find both kinds within this book. Concentrating on a mantra is also called mantra-yoga, especially when it is for our spiritual upliftment, or to unite us with the Supreme. Mantra-yoga, or the art of focusing on the sound vibrations in mantras or prayers, is actually a mystical tradition found in almost every spiritual path in the world. It may involve the softly spoken repetition of a prayer or mantra for one's own meditation, or it may be the congregational singing of spiritually uplifting songs, prayers, or sacred names of the Supreme Being. It all involves the same process, but in the Eastern tradition it is called mantra-yoga because it is the easy process of focusing our minds on the Supreme through His names, which helps spiritualize our consciousness. *Man* means the mind, *tra* means deliverance. Therefore, a spiritual mantra is the pure sound vibration for delivering the mind from material to spiritual consciousness. This is the goal of any spiritual path. Although all spiritual traditions have their own prayers or mantras, the Vedic Sanskrit mantras are especially powerful and effective in uniting us with the spiritual realm. However, a complete yoga process is generally a blend of a few yoga systems, such as ashtanga-yoga with bhakti-yoga, and bhakti-yoga with mantra-yoga. Therefore, some yoga systems also include mantra-yoga, or the process of concentrating on the sound vibration within a mantra. This is especially important in this age of Kali-yuga.

Many years ago the brahmana priests could accomplish many kinds of wondrous deeds simply by correctly chanting particular mantras. Many of these mantras still exist, but it is very difficult to find those who can chant them accurately. This is actually a safety measure because if the wish-fulfilling mantras were easily chanted, there would no doubt be many people who would misuse them. But other mantras that are available can easily help purify one's consciousness, give spiritual enlightenment, and put one in touch with the Supreme.

In *Bhagavad-gita* (10.25) Sri Krishna explains that He is the transcendental *om* mantra and that the chanting of *japa* (chanting a mantra quietly for one's own meditation) is the purest of His representations and sacrifices. It is understood that by chanting *japa* and hearing the holy sounds of the mantra, one can come to the platform of spiritual realization. This is the process of mantra-yoga. However, even though the mantra is powerful in itself, when the mantra is chanted by a great devotee, it becomes more powerful. This is also the effect when a disciple is fortunate enough to take initiation or *diksha* from a spiritually potent master who gives him a mantra for spiritual purposes. Then the disciple can make rapid progress by utilizing the mantra.

Sanskrit mantras often consist of eternal sound energies that have always existed, both within the universe as well as beyond it, and before its manifestation and after its annihilation. Such special mantras are part of the eternal sound vibration called *shabda-brahma*.

When it comes to mantras, the *Vedas* mention three types: *vedic*, *tantric* and *puranic*. These can be further divided into *sattvic*, *rajasic* and *tamasic*. The mantras that are *sattvic* or in the mode of goodness are chanted for light, wisdom, compassion, divine love, or God realization. They help bring peace, destroy karma, and bring one to perfection after death. The mantras that are *rajasic* or in the mode of passion are chanted for material benedictions, like blessings for a healthy child, prosperity, successful business, and so on. However, such mantras do not help one rise above karma, but force one to take rebirth in order to acquire the results of their karma. The mantras that are *tamasic* or in the mode of ignorance or darkness are also called "black magic." These are used for the deliberate manipulation of the material energy for one's own purpose. Thus, they are what could be called sinful, and are often used to call spirits or to assist one to perform deeds that may bring harm to others for one's own benefit.

Some mantras hold certain powers in their vibratory formulas that are directly related to particular Deities, divine personalities, or forms of God. In fact, they may represent the Deity in full. When they do, they are considered non-different from the Deity and the sound vibrations are spiritual in nature. By the repetition of the mantra, the person who chants it invokes the energy and mercy of that Deity. Thus, the Deity reveals Himself or Herself to the *sadhaka*, who then overcomes illusion and realizes the spiritual position of the Deity and his or her relationship with the Deity. The six kinds of mantras used in this connection are:

1. Dhyana Mantras–mantras for meditation to mentally invoke the Deity's form, abode or pastimes.
2. Bija Mantras–the seed mantras or seed words that are used for meditation and purification of the articles used in worship. Mantras often begin with these. They include such *bijas* or seed mantras as *Aim* and *Shrim*, which are often connected to the feminine or Devi. Or *Klim* which helps arouse the force of attraction to the object addressed in the mantra. Or *Krim* which is often connected to Kali or Devi, or *Gum* which is in association with Ganesh. The *bija* or seed mantras are derived from the 50 prime sounds which invoke various levels of energy and also the nature of the elements, such as water, air, earth, fire, etc., and are related to *om*.
3. Mula Mantras–root mantras are the essence of the Deity, used when offering certain articles during the worship to address the Lord or Deity.
4. Stutis and Stotras–mantras or prayers chanted before, during and after the worship to glorify the Lord's name, form, qualities, and pastimes.
5. Pranama Mantras–prayers offering obeisances to great personalities or to the Lord, often used at the end of worship.
6. Gayatri Mantras–Vedic or Pancharatrika mantras used to worship or invoke the blessings of the Lord, or to focus the mind on God, and for invoking different moods, energies, or powers.

The Vedic mantras, such as those coming from the four *samhitas* of the *Rig*, *Sama*, *Yajur*, and *Atharva Vedas*, are eternal or spiritual sound vibrations. They are not composed by any man at some particular point in history. They are part of the *shabda-brahma*, the eternal sound vibration. These mantras are like seeds of vast amounts of power and knowledge that are held within them. Thus, many scriptures explain that such powers cannot be fully revealed to someone unless such mantras have been received through the process of *diksha* or initiation from a spiritual master.

Besides this, the results of chanting a mantra depend on the chanter's conception or intent in the mind while chanting it. Thus, one must know the meaning or purpose of the mantra while reciting it. If one thinks the mantra is for attaining material goals, the person may get that. But if the inner purpose of the mantra is known to deliver one to the spiritual world, and a person chants it sincerely for that purpose, then that will be the reward rather than something minor or material, as long as the person does not prematurely give up chanting it.

Most Sanskrit mantras have several principles that you find in them. First, they are often handed down or revealed by sages or authorities who have attained self-realization by its use. They also generally use a particular meter or rhythm while chanting it. Plus, the mantra often represents a certain Deity. It also has a *bija* or seed word that gives it additional power, and the sound formula it contains has a special *shakti* or energy. And finally, constant repetition of the mantra will open or activate the key of it which then can reveal pure consciousness in the one who has been initiated into its use. The practice of repeating or chanting it for one's personal use is called *japa*. The *japa* or chanting it a required number of times is often what triggers its power within the consciousness of the chanter in which it reaches its *siddha*, or perfection and goal.

The mantra is thus a point of meditation for the mind, but also a formula or transcendental sound vibration, like the holy name of God, that releases its energy into one's consciousness. Thus it prepares one for perceiving higher states of reality. With constant practice of the appropriate mantra, and with the proper pronunciation and devotional mood, the mantra can reveal the Absolute Truth to the practitioner as well as one's own spiritual form and relationship that you may have with the Supreme Being.

This is why it is best that one should receive and be initiated into the chanting of the mantra by a qualified guru. Then the mantra will be especially effective and powerful, and carry special means of invoking realizations into the devotee who uses it.

Mantras can be divided into two additional categories, namely *saguna* and *nirguna*. *Saguna* mantras (those that describe personal traits) often are like prayers that invoke certain Deities or characteristics of the Absolute. *Nirguna* mantras (those that refer to the nature of the Absolute without qualities) describe the person's identification with the Absolute.

Mantras can be used in different ways. They can be chanted in whispers, or out loud, or silently within the mind. Generally each mantra has a recommendation as to which way works best. Some mantras, like the Hare Krishna mantra, can be used in any of these ways, as well as sung as a song with a group or congregation. Generally, this is done with a lead singer who sings the mantra in a particular melody, and then everyone else sings it afterwards.

Some mantras are meant to be chanted only within the mind because their vibration or wavelength is beyond ordinary sound. So the silent method helps invoke the energy within the consciousness. However, to first whisper it or softly speak the mantra correctly may help one be able to chant it silently and make a stronger connection with the mantra.

The repeated chanting of a mantra is called *japa*. It is explained in the Vedic texts that in this age of Kali-yuga the process of chanting *japa* or mantra meditation is much more effective than practicing other spiritual paths that include meditating on the void or Brahman effulgence, or trying to control the life air within the body as in raja-yoga. Plus, only a very few can become perfect at raising the *kundalini* force up through the various *chakras*, or moving the life air up to the top of the head for enlightenment, and then get it to leave the body at the right time to achieve full liberation. And meditating on the void becomes useless as soon as there is the slightest external distraction, which in this age of Kali-yuga is a continuous thing. Therefore, the most effective means of focusing the consciousness is to concentrate on the sound vibration of a mantra.

Using a mantra for *japa* meditation is a process to help rid ourselves of unwanted thoughts and to retain the one thought upon which we are concentrating. It helps us purify the mind of that which obstructs knowledge of our true self. As our concentration on the mantra frees our mind from random thoughts, and as the sound vibration of it raises the frequency level upon which we operate, our consciousness can become clear to observe our real nature. In the word *japa*, the letter "*pa*" stands for that which removes or destroys all impurities and obstructions. The letter "*ja*" stands for that which puts an end to the cycle of birth and death. *Japa*, therefore, is a means of liberation when the proper mantra is used for destroying the mental impurities and negative and materialistic desires and impressions that exist in the mind and consciousness.

There are two mantras that are especially recommended in the Vedic literature to accomplish this. One is *omkara* or the *om* mantra, and the other is Hare Krishna, Hare Krishna, Krishna Krishna, Hare Hare/Hare Rama, Hare Rama, Rama Rama, Hare Hare, which is known as the *maha* or great mantra. It is explained that these two mantras can deliver one to the realm beyond material existence. But there are ways to use these mantras, which we will explain next. Many of the instructions that we describe for these mantras also work most effectively for the others that are included in this book.

CHAPTER TWO

The Om Mantra

Omkara (*pranava*) is considered to be the sound incarnation of the Supreme Personality of God and is identical with the Supreme Lord. It is one of the most important of all mantras, and is often used at the beginning of many of the Vedic mantras or *stotras* that we find. Thus, it is important to know its inner meaning and how it is meant to be pronounced.

Om is considered to be beginningless, changeless, supreme, and free from any external contamination. The *Narada-pancharatra* states: "When the transcendental sound vibration is practiced by a conditioned soul, the Supreme Lord is present on his tongue." The *Atharva-veda* and the *Mandukya Upanishad* both mention the importance of *omkara*. *Omkara* is said to be the beginning, middle and end, and is eternal, beyond all material restrictions or contaminations.

The *om* mantra is a most sacred syllable in Vedic culture. The *Vedas* glorify *om* as the origin of the *Vedas*, or the seed from which all of the *Vedas* grew. This is why *om* precedes every Vedic mantra. *Om* expands into the *vyahritis* (*bhuh*, *bhuvah* and *svaha*) that indicate the three planetary levels of the universe, or the whole creation. The *vyahritis* expand into the Brahma Gayatri mantra, and this expands into all of the Vedic literature.

Om is the sound substance of the Absolute, the seed of the universal manifestation, and connected to the infinite Brahman. It is a name of God. It is also composed of the letters A, U and M, AUM. Several meanings for these have been written in the Sanskrit texts. "A" represents that which is observed in the state of wakefulness, or the experience of the body and senses. "U" represents that which is observed in the dream state, or the inner astral realm. "M" represents that which is in the state of deep sleep as well as that which is beyond the perception of the senses in the wakeful state. The silence, which is like the fourth letter of AUM, is the basis and underlying reality found in all states of consciousness, whether waking, dreaming or deep sleep. This is the Brahman, which is all that is manifested and all that is unmanifest.

It is also said by some that the letters of AUM represent Brahma, Vishnu and Shiva, or the principles of universal creation, maintenance and destruction. The idea is that the vibration of AUM was the initial cause that lead to the creation, and continues the cycles of maintenance and destruction of the universe.

However, *om* also reveals itself according to the depth of consciousness and realizations of the practitioner or *sadhaka*. For example, it is also described by the Gosvamis of Vrindavana that, on a different level, the letter A (*a-kara*) refers to the Supreme Being, Krishna, the master of all living beings and all material and spiritual worlds. He is the Supreme Leader. The letter U (*u-kara*) represents Radharani, or the pleasure potency or spiritual energy of the Supreme, otherwise known as the feminine aspect of God. The M (*ma-kara*) represents the living beings, the marginal energy of the Supreme. Thus, *om* is the complete combination of the Absolute Truth. In other words, *omkara* represents the Supreme Being, His name (Krishna), fame, pastimes, entourage, expansions, energies, and everything else. Thus, *om* is also the resting place of everything and the full understanding of the *Vedas* and all Vedic knowledge.

Further information relates that *omkara*, as the representation of the Supreme Lord, delivers one back to the spiritual dimension if one remembers or chants it at the time of death. Srila Jiva Gosvami, in his *Bhagavat-sandarbha*, says that *omkara* is considered the sound vibration of the holy name of the Supreme Lord. The *Srimad-Bhagavatam* also begins with *omkara*. Thus it is considered the seed of deliverance from the material world. Since the Supreme is absolute, then both He and His name are the same. Contact with the name is also contact with the Lord Himself.

The image of *om* looks something like the number 3 with an extra curve. The largest lower curve represents the waking state. The upper curve signifies deep dreamless sleep. The additional lower curve is the dream state. [Some say the large lower curve is the dream state, the upper curve is the waking state, and the side lower curve is the deep dreamless sleep.] The dot represents the Absolute Reality which is separated from the other curves (or states of consciousness) by a half-circle. This half-circle signifies *maya*, the illusion or material energy which separates the Absolute Reality from the different levels of material consciousness. It is *maya* which keeps us focused on various states of consciousness within the realm of the material manifestation which then veils the Absolute from our experience or awareness. The half-circle, being open on top, indicates the infinite and unbounded nature of the Absolute, which is always separate from *maya*.

Om, therefore, is the summation of the indescribable reality. It is the encapsulated form of all that is. When AUM is pronounced properly, the "A" begins from the base of the spine, the Muladhara Chakra. As the sound moves up, the "A" or *A-kara* activates the area of the naval and the digestive system.

The "U" sound comes from the heart area, so our blood circulation becomes activated. The heart gets the extra supply of oxygen, which then spreads through other parts of the body. The sound of "U" is pronounced in the throat region, ending at the tongue's tip. The "M" is focused at the lips, or the end of the vocal mechanism. It goes in our head and comes out through our nose, which stimulates the vibrations in the brain. This also helps activate the pituitary gland and helps the over-all improvement of the body. Plus the psychic abilities are awakened. Thus, when *om* is chanted or pronounced correctly, it includes all the sounds or vowels of the alphabet.

In the last part of the mantra is the silence into which the *om* culminates. It is the *om* without the distinction of parts. It has no name and thus does not come under the purview of empirical usage. It is the self or pure consciousness, the *turiya*, which transcends all distinctions.

Om is also said to be the sound of the universe, or the sound of the energy which flows through it. Thus, to meditate on *om* in deep attention leads one's mind into profound states of higher consciousness. *Omkara* is unlimited, transcendental, and indestructible. As such, it is not so easy for the average person to understand all the intricacies of *om* or to chant it properly, and, thus, reach the *siddha* or perfection by chanting it.

Actually, the chanting of *omkara* is generally practiced by those engaged in the mystic yoga process. However, anyone who chants Vedic verses will also be chanting *om*, because *om* is often included as a *bija* or seed mantra at the beginning of many such verses or mantras. By chanting *om* and controlling the breathing perfectly, which is mostly a mechanical way of steadying the mind, one is eventually able to go into trance or *samadhi*. Through this system, one gradually changes the tendencies of the materially absorbed mind and makes it spiritualized. But this takes many years to perfect and such a slow process is hardly practical in this age for the average person. If one is not initiated into the brahminical way of knowledge, he will find it difficult to understand the depths of *omkara* and will not likely be able to get the desired results from chanting it. Therefore, it is not advised that people in general chant *omkara* in this age of Kali-yuga with the expectation of using it to reach full spiritual perfection because they are often not qualified or unable to chant it properly to attain the inner depths of spiritual completion. But there is no harm in trying or in using it, as there are no adverse effects as with some mantras.

OM MEDITATION TECHNIQUE

The correct procedure for chanting *om* is as follows:

1. Sit in your meditation posture with eyes closed and your mind at peace. The head, neck and spine must be straight. Prepare yourself appropriately with relaxation, deep breathing and *pranayama*,

2. When ready, take in a deep breath slowly until it reaches the naval, hold it comfortably,

3. Then begin to utter *om* with a long exhale, going ooooooommmmmm or aaaaauuuuummmmmm. You first chant the "A" or "aaahhh" sound during the main portion of the exhale, and then go to pronouncing the "U" or "uh" sound, and conclude with the "M" sound. The "A" is chanted through parted lips, slowly ascending in volume. The "U" is chanted through lips that are closer together. The time taken for chanting the "U" should be double the time taken for chanting "A". The last sound "M" is uttered through the nose with lips closed. The time for chanting "M" should be double that for "U". As you chant the "M" the volume of the sound should descend as slowly as it rose during the "A", taking as much time as it took to ascend.

4. Chant it like this several times for a total of at least nine times.

5. As you chant, do it more quietly until it is a whisper, bringing your awareness deeper within yourself each time.

6. Then chant even more deeply, but only mentally, not out loud. Let the sound pervade and resonate in your mind. It should be the only thing that you hear.

7. The next step is when this form of meditation gets more difficult. Now cease the mental chanting while still listening to the sound within your awareness. Let yourself flow into that sound, losing all other identity and all other awareness. Nothing else exists. Only you and *om*, the vibration of God. Your focus on it should be steady and without effort, as if you are simply flowing with it. Within that vibration is all there is. If you can reach this level of awareness, then for several minutes or as long as you can, if you are aware of time at all, sit in that awareness of God, the Absolute, the Pure, the Omniscient and Supreme Being. Let that awareness fill your being completely, and thus make you complete as part of the Complete Whole.

Herein you may begin to see that to really reach the full perfection of this form of meditation is not so easy for most people. This is why some sages feel, and some references in *shastra* state, that this can be a nice preliminary form of practice, but should not be expected to take people to the deepest level of realization simply because most people in the age of Kali-yuga will find it too difficult. There are simply too many distractions to reach the desired success with it, especially for step number seven, and the mental strength and concentration needed are rarely to be found these days. Nonetheless, people can still use it as best they can, and different results will be determined by the particular consciousness of each individual.

The mantra that is especially meant to be chanted in this age is easy and actually more directly connected with the Supreme than the sound vibration of *omkara* because it contains the holy names and the same spiritual energy of the Lord. It can be used in any number of ways to help focus the minds of people on all levels of awareness. This mantra for Kali-yuga is the *maha-mantra*, or great mantra for deliverance, which is Hare Krishna, Hare Krishna, Krishna Krishna, Hare Hare/Hare Rama, Hare Rama, Rama Rama, Hare Hare.

CHAPTER THREE

Chanting the Hare Krishna Maha-Mantra

There are many Vedic references that specifically recommend the chanting of the Hare Krishna *maha-mantra* as the most effective and advantageous means of reaching spiritual realization and counteracting all the problems of this age. Some of these verses are the following:

These sixteen words--Hare Krishna, Hare Krishna, Krishna Krishna, Hare Hare/Hare Rama, Hare Rama, Rama Rama, Hare Hare--are especially meant for counteracting the ill effects of the present age of quarrel and anxiety. (*Kali-santarana Upanishad*)

All mantras and all processes for self-realization are compressed into the Hare Krishna *maha-mantra*. (*Narada-pancharatra*)

Chant the holy names, chant the holy names, chant the holy names. In this age of Kali [the age of quarrel and confusion] without a doubt there is no other way, there is no other way, there is no other way. (*Brihan-naradiya Purana* 38.126)

In this age there is no use in meditation, sacrifice and temple worship. Simply by chanting the holy name of Krishna--Hare Krishna, Hare Krishna, Krishna Krishna, Hare Hare/Hare Rama, Hare Rama, Rama Rama, Hare Hare--one can achieve perfect self-realization. (*Vishnu Purana* 6.2.17)

The self-realization which was achieved in the Satya millennium by meditation, in the Treta millennium by the performance of different sacrifices, and in the Dvapara millennium by opulent worship of Lord Krishna [as the Deity in the temple], can be achieved in the age of Kali simply by chanting the holy names, Hare Krishna. (*Bhag.*12.3.52)

(Verses similar to this are also found in the *Padma Purana,* Uttara-khanda 72.25, and the *Brihan-naradiya Purana* 38.97)

Living beings who are entangled in the complicated meshes of birth and death can be freed immediately by even unconsciously chanting the holy name of Krishna, which is feared by fear personified. (*Bhag.*1.1.14)

When instructing King Pariksit, the great sage Shukadeva Gosvami said, "O King, constant chanting of the holy name of the Lord after the ways of the great authorities is the doubtless and fearless way of success for all, including those who are free from all material desires, those who are desirous of all material enjoyment, and also those who are self-satisfied by dint of transcendental knowledge. What is the value of a prolonged life which is wasted, inexperienced by years in this world? Better a moment of full consciousness, because that gives one a start in searching after his supreme interest." [1]

The reason that chanting the Lord's names is such an effective process is because the Lord and His names are identical: they are the same spiritual energy. So instead of trying to first empty the mind of all thoughts and desires, which is a typical part of the process of meditation, we simply fill the mind with the spiritual vibration of the holy names of the Supreme. By chanting Hare Krishna we are in immediate contact with God. If we chant someone else's name, we cannot enjoy their association because the name and the person are different. For example, by chanting "water, water, water," we do not quench our thirst because water and the name are two different things. But in the spiritual world everything is absolute. Krishna is nondifferent from His names and, therefore, we can feel His presence simply by chanting His names. This is further elaborated in the *Caitanya-caritamrita* that explains that there is no difference between the Lord's name, form, or personality, and they are all transcendentally sweet. Krishna's name is the same as Krishna Himself, and is not material in any way. It gives spiritual benedictions and is full of pleasure. But in the material world everything is different. [2] Furthermore, the *Caitanya-cartamrita* also explains that the Hare Krishna *maha-mantra* is said to be the sound incarnation of Krishna, and anyone who chants this mantra is in direct association with Krishna and is delivered from the clutches of the material energy. [3]

It is explained that because chanting the names of God brings us in direct contact with God in proportion to the chanter's purity, this process of self-realization is the way of success for everyone. The *Bhagavatam* discloses that the chanting of God's names in the manner of the great authorities is the doubtless way to spiritual success for everyone, no matter whether they are full of material desires or free of all desires or are self-satisfied because of their spiritual knowledge.[4]

Simply by relying on the chanting of the holy names of God, one need not depend upon other processes, rituals, paraphernalia, or persons. One does not even have to be initiated by a spiritual master to chant the *maha-mantra*. As the *Caitanya-caritamrita* says, one does not have to take initiation, but only has to chant the holy names. Thus, deliverance is available to even the lowest of people.[5] Furthermore, Rupa Gosvami writes about the potency of the holy name in his *Padyavali*:

> The holy name of Lord Krishna is an attractive feature for many saintly, liberal people. It is the annihilator of all sinful reactions and is so powerful that save for the dumb who cannot chant it, it is readily available to everyone, including the lowest type of man, the *chandala*. The holy name of Krishna is the controller of the opulence of liberation, and it is identical with Krishna. Simply by touching the holy name with one's tongue, immediate effects are produced. Chanting the holy name does not depend on initiation, pious activities, or the *purascarya* regulative principles generally observed before initiation. The holy name does not wait for all these activities. It is self-sufficient. (*Padyavali* 29)

Herein is evidence that the Hare Krishna *maha-mantra* is so powerful that one who sincerely takes shelter of it, regardless of their condition, will attain all the desired results of connection with the Supreme. The *Skanda Purana* gives further evidence of how powerful is the *maha-mantra*:

> The name of the Lord need not be chanted with regard to place, time, circumstantial conditions, preliminary self-purification or any other factors. Rather, it is completely independent of all other processes and rewards all the desires of those who eagerly chant it. (*Skanda Purana*)

Therefore, without a doubt, the Hare Krishna mantra is the most potent mantra one can utilize for spiritual upliftment. The *Caitanya-caritamrita* also points out that one is freed of all sinful reactions simply by chanting Krishna's names. And all the nine types of devotional service are completed by this process. Thus, in Kali-yuga only the chanting of the holy names is necessary for worshiping the Lord.[6] However, if one is not able to chant purely or follow the regulations for chanting, it is recommended that one get further guidance from a bona fide spiritual master.

In Kali-yuga, the chanting of the holy names is certainly the most practical and effective process for the conditioned souls. It is also the easiest process whether one finds himself in Kali-yuga, Satya-yuga, Treta-yuga, or Dvapara-yuga. Regardless of what age one may be living in, the process of chanting the holy names is always recommended for everyone. "The names of the Supreme Lord who has the disc as His weapon should be glorified always and everywhere."[7] But since the age of Kali is the most difficult, where men have short durations of life, it is also the most fortunate age. This is explained in *Srimad-Bhagavatam* which states that those who are wise know the value of this age of Kali because, in spite of the fallen nature of this age, the spiritual perfection of life can be attained by the easy process of *sankirtana*, the congregational chanting of Krishna's holy names. No better position can be found to attain freedom from material existence and entrance into the spiritual kingdom than joining the Lord's *sankirtana* movement.[8]

Even those living in other ages desire to take birth in Kali-yuga to take advantage of this special concession of a speedy delivery from the cycle of birth and death through the process of *sankirtana*. This is confirmed in *Srimad-Bhagavatam* where we find it said that those who live during Satya-yuga and other ages wish to be born in Kali-yuga just to take advantage of associating with the devotees of Lord Narayana, who are especially found in South India.[9]

The *Srimad-Bhagavatam* (11.5.32) relates that intelligent persons perform congregational singing of Krishna's names to worship the incarnation of Krishna who sings His own names, and who is accompanied by His associates and confidential companions [indicating Lord Chaitanya].[10] Therefore, as the *Caitanya-caritamrita* specifically says, the essence of all scriptural teachings is that the only religious principle in the age of Kali is to chant the Lord's holy names, which are the basis of all Vedic hymns.[11] "In this way, the most perfect penance to be executed in this world is the chanting of the name of Lord Sri Hari. Especially in the age of Kali, one can satisfy the Supreme Lord Vishnu by performing *sankirtana*."[12]

The fact of the matter, as further related in the *Bhagavatam*, is that regardless of what one's present situation is, if a person once speaks about the activities and chants the holy names of the Supreme, or hears about and remembers Him, he becomes eligible to engage in the Vedic rituals. And how much more glorious are those who regularly chant the holy names. Such people are indeed worshipable, for they must have performed all kinds of austerities, achieved the characteristics of the Aryans, studied the *Vedas*, bathed at all the holy places of pilgrimage, and done whatever else is required.[13]

When the great sage Narada Muni was explaining to Srila Vyasadeva the means by which he became enlightened, he said, "It is personally experienced by me that those who are always full of cares and anxieties due to desiring contact of the senses with their objects can cross the ocean of nescience [illusory darkness] on a most suitable boat--the constant chanting of the transcendental activities of the Personality of Godhead. It is true that by practicing restraint of the senses by the yoga system one can get relief from the disturbances of desire and lust, but this is not sufficient to give satisfaction to the soul, for this [satisfaction] is derived from devotional service to the Supreme Personality."[14]

Lord Krishna goes on to explain to Uddhava that in the association of saintly devotees, there is always the discussion about Him, and those who partake in such hearing and chanting about the Lord's glories are certainly purified of all sins. In this way, whoever hears, chants and respectfully opens his heart to these topics about the Lord becomes faithfully dedicated to Him. Thus, he achieves devotional service to Lord Krishna. Then, as Lord Krishna Himself asks, "What more remains to be accomplished for the perfect devotee after achieving devotional service unto Me, the Supreme Absolute Truth, whose qualities are innumerable and who am the embodiment of all ecstatic experience?"[15]

As further related by Sukadeva Gosvami, "A person who with faith engages in chanting the glories of these various pastimes and incarnations of Vishnu, the Lord of lords, will gain liberation from all sins. The all-auspicious exploits of the all-attractive incarnations of Lord Shri Krishna, the Supreme Personality of Godhead, and also the pastimes He performed as a child, are described in this *Srimad-Bhagavatam* and in other scriptures. Anyone who clearly chants these descriptions of His pastimes will attain transcendental loving service unto Lord Krishna, who is the goal of all perfected sages."[16]

Sri Suta Gosvami relates that in a conversation between Narada Muni and Sanatkumara, Sanatkumara explained the way to attain freedom from this world, even for the most wayward sinners. Even all those mean men who are destitute of all good ways of behavior, who are of a wicked mind, who are outcaste, who deceive the world, who are intent upon religious hypocrisy, pride, drinking liquor, and wickedness, who are sinful and cruel, who are interested in another man's wealth, wife and sons, become pure if they resort to the lotus-like feet of Vishnu. The name of Vishnu, sure to succeed here, protects those sinful men who transgress even Him who causes divinity, who gives salvation to the immobile beings and the mobile beings. A man who has done all kinds of sins is freed if he resorts to Vishnu. If a contemptible, wicked biped would commit sin against Vishnu, and by chance resorts to His name, he is emancipated due to the (power of the) name (of Vishnu). However, a man falls down due to his sin against (Vishnu's) name, which is the friend of all.[17]

The sage Kavi instructed King Nimi that the holy names of the Supreme Lord are all-auspicious because they describe His transcendental birth and pastimes, which He performs for the upliftment and salvation of all conditioned souls. For this reason the Lord's holy names are sung throughout the world. By chanting these holy names of the Supreme, one reaches the level of love of God, in which one becomes fixed as an eternal servant of the Lord. Then such a devotee becomes very attached to a particular name and form of the Lord in his service. As his heart melts in ecstatic love, he may laugh loudly or cry or shout. Sometimes he may even sing or dance like a madman in such ecstasy because he becomes indifferent to the opinion of others.[18]

In this way, we can begin to understand how elevated the writer of the Vedic scripture considers those who have adopted the process of chanting Krishna's holy names. However, for those who do not like the chanting of the holy names and blaspheme the process and criticize or try to restrain those who do chant, we can understand that their sentiment is due to their sinful and offensive activities. Such people are said to have no intelligence and work for no useful purpose and simply contribute to the chaos and confusion within society. The *Bhagavatam* (3.9.7) confirms that those who do not engage in the blessed chanting and hearing about the activities of the Supreme are bereft of intelligence and good fortune. They perform sinful activities to enjoy sensual pleasure that lasts only for a short time.

LORD VISHNU'S NAMES ARE MORE POWERFUL THAN THE GREATEST HOLY PLACES

The power of the Lord's holy names is exhibited in the following story. It is described in the *Padma Purana* that many years ago when asked by the sages at the forest of Naimisharanaya which one single act will bring the fruit of visiting the many holy places, Suta Gosvami answered in this way: Out of so many rituals and rites that are prescribed, only one is superior. There is no doubt that one who has devotion to Lord Vishnu has undoubtedly conquered everything. Hari, [Vishnu, Krishna], the Lord of all gods, should alone be propitiated. The goblin of sin will perish by means of the great sacred hymns in the form of the names of Vishnu. There is no doubt that those with pure hearts, going around Vishnu even once, get (the fruit of) having bathed at all the holy places. A man would obtain the fruit of (having visited) all holy places by seeing Vishnu's image. Chanting the excellent name of Vishnu, a man would obtain (the result) of having chanted all the sacred hymns. A man having once smelt the tulasi plant, the grace of Vishnu, does not see the huge and terrible face of Yama [Yamaraja, the lord of death]. A man having (but) once saluted Krishna does not drink the mother's milk [does not need to be reborn again]. I always repeatedly salute them whose mind is (fixed) on the feet of Vishnu. Even [those of lower tribes, such as] pulkasas, chandalas, or other mleccha tribes, who serve the feet of Vishnu alone are fit to be saluted. Then what about the meritorious and devoted brahmanas and royal sages? Having placed one's devotion in Vishnu, a person does not experience confinement in the womb (is not reborn). A man who with high sounds chants the name of Vishnu purifies the world as does the Ganga [Ganges River]. There is no doubt that a man is freed from sins like murder of a brahmana by seeing (the image of), touching (the feet of), reciting (the name of), and devoting oneself (to Vishnu). Circumambulating (the image of) Hari [Vishnu, Krishna], and loudly chanting His names in a sweet and melodious voice, accompanied with clapping of the hands, a man has struck the sin of murdering a brahmana from his hands. A man becomes pure by just seeing Him, who having narrated His story, would listen to a narrative about Him. Then, O best of sages, how can there be the slightest doubt about such a person's sins.[19]

"O great sages, Vishnu's name is the best holy place of all holy places. Those who have uttered the name of Krishna make the world a holy place. Therefore, O best of sages, they consider nothing more meritorious than this. A man using and holding on his head the remains of offered flowers to Vishnu, would beckon Vishnu, who is the destroyer of grief due to fear of Yamaraja. Undoubtedly, Vishnu (alone) is to be worshiped and saluted. Therefore, see and worship Vishnu only who has no beginning or end, who is the soul (of everything), and who is unmanifest. Those who look upon Vishnu and another deity as equal, go to terrible hells. Vishnu would not care for them. Vishnu, the Lord Himself, liberates a fool or a chandala to whom Vishnu is dear. There is none greater than Vishnu, who is like a wild fire for (burning) heaps of sins. A man, even after having committed a terrible sin, is freed by the name of Vishnu. Lord Vishnu, the Father of the worlds, has put greater strength than Himself into His name. Therefore a man looking highly upon Vishnu's name should be devoted to Hari. The name of Vishnu is a great destructive weapon like the thunderbolt in rending the mountain of sins. His feet are fruitful and move for that (only). The hands that worship Him are alone said to be blessed. That head which bends before Hari (Vishnu) is the best part of the body. That is (really) the tongue that extols Vishnu. That is the mind which follows His feet. That is the hair that bristles [stands up in ecstasy] at the utterance of His name. Those are the tears that are shed due to devotion to Lord Vishnu. Oh, people are very much duped by their faults if they do not resort to (Him) by merely chanting His names. Those who though having got a tongue do not utter the name of Vishnu, easily fall [back into the cycles of birth and death] even after having secured the stairway to liberation. Therefore, a man should carefully (please) Lord Vishnu by means of worldly and religious rites [devotional service]. Lord Vishnu is pleased with worldly and religious rites, not otherwise. The worship of Vishnu is said to be a holier place than a holy place. A man obtains that fruit by serving Vishnu which he obtains by bathing at and drinking (the water from) all the holy places. Only blessed men worship Vishnu by means of worldly and religious rites [devotional service]. Therefore, O sages, worship Krishna (Vishnu), who is the most auspicious.[20]

THE POWER OF THE MAHA-MANTRA: HOW IT WORKS

It may be somewhat surprising for the average Westerner to hear about the power within the vibrations of words or mantras, but the potency is real. For example, any numerologist will tell you that each letter has a particular value and a group of letters pronounced as a word invokes the power of those letters. Therefore, someone's name contains the subtle formula for signifying to varying degrees one's characteristics, qualities and future. By associating with particular sound vibrations one becomes influenced by them.

A good example of this is when one country tries to take over another in war, or one political party tries to defeat another. The first thing they try to do is take over the lines of communication and the media, such as radio, television, and newspapers. By sending out its propaganda through sound, a government can influence people's minds and stay in power, or a political party can remove the leaders of the opposition. In the latter case, a new government may become established.

According to the predominant types of sound vibration people associate with through T.V. and radio, or in reading articles in magazines and newspapers, they become attracted to certain things or drawn towards certain viewpoints. When television shows, songs on the radio, stories in magazines, and advertising everywhere propagates the concern for temporary sense gratification, then people lose their interest in the real goal of life. They simply become absorbed in the thoughts of whatever type of sound vibration enters their consciousness. When nonsensical sound vibrations enter and contaminate the ether, the air, water, and the very molecular structure of each and every person, place and thing, then we cannot expect anything else but continued and worsening turmoil and perplexities in the world.

Let us try to understand how this happens. First of all, energy pervades the atmosphere of this creation in the form of vibrations, as in sound waves, light waves, radio waves, and so on. The mind can especially be affected by the kind of energy or vibration it picks up or tunes into. The function of the mind is twofold: it joins thoughts and concepts into theories and goals or desires, and it simplifies or interprets experiences that are gathered through the senses. This is controlled by sound vibration or thought waves. For example, when you hear the following words, an image will form in your mind: dog, cat, insect, man, woman, politician, automobile, and sunset. We can take the experiment a little further when we say, snarling dog, sleeping cat, biting insect, ugly old man, beautiful voluptuous woman, conniving politician, sleek automobile, and tranquil red sunset.

The second set of words may have brought images to your mind that were completely different than the first set. This is all due to sound which triggers the mind to react and form thoughts or images related to the words by interpreting past experiences. Such thoughts and images may also form into goals or desires of what we want to attain or wish to avoid. When throughout our life we are bombarded by different kinds of sound waves, whether from schoolbooks in our early years, or to present-day radio, television, and movies, our consciousness is led through particular changes and different levels of development. This might be controlled by others so that we act in a certain way according to someone else's design, whether we know it or not. If you start listening to the radio all the time and all they play are songs about making love under the apple tree, you will not have to tell anyone what you will be thinking about. It is not difficult to figure out. This is how we are controlled by sound.

Another example is that sometime we may be feeling peaceful and decide to spend a nice, quiet evening watching television. After several hours of being exposed to all kinds of sound vibration in the form of game shows, cop shows, comedy, soap opera, news, and a multitude of advertising, we may wake up the next morning unrested, agitated, and disturbed without knowing why. But the kind of energy we imbibed through sound will continue to have an affect on us later. In this way, the kind of sound vibration we associate with can make a big difference on our consciousness.

There are, however, many kinds of beneficial sound vibrations that we can utilize. A friend of mine once cut his finger down to the bone while he was in India. It was a serious cut and he was not able to do much to stop the bleeding. He told one of the Indian men nearby who took him into his house. The man put some mustard seed oil on the cut and stroked it with his finger while chanting a certain mantra. At that point the bleeding stopped. He did it again and the cut closed. The man did it a third time and, to my friend's amazement, the cut on his finger was practically healed. Some farmers also use mantras to produce better crops. Plants are very sensitive to vibrations and different sounds can assist plants in their growth.

In the Vedic literature there are, of course, many stories that describe the use of mantras. The brahmana priests produced many kinds of magical results by using them. They could even curse others or, if necessary, kill someone with the use of mantras. The warriors or kings could also attach a *brahmastra* weapon to the arrows they shot. A *brahmastra* is a weapon equivalent to the atomic bombs of today, but were produced by perfectly chanting particular mantras. However, the *brahmastra* could also be called back by using a different mantra and the extent of damage could also be controlled. They were not like the bombs of today that, when released, are completely uncontrollable and kill and hurt everyone and anyone in its range.

There are many other kinds of sound vibrations, mantras, or prayers that can be used for gaining money, maintaining health, defeating enemies, getting good luck, subduing evil spirits, counteracting snake bite, and so on. There are countless mantras or prayers for temporary results, not only in the Vedic culture but in other cultures as well. The most powerful mantras are those that can completely free one from this material world and the cycle of birth and death and allow one to enter the spiritual realm. As already established, there is no mantra more powerful for this purpose than the Hare Krishna *maha-mantra*.

The way the *maha-mantra* works is a science. One thing we must first understand is that there are channels by which the Infinite descends into this world. One channel is through transcendental sound. The *maha-mantra* is a purely spiritual vibration. It cannot be chanted with a material tongue nor heard with a material ear. In this way, the holy name reserves the right of not being exposed to organic senses or understood by someone in materialistic consciousness. However, the Infinite has the power of making Himself known to the finite mind. When He reveals Himself to His devotee, the devotee experiences the perception of God. This is called Self-realization and transcendental revelation. This can be attained through the process of purely chanting the *maha-mantra*.

The holy names are not revealed simply through Vedic writings, but they are revealed to the world through the spiritual tongues of the pure devotees. Such pure devotees are the real spiritual masters of everyone in the universe. But if the guru is not genuine, then the sound or mantra, though seeming to sound the same, will not produce the real effect.

The audience of the pure devotee hears the name of Krishna but may not fully recognize or comprehend it. Yet the name enters the ear and vibrates the eardrum which touches our mind. There is still not genuine spiritual realization at this point because the soul remains untouched. Yet the name begins to affect our mind by cleansing the dust within. This dust is the materialistic consciousness that causes forgetfulness of our real spiritual identity. This forgetfulness manifests in forms of bodily attachment, lust, greed, envy, anger, etc. Therefore, by chanting the *maha-mantra* we wash our mind and enable it to get free of the contaminating dust. Then the mind and intelligence become very clear and sharp. Plus when the Supersoul hears our sincere attempt to chant the holy names, He will also assist us in clearing away any obstacles in our path. Thus, our ability increases to delve more deeply into spiritual understanding and to acquire a taste for the holy names.

The mind is the connecting link between the body and the spirit soul within. The soul, which does not actively engage in any material activities, remains in a state of suspended animation while covered by illusion, as in the case of a materially conditioned person who engages in material activities. Through the vehicle of the mind, the senses act and we perceive things around us and form theories. If the mind is unclear or dusty due to the influence of the material energy, we then become confused about the goal of life and may engage in so many material pursuits. When the mind is cleansed or purified by associating with the Infinite in the form of the *maha-mantra*, all our material concoctions are forced out. By inundating our mind with the transcendental sound of the holy names, all of our misconceptions, which is the cause of our material suffering, are completely conquered, leaving no more enemies within the mind. Then the mind reflects the quality and nature of the soul.

The holy sound of Hare Krishna, as uttered by the pure devotee, moves our intellect and we begin to consider the Vedic philosophy. When the intelligence is thus energized by spiritual knowledge, the transcendental sound vibration, after cutting through the senses, mind, and intelligence, makes contact with the soul. Thus, we are able to hear the holy name with our real spiritual ear, and actual spiritual revelation and Self-realization is open to us. Then the soul, having made contact with the Supreme or Supersoul through the form of transcendental sound, recapitulates, sending the vibration back through our intelligence, mind and senses. At that time, when we chant Hare Krishna, the Supreme Infinite Lord is there in the vibration and our whole being experiences a deluge of unlimited spiritual ecstasy.

From this level of spiritual realization, we can enter into the understanding of the very cause of everything that exists. The mind, body, and soul, and even material nature itself can be changed into transcendental energy by one pure exclamation of Hare Krishna. This is very important to understand because when everything becomes saturated with this transcendental sound, the result is total transformation of energy. Thus, what is material can be changed into something spiritual. If this can be done on a grand scale, the material world can be transformed into the spiritual world.

Another example of how the holy names of Krishna work, and how powerful they are, can be cited from the *Srimad-Bhagavatam*, Sixth Canto, in the story of Ajamila. Ajamila was born of good parents who trained him in knowledge of the *Vedas* to become a perfect brahmana. Yet one time, while walking along the road, he happened to see a man and a prostitute in a state of intoxication, frolicking in the grass. The woman was not covered properly and was uninhibitedly engaging in amorous pastimes with the man. Upon seeing this, Ajamila became very agitated and later sought the company of the prostitute. He left his young beautiful wife and lived with the prostitute, giving up all regulative principles. He begot ten sons in the womb of the prostitute and named the youngest son Narayana, a name of one of the expansions of Krishna.

To maintain himself and his family, Ajamila cheated others in gambling or by robbing them. While he spent his time in abominable, sinful activities, eighty-eight years of his life passed by. Since his youngest son was born while Ajamila was very old, Narayana was very dear to him. Because of the child's awkward manners and speech, Ajamila delighted in the child's activities. When Ajamila ate or drank, he always did so with his son, Narayana. Ajamila, however, could not understand that the length of his life was decreasing and death was approaching. When the time of death arrived for Ajamila, he began to think only of his son.

At the moment of death, Ajamila became extremely frightened when he saw three persons with deformed bodies, fierce, twisted faces, and their hair standing erect. These were the Yamadutas, the soldiers of Yamaraja, the lord of death. With a noose in their hands, they had come to take him to Yamaraja. Because of attachment to his son, Ajamila fearfully began to call him loudly by his name, Narayana.

Just then the Vishnudutas, soldiers of Lord Vishnu, arrived when they heard the holy name of their master from the mouth of the dying Ajamila. Ajamila had certainly chanted the name of Narayana without offense because he had chanted in complete anxiety. The Yamadutas were snatching the soul from the heart of Ajamila, but the messengers of Lord Vishnu forcefully stopped them from doing so. The Yamadutas inquired why they were being stopped from taking Ajamila. The Vishnudutas then asked the Yamadutas that if they were really servants of Lord Yamaraja, then explain the meaning of religious and irreligious principles.

The Yamadutas replied that from their master, Yamaraja, they had heard that which is prescribed in the *Vedas* constitutes religious principles, and the opposite is irreligion. They continued to explain that Lord Narayana is situated in His own abode in the spiritual world, but controls the entire cosmic creation.

The sun, fire, sky, air, demigods, moon, evening, day, night, directions, water, land, and Supersoul Himself all witness the activities of the living entities. Those that deserve punishment are those who are confirmed by these witnesses as having engaged in unrighteous activities. Everyone engaged in fruitive activities deserves punishment in proportion to their sinful acts. In this way, they must enjoy or suffer the corresponding reactions of their karma in the next life.

The Yamadutas continued to explain the laws of karma and the position of the living entity, pointing out that in considering the sinful life of Ajamila, they had the right to take him to hell in order to rectify his sinful behavior.

The Vishnudutas, however, stated that Ajamila had already atoned for all of his sinful actions, not only for this one life but for those performed in millions of lives, simply by chanting the holy name of Narayana in a helpless condition. Even though he had not chanted purely, he chanted without offense, and, therefore, was now pure and eligible for liberation. Throughout Ajamila's life, he called the name Narayana. Although calling his son, by chanting the name Narayana, he sufficiently atoned for the sinful actions of millions of lives. At the time of death, Ajamila had helplessly and very loudly chanted the holy name of the Lord. That chanting alone had already freed him from the reactions of all sinful life. Therefore, the soldiers of Lord Vishnu forbade the servants of Yamaraja to take Ajamila for punishment in hell. Anyone who takes shelter of the Supreme through His holy names can similarly be saved from the dark future of sinful reactions after death.

Although *Srimad-Bhagavatam* relates the full story of Ajamila and how he witnessed the discussion between the Yamadutas and Vishnudutas and then went on to achieve ultimate spiritual perfection by taking to the process of bhakti-yoga, our short summary here is to show the potency of the holy names. Ajamila is not much different than most people in this age of Kali who are attracted to sinful activities. Therefore, we should seriously try to understand and take advantage of the chanting of the holy names, for by doing so even the greatest sins we may have committed can be atoned, as the following verses explain:

Simply by chanting one holy name of Hari, a sinful man can counteract the reactions to more sins than he can commit. (*Brihad-vishnu Purana*)

As when all small animals flee in fear when a lion roars, similarly all one's sinful reactions leave when a person chants the Lord's holy names while in a helpless condition or even if he has no desire to do so. (*Garuda Purana*)

The path to liberation is guaranteed when a person once chants the holy name of Lord Hari. (*Skanda Purana*)

The *Srimad-Bhagavatam* explains that chanting the holy names can negate the reactions of the most serious of sins, and, therefore, everyone should take this seriously and join the *sankirtana* movement, which is the most auspicious activity in the universe.[21] And the *Caitanya-caritamrita* discloses that beyond dissolving one's entanglement in material existence, by chanting Krishna's names one develops attraction and awakens his love for Krishna.[22]

From these verses we can understand that there is no impediment for everyone to readily utilize the holy names to purify themselves of even the worst sins, providing they are sincere and chant purely. Even those who cannot speak properly can repeat the *maha-mantra* within their minds. From those who are the most saintly to those who are in the most abominable position, all have the opportunity of chanting the holy names to begin the escape from karmic reactions and to free themselves from material entanglement.

As described in *Srimad-Bhagavatam*, the chanting of the names of the Supreme is the best atonement for one who is a thief, a drunkard, a killer of *brahmanas*, or one who kills women or kings or cows or his own parents, or for any other kind of sins. Simply by chanting the holy names one attracts the attention of the Supreme who gives that person special protection.[23]

Herein we can discern that attracting the attention of the Supreme by chanting His holy names is the best means of protecting ourselves from our past impurities. This does not mean we can continue doing such sinful acts, but when we have stopped them and felt remorse, then we can engage in sincere chanting of the Lord's holy names. When the Supreme is pleased with someone, what can they not accomplish? Anything can be done by one who becomes spiritually powerful. Therefore, out of all the various processes of atonement that are prescribed by different scripture, engaging in the chanting of the holy names is best because it actually uproots the material desires in the heart. As the *Bhagavatam* confirms, the various processes of atonement are not complete if one's mind still runs back to unwanted material habits. Therefore, those who want freedom from their karmic reactions, chanting of the names and pastimes of the Supreme is the best because it completely purifies the mind.[24] It further relates that chanting the holy names of the Lord before dying by some misfortune is enough to deliver a person from having to enter hell to suffer for his bad karmic reactions.[25]

Not only is the name of the Lord so powerfully effective on one who seriously chants it, despite the fact that he may have been sinful in his past, the name also acts on one who chants it in a very casual manner. The *Bhagavatam* points out that even if one chants the holy names neglectfully, jokingly, or simply for entertainment, the holy names are nonetheless effective enough to free the person from unlimited sins, just as a powerful medicine is effective whether a patient who takes it understands it or not.[26]

Even making an offense to God Himself or to the holy names, such offenses can be mitigated by taking shelter of chanting the Lord's holy names. This is related in the *Padma Purana* as follows: When somehow a sin or blemish is committed against the name of Vishnu, the person should always recite the name and sincerely seek its refuge only. Lord Vishnu's names alone remove the sin of those who have committed a sin or offence against the names since they alone, continuously recited, bring wealth. It is the name alone, when recited without interruption, when remembered or heard, either in a pure form or with incorrect syllables, would protect a man. This alone is the truth. Of course, if it is resorted to hypocritically or for greed born of love for body or wealth, it would not quickly produce the desired result. O Narada, this great secret, which removes all inauspiciousness, and keeps off all sins, was formerly heard (by me) from Shiva. O Narada, even those who are intent on committing sins [but refrain from such], but who know the names of Vishnu would be liberated merely by reciting them.[27]

Pondering all these points, Lord Yamaraja, in the *Srimad-Bhagavatam*, concludes that all intelligent men take to devotional service by chanting the holy names of the Supreme because even if they accidentally perform some sinful act, they are protected since the chanting of the Hare Krishna mantra obliterates all sinful reactions.[28]

ATTAINING LIBERATION THROUGH CHANTING

In the previous segment it is mentioned that there are certain channels through which the Infinite descends. Similarly, there are certain channels that the living beings can use to escape material existence and return to the spiritual realm. Of course, the final goal of any religious process or yoga system is to get free from material entanglement and enter directly into spiritual existence. This happens easily for one who learns how to purely chant the holy names. This is verified in the *Caitanya-caritamrta* which states that the chanting of the Hare Krishna mantra vanquishes all sins and makes way for the performance of devotional service to begin. The chanting of this *maha-mantra* gives so much spiritual advancement that one easily ends his material existence and attains love of God.[29]

From everything that has been described so far about the glories of the holy name, such as its potency to purify the mind, to relieve us of material activities and the reactions to sinful acts, as well as to put us in direct contact with the Supreme and reawaken our attraction for Him, it is obvious, especially for this age of Kali-yuga, that the most worshipable object is the Lord's holy names, especially as found in the Hare Krishna *maha-mantra*. The *Bhagavatam* also confirms this by stating that the topmost religious principle for the entire human race is to engage in devotional service beginning with the chanting of the Lord's holy names. Therefore, those who chant the holy names have reached the ultimate position in civilized life and, if they continue on the path, will attain further realizations in spiritual life up to reaching the platform of pure, unadulterated devotional service.[30]

All such transcendental opulences, as stated in the above verses, are attained simply by chanting the Hare Krishna *maha-mantra* without offenses. In this way, one attains the supreme spiritual bliss. The *Caitanya-caritamrita* explains that by chanting the spiritual names of Krishna one tastes spiritual ecstasy when his love for Krishna awakens. Then one attains Krishna's direct association and feels like he is in an ocean of love.[31]

The name "Krishna" literally means "the greatest pleasure," or "He who is all-attractive." All living entities are looking for pleasure and happiness. God is the storehouse of all pleasure and whatever happiness we feel in this material world is simply due to contact with His energy. However, by chanting His holy names, we can transcend whatever temporary pleasure is found on the material platform and experience actual spiritual happiness by coming in direct contact with the Supreme, the source of all pleasure. The *Caitanya-caritamrita* verifies that simply by chanting the Hare Krishna mantra a person is freed from material life and will be able to see the Lord.[32]

The mystery behind these names of God is further explained in the *Sri Caitanya Upanishad*, texts 12-14. It explains that the names of the Supreme that are used in the Hare Krishna mantra have specific meanings. *Hari* refers to "He who unties the knot of a person's material desires." Krishna is divided into *Krish*, which means "He who is attractive to everyone," and *Na*, which means "the greatest spiritual pleasure." And *Rama* means "He who is full of spiritual bliss and attracts all others." The Hare Krishna mantra consists of the repetition of these names of the Supreme (Hare Krishna, Hare Krishna, Krishna Krishna, Hare Hare/Hare Rama, Hare Rama, Rama Rama, Hare Hare) and is the best of all mantras and most confidential of secrets. Those who are serious about making spiritual progress continually chant these holy names and cross over material existence.

For one who takes shelter of the *maha-mantra*, he is sure to reach the Supreme because such mystic meditation engages the mind and intelligence in Krishna. By such continued remembrance of Krishna, even though one may seem to be engaged in so many duties, one regains his spiritual consciousness which is the prerequisite for entering back into the spiritual world. As Sri Krishna explains in *Bhagavad-gita*, a person should think of Him as Krishna and carry out one's duty with the mind and intelligence fixed on Him. Thinking and meditating on Krishna in this undeviated way, one can be sure to reach the divine Supreme Spirit.[33]

From this information we can understand that if we can continue setting some time aside everyday for chanting the *maha-mantra* and spiritualizing our consciousness, we will be prepared for entering the spiritual realm after death. This is the most important aspect of any yoga or religious system--being free from material consciousness and remembering the Supreme at the time we give up our body. This requirement is easily fulfilled simply by remembering the Lord through chanting His holy names. This is confirmed in the *Srimad-Bhagavatam* which declares that one who takes shelter of Krishna by invoking His spiritual names at the time of leaving the body is cleansed of many lifetimes of sin and attains Krishna without fail.[34]

The most practical example of this is Ajamila, as previously discussed. The *Bhagavatam* describes that at the time of death Ajamila chanted the Lord's name and returned to the spiritual world, although he was calling for his son, Narayana, and had spent a lifetime in sinful activity.[35] So where is the doubt that if one seriously chants the Lord's holy name he will return to the spiritual world? Therefore, as the *Bhagavatam* elaborates, for one who is serious about attaining freedom from material existence, there is nothing more effective than chanting the holy names of the Supreme and discussing His pastimes and qualities. Other processes are not as complete and leave one's mind tainted with passion and ignorance.[36] Furthermore, all of one's sinful karmic reactions are wiped out simply by chanting the Lord's names and glorifying His qualities and activities. Even if one cannot properly pronounce the holy name, a person will achieve liberation if he chants without offense.[37]

GOD INAUGURATES CHANTING THE HOLY NAMES

We should not think that *sankirtana*, the group chanting of the Lord's holy names, is simply part of the system of mantra-yoga, or is merely a formula that has been passed down through the ages like other yoga systems. Nor is it a ritual, ceremony, or activity meant for producing good karma or positive fruitive results. Neither is it merely a way to focus the mind and achieve peace and tranquility. It is more than any of these.

As previously explained, there is a system of self-realization especially recommended for each age. In the age of Kali, people are not attracted to spiritual pursuits and are often rebellious against anything that seems to restrict or stifle their freedom to do anything they want. Since in this age we are so easily distracted by so many things and our mind is always in a whirl, we need an easy path. Therefore, the Vedic *shastra* explains that God has given us an easy way to return to Him in this age. It is almost as if He has said, "Since you are My worst son, I give you the easiest process." The *Caitanya-caritamrita* confirms this and says that the Supreme Being descends as Sri Caitanya, with a golden complexion, to simply spread the glories of chanting the holy names, which is the only religious principle in this age of Kali.[38] In this way, God Himself has given the method of chanting His holy names as the most effective means to reach His spiritual abode.

The Lord always descends to establish the codes of religion. This is confirmed in *Bhagavad-gita* where Lord Krishna explains that although He is unborn and the Lord of all living beings, He still descends in His spiritual form to re-establish proper religious principles and annihilate the miscreants whenever there is a decline of religion and a rise in irreligious activity.[39]

Though there are many incarnations or avatars of God, all avatars are known and predicted in the Vedic literature. Each incarnation performs many wonderful pastimes. But in Kali-yuga the Lord descends as His own devotee in the form of Sri Chaitanya in order to show the perfect example of how devotional service should be performed, and to stress the chanting of the Hare Krishna mantra for this age by inaugurating the process of the *sankirtana* movement.

A few of the predictions of the appearance of Lord Chaitanya can be found in many Vedic texts. One of them is from the *Svetasvatara Upanishad* (3.12): "The Supreme Personality of God [Purusha] is Mahaprabhu [great master], the propagator of transcendental enlightenment." Another is from the *Vayu Purana*: "In the age of Kali I shall descend as the son of Sacidevi to inaugurate the *sankirtana* movement." The *Bhagavatam* also describes how intelligent men sing the holy names to worship the incarnation of God who is accompanied by His associates and always sings the names of Krishna.[40] And in *Caitanya-*

caritamrita the Supreme Lord Himself describes how He will appear as His own devotee to perform and teach devotional service by inaugurating the *sankirtana* movement, which is the religion for this age.[41]

The *Sri Caitanya Upanishad* (texts 5-11) of the *Atharva-veda* contains the most detailed prediction of Lord Chaitanya's appearance and activities. When Pippalada asked his father, Lord Brahma, how the sinful living entities will be delivered in Kali-yuga and who should be the object of their worship and what mantra should they chant to be delivered, Brahma told him to listen carefully and he would describe what will take place in the age of Kali. Brahma said that the Supreme Lord Govinda, Krishna, will appear again in Kali-yuga as His own devotee in a two-armed form with a golden complexion in the area of Navadvipa along the Ganges. He will spread the system of devotional service and the chanting of the names of Krishna, especially in the form of the Hare Krishna *maha-mantra*: Hare Krishna, Hare Krishna, Krishna Krishna, Hare Hare/Hare Rama, Hare Rama, Rama Rama, Hare Hare.

These and other predictions confirm the fact that Sri Chaitanya Mahaprabhu would appear to specifically propagate the chanting of the holy names. Of course, now we have complete descriptions and elaborations on His life, activities, and philosophy, as had been written by His close associates. This verifies the fact that the chanting of the *maha-mantra* is the rare and special opportunity given by God for all to be relieved from the problems of the age of Kali and of material life in general. As confirmed in the *Caitanya-caritamrita*, it is Sri Krishna Chaitanya who inaugurates the congregational chanting of the holy names, which is the most sublime of all spiritual sacrifices. Intelligent people will worship Him through this means, while other foolish people will continue in the cycle of repeated birth and death in this material world.[42]

In another place in the *Caitanya-caritamrita* Sri Chaitanya specifically tells Svarupa Damodara and Ramananda Raya that chanting the holy names is the most practical way to attain salvation from material existence in this age, and anyone who is intelligent and takes up this process of worshiping Krishna will attain the direct shelter of Krishna.[43]

HOW TO CHANT THE MAHA-MANTRA

There are no hard and fast rules for chanting the Hare Krishna *maha-mantra*. One can chant anywhere, anytime, in any situation. In fact, the *Caitanya-caritamrita* describes that chanting the holy name at any time or place, even during sleep or while eating, brings one all perfection.[44] However, there are different stages of chanting. The first stage of chanting is the offensive stage, when we often still hold on to our attachments, have little taste for chanting, and are working at clearing our mind of unwanted things. The second stage is offenseless chanting, after we have made a little progress and are starting to get a taste for the holy names. Then is the third or pure stage of chanting, which is when the chanting becomes extremely powerful. This is when we have a strong taste or attraction for the Lord's holy names, and can become absorbed in the hearing and chanting of them.

The proper way to chant is to give up all of our internal thoughts. As mentioned before, it is almost impossible to meditate on the void and empty our mind of all thinking. Our mind is always being pulled here and there by something. But the chanting process is easy because we simply concentrate on the mantra. However, our meditation on the mantra will be most effective if we can avoid the internal dialogue we always have within our mind. We should not be chanting while we make plans for the day, or while focusing our attention on other things. The *maha-mantra* is the Supreme in the incarnation of sound. Therefore, we must chant with complete respect and veneration. We must give the mantra our full attention, otherwise the chanting is considered offensive. The process is to simply chant and hear. That is all. If we can do that, then we will make rapid progress and quickly attain the second stage of chanting, which is the offenseless stage.

As one progresses through the second stage, a person begins to get a taste for the chanting, and begins to feel the nectar of joy and bliss within the names. As a person enters the third or pure stage of chanting, the layers of ignorance that keeps one from realizing their spiritual identity are peeled away. At the fullest point, one gains direct perception of their spiritual identity and relationship with God, and is immediately liberated while still in the material body. The Lord reveals Himself to such a sincere devotee and the devotee relishes the taste of transcendental life. As Srila Rupa Gosvami states in his *Sri Upadesamrita* (text 7), everything about Krishna is spiritually sweet, such as His names, qualities and activities. But one who suffers from the disease of ignorance cannot taste this sweetness. Yet by chanting the names everyday, a person can destroy this disease and relish the natural sweetness of Krishna's names.

The Hare Krishna mantra is said to contain everything for both material and spiritual well-being. So if one chants Hare Krishna with material desires, he can attain these, as long as they are not too contrary to one's real well-being. And if one wants *mukti*, or liberation from the material world, he can also get that. Then again if one chants the Hare Krishna *maha-mantra* understanding that Radha and Krishna are personally present there enjoying intimate pastimes in Vrindavana, then one can attain Their eternal loving service. Ultimately, the content of the mantra cannot be separated from the *sadhaka's* or practitioner's mentality. Both have a part to play at what will be attained through the use of it.

The essential state of mind that one should have while chanting the *maha-mantra* is described by Sri Chaitanya Mahaprabhu Himself in the third verse of His *Siksastaka* prayers:

One should chant the holy name of the Lord in a humble state of mind, thinking oneself lower than the straw in the street; one should be more tolerant than a tree, devoid of all sense of false prestige and should be ready to offer all respect to others. In such a state of mind one can chant the holy name of the Lord constantly.

The names of God come directly from the spiritual world, Vaikuntha, which means the place of no anxiety. Therefore, the more we are absorbed in *kuntha*, or anxiety caused by material pursuits, the longer it will take for us to reach the Vaikuntha platform. But the more we associate with the Vaikuntha vibration of the *maha-mantra*, the sooner we will progress to the stage of experiencing the ecstasy that comes from awakening our transcendental love for the Supreme. The *Caitanya-caritamrita* confirms that bodily transformations of spiritual ecstasy, such as trembling, perspiration, a faltering voice, and tears, may manifest when one's spiritual love for the Lord is actually awakened.[45]

To begin progressing on the path of chanting the *maha-mantra*, or other mantras, it is prescribed that the practitioner chant on beads called *japa-mala*, similar to a rosary. This consists of 108 beads with one extra head bead, which is larger than the others. This represents the 108 *Upanishads*, or, as described elsewhere, Krishna in the form of the head bead surrounded by 108 of His most advanced devotees, the *gopis* of Vrindavana.

You may be able to purchase a set of *japa* beads at certain import shops or temples. If you cannot find them anywhere, you can also make them. Simply go to a crafts shop and purchase 108 beads of the same size and one larger bead of your choice for the Krishna bead. Also get a length of durable nylon cord. String the 108 beads with a knot in between each one and bring the two ends of the cord through one hole of the Krishna bead and out the other side where you tie the two ends of the cord together in a firm knot. Then cut the remaining lengths of the cord so you have a small tassel. Now you have got your own set of beads for *japa* meditation.

One chants the Hare Krishna mantra once on each bead from the head bead all the way around the 108 beads. This is one round, or one *mala*. Then without chanting on the Krishna bead, turn the beads around in your hand and go in the opposite direction and chant another round. One should set a certain amount of time each day, preferably in the morning, to peacefully sit down or walk and chant the particular number of rounds you have set for yourself. One may chant two rounds, four rounds, or whatever one can do.

For those who are serious, it is prescribed that they chant a total of at least sixteen rounds everyday. With a little practice, this normally takes about two hours. Two rounds will take about fifteen minutes. But one should set a fixed number of rounds to chant everyday. Then one can also spend some time reading spiritual texts, such as *Bhagavad-gita* or *Srimad-Bhagavatam* to enhance his or her spiritual development. A daily program of chanting and reading will produce definite results very quickly.

As with any form of meditation, it is best to do your chanting in the early morning when it is quiet and peaceful, and before your mind starts with the activities of the day. However, you can do it anytime or even at a few different times, such as in the morning and again in the evening to put things back into perspective, especially if you have had a busy or difficult day.

When you are ready to use the mantra, it does not hurt to calm the mind through the basic steps of preparation for meditation such as a few *pranayama* breathing techniques and so on. This is, after all, steps for preparing to attain deeper levels of awareness and consciousness, although this may not be necessary but can be helpful. Then take your *japa* beads and begin intently chanting the Hare Krishna mantra. When the mind is calm and focused, it especially will be able to concentrate on the vibrations of the mantra. As you chant it with your voice, it is received through the ear and considered by the intelligence. From there it goes deeper into the consciousness. Let no other thoughts enter the mind so that the mantra is all there is. Dive deep into the sound of your chanting and feel the vibration of the holy names and the divine energy they emit.

As you become regulated at this, doing it everyday, changes will begin to manifest in your consciousness that may be imperceptible at first, while other changes begin that will be noticeable from the start. You will often notice an internal energy within you that was not there before. Amongst other things, you may feel more sure of your own position and purpose in life, and a closer affinity with God and all beings. Of course, this is just the beginning, so if you do this regularly, deeper insights and realizations will occur as your consciousness acquires more clarity and purification.

This short description does not include that you could also get a real taste for the nectar within the Lord's holy names themselves as you can begin to perceive a reciprocation between yourself and the Lord in His names every time you begin to chant. This takes on a whole different side of spiritual growth that more closely links one to God, which, after all, is the whole purpose of any sort of yoga or religion.

CONCLUSION

This chapter contains descriptions of the glories and effectiveness of chanting the *maha-mantra*. Those who are intelligent will certainly add this spiritual practice to their lives. By taking it seriously, they will soon notice a change in their disposition. They may feel more peaceful, content, happy, etc. One trait that is always noticeable in a person who seriously takes to bhakti-yoga and the chanting of the *maha-mantra* is a decrease in such feelings as anxiety and distress, up to the point of complete fearlessness. Once someone is no longer afraid of death, then what is there to be afraid of in this material world? One loses such fear when he or she is spiritually Self-realized and knows he or she is not this body and, therefore, not actually subject to death, but merely undergoes a transformation of giving up the body. And by taking shelter of the protection of the holy names of Krishna, one will remain spiritually safe in any condition of life.

It is unfortunate that many people in the world are either not aware of this transcendental knowledge or have no taste for it. For such people, extensive material engagements and plan-making are their primary occupation. But this kind of activity is like working hard for nothing because in the end one is awarded only with death, in which all material assets are lost. As stated in *Srimad-Bhagavatam*, nondevotees engage in very troublesome work and cannot sleep well at night because they are absorbed in worldly plans. By providence their ambitions are frustrated and they continue in the cycle of repeated birth and death in material existence.[46]

The only way, therefore, to get release from such material problems and be free from the contamination of the age of Kali-yuga is to take up the practice of bhakti-yoga and regularly chant the Hare Krishna *maha-mantra* while observing the regulations as best as one can. By chanting the *maha-mantra* with faith, a person will eventually purify his or her consciousness and reach success. As more people begin to chant the holy names, the troubles and upheavals found everywhere in the world will diminish, and this age of Kali-yuga can become like the peaceful and bountiful Satya-yuga--the golden age. This is actually the prediction made by Lord Sri Chaitanya Mahaprabhu, who said that love of God will one day inundate the world and drown everyone, regardless of who or what they are.[47] Then many beneficial changes in this world will be seen. Therefore, the best thing any of us can do is to take it seriously.

> Let there be all victory for the chanting of the holy name of Lord Krishna, which can cleanse the mirror of the heart and stop the miseries of the blazing fire of material existence. That chanting is the waxing moon that spreads the white lotus of good fortune for all living entities. It is the life and soul of all education. The chanting of the holy name of Krishna expands the blissful ocean of transcendental life. It gives a cooling effect to everyone and enables one to taste full nectar at every step. (*Siksastaka* 1, written by Sri Chaitanya Mahaprabhu)

CHAPTER NOTES
1. *Srimad-Bhagavatam* 2.1.11-13
2. *Caitanya-caritamrita*, Madhya-lila 17.131-133
3. Ibid., Adi-lila 17.22 and *Padma Purana*
4. *Srimad-Bhagavatam* 2.1.11
5. *Caitanya-caritamrita*, Madhya-lila 15.108
6. Ibid., Madhya-lila, 15.107
7. *Vaisakha-mahatmya* section of the *Padma Purana*
8. *Srimad-Bhagavatam* 11.5.36-37 and 12.3.51
9. Ibid., 11.5.38
10. Ibid., 11.5.32
11. *Caitanya-caritamrita*, Adi-lila, 7.74
12. *Caturmasya-mahatmya* section of the *Skanda Purana*
13. *Srimad-Bhagavatam* 3.33.6-7
14. Ibid., 1.6.34-35
15. Ibid., 11.26.28-30
16. Ibid., 11.31.27-28
17. *Padma Purana* 4.25.8-13

18. *Srimad-Bhagavatam* 11.2.39-40

19. *Padma Purana* 3.50.1-17

20. Ibid., 3.50.17-39

21. *Srimad-Bhagavatam* 6.3.31

22. *Caitanya-caritamrita*, Madhya-lila, 15.109

23. *Srimad-Bhagavatam* 6.2.9-10

24. Ibid., 6.2.12

25. Ibid., 6.2.15

26. Ibid., 6.2.14, 19

27. *Padma Purana* 4.25.22-27

28. *Srimad-Bhagavatam* 6.3.26

29. *Caitanya-caritamrita*, Adi-lila, 8.26, 28

30. *Srimad-Bhagavatam* 6.3.22

31. *Caitanya-caritamrita*, Antya-lila, 20.14

32. Ibid., Adi-lila, 7.73

33. *Bhagavad-gita* 8.7-8

34. *Srimad-Bhagavatam* 3.9.15

35. Ibid., 6.2.49

36. Ibid., 6.2.46

37. Ibid., 6.3.24

38. *Caitanya-caritamrita*, Adi-lila, 3.40

39. *Bhagavad-gita* 4.6-8

40. *Srimad-Bhagavatam* 11.5.32

41. *Caitanya-caritamrita*, Adi-lila, 3.19-20

42. Ibid., Adi-lila, 3.77-78

43. Ibid., Antya-lila, 20.8-9

44. Ibid., Antya-lila, 20.18

45. Ibid., Adi-lila, 8.27

46. *Srimad-Bhagavatam* 3.9.10

47. *Caitanya-caritamrita*, Adi-lila, 7.26

CHAPTER FOUR

Standard Songs Used in the Hare Krishna Temples

This chapter contains the words to songs and mantras used most often in the daily programs of the Krishna temples around the world.

Obeisances to Srila Bhaktivedanta Swami Prabhupada

(Said upon entering the temple room by his disciples, and sung during many arati ceremonies.)

nama om vishnu-padaya
krishna-preshthaya bhu-tale
shrimate bhaktivedanta-
svamin iti namine

namas te sarasvate deve
gaura-vani-pracharine
nirvishesha-shunyavadi-
pashcatya-desha-tarine

Translation

I offer my respectful obeisances unto His Divine Grace A. C. Bhaktivedanta Swami Prabhupada, who is very dear to Lord Krishna, having taken shelter at His lotus feet.

Our respectful obeisances are unto you, O spiritual master, servant of Sarasvati Gosvami. You are kindly preaching the message of Lord Chaitanyadeva and delivering the Western countries, which are filled with impersonalism and voidism.

Sri Sri Gurvashtaka

(Glories of the Spiritual Master, sung for early morning mangala arati,
by Srila Vishvanatha Chakravarti Thakura)

(1) samsara-davanala-lidha-loka
tranaya karunya-ghanaghanatvam
praptasya kalyana-gunarnavasya
vande guroh shri-charanaravindam

(2) mahaprabhoh kirtana-nritya-gita-
vaditra-madyan-manaso rasena
romancha-kampashru-taranga-bhajo
vande guroh shri-charanaravindam

(3) shri-vigraharadhana-nitya-nana-
shringara-tan-mandira-marjanadau
yuktasya bhaktamsh cha niyunjato 'pi
vande guroh shri-charanaravindam

(4) chatur-vidha-shri-bhagavat-prasada-
svadv-anna-triptan hari-bhakta-sanghan
kritvaiva triptim bhajatah sadaiva
vande guroh shri-charanaravindam

(5) shri-radhika-madhavayor apara-
madhurya-lila-guna-rupa-namnam
prati-kshanasvadana-lolupasya
vande guroh shri-charanaravindam

(6) nikunja-yuno rati-keli-siddhyai
ya yalibhir yuktir apekshaniya
tatrati-dakshyad ati-vallabhasya
vande guroh shri-charanaravindam

(7) sakshad-dharitvena samasta-shastrair
uktas tatha bhavyata eva sadbhih
kintu prabhor yah priya eva tasya
vande guroh shri-charanaravindam

(8) yasya prasadad bhagavat-prasado
yasyaprasadan na gatih kuto 'pi

dhyayan stuvams tasya yashas tri-sandhyam
vande guroh shri-charanaravindam

(9) srimad-guror ashtakam etad ucchair
brahme muhurte pathati prayatnat
yas tena vrindavana-natha-sakshat-
sevaiva labhya janusha 'nta eva

Translation

(1) The spiritual master is receiving benediction from the ocean of mercy. Just as a cloud pours water on a forest fire to extinguish it, so the spiritual master delivers the materially afflicted world by extinguishing the blazing fire of material existence. I offer my respectful obeisances unto the lotus feet of such a spiritual master, who is an ocean of auspicious qualities.

(2) Chanting the holy name, dancing in ecstasy, singing, and playing musical instruments, the spiritual master is always gladdened by the sankirtana movement of Lord Chaitanya Mahaprabhu. Because he is relishing the mellows of pure devotion within his mind, sometimes his hair stands on end, he feels quivering in his body, and tears flow from his eyes like waves. I offer my respectful obeisances unto the lotus feet of such a spiritual master.

(3) The spiritual master is always engaged in the temple worship of Shri Shri Radha and Krishna. He also engages his disciples in such worship. They dress the Deities in beautiful clothes and ornaments, clean Their temple, and perform other similar worship of the Lord. I offer my respectful obeisances unto the lotus feet of such a spiritual master.

(4) The spiritual master is always offering Krishna four kinds of delicious food [analyzed as that which is licked, chewed, drunk, and sucked]. When the spiritual master sees that the devotees are satisfied by eating bhagavat-prasada, he is satisfied. I offer my respectful obeisances unto the lotus feet of such a spiritual master.

(5) The spiritual master is always eager to hear and chant about the unlimited conjugal pastimes of Radhika and Madhava, and Their qualities, names, and forms. The spiritual master aspires to relish these at every moment. I offer my respectful obeisances unto the lotus feet of such a spiritual master.

(6) The spiritual master is very dear, because he is expert in assisting the gopis, who at different times make different tasteful arrangements for the perfection of Radha and Krishna's conjugal loving affairs within the groves of Vrindavana. I offer my respectful obeisances unto the lotus feet of such a spiritual master.

(7) The spiritual master is to be honored as much as the Supreme Lord, because he is the most confidential servitor of the Lord. This is acknowledged in all revealed scriptures and followed by all authorities. Therefore I offer my humble obeisances unto the lotus feet of such a spiritual master, who is a bona fide representative of Shri Hari [Krishna].

(8) By the mercy of the spiritual master one receives the benediction of Krishna. Without the grace of the spiritual master, one cannot make any advancement. Therefore, I should always remember and praise the spiritual master. At least three times a day I should offer my respectful obeisances unto the lotus feet of my a spiritual master.

(9) That person who very attentively recites this ashtakam to Sri Gurudeva during the brahma muhurta is sure to achieve direct service to the lotus feet of Sri Krishna, the very life and soul of Vrindavana (Vrindavana-natha), upon attaining his vastu-siddhi, or pure spiritual form.

Additional Prayers Sung During Mangala Arati

The Pancha-Tattva Maha Mantra

(Jaya) shri-krishna-chaitanya
prabhu nityananda
shri-advaita gadadhara
shrivasadi-gaura-bhakta-vrinda

I offer my obeisances unto the Supreme Lord, Shri Krishna Chaitanya Mahaprabhu, along with His associates, Lord Nityananda, Shri Advaita Acharya, Gadadhara, Shrivasa and all the devotees of the Lord. (This mantra is very important and is known as the Pancha-tattva Maha-mantra. In order to derive the full benefit of chanting the Hare Krishna maha-mantra, we must first take shelter of Shri Chaitanya Mahaprabhu, learn the Pancha-tattva mantra, and then chant the Hare Krishna maha-mantra. That will be very effective. So this mantra is sung

in most kirtanas before singing Hare Krishna, as well as before chanting
japa.)

The Hare Krishna Maha-mantra

Hare Krishna Hare Krishna
Krishna Krishna Hare Hare
Hare Rama Hare Rama
Rama Rama Hare Hare

Translation

"Oh Lord Krishna, Oh energy of the Lord, please engage me in
Your devotional service." (This should be chanted exactly like a small child
crying for it's mother. The transcendental sound vibration of this mantra is
the essence of all the *Vedas* and non-different from Lord Krishna
personally. In the temples, this mantra is sung during some portion of
almost all kirtanas.)

Prema-Dhvani or Pranam Prayers

(These prayers are recited after the arati, while everyone joins in
with the "Jaya" at the end of each line. This is a very basic rendition, while
additional lines and obeisances to other personalities and holy places can
be said as well.)
1. Jaya-nitya-lila-pravishta om Vishnu-pada paramahamsa
parivrajakacharya ashtottara-shata Shri Srimad His Divine Grace Srila
A. C. Bhaktivedanta Swami Maharaja Prabhupada ki jaya.
2. Jaya om Vishnu-pada paramahamsa parivrajakacharya ashtottara-shata
Shri Srimad Bhaktisiddhanta Sarasvati Goswami Maharaja Prabhupada
ki jaya.
3. Ananta-kotivaishnava-vrinda ki jaya.
4. Namacharya Haridasa Thakura ki jaya
5. Iskcon founder acharya Srila Prabhupada ki jaya.
6. Premse kaho Shri-Krishna-Chaitanya, Prabhu Nityananda, jaya
Advaita, Gadadhara, Shrivasadi-gaura-bhakta-vrinda ki jaya.
7. Shri-Shri-Radha-Krishna Gopa-Gopinatha, Shyama Kund, Radha
Kund, Girigovardhana ki jaya.
8. Vrindavana-dhama ki jaya.
9. Mathura-dhama ki jaya.
10. Navadvipa-dhama ki jaya.

11. Jagannatha-puri dhama ki jaya.

12. Ganga-mayi ki jaya

13. Yamuna-mayi ki jaya.

14. Tulasi-devi ki jaya.

15. Bhakti-devi ki jaya.

16. Sankirtana-yajna ki jaya.

17. Brihad-mridanga ki jaya.

18. Samaveta-bhakta-vrinda ki jaya.

19. Gaura-premananda Hari Hari bol,

20. All glories to the assembled devotees. (Hare Krishna) All glories to the assembled devotees. (Hare Krishna) All glories to Sri Guru and Gauranga.

Shri Nrisimha Pranam

(Obeisances to Lord Nrisimha, sung at the end of arati)

namas te narasimhaya
prahladahlada-dayine
hiranyakashipor vakshah-
shila-tanka-nakhalaye

ito nrisimhah parato nrisimho
yato yato yami tato nrisimhah
bahir nrisimho hridaye nrisimho
nrisimham adim sharanam prapadye

tave kara-kamala-vare nakham
adbhuta-shringam
dalita-hiranyakashipu-tanu-bhrigam
keshava-dhrita-narahari-rupa jaya jagadisha hare

Translation

I offer my obeisances to Lord Narasimha, who gives joy to Prahlada Maharaja and whose nails are like chisels on the stonelike chest of the demon Hiranyakashipu.

Lord Nrisimha is here and also there. Wherever I go Lord Nrisimha is there. He is in the heart and is outside as well. I surrender to Lord Nrisimha, the origin of all things and the supreme refuge.

O Keshava! O Lord of the universe! O Lord Hari, who have assumed the form of half-man, half-lion! All glories to You! Just as one can easily crush a wasp between one's fingernails, so in the same way the body of the wasp-like demon, Hiranyakashipu, has been ripped apart by the wonderful pointed nails on Your beautiful lotus hands. (This verse is from Shri Dasavatara-stotra, the Gita-govinda, written by Jayadeva Gosvami.)

Tulasi-arati Kirtana

vrindayai tulasi-devyai
priyayai keshavasya cha
vishnu-bhakti-prade devi
satyavatyai namo namaha

Translation

(The first mantra is offering of obeisances to Shrimati Tulasi Devi. Srila Prabhupada explains that the Tulasi tree is a pure devotee of Krishna in the body of a plant. Worship of the Tulasi plant is very important in devotional service.) "I offer my repeated obeisances unto Vrinda, Shrimati Tulasi Devi, who is very dear to Lord Keshava. O goddess, you bestow devotional service to Lord Krishna and possess the highest truth."

namo namah tulasi krishna-preyasi namo namaha
radha-krishna-seva pabo ei abhilashi
ye tomara sharana loy, tara vancha purna hoy
kripa kori' koro tare brindavana-basi
mor ei abhilash bilas kunje dio vas
nayane heribo sada jugala-rupa-rashi
ei nivedana dharo sakhir anugata koro
seva-adhikara diye koro nija dasi
dina krishna-dase koy ei jena mora hoy
shri-radha-govinda-preme sada jena bhasi

Translation

O Tulasi, beloved of Krishna, I bow before you again and again. My desire is to obtain the service of Shri Shri Radha-Krishna.

Whoever takes shelter of you has his wishes fulfilled. Bestowing your mercy on him, you make him a resident of Vrindavana.

My desire is that you will also grant me a residence in the pleasure groves of Shri Vrindavana-dhama. Thus, within my vision I will always behold the beautiful pastimes of Radha and Krishna.

I beg you to make me a follower of the cowherd damsels of Vraja. Please give me the privilege of devotional service and make me your own maidservant.

This very fallen and lowly servant of Krishna prays, "May I always swim in the love of Shri Radha and Govinda."

Devotees circumambulate the Tulasi plant while singing the following prayer:

> yani kani cha papani
> brahma-hatyadikani cha
> tani tani pranashyanti
> pradakshina pade pade

"By the circumambulation of Shrimati Tulasi Devi all the sins that one may have committed are destroyed at every step, even the sin of killing a brahman."

The Ten Offenses in Chanting the Holy Names

The general order of prayers in many temples is that after the Tulasi puja, the ten offenses in chanting Hare Krishna *japa* are recited, usually together with whoever is at the morning program, as follows:

1. To blaspheme the devotees who have dedicated their lives to the propagation of the holy names of the Lord.
2. To consider the names of the demigods like lord Shiva or lord Brahma to be equal to, or independent of, the name of Lord Vishnu.
3. To disobey the orders of the spiritual master.
4. To blaspheme the Vedic literature or literature in pursuance of the Vedic version.
5. To consider the glories of chanting Hare Krishna as imagination.
6. To give mundane interpretation of the holy name of the Lord.
7. To commit sinful activities on the strength of chanting the holy names of the Lord.

8. To consider the chanting of Hare Krishna as one of the auspicious, ritualistic activities which are offered in the Vedas as fruitive activities (karma-kanda).

9. To instruct a faithless person about the glories of the holy name.

10. To not have complete faith in the chanting of the holy names and to maintain material attachments even after understanding so many instructions on this matter. It is also offensive to be inattentive while chanting.

Anyone who claims to be a Vaishnava must carefully guard against these ten offenses in order to quickly achieve the desired success, Krishna Prema!

Now let us offer are respectful obeisances unto all the Vaishnavas, devotees of the Lord. They are just like desire trees who can fulfill the desires of everyone and they are full of compassion for the fallen conditioned souls.

Shri Vaishnava Pranam

(Obeisances to fellow devotees often said after the early *aratis* and before doing *japa*)

vancha-kalpatarubhyash cha
kripa-sindubhya eva cha
patitanam pavanabhyo
vaishnavebhyo namo namaha

Translation

I offer my respectful obeisances unto all the Vaishnavas, devotees of the Lord. They are just like desire trees who can fulfill the desires of everyone and they are full of compassion for the fallen conditioned souls.

Sri Sri Shikshashtaka
by Lord Chaitanya Mahaprabhu

Lord Chaitanya Mahaprabhu did not do much writing, but was widely renowned as a scholar in His youth. Nonetheless, He did leave these eight verses known as Sikshashtaka. These explain the essence of His mission and the philosophy of devotional service to Lord Krishna. See the article on Lord Chaitanya to learn more about Him.

(1)

cheto-darpana-marjanam bhava-maha-davagni-nirvapanam
shreyah-kairava-chandrika-vitaranam vidya-vadhu-jivanam
anandambhdhi-vardhanam prati-padam purnamritasvadanam
sarvatma-snapanam param vijayate shri-krishna-sankirtanam

Glory to the Shri Krishna sankirtana (congregational chanting of
the Lord's holy names), which cleanses the heart of all the dust accumulated
for years and extinguishes the fire of conditional life, of repeated birth and
death. That sankirtana movement is the prime benediction for humanity at
large because it spreads the rays of the benediction moon. It is the life of all
transcendental knowledge. It increases the ocean of transcendental bliss,
and it enables us to fully taste the nectar for which we are always anxious.

(2)

namnam akari bahudha nija-sarva-shaktis
tatrarpita niyamitah smarane na kalaha
etadrishi tava kripa bhagavan mamapi
durdaivam idrisham ihajani nanuragahah

O my Lord, Your holy name alone can render all benediction to
living beings, and thus You have hundreds and millions of names, like
Krishna and Govinda. In these transcendental names, you have invested all
Your transcendental energies. There are not even hard and fast rules for
chanting these names. O my Lord, out of kindness You enable us to easily
approach you by Your holy names, but I am so unfortunate that I have no
attraction for them.

(3)

trinad api sunicena
taror api sahishnuna
amanina manadena
kirtaniyah sada harihi

One should chant the holy name of the Lord in a humble state of
mind, thinking oneself lower than the straw in the street; one should be
more tolerant than a tree, devoid of all sense of false prestige, and should
be ready to offer all respect to others. In such a state of mind one can chant
the holy name of the Lord constantly.

(4)

na dhanam na janam na sundarim
kavitam va jagad-isha kamaye
mama janmani janmanishvare
bhavatad bhaktir ahaituki tvayi

O almighty Lord, I have no desire to accumulate wealth, nor do I desire beautiful women, nor do I want any number of followers. I only want your causeless devotional service, birth after birth.

(5)

ayi nanda-tanuja kinkaram
patitam mam vishame bhavambudhau
kripaya tava pada-pankaja-
sthita-dhuli-sadrisham vichintaya

O son of Maharaja Nanda [Krishna], I am Your eternal servitor, yet somehow or other I have fallen into the ocean of birth and death. Please pick me up from this ocean of death and place me as one of the atoms at Your lotus feet.

(6)

nayanam galad-ashru-dharaya
vadanam gadgada-ruddhaya gira
pulakair nichitam vapuh kada
tava nama-grahane bhavishyati

O my Lord, when will my eyes be decorated with tears of love flowing constantly when I chant Your holy name? When will my voice choke up, and when will the hairs of my body stand on end at the recitation of Your name?

(7)

yugayitam nimeshena
chakshusha pravrishayitam
shunyayitam jagat sarvam
govinda-virahena me

O Govinda! Feeling Your separation, I am considering a moment to be like twelve years or more. Tears are flowing from my eyes like torrents of rain, and I am feeling all vacant in the world in Your absence.

(8)

ashlishya va pada-ratam pinashtu mam
adarshanan marma-hatam karotu va
yatha tatha va vidadhatu lampato
mat-prana-nathas tu sa eva naparaha

I know no one but Krishna as my Lord, and He shall remain so even if He handles me roughly by His embrace or makes me brokenhearted by not being present before me. He is completely free to do anything and everything, for He is always my worshipful Lord, unconditionally.

Jaya Radha-Madhava
(Sung before morning class, written by Shrila Bhaktinoda Thakura)

jaya radha-madhava kunja-bihari
gopi-jana-vallabha giri-vara-dhari
yashoda-nandana braja-jana-ranjana
jamuna-tira-vana-chari

Translation

Krishna is the lover of Radha. He displays many amorous pastimes in the groves of Vrindavana, He is the lover of the cowherd maidens of Vraja, the holder of the great hill named Govardhana, the beloved son of Mother Yashoda, the delighter of the inhabitants of Vraja, and He wanders in the forests along the banks of the River Yamuna.

(Srila Prabhupada was very fond of this song and sang it just before his lectures. In Allahabad and Gorakhpur, Srila Prabhupada fell into a trance after singing the first two lines, and after some time he came back into external consciousness and said: "Now just chant Hare Krishna." Srila Prabhupada said that this song is "a picture of Vrindavana. Everything is there--Shrimati Radharani, Vrindavana, Govardhana, Yashoda, and all the cowherd boys.")

Mantras Chanted Before Class

Om namah bhagavate vasudevaya
I offer my obeisances to the Supreme Personality of Godhead, Vasudeva.

narayanam namaskritya
naram chaiva narottamam
devim sarasvatim vyasam
tato jayam udirayet

Before reciting this Srimad-Bhagavatam, which is the very means of conquest, one should offer respectful obeisances unto the Personality of Godhead, Narayana, unto Nara-narayana Rishi, the supermost human being, unto Mother Sarasvati, the goddess of learning, and unto Srila Vyasadeva, the author. (Srimad-Bhagavatam 1.2.4)

Shrinvatam sva-kathah krsnah
punya-shravana-kirtanah
hridy antah stho hy abhadrani
vidhunoti suhrit satam

Sri Krishna, the Personality of Godhead, who is the Paramatma in everyone's heart and the benefactor of the truthful devotee, cleanses desire for material enjoyment from the heart of the devotee who has developed the urge to hear His messages, which are in themselves virtuous when properly heard and chanted. (Srimad-Bhagavatam 1.2.17)

nashta-prayeshu abhadreshu
nuyam bhagavata-sevaya
bhagavaty uttama-shloke
bhaktir bhavati naishthiki

By regular attendance in classes on the Bhagavatam and by rendering service to the pure devotee, all that is troublesome to the heart is almost completely destroyed, and loving service unto the Personality of Godhead, who is praised with transcendental songs, is established as an irrevocable fact.

Mantras Chanted Before Class Commentary

Sri Guru Pranama
Om ajnana-timirandhasya   jnananjana-shalakaya
chakshur unmilitam yena   tasmai shri-guruve namaha

I was born in the darkest of ignorance, and my spiritual master opened my eyes with the torch of knowledge. I offer my respectful obeisances unto him.

Sri Rupa Pranama
shri-chaitanya-mano 'bhishtam   sthapitam yena bhu-tale
svayam rupah kada mahyam   dadati sva-padantikam

When will Srila Rupa Gosvami Prabhupada, who has established within this material world the mission to fulfill the desire of Lord Chaitanya, give me shelter under his lotus feet?

Mangalacharana
vande 'ham shri-guroh shri-yuta-pada-kamalam shri-gurun vaishnavams cha
shri-rupam sagrajatam saha-gana-raghunathanvitam tam sa-jivam
sadvaitam savadhutam parijana-sahitam krishna-chaitanya-devam
shri-radha-krishna-padan saha-gana-lalita-shri-vishakhanvitamsh cha

I offer my respectful obeisances unto the lotus feet of my spiritual master and unto the feet of all Vaishnavas. I offer my respectful obeisances unto the lotus feet of Shrila Rupa Gosvami along with his elder brother Sanatana Gosvami, as well as Raghunatha Dasa and Raghunatha Bhatta, Gopala Bhatta, and Shrila Jiva Gosvami. I offer my respectful obeisances to Lord Krishna Chaitanya and Lord Nityananda, along with Advaita Acharya, Gadadhara, Shrivasa, and other associates. I offer my respectful obeisances to Shrimati Radharani, and Shri Krishna along with Their associates, Shri Lalita and Vishakha.

Sri Krishna Pranama
he krishna karuna-sindho   dina bandho jagat pate
gopesha gopika-kanta   radha-kanta namo 'stu te

O my dear Krishna, You are the friend of the distressed and the source of creation. You are the master of the gopis and the lover of Radharani. I offer my respectful obeisances unto You.

Sri Radha Pranama
tapta-kanchana-gaurangi   radhe vrindavaneshvari
vrishabhanu-sute devi   pranamami hari-priye

I offer my respects to Radharani whose bodily complexion is like molten gold and who is the Queen of Vrindavana. You are the daughter of King Vrishabhanu, and You are very dear to Lord Krishna.

Sri Vaishnava Pranama
vancha-kalpatarubhyash cha   kripa-sindhubhya eva cha
patitanam pavanebhyo   vaishnavebhyo namo namaha

I offer my respectful obeisances unto all the Vaishnava devotees of the Lord who can fulfill the desires of everyone, just like desire trees, and who are full of compassion for the fallen souls.

Pancha-tattva Maha-mantra
shri krishna chaitanya prabhu nityananda
shri advaita gadadhara shrivasadi-gaura-bhakta-vrinda

I offer my obeisances to Shri Krishna Chaitanya, Prabhu Nityananda, Sri Advaita, Gadadhara, Shrivasa and all others in the line of devotion.

Hare Krishna, Hare Krishna, Krishna Krishna, Hare Hare
Hare Rama, Hare Rama, Rama Rama, Hare Hare

Additional Pranama Mantras
(These, along with the previous ones listed above, are often used during pushpa abhisheka ceremonies)

Sri Bhaktisiddhanta Sarasvati Pranati
namo om vishnu-padaya krishna-preshthaya bhutale
shrimate bhaktisiddhanta-sarasvati namine

I offer my respectful obeisances unto His Divine Grace Bhaktisiddhanta Sarasvati, who is very dear to Lord Krishna, having taken shelter of His lotus feet.

shri-varshabhanavi-devi-dayitaya kripabdhaye
krishna-sambandha-vijnana-dayine prabhave namaha

I offer my respectful obeisances to Sri Varshabhanavi-devi-dayita dasa [another name of Srila Bhaktisiddhanta Sarasvati], who is favored by Srimati Radharani and who is the ocean of transcendental mercy and the deliverer of the science of Krishna.

madhuryojjvala-premadhya-sri-rupanuga-bhaktida-
sri-gaura-karuna-shakti-vigrahaya namo 'stu te

I offer my respectful obeisances unto you, the personified energy of Sri Chaitanya's mercy, who delivers devotional service which is enriched with conjugal love of Radha and Krishna, coming exactly in the line of revelation of Srila Rupa Goswami.

namas te gaura-vani-shri-murtaye dina-tarine
rupanuga-viruddhapasiddhanta-dhvanta-harine

I offer my respectful obeisances unto you, who are the personified teachings of Lord Chaitanya. You are the deliverer of the fallen souls. You do not tolerate any statement which is against the teachings of devotional service enunciated by Srila Rupa Goswami.

Srila Gaurakishora Pranati
namo gaura-kishoraya sakshad-vairagya-murtaye
vipralambha-rasambhode padambujaya te namaha

I offer my respectful obeisances unto Gaurakishora dasa Babaji Maharaja [the spiritual master of Bhaktisiddhanta Sarasvati], who is renunciation personified. He is always merged in a feeling of separation and intense love of Krishna.

Srila Bhaktivinoda Pranati
namo bhaktivinodaya sac-cid-ananda-namine
gaura-shakti-svarupaya rupanuga-varaya te

I offer my respectful obeisances unto Saccidananda Bhaktivinoda, who is transcendental energy of Chaitanya Mahaprabhu. He is a strict follower of the Gosvamis, headed by Srila Rupa.

Srila Jagannatha Pranati
gauravirbhava-bhumes tvam nirdeshta saj-jana-priyaha
vaishnava-sarvabhaumah sri-jagannathaya te namaha

I offer my respectful obeisances to Jagannatha dasa Babaji, who is respected by the entire Vaishnava community and who discovered the place where Lord Chaitanya appeared.

Sri Gauranga Pranama
namo maha-vadanyaya krishna-prema-pradaya te
krishnaya krishna-chaitanya-namne gaura-tvise namaha

O most munificent incarnation! You are Krishna Himself appearing as Sri Krishna Chaitanya Mahaprabhu. You have assumed the golden color of Srimati Radharani, and You are widely distributing pure love of Krishna. We offer our respectful obeisances unto You.

Sri Pancha-tattva Pranama
pancha-tattvatmakam krishnam bhakta-rupa-svarupakam
bhaktavataram bhaktakhyam namami bhakta-shaktikam

I offer my obeisances unto the Supreme Lord, Krishna, who is nondifferent from His features as a devotee, devotional incarnation, devotional manifestation, pure devotee, and devotional energy.

Sambandhadhideva Pranama
jayatam suratau pangor mama manda-mater gati
mat-sarvasva-padambhojau radha-madana-mohanau

Glory to the all-merciful Radha and Madana-mohana! I am lame and ill advised, yet they are my directors, and Their lotus feet are everything to me.

Abhidheyadhideva Pranama
divyad-vrindaranya-kalpa-drumadhaha
shrimad-ratnagara-simhasana-sthau
shrimad-radha-shrila-govinda-devau
preshthalibhih sevyamanau smarami

In a temple of jewels in Vrindavana, underneath a desire tree, Sri
Sri Radha-Govinda, served by their most confidential associates, sit upon
an effulgent throne. I offer my humble obeisances unto Them.

Prayojanadhideva Pranama
shriman rasa-rasarambhi vamshi-vata-tata-sthitaha
karshan venu-svanair gopir gopinathaha shriye 'stu naha

Sri Srila Gopinatha, who originated the transcendental mellow of
the rasa dance, stands on the shore in Vamshivata and attracts the attention
of the cowherd damsels with the sound of His celebrated flute. May they
all confer upon us their benediction.

From the Brahma-samhita
(Sung during the greeting of the Deities)

venum kvanantam aravinda-dalayataksham
barhavatamsam asitambuda-sundarangam
kandarpa-koti-kamaniya-vishesha-shobham
govindam adi-purusham tam aham bhajami

angani yasya sakalendriya-vittimanti
pasyanti panti kalayanti chiram jaganti
ananda-chin-maya-saduj-jvala-virgrahasya
govindam adi-purusham tam aham bhajami

Sri Guru-vandana
(Sung during Guru-puja, worship of the spiritual master, by Shrila
Narottama dasa Thakura)

(1) shri-guru-charana-padma, kevala-bhakati-sadma
bando mui savadhana mate
jahara prasade bhai, e bhava toriya jai,
krishna-prapti hoy jaha ha'te

(2) guru-mukha-padma-vakya, chittete koriya aikya
ar na koriho mane asha
shri-guru-charane rati, ei se uttama-gati
je prasade pure sarva asha

(3) chakhu-dan dilo jei, janme janme prabhu sei
divya-jnan hride prokashito
prema-bhakti jaha hoite, avidya vinasha jate
vede gay jahara charito

(4) shri-guru karuna-sindhu, adhama janara bandhu
lokanath lokera jivana
ha ha prabhu koro doya, deho more pada-chaya
ebe jasha ghushuk tribhavana

jaya jaya prabhupada! jaya jaya gurudeva!

Translation

(1) The lotus feet of our spiritual master are the only way by which we can attain pure devotional service. I bow to his lotus feet with great awe and reverence. By his grace one can cross the ocean of material suffering and obtain the mercy of Krishna.

(2) My only wish is to have my consciousness purified by the words emanating from his lotus mouth. Attachment to his lotus feet is the perfection that fulfills all desires.

(3) He opens my darkened eyes and fills my heart with transcendental knowledge. He is my Lord birth after birth. From him ecstatic prema emanates; by him ignorance is destroyed. The Vedic scriptures sing of his character.

(4) Our spiritual master is the ocean of mercy, the friend of the poor, and the lord and master of the devotees. O master! Be merciful unto me. Give me the shade of your lotus feet. Your fame is spread all over the three worlds. We take shelter of your lotus feet. You are the friend of the most fallen.
All glories to Srila Prabhupada! All glories to Gurudeva!

Sri Nama-Kirtana

(Another nice song sung anytime, but often after greeting the Deities,
by Shrila Bhaktivinoda Thakura)

(1) yashomati-nandana, braja-baro-nagara
gokula-ranjana kana
gopi-parana-dhana, madana-manohara
kaliya-damana-vidhana

(2) amala harinam amiya-vilasa
vipina-purandara, navina nagara-bora
bamshi-badana suvasa

(3) braja-jana-palana, asura-kula-nashana
nanda-godhana-rakhowala
govinda madhava, navanita-taskara
sundara nanda-gopala

(4) jamuna-tata-chara, gopi-basana-hara
rasa-rasika kripamoya
shri-radha-vallabha, brindabana-natabara
bhakativinod-ashraya

Translation

(1) Lord Krishna is the beloved son of mother Yashoda; the transcendental lover in the land of Vraja; the delight of Gokula; Kana [a nickname of Krishna]; the wealth of the lives of the gopis. He steals the mind of even Cupid and punishes the Kaliya serpent.

(2) These pure, holy names of Lord Hari are full of sweet, nectarean pastimes. Krishna is the Lord of the twelve forests of Vraja. He is ever-youthful and is the best of lovers. He is always playing on a flute, and He is an excellent dresser.

(3) Krishna is the protector of the inhabitants of Vraja; the destroyer of various demoniac dynasties; the keeper and tender of Nanda Maharaja's cows; the giver of pleasure to the cows, land, and spiritual senses; the husband of the goddess of fortune; the butter thief; and the beautiful cowherd boy of Nanda Maharaja.

(4) Krishna wanders along the banks of the River Yamuna. He stole the garments of the young damsels of Vraja who were bathing there. He delights in the mellows of the rasa dance; He is very merciful; the lover and beloved of Shrimati Radharani; the great dancer of Vrindavana; and the shelter and only refuge of Thakura Bhaktivinoda.

Govinda Jaya Jaya
(Another nice song that is often used)

govinda jaya jaya gopala jaya jaya
radha-ramana hari govinda jaya jaya

Translation

All glories to Lord Govinda (the giver of pleasure to the senses and cows) and Lord Gopala (the transcendental Cowherd Boy). All glories to Radha-Ramana (another name of Krishna), Hari (Lord Krishna who takes away the material attachments of the devotees) and Govinda.

Prasada-sevaya
(Sung before honoring the Lord's prasada--from Gitavali)

Sharira abidya-jal, jodendriya tahe kal,
jiva phele vishaya-sagore
ta'ra madhye jihwa ati, lobhamoy sudurmati,
ta'ke jeta kathina samsare

krishna baro doyamoy, koribare jihwa jay,
swa-prasad-anna dilo bhai
sei annamrita pao, radha-krishna-guna gao,
preme dako chaitanya-nitai

1. This material body is a network of ignorance, and the senses are one's deadly enemies, for they throw the soul into this ocean of material sense enjoyment. Among those senses the tongue is the most voracious and uncontrollable; it is very difficult to conquer the tongue in this world.

2. Lord Krishna is very merciful and has given us the remnants of His own food just to control the tongue. Now please accept that nectarean Krishna-prasada and sing the glories of Their Lordships Sri Sri Radha and Krishna, and in love call out "Chaitanya Nitai!"

Glorification of the Lord's Prasada
(from the *Mahabharata*)

maha-prasade govinde
nama-brahmani-vaishnava
svalpa-punya-vatam rajan
vishvaso naiva jayate

"O King, for those who have amassed very few pious activities, their faith in maha-prasada, in Sri Govinda, in the Holy Name and in the Vaishnava is never born [again]."

ADDITIONAL KIRTANS

From Shri Shri Shad-goswamy-ashtaka
(Verse 2 is sung before reading The Nectar of Devotion)

Verse 1
krishnotkirtana-gana-nartana-parau premamritambho-nidhi
dhiradhira-jana-priyau priya-karau nirmatsarau pujitau
sri-chaitanya-kripa-bharau bhuvi bhuvo bharavahantarakau
vande rupa-sanatanau raghu-yugau sri-jiva-gopalakau

I offer my respectful obeisances unto the six Gosvamis, namely Sri Rupa Gosvami, Sri Sanatana Gosvami, Sri Raghunatha Bhatta Gosvami, Sri Raghunatha dasa Gosvami, Sri Jiva Gosvami, and Sri Gopala Bhatta Gosvami, who are always engaged in chanting the holy name of Krishna and dancing. They are just like the ocean of love of God, and they are popular both with the gentle and with the ruffians, because they are not envious of anyone. Whatever they do, they are all-pleasing to everyone, and they are fully blessed by Lord Chaitanya. Thus they are engaged in missionary activities meant to deliver all the conditioned souls in the material universe.

Verse 2

nana-sastra-vicharanaika-nipunau sad-dharma-samsthapakau
lokanam hita-karinau tri-bhuvane manyau saranyakarau
radha-krsna-padaravinda-bhajananandena mattalikau
vande rupa-sanatanau raghu-yugau sri-jiva-gopalakau

I offer my respectful obeisances unto the six Gosvamis, namely Sri Rupa
Gosvami, Sri Sanatana Gosvami, Sri Raghunatha Bhatta Gosvami, Sri
Raghunatha dasa Gosvami, Sri Jiva Gosvami, and Sri Gopala Bhatta
Gosvami, who are very expert in scrutinizingly studying all the revealed
scriptures with the aim of establishing eternal religious principles for the
benefit of all human beings. Thus they are honored all over the three worlds
and they are worth taking shelter of because they are absorbed in the mood
of the gopis and are engaged in the transcendental loving service of Radha
and Krishna.

Verse 3

sri-gauranga-gunanuvarnana-vidhau sraddha-samrddhy-anvitau
papottapa-nikrntanau tanu-bhrtam govinda-ganamrtaih
anandambudhi-vardhanaika-nipunau kaivalya-nistarakau
vande rupa-sanatanau raghu-yugau sri-jiva-gopalakau

I offer my respectful obeisances unto the six Gosvamis, namely Sri Rupa
Gosvami, Sri Sanatana Gosvami, Sri Raghunatha Bhatta Gosvami, Sri
Raghunatha dasa Gosvami, Sri Jiva Gosvami, and Sri Gopala Bhatta
Gosvami, who are very much enriched in understanding of Lord Chaitanya
and who are thus expert in narrating His transcendental qualities. They can
purify all conditioned souls from the reactions of their sinful activities by
pouring upon them transcendental songs about Govinda. As such, they are
very expert in increasing the limits of the ocean of transcendental bliss, and
they are the saviors of the living entities from the devouring mouth of
liberation.

Verse 4

tyaktva turnam asesa-mandala-pati-srenim sada tuccha-vat
bhutva dina-ganesakau karunaya kaupina-kanthasritau
gopi-bhava-rasamrtabdhi-lahari-kallola-magnau muhur
vande rupa-sanatanau raghu-yugau sri-jiva-gopalakau

I offer my respectful obeisances unto the six Gosvamis, namely Sri Rupa Gosvami, Sri Sanatana Gosvami, Sri Raghunatha Bhatta Gosvami, Sri Raghunatha dasa Gosvami, Sri Jiva Gosvami, and Sri Gopala Bhatta Gosvami, who kicked off all association of aristocracy as insignificant. In order to deliver the poor conditioned souls, they accepted loincloths, treating themselves as mendicants, but they are always merged in the ecstatic ocean of the gopis' love for Krishna and bathe always and repeatedly in the waves of that ocean.

Verse 5

kujat-kokila-hamsa-sarasa-ganakirne mayurakule
nana-ratna-nibaddha-mula-vitapa-sri-yukta-vrndavane
radha-krsnam ahar-nisam prabhajatau jivarthadau yau muda
vande rupa-sanatanau raghu-yugau sri-jiva-gopalakau

I offer my respectful obeisances unto the six Gosvamis, namely Sri Rupa Gosvami, Sri Sanatana Gosvami, Sri Raghunatha Bhatta Gosvami, Sri Raghunatha dasa Gosvami, Sri Jiva Gosvami, and Sri Gopala Bhatta Gosvami, who were always engaged in worshiping Radha-Krishna in the transcendental land of Vrindavana where there are beautiful trees full of fruits and flowers which have under their roots all valuable jewels. The Gosvamis are perfectly competent to bestow upon the living entities the greatest boon of the goal of life.

Verse 6

sankhya-purvaka-nama-gana-natibhih kalavasani-krtau
nidrahara-viharakadi-vijitau chatyanta-dinau cha yau
radha-krsna-guna-smrter madhurimanandena sammohitau
vande rupa-sanatanau raghu-yugau sri-jiva-gopalakau

I offer my respectful obeisances unto the six Gosvamis, namely Sri Rupa Gosvami, Sri Sanatana Gosvami, Sri Raghunatha Bhatta Gosvami, Sri Raghunatha dasa Gosvami, Sri Jiva Gosvami, and Sri Gopala Bhatta Gosvami, who were engaged in chanting the holy names of the Lord and bowing down in a scheduled measurement. In this way they utilized their valuable lives and in executing these devotional activities they conquered over eating and sleeping and were always meek and humble enchanted by remembering the transcendental qualities of the Lord.

Verse 7
radha-kunda-tate kalinda-tanaya-tire cha vamsivate
premonmada-vasad asesa-dasaya grastau pramattau sada
gayantau cha kada harer guna-varam bhavabhibhutau muda
vande rupa-sanatanau raghu-yugau sri-jiva-gopalakau

I offer my respectful obeisances unto the six Gosvamis, namely Sri Rupa
Gosvami, Sri Sanatana Gosvami, Sri Raghunatha Bhatta Gosvami, Sri
Raghunatha dasa Gosvami, Sri Jiva Gosvami, and Sri Gopala Bhatta
Gosvami, who were sometimes on the bank of the Radha-kunda lake or the
shores of the Yamuna and sometimes at Vamsivata. There they appeared
just like madmen in the full ecstasy of love for Krishna, exhibiting different
transcendental symptoms in their bodies, and they were merged in the
ecstasy of Krishna consciousness.

Verse 8
he radhe vraja-devike cha lalite he nanda-suno kutah
sri-govardhana-kalpa-padapa-tale kalindi-vane kutah
ghosantav iti sarvato vraja-pure khedair maha-vihvalau
vande rupa-sanatanau raghu-yugau sri-jiva-gopalakau

I offer my respectful obeisances unto the six Gosvamis, namely Sri Rupa
Gosvami, Sri Sanatana Gosvami, Sri Raghunatha Bhatta Gosvami, Sri
Raghunatha dasa Gosvami, Sri Jiva Gosvami, and Sri Gopala Bhatta
Gosvami, who were chanting very loudly everywhere in Vrindavana,
shouting, "Queen of Vrindavana, Radharani! O Lalita! O son of Nanda
Maharaja! Where are you all now? Are you just on the hill of Govardhana,
or are you under the trees on the bank of the Yamuna? Where are you?"
These were their moods in executing Krishna consciousness.

Recited Before Reading Krishna Book

krishna krishna krishna krishna krishna krishna krishna he
krishna krishna krishna krishna krishna krishna krishna he
krishna krishna krishna krishna krishna krishna raksha mam
krishna krishna krishna krishna krishna krishna pahi mam
rama raghava rama raghava rama raghava raksha mam
krishna keshava krishna keshava krishna keshava pahi mam

O Lord Krishna, please protect me and maintain me. O Lord Rama, descendant of King Raghu, please protect me. O Krishna, O Keshava, killer of the Keshi demon, please maintain me.

Nama-Sankirtana

1
hari harayenamah krishna yadavaya namaha
yadavaya madhavaya keshavaya namaha

2
gopala govinda rama shri-madhusudana
giridhari gopinatha madana-mohana

3
shri-chaitanya-nityananda shri-adwaita-sita
hari guru vaishnava bhagavata gita

4
shri-rupa-sanatana bhatta-raghunatha
shri-jiva gopala-bhatta dasa-raghunatha

5
ei chay gosair kori charana vandan
jaha hoite bighna-nash abhishta-puran

6
ei chay gosai jar-mui tar das
ta-sabara pada-renu mora pancha-gras

7
tadera charana-sebi-bhakta-sane bas
janame janame hoy e abhilash

8
ei chay gosai jabe braje koila bas
radha-krishna-nitya-lila korila prakash

9
anande bolo hari bhaja brindaban
shri-guru-vaishnava-pade mayaiya man

10
shri-guru-vaishnava-pada-padma kori ash
narottama dasa kohe nama-sankirtana

1. O Lord Hari, O Lord Krishna, I offer my obeisances to You, who are known as Hari, Yadava, Madhava, and Keshava.

2. O Gopala, Govinda, Rama, Shri Madhusudana, Giridhari, Gopinatha, and Madana-mohana.

3. All glories to Shri Chaitanya and Nityananda. All glories to Shri Adwaita Acharya and His consort, Shri Sita Thakurani. All glories to Lord Hari, to the spiritual master, the Vaishnavas, Srimad-Bhagavatam, and Srimad Bhagavad-gita.

4. All glories to Shri Rupa Goswami, Sanatana Goswami, Raghunatha Bhatta Goswami, Shri Jiva Goswami, Gopala Bhatta Goswami, and Raghunatha Dasa Goswami.

5. I offer my obeisances to the feet of these Six Goswamis. Bowing to them destroys all obstacles to devotion and fulfills all spiritual desires.

6. I am the servant of that person who is a servant of these Six Goswamis. the dust of their lotus feet is my five kinds of foods.

7. This is my desire: that birth after birth I may live with those devotees who serve the lotus feet of these Six Goswamis.

8. When these Six Goswamis lived in Vraja, they revealed the lost holy places and explained the eternal pastimes of Radha and Krishna.

9. Just shout the names of Lord Hari in great ecstasy and worship the transcendental realm of Vrindavana while absorbing your mind in meditation upon the divine feet of the spiritual master and the Vaishnavas.

10. Desiring to serve the lotus feet of Shri Guru and the Vaishnavas, Narottama Dasa sings this sankirtana of the holy names of Lord Hari.

Gaura-Arati
(The evening arati song, by Shrila Bhaktivinoda Thakura)

(kiba) jaya jaya gorachander aratiko shobha
jahnavi-tata-vane jaga-mana-lobha

(Refrain:) jaga-mana-lobha
gauranger arotik shobha
jaga-mana-lobha

dakhine nitaichand, bame gadadhara
nikate adwaita, shrinivasa chatra-dhara

bosiyache gorachand ratna-simhasane
arati koren brahma-adi devi-gane

narahari-adi kori' chamara dhulaya
sanjaya-mukunda-basu-ghosh-adi gaya

shanka baje ghanta baje karatala
madhura mridanga baje parama rasala

(Refrain:) madhur madhur madhur baje
shanka baje ghanta baje
madhur madhur madhur baje

(kiba) bahu-koti chandra jini' vadana ujjvala
gala-deshe bana-mala kore jhalamala

shiva-shuka-narada preme gada-gada
bhaktivinoda dekhe gorara sampada

(Repeat first verse of song)

Translation

All glories, all glories to the beautiful arati ceremony of Lord Chaitanya. This Gaura-arati is taking place in a grove on the banks of the Jahnavi [Ganges] and is attracting the minds of all living entities in the universe.

On Lord Chaitanya's right side is Lord Nityananda, and on His left side is Shri Gadadhara. Nearby stand Shri Advaita, and Shrivasa Thakura is holding an umbrella over Lord Chaitanya's head.

Lord Chaitanya has sat down on a jeweled throne, and the demigods, headed by Lord Brahma, perform the arati ceremony.

Narahari Sarakara and other associates of Lord Chaitanya fan Him with chamaras, and devotees headed by Sanjaya Pandita, Mukunda Datta, and Vasu Ghosha sing sweet kirtana.

Conchshells, bells, and karatalas resound, and the mridangas play very sweetly. This kirtana music is supremely sweet and relishable to hear.

The brilliance of Lord Chaitanya's face conquers millions upon millions of moons, and the garland of forest flowers around His neck shines.

Lord Shiva, Sukadeva Gosvami, and Narada Muni are all there, and their voices are choked with the ecstasy of transcendental love. Thus Thakura Bhaktivinoda envisions the glory of Lord Shri Chaitanya.

Shri Damodarashtaka

(Sung every morning during the month of Kartika (October-November) (found in the Padma Purana of Krsna Dvaipayana Vyasa, spoken by Satyavrata Muni in a conversation with Narada Muni and Saunaka Rsi.) "In the month of Kartika one should worship Lord Damodara and daily recite the prayer known as Damodarastaka, which has been spoken by the sage Satyavrata and which attracts Lord Damodara." (Sri Hari-bhakti-vilasa 2.16.198)

(1)
namamisvaram sac-cid-ananda-rupam
lasat-kundalam gokule bhrajamanam

yasoda-bhiyolukhalad dhavamanam
paramrstam atyantato drutya gopya

(2)
rudantam muhur netra-yugmam mrjantam
karambhoja-yugmena satanka-netram
muhuh svasa-kampa-trirekhanka-kantha-
sthita-graivam damodaram bhakti-baddham

(3)
itidrk sva-lilabhir ananda-kunde
sva-ghosam nimajjantam akhyapayantam
tadiyesita-jnesu bhaktair jitatvam
punah prematas tam satavrtti vande

(4)
varam deva moksam na moksavadhim va
na chanyam vrne 'ham varesad apiha
idam te vapur natha gopala-balam
sada me manasy avirastam kim anyaih

(5)
idam te mukhambhojam atyanta-nilair
vrtam kuntalaih snigdha-raktais cha gopya
muhus cumbitam bimba-raktadharam me
manasy avirastam alam laksa-labhaih

(6)
namo deva damodarananta visno
prasida prabho duhkha-jalabdhi-magnam
krpa-drsti-vrstyati-dinam batanu
grhanesa mam ajnam edhy aksi-drsyah

(7)
kuveratmajau baddha-murtyaiva yadvat
tvaya mocitau bhakti-bhajau krtau cha
tatha prema-bhaktim svakam me prayaccha
na mokse graho me 'sti damodareha

(8)
namas te 'stu damne sphurad-dipti-dhamne
tvadiyodarayatha visvasya dhamne
namo radhikayai tvadiya-priyayai
namo 'nanta-lilaya devaya tubhyam

(1) To the Supreme Lord, whose form is the embodiment of eternal existence, knowledge, and bliss, whose shark-shaped earrings are swinging to and fro, who is beautifully shining in the divine realm of Gokula, who [due to the offense of breaking the pot of yogurt that His mother was churning into butter and then stealing the butter that was kept hanging from a swing] is quickly running from the wooden grinding mortar in fear of mother Yasoda, but who has been caught from behind by her who ran after Him with greater speed - to that Supreme Lord, Sri Damodara, I offer my humble obeisances.

(2) [Seeing the whipping stick in His mother's hand,] He is crying and rubbing His eyes again and again with His two lotus hands. His eyes are filled with fear, and the necklace of pearls around His neck, which is marked with three lines like a conchshell, is shaking because of His quick breathing due to crying. To this Supreme Lord, Sri Damodara, whose belly is bound not with ropes but with His mother's pure love, I offer my humble obeisances.

(3) By such childhood pastimes as this He is drowning the inhabitants of Gokula in pools of ecstasy, and is revealing to those devotees who are absorbed in knowledge of His supreme majesty and opulence that He is only conquered by devotees whose pure love is imbued with intimacy and is free from all conceptions of awe and reverence. With great love I again offer my obeisances to Lord Damodara hundreds and hundreds of times.

(4) 0 Lord, although You are able to give all kinds of benedictions, I do not pray to You for the boon of impersonal liberation, nor the highest liberation of eternal life in Vaikuntha, nor any other boon [which may be obtained by executing the nine processes of bhakti]. O Lord, I simply wish that this form of Yours as Bala Gopala in Vrndavana may ever be manifest in my heart, for what is the use to me of any other boon besides this?

(5) 0 Lord, Your lotus face, which is encircled by locks of soft black hair tinged with red, is kissed again and again by Mother Yasoda, and Your lips

are reddish like the bimba fruit. May this beautiful vision of Your lotus face be ever manifest in my heart. Thousands and thousands of other benedictions are of no use to me.

(6) 0 Supreme Godhead, I offer my obeisances unto You. O Damodara! O Ananta! O Visnu! O master! O my Lord, be pleased upon me. By showering Your glance of mercy upon me, deliver this poor ignorant fool who is immersed in an ocean of worldly sorrows, and become visible to my eyes.

(7) 0 Lord Damodara, just as the two sons of Kuvera - Manigriva and Nalakuvara - were delivered from the curse of Narada and made into great devotees by You in Your form as a baby tied with rope to a wooden grinding mortar, in the same way, please give to me Your own prema-bhakti. I only long for this and have no desire for any kind of liberation.

(8) 0 Lord Damodara, I first of all offer my obeisances to the brilliantly effulgent rope which binds Your belly. I then offer my obeisances to Your belly, which is the abode of the entire universe. I humbly bow down to Your most beloved Srimati Radharani, and I offer all obeisances to You, the Supreme Lord, who displays unlimited pastimes.

Saparshada-bhagavad-viraha-janita-vilapa
(Lamentation Due to Separation from the Lord and His Associates)
(Sung on the disappearance days of saints)

1
ye anila prema-dhana karuna prachura
heno prabhu kotha gela acharya-thakura

2
kaha mora svarupa rupa kaha sanatana
kaha dasa raghunatha patita-pavana

3
kaha mora bhatta-yuga kaha kaviraja
eka-kale kotha gela gora nata-raja

4

pashane kutibo matha anale pashibo
gauranga gunera nidhi kotha gele pabo

5

se-saba sangira sange ye koilo vilasa
se-sanga na paiya kande narottama dasa

1. He who brought the treasure of divine love and who was filled with compassion and mercy--where has such a personality as Shrinivasa Acharya gone?

2. Where are my Svarupa Damodara and Rupa Goswami? Where is Sanatana? Where is Raghunatha dasa, the savior of the fallen?

3. Where are my Raghunatha Bhatta and Gopala Bhatta, and where is Krishnadasa Kaviraja? Where did Lord Gauranaga, the great dancer, suddenly go?

4. I will smash my head against the rock and enter into the fire. Where will I find Lord Gauranga, the reservoir of all wonderful qualities?

5. Being unable to obtain the association of Lord Gauranga accompanied by all of these devotees in whose association He performed His pastimes, Narottama Das simply weeps.

Putting on Tilaka

In the Uttara-khanada of the Padma Purana, Lord Shiva says to Parvati that in the middle of the "V" of the Vaishnava tilaka mark there is a space and in that space reside Lakshmi and Narayana. Therefore, the body that is decorated with tilaka should be considered a temple of Lord Vishnu. The Padma Purana also states:

vama-parshve sthito brahma
dakshine cha sadashivaha
madhye vishnum vijaniyat
Tasman madhyam na lepayet

"On the left side of the tilaka Lord Brahma is situated, and on the right side is Sadashiva, but one should know that in the middle dwells Lord Vishnu. Therefore one should not smear the middle section."

One should pour a little water into the palm of his left hand and rub gopi-chandana (mud from Dwaraka) into it. When making Tilaka the following mantra from the Uttara Khanda of the Padma Purana:

lalate keshavam dhyayen
narayanam athodare
vaksha-sthale madhavam tu
govindam kantha-kupake

vishnum cha dakshine kukshau
bahau cha madhusudanam
trivikramam kandare tu
vamanam vama-parshvake

shridharam vama-bahau tu
hrishikesham cha kandhare
pristhe tu padma-nabham cha
katyam damodaram nyaset

tat prakshalana-toyam tu
vasudeveti murdhani

In accordance with the above mentioned mantra one should apply the gopi-chandana with the ball of the middle finger tip to make the tilaka marks on the twelve parts of the body. According to the Brahmanda Purana, one should not use the fingernail to make the space in the middle of the tilaka. One should place a thin damp cloth over the finger and make the space with that. Thus, when the tilaka is applied, the following mantras should be chanted:
The forehead--om keshavaya namaha
The belly--om narayanaya namaha
The chest--om madhavaya namaha
The throat--om govindaya namaha
The right side of the waist--om vishnave namaha
The right upper arm--om madhusudanaya namaha
The right shoulder--om trivikramaya namaha
The left side of the waist--om vamanaya namaha

The left upper arm--om shridharaya namaha
The left shoulder--om hrishikeshaya namaha
The upper back--om padmanabhaya namaha
The lower back--om damodaraya namaha

Finally, after washing one's had, whatever water is left should be wiped on the top of the head in the region of the shikha (tuft of hair) with the mantra: om vasudevaya namaha.

In the *Padma Purana* it is stated:

> nasadi-kesha-paryantam
> urdhva-pundram sushobhanam
> madhye chidra-samayuktam
> tad vidyad dhari-mandiram

"That marking (of tilaka), which begins from the root of the nose and extends up to the hairline, which has a space in it and is very beautiful, is known as urdhva-pundra (tilaka). One should know it to be a temple of Lord Hari [Vishnu]." The Padma Purana also mentions that the tilaka marking should only extend three quarters of the way down the nose from the root of the nose, which is located between the eyebrows. The space in the middle of the tilaka should begin from between the eyebrows and extend up to the hairline. The marking on the nose and forehead should be connected. That is a perfect tilaka marking.

CHAPTER FIVE

Prayers to Lord Krishna for Blessings, Purity and Auspiciousness

smrite sakala-kalyana
bhajanam yatra jayate
purusham tam ajam nityam
vrajami sharanam harim

"I take shelter of Lord Hari, who is the unborn, eternal Supreme Personality of Godhead. Upon remembering Him, a reservoir of all auspiciousness is produced."

(Om) yam brahma vedanta-vido vadanti
pare pradhanam purusham tathanye
vishvodgateh karanam ishvaram va
tasmai namo vighna-vinashaya

"Obeisances unto Him who is the destroyer of all obstacles, who the knowers of Vedanta describe as the Supreme Brahman, and who others describe as the pradhana, or totality of mundane elements. Some describe Him as the supreme male person, or purusha, while others describe Him as the Supreme Lord and the cause of the creation of the universe." (*Vishnu Purana*)

om tad vishnoh paramam padam sada
pashyanti surayo diviva chakshur-atatam
tad vipraso vipanyavo jagrivamsaha
samindhate vishnor yat paramam padam

"Just as the sun's rays in the sky are extended to the mundane vision, so in the same way the wise and learned devotees always see the supreme abode of Lord Vishnu. Because those highly praiseworthy and spiritually awake brahmanas are able to see the spiritual world, they are also able to reveal that supreme abode of Lord Vishnu." (*Rig Veda* 1.22.20)

om krishno vai sac-cid-ananda-ghanaha krishna adi-purushaha
krishnaha purushottamaha krishno ha u karnadi-mulam krishnaha sa
ha sarvaih karyaha krishnaha kasham-krid-adisha-mukha-prabhu
pujyaha krishno 'nadis tasminn ajandantar-bahye yan
mangalam tal labhate kriti

"Lord Krishna is the color of a new rain cloud, therefore He is compared to a transcendental cloud full of eternity, bliss and cognizance. He is the original and supreme person. He is the origin of all activities and the one and only Lord of all. He is the worshipful Lord of the best of demigods, the controller of Brahma, Vishnu and Shiva. Krishna is without any beginning. Whatever auspiciousness is found within or beyond this universe the devotee obtains in Krishna alone" (*Rig Veda, Krishna Upanishad*)

(Om) madhavo madhavo vaci
madhavo madhavo hridi
smaranti sadhavaha sarve
sarva-karyeshu madhavam

"Lord Madhava is in one's words and Lord Madhava is in one's heart. All the saintly persons remember Lord Madhava, the husband of the goddess of fortune, in all their undertakings." (*Narasimha Purana*)

(Om) svasti no govindah svasti no 'cyutanantau
svasti no vasudvo vishnur dadhatu
svasti no narayano naro vai
svasti nah padmanabhaha puroshottamo dadhatu
svasti no vishvakseno vishveshvaraha
svasti no hrishikesho harir dadhatu
svasti no vainateyo harih
svasti no 'njana-suto hanur bhagavato dadhatu
svasti svasti sumangalaih kesho mahan
shri-krishnaha sac-cid-ananda-ghanaha sarveshvareshvaro dadhatu

"May Lord Govinda, Acyuta, Ananta Shesha, Vasudeva and Lord Vishnu bestow auspiciousness upon us. May Nara-Narayana, Padmanabha and Purushottama bestow auspiciousness upon us. May Vishvaksena, the Lord of the universe, Hrishikesh and Lord Hari bestow auspiciousness upon us. May Garuda and the son of Anjana, who is the great devotee of Lord Rama, Hanuman, bestow auspiciousness upon us. May the great and only Lord of auspiciousness, Sri Krishna, who is like a transcendental cloud full of eternity, knowledge and bliss and who is the Lord of all the demigods, bestow upon us all prosperity and auspiciousness." (*Rig Veda, Krishna Upanishad*)

karotu svasti me krishnaha
sarva-lokeshvareshvaraha
karshnadayash cha kurvantu
svasti me loka-pavanaha

"May Lord Krishna, the Lord of the demigods, the presiding controller of all the worlds, bestow auspiciousness upon me. May His devotees, who are the saviors of all people, bestow benedictions of auspiciousness upon me." (*Sammohana Tantra*)

krishno mamaiva sarvatra
svasti kuryat shriya samam
tathaiva cha sada karshnihi
sarva-vighna-vinashanaha

"May Lord Krishna along with His beloved Radha bring about prosperity and auspiciousness at all times. In the same way may the devotee of Krishna, who is able to destroy all obstacles, always bring about auspiciousness." (*Vishnu Yamala Samhita*)

Atharva Vediya Gopala-tapani Upanishad, Purva Vibhaga
(verses 36-47)

om namo vishva-rupaya
vishva-sthity-anta-hetave
vishveshvaraya vishvaya
govindaya namo namaha

"Lord Brahma, speaking to the great sages and saints, prayed to Lord Krishna as follows: I offer my humble obeisances to Lord Krishna, who is the giver of pleasure to the cows, whose external form is the form of the universe, who is the cause of the maintenance and dissolution of the material universe, and who is the Lord of the universe."

namo vijnana-rupaya
paramananda-rupine
krishnaya gopi-nathaya
govindayah namo namah

"I offer my obeisances to Lord Krishna, who is the giver of pleasure to the cows, who is the Lord of the gopis and who is the embodiment of unlimited knowledge and the highest bliss."

namah kamala-netraya
namah kamala-maline
namah kamal-nabhaya
kamala-pataye namaha

"I offer my obeisances to Krishna, who possesses lotus-petal eyes, who wears a garland of sweet-smelling lotus flowers, who has a lotus navel and who is the Lord of the gopis, who are as beautiful as lotus flowers."

barhapidabhiramaya
ramayakuntha-medhase
rama-manasa-hamsaya
govindaya namo namaha

"I offer my obeisances to Lord Govinda, who looks very beautiful wearing a peacock feather upon His head. His plenary expansion is Lord Ramachandra, His intelligence is eternal and ever-fresh, and He is the swan that swims in the mind of Lakshmi-devi."

kamsa-vamsha-vinashaya
keshi-chanura-ghatine
vrishabha-dhvaja-vandyaya
partha-sarathaye namaha

"I offer my obeisances unto Krishna, who is the destroyer of the dynasties of demons headed by King Kamsa. He is the slayer of the Keshi demon and the wrestler Chanura. He is offered prayers by Lord Shiva, whose chariot flag is marked with the insignia of Nandi, the bull, and He is the chariot driver of the son of Pritha, Arjuna."

venu-vadana-shilaya
gopalayahi-mardine
kalindi-kula-lolaya
lola-kundala-dharine

"I offer my obeisances to Krishna, who is accustomed to playing on a flute, who is the protector of the cows and the chastiser of the Kaliya serpent. He is fond of wandering here and there on the banks of the Yamuna and He is beautified by wearing swinging earrings."

ballavi-vadanambhoja-
maline nritya-shaline
namah pranata-palaya
shri-krishnaya namo namaha

"I offer my obeisances again and again unto Shri Krishna, who wears a garland of kisses from the lotus mouths of the gopis. He is conversant with the art of dancing and is the protector of the surrendered souls."

namah papa-pranashaya
govardhana-dharaya cha
putana-jivitantaya
trinavartasu-harine

"I offer my obeisances unto Lord Krishna, who is the destroyer of the sins of the fallen souls. He is the lifter of Govardhan Hill, He brought about the end to the life of Putana and He took away the life of the demon Trinavarta."

nishkalaya vimohaya
shuddhayashuddha-vairine
advitiyaya mahate
shri-krishnaya namo namaha

"I offer my humble obeisances again and again unto the great Lord Krishna, who is beyond the illusion of maya and from whom that illusion comes. He is the supreme pure, the enemy of the demons and is one without a second."

prasida paramananda
prasida parameshvara
adhi-vyadhi-bhujangena
dashtam mam uddhara prabho

"O Supreme Lord, O reservoir of the highest pleasure, be pleased upon me. I have been bitten by the poisonous snake of mental and bodily miseries. Therefore, O Lord, please deliver me."

shri-krishna rukmini-kanta
gopi-jana-manohara
samsara-sagare magnam
mam uddhara jagad-guro

"O Lord Krishna, O lover of Rukmini, O attractor of the minds of the gopis, please uplift me, for I am immersed in the ocean of birth and death, O spiritual preceptor of the universe."

keshava klesha-harana
narayana janardana
govinda paramananda
mam samuddhara madhava

"O Lord Keshava, O destroyer of the three-fold miseries, O only refuge of all souls, O destroyer of the Jana demons, O Govinda, O reservoir of pleasure, please uplift me who am fallen, O husband of the goddess of fortune."

he krishna karuna-sindho
dina-bandho jagat-pate
gopesha gopika-kanta
radha-kanta namo 'stu te

"O my dear Krishna, You are the friend of the distressed, the ocean of mercy, and the Lord of creation. You are the master of the cowherdsmen and the lover of the gopis, especially Radharani. I offer my respectful obeisances unto You."

Mere Man Mandir

This song prays that Lord Krishna, Giridhari, the lifter of Govardhan Hill, will appear to us in the temple (mandir) of our mind (man).

Mere man mandir mein ek bar tum a jao Giridhari
Giridhari Banavari
Manmohan kunjavihari pyare a jao Giridhari

O Giridhari! I am begging You to enter, just once, into the temple of my mind. O Giridhari, O Banavari, You who reside in the groves of Vrindavan and attract our minds towards You. O beloved Giridhari, please come to me.

Bahut bar he ter lagai
karuna nainan mein ghir ai
ye roya ek dukhari pyare a jao Giridhari

So many times have I called out to You with eyes over-flowing with tears. This most unhappy person is pleading before You. So please, O beloved Giridhari, please come to me.

mag johat ankhiyan pathrai
dar dar par maya takarai
ye dekho dasha hamari pyare a jao Giridhari

Simply waiting for You my eyes have become weary. Maya is attacking me at every step. Just see my pitiable condition, O beloved Giridhari, and please come to me.

thori kripa idhar barsao
prem boond pyase ko pao
mein aya ek bhikhari pyare a jao Giridhari

Please shower some of Your mercy here also. Being extremely thirsty, let me drink just a drop of your love. I am nothing but a beggar, begging from you. O beloved Giridhari, please come to me.

bhaint nahin mein kuch bhi laya
khali nath tere dar aya
mein tera prem pujari pyare a jao Giridhari

I have brought You no gifts, my Lord, and have come empty-handed at Your doorstep. I worship You with my love, so O beloved Giridhari, please come to me.

pyar karo chahe thukara do
pas bulao dur bhaga do
mein sab vidhi sharon tihari pyare a jao Giridhari

You are free to love me or reject me. You may call me near or You may send me away. In any condition of life, I am a soul surrendered unto You, please, O beloved Giridhari, please come to me.

Sri Dasavatara-stotra
By Jayadeva Gosvami
These are verses glorifying the ten main incarnations of Lord Keshava, Krishna, from the *Gita-Govinda*. These show that Lord Krishna is the source of all other incarnations of God.

(1)
pralaya-payodhi-jale dhritavan asi vedam
vihita-vahitra-charitram akhedam
keshava dhrita-mina-sharira jaya jagadisha hare

O Keshava! O Lord of the universe! O Lord Hari, who have assumed the form of a fish. All glories to You. You easily acted as a boat in the form of a giant fish just to give protection to the Vedas, which had become immersed in the turbulent sea of devastation.

(2)
kshitir iha vipulatare tishthati tava prishthe
dharani-dharana-kina-chakra-garishthe
keshava dhrita-kurma-sharira jaya jagadisha hare

O Keshava! O Lord of the universe! O Lord Hari, who have assumed the form of a tortoise. All glories to You. In this incarnation as a divine tortoise the great Mandara Mountain rests upon your gigantic back as a pivot for churning the ocean of milk. From holding up the huge mountain a large scar-like depression is put in Your back, which has become most glorious.

(3)
vasati dashana-shikhare dharani tava lagna
shashini kalanka-kaleva nimagna
Keshava dhrita-shukara-rupa jaya jagasihsa hare

O Keshava! O Lord of the universe! O Lord Hari, who have assumed the form of a boar. All glories to You. The earth, which had become immersed in the Garbhodaka Ocean at the bottom of the universe, sits fixed upon the tip of Your tusk like a spot upon the moon.

(4)
tava kara-kamala-vare nakham adbhuta-shringam
dalita-hiranyakashipu-tanu-bhringam
keshava dhrita-narahari-rupa jaya jagadisha hare

O Keshava! O Lord of the universe! O Lord Hari, who have assumed the form of half-man, half-lion. All glories to You. Just as one can easily crush a wasp between one's fingernails, so in the same way the body of the wasp-like demon Hiranyakashipu has been ripped away by the wonderful pointed nails on Your beautiful lotus hands.

(5)
chalayasi vikramane balim adbhuta-vamana
pada-nakha-nira-janita-jana-pavana
keshava dhrita-vamana-rupa jaya jagadisha hare

O Keshava! O Lord of the universe! O Lord Hari, who have assumed the form of a dwarf-brahmana. All glories to You. O wonderful dwarf, by Your massive steps You deceive King Bali, and by the Ganges water that has emanated from the nails of Your lotus feet, You deliver all living beings within this world.

(6)
kshatriya-rudhira-maye jagad-apagata-papam
snapayasi payasi shamita-bhavan-tapam
keshava dhrita-bhrigupati-rupa jaya jagadisha hare

O Keshava! O Lord of the universe! O Lord Hari, who have
assumed the form of Bhrigupati [Parashurama]. All glories to You. At
Kurukshetra You bathe the earth in the rivers of blood from the bodies of
the demoniac kshatriyas [rulers] that You have slain. The sins of the world
are washed away by You, and because of You people are relieved from the
blazing fire of material existence.

(7)
vitarasi dikshu rane dik-pati-kamaniyam
dasha-mukha-mauli-balim ramaniyam
keshava-dhrita-rama-sharira jaya jagadisha hare

O Keshava! O Lord of the universe! O Lord Hari, who have
assumed the form of Ramachandra. All glories to you. In the battle of
Lanka You destroy the ten-headed demon Ravana and distribute his heads
as a delightful offering to the presiding deities of the ten directions, headed
by Indra. This action was long desired by all of them, who were much
harassed by this monster.

(8)
vahasi vapushi vishade vasanam jaladabham
hala-hati-bhiti-milita-yamunabham
keshava dhrita-haladhara-rupa jaya jagadisha hare

O Keshava! O Lord of the universe! O Lord Hari, who have
assumed the form of Balarama, the wielder of the plow. All glories to You.
On Your brilliant white body You wear garments the color of a fresh blue
rain cloud. These garments are colored like the beautiful dark hue of the
River Yamuna, who feels great fear due to the striking of Your plowshare.

(9)
nindasi jajna-vidher ahaha shruti-jatam
sadaya-hridaya darshita-pashu-ghatam
keshava dhrita-buddha-sharira jaya jagadisha hare

O Keshava! O Lord of the universe! O Lord Hari, who have assumed the form of Buddha. All glories to You. O Buddha of compassionate heart, you descry the slaughtering of poor animals performed according to the rules of Vedic sacrifice.

(10)

mleccha-nivaha-nidhane kalayasi karavalam
dhumaketum iva kim api karalam
keshava dhrita-kalki-sharira jaya jagadisha hare

O Keshava! O Lord of the universe! O Lord Hari, who have assumed the form of Kalki. All glories to You. You appear like a comet and carry a terrifying sword for bringing about the annihilation of the wicked barbarian men at the end of Kali-yuga.

(11)

shri-jayadeva-kaver idam uditam udaram
shrinu sukha-dam shubha-dam bhava-saram
keshava dhrita-dasha-vidha-rupa jaya jagadisha hare

O Keshava! O Lord of the universe! O Lord Hari, who have assumed these ten different forms of incarnation. All glories to You. O readers, please hear this hymn of the poet Jayadeva, which is most excellent, an awarder of happiness, a bestower of auspiciousness, and is the best thing in this dark world.

(12)

vedan uddharate jaganti vahate bhu-golam udbibhrate
daityam darayate balim chalayate kshatra-kshayam kurvate
paulastyam jayate halam kalayate karunyam atanvate
mlecchan murchayate dashakriti-krite krishnaya tubhyam namaha

O Lord Krishna, I offer my obeisances unto You, who appear in the forms of these ten incarnations. In the form of Matsya You rescue the Vedas, and as Kurma You bear the Mandara Mountain on Your back. As Varaha You lift the earth with your tusk, and in the form of Narasimha you tear open the chest of the daitya Hiranyakashipu. In the form of Vamana You trick the daitya king Bali by asking him for only three steps of land, and then You take away the whole universe from him by expanding your steps. As Parashurama you slay all of the wicked kshatriyas, and as

Ramachandra You conquer the rakshasa king Ravana. In the form of Balarama You carry a plow with which You subdue the wicked and draw toward you the River Yamuna. As Lord Buddha You show compassion toward all the living beings suffering in this world, and at the end of the Kali-yuga You appear as Kalki to bewilder the mlecchas [degraded low-class men].

108 Names of Krishna

OM SHRI KRISHNAYA NAMAHA
Salutations to Lord Shri Krishna

OM KAMALA NATHAYA NAMAHA
To Kamala's (Goddess Lakshmi's) spouse

OM VAASUDEVAYA NAMAHA
To Vasudeva (Vasudev's son, Krishna)

OM SANATANAYA NAMAHA
To the Eternal One

OM VASUDEVAYA NAMAHA
To the Son of Vasudeva

OM PUNYAYA NAMAHA
To the Meritorious One

OM LILA-MANUSHA-VIGRAHAYA NAMAHA
To Him who has assumed a human form to perform His pastimes

OM SHRIVATSA KAUSTHUBHA-DHARAYA NAMAHA
To the Lord who wears the Shri Vatsa (representing Shri Lakshmi) and the Kaustubha gem

OM YASHODA-VATSALAYA NAMAHA
To Mother Yashoda's darling child

OM HARAYE NAMAHA
To Shri Hari

OM
CHATURBHUJATTA-CHAKRASI-GADA-SHANKADHYAYUDHA
YA NAMAHA
To the Four-armed One who carries the weapons of disc, conch and club

OM DEVAKI NANDANAYA NAMAHA
To Mother Devaki's son

OM SHRISAYA NAMAHA
To the abode of Shri (Lakshmi)

OM NANDAGOPA PRIYATMAJAYA NAMAHA
To Nanda Gopa's darling child

OM YAMUNAVEGA SAMHARINE NAMAHA
To the Lord who destroyed the speed of the river Yamuna

OM BALABHADRA PRIYANUJAYA NAMAHA
To Balabhadra's (Balarama's) dear younger brother

OM PUTANA JIVITA HARAYA NAMAHA
To the Destroyer of the demoness Putana

OM SHAKATASURA BHANJANAYA NAMAHA
To the Lord who destroyed the demon Sakatasura

OM NANDAVRAJA JANA NANDINE NAMAHA
To the Lord who brought great happiness to Nanda and the people of
Vraja

OM SACHIDANANDA VIGRAHAYA NAMAHA
To the Lord who is the embodiment of Existence, Awareness and Bliss

OM NAVANITA VILIPTANGAYA NAMAHA
To the Lord whose body is smeared with butter

OM NAVANITA NATAYA NAMAHA
To the One who danced to get butter

OM ANAGHAYA NAMAHA
To the sinless One

OM NAVANITA NAVAHARAYA NAMAHA
To the Lord who invented a new form of food-butter
(because He consumed large quantities of it)

OM MUCHUKUNDA PRASADAKAYA NAMAHA
to the Lord who blessed (gave salvation) to King Muchukunda

OM SHODASHA STHRI SAHASRESHAYA NAMAHA
To the Lord of sixteen thousand wives

OM TRIBHANGI LALITAKRITAYE NAMAHA
To the Lord who poses bent in three places

OM SUKAVAG AMRITABHDHINDAVE NAMAHA
To the ocean of nectar in the form of Sukadeva's words (spoken as
Srimad-Bhagavatam)

OM GOVINDAYA NAMAHA
To the Lord of the cows

OM YOGINAM PATAYE NAMAHA
To the Lord of the yogis

OM VATSA VATACHARAYA NAMAHA
To the Lord who roamed (in Vrindavana) with the company of calves
and friendly cowherd boys

OM ANANTAYA NAMAHA
To the Infinite One

OM DHENUKASURA MARDANAYA NAMAHA
To the Lord who killed the demon Dhenukasura

OM TRINIKRITA TRINAVARTAYA NAMAHA
To the Lord who destroyed the whirlwind demon Trinavarta

OM YAMALARJUNA BHANJANAYA NAMAHA
To the Lord who broke the two Yamalarjuna trees

OM UTTALA TALABHETTRE NAMAHA
To the Lord who broke the huge trees

OM TAMALA SHYAMALA KRITAYE NAMAHA
To the Lord who is a beautiful as the dark Tamala tree

OM GOPA GOPISHVARAYA NAMAHA
To the Lord of Gopas and Gopis

OM YOGINE NAMAHA
To the greatest Yogi

OM KOTI SURYA SAMAPRABHAYA NAMAHA
To the Lord who is as lustrous as a million suns

OM ILAPATAYE NAMAHA
To the Lord of the Earth

OM PARASMAI JYOTISHE NAMAHA
To the One who is the Supreme Light

OM YADAVENDRAYA NAMAHA
To the Lord of the Yadavas

OM YADUDVAHAYA NAMAHA
To the Leader of the Yadus

OM VANAMALINE NAMAHA
To the Lord who wears a sylvan garland

OM PITA VASASE NAMAHA
To the Lord who wears yellow robes

OM PARIJATAPA HARAKAYA NAMAHA
To the Lord who removed the parijatha flower (from India's garden)

OM GOVARDHANACHALO DHARTRE NAMAHA
To the Lord who lifted Govardhan Hill

OM GOPALAYA NAMAHA
To the protector of cows

OM SARVA PALAKAYA NAMAHA
To the protector of all beings

OM AJAYA NAMAHA
To the all-victorious Lord

OM NIRANJANAYA NAMAHA
To the Lord who is untainted

OM KAMA JANAKAYA NAMAHA
To the Lord who generates desires in the worldly-minded

OM KANCHA LOCHANAYA NAMAHA
To the Lord who has beautiful eyes

OM MADHUGHNE NAMAHA
To the Lord who killed the demon Madhu

OM MATHURA NATHAYA NAMAHA
To the Lord of the holy place of Mathura

OM DVARAKA NAYAKAYA NAMAHA
To the Lord of Dwaraka

OM BALINE NAMAHA
To the all-powerful Lord

OM BRINDAVANANTA SANCARINE NAMAHA
To the Lord who roamed around Vrindavana

OM TULASIDAMA BHUSHANAYA NAMAHA
To the Lord who adorns Himself with tulasi leaf garlands

OM SYAMANTAKA MANER HARTRE NAMAHA
To the Lord who stole the Syamantaka gem

OM NARA NARAYANATMAKAYA NAMAHA
To the Lord who has the twin forms of Nara and Narayana

OM KUBJA KRISHTAMBARADHARAYA NAMAHA
To the Lord who wore the ointment offered by Kubja, the hunchbacked
lady

OM MAYINE NAMAHA
To the Lord of Maya (the illusion)

OM PARAMAPURUSHAYA NAMAHA
To the Supreme Person

OM MUSHTIKASURA CHANURA
MALLAYUDHA-VISHARADAYA NAMAHA
To the expert wrestler who wrestled with the two demons, Mushtika and
Chanura

OM SAMSARA VAIRINE NAMAHA
To the enemy of Samsara (the cycle of births and deaths)

OM KAMSARAYE NAMAHA
To the enemy of King Kamsa (who wanted to kill Krishna)

OM MURARAYE NAMAHA
To the enemy of the demon Mura

OM NARAKANTAKAYA NAMAHA
To the destroyer of the demon Naraka

OM ANADI BRAHMACHARINE NAMAHA
To the beginningless Absolute

OM KRISHNA VYASANA KARSHAKAYA NAMAHA
To the One who removed Draupadi's distress

OM SHISHUPALA SHIRASCETTRE NAMAHA
To the Lord who removed Sisupala's head

OM DURYODHANA KULANTAKAYA NAMAHA
To the destroyer of the dynasty of Durodhana

OM VIDURAKRURA VARADAYA NAMAHA
To the Lord who gave boons to Vidura and Akrura

OM VISHVARUPA PRADARSHAKAYA NAMAHA
To the Lord who revealed His Viswarupa (the Universal Form)

OM SATYAVACHE NAMAHA
To the Lord who utters only truth

OM SATYA SANKALPAYA NAMAHA
To the Lord of true resolve

OM SATYABHAMA RATAYA NAMAHA
To the Lover of Satyabhama

OM JAYINE NAMAHA
To the Lord who is ever victorious

OM SUBHADRA PURVAJAYA NAMAHA
To the elder brother of Subhadra

OM VISHNAVA NAMAHA
To Lord Vishnu

OM BHISHMA MUKTI PRADAYAKAYA NAMAHA
To the Lord who bestowed salvation on Bhishma

OM JAGADGURAVE NAMAHA
To the Lord who is Guru to the whole world

OM JAGANNATHAYA NAMAHA
To the Lord of the whole world

OM VENUNADA VISHARADAYA NAMAHA
To the Lord who is an expert in playing flute music

OM VRISHABHASURA VIDHVAMSINE NAMAHA
To the Lord who destroyed the demon Vrishaba

OM BANASURA KARANTAKAYA NAMAHA
To the Lord who chopped off the hands of the demon Banasura

OM YUDHISTHIRA PRATISHTHATRE NAMAHA
To the Lord who established Yudhisthir (as the king)

OM BARHI BARHAVATAMSAKAYA NAMAHA
To the One who is adorned with effulgent peacock feathers

OM PARTHASARATHAYE NAMAHA
To Partha Sarathi, the chariot driver of Arjuna

OM AVYAKTAYA NAMAHA
To the Lord who is difficult to comprehend

OM GITAMRITA MAHODADHAYE NAMAHA
To the Ocean containing the nectar of the Bhagavad-gita

OM KALIYAPHANI MANIKYA RANJITA SHRI PADAMBHUJAYA
NAMAHA
To the Lord whose lotus feet are adorned with the gems from the hoods
of the serpent Kaliya

OM DAMODARAYA NAMAHA
To the One who was tied with a grinding stone around His waist

OM YAJNABHOKTRE NAMAHA
To the Lord who consumes sacrificial offerings

OM DANAVENDRA VINASHAKAYA NAMAHA
To the destroyer of the Lord of Asuras

OM NARAYANAYA NAMAHA
To Lord Narayana

OM PARABRAHMANE NAMAHA
To the Supreme Brahman

OM PANNAGASHANA VAHANAYA NAMAHA
To the Lord who has a serpent (Adisesha) as His seat

OM JALAKRIDASAMASHAKTA GOPI VASTRAPAHARAKAYA
NAMAHA
To the Lord who (playfully) hid the clothes (left on the shore) of the
Gopis who were engrossed in playing in the waters of the Yamuna river

OM PUNYA-SHLOKAYA NAMAHA
To the Lord whose praises bestow merit

OM TIRTHAPADAYA NAMAHA
To the One whose feet are holy

OM VEDAVEDYAYA NAMAHA
To the source of the Vedas

OM DAYANIDHAYE NAMAHA
To the Treasure of compassion

OM SARVA BHUTATMAKAYA NAMAHA
To the Soul of the elements

OM SARVAGRAHA RUPINE NAMAHA
To the All-formed One

OM PARATPARAYA NAMAHA
To the One who is highest than the highest

Sri Nanda-Nandanastakam
An Old Prayer to Lord Krishna, author unknown

I offer pranama to Sri Nandanandana (the son of Nanda Maharaja,
Krishna), whose face is extremely delightful, from whose beautiful ears
hang jewelled earrings, and whose entire body is anointed with fragrant
chandana.

I offer pranama to Sri Nandanandana, whose eyes are more beautiful than the fully-bloomed lotus, whose head is beautifully adorned with an arrangement of peacock feathers, and who enchants millions of Cupids.

I offer pranama to Sri Nandanandana, from whose beautiful nose hangs an elephant-pearl, whose teeth are brilliantly shining, and whose bodily complexion is more beautiful and lustrous than a fresh rain cloud.

I offer pranama to Sri Nandanandana, whose lotus hands hold the flute, whose lingering gait defeats even that of an impassioned elephant, and whose dark limbs are beautified by a yellow shawl.

I offer pranama to Sri Nandanandana, whose three-fold bending posture is exquisitely elegant, the effulgence of whose toe-nails puts to shame even the moon, and who wears invaluable jewels and ornaments.

I offer pranama to Sri Nandanandana, whose body exudes an extraordinarily beautiful fragrance and whose broad chest is adorned with the kaustubha jewel and the mark of Srivatsa.

I offer pranama to Sri Nandanandana, Vrindavana's expert lover who dresses in a manner that enhances His charming, playful pastimes, and who pulverized the pride of Indra.

I offer pranama to Sri Nandanandana, who as the lover of the Vraja gopis perpetually delights them and who enchants the minds of all living entities.

Whoever regularly recites this Sri Nanda-Nandanastakam with deep faith will easily cross the seemingly insurmountable ocean of material existence and attain eternal residence at the lotus feet of Sri Krishna.

The Krishna Arati

Aaratii Yugala Kishora Kii Kiijai |
Tana Mana Dhana Sab Arpana Kiijai ||

Let us chorus this prayer and wave lights to the two adolescents, Radha and Krishna and offer our body mind and all our riches (to win their gracious favour).

Ravi Shashi Koti Vadana Kii Shobhaa |
Taahi Nirakha Meraa Mana Lobhaa ||
When I look at them, my mind is enamoured of the beauty of their faces
which matches that of a myriad of suns and Moons.

Gaura Shyaama Mukha Nikhrata Riijhai 1
Prabhu Ko Ruupa Nayana Bhara Pijai ||
When one beholds the two faces, one fair and the other dark, one is
instantly fascinated. The poet calls upon all to satiate their eyes with the
beauty of the Lord's countenance.

Kanchanna Thaala Kapuura Kii Baatii |
Hari Aaye Nirmala Bahii Chaatii ||.
Wave the golden platter with camphor burning in it before the Lord who,
manifesting himself, cleanses the heart of all its impurities.

Phuulana Kii Seja Phuulana Kii Maalaa |
Ratna Sinhaasana Baithe Nandalaalaa ||
The Lord, the beloved son of Nanda, sleeps on a couch of flowers and
wears a wreath of blossoms. He has ensconced himself on a throne made
of gems.

Mora Mukuta Kara Muralii Sohai |
Natavara Vesha Dekha Mana Mohai ||
A crown of peacock feathers on his head and a flute in his hand are the
adornments of this showman whose appearance fascinates the mind.

Anga Niila Piita Pata Saarii |
Kunja Bihaarii Giravaradhaarii ||
The body of the Lord, a dawdler in bowers and groves and upholder of a
great mountain, is all blue and yellow silken are his clothes.

Shri Purushottama Girivara Dhaarii |
Aaratii Karata Sakala Nar Naarii ||
Every woman of Vraja, who adores him with festal lights, sings of Lord
Krishna, the upholder of the best of mountains and supreme amongst men.

Nanda Nandana Vrushahaanu Kishorii |
Paramaananda Svaamii Avichala Jodii ||

Inseparable says Swami Paramananda, is the company of Krishna, delight of Nanda and Radha, the youthful daughter of Vrushabhanu.

Krishna Chalisa

Krishna Chalisa means a prayer of "forty verses", which praise and entreat Sri Krishna with devotion. They are recited over and over again to recall the virtues of Krishna, the Lord, in order to aid the disciple to meditate on good and righteous qualities.

ll Doha ll
Banshi Shobhit Kar Madhur, Neel Jalad Tanu Shyam l
Arun Adhar Janu Bimba Phal, Nayan Kamal Abhiraam ll
Puran Indu Arvind Mukha, Pitaambar Shubha Saaj l
Jai Manmohan Madan Chhavi, Krishnachandra Maharaj ll

The sweet sounding flute embellishes your hands, your body dark of hue is like the blue lotus. Your crimson lips are like the bimba fruit, and your eyes are like the pleasing lotuses. Your face is like a fresh- blossoming lotus and radiating like the full moon, and you are beautifully attired in your yellow silken costume.

ll Chaupai ll
Jai Yadunandan Jai Jagvandan, Jai Vasudev Devki Nandan
Jai Yashoda Sut Nanda Dulaare, Jai Prabhu Bhaktan Ke Rakhavaare

Glory, glory to the son of the Yadav race, glory to one who is universally adored; glory to the son of Vasudeva and Devaki. Glory to the beloved son of Yashoda and Nanda, glory to you, O Lord, the protector of your devotees.

Jai Natanaagar Naag Nathaiyaa, Krishna Kanhaiya Dhenu Charaiya
Puni Nakh Par Prabhu Girivar Dhaaro, Aao Deenan Kasht Nivaaro

Glory to the most accomplished player, the subduer of the Naag (cobra snake, you are indeed Kanhaiya, the cowherd. O Lord! You uplifted the Govardhan mountain on the nail of your small finger, Pray come and free the helpless from their distress.

Bansi Madhur Adhar Dhari Teri, Hove Puran Manorath Meri
Aao Hari Puni Maakhan Chaakho, Aaj Laaj Bhaktan Ki Raakho

O Lord, you have the sweet flute touching your lips, Pray fulfill our wishes. Come again, O Lord to eat makkhan (cream), And protect your devotee's honor this day.

Gol Kapol Chibuk Arunaare, Mridul Muskaan Mohini Daare
Ranjit Raajiv Nayan Vishaalaa, Mor Mukut Vaijayanti Maalaa

With reddish chubby cheeks, Your smile is gentle (soft and sweet) and bewitching. You have large lotus-like eyes, you wear crown adorned with peacock feather and you wear Vaijayanti garland.

Kundal Shravan Peetpat Aache, Kati Kinkini Kaachhan Kaachhe
Neel Jalaj Sundar Tanu Sohe, Chhavi Lakhi Sur Nar Muni Mana Mohe

Your ears are elegantly adorned with gold ear-rings, while the trinkets on your corset and the lovely kachani are looking graceful. Gods and humans and sages are entranced at the sight of your beautiful and magnificent body which is like the blue lotus.

Mastak Tilak Alak Ghunghraale, Aao Shyaam Bansuri Vaale
Kari Pai Paan, Putanaahin Taaryo, Akaa Bakaa Kaaga Sur Maaryo

Your forehead is decorated with tilak with lovely braided hair on your head; Please come, O Shyam, the flute player. You liberated the demoness Putana when as a baby, you sucked the dreadful breast of Putana drawing out poison along with her life. Also you killed many a demons like Akaasur, Bakaasur and Kagaasur.

Madhuvan Jalat Agni Jab Jvaala, Bhaye Sheetal ,Lakhitahin Nandalala
Surpati Jab Brij Chadhyo Risaai, Musar Dhaar Baari Barsaai

When wild fire broke out in the forest Madhuvan, Nandalala swallowed up that fierce conflagration and restored the cool. The ruler of gods, Indra, was angered, and Indra produced over Vraj a deluge causing the rains to come down in torrents of cataclysmic and violent downpour.

Lagat-Lagat Brij Chahan Bahaayo, Govardhan Nakhdhari Bachaayo.
Lakhi Yashodaa Man Bhram Adhikaai, Mukh Mahan Chaudah Bhuvan
Dikhaai

When entire Vraj was being drowned, the Lord saved Vraj by
uprooting with one hand Mount Govardhan and sheltering Vraj under it.
For removing doubts in mother Yashoda's mind, you displayed, within your
mouth, the fourteen spheres.

Dusht Kansa Ati Udham Machaayo, Koti Kamal Kahan Phul Mangaayo.
Naathi Kaaliyahin Tab Tum Linhen, Charanchinh Dai Nirbhay Kinhe

When wicked Kansa was causing great havoc, and demanded that
a crore of lotus flowers be sent to him. By overpowering and subduing
Kaliya, you provided safety for all.

Kari Gopin Sang Raas Vilaasa, Sab Ki Puran Kari Abhilashaa
Ketik Mahaa Asur Sanhaaryo, Kansahi Kesh Pakadi Dai Maaryo

You fulfilled the desires of all the Gopis by playing Raas with
them. You eliminated innumerable powerful demons, and with Kansa,
grasping him tightly by the hair, you dragged him hard and killed him.

Maatu Pitaa Ki Bandi Chhudaayi, Ugrasen Kahan Raaj Dilaayi
Mahi Se Mritak Chhaho Sut Laayo, Matu Devaki Shok Mitaayo

Having secured the release of his mother and father from bondage,
you restored to Ugrasen his lost kingdom. You brought back the six dead
sons of Devaki from the underworld and freed her from grief.

Bhomaasur Mura Daitya Sanhaari, Laaye Shatdash Sahas Kumaari
Dai Bhinhin Trincheer Sanhaara, Jaraasindhu Raakshas Kahan Maara

You killed the demon Bhomasur and also the demon Mura; and
freed sixteen thousand maidens who were kept in bondage by Narkasur. By
a cryptic signal by splitting a twig you instructed Bhima as to how
Jarasandha can be slain.

Asur Vrikaasur Aadik Maaryo, Bhaktan Ke Tab Kasht Nivaariyo
Deen Sudaamaa Ke Dukh Taaryo, Tandul Teen Muthi Mukh Daaryo

By killing many demons like Vrikaasur, you eased the distress of your devotees. You removed poor Sudama's poverty, and you ate with relish three handfuls of beaten rice.

Prem Ke Saag Vidura Ghar Maange, Duryodhan Ke Mevaa Tyaage
Laakhi Premki Mahimaa Bhaari, Naumi Shyam Deenan Hitkaari

You ate simple vegetables at the house of devotees like Vidur in preference to the rich fare at Duryodhan's palace. O Shyama! O compassionate to the poor! Having witnessed your abounding grace and glory, I bow to you.

Bhaarath Ke Paarath Rath Haanke, Liye Chakra Kar Nahin Bal Thaake
Nij Gitaa Ke Gyaan Sunaaye, Bhaktan Hriday Sudhaa Barsaaye

You drove chariot during the battle of Mahabharata; you remained unwearied with the discus in your hand. You communicated the wisdom of the Gita and let the hearts of your devotees abound with the nectar of love.

Meera Thi Aisi Matvaali, Vish Pee Gayi Bajaakar Taali
Raanaa Bhejaa Saamp Pitaari, Shaaligraam Bane Banvaari

Mira, your devotee, was so totally engrossed with unbounded devotion to you, that brimming with joy she even drank poison. When O Banavaari, the Rana sent a basket containing a snake, you assumed the form of a Shaligram stone.

Nij Maayaa Tum Vidhihin Dikhaayo, Urate Sanshay Sakal Mitaayo
Tav Shat Nindaa Kari Tatkaalaa, Jivan Mukt Bhayo Shishupaalaa

By revealing your illusory powers to Brahma, you dispelled all his misgivings. When Shishupala reviled you, you terminated his life.

Jabahin Draupadi Ter Lagaai, Deenanaath Laaj Ab Jaai
Asa Anaatha Ke Naath Kanhaiyaa, Dubat Bhanvar Bachaavat Naiyaa

When Draupadi sought your help by pleading, 'O Lord of the distressed! My honor is at stake!' You are, O Kanhaiya, so great a guardian of the helpless orphan that you rescue every sinking boat from the whirlpool of life.

Sundardaas Aas Ura Dhaari, Dayadrishti Keeje Banwaari
Naath Sakal Mam Kumati Nivaaro, Chhamobegi Apraadh Hamaaro

O Lord! Sundardas, an inmate of the hermitage of Durvasa, beseeches You to grant his wishes. O Lord! Dispel all ignorance from his heart and forgive him his faults.

Kholo Pat Ab Darshan Deeje, Bolo Krishna Kanhaiya Ki Jai

May you reveal yourself to him by opening the door of his heart. May we all sing 'Victory, victory to you, Lord Krishna, glory to Kanhaiya!'

ll Doha ll
Krishna chandra ke naam Se, hot praphullit gaay,
tan ghaatak paatak tarat, rog duri hoy jaay.
Chaalisaa jo nit padhai, Kathin kasht kati jaai,
dhan jan bal vidyaa badhaai, nit nar sukh sarsai.
Yah chalisa Krishna ka, path kare ur dhaari,
asht siddhi nav niddhi phal, lahe padaarath chaari.

Whoever with cheerfulness sings this song will have his (or her) three types of troubles removed and will be freed from sins and diseases. Those who recite this Krishna Chalisa with faith and devotion can acquire eight siddhis (supernatural powers through Yoga, viz., anima, mahima, garima, laghima, prapti, prakamya, ishitva and vashitva) and the nine types of treasures.

Om Namo Bhagavate Vasudevaya

Sri-Harer Namastakam

In the above prayers by Lord Chaitanya, there is the mention of the importance of the chanting of the holy names of Lord Krishna. This prayer/song on the glories of the holy name of Lord Hari, Krishna, elaborates on that sentiment and is a great source of knowledge and meditation for our spiritual advancement.

(1)

madhuram madhurebhyo' pi
mangalebhyo' pi mangalam
pavanam pavanebhyo' pi
harer namaiva kevalam

The holy name of Sri Hari (Krishna) is alone the sweetest of all sweet things. It is the most auspicious of all auspicious things and is the greatest purifier of all purifying things.

(2)

abrahma-stamba-paryantam
sarva maya-mayam jagat
satyam satyam punah satyam
harer namaiva kevalam

The entire material creation from Brahma down to the clump of grass is a product of the illusory energy of the Supreme. Sri Harinama is alone reality.

(3)

sa guruh sa pita chapi
sa mata bandhavo' pi saha
shikshayech chet sada smartum
harer namaiva kevalam

If someone teaches us to remember the holy name of Hari alone, then that person is our preceptor, father, mother and friend.

(4)

nihshwase nahi vishvasaha
kada ruddho bhavishyati
kirtaniya mato balyad
harer namaiva kevalam

There is no certainty in when our last breath will come. Therefore the name of Hari must be exclusively chanted from one's very childhood.

(5)

harih sada vaset tatra
yatra bhagavata janaha

gayanti bhakti-bhavena
harer namaiva kevalam

Sri Hari eternally dwells in that place where great souls chant His holy name alone with great devotion.

(6)
aho duhkham maha-duhkham
duhkhad duhkhataram yataha
kachayam vismritam ratna
harer namaiva kevalam

Alas, what a sadness, what a great sorrow, it is more painful than any misery, that this jewel of the Harinama [the holy name of Lord Hari] has been mistaken as a piece of glass and has thus been forgotten by the general mass of people.

(7)
diyatam diyatam karno
niyatam niyatam vachaha
giyatam giyatam nityam
harer namaiva kevalam

Hear again and again, utter over and over, eternally sing and sing again the name of Hari alone.

(8)
trina-kritya jagat sarvam
rajate sakala-param
chid-ananda-mayam shuddham
harer namaiva kevalam

It is the Harinama alone which is full of ecstasy and divine knowledge. It is the supreme pure and reigns supreme over all, making the entire universe seem as insignificant as a blade of grass.

Man Radhe Krishna
This song asks our mind to simply focus and become absorbed on chanting the names of Radha and Krishna.

man Radhe Krishna, Radhe Krishna, Radhe Krishna bol
Radhe Krishna bol re, Radha Krishna bol

Vrindavan mein khelan avein
lata pata phoolan barsavein
madhu dhara ki nadi bahavein
man phool bichhi galiyan mein dole

Yamuna darshan karne ai
van ki chata badi sukhdai
hans mandali vahan ghir ai
kamalan ki mala le ai
man dekh yugal chavi kare kilol
Radhe kare kilol, Shyama kare kilol

Please, O mind, simply chant Radhe Krishna, Radhe Krishna, Radhe Krishna! Please chant Radhe Krishna, chant Radhe Krishna.

When Lord Krishna comes to play in Vrindavana, the creepers shower a rain of leaves and flowers. Honey flows from the flowers like a river and the mind meanders through lanes strewn with the blossoms.

Yamunadevi has come to behold the beautiful form of Krishna. The beauty of the forest brings great pleasure. Flocks of swans have wandered there, bringing with them a garland of lotus flowers. Beholding the beautiful forms of Radha and Krishna, the mind is singing. O Radha, my mind is singing. O Shyama [Krishna], my mind is singing.

CHAPTER SIX

The Govindam Prayers from the Brahma Samhita

These prayers are by Lord Brahma after his realization of Lord Krishna's supreme nature. They hold much spiritual insight and are chanted to invoke the spiritual atmosphere while engaged in devotional activities. They compose verses 1 and 29-55 of the *Brahma-samhita*.

> ishvarah paramah krishnah
> sac-cid-ananda-vigrahaha
> anadir adir govindaha
> sarva-karana-karanam

Krishna, Who is known as Govinda, is the Supreme Personality of Godhead. He has an eternal blissful spiritual body. He is the Origin of all. He has no other origin and He is the Prime Cause of all causes.

> chintamani prakara-sadmasu kalpa-vriksha-
> laksavriteshu surabhir abhipalayantam
> lakshmi-sahasra-shata-sambhrama-sevyamanam
> govindam adi-purusham tam aham bhajami

I worship Govinda, the Primeval Lord, the First Progenitor Who is tending the cows, yielding all desires, in abodes built with spiritual gems, surrounded by millions of purpose-trees, always served with great reverence and affection by hundreds of thousands of Lakshmis or Gopis.

> Venum kvanantam aravinda-dalayataksam
> barhavatam samasitambuda-sundarangam
> kandarpa-koti-kamaniya vishesha-shobham
> govindam adi-purusham tam aham bhajami

I worship Govinda, the Primeval Lord, Who is adept in playing on His flute, with blooming eyes like lotus petals, with head bedecked with peacock's feather, with the figure of beauty tinged with the hue of blue clouds, and His unique loveliness charming millions of cupids.

alola-chandraka-lasad-vanamalya-vamshi-
ratnangadam pranaya-keli-kala-vilasam
shyamam tribhanga-lalitam niyata-prakasham
govindam adi-purusham tam aham bhajami

I worship Govinda, the Primeval Lord, round Whose neck is swinging a garland of flowers beautified with the Moon-locket, Whose two hands are adorned with the flute and jeweled ornaments, Who always revels in pastimes of love, Whose graceful three-fold bending form of Shyamasundara is eternally manifest.

angani yasya sakalendriya-vrittimanti
pashyanti panti kalayanti chiram jaganti
ananda-chinmaya-sad-ujjvala-vigrahasya
govindam adi-purusham tam aham bhajami

I worship Govinda, the Primeval Lord, Whose transcendental form is full of bliss, truth, substantiality and is thus full of the most dazzling splendour. Each of the limbs of that Transcendental Figure possesses in Himself, the fullfledged functions of all the organs, and eternally sees, maintains and manifests the infinite universes, both spiritual and mundane.

advaitam achyutam anadim ananta-rupam
adyam purana-purusham navayauvanam cha
vedesu durlabham adurlabham atma-bhaktau
govindam adi-purusham tam aham bhajami

I worship Govinda, the Primeval Lord, Who is inaccessible to the Vedas, but obtainable by pure unalloyed devotion of the soul, Who is without a second, Who is not subject to decay and is without a beginning, Whose Form is endless, Who is the beginning, Whose Form is endless, Who is the beginning, and the eternal Purusha; yet He is a Person possessing the beauty of blooming youth.

> panthas tu koti-shata-vatsara-sampragamyo
> vayor athapi manaso muni-pungavanam
> so 'pyasti yat prapada-simny avichintya-tattve
> govindam adi-purusham tam aham bhajami

I worship Govinda, the Primeval Lord, only the tip of the toe of whose lotus feet is approached by the yogis who aspire after the transcendental and betake themselves to pranayama by drilling the respiration; or by the jnanins who try to search out the nondifferentiated Brahman by the process of elimination of the mundane extending over thousands of millions of years.

> eko 'py asau rachayitum jagad-anda-kotim
> yac chaktir asti jadad-anda-chaya yad-antah
> andantara-stha-paramanu-chayantara-stham
> govindam adi-purusham tam aham bhajami

He is an undifferentiated Entity as there is no distinction between potency and the Possessor thereof. In His work of creation of millions of worlds, His potency remains inseparable. All the universes exist in Him and He is present in His fullness in everyone of the atoms that are scattered through the universe, at one and the same time. Such is the Primeval Lord whom I adore.

> yad bhava-bhavita dhiyo manujas tathaiva
> samprapya rupa-mahimasanayanabhushaha
> suktair yam eva nigama-prathitaih stuvanti
> govindam adi-purusham tam aham bhajami

I adore the same Govinda, the Primeval Lord, in Whose praise men, who are imbued with devotion, sing the mantra-suktas contained in the Vedas, by gaining their appropriate beauty, greatness, thrones, conveyances and ornaments.

> ananda-chinmaya-rasa-pratibhavitabhis-
> tabhir ya eva nija-rupataya kalabhihi
> goloka eva nivasaty akhilatma-bhuto
> govindam adi-purusham tam aham bhajami

I worship Govinda, the Primeval Lord, residing in His own realm, Goloka, with Radha, resembling His own spiritual figure, the Embodiment of the Ecstatic potency possessed of the sixty-four artistic activities, in the company of Her confidants (sakhis), embodiments of the extensions of her body, permeated and vitalized by His ever-blissful spiritual rasa.

> premanjana-cchurita-bhakti-vilochanena
> santah sadaiva hridayeshu vilokayanti
> yam shyama-sundaram achintya-guna-svarupam
> govindam adi-purusham tam aham bhajami

I worship Govinda, the Primeval Lord, Who is Shyamasundara, Krishna Himself with inconceivable innumerable attributes, whom the pure devotees see in their heart of hearts, with the eye of devotion tinged with the salve of love.

> ramadi-murtishu kala-niyamena tishthan
> nanavataram akarod bhuvaneshu kintu
> krishnah svayam samabhavat paramaha puman yo
> govindam adi-purusham tam aham bhajami

I worship Govinda, the Primeval Lord, Who manifested Himself personally as Krishna and the different avataras in the world in the forms of Rama, Nrisimha, Vamana, etc., as His subjective portions.

> yasya prabha prabhavato jagad-anda-koti-
> kotisu ashesha-vasudhadi-vibhuti-bhinnam
> tad brahma nishkalam anantam ashesha-bhutam
> govindam adi-purusham tam aham bhajami

I worship Govinda, the Primeval Lord, whose effulgence is the source of the nondifferentiated Brahman mentioned in the Upanishads, being differentiated from the infinity of glories of the mundane universe, appears as the Indivisible, Infinite and Limitless Truth.

> maya hi yasya jagad-anda-shatani sute
> traigunya-tad-vishaya-veda-vitayamana
> sattvavalambi-para-sattva-visuddha-sattvam
> govindam adi-purusham tam aham bhajami

I worship Govinda, the Primeval Lord, Who is the Absolute Substantive Principle being the ultimate entity in the form of the Support of all existence, Whose external potency embodies the three-fold mundane qualities, viz., sattva, rajas, and tamas and diffuses the Vedic knowledge regarding the mundane world.

> ananda-chinmaya-rasatmataya manahsu
> yah praninam pratiphalam smaratam upetya
> lilayitena bhuvanani jayaty ajasram
> govindam adi-purusham tam aham bhajami

I worship Govinda, the Primeval Lord, Whose glory ever triumphantly dominate the mundane world by the activity of His own pastimes, being reflected in the minds of recollecting souls as the Transcendental Entity of ever-blissful cognitive rasa.

> goloka-namni nija-dhamni tale cha tasya
> devi-mahesha-hari-dhamasu teshu teshu
> te te prabhava-nichaya vihitash cha yena
> govindam adi-purusham tam aham bhajami

Lowest of all is located Devi-dhama (mundane world), next above it is Mahesha-dhama (abode of Mahesh, Shiva); above Mahesh-dhama is placed Hari-dhama (abode of Hari) and above them all is located Krishna's own realm named Goloka. I adore the Primeval Lord Govinda, who has allotted their respective authorities to the rules of those graded realms.

> srishti-sthiti-pralaya-sadhana-shaktir eka
> chayeva yasya bhuvanani vibharti durga
> icchanurupam api yasya che cheshtate sa
> govindam adi-purusham tam aham bhajami

The external potency Maya who is of the nature of the shadow of the Chit potency, is worshiped by all people as Durga, the creating, preserving and destroying agency of this mundane world. I adore the Primeval Lord Govinda in accordance with Whose will Durga conducts herself.

> kshiram yatha dadhi vikara-vishesha-yogat
> sanjayate na hi tatah prithag asti hetoho

yah shambhutam api tatha samupaiti karyad
govindam adi-purusham tam aham bhajami

Just as milk is transformed into curd (yogurt) by the action of acids, but yet
the effect "curd" is neither the same as, nor different from, its cause, viz.,
milk, so I adore the Primeval Lord Govinda of whom the state of Sambu is
transformation for the performance of the work of destruction.

diparchir eva hi dashantaram abhyupetya
dipayate vivrita-hetu-samana-dharma
yas tadrig eva hi cha vishnu-taya vibhati
govindam adi-purusham tam aham bhajami

The light of one candle being communicated to other candles, although it
burns separately in them, is the same in its quality. I adore the Primeval
Lord Govinda who exhibits Himself equally in the same mobile manner in
His various manifestations.

yah karanarnava-jale bhajati sma yoga-
nidram ananta-jagad-anda-saroma-kupaha
adhara-shaktim avalambya param sva-murtim
govindam adi-purusham tam aham bhajami

I adore the Primeval Lord Govinda who assumes His own great subjective
form, who bears the name of Shesha. Replete with the all-accommodating
potency, and reposing in the causal ocean with the infinity of the world in
the pores of His hair, He enjoys creative sleep (yoga-nidra).

yasyaika-nishvasita-kalam athavalambya
jivanti loma-vilaja jagad-anda-nathaha
vishnur mahan sa iha yasya kala-vishesho
govindam adi-purusham tam aham bhajami

Brahma and other lords of the mundane worlds, appearing from the pores
of hair of Maha-Vishnu, remain alive as long as the duration of one
exhalation of the latter (Maha-Vishnu). I adore the Primeval Lord Govinda
of Whose subjective personality Maha-Vishnu is the Portion of a Portion
[of the Surpeme].

bhasvan yathashma-shakaleshu nijeshu tejaha
sviyam kiyat prakatayaty api tadvad atra
brahma ya esa jagad-anda-vidhana-karta
govindam adi-purusham tam aham bhajami

I adore the Primeval Lord Govinda from Whom the separated subjective portion Brahma receives his power for the regulation of the mundane world, just as the Supreme manifests some portion of His own light in all effulgent gems that bear the names of Surya-kanta, etc.

yat-pada-pallava-yugam vinidhaya kumbha-
dvandve pranama-samayesa ganadhirajaha
vighnan vihantum alam asya jagat-trayasya
govindam adi-purusham tam aham bhajami

I adore the Primeval Lord Govinda, Whose lotus feet are always held by Ganesh upon the pair of tumuli protruding from his elephant head in order to obtain power for his function of destroying all the obstacles on the path of progress of the three-worlds.

agnir mahi gaganam ambu marud-dishash cha
kalas tathatma-manasiti jagat-trayani
yasmad bhavanti vibhavanti vishanti yam cha
govindam adi-purusham tam aham bhajami

The three-worlds are composed of the nine elements, viz., fire, earth, ether, water, air, direction, time, soul and mind. I adore the Primeval Lord Govinda from Whom they originate, in Whom they exist and into Whom they enter at the time of the Universal Cataclysm.

yac chakshur esha savita sakala-grahanam
raja samasta-sura-murtir ashesha-tejaha
yasyajnaya bhramati sambhrita-kala-chakro
govindam adi-purusham tam aham bhajami

The sun, who is the king of all the planets, full of infinite effulgence, the image of the good soul, is the eye of this world. I adore the Primeval Lord Govinda in pursuance of Whose order the sun performs his journey mounting the wheel of time.

dharmo 'tha papa-nichayah shrutayas tapamshi
brahmadi-kita-patagavadhayash cha jivaha
yad datta-matra-vibhava-prakata-prabhava
govindam adi-purusham tam aham bhajami

I adore the Primeval Lord Govinda, by Whose conferred power are maintained the manifested potencies that are found to exist in all virtues, in the Vedas, in the penances and in all jivas from Brahma down to the meanest insect.

yas tv indra-gopam athavendra-maho sva-karma-
bandhanurupa-phala-bhajanam atanoti
karmani nirdahati kintu cha bhakti-bhajam
govindam adi-purusham tam aham bhajami

I adore the Primeval Lord Govinda, Who burns up to their roots all fruitive activities of those who are imbued with devotion and impartially ordains for each the due enjoyment of the fruits of one's activities, of all those who walk in the path of work, in accordance with the chain of their previously performed works, no less in the case of the tiny insect that bears the name of "Indragopa" than in that of Indra, king of the devas.

yam krodha-kama-sahaja-pranayadi-bhiti-
vatsalya-moha-guru-gaurava-sevya-bhavaihai
sanchintya tasya sadrishim tanum apurete
govindam adi-purusham tam aham bhajami

I adore the Primeval Lord Govinda, the meditators of Whom, by meditating upon Him under the sway of wrath, amorous passion, natural friendly love, fear, parental affection, delusion, reverence and willing service, attain to bodily forms befitting the nature of their contemplation.

CHAPTER SEVEN

Prayers to Sri Sri Radha and Lord Krishna

Provides a beautiful selection of verses, and two peerless mantras from the *Sri Sanatkumara-samhita* as advised by Lord Sadashiva.

tato vrindavanam dhayet
paramananda-vardhanam
sarvartu-kusumopetam
patatri-gana-naditam

bhramad-bhramara-jhankara
mukhari-krita-din-mukham
kalindi-jala-kallola-
sangi-martua-sevitam

nana-pushpa-latalbaddha-
vriksha-sandaish cha manditam
kamalotpala-kahlara-
dhuli-dhusaritantaram

tan-madhye ratna-bhumim cha
suryayuta-sama-prabham
tatra kalpatarudyanam
niyatam prema-varshinam

manikya-shikharalambi
tan-madhye mani-mandapam
nana-ratna-ganaish chitram
sarvartu-suvirajitam

nana-ratna-lasac-chitra-
vitanair upashobhitam
ratna-torana-gopura-
manikyacchadananvitam

koti-surya-samabhasam
vimuktam shat-tarangakaih

tan-madhye ratna-khachitam
svarna-simhasanam mahat
kamalotpala-kahlara-
dhuli-dhusaritantaram

"Vrindavana-dhama is a place of ever-increasing joy. Flowers and fruits of all seasons grow there, and that transcendental land is full of the sweet sound of various birds. All directions resound with the humming of bumblebees, and it is served with cool breezes and the waters of the Jamuna. Vrindavana is decorated with wish-fulfilling trees wound with creepers and beautiful flowers. Its divine beauty is ornamented with the pollen of red, blue and white lotuses. The ground is made of jewels whose dazzling glory is equal to a myriad of suns rising in the sky at one time. On that ground is a garden of desire trees, which always shower divine love. In that garden is a jeweled temple whose pinnacle is made of rubies. It is decorated with various jewels, so it remains brilliantly effulgent through all seasons of the year. The temple is beautified with bright-colored canopies, glittering with various gems, and endowed with ruby-decorated coverings and jeweled gateways and arches. Its splendor is equal to millions of suns, and it is eternally free from the six waves of material miseries. In that temple there is a great golden throne inlaid with many jewels. In this way one should meditate on the divine realm of the Supreme Lord, Sri Vrindavana-dhama." (*Gautamiya Tantra* 4)

divyad-vrindaranya-kalpa-drumadhah-
shrimad-ratnagara-simhasana-sthau
shri-shri-radha-shrila-govinda-devau
preshthalibhih sevyamanau smarami

"I mediate on Shri Shri Radha and Govinda, who sit on an effulgent throne underneath a desire tree in a temple of jewels in Vrindavana. They

are being served by Their most confidential associates, the gopis."
(*Chaitanya-charitamrita*, Adi-lila, 1.16)

> sat-pundarika-nayanam
> meghabham vaidyutambaram
> dvi-bhujam jnana-mulradhyam
> vana-malinam ishvaram

> divyalankaranopetam
> sakhibhih pariveshtitam
> chid-ananda-ghanam krishnam
> radhalingita-vigraham

> shri krishnam shri-ghana-shyamam
> purnananda-kalevaram
> dvi-bhujam sarva-devesham
> radhalingita-vigraham

"I meditate on the Supreme Lord, Shri Krishna, who possesses beautiful lotus eyes, whose color is that of a new cloud, whose clothes are like lightning, who possesses two arms and a beautiful forest garland, and whose hand is indicating divine knowledge by exhibiting the jnana-mudra. That Krishna is decorated with glittering ornaments and is surrounded by all the cowherd friends of Shrimati Radharani. While being embraced by Shrimati Radharani Herself, His form is intensified consciousness and bliss. Shri Krishna, who is intensely bluish-black, in His two-armed form, is the Lord of all the demigods, and His body is full of transcendental bliss."

> samsara-sagaran natha
> putra-mitra-grihanganat
> goptarau me yuvam eva
> prapanna-bhaya-bhanjanau

"O Radha-Krishna, You are my protectors from the ocean of material existence which is characterized by sons, friends, household and land. Therefore You are known as the destroyers of the fear of those who are surrendered unto You."

yo 'ham mamasti yat-kinchid
iha loka paratra cha
tat sarvam bhavato 'dyaiva
charaneshu samarpitam

"O Your Lordships, myself and whatever little bit is mine in this world and in the next, all that I now offer unto Your lotus feet."

aham apy aparadhanam
alayas tyakta sadhanaha
agatis cha tato nathau
bhavantau me para gatih

"O Your Lordships, I am certainly the abode of many offenses, and am completely devoid of the practice of devotional service; neither do I have any resort or shelter. Therefore, I am taking You as my ultimate goal."

tavasmi radhika-natha
karmana manasa gira
krishna-kante tavaivasmi
yuvam eva gatir mama

sharanam vam prapanno 'smi
karuna-nikarakarau
prasadam kuru dasyam bho
mayi dushte 'paradhini

"O Lord of Shrimati Radharani, I am Yours; my actions, mind and words. O lover of Shri Krishna, Shrimate Radharani, I belong to You alone. You both are my only shelter. O Radha and Krishna, ocean of mercy, I am taking shelter of You. Please be pleased upon me and make me Your servant, although I am such a fallen offender."

mat-samo nasti papatma
naparadhi cha kashchana
parihare 'pi lajja me
kim bruve purushottama

yuvatinam yatha yuni
yunam cha yuvatuu yatha

mano 'bhiramate tadvan
mano me ramatam tvayi

"O Purushottama, there is no sinful person or offender who is equal
to me. How can I describe my shame? Just as the minds of young ladies
take pleasure in a young man, and the minds of young men take pleasure in
a young woman, kindly let my mind take pleasure in You alone."

bhumau skhakita-padanam
bhumir evavalambanam
tvayi jataparadhanam
tvam eva sharanam prabho

"Just as the ground is the only support for those whose feet have
slipped, so also You alone are the only shelter, even for those who have
committed offense to You."

govinda-vallabhe radhe
prarthaye tvam aham sada
tvadiyam iti janatu
govindo mam tvaya saha

"O Shrimati Radharani, the dearest of Lord Govinda, this is always
my request to You--please let Lord Govinda, along with Yourself, consider
me to be one of Your assistants."

radhe vrindavanadhishe
karunamrita-vahini
kripaya nija-padabja-
dasyam mahyam pradiyatam

"O Shrimati Radharani, O Queen of Vrindavana, You are a river
flowing with the nectar of mercy. Please be kind upon me, and give me a
little service at Your lotus feet."

Two Peerless Mantras From the Sri Sanatkumara-samhita

In the *Sri Sanatkumara-samhita*, from the ancient Skanda Purana,
we find a conversation between the great sage Sri Narada and Lord

Sadashiva, the master of the demigods. Starting at text number 26 to text 30, Narada Muni asks Lord Sadashiva, "O master please tell what method the people of Kali-yuga may adopt to easily attain the transcendental abode of Lord Hari [Krishna]. O Lord, what mantra will carry the people from this world of birth and death? So everyone may benefit, please tell it to me. O Lord, of all mantras what mantra needs no purashcharana, no nyasa, no yoga, no samskara, and no other thing? A single utterance of the Lord's holy name gives the highest result. O master of the demigods, if I am competent to hear it, please kindly tell me the Lord's holy name."

In texts 31-35 , Lord Sadashiva gives his answer: Lord Sadashiva said: "O fortunate one, your question is excellent. O you who wish for the welfare of all, I will tell you the secret chintamani [wish-fulfilling] jewel of all mantras. I will tell you the secret of secrets, the most confidential of all confidential things. I will tell you what I have not told either the goddess or your elder brothers. I will tell you two peerless Krishna mantras that are the crest-jewels of all mantras. One mantra is:

"'Gopijana-vallabha-charanau sharanam prapadye.' (I take shelter of the feet of He who is the gopi's beloved) This mantra has three compound words, five individual words and sixteen syllables.

"The second mantra is: 'Namo gopijana-vallabhabhyam.' (Obeisances to the divine couple, who are dear to the gopis) This mantra has two words and ten syllables.

In texts 36-41, Lord Sadashiva continues: "One who either with faith or without faith once chants this five-word mantra resides among Lord Krishna's gopi-beloveds. Of this there is no doubt. In chanting these mantras there is no need of purshcharana, nyasa, ari-shuddhi, mitra-shuddhi, or other kinds of purification. In chanting these mantras there is no restriction of time or place. All, from the lowest outcaste to the greatest sage, are eligible to chant this mantra. Women, shudras, and all others are eligible. The paralyzed, mute, blind, and lame are eligible. The Andhras, Hunas, Kiratas, Pulindas, Pukkashas, Abhiras, Yavanas, Kankas, Khashas, and all others born from sinful wombs are also eligible. They who are overcome with pride and ego, who are intent on committing sins, who are killers of cows and brahmanas, and who are the greatest of sinners, are also eligible. They who have neither knowledge nor renunciation, they who have never studied the shruti-shastra and other scriptures, and all others, whoever they may be, are also eligible to chant these mantras."

Then in texts 42-48 Lord Sadashiva explains who is not eligible and who should not be told these sacred mantras or the purpose of them:

"Anyone who has devotion to Lord Krishna, the master of all masters, is eligible to chant these mantras, but they who have no devotion, even they may be the greatest of sages, are not eligible. They who have performed many yajnas, given charity, visited all holy places, been devoted to speaking the truth, accepted the renounced order, traveled to the farther shore of the Vedas and Vedangas, devotedly served the brahmanas, taken birth in good families, and performed austerities and vows, but are not devoted to Lord Krishna, are not eligible to chant these mantras. Therefore these mantras should not be spoken to one who is not devoted to Lord Hari, nor to one who is ungrateful, proud, or faithless, nor to an atheist or a blasphemer. One should not speak these mantras to one who does not wish to hear them, nor to one who has not stayed for one year in the speaker's ashrama. One should carefully give these mantras to one who is free from hypocrisy, greed, lust, anger, and other vices, and who is sincerely devoted to Lord Krishna. The sage of this mantra is Lord Sadashiva. The meter is Gayatri. The Deity is Lord Krishna, the beloved of the gopis. The purpose is to attain service to dear Lord Hari."

In text 53 Lord Sadashiva says: "By once chanting this mantra one attains success. Of this there is no doubt. Still, for the purpose of chanting japa one should chant this mantra ten times daily."

In texts 54-77 of the Sri Sanatkumara-samhita, Lord Sadashiva describes the most nectarean meditation of the mantras, after which he continues with many additional topics in regard to the pastimes of Radha and Krishna and the importance of the land of Vrindavana:

"O best of brahmanas, now I will tell you the meditation of this mantra. I meditate on two-armed Lord Krishna, who is dark like a monsoon cloud, dressed in yellow garments, garlanded with forest flowers... crowned with a peacock feather, and garlanded with lotus whorls, whose face is splendid like ten million moons, whose eyes move restlessly... whose forehead is marked with tilaka of sandal paste and musk... who is splendid with earrings like two rising suns, whose perspiration-anointed cheeks are like two glistening mirrors... who with raised eyebrows playfully glances at His beloved's face, the tip of whose graceful raised nose is decorated with a glistening pearl... whose bimba-fruit lips are splendid in the moonlight of His teeth, whose hands are splendid with bracelets, armlets, and jewel rings... who holds a flute in His left lotus hand, whose waist is splendid with a graceful belt, whose feet are splendid with graceful anklets... whose eyes are restless with the nectar of amorous pastimes, who jokes with His beloved, making Her laugh again and again... and who stays with Her on a jewel throne under a kalpa-vriksha tree in Vrindavana forest. In this way one should meditate on Lord Krishna and His beloved."

"On the Lord's left side one should meditate on Sri Radha, who is dressed in blue garments, who is splendid like molten gold... who with the edge of Her garment covers Her graceful lotus smile, whose restless chakori-bird eyes dance on Her beloved's face... who with Her forefinger and thumb places betel nuts and crushed betel leaves in Her beloved's lotus mouth... whose full, raised breasts are decorated with a glistening pearl-necklace, whose waist is slender, whose broad hips are decorated with tinkling ornaments... who is decorated with jewel earrings, finger rings, toe rings, bracelets, armlets, and tinkling golden anklets... whose limbs are graceful with the best of beauty, who is always in the prime of youth, and who is always plunged in the nectar of bliss. O king of brahmanas, Her friends, whose age and qualities are like Hers, devotedly serve Her with chamaras, fans, and other articles."

"Please hear, O Narada, and I will tell you the meaning of these mantras. The material world is manifested by the Lord's maya potency and other external potencies. The spiritual world is manifested by the Lord's chit potency and other internal and everlasting spiritual potencies. The protector of these potencies is said to be the gopi Sri Radha, who is Lord Krishna's beloved. The transcendental goddess Sri Radha is the direct counterpart of Lord Sri Krishna. She is the central figure for all the goddesses of fortune. She is the pleasure potency of Lord Krishna. The wise say that She is the pleasure potency of Lord Krishna. Durga and the other goddesses in the world of the three modes are a million-millionth part of one of Her expansions. She is directly Goddess Maha-Lakshmi and Lord Krishna is Lord Narayana. O best of sages, there is not the slightest difference between Them. O best of sages, what more can I say? Nothing can exist without them. This universe made of spirit and matter together is Their potency. She is Durga and Lord Hari is Shiva. Lord Krishna is Indra and She is Shachi. She is Savitri and Lord Hari is Brahma. She is Dhumorna and Lord Hari is Yama. O Narada, please know that everything is Their potency. Even if I had many hundreds of years, I could not describe all Their glories."

CHAPTER EIGHT

Prayers to Srimati Radharani, the Queen of Goddesses

This presents the *Sri Prarthana-paddhati*, the *Radha-Stuti* prayers, two versions of the *Sri Radhikhastakam*, *Sri Radha-Kundastakam* (prayers to the Radha-kund), *Radha Kripa Kataksha*, *Sri Sri Gandharva Samprarthanastakam*, *Catu-puspanjalih* [Stavamala], *Sri Vilapa Kusumanjali*, The 16 Names of Sri Radha, The 108 Names of Shrimati Radhika, and The 1008 Names of Srimati Radharani.

Sri Prarthana-paddhati [Stavamala]

In his Sri Prarthana-paddhati [Stavamala], Srila Rupa goswami prays:

"O Queen of Vrndavana, O Radharani, Your complexion is like molten gold, Your doe-like eyes are captivatingly restless, a million full and brilliant moons wane before Your lustrous countenance, and a blue sari, having stolen the hue of a fresh rain-laden cloud, has enwrapped Your exquisite form. O Radha, You are the crest-jewel of all the dallying damsels of Vrndavana, fragrant and pristine like a budding jasmine flower. Your sublime form is adorned with priceless jewelry, and you are the best of all the charming and intelligent gopis. You are decorated with all wonderful excellences and surrounded by eight dedicated and beloved cowherd girls known as the asta-sakhis.

"The ambrosia of Your beautiful lips, red as the bimba fruit, is life-giving syrup to Krsna. O Radha, I am rolling on the banks of the Yamuna, my poor heart filled with anticipation, praying to You with all humility. I am guilty of being an offender, a rascal, a useless wretch--yet I beg You to kindly engage me in even the smallest service to Your lotus feet. O most merciful Lady, it will not become You to ignore this most distressed soul, for Your heart is always overflowing with compassion and love."

Radha-Stuti

radha raseshvari ramya
rama cha paramatmanah
rasodbhava krishna-kanta
krishna-vaksha-sthala-sthita

"Beautiful Shrimate Radharani is the queen and the origin of the
rasa dance. She is the giver of pleasure to Krishna, who is the Supersoul in
the hearts of all. She is the lover of Krishna and is always situated upon the
chest of the Lord."

krishna-pranadhidevi cha
maha-vishnoh prasur api
sarvadya vishnu-maya cha
satya nitya sanatani

"She is the presiding Deity of Krishna's very life, and She is the
first of all persons, the energy of Lord Vishnu, the embodiment of
truthfulness--eternal and ever-youthful."

brahma-svarupa parama
nirlipta nirguna para
vrinda vrindavane tvam cha
viraja-tata-vasini

"Her form is spiritual, therefore She is transcendental and beyond
mundane qualities. She is divine energy and is unattached. O Radha, in
Vrindavana You are the leader of the gopis, and You reside on the banks
of the Viraja River."

goloka-vasini gopi
gopisha gopa-matrika
sananda paramananda
nanda-nandana-kamini

"She is a resident of Goloka Vrindavana and is a cowherd damsel.
She is the queen of the gopis and the divine mother of the cowherd boys.
She is joyful and always experiencing the highest bliss, and She incites
lusty desires in the heart of the son of Nanda (Lord Krishna)."

vrishabhanu-suta shanta
kanta purnatama tatha
kamya kalavati-kanya
tirtha-putra sati shubha

"Radha is the daughter of Maharaja Vrishabhanu. She is very peaceful and lovely. She is completely contented and fulfilled, very pleasing and is the daughter of Kalavati. She is the purifier of the tirthas (holy places) and She is most auspicious and chaste to Lord Krishna."

samsara-sagare ghore
bhitam mam sharanagatam
sarvebhyo 'pi vinirmuktam
kuru radhe surshvari

"O Radha, I have fallen into the horrible ocean of birth and death and am frightened, but I am seeking Your shelter. O queen of the demigods, please free me from all fears."

tvat-pada-padma-yugale
pada-padmalayarcite
dehi mahyam param bhaktim
krishnena parisevite

"O Radhika, please give me transcendental devotional service to Your lotus feet, which are worshiped by Lord Brahma and Lakshmi, and which are served even by Lord Krishna."

tapta-kanchana-gaurangi
radhe vrindavaneshvari
vrishabhanu-sute devi
pranamami hari-priye

"O Shrimati Radharani, I offer my respects to You whose bodily complexion is like molten gold. O Goddess, You are the queen of Vrindavana. You are the daughter of King Vrishabhanu, and are very dear to Lord Krishna."

mahabhava-svarupa tvam
krishna-priya-variyasi

prema-bhakti-prade devi
radhike tvam namamy aham

"O Shrimate Radharani, You are the exalted form of mahabhava, therefore You are the most dear to Krishna. O Goddess, You alone are able to bestow pure love for the Supreme Lord; therefore I offer my humble obeisances unto You."

Shri Radhikastakam
Eight Prayers Glorifying Sri Radhika
by Shrila Raghunatha dasa Gosvami

Text 1
rasa-valita-mrgaksi-mauli-manikya-laksmih
pramudita-muravairi-prema-vapi-marali
vraja-vara-vrsabhanoh punya-girvana-valli
snapayatu nija-dasye radhika mam kada nu

When will Sri Radhika, who is a splendid ruby in the crown of all nectarean doe-eyed girls, a swan swimming in the lake of love for jubilant Lord Krsna, and a celestial vine sprouted from Vraja's exalted King Vrsabhanu, bathe me in Her service?

Text 2
sphurad-aruna-dukula-dyotitodyan-nitamba-
sthalam abhi vara-kanci-lasyam ullasayanti
kucha-kalasa-vilasa-sphita-mukta-sara-srih
snapayatu nija-dasye radhika mam kada nu

When will Sri Radhika, who makes the sash of bells dance on Her hips splendid with red silk, and whose necklace of large pearls plays on the waterpots of Her breasts, bathe me in Her service?

Text 3
sarasija-vara-garbhakharva-kantih samudyat-
tarunima-ghanasaraslista-kaishora-sidhuh
dara-vikasita-hasya-syandi-bimbadharagra
snapayatu nija-dasye radhika mam kada nu

When will Sri Radhika, who is as splendid as a great lotus whorl, who is new nectar mixed with the camphor of youth, and whose bimba fruit lips blossom with a gentle smile, bathe me in Her service?

Text 4

ati-chatulataram tam kananantar milantam
vraja-nrpati-kumaram viksya sanka-kulaksi madhura-mridu-vacobhih
samstuta netra-bhangya
snapayatu nija-dasye radhika mam kada nu

When will Sri Radhika, who, accidentally meeting restless Krsna in the outskirts of the forest, stared at Him with suspicious eyes as he cast amorous glances at Her and flattered Her with many sweet and gentle words, bathe me in Her service?

Text 5

vraja-kula-mahilanam prana-bhutakhilanam
pasupa-pati-grhinyah krsna-vat-prema-patram
su-lalita-lalitantah-sneha-phullantaratma
snapayatu nija-dasye radhika mam kada nu

When will Sri Radhika, who the girls of Vraja love as much as their own lives, who the gopa queen Yasoda loves as much as Lord Krsna, and who makes the heart of charming lalita blossom with love, bathe me in Her service?

Text 6

niravadhi sa-visakha sakhi-yutha-prasunaih
srajam iha rachayanti vaijayantim vanante agha-vijaya-varorah-preyasi
sreyasi sa
snapayatu nija-dasye radhika mam kada nu

When will Sri Radhika, who in the company of Visakha at the forest's edge strings a Vaijayanti garland from the flowers of many trees, and who is the beautiful beloved resting on Lord Krsna's handsome chest, bathe me in Her service?

Text 7
prakatita-nija-vasam snigdha-venu-pranadair
druta-gati-harim arat prapya kunje smitaksi sravana-kuhara-kandum
tanvati namra-vaktra
snapayatu nija-dasye radhika mam kada nu

When will Sri Radhika, who smelling the fragrance of Lord Krsna and hearing the sweet sounds of His flute, ran to Him in the forest grove and, scratching Her ears, approached Him with smiling eyes and lowered face, bathe me in Her service?

Text 8
amala-kamala-raji-sparsa-vata-prasite
nija-sarasi nidaghe sayam ullasiniyam parijana-gana-yukta kridayanti
bakarim
snapayatu nija-dasye radhika mam kada nu

When will Sri Radhika, who on a summer evening happily plays with Lord Krsna by Her own lake cooled by breezes touching the many splendid lotuses, bathe me in Her service?

Text 9
pathati vimala-ceta mista-radhastakam yah
parihrita-nikhilasa-santatih katarah san pasupa-pati-kumarah kamam
amoditas tam
nija-jana-gana-madhye radhikayas tanoti

Pleased with any person who, abandoning all hope of material happiness, and overwhelmed (with love), reads this sweet Sri Radhastaka with a pure heart, the prince of Vraja (Krsna) of His own accord places him among Sri Radha's personal associates.

Sri Radhikastakam
by Srila Krsnadas Kaviraja Gosvami

kumkumakta kanchanabja garvahari gaurabhapitananci tavja gandha kirti
nindi saurabhaballavesa
sunu sarva banchitartha sadhikamahyamatma pada padma dasya-dastu
radhika

kauravinda-kanti-nindi-citrapatta satikakrsna matta bhringa keli
phulla-puspa batikakrsna nitya
sangamartha padma bandhu radhikamahyamatma pada padma
dasya-dastu radhika

saukumarya srista pallavali kirti nigrahachandra-chandanotpalendu
sevya sita vigrahasvabhimarsa
vallabhisa kama-tapa badhikamahyamatma pada padma dasya-dastu
radhika

visva-vandya yaubatabhi-vanditapi ya ramarupa-navya-yavnadi sampada
na yaisamasilahardya
lilaya cha sa yatosti nadhikamahyamatma pada padma dasya-dastu
radhika

rasalasya gita narma satkalali-panditaprema-ramya rupavesa sadgunali
manditavisva-navya-gopa-
yosidalito'pi yadhikamahyamatma pada padma dasya-dastu radhika

nitya-navya rupa keli krsnabhava sampadakrsna-raga-bandha-gopa
yaubatesu kampadakrsna-rupa
vesa keli lagna sat-samadhikamahyamatma pada padma dasya-dastu
radhika

sveda-kampa-kantakasru gadgadadi sancitamarsa harsa vamataki bhava
bhusanancitakrsna-netra
tosi-ratna mandanali dadhikamahyamatma pada padma dasya-dastu
radhika

ya ksanardha krsna-viprayoga santotoditaneka-dainya chapaladi
bhavavrinda moditayatnalabdha
krsna sanga nirgatakhiladhikamahyamatma pada padma dasya-dastu
radhika

astakena yastanena nanti krsna ballabhamdarsanepi sailajedi yosidali
durlabhamkrsna sanga
nanditatma dasya sidhu bhajanammahyamatma pada padma dasya-dastu
radhika

Translation

"May that Srimati Radhika--whose bodily complexion snatches away the pride of a golden lotus flower tinged with kunkuma, whose bodily fragrance reproaches the fame of a fragrant lotus sprinkled with saffron powder, and who fulfills all the desires of the prince of Vraja, Sri Krishna--always bestow upon me the service of Her lotus feet.

"May that Srimati Radhika--whose dazzling, colorful silk sari defeats the splendour of coral, who is a garden of all varieties of blooming flowers which attract the maddened bumblebee Sri Krishna who comes to play amongst Her flowers, and who worships the sun-god in order to meet with Krishna eternally--always bestow upon me the service of Her lotus feet.

"May that Srimati Radhika--whose softness defeats the fame of delicate budding flowers, whose body's coolness is worshipable for the moon, sandalwood-paste, the lotus, and camphor, and whose touch dispels the heat of Gopijanavallabha, Sri Krishna's amorous desires--always bestow upon me the service of Her lotus feet.

"Although Lakshmi-devi is honored by all the worshipable damsels of the universe, the opulence of her great beauty and ever-fresh youthfulness is overshadowed by that of Srimati Radhika. Nor can Lakshmi-devi surpass Her by her natural loving and playful disposition. May that Srimati Radhika always bestow upon me the service of Her lotus feet.

"May that Srimati Radhika--who is expert in all the celestial arts of the rasa-lila, like dancing, singing and joking; who is adorned with supernatural prema, enchanting beauty, wonderful dresses and ornaments, and all divine virtues; and who is the topmost youthful maiden of Vraja--always bestow upon me the service of Her lotus feet.

"May that Srimati Radhika--who by Her ever-fresh beauty, ever-fresh playfulness, and ever-fresh wealth of affection causes all the young maidens of Vraja, who are abound in love to Sri Krishna, to tremble in anxiety; and who is immersed in samadhi (meditation) upon Sri Krishna's beauty, attire, and playful pastimes--always bestow upon me the service of Her lotus feet.

"May that Srimati Radhika--who in divine ecstasy manifests perspiration, hairs standing on end, trembling tears, and a choked voice; who is adorned with indignation, joy, and contrariness; and who wears splendid jewel-studded ornaments which delight Sri Krishna's eyes--always bestow upon me the service of Her lotus feet.

"May that Srimati Radhika--who upon being separated from Sri Krishna for even half a moment becomes distressed by the ever-arising feelings of Her own lowliness and great restlessness, and who upon meeting Krishna through the intense efforts of one of Their messengers is relieved of all Her mental anguish--always bestow upon me the service of Her lotus feet.

"Srimati Radhika, whose darshana (audience) is rarely attained even by Parvati-devi and other goddesses, who gives great pleasure to Her sakhis (confidential servants), who Herself becomes elated upon meeting with Sri Krishna, and who is Krishna's dearest lover, very quickly makes that person who prays to Her singing this astaka a recipient for the nectar of Her service. This astaka is recited in the poetic meter known as 'Tunaka'."

Sri Radha-Kundastakam
[The Glories of Srimati Radhika's Kund, Pond]
by Srila Raghunatha dasa Gosvami

"After the killing of Aristasura, Srimati Radhika and Her sakhis exchanged many joking words with Sri Krishna concerning the necessary atonement for one who has committed the offence of killing a bull. As a result, the Queen of Vrindavana, Srimati Radhika, and Her sakhis joyfully excavated and filled Sri Radha-kunda with their own hands. May that immensely fragrant Radha-kunda be my shelter.

"In the land of the hearts of those who bathe in Radha-kunda, a desire tree of the superlative prema, which is not attainable even for Krishna's principal queens in Dvaraka, will arise. May that supremely charming Radha-kunda be my shelter.

"For the pleasure of Srimati Radhika, even Sri Krishna Himself, yearning to attain Her merciful sidelong glance, regularly bathes in

Radha-kunda, carefully observing all the appropriate rituals. May that supremely enchanting Radha-kunda be my shelter.

"May that supremely enchanting Radha-kunda, which the moon of Vraja, Sri Krishna, loves as much as He loves the crown-jewel amongst the sweet girls of Vraja, Srimati Radhika, and which He has made known by the name of Radhika Herself, be my shelter.

"The mercy obtained by serving Radha-kunda makes the desire-creeper of prema for the prince of Vraja sprout and is celebrated for bearing the flower of service to the svamini Srimati Radhika. May that supremely charming Radha-kunda be my shelter.

"Gloriously manifest on the banks of Radha-kunda are eight kunjas (groves) named after Radhika's principal sakhis. Acting as stimuli for the amorous pastimes of the Divine Couple, these kunjas are filled with the sweet humming of bumblebees and are desired by everyone. May that supremely enchanting Radha-kunda be the shelter of my life.

"Situated on an exquisite dais on the bank of Radha-kunda and accompanied by Her beloved sakhis, our svamini Srimate Radhika charmingly engages in sweet, joking words with Sri Krishna, the moon of Vraja. These playful verbal exchanges are enhanced by the suggestion of so many innuendoes. May that Radha-kunda be the shelter of my life.

"May that very charming and especially fragrant Radha-kunda, where intoxicated with love the Divine Couple and the sakhis daily sport with great joy in the water so fragrant with exquisite lotus flowers, be the sole shelter of my life.

"To that devotee who, in a resolute mood of aspiring to serve Srimati Radhika, reads this charming prayer describing Sri Radha-kunda, even in their present body Sri Krishna will quickly grant them darshana of not only His beloved Radhika, but also of their many variegated amorous pastimes. Witnessing these pastimes and envisioning himself serving Yugala-kishora (Krishna) in various ways, such a devotee will feel immense jubilation. This astaka is recited in the poetic meter known as 'Malini'."

Sri Sri Radha-Kripa-Kataksha Stava Raja

Spoken by Lord Shiva to Parvati in the Tantra named
Urdhvamnaya-Tantra

This is the most famous stotra in Sri Vrindavana; all the sadhus and devoted matajis [ladies] know it by heart, and it is recited daily in most temples and nearby villages; indeed, this prayer is regarded as the very heart of Vrindavana. It is also known as:

The King of Prayers which Petitions the Most Merciful Side-long Glance from Srimati Radharani

Verse 1
Munindra-vrinda-vandite! Tri-loka-shoka-harini
Prasanna-vaktra-pankaje! Nikunja-bhu-vilasini!
Vrajendra-bhanu-nandini! Vrajendra-sunu-sangate!
Kada karishyasiha mam kripa-kataksha-bhajanam?

Oh You who are adored by all the best sages!
Oh You who takes away all the miseries of the three material worlds!
Oh You whose face joyfully blooms just like a lotus flower!
Oh You who delights in playing love-sports throughout the secret forest bower-houses!
Oh most charming daughter of Vrishabhanu, the best of kings!
Oh closest heart-felt companion of the son of the King of Vraja!
When, oh when will You make me the object of Your side-long glance of causeless mercy?

Verse 2
Ashoka-vriksha-vallari-vitana-mandapa-sthite!
Pravala-vala-pallava-prabharunanghri-komale!
Varabhaya-sphurat-kare! Prabhuta-sampadalaye!
Kada karishyasiha mam kripa-kataksha-bhajanam?

Oh You who are situated in a pavilion beneath a canopy of creepers spread over the branches of the blooming ashoka trees!
Oh You whose soft and delicate feet radiate with the pinkish glow of freshly sprouted coral-like tree-buds!

Oh You whose upraised hand bestows upon Your devotees the benediction of absolute fearlessness!
Oh fountainhead of profuse divine opulences!
When, oh when will You shower upon me Your side-long glance of overflowing grace?

Verse 3

Ananga-ranga-mangala-prasanga-bhangura-bhruvam
Savibhramam-sasambhramam driganta-vana-patanaih
Nirantaram vashi-krita-pratita-nanda-nandane!
Kada karishyasiha mam kripa-kataksha-bhajanam?

Oh You who continuously subdues the Son of Nanda into complete surrender unto Yourself by piercing Him with the arrows of loving glances shot from the very corners of Your eyes—
Glances laden with amorous delusions which inspire Him with feelings of most reverential submission, further stimulated by Your crookedly-bending eyebrows that dance with the most auspicious sportive interest of the God of love!
When oh when will You make me the object of Your side-long glance of causeless mercy?

Verse 4

Tadit-suvarna-champaka-pradipta-gaura-vigrahe!
Mukha-prabha-parasta-koti-sharadendu-mandale!
Vichitra-chitra-sancharach-chakora-shava-lochane!
Kada karishyasiha mam kripa-kataksha-bhajanam?

Oh You whose form is fair-complexioned with the brilliant hue of lightning, pure gold, and champaka flowers!
Oh You whose facial splendor eclipses the aura of millions of autumn moons!
Oh You whose eyes restlessly move to and fro like the young chakora birds and thus make astonishing expressions from moment-to-moment!
When, oh when will You shower upon me Your side-long glance of over-flowing grace?

Verse 5

Madonmadati-yauvane! Pramoda-mana-mandite!
Priyanuraga-ranjite! Kala-vilasa-pandite!

Ananya-dhanya-kunja-rajya-kama-keli-kovide!
Kada karishyasiha mam kripa-kataksha-bhajanam?

Oh You who are madly intoxicated with Your own eternal youth!
Oh You who are decorated by the great delight of Your mood of jealous pouting!
Oh You who are dyed in pure loving affection for Your Beloved!
Oh You who are most expert in all the various arts of amorous loving expressions!
Oh You who are most learned in designing loving sports within the matchless opulent kingdom of glorious forest groves!
When, oh when will You make me the object of Your side-long glance of causeless mercy?

Verse 6
Ashesha-hava-bhava-dhira-hira-hara-bhushite!
Prabhuta-shata-kumbha-kumbha kumbhi-kumbha-sustani!
Prashasta-manda-hasya-churna-purna-saukhya-sagare!
Kada karishyasiha mam kripa-kataksha-bhajanam?

Oh You who are decorated by the diamond necklace of limitless feminine charms like amorous gestures, ecstatic moods, and gentle mannerisms!
Oh You whose breasts are plump like the purest golden water jugs, or like the cranial globes of a young elephant!
Oh You who are like the swelling ocean of happiness full of (not water, but) the soft pollen of Your most praise-worthy mild sweet smile!
When, oh when will You shower upon me Your side-long glance of over-flowing grace?

Verse 7
Mrinala-vala-vallari-taranga-ranga-dor-late!
Latagra-lasya-lola-nila-lochanavalokane!
Lalal-lulan-milan-manojna-mugdha-mohanashrite!
Kada karishyasiha mam kripa-kataksha-bhajanam?

Oh You whose creeper-like arms rhythmically wave and flow like fresh young lotus stems in the ripples of a river!
Oh You whose restless, roving glance of deep blue eyes dances seductively like vine-tips in the breeze!

Oh You whose playful frolics and alluring movements induce lovely meetings and fascinate Mohan [Krishna] Himself to take refuge in Your charm!

When, oh when will You make me the object of Your side-long glance of causeless mercy?

Verse 8
Suvarna-malikanchita-tri-rekha-kambu-kanthage!
Tri-sutra-mangali-guna-tri-ratna-dipti-didhite!
Salola-nila-kuntala-prasuna-guccha-gumphite!
Kada karishyasiha mam kripa-kataksha-bhajanam?

Oh You whose smooth conchshell-like neck, marked with three lines, is decorated with a pure golden necklace!

Oh You who shines in the splendorous auras of Your three-stranded necklace, woven with small jasmine garlands, and decorated with the three jewels diamond, emerald and pearl!

Oh You whose flowing deep blue-black locks are interwoven with bunches of colorful flower blossoms!

When, oh when will You shower upon me Your side-long glance of over-flowing grace?

Verse 9
Nitamba-bimba-lambamana-pushpa-mekhala-gune!
Prashasta-ratna-kinkini-kalapa-madhya-manjule!
Karindra-shunda-dandikavaroha-saubhagoruke!
Kada karishyasiha mam kripa-kataksha-bhajanam?

Oh You whose rounded hips are decorated by a belt of dangling flowers!

Oh You whose charmingly thin waist is decorated by groups of superexcellent tiny tinkling jewel-bells!

Oh You whose most beautiful thighs taper gracefully like the trunk of the king of elephants!

When, oh when will You make me the object of Your side-long glance of causeless mercy?

Verse 10
Aneka-mantra-nada-manju-nupura-rava-skhalat
Samaja-raja-hamsa-vamsha-nikvanati-gaurave!

Vilola-hema-vallari-vidambi-charu-chankrame!
Kada karishyasiha mam kripa-kataksha-bhajanam?

Oh You whose most captivating ankle bells are resounding various Vedic
mantras as You walk, and which possess additional superexcellence in
resembling the warbling of a flock of most noble swans!
Oh You whose pleasant bodily movements put to shame the swaying dance
of golden forest creepers!
When, oh when will You shower upon me Your side-long glance of
over-flowing grace?

Verse 11
Ananta-koti-vishnu-loka-namra-padmajarchite!
Himadrija-pulomaja-virinchija-vara-prade!
Apara-siddhi-vriddhi-digdha-sat-padanguli-nakhe!
Kada karishyasiha mam kripa-kataksha-bhajanam?

Oh You who is humbly bowed to by all the Lord Brahmas of countless
millions of universes created by Lord Vishnu!
Oh You who is the bestower of boons to the daughter of the Himalayas
(Parvati), to the daughter of Puloma (Indra's wife Saci), and to Brahma's
wife (Sarasvati)!
Oh You whose toenails glow with the radiance of boundless mystic
perfections and opulent prosperities!
When, oh when will You make me the object of Your side-long glance of
causeless mercy?

Verse 12
Makheshvari! Kriyeshvari! Svadheshvari! Sureshvari!
Triveda-bharatishvari! Pramana-shasaneshvari!
Rameshvari! Kshameshvari! Pramoda-kananeshvari!
Vrajeshvari! Vrajadhipe! Sri Radhike! Namo 'stu te!

Oh Goddess of Vedic sacrifices!
Oh Goddess of all pious activities!
Oh Goddess of all that is natural and spontaneous!
Oh Goddess of all the demigods and goddesses!
Oh Goddess of all the knowledge of the three Vedas!
Oh Goddess of the enforcement of universal law!
Oh Goddess of all the goddesses of fortune!

Oh Goddess of forgiveness!
Oh Goddess of the most pleasurable forest of Vrindavana!
Oh Goddess of the entire realm of Vraja!
Oh one and only authority of Vraja!
Oh Sri Radhika!
I offer my most respectful obeisances unto You!

Verse 13
Iti mamadbhutam stavam nishamya bhanu-nandini!
Karotu santatam janam kripa-kataksha-bhajanam
Bhavet tadaiva sanchita-trirupa-karma-nashanam
Bhavet tade vrajendra-sunu-mandala-praveshanam

"May Sri Vrishabhanu-nandini, upon hearing my most astonishing prayer being recited by someone, make that person the constant object of Her most merciful side-long glance. Then, at that time, one will feel that all the effects of three types of karma (whether entangling one in the past, present or future) has been completely destroyed. And at such a time, one will finally gain entrance into the assembly of Nanda-nandana's [Krishna's] eternal loving associates."

Verse 14
Rakayam cha sitashtamyam
Dashamyan cha vishuddha-dhihi
Ekadashyam trayodashyam
Yah pathet sadhakah sudhihi

Verse 15
Yam yam kamayate kamam
Tam tam prapnoti sadhakaha
Radha-kripa-katakshena
Bhaktih syat prema-lakshana

"That practicing devotee (sadhaka) of purified intelligence, who recites this stava with a fixed mind on the lunar days—full moon, bright ashtami (waxing eighth day), dashami (tenth day), ekadashi (eleventh day), or trayodashi (thirteenth day)—finds that each and every desire that one had will be fulfilled without fail. And by the most merciful side-long glance of Sri Radha, one will obtain devotional service which has a very special quality of pure, ecstatic love (Prema)."

Verse 16
Uru-dagne nabhi-dagne
Hrid-dagne kantha-dagnake
Radha-kunda-jale sthitva
Yah pathet sadakah shatam

Verse 17
Tasya sarvartha-siddhah syad
Vak-samarthya tato labhet
Aishvaryam cha labhet sakshad
Drisha pashyati radhikam

"That practicing devotee (sadhaka) who recites this stava 100 times while situated in the waters of Sri Radha-kunda up to the thighs, navel, chest or neck, attains complete perfection in all the four purusarthas or goals of human existence—namely dharma (religiosity), artha (economic success), kama (fulfillment of desires), and moksha (liberation from material existence). One also attains the power by which everything spoken will come true. One becomes very opulent due to attaining transcendental majesty, and gets to meet Sri Radhika face to face, seeing Her even with one's present eyes."

Verse 18
Tena sa tat-kshanad eva
Tushta date maha-varam
Yena pashyati netrabhyam
Tat-priyam shyama-sundaram

"Thereby Sri Radhika becomes so pleased that She instantly bestows a great benediction. And that benediction is—one also sees Her own beloved Syamasundara with one's very own eyes."

Verse 19
Nitya-lila-pravesham cha
Dadati hi vrajadhipaha
Atah parataram prapyam
Vaishnavanam na vidyate

"Then that very Lord of Vraja-dhama grants one entrance into His own eternal pastimes of ecstatic daily sports. And other than attaining this goal, there is nothing but nothing else which is really hankered for by the true Vaishnavas."

Sri Sri Gandharva Samprarthanastakam
by Srila Rupa Goswami

vrindavane viharator iha kile-kunje
matta-dvipa-pravara-kautuka-vibhramena |
sandarshayasva yuvayor vadanaravinda-
dvandvam vidhehi mayi devi kripam prasida ||1||

1. O Goddess! Be merciful to me and reveal Your lotus face to me when You and Sri Krishna play in the play-groves of Vrindavana, enjoying like intoxicated, blissful Lordly elephants!

ha devi kaku-bhara-gadgadayadya vacha
yace nipatya bhuvi dandavad udbhatartih |
asya prasadam abudhasya janasya kritva
gandharvike nija-gane gananam vidhehi ||2||

2. O Goddess! In great distress I prostrate myself before You, falling on the ground, praying piteously unto You with faltering voice. O Gandharvike! After You bestowed Your mercy on this fool, count him (her) amongst Your own people!

shyame rama-ramana-sundarata-varishtha-
saundarya-mohita-samasta-jagaj-janasya |
shyamasya vama-bhuja-baddha-tanum kadaham
tvam indira-virala-rupa-bharam bhajami ||3||

3. O Syame (Sri Radhe)! When will I worship You as Indira (Laksmi), when Your beautiful body is bound up by Syama's left arm? Krishna's beauty enchants all the people of the world and is even greater than that of Rama-ramana (Lord Visnu, Laksmi's husband).

tvam pracchadena mudira-cchavina pidhaya
manjira-mukta-charanam cha vidhaya devi |
kunje vrajendra-tanayena virajamane
naktam kada pramuditam abhisarayishye ||4||

4. O Goddess! When can I arrange for Your blissful nocturnal meeting with the son of the king of Vraja in the grove by covering Your body with a cloud-blue sari and by removing the ankle-bells from Your feet?

kunje prasuna-kula-kalpita-keli-talpe
samvishtayor madhura-narma-vilasa-bhajoh |
loka-trayabharanayosh charanambujani
samvahayishyati kada yuvayor jano'yam ||5||

5. When will this person serve Your lotus feet, that adorn the three worlds by massaging them, as You are sitting together on a play-bed made of flowers in a grove, while You are making sweet jokes with each other?

tvat-kunda-rodhasi vilasa-parishramena
svedambu-cumbi-vadanambu-ruha-shriyo vam |
vrindavaneshvari kada taru-mula-bhajo
samvijayami chamari-chaya-chamarena ||6||

6. O Queen of Vrindavana! When can I fan You with a yaktail fan with a jewelled rod when You and Sri Krishna are sitting under a tree, Your lotus-like faces beautified by drops of perspiration from fatigue after Your pastimes on the shore of Your pond (Sri Radha Kund)?

linam nikunja-kuhare bhavatim mukunde
citraiva sucitavatim rucirakshi naham |
bhugnam bhruvam na rachayeti mrisharusham tvam
agre vrajendra-tanayasya kada nu neshye ||7||

7. O beautiful-eyed One! It was not me who told Mukunda in which corner of the kunja You were hiding! Citra did it! Don't frown Your eyebrows at me in false anger! When can I take You before the son of the king of Vraja?

vag-yuddha-keli-kutuke vraja-raja-sunum
jitvonmadam adhika-darpa-vikasi-jalpam |
phullabhir alibhir analpam udiryamana-
stotram kada nu bhavatim avalokayishye ||8||

8. When You defeat Krishna in a joking argument, You show even greater pride, extending Your proud words to Your blooming friends, who will praise You. When will I see You like this?

yah ko'pi sushthu vrishabhanu-kumarikayah
samprarthanashtakam idam pathati prapannah
sa preyasa saha sametya dhrita-pramoda
tatra prasada-laharim urarikaroti

Anyone who nicely recites these eight prayers to the daughter of king
Vrisabhanu will be accepted by Her in a wave of mercy and She will
joyfully appear before her with Her lover.

iti shri-gandharva-samprarthanashtakam sampurnam
Thus ends the Gandharva Samprarthanastakam.

Catu-puspanjalih [Stavamala]
Rupa Goswami prays to Srimati Radharani in his Catu-puspanjalih
[Stavamala] as follows:

"O Queen of Vrndavana, Sri Radha, I worship You. Your fair
complexion is more resplendent than molten gold, the color of Your sari the
hue of a blue lotus flower. Your beautiful braided hair is long and
raven-black, its coiffure studded with many brilliant gems, like the shining
black hood of a cobra.

"Even the beautiful lotus in full bloom or the rising full moon
offers no comparison to Your breathtaking face, for it is much more
exquisite. Your shining forehead is marked by a tidy saffron tilaka.

"The arches of Your elegant eyebrows put to shame Cupid's bow.
Your cascading black tresses sway, and the dark mascara on Your roving
eyes makes them look like restless black partridges.

"Your fine nose is decorated by a ring studded with the noblest
pearl, and Your lips are more charming than bright red tulips. Your
sparkling, even teeth are like rows of spotlessly white jasmine buds.

"The golden earrings that dangle gracefully from Your ears like a
pair of Laburnum flowers are inlaid with many precious gems. The gentle
cleft of Your delicate chin is decorated with a dot of musk, and an
intricately bejewelled necklace sparkles on You with regal splendor.

"Your nicely formed arms are like lotus stems, adorned with fine
and precious gems, and the two armlets inlaid with blue sapphires softly
jingle with Your slightest movements, pleasing all ears with their sweet
music.

"Your hands are beautiful and soft, like the lotus, and Your fingers are decorated with rings mounted with precious jewels. Your breasts are adorned with a large necklace finely set with stones and gems.

"The central jewel of Your regal necklace sits atop a line of dark gems that grow gradually larger in size. One could mistake it for a black snake carrying a gem on its hood. You are slender around the waist, and Your belly is concave because it must carry the burden of Your full breasts. It is marked by three lines like entwining creepers.

"A tinkling girdle of gold inset with precious stones adorns Your broad flaring hips, and Your shapely thighs put to shame the pride of the golden trunks of banana trees.

"Your kneecaps are so delicate and well-formed that they are far more attractive than round golden caskets studded with gems. The ankle-bells on Your finely formed feet sing an eternal melody, and the pink lotuses that blossom in autumn bow their heads in ardent worship to the beauty of Your lotus feet.

"The brilliance of millions upon millions of full moons pales before the opalescent nails of Your lotus feet. Innumerable ecstatic symptoms are Your natural embellishments, and You become stunned and perspire freely when Your yearning sidelong looks from afar intimately traverse Krsna's body. Uncontrollable erotic waves overcome You, and when You meet with Your beloved Krsna You are swept away in a surge of sublime ecstasy. O Queen of Vrndavan, You are the reservoir of all divine qualities, and I therefore worship Your lotus feet.

"O Srimati Radharani, all the symptoms of the very highest ecstasy, maha-bhava, become simultaneously manifest in You, and Your heart is benumbed. You are the ocean of unlimited transcendental emotions found only in perfect heroines, and everyone is amazed when You exhibit these ecstatic emotions.

"All the charming and captivating traits which make a heroine perfect are offering their obeisances to Your lotus feet in silent praise. The great beauty Laksmi-devi, the goddess of fortune, is humbly praying to attain residence on the toenails of Your lotus feet.

"You are the crest jewel of the damsels of Vraja, an eternal resident of Gokula, the most beloved object of the gopis. Your gentle smile acts as the life sustaining salve for Lalita and other sakhis.

"When Your roving eyes glance on Krsna with a sidelong look, it acts on Him like a drop of ambrosia, maddening and inciting Him with love. You are the apple of Your father king Vrisabhanu's eyes, and the soothing rays of Your moonlike activities exhilarate him.

"Your heart is like an ocean which is overflooding with waves of compassion. Therefore, O Radhika! Shower Your mercy, and be pleased with this person who is begging to become Your maidservant.

"O Radha my mistress! When will I be fortunate to see that after a lover's quarrel, when Krsna tries to pacify You, His indignant lady-love, with sweet cajoling words, in which He is truly expert, and begs You for a lovers' tryst, You are really pleased within but nonetheless turn Your face away and look at Krsna from the corner of Your eyes.

"O Divine Lady! Will that day ever come? When Lord Krsna, who is adept at everything, strings a charming garland of myrtle blossoms and slips it over Your head and His electric touch sends waves of ecstasy pulsating through You, and You begin to perspire profusely, when will I be fortunate enough to gently fan You with a palm leaf fan?

"O divine Lady! O beautiful Queen! When after Your hours of pleasure with Krsna Your intricately made-up hair becomes dishevelled and You need someone to set it properly again, when will You instruct this maidservant to do this service?

"O Divine beauty with cherry lips! Will I be able to see the wonderful dalliances between You and Krsna? When I place betel-nut pan into Your lotus mouth, Krsna tries to take it out of Your mouth and chew the same pan.

"O Srimati Radha! Among all the beloved gopis of Krsna You are His most cherished jewel. Therefore kindly be pleased with me and quickly shower Your mercy by including me amongst Your family members.

"O Queen of Vraja! I beg repeatedly at Your lotus feet for Your compassionate grace. Please allow me to become Your maid-in-attendance (sakhi) and confidante, so that when You become indignant after a lover's quarrel Krsna will approach me, knowing that I am Your sakhi, and flatter me to take Him to You; then I will take His hand and guide Him to You.

"Anyone who reads this prayer, named Catuspuspanjali, dedicated to Radharani, the Queen of Vrndavana, with faith and devotion, will very soon receive Her mercy directly."

Vilapa Kusumanjali
by Srila Raghunatha dasa Goswami
Special Prayers

tvad-alokana-kalahi-*
damsair eva mrtam janam

tvat-padabja-milal-laksa-
bhesajair devi jivaya

TRANSLATION

O Radharani, the queen of Vrndavana, with the medicine of the red lac from Your lotus feet, please bring back to life this person now dead from the bites of the black snake of not seeing You. (Vilapa-kusmanjali by RDG)

tavaivaasmi tavaivaasmi
na jivaami tvayaa vinaa
iti vijnaaya devi tvam
naya mam charanaantikam

I am Yours alone! I am Yours alone! I cannot live without You! O queen, please understand this and bring me to Your feet.

Shrila Raghunatha dasa Goswami writes further in the Vilapa-kusumanjali: "O Supreme Ladyship, Queen of my heart, Radha! Laksmi-devi the goddess of fortune does not possess even a drop of the beauty that exudes from Your exquisite toenails, therefore if You do not grant me the proper vision to perceive Your transcendental pastimes, then what use do I have for this life, which is burning in the fire of excruciating sorrow?

"O merciful Lady! Indeed, lately I am floating in a nectarean ocean of hope, and passing time in hardship and pain, but if You do not shower mercy upon me then this life, living in Vrndavana, and even Lord Krsna are all meaningless to me." 101-102

"The Queen of Vraja is my mistress. O Lady mistress, O Radha, I am Your maidservant, but the flames of intense separation are incinerating my heart and I grow feeble from profuse crying. Finding no other means, I am therefore sitting somewhere in Govardhana and composing these verses in deep lamentation.

"O dallying damsel of Vraja, Sri Radhika, I am sucked into an ocean of grief and my condition is so miserable! Kindly send me Your mercy in the form of an infallible boat and save me from this whirlpool. Please give me sanctuary at Your lotus feet."

"O Radha-kunda, pond of sublime joy, my mistress Srimati Radhika is always absorbed in divine amorous pastimes with her beloved paramour Sri Krsna on your banks, and you have endeared yourself to this Divine Couple more than anything else They cherish. Please, therefore, be merciful upon me and allow me but a moments vision of the object of my greatest adoration, Srimati Radharani.

SRI VILAPA KUSUMANJALI

1. O friend Rupa Manjari, although you are a famous and important person in this town, still you cannot see the face of the Supreme Personality of Godhead standing before you. Your husband is not here, and yet there is a mark on the bimba fruits of your lips as if someone has bitten them. Did a great parrot bite them?

2. O lotus tree, on the pretext of this bunch of new blossoms you are now broadly smiling in this forest. You have every right to be proud. After all, the black Krishna bee has left all the fragrant flower vines and He is now searching for the pathway to you.

3. O Rati manjari, in the king of Vraja's city, where many gopis live, you are the most pious of all. That is why you are now going to a cave, requested by your queen to search for the favourite belt She forgot in the midst of many pastimes.

4. Let me surrender to my spiritual master, Yadunandana Acharya. A powerful and dear devotee of the Supreme Lord, Yadunandana, he sprinkled the nectar of his mercy on me.

5. I worship Lord Chaitanyachandra, the supremely independent ocean of great mercy, who with His ropes of mercy quickly lifted me from the endlessly troublesome great dry well of household life, from which escape is very difficult, who gave me the shelter of His lotus feet, which rebuke the lotuses, and who gave me to Svarupa Damodar Goswami.

6. I was unwilling to drink the nectar of devotional service possessed of renunciation, but Sanatana Goswami, out of his causeless mercy, made me drink, even though I was otherwise unable to do so. Therefore he is an ocean of mercy. He is very much compassionate on fallen souls like me, and thus it is my duty to offer my respectful obeisances unto his lotus feet.

7. O queen, a certain maidservant, overwhelmed with love and her heart burning in the great fire of separation, laments in the following verses.

8. O queen, please rescue this unfortunate person, drowning in an ocean of pain. Place him on the strong boat of your mercy and carry him to the wonderful realm of Your lotus feet.

9. O queen, with the medicine of the red lac from Your lotus feet, please bring back to life this person now dead from the bites of the black snake of not seeing You.

10.O queen, with the nectar of a moment's glance please restore the life of this gopi maidservant of Your lotus feet, who now burns in the great forest fire of separation from You.

11. O beautiful faced one, when, even in a dream, will I, by decorating my head with the splendid perfumed powder of Your lotus feet, attain the goal of my life?

12. O beautiful one, when will the sound of your anklebells, sprinkling drops from an ocean of nectar, cure my deafness?

13. O queen, with the two bumblebees of the corners of Your eyes, which in the moonlit rendezvous anxiously wander over each direction as if the forest were a jungle of blue lotuses, will You glance upon this person?

14. O queen of Vrndavan, since Rupa manjari filled my eyes with light in the land of Vraja, I have yearned to see the red lac decorating Your lotus feet.

15. O queen whose eyes are as beautiful as two blossoming lotus flowers, when Your lake, filled with sweet water and splendid with many blossoming lotus flowers and buzzing bees, appeared before my eyes I at once began to yearn for the nectar of direct service to You.

16. O queen, I shall never ask You for anything other than direct service to your lotus feet. I offer my respectful obeisances to Your friendship. I offer my respectful obeisances to Your friendship again and again. May I find Your service as sweet as nectar. May I find Your service as sweet as nectar.

17. O queen whose fair complexion scratches with its nails the pride of yellow turmeric, when, happily marking my arms with auspicious markings embraced by charming red lac, will You give me the dear service of Your lotus feet.

18. O queen, when with great love and happiness will I daily rinse the drains of Your house with pure water, dry them with my own hair, and then scent Your garden pavilion with an abundance of sweetly fragrant incense?

19. When, at Your house early in the morning, will I carefully wash Your two lotus feet with camphor-scented water and then dry them with my hair?

20. When will this maidservant brush Your teeth with a twig, wash Your lotus feet, and, when You have entered another room, massage You with scented oil?

21. O queen whose lotus face defeats the moon, when, with jars of water scented with flowers and camphor and brought by one of Your charming and affectionate friends, will I carefully bathe You?

22. O moon-faced one, will I with a silken towel slowly and carefully dry the water from Your beautiful, delicate limbs, and the two fishes of Your eyes happily and restlessly swim from one direction to another, will I be

allowed, the hairs on my body standing up in bliss, to cover Your hips with a matchless red silk cloth, and all Your limbs, from Your head down, with a beautiful blue sari?

23. O beloved of the prince of Vraja, when, after washing Your lotus feet, will this person, with the many beautiful small garlands artistically fashioned by Narmada devi, lovingly braid Your hair?

24. O queen, when will I happily place on Your forehead beautiful musk tilaka as splendid as the full moon, on Your limbs glistening kunkuma, and on Your breasts wonderful pictures in fragrant colors?

25. O queen, will I, drawing a line of red sindura with a jeweled salaka, decorate the part in Your hair?

26. O queen, with a steady hand will I artistically decorate You with the aromatic red tilaka dots that are the most powerful aphrodisiac to madden Lord Krishna?

27. O beautiful one, will I happily decorate with beautiful earrings Your ears, which are the god of love's two ropes for binding the regal mad elephant of the prince of Vraja's heart?

28. O beautiful queen, although I carefully placed this garment over Your breasts to cover them from Krishna's gaze, He has not understood my intention. Tightly embracing You, He has Himself become the garment covering the two treasures dearer than His own life.

29. O golden-complexioned one, will this maidservant place lovely necklaces of pearls and jewels on Your beautiful breasts, Lord Mukunda's pillows when He is sleepy and fatigued?

30. O lotus-eyed one, at some time will I adorn Your fingers with glittering rings and Your two graceful arms, which are so dear to Lord Hari, with blue armlets studded with jewels?

31. O beautiful-eyed one, will I soon worship Your two lotus feet with jeweled anklets and the petals of Your lotus feet with toe-rings? With a splendid belt will I soon worship Your hips, the sacred pilgrimage place of Lord Krishna?

32. Bowed down with intense bliss, with two jeweled armlets will I decorate Your two graceful lotus arms, which expertly destroy the peacefulness of the swan of Lord Krishna's heart?

33. O beautiful one, will this person some day worship with a valuable necklace Your neck, which attained all good fortune when it was touched by the arm of Lord Gokulacandra in the festival of the rasa dance?

34. O beautiful-faced one, will I make the Syamantaka jewel, which after the death of proud Sankhacuda, was given by Balarama to cheerful-hearted Madhumangala, which Madhumangala with his own hand gave to You, and

which since has become the friend of the Kaustubha jewel, the central jewel of Your necklace?

35. O slender-waisted one, when, fearing that Your very slender waist might break, will I very carefully tie it with a new golden belt splendid with flower-cluster tassels at each end?

36. O golden one, when will Your nose, which defeats the sesame flower, receive from my hand a beautiful golden honey-pearl that agitates the great bumblebee of Lord Krishna?

37. O golden one, when, by Your order, will I place on Your left arm a silken band tied with jewels and flowers?

38. O restless-eyed one, the rings I place in Your ears made Lord Krishna, who agitates all the gopis, aimlessly wander in a circle.

39. O fawn-eyed one, when will I place a dot of splendid musk on Your chin, the temple of Mukunda's happiness?

40. O queen, when will I decorate Your pearl-like teeth with ruby-like red lines?

41. O girl with the golden lips, will the Krishna-parrot bite the nectar bimba fruits of Your lips, splendid with red khadira and camphor, placed by Me?

42. When will this person worship with black kajjala Your two eyes, which defeat the khanjana birds, and which, with the slightest movement from their corners, in a moment tightly bind the regal elephant of Lord Krishna?

43. His head reddened by the marks of Your feet as He tries to soothe Your jealous anger Lord Krishna has become extremely handsome. When, decorated with nectar red lac by me, will Your feet become very splendid?

44. O graceful artist, O queen, when will this maidservant happily place a sweet jasmine-garland filled with humming bees on Your gracefully sloping shoulders, touched in the rasa dance by Lord Krishna, who has become a moon shining with amorous passion?

45. O girl with charming limbs, O girl with a beautiful face, will this maidservant nearby hand You the articles of worship when, surrounded by Your friends, You are eager at heart to devotedly worship the sun-god on an alter of suryamani jewels?

46. O girl with beautiful thighs, employing the hands of Your friends, such as myself, will You place before Lord Krishna the many delicious foods You very carefully cooked by the order of the queen of Vraja?

47. O beautiful one, when, lovingly touching her forehead to the forehead of they, like me, who had brought the feast, will the jubilant queen of Vraja, like a loving mother, ask me, because I am Your maidservant, about Your welfare?

48. O queen, will I place before You the prasadam remnants tasted by the lotus mouth of Lord Krishna and respectfully brought by Danistha-gopi.

49. O girl whose limbs are anointed with kunkuma, when will I carefully feed You, Lalita, and Your other friends many kinds of ambrosia foods and nectar drinks mixed with the remnants of what was directly tasted by Lord Krishna?

50. O restless-eyed one, when will I lovingly give You sweet drinking-water scented with fresh patala flowers and camphor, water to rinse Your mouth, a toothbrush twig, and other things?

51. O queen, when, with great love, will I carefully light an abundance of aromatic incense, fan You, and perform other suitable services as You take Your meal?

52. O sweet-limbed girl, when, the hairs of my body standing upright in ecstasy, will I place a betel leaf filled with betel nuts and camphor into the lotus flower of Your mouth?

53. O queen, O beloved of Lord Krishna, will Lalita worship you with an arati lamp as Your other friends worship You with auspicious new songs and flowers and this maidservant, thinking You millions of times more dear than her own life's breath, worships You with a camara whisk?

54. O queen, when, eloquently joking with Lalita and Your other friends, will You decorate with a nap the charming pastime-bed I made with my own hands?

55. O merciful one, O girl with the beautiful heart, will the beautiful and auspicious time come when this maidservant massages Your feet and Rupa manjari massages Your two lotus hands?

56. O girl with the beautiful face, on the strength of some good fortune will I, as a vine of devotion here, in a secret place with Your affectionate friends, attain the remnants You had spit out and the waves of nectar water that washed Your lotus feet?

57. O queen, during Your meal will You take some nectar from Your own lotus mouth and lovingly give it to me, whose heart has gone to You?

58. O queen, will my two eyes someday attain You as, stumbling because of the happiness rising in Your heart, and the hairs of Your body standing erect, You walk to the town of Vraja's king in order to prepare a nectar feast for Lord Madhava?

59. Will Rupa manjari lead You on the path with Lalita and Visakha at Your two sides, Your friends all around, and me holding Your delicate waist from behind?

60 - 61. When will Danistha, seeing it in the distance, affectionately lead You, in my presence, to Nandisvara, the great abode of the king of Vraja,

which is filled with affectionate gopi friends, which is even more important than the Govardhana Hill worshipped by Vraja, which is very dear to the prince of Vraja, and which is filled with the tumultuous sounds of the eloquent gopas and the lowing of the surabhi cows?

62. O sweet one, O talented one, when, washing Your auspicious lotus feet, entering the kitchen, bowing down before the queen of Vraja and the other elder gopis, and cooking a nectar feast, will You plunge me into an ocean of bliss?

63. O queen, when will You be seen, Your head bowed and Your face blossoming with happiness as You place the ambrosia foods and nectar drinks for Lord Madhava in the hand of Rohini devi?

64. O sweet girl, when will Your lotus face, its passionate sidelong glances seen by Lord Madhava during the feast in the company of His elders, fill me with happiness?

65. When will You be seen as You gaze at the prince of Vraja, His cheeks sweet with a smile, as He wanders in the forest fulfilling His vow to protect the surabhi cows, or as He is embraced by His mother, her heart overwhelmed?

66. O girl bashful at heart, O girl with the beautiful face, seeing You happily taking Your meal, according to Your promise, with your dear friends and with the queen of Vraja, who is more affectionate than millions and trillions of mothers, will I at once attain bliss in my heart?

67. O girl whose eyes are restless as khanjana birds, seeing You with an embrace, with kissing Your head, and with many loving glances, loved by the queen of Vraja as if You were her own daughter, will I celebrate a great festival of transcendental bliss in my heart?

68. O friend Rupa manjari, will I, following behind, lead our queen, now a dancing arena for waves of amorous passion, Her large eyes wide open, and your arm affectionately placed about the vine of Her waist, to the pastime forest grove decorated by the presence of Lord Hari?

69. O friend, within my sight will Queen Radha with You decorate Her beloved with flower ornaments in a forest cottage by the shore of Her lake?

70. O beautiful one, hearing from the parrot Vichaksana of Your rendezvous with the prince of Vraja, will I happily decorate You with elegant garments, flower earrings, and necklaces?

71. O queen, when will I decorate the splendid doorway with garlands of many flowers filled with buzzing bees and with many splendid pictures of Kama drawn in kunkuma? O moon-faced girl, when will I decorate the bed in the cottage named Madananandada with networks of flowers?

72. O girl as fair as gold, will I happily and gently massage Your lotus feet as You rest Your head against the arm of the prince of Vraja, His lotus feet worshipped by Rupa manjari's hands?

73. Will I see You, Your eyebrows knitted and Your eyes burning with pride as Lord Madhusudana, the crown on the heads of expert jesters, stops You near Govardhana Hill on the pretext of collecting a toll?

74. O sweet-faced girl, when, seeing Lord Mukunda because of the breeze carrying the fragrance of Your slender form on some pretext leave the pastime-bed Chandravali with her own hand decorated with jasmine flowers, and, like a black bee, meet You at the lake shore, will I shine with pride?

75. O sweet, moon-faced girl, when will we see the new pastimes You enjoy with the Lord of Your life and with Your friends at Your sweet lake filled everywhere with the humming of intoxicated bees, the cooing of birds, and hosts of splendid, blossoming lotuses?

76. O girl with the beautiful thighs, when will Lord Krishna, who floods me with an ocean of bliss, happily decorate You with many kinds of flowers on the splendid lake shore crowded with blossoming flowers and forests full of humming bees?

77. As Her limbs blossom with happiness, will my queen's hair, decorated by jubilant, trembling Lord Hari with many types of slightly blossomed flowers, many large gunjas, and many splendid peacock feathers, all hastily brought by a certain happy girl, bring bliss to my eyes?

78. O girl with the beautiful face, seeing Lord Madhava struck with a lotus flower by intoxicated You in a flurry of amorous pastimes, will I try to hide the smile on my face?

79. When, O girl with the beautiful face, as You sing sweet love songs with the prince of Vraja, Your splendid graceful shoulder embraced by His long arms and He embraced by Your beautiful arms, will You give me transcendental bliss?

80. O queen, when will I hide the flute that You won from Lord Hari in the dice game, broke, and tossed to me?

81. O girl with the beautiful face, when, the hairs of my body standing up in ecstasy, will I fan You as You lay on a pastime bed of jasmine flowers in the temple of bliss of amorous love, smiling and conversing very sweetly with Your beloved?

82. O queen, O girl whose face is a blossoming lotus flower, O personification of shyness, when, Your two lotus feet exhausted by walking from the rendezvous, will You affectionately call this shameless person by name and engage her in massaging them?

83. "O granddaughter Radha, the time for You to worship the sungod has come! Where are You." Will Mukhara devi, appearing like the personification of nectar as she angrily speaks in this way, delight me?

84. O queen with my eyes and ears will I serve the nectar of Your words scented with the camphor of Your smile?

85. O pious one, when, picking flowers with Your sweet and crooked friends, You pretend to quarrel with the Lord of Your life and You angrily leave Him, will You fill me with boundless happiness?

86. O merciful one, sweetly begged by Madhava with many unbearable appeals, will this agitated person fall down before Lalita's feet to break Your jealous anger?

87. O wise and solemn one, will Your coronation as the queen of Vrndavan forest, jubilantly performed by Paurnamasi with a great festival of auspicious singing, dancing and the music of vinas and other instruments, and with many pitchers of pure, scented water, be seen by me?

88. O girl with the beautiful face, when on the full moon day of the month of Sravana Your brother Sridama pleases the miser Jatila by giving her ten thousand cows and then takes You home for a visit, will, as You melt with weeping from both happiness and sorrow, Your parents lovingly embrace You in my presence?

89. O merciful one, when, because I feel shy before Your friends, will You take me to a cave in the king of mountains and there tutor me in the art of melodious singing?

90. O queen, when, requested by Lalita devi, will You affectionately ask me, my head bowed with shyness in the assembly, to recite many splendid and sweet poems?

91. O queen, when, on the shore of Your lake, in a grove filled with humming bees, will You teach me to play the kacchapi lute?

92. O queen, when, because Your friends are too shy to act, will You hint that I should restring the favourite necklace, broken in Your pastimes?

93. O queen, when, after looking in all directions, will You take the chewed betel nuts from Your mouth and affectionately place them in mine?

94. O girl with the moon face, with clever hints will You send me to quickly get the favorite charming sash forgotten in the amorous passionate battle with the Lord of Your life?

95. O grave and sober one, after angrily punishing this person for a very slight fault, will You again glance on her with a little mercy when Lalita brings her before You?

96. I am Yours! I am Yours! I cannot live without You! O queen, please understand this and bring me to Your feet.

97. O restless-eyed girl, Your lake is the eternal home of You and Your beloved. My residence is there. There I stay.

98. O beautiful lake, my queen eternally enjoys amorous pastimes with Her beloved on your shore. If you are most dear to Them, then, please mercifully show me now the girl who is my life and soul.

99. My queen will not leave your company for even a moment. Because You are both the same age you are the realm of Her playful joking pastimes. O girl with the beautiful face, O Visakha, please show me my queen and save the life of me, on the verge of death because I am separated from Her.

100. O Lord, O nectar moon of Gokula, O Lord whose cheerful face is a lotus flower, O sweetly-smiling one, O Lord melting with compassion, so I may serve You both with love please lead me to the place where Your beloved enjoys loving pastimes with You.

101. My queen, even a drop of the beauty of the tip of whose lotus toenail the goddess of fortune is not able to attain, if You do not give charity to my eyes, then what is the use of my life, ablaze with a great forest-fire of sufferings?

102. For me somehow the present moment is flooded by a nectar ocean of many hopes. If You do not give me Your mercy, then of what use to me are this life, the land of Vraja, and Sri Krishna, the enemy of Baka?

103. O merciful one, if You will not give Your great mercy to suffering me, then what is the use of all these words? What will my long service to Your lake accomplish?

104. O affectionate one, I pray that this Vilapa-kusumanjali (Handful of Flowers in the Form of a Lament), which, with much weeping to attain Your loving service, and with a heart burning with pain, I take from my chest and place at Your lotus feet, may give You a little pleasure.

The 16 Names of Shri Radha

by Lord Narayana in the *Brahma Vaivarta Purana*, Shri Krishna Janma Khanda 17.220-240:

Radha - She who is the bestower of ultimate divine bliss.
Rasesvari - She Who is the Goddess of the rasa dance.
Rasa-Vasini - She Who always lives with the rasa dance.
Rasikesvari - She Who is the Goddess of those who relish divine mellows.
Krsna-Pranadhika - She Who is dearer to Krishna than His own life.
Krsna-Priya - She Who is Krishna's most dearly beloved companion.

Krsna-Svarupini - She Whose form resembles Krishna is so many ways.
Krsna-Vamanga-sambhuta - She Who is generated from Krishna left side.
Paramananda Rupini - She Who is the personification of supreme ecstasy.
Krsna - She Who bestows the best form of supreme liberation.
Vrindavani - She Who lives in Vrindavana.
Vrinda - She Who always lives in the company of Her girlfriends.
Vrindavana-Vinodini - She Who enjoys many pleasures in Vrindavana.
Chandravali - She Whose form has many moons.
Chandra-Kamta - She Who effulgence is like the moon.
Sarac-chandra-Prabhanana - She Whose face glows like the full moon of August.

108 Names of Shrimati Radhika
SRI SRI RADHIKA ASTOTTARA SATA NAMA STOTRAM
by Srila Raghunatha Dasa Goswami

aviksatmesvari kascid vrndavana-mahesvarim
tat padamboja-maka gati dasyati katara
patita tat-saras tire ruda tyartha-ravakulam
tac chri-vaktreksanavaptyai namanyetani sanjagau

Some maidservant, unable to find her mistress, has fallen on the bank of Radhakunda, crying in great anxiety, being very eager to take exclusive shelter of Her lotus feet, glorifying Her by singing the following names of Her:

radha gandharvika a-kamita
gandharva radhika chandrakantir madhava-sangini

1. Radha, 2. Gandharvika by the prince of Vraja, 4. Who is worshipped by the Gandharva-angels, 5. Whose luster is like the moon, 6. Who accompanies Madhava.

damodaradvaita-sakhi kartikotkirtidesvari
mukunda dayita-vrnda dhammilla mani-manjari

7. Damodar's unrivalled queen who bestows fame on the Kartika month, 9. The crestjewel of Mukunda's ladyfriends.

bhaskaropasika varsabhanavi vrsabhanuja
ananga manjari jyestha sridama varajottama

10. Who worships the sun, 11. Who belongs to King Vrisabhanu, 12. Who is born from King Vrisabhanu, 13. Ananga Manjari's older sister, 14. Sridama's younger sister, 15. The greatest (fem.)

kirtida-kanyaka matr-sneha-piyusa-putrika
visakha-savayah prestha visakha jivitadhika

16. Kirtida's daughter, 17. Who is the nectarean object of Her mother's affection, 18. Who is of the same age as Visakha, 19. Who is dearer than life to Visakha.

pranadvitiya lalita vrndavana viharini
lalita prana-laksaika-raksa vrndavanesvari

20. Who is none other than Lalita's very life, 21. Enjoys in Vrindavana, 22. Who saves Lalita's life lakhs of times, 23. Queen of Vrndavana.

vrajendra-grhini krsna-praya-sneha-niketanam
vraja go-gopa-gopali jiva-matraika-jivanam

24. Who is as dear to Mother Yasoda as Krsna, 25. Who is the only life of the life of the cows, cowherdsmen and cowherdgirls of Vraja.

snehalabhira-rajendra vatsalacyuta-purva-ja
govinda pranayadhara surabhi sevanotsuka

26. Who is the object of King Nanda's affection, 27. Who gets parental affection from Balaram, 28. Who is the object of Govinda's love (Govinda is eager to serve His surabhi cows).

dhrta nandisvara-ksema gamanotkanthi-manasa
sva-dehadvaitata drsta dhanistha dhyeya-darsana

29. Who is very eager to go to Nandisvara for serving Krsna, 30. Who is regarded as non-different from her by Dhanistha and seen in her meditations, (Dhanistha is Yasoda's maidservant).

gopendra-mahisi paka-sala-vedi prakasika
ayur-varddha-karaddhana rohini gTRa-mastaka

31. Who is seen in Mother Yasoda's kitchen, 32. Whose cooked grains increase Krsna's life, 33. Whose head is smelt by Rohini.

subala nyasta sarupya subala priti-tosita
mukhara-drk sudha-naptri jatila drsti-bhasita

34. Who has bestowed a form equal to Hers to Subala, 35. Who is very fond of Subala, 36. Who is nectar in Mukhara's eyes, 37. Who is afraid to see Her mother-in-law, Jatila.

madhumangala narita-smita-chandrika
paurnamasi bahih khelat prana-panjara sarika

38. Who smiles moonbeams after hearing Madhumangala's jokes, 39. The she-parrot of Whose heart is caught in Paurnamasi's cage.

sva ganadvaita jivatuh sviyahankara-vardhini
sva ganopendra padabja sparsa-lambhana harsini

40. Who is the oiends, 41. Who increases the pride of Her relatives, 42. Who is very happy to touch Upendra's feet with Her friends.

sviya vrndavanodyana paliki krta-vrndaka
jnata vrndatavi sarva lata-taru-mrga-dvija

43. Who has placed Vrinda in charge of Vrindavana's gardens, 44. Who is known by all the vines, trees, deer and birds of Vrindavana.

isac chandana samghrsta nava-kasmira-deha-bhah
java-puspa pritha-hari patta chinarunambara

45. Whose body shines with fresh vermillion ground with some sandalpaste, 46. Whose silken dress shines more reddish than the java flower.

charanabja-tala-jyotir arunakrta-bhutala
hari chitta chamatkari charu nupura nihsvana

47. Whose lotus the surface of the earth shines crimson-red, 48. Who astonishes Hari's mind with the sweet sound of Her anklebells.

krsna-sranti-hara sroni pitha-valgita ghantika
krsna sarvasva pinodyat kuchanchan mani-malika

49. The nice sounds of whose waistbells remove Krsna's fatigue, 50. The pearl necklace on whose firm, raised breasts is everything to Krsna.

nana-ratnollasad sankha-cuda charu bhuja-dvaya
syamantaka-mani bhrajan mani-bandhati-bandhura

51. Whose two beautiful arms are adorned with conchshell bangles inset with various jewels, 52. On Whose wrist the beautiful Syamantaka jewel shines.

suvarna darpana- ullanghi mukha-mandala
pakka dadima bijabha dantakrstaghabhic chuka

53. The shining of Whose face defeats that of a golden mirror, 54. Whose teeth, that shine like ripe pomegranate seeds, attract the parrot-like Aghabhit (Krsna).

abja-ragadi srstasana
saubhagya kajjalankakta netranandita khanjana

55. Whose ruby earrings are shaped like lotus buds, 56. Whose wagtail-like eyes are anointed with beautiful eyeliner, giving great joy to the eyes.

suvrtta mauktikamukta nasika tilapuspika
sucharu nava-kasturi tilakancita-bhalaka

57. Whose nose, that is beautiful as a sesame flower, is adorned with a round pearl, 58. Whose forehead is adorned with beautiful tilak made of fresh musk.

divya veni vinirdhuta keki-pincha-vara-stutih
netranta-sara vidhvamsakrta chanurajid dhrtih

59. Whose divine hair braid is worshiped by peacock feathers (being defeated in beauty), 60. The arrows of Whose glances destroy the patience of Krsna, Who defeated the Chanura wrestler.

sphurat kaisora-tarunya sandhi-bandhura-vigraha
madhavollasakonmatta pikoru madhura-svara

61. Who is blooming teenage beauty personified, 62. Who pleases Madhava, 63. Who maddens Madhava with Her sweet, cuckoo-like voice.

pranayuta-sata prestha madhavotkirti-lampata
krsnapanga-tarangodyat smita-piyusa-budbuda

64. Who is more attached to Madhava's great glories than to millions of lives, 65. Whose nectars provide bubbles on the waves of Krsna's glances.

punjibhuta jagallajja vaidagdhi-digdha-vigraha
karuna vidravad deha murtiman madhuri-ghata

66. Who is the height of cleverness, embarrassing the whole world, 67. Whose body melts in kindness, 68. Who is abundant sweetness personified.

jagad-gunavati-varga giyamana gunocchaya
sacyadi subhaga-vrnda vandyama-saubhaga

69. Whose glories are loudly sung by all the great ladies of the world, 70. Who is incessantly praised by beautiful ladies like Saci.

vina-vadana sangita rasalasya visarada
narada pramukhodgita jagad anandi sad-yasah

71. Who is expert in singing and playing vina in the rasa dance, 72. Whose pure glories are sung by sages headed by Narada, giving joy to the world.

govardhana-guha geha grhini kunja-mandana
chandamsu-nandini baddha bhagini-bhava-vibhrama

73. She is the housewife in the caves in Govardhana, 74. She decorates the kunja, 75. She has a sisterly relationship with Yamuna (Yamuna is the

daughter of the sun and Radha is the daughter of Vrisabhanu, the sun in Taurus).

divya kundalata narma sakhya-dama-vibhusita
govardhanadharahladi srngara-rasa-pandita

76. She is adoring Kundalata's friendship, 77. She is the professor in amorous rapture, giving joy to the holder of Govardhana.

girindra-dhara vaksah srih sankhacudari-jivanam
gokulendra-suta-prema kama-bhupendra-pattanam

78. She is always present at the chest of the holder of Govardhan, 79. She is the life of the enemy of Sankhacuda, 80. She is the settlement of Cupid for the love of the son of Gokulendra.

vrsa-vidhvamsa nti sva-nirmita sarovara
nija kunda-jala-krida jita sankarsananuja

81. Who made Her own pond after the killer of Arista mocked Her, 82. Who defeats Sankarsana's younger brother in sports in Her own pond.

mura-mardana mattebha vihara-mrta-dirghika
girindra-dhara-parindra rati-yuddhoru simhika

83. She is the ambrosial pond of enjoyment for the intoxicated elephant who defeated Mura, 84. She is a powerful lioness fighting amorous sports with the king of lions, the holder of the best of mountains.

sva tanu-saurabhonmatti krta mohana madhava
dor-mulocchalana krida vyakuli-krta kesava

85. Who enchants by bodily fragrance, 86. Who agitates Kesava by playfully showing Her armpit.

nija kunda-tati kunja klrpta keli kalodyama
divya malli-kulollasi sayyakalpita vigraha

87. Who expands Her artful plays in the kunja on the bank of Her own pond, 88. Who makes a bed of divine jasmine flowers there with joy.

krsna vama-bhuja nyasta charu daksina gandaka
savya bahu-lata baddha krsna daksina sad-bhuja

89. Who places Her beautiful right cheek on Krsna's left arm, 90. Who holds Krsna's right arm with Her left vine-like arm.

krsna daksina charuru slista vamoru-rambhika
girindra-dhara drg-vaksor mardi-sustana-parvata

91. Whose beautiful, broad, banana-like left hip touches Krsna's right hip, 92. Whose nice, mountain-like breasts are being massaged by the Holder of Govardhana.

govindadhara piyusa vasitadhara-pallava
sudha-sanchaya charukti sitali-krta madhava

93. Whose leaf-like lips are scented by the nectar of Govinda's lips, 94. Whose beautiful words distribute nectar, cooling Madhava off.

govindodgirna tambula raga rajyat kapolika
krsna sambhoga saphali-krta manmatha sambhava

95. Whose cheeks are colored by the pan from Govinda's lips, 96. Who realizes Krsna's fancies of amorous enjoyments.

govinda marjitoddanmukha
visakha vijita krida-santi nidralu-vigraha

97. The profuse perspiration from whose face is wiped off by Govinda, 98. Who is being fanned by Visakha when She falls asleep after playing with Krsna.

govinda-charana-nyasta kaya-manasa jivana
svapranarbuda nirmanchya hari pada-rajah kana

99. Who has placed Her life, body and mind at Govinda's lotus feet, 100. Who worships the dust of Hari's lotus feet with billions of hearts.

anumatracyutadarsa sayyamanatma lochana
nitya-nutana govinda vaktra-subhramsu-darsana

101. Who curses Her eyes for every second that they do not see Acyuta,
102. Who beholds Govinda's ever-fresh moonlike face.

nihsima hari-madhurya saundaryadyeka-bhogini
sapatnya dhama murali-matra bhagya kataksini

103. Who is the only enjoyer of Hari's endless sweetness and beauty, 104.
Who can only blink at the fortune of Her co-wife, the Murali flute.

gadha buddhi-bala krida jita vamsi-vikarsini
narmokti chandrikotphulla krsna kamabdi-vardhini

105. Who takes Krsna's flute after defeating Him in a gambling match, 106.
Who increases the ocean of Krsna's desires by the full moonbeams of Her
joking words.

vraja-chandrendridhu-salika
krsna sarvendriyonmadi radhetyaksara-yugmaka

107. Who is the moonlike resting place for all the senses of the moon of
Vraja (Sri Krsna), 108. The two syllables of Whose name Ra-dha madden
all of Krsna's senses.

idam sri radhika namnam astottara satojjvalam
sri radhalambhakam nama stotram charu-rasayanam
yo dhite parama pritya dinah katara-manasah
sa natham acirenaiva sa natham iksate dhruvam

Whoever recites these 108 names of Sri Radha, that consists of all
beautiful, nectarean Radha-nama, with great love, humility and eagerness,
will certainly and swiftly behold her Mistress.

iti srimad raghunatha dasa gosvami viracita stavavalyam
sri radhika-stottara-sata nama stotram sampurnam.

Thus ends Srimad Raghunatha Dasa Gosvami's Sri Radhika's 108
names-prayer.

Sri Radha Sahasra-nama Stotra

The Thousand Names of Radharani

[From the Narada Pancharata, translated by Bhaktivinoda Thakura, translated into English by Kusakratha Prabhu]

(Sri Radha Sahasra-nama was originally spoken by Lord Shiva to Parvati devi, recorded in the 5th Chapter of Sri Narada Pancharatra.)

Texts 1 and 2

Sri Parvati said: O lord of lords, O master of the universe, O master kind to your devotees, if you are kind to me, if you have mercy for me, then, O lord, please tell me all you have heard, the most secret of secrets in your effulgent heart.

Texts 3 and 4

O lord of lords, the transcendental thousand names of Goddess Sri Radha-gopi, which inspire pure devotional service, and which you have never told anyone, please tell to me. Why is the Goddess, who creates and destroys the universes, a gopi?

Text 5

Lord Siva said: O goddess, O queen, please hear this auspicious and very wonderful truth, which destroys sins: For Her their are neither births nor material activities.

Text 6

When Lord Hari, out of a sense of duty, performs activities (in the material world), she, desiring to be near Him, assumes many different forms.

Text 7

I have already explained why She is a gopi. O goddess, now please hear Her thousand names.

Text 8

What I have never spoken in the Tantras and what they who yearn for liberation cherish, out of love for you, I will now speak.

Text 9

Day and night this knowledge is as dear to me as life. O daughter of the mountain king, please hear and regularly chant (these thousand names) as far as you are able.

Text 10

By Her kindness Krsna, the master of Goloka, is the Supreme Master. Narada is the sage of Her thousand holy names.

Text 11

Radha, who grants the four goals of life, is said to be the Supreme Goddess.

(Her thousand names follow)

Text 11
om sri-radha radhika krsna-
vallabha krsna-samyuta

Om. She is Lord Krsna's greatest worshiper (sri-radha and radhika), Lord Krsna's beloved (krsna-vallabha), and Lord Krsna's constant companion (krsna-samyuta).

Text 12
vrndavanesvari krsna-
priya madana-mohini
srimati krsna-kanta cha
krsnananda-pradayini

She is the queen of Vrndavana (vrndavanesvari), the beloved of Lord Krsna (krsna-priya), more charming than Kamadeva (madana-mohini), beautiful (srimati), Lord Krsna's beloved (krsna-kanta), and the giver of bliss to Lord Krsna (krsnananda-pradayini).

Text 13
yasasvini yasogamya
yasodananana-vallabha
damodara-priya gopi
gopananda-kari tatha

She is famous (yasasvini and yasogamya), the beloved of Yasoda's son (yasodananana-vallabha), dear to Lord Damodara (damodara-priya), a cowherd girl (gopi), and the giver of happiness to the gopas (gopananda-kari).

Text 14
krsnanga-vasini hrdya
hari-kanta hari-priya
pradhana-gopika gopa-
kanya trailokya-sundari

Her residence is on Lord Krsna's limbs (krsnanga-vasini). She is
charming (hrdya). She is Lord Hari's beloved (hari-kanta and hari-priya),
the most important gopi (pradhana-gopika), the daughter of a gopa
(gopa-kanya), and the most beautiful girl in the three worlds (trailokya-
sundari).

Text 15
vrndavana-vihari cha
vikasita-mukhambuja
gokulananda-kartri cha
gokulananda-dayini

She enjoys pastimes in Vrndavana (vrndavana-vihari), Her face is a
blossoming lotus (vikasita-mukhambuja), and she brings happiness to
Gokula (gokulananda-kartri and gokulananda-dayini).

Text 16
gati-prada gita-gamya
gamanagamana-priya
visnu-priya visnu-kanta
visnor anga-nivasini

She gives the goal of life (gati-prada), is approached by chanting her
holy names (gita-gamya), is the beloved of the omniprescent Supreme
Personality of Godhead (gamanagamana-priya), is Lord Visnu's beloved
(visnu-priya and visnu-kanta), and resides on Lord Visnu's limbs (visnor
anga-nivasini).

Text 17
yasodananda-patni cha
yasodananda-gehini
kamari-kanta kamesi
kama-lalasa-vigraha

She is the wife of Yasoda's son (yasodananda-patni and yasodananda-
gehini), the beloved of lust's enemy (kamari-kanta), Lord Krsna's

amorous queen (kamesi), and Lord Krsna's passionate lover (kama-lalasa-vigraha).

Text 18

jaya-prada jaya jiva
jivananda-pradayini
nandanandana-patni cha
vrsabhanu-suta siva

She is the giver of victory (jaya-prada) and She is victory itself (jaya). She is life (jiva), the giver of happiness to the living entities (jivananda-pradayini), the wife of Nanda's son (nandanandana-patni), King Vrsabhanu's daughter (vrsabhanu-suta), and auspicious (siva).

Text 19

ganadhyaksa gavadhyaksa
gavam gatir anuttama
kanchanabha hema-gatri
kanchanangada-dharini

She is the leader of the gopis (ganadhyaksa), the ruler of the cows (gavadhyaksa and gavam gati), and without superior (anuttama). She has a golden complexion (kanchanabha), Her limbs are golden (hema-gatri), and She wears golden armlets (kanchanangada-dharini).

Text 20

asoka sokorahita
visoka soka-nasini
gayatri vedamata cha
vedatita vid-uttama

She never laments (asoka, sokorahita, and visoka), she ends lamentation (soka-nasini). She is the Gayatri mantra (gayatri), the mother of the Vedas (veda-mata), beyond the Vedas (vedatita), and the wiseset philosopher (vid-uttama).

Text 21

niti-sastra-priya niti-
gatir matir abhistada
veda-priya veda-garbha
veda-marga-pravardhini

She is an eager student of the scriptures describing ethics (niti-sastra-priya). She is the perfect moralist (niti-gati), the most thoughtful philosopher (mati), the fulfiller of desires (abhistada), an eager student of the Vedas (veda-priya), the mother of the Vedas (veda-garbha), and the teacher of the Vedas' path (veda-marga-pravardhini).

Text 22
veda-gamya veda-para
vicitra-kanakojjvala
tathojjvala-prada nitya
tathaivojjvala-gatrika

She is approached by Vedic study (veda-gamya). She is the supreme goal described in the Vedas (veda-para). She is splendid with wonderful golden ornaments (vicitra-kanakojjvala), glorious (ujjvala-prada), and eternal (nitya), and Her limbs are filled with glory (ujjvala-gatrika).

Text 23
nanda-priya nanda-suta-
radhyanandaprada subha
subhangi vimalangi cha
vilasiny aparajita

She is dear to Maharaja Nanda (nanda-priya), worshiped by Nanda's son (nanda-sutaradhya), delightful (ananda-prada), beautiful (subha), with beautiful limbs (subhangi), with splendid limbs (vimalangi), playful (vilasini), and unconquerable (aparajita).

Text 24
janani janmasunya cha
janma-mrtyu-jarapaha
gatir gatimatam dhatri
dhatranandapradayini

She is the mother of all (janani), without birth (janma-sunya), the remover of birth, death, and old-age (janma-mrtyu-jarapaha), the supreme goal of the aspiring devotees (gatir gatimatam), the mother of all (dhatri), and the giver of bliss to the Supreme Creator (dhatranandapradayini).

Text 25
jagannatha-priya saila-

vasini hema-sundari
kisori kamala padma
padma-hasta payoda-da

She is dear to the Lord of the universes (jagannatha-priya), She resides
on a hill (saila- vasini), is beautiful and golden (hema-sundari), is
youthful (kisori), like a lotus flower (kamala and padma), her hands are
lotuses (padma-hasta), and She is buxom (payoda-da).

Text 26
payasvini payo-datri
pavitra sarva-mangala
maha-jiva-prada krsna-
kanta kamala-sundari

She is buxom (payasvini and payo-datri), pure (pavitra), all-auspicious
(sarva-mangala), the great giver of life (maha-jiva-prada), Lord Krsna's
beloved (krsna-kanta), and beautiful as a lotus (kamala-sundari).

Text 27
vicitra-vasini citra-
vasini citra-rupini
nirguna su-kulina cha
niskulina nirakula

She is wonderfully fragrant (vicitra-vasini and citra-vasini), wonderfully
beautiful (citra-rupini), free of the modes of material nature (nirguna),
born in a pious family (su-kulina), not born in any family of the material
world (niskulina), and free from all distrees (nirakula).

Text 28
gokulantara-geha cha
yogananda-kari tatha
venu-vadya venu-ratih
venu-vadya-parayana

Her home is in Gokula (gokulantara-geha). She delights Lord Krsna
when She meets Him (yogananda-kari). She plays the flute (venu-vadya),
enjoys playing the flute (venu-rati), and is fond of playing the flute
(venu-vadya-parayana).

Text 29
gopalasya priya saumya-
rupa saumya-kulodvaha
mohamoha vimoha cha
gati-nistha gati-prada

She is Lord Gopala's beloved (gopalasya priya). She is gentle and noble (saumya-rupa), born in an exalted family (saumya-kulodvaha), charming (moha and vimoha), and free from bewilderment (amoha), and She gives the goal of life (gati-nistha and gati-prada).

Text 30
girbana-vandya girbana
girbana-gana-sevita
lalita cha visoka cha
visakha chitra-malini

The demigods offer repsectful obeisances to Her (girbana-vandya). She is divine (girbana), served by the demigods (girbana-gana-sevita), playful and charming (lalita), free from lamentation (visoka), the star Visakha (visakha), and decorated with wonderful garlands (citra-malini).

Text 31
jitendriya suddha-sattva
kulina kula-dipika
dipa-priya dipa-datri
vimala vimalodaka

She has conquered Her senses (jitendriya). She is situated in pure goodness (suddha-sattva), born in a noble family (kulina), the lamp illuminating Her family (kula-dipika), fond of lamps (dipa-priya), the giver of the lamp (dipa-datri), pure (vimala), and the sacred river (vimalodaka).

Text 32
kantara-vasini krsna
krsnachandra-priya matih
anuttara duhkha-hantri
duhkha-kartri kulodvaha

She lives in a forest (kantara-vasini). She is Lord Krsna's beloved (krsna

and krsnachandra-priya). She is thoughtfulness (mati), unsurpassed
(anuttara), the remover of sufferings (duhkha-hantri), the creator of
sufferings (duhkha-kartri), and the noblest in Her family (kulodvaha).

Text 33
matir laksmir dhrtir lajja
kantih pustih smrtih ksama
ksirodasayini devi
devari-kula-mardini

She is thoughtfulness (mati), Goddess Laksmi (laksmi), perseverance
(dhrti), modesty (lajja), beauty (kanti), fulfillment (pusti), memory
(smrti), patience (ksama), she who lies down on the ocean of milk
(ksirodasayini), the goddess (devi), and the crusher of Lord Krsna's
enemies (devari-kula-mardini).

Text 34
vaisnavi cha maha-laksmih
kula-pujya kula-priya
samhartri sarva-daityanam
savitri veda-gamini

She is Lord Visnu's consort (vaisnavi), Goddess Maha-Laksmi (maha-
laksmi), worshiped by Her family (kula-pujya), dear to Her family (kula-
priya), the destroyer of all the demons (samhartri sarva-daityanam), the
gayatri mantra (savitri), and a follower of the Vedas (veda-gamini).

Text 35
vedatita niralamba
niralamba-gana-priya
niralamba-janaih pujya
niraloka nirasraya

She is beyond the Vedas (vedatita), liberated (niralamba), dear to the
liberated (niralamba-gana-priya), worshiped by the liberated (niralamba-
janaih pujya), unseen by conditioned souls (niraloka), and independent
(nirasraya).

Text 36
ekanga sarvaga sevya
brahma-patni sarasvati

rasa-priya rasa-gamya
rasadhisthatr-devata

She has one form (ekanga). She is all-pervading (sarvaga), the supreme
object of worship (sevya), Brahma's wife (brahma-patni), Goddess
Sarasvati (sarasvati), fond of the rasa dance (rasa-priya), the girl Lord
Krsna approaches in the rasa dance (rasa-gamya), and the predominating
Deity of the rasa dance (rasadhisthatr-devata).

Text 37
rasika rasikananda
svayam rasesvari para
rasa-mandala-madhyastha
rasa-mandala-sobhita

She enjoys the transcendental mellows (rasika) and tastes the bliss of the
transcendental mellows (rasikananda). She is the queen of the rasa dance
(svayam rasesvari), transcendental (para), the girl who stays in the
middle of the rasa dance circle (rasa-mandala-madhyastha), and the girl
who beautifies the rasa dance circle (rasa-mandala-sobhita).

Text 38
rasa-mandala-sevya cha
rasa-krida manohara
pundarikaksa-nilaya
pundarikaksa-gehini

She is served in the rasa dance circle (rasa-mandala-sevya), and She
enjoys the pastime of the rasa dance (rasa-krida). She is beautiful
(manohara), Her dark eyes are lotus flowers (pundarikaksa-nilaya), and
She is the wife of lotus-eyed Krsna (pundarikaksa-gehini).

Text 39
pundarikaksa-sevya cha
pundarikaksa-vallabha
sarva-jivesvari sarva-
jiva-vandya parat para

She is served by lotus-eyed Krsna (pundarikaksa-sevya), dear to lotus-
eyed Krsna (pundarikaksa-vallabha), the queen of all living entities
(sarva-jivesvari), worshiped by all living entities (sarva-jiva-vandya),
and greater than the greatest (parat para).

Text 40
prakrtih sambhu-kanta cha
sadasiva-manohara
ksut pipasa daya nidra
bhrantih srantih ksamakula

She is the goddess of the material nature (prakrti), and the beautiful wife
of Lord Siva (sambhu-kanta and sadasiva-manohara). She is hunger
(ksut), thirst (pipasa), mercy (daya), sleep (nidra), bewilderment
(bhranti), exhaustion (sranti), and patience (ksamakula).

Text 41
vadhu-rupa gopa-patni
bharati siddha-yogini
satya-rupa nitya-rupa
nityangi nitya-gehini

She is a young girl (vadhu-rupa), the wife of a gopa (gopa-patni), the
goddess of eloquence (bharati), and perfect in the science of yoga
(siddha-yogini). Her form is eternal (satya-rupa, nitya-rupa, and
nityangi), and She is Lord Krsna's wife eternally (nitya-gehini).

Text 42
sthana-datri tatha dhatri
maha-laksmih svayam-prabha
sindhu-kanya sthana-datri
dvaraka-vasini tatha

She gives Her devotees their homes (sthana-datri). She is the mother
(dhatri), Goddess Maha-Laksmi (maha-laksmi), self-effulgent (svayam-
prabha), the daughter of the milk ocean (sindhu-kanya), and she who
resides in Dvaraka (dvaraka-vasini).

Text 43
buddhih sthitih sthana-rupa
sarva-karana-karana
bhakti-priya bhakti-gamya
bhaktananda-pradayini

She is intelligence (buddhi), steadiness (sthiti and sthana-rupa), the
cause of all causes (sarva-karana-karana), fond of serving Lord Krsna
(bhakti-priya), approached by devotional service (bhakti-gamya), and the

giver of bliss to the devotees (bhaktananda-pradayini).

Text 44
bhakta-kalpa-drumatita
tathatita-guna tatha
mano-'dhisthatr-devi cha
krsna-prema-parayana

She is more than a kalpa-vrksa tree for the devotees (bhakta-kalpa-drumatita), the possessor of the greatest transcendental virtues (atita-guna), the predominating Deity of the heart (mano-'dhisthatr-devi), and the girl completely in love with Lord Krsna (krsna-prema-parayana).

Text 45
niramaya saumya-datri
tatha madana-mohini
ekanamsa siva ksema
durga durgati-nasini

She is free from all disease (niramaya), the most gentle, kind, and generous (saumya-datri), more charming than Kamadeva (madana-mohini), one without a second (eka and anamsa), the wife of Lord Siva (siva and durga), happiness and auspiciousness personified (ksema), and the person who destroys all calamities (durgati-nasini).

Text 46
isvari sarva-vandya cha
gopaniya subhankari
palini sarva-bhutanam
tatha kamanga-harini

She is the supreme controller (isvari), worshiped by all (sarva-vandya), reclusive (gopaniya), the giver of auspiciousness (subhankari), the protectress of all living entities (palini sarva-bhutanam), and the wife of Lord Siva who destroyed Kamadeva's body (kamanga-harini).

Text 47
sadyo-mukti-prada devi
veda-sara parat para
himalaya-suta sarva
parvati girija sati

She is the person who quickly gives liberation (sadyo-mukti-prada), the goddess (devi), the essence of the Vedas (veda-sara), greater than the greatest (parat para), and Goddess Parvati (himalaya-suta, sarva, parvati, girija, and sati).

Text 48
daksa-kanya deva-mata
manda-lajja hares tanuh
vrndaranya-priya vrnda
vrndavana-vilasini

She is Daksa's daughter (daksa-kanya), the demigods' mother (deva-mata), bold (manda-lajja), Lord Hari's own transcendental form (hares tanuh), fond of Vrndavana (vrndaranya-priya), goddess Vrnda (vrnda), and the girl who enjoys pastimes in Vrndavana (vrndavana-vilasini).

Text 49
vilasini vaisnavi cha
brahmaloka-pratisthita
rukmini revati satya-
bhama jambavati tatha

She is playful (vilasini), Lord Visnu's companion (vaisnavi), the predominating goddess of the spiritual world (brahmaloka-pratisthita), Rukmini (rukmini), Revati (revati), Satyabhama (satyabhama), and Jambavati (jambavati).

Text 50
sulaksmana mitravinda
kalindi jahnu-kanyka
paripurna purnatara
tatha haimavati gatih

She is Sulaksmana (sulaksmana), Mitravinda (mitravinda), Kalindi (kalindi), Jahnavi (jahnu-kanyka), most perfect (paripurna and purnatara), Goddess Parvati (haimavati), and the supreme goal of life (gati).

Text 51
apurva brahma-rupa cha
brahmanda-paripalini

brahmanda-bhanda-madbyastha
brahmanda-bhanda-rupini

She is unprecedented (apurva), spiritual (brahma-rupa), the protectress
of the universe (brahmanda-paripalini), the goddess who enters the
material universe (brahmanda-bhanda-madbyastha), the goddess who
Herself is the material universe (brahmanda-bhanda-rupini).

Text 52
anda-rupanda-madhyastha
tathanda-paripalini
anda-bahyanda-samhartri
siva-brahma-hari-priya

She is the goddess who is the material universe (anda-rupa), the goddess
who has entered the material universe (anda-madhyastha), the
protectress of the material universe (anda-paripalini), the goddess who is
beyond the material universe (anda-bahya), the destroyer of the material
universe (anda-samhartri), and she who is dear to Siva, Brahma, and
Visnu (siva-brahma-hari-priya).

Text 53
maha-visnu-priya kalpa-
vrksa-rupa nirantara
sara-bhuta sthira gauri
gaurangi sasi-sekhara

She is Lord Maha-Visnu's beloved (maha-visnu-priya), a kalpa-vrksa tree
(kalpa-vrksa-rupa), eternal (nirantara and sthira), the best (sara-bhuta),
fair (gauri and gaurangi), and Lord Siva's wife (sasi-sekhara).

Text 54
sveta-champaka-varnabha
sasi-koti-sama-prabha
malati-malya-bhusadhya
malati-malya-dharini

She is fair as a sveta champaka flower (sveta-champaka-varnabha),
splendid as millions of moons (sasi-koti-sama-prabha), and decorated
with jasmine garlands (malati-malya-bhusadhya and malati-malya-
dharini).

Text 55
krsna-stuta krsna-kanta
vrndavana-vilasini
tulasy-adhisthatr-devi
samsararnava-para-da

She is praised by Krsna (krsna-stuta) and loved by Krsna (krsna-kanta).
She enjoys pastimes in Vrndavana (vrndavana-vilasini). She is Goddess
Tulasi (tulasy-adhisthatr-devi). She carries one to the farther shore of the
ocean of birth and death (samsararnava-para-da).

Text 56
saradaharadambhoda
yasoda gopa-nandini
atita-gamana gauri
paranugraha-karini

She gives what is the best (sarada). She gives food (aharada). She gives
water (ambhoda). She gives fame (yasoda). She is a gopa's daughter
(gopa-nandini), very graceful (atita-gamana), fair (gauri), and kind to
others (paranugraha-karini).

Text 57
karunarnava-sampurna
karunarnava-dharini
madhavi madhava-mano-
harini syama-vallabha

She is a flooding ocean of mercy (karunarnava-sampurna and
karunarnava-dharini). She is Lord Krsna's beloved (madhavi and syama-
vallabha), and she charms Lord Krsna's heart (madhava-mano-harini).

Text 58
andhakara-bhaya-dhvasta
mangalya mangala-prada
sri-garbha sri-prada srisa
sri-nivasacyutapriya

She removes the fear of darkness (andhakara-bhaya-dhvasta). She is
auspicious (mangalya), the giver of auspiciousness (mangala-prada), the
mother of all beauty (sri-garbha), the giver of beauty (sri-prada), the
queen of beauty (srisa), the abode of beauty (sri-nivasa), and the beloved

of the infallible Supreme Personality of Godhead (acyutapriya).

Text 59
sri-rupa sri-hara srida
sri-kama sri-svarupini
sridamananda-datri cha
sridamesvara-vallabha

She is the form of beauty (sri-rupa and sri-svarupini), the remover of beauty (sri-hara), the giver of beauty (srida), the desire for beauty (sri-kama), the giver of bliss to Sridama (sridamananda-datri), and dear to Sridama's master (sridamesvara-vallabha).

Text 60
sri-nitamba sri-ganesa
sri-svarupasrita srutih
sri-kriya-rupini srila
sri-krsna-bhajananvita

She has beautiful hips (sri-nitamba). She is the beautiful queen of the gopis (sri-ganesa). She is beautiful (sri-svarupasrita and srila). She is the Vedas (sruti) and the activities of devotional service (sri-kriya-rupini). She devotedly worships Sri Krsna (sri-krsna-bhajananvita).

Text 61
sri-radha srimati srestha
srestha-rupa sruti-priya
yogesa yoga-mata cha
yogatita yuga-priya

She worships Lord Krsna (sri-radha). She is beautiful (srimati). She is the best (srestha and srestha-rupa). She is dear to the Vedas (sruti-priya), the queen of yoga (yogesa), the mother of yoga (yoga-mata), beyond yoga (yogatita), and dear to the two divine persons (yuga-priya).

Text 62
yoga-priya yoga-gamya
yogini-gana-vandita
java-kusuma-sankasa
dadimi-kusumopama

She is dear to yoga (yoga-priya), approached by yoga (yoga-gamya), worshiped by the yoginis (yogini-gana-vandita), glorious as a rose (java-kusuma-sankasa), and glorious as a pomegranate (dad imi-kusumopama).

Text 63
nilambaradhara dhira
dhairya-rupa-dhara dhritih
ratna-simhasana-stha cha
ratna-kundala-bhusita

She wears blue garments (nilambara-dhara). She is very sober and serious (dhira and dhairya-rupa-dhara). She is seriousness (dhriti). She sits on a jewel throne (ratna-simhasana-stha) and She is decorated with jewel earrings (ratna-kundala-bhusita).

Text 64
ratnalankara-samyukta
ratna-malya-dhara para
ratnendra-sara-haradhya
ratna-mala-vibhusita

She wears jewel ornaments (ratnalankara-samyukta), a necklace of jewels (ratna-malya-dhara and ratna-mala-vibhusita), and a necklace of the kings of jewels (ratnendra-sara-haradhya). She is transcendental (para).

Text 65
indranila-mani-nyasta-
pada-padma-subha sucih
karttiki paurnamasi cha
amavasya bhayapaha

Her lotus feet are beautiful with sapphire ornaments (indranila-mani-nyasta-pada-padma-subha) and She is beautiful (suci). She is the month of Karttika (karttiki), the full-moon day (paurnamasi), the new-moon day (amavasya), and the remover of fears (bhayapaha).

Text 66
govinda-raja-grhini
govinda-gana-pujita
vaikuntha-natha-grhini
vaikuntha-paramalaya

She is Lord Govinda's queen (govinda-raja-grhini) and She is worshiped by Lord Govinda's devotees (govinda-gana-pujita). She is the queen of Vaikuntha's king (vaikuntha-natha-grhini) and She resides in the supreme abode of Vaikuntha (vaikuntha-paramalaya).

Text 67

vaikunthadeva-devadhya
tatha vaikuntha-sundari
mahalasa vedavati
sita sadhvi pati-vrata

She is glorious in the comopany of Vaikuntha's supreme king (vaikuntha-deva-devadhya) and She is the beautiful goddess of Vaikuntha (vaikuntha-sundari). She is languid (mahalasa), wise (vedavati), saintly (sadhvi), and devoted to Her Lord (pati-vrata). She is Goddess Sita (sita).

Text 68

anna-purna sadananda-
rupa kaivalya-sundari
kaivalya-dayini srestha
gopinatha-manohara

She is Goddess Durga (anna-purna). Her form is full of eternal bliss (sadananda-rupa). She is the most beautiful (kaivalya-sundari), the giver of liberation (kaivalya-dayini), the best (srestha), and the girl who charms Lord Gopinatha's heart (gopinatha-manohara).

Text 69

gopinathesvari chandi
nayika-nayananvita
nayika nayaka-prita
nayakananda-rupini

She is Lord Gopinatha's queen (gopinathesvari). She is passionate (chandi). She has the eyes of a beautiful heroine (nayika-nayananvita). She is a beautiful heroine (nayika). She is dear to the hero Krsna (nayaka-prita). She delights the hero Krsna (nayakananda-rupini).

Text 70

sesa sesavati sesa-
rupini jagad-ambika

gopala-palika maya
jayanandaprada tatha

She reclines on Lord Sesa (sesa, sesavati, and sesa-rupini). She is the
mother of the universe (jagad-ambika), the protectress of the cowherd
people (gopala-palika), the Lord's illusory potency (maya), and she who
gives the bliss of victory (jayanandaprada).

Text 71

kumari yauvanananda
yuvati gopa-sundari
gopa-mata janaki cha
janakananda-karini

She is a young girl (kumari and yuvati), filled with the bliss of
youthfulness (yauvanananda), a beautiful gopi (gopa-sundari), the
mother of the gopas (gopa-mata), the daughter of King Janaka (janaki),
and the girl who gives bliss to King Janaka (janakananda-karini).

Text 72

kailasa-vasini rambha
vairagyakula-dipika
kamala-kanta-grhini
kamala kamalalaya

She is the Goddess who resides on Mount Kailasa (kailasa-vasini). She
is the apsara Rambha (rambha). She is a glowing lamp of renunciation
(vairagyakula-dipika). She is Lord Narayana's wife (kamala-kanta-
grhini). She is the goddess of fortune (kamala) and the abode where the
goddess of fortune resides (kamalalaya).

Text 73

trailokya-mata jagatam
adhisthatri priyambika
hara-kanta hara-rata
harananda-pradayini

She is the mother of the three worlds (trailokya-mata), the predominating
Deity of the universes (jagatam adhisthatri), the beloved (priya), the
mother (ambika), the beloved of Lord Siva (hara-kanta and hara-rata),
and She who gives bliss to Lord Siva (harananda-pradayini).

Text 74
hara-patni hara-prita
hara-tosana-tatpara
haresvari rama-rata
rama ramesvari rama

She is Lord Siva's wife (hara-patni), Lord Siva's beloved (hara-prita), devoted to pleasing Lord Siva (hara-tosana-tatpara), Lord Siva's queen (haresvari), Lord Rama's beloved (rama-rata and rama), and Lord Rama's queen (ramesvari).

Text 75
syamala citra-lekha cha
tatha bhuvana-mohini
su-gopi gopa-vanita
gopa-rajya-prada subha

She is Lord Krsna's beloved (syamala), wonderfully beautiful (citra-lekha), the enchantress of the three worlds (bhuvana-mohini), a beautiful gopi (su-gopi and gopa-vanita), she who gives a kingdom to the gopas (gopa-rajya-prada), and beautiful (subha).

Text 76
angavapurna maheyi
matsya-raja-suta sati
kaumari narasimhi cha
varahi nava-durgika

She is beautiful (angavapurna), the queen of the earth (maheyi), the daughter of Matsyaraja (matsya-raja-suta), saintly (sati), a young girl (kaumari), Lord Nrsimha's beloved goddess of fortune (narasimhi), Lord Varaha's beloved (varahi), and the mother of the nine Durgas (nava-durgika).

Text 77
chanchala chanchalamoda
nari bhuvana-sundari
daksa-yajna-hara daksi
daksa-kanya su-lochana

She is fickle (chanchala and chanchalamoda), appears to be a human girl (nari), is the most beautiful girl in the worlds (bhuvana-sundari), stopped

Daksa's yajna (daksa-yajna-hara), is Daksa's daughter (daksi and daksa-kanya), and has beautiful eyes (su-lochana).

Text 78

rati-rupa rati-prita
rati-srestha rati-prada
ratir laksmana-geha-stha
viraja bhuvanesvari

She is beautiful (rati-rupa), delightful (rati-prita and rati-prada), the most delightful (rati-srestha) happiness (rati), the goddess who stays in Laksmana's home (laksmana-geha-stha), free from the world of matter (viraja), and the queen who rules the worlds (bhuvanesvari).

Text 79

sankhaspada harer jaya
jamatr-kula-vandita
bakula bakulamoda-
dharini yamuna jaya

She has countless transcendental abodes (sankhaspada). She is Lord Hari's wife (harer jaya). She is worshiped by Her in-laws (jamatr-kula-vandita). She is beautiful as a bakula flower (bakula) and fragrant as a bakula flower (bakulamoda-dharini). She is the Yamuna river (yamuna) and the goddess of victory (jaya).

Text 80

vijaya jaya-patni cha
yamalarjuna-bhanjini
vakresvari vakra-rupa
vakra-viksana-viksita

She is the goddess of victory (vijaya), the wife of the Lord of victory (jaya-patni), the beloved of He who broke the yamalarjuna trees (yamalarjuna-bhanjini), the queen of the crooked and deceptive (vakresvari), graceful (vakra-rupa), and a girl expert at crooked glances (vakra-viksana-viksita).

Text 81

aparajita jagannatha
jagannathesvari yatih

khechari khechara-suta
khecharatva-pradayini

She is unconquerable (aparajita), the queen of the universes
(jagannatha), she who controls the king of the universes
(jagannathesvari), renounced (yati), a goddess who lives in the celestial
worlds (khechari khechara-suta), and one who brings others to the
celestial worlds (khecharatva-pradayini).

Text 82
visnu-vaksah-sthala-stha cha
visnu-bhavana-tatpara
chandra-koti-sugatri cha
chandranana-manohari

She rests on Lord Visnu's chest (visnu-vaksah-sthala-stha) and is rapt in
meditation on Lord Visnu (visnu-bhavana-tatpara). She is beautiful as
millions of moons (chandra-koti-sugatri) and Her moonlike face is very
beautiful (chandranana-manohari).

Text 83
seva-sevya siva ksema
tatha ksema-kari vadhuh
yadavendra-vadhuh sevya
siva-bhakta sivanvita

She should be served with devotion (seva-sevya). She is Lord Siva's
beloved (siva). She is patience (ksema), patient (ksema-kari), a beautiful
girl (vadhu), the wife of the Yadavas' king (yadavendra-vadhu), the
object of devotional service (sevya), a great devotee of Lord Siva (siva-
bhakta), and Lord Siva's companion (sivanvita).

Text 84
kevala nisphala suksma
maha-bhimabhayaprada
jimuta-rupa jaimuti
jitamitra-pramodini

She is liberated (kevala), free from the fruits of karma (nisphala), subtle
(suksma), terrifying (maha-bhima), the giver of fearlessness
(abhayaprada), the sustainer (jimuta-rupa), Lord Visnu's beloved
(jaimuti), and the girl who delights Lord Visnu (jitamitra-pramodini).

Text 85
gopala-vanita nanda
kulajendra-nivasini
jayanti yamunangi cha
yamuna-tosa-karini

She is Lord Gopala's beloved (gopala-vanita), dear to King Nanda
(nanda), of noble birth (kulaja), the resident of a king's palace (indra-
nivasini), glorious (jayanti), a girl who stays by the Yamuna
(yamunangi), and a girl who pleases the Yamuna (yamuna-tosa-karini).

Text 86
kali-kalmasa-bhanga cha
kali-kalmasa-nasini
kali-kalmasa-rupa cha
nityananda-kari krpa

She breaks and destroys the sins of Kali-yuga (kali-kalmasa-bhanga and
kali-kalmasa-nasini). She is expert at enjoying pastimes of quarreling
with Lord Krsna (kali-kalmasa-rupa). She brings Lord Krsna eternal
bliss (nityananda-kari). She is kindness personified (krpa).

Text 87
krpavati kulavati
kailasachala-vasini
vama-devi vama-bhaga
govinda-priya-karini

She is merciful (krpavati), born in a very respectable and noble family
(kulavati), the goddess who resides on Mount Kailasa (kailasachala-
vasini), beautiful (vama-devi and vama-bhaga), and she who delights
Lord Govinda (govinda-priya-karini).

Text 88
nagendra-kanya yogesi
yogini yoga-rupini
yoga-siddha siddha-rupa
siddha-ksetra-nivasini

She is the daughter of Nagaraja (nagendra-kanya), the queen of yoga
(yogesi) a performer of yoga (yogini), yoga personified (yoga-rupini),
the perfection of yoga (yoga-siddha), the perfection of yoga personified

(siddha-rupa), and she who resides in a sacred place (siddha-ksetra-nivasini).

Text 89
ksetradhisthatr-rupa cha
ksetratita kula-prada
kesavananda-datri cha
kesavananda-dayini

She is the predominating Deity of sacred places (ksetradhisthatr-rupa), beyond all places in this world (ksetratita), born in a noble family (kula-prada), and the giver of happiness to Lord Kesava (kesavananda-datri and kesavananda-dayini).

Text 90
kesava kesava-prita
kesavi kesava-priya
rasa-krida-kari rasa-
vasini rasa-sundari

She is Lord Kesava's beloved (kesava, kesava-prita, kesavi, and kesava-priya), the enjoyer of the rasa-dance pastimes (rasa-krida-kari), the girl who stays in the rasa-dance arena (rasa- vasini), and the beautiful girl of the raasa dance (rasa-sundari).

Text 91
gokulanvita-deha cha
gokulatva-pradayini
lavanga-namni narangi
naranga-kula-mandana

She stays in Gokula (gokulanvita-deha), gives residence in Gokula to others (gokulatva-pradayini), has a name beautiful as a a lavangha flower (lavanga-namni), is amorous (narangi), and is the transcendental decoration of amorous Krsna (naranga-kula-mandana).

Text 92
ela-lavanga-karpura-
mukha-vasa-mukhanvita
mukhya mukhya-prada mukhya-
rupa mukhya-nivasini

She is anointed with ela, lavanga, karpura and many other fragrances (ela-lavanga-karpura-mukha-vasa-mukhanvita), is the most exalted of young girls (mukhya), gives the most valuable thing (mukhya-prada), has the most beautiful form (mukhya-rupa), and lives in the best abode (mukhya-nivasini).

Text 93

narayani kripatita
karunamaya-karini
karunya karuna karna
gokarna naga-karnika

She is Lord Narayana's beloved (narayani). She is supremely merciful (krpatita, karunamaya-karini, karunya, and karuna). She is the sacred place Gokarna (gokarna), Karna (karna), and Naga-karnika (naga-karnika).

Text 94

sarpini kaulini ksetra-
vasini jagad-anvaya
jatila kutila nila
nilambaradhara subha

She is graceful (sarpini), born in a noble family (kaulini), a resident of holy places (ksetra-vasini), the mother of the universes (jagad-anvaya), an ascetic (jatila), crooked (kutila), beauiful (nila and subha), and dressed in blue garments (nilambaradhara).

Text 95

nilambara-vidhatri cha
nilakantha-priya tatha
bhagini bhagini bhogya
krsna-bhogya bhagesvari

She is dressed in blue garments (nilambara-vidhatri). She is Lord Siva's beloved (nilakantha-priya). She is beautiful (bhagini, bhagini, and bhogya), Lord Krsna's happiness (krsna-bhogya), and the queen of transcendental opulences (bhagesvari).

Text 96

balesvari balaradhya
kanta kanta-nitambini

nitambini rupavati
yuvati krsna-pivari

She is Lord Balarama's queen (balesvari), worshiped by Lord Balarama (balaradhya), beautiful (kanta and rupavati), a girl with beautiful hips (kanta-nitambini nitambini), youthful (yuvati), and Lord Krsna's beloved (krsna-pivari).

Text 97
vibhavari vetravati
sankata kutilalaka
narayana-priya salila
srkkani-parimohita

She is amorous (vibhavari). She holds a stick (vetravati). She is slender (sankata). Her hair is curly (kutilalaka). She is Lord Narayana's beloved (narayana-priya). She resides on a hill (salila). With the movements of Her mouth She ecnhants Lord Krsna (srkkani-parimohita).

Text 98
drk-pata-mohita pratar-
asini navanitika
navina nava-nari cha
naranga-phala-sobhita

With a glance She enchants Lord Krsna (drk-pata-mohita). She eats breakfast early (pratar-asini) and churns butter (navanitika). She is young (navina nava-nari), and she is splendid as a naranga fruit (cha naranga-phala-sobhita).

Text 99
haimi hema-mukhi chandra-
mukhi sasi-su-sobhana
ardha-chandra-dhara chandra-
vallabha rohini tamih

She is splendid as gold (haimi). Her face is golden (hema-mukhi). Her face is like the moon (chandra-mukhi). She is beautiful as the moon (sasi-su-sobhana), like a graceful half-moon (ardha-chandra-dhara), dear to moonlike Krsna (chandra-vallabha), a beautiful young girl (rohini), and splendid as the night (tami).

Text 100
timingla-kulamoda-
matsya-rupanga-harini
karani sarva-bhutanam
karyatita kisorini

She became the beloved of Lord Matsya and delighted the timingilas
(timingla-kulamoda-matsya-rupanga-harini). She is the mother of all
living entities (karani sarva-bhutanam). She is beyond all material duties
(karyatita). She is a beautiful young girl (kisorini).

Text 101
kisora-vallabha kesa-
karika kama-karika
kamesvari kama-kala
kalindi-kula-dipika

She is youthful Krsna's beloved (kisora-vallabha). She has beautiful hair
(kesa-karika). She is passionate (kama-karika), the queen of amorous
pastimes (kamesvari), expert at amorous pastimes (kama-kala), and the
lamp that splendidly shines on the Yamuna's shore (kalindi-kula-dipika).

Text 102
kalindatanaya-tira-
vasini tira-gehini
kadambari-pana-para
kusumamoda-dharini

She has made Her home on the Yamuna's shore (kalindatanaya-tira-
vasini and tira-gehini). She is fond of drinking kadambari nectar
(kadambari-pana-para). She is fragrant with many flowers
(kusumamoda-dharini).

Text 103
kumuda kumudananda
krsnesi kama-vallabha
tarkali vaijayanti cha
nimba-dadima-rupini

She is like a kumuda flower (kumuda). She is pleased by the kumuda
flowers (kumudananda). She is Lord Krsna's queen (krsnesi) and
passionate lover (kama-vallabha). She is an expert logician (tarkali). She

is glorious (vaijayanti). Her form is like a nimba or a pomegranate tree (nimba-dadima-rupini).

Text 104
bilva-vrksa-priya krsnam-
bara bilvopama-stani
bilvatmika bilva-vapur
bilva-vrksa-nivasini

She is fond of the bilva tree (bilva-vrksa-priya). She is Lord Krsna's garment (krsnambara). Her breasts are like bilva fruits (bilvopama-stani). Her form is like a bilva tree (bilvatmika and bilva-vapuh). She stays under a bilva tree (bilva-vrksa-nivasini).

Text 105
tulasi-tosika taiti-
lananda-paritosika
gaja-mukta maha-mukta
maha-mukti-phala-prada

She pleases tulasi (tulasi-tosika). She pleases Taitilananda (taitilananda-paritosika). She is decorated with gaja pearls (gaja-mukta, maha-mukta, and maha-mukti-phala-prada).

Text 106
ananga-mohini sakti-
rupa sakti-svarupini
pancha-sakti-svarupa cha
saisavananda-karini

She is is charming and passionate (ananga-mohini). She is Lord Krsna's transcendental potency (sakti-rupa and sakti-svarupini). She is the personification of five transcendental potencies (pancha-sakti-svarupa). She is filled with the happiness of youth (saisavananda-karini).

Text 107
gajendra-gamini syama-
latananga-lata tatha
yosit-sakti-svarupa cha
yosid-ananda-karini

She is graceful as an elephant (gajendra-gamini). She is a flowering vine

of beauty (syama-lata) and a flowering vine of passionate desires
(ananga-lata). She is the personification of feminine power (yosit-sakti-
svarupa) and feminine bliss (yosid-ananda-karini).

Text 108

prema-priya prema-rupa
premananda-tarangini
prema-hara prema-datri
prema-saktimayi tatha

She passionately loves Lord Krsna (prema-priya). She is the form of all
transcendental love (prema-rupa). She is an ocean filled with waves of
transcendental love (premananda-tarangini). She is the giver of
transcendental love (prema-hara and prema-datri). She is full of the
power of transcendental love (prema-saktimayi).

Text 109

krsna-premavati dhanya
krsna-prema-tarangini
prema-bhakti-prada prema
premananda-tarangini

She loves Lord Krsna (krsna-premavati). She is fortunate (dhanya). She
is an ocean filled with waves of love for Lord Krsna (krsna-prema-
tarangini). She gives loving devotional service (prema-bhakti-prada).
She is transcendental love (prema). She is an ocean filled with waves of
the bliss of transcendental love (premananda-tarangini).

Text 110

prema-krida-paritangi
prema-bhakti-tarangini
premartha-dayini sarva-
sveta nitya-tarangini

Her limbs are filled with amorous playfulness (prema-krida-paritangi).
She is an ocean filled with waves of loving devotional service (prema-
bhakti-tarangini). She gives a great wealth of transcendental love
(premartha-dayini). She is fair (sarvasveta), and She is an ocean of
eternity (nitya-tarangini).

Text 111

hava-bhavanvita raudra
rudrananda-prakasini
kapila srnkhala kesa-
pasa-sambandhini ghati

She is expert at flirting with Lord Krsna (hava-bhavanvita). She is Lord
Siva's beloved (raudra). She delights Lord Siva (rudrananda-prakasini).
She is fair (kapila). She is the shackle that binds Lord Krsna (srnkhala).
She carefully braids Her hair (kesa-pasa-sambandhini). She carries a jug
(ghati).

Text 112

kutira-vasini dhumra
dhumra-kesa jalodari
brahmanda-gochara brahma-
rupini bhava-bhavini

She lives in a cottage (kutira-vasini). She is Goddess Durga (dhumra).
Her hair is dark as smoke (dhumra-kesa). She resides in the milk-ocean
(jalodari). She has descended to the material world (brahmanda-
gochara). Her form is spiritual (brahma-rupini). She is full of
transcendental love (bhava-bhavini).

Text 113

samsara-nasini saiva
saivalananda-dayini
sisira hema-ragadbya
megha-rupati-sundari

She destroys the cycle of repeated birth and death (samsara-nasini). She
is Lord Siva's beloved (saiva). She bears the pleasing fragrance of
saivala (saivalananda-dayini). She is pleasantly cool (sisira), Her
complexion is golden (hema-ragadbya), Her form is glorious as a cloud
(megha-rupa), and She is very beautiful (ati-sundari).

Text 114

manorama vegavati
vegadhya veda-vadini
dayanvita dayadhara
daya-rupa susevini

She is beautiful (manorama), quick (vegavati and vegadhya), eloquent in speaking the Vedas (veda-vadini), merciful (dayanvita, dayadhara, and daya-rupa), and the proper object of devotional service (susevini).

Text 115
kisora-sanga-samsarga
gaura-chandranana kala
kaladhinatha-vadana
kalanathadhirohini

She meets youthful Krsna (kisora-sanga-samsarga), Her face is a brilliant moon (gaura-chandranana), She is a crescent moon (kala), Her face is a full moon (kaladhinatha-vadana), and She is glorious as a full moon (kalanathadhirohini).

Text 116
viraga-kusala hema-
pingala hema-mandana
bhandira-talavana-ga
kaivarti pivari suki

She is renounced (viraga-kusala), Her complexion is golden (hema-pingala), She is decorated with golden ornaments (hema-mandana), She goes to Bhandiravana and Talavana (bhandira-talavana-ga), She catches the fish that is Sri Krsna (kaivarti), She is a beautiful young girl (pivari), and She is graceful (suki).

Text 117
sukadeva-gunatita
sukadeva-priya sakhi
vikalotkarsini kosa
kauseyambara-dharini

Her virtues are beyond the power of Sukadeva Gosvami to describe (sukadeva-gunatita), She is dear to Sukadeva Gosvami (sukadeva-priya), She is friendly (sakhi), She picks up the fallen and unhappy (vikalotkarsini), She is a treasure-house of transcendental opulences (kosa), and She is dressed in elegant silk garments (kauseyambara-dharini).

Text 118
kosavari kosa-rupa
jagad-utpatti-karika
srsti-sthiti-kari samha-
rini samhara-karini

She is a treasure-house of transcendental opulences (kosavari and kosa-rupa), the mother of the universes (jagad-utpatti-karika), the creature and maintainer of the universes (srsti-sthiti-kari), and the destroyer of the universes (samharini and samhara-karini).

Text 119
kesa-saivala-dhatri cha
chandra-gatri su-komala
padmangaraga-samraga
vindhyadri-parivasini

Her hair is dark moss (kesa-saivala-dhatri), and Her limbs are moons (chandra-gatri). She is very gentle and delicate (su-komala), She is anointed with lotus cosmetics (padmangaraga-samraga), and She has a home in the Vindhya Hills (vindhyadri-parivasini).

Text 120
vindhyalaya syama-sakhi
sakhi samsara-ragini
bhuta bhavisya bhavya cha
bhavya-gatra bhavatiga

She has a home in the Vindhya Hills (vindhyalaya), is the intimate friend of Lord Krsna (syama-sakhi), is friendly (sakhi), loves the world (samsara-ragini), existed in the past (bhuta), will continue to exist in the future eternally (bhavisya), and exists in the present (bhavya). Her limbs are beautiful (bhavya-gatra), and She is beyond the material world of repeated birth and death (bhavatiga).

Text 121
bhava-nasanta-kariny a-
kasa-rupa su-vesini
rati-ranga-parityaga
rati-vega rati-prada

She puts an end to the cycle of repeated birth and death (bhava-nasanta-karini), Her form is spiritual and subtle (akasa-rupa), She is beautifully dressed (su-vesini), She left the arena of amorous pastimes (rati-ranga-parityaga, and She enjoys the happiness of amorous pastimes (rati-vega and rati-prada).

Text 122
tejasvini tejo-rupa
kaivalya-patha-da subha
mukti-hetur mukti-hetu-
langhini langhana-ksama

She is splendid and powerful (tejasvini and tejo-rupa), gives the path of liberation (kaivalya-patha-da), is beautiful (subha), is the cause of liberation (mukti-hetur), jumps over impersonal liberation (mukti-hetu-langhini), and is tolerant of offenses (langhana-ksama).

Text 123
visala-netra vaisali
visala-kula-sambhava
visala-grha-vasa cha
visala-vadari ratih

She has large eyes (visala-netra), comes from an exalted family (vaisali, visala-kula-sambhava, visala-grha-vasa, and visala-vadari), and is transcendental happiness personified (rati).

Text 124
bhakty-atita bhakta-gatir
bhaktika siva-bhakti-da
siva-sakti-svarupa cha
sivardhanga-viharini

By serving Her one crosses beyond the world of repeated birth and death (bhakty-atita), She is the goal of devotional service (bhakta-gati), She is devotional service (bhaktika), She gives auspicious devotional service (siva-bhakti-da), She is an auspicious potency of the Lord (siva-sakti-svarupa), and She enjoys pastimes as the beloved who is half the body of the auspicious Lord (sivardhanga-viharini).

Text 125
sirisa-kusumamoda
sirisa-kusumojjvala
sirisa-mrdhvi sairisi
sirisa-kusumakrtih

She is fragrant as a sirisa flower (sirisa-kusumamoda), splendid as a
sirisa flower (sirisa-kusumojjvala), soft as a sirisa flower (sirisa-mrdhvi),
glorious as a sirisa flower (sairisi), and beautiful as a sirisa flower
(sirisa-kusumakrti).

Text 126
vamanga-harini visnoh
siva-bhakti-sukhanvita
vijita vijitamoda
gagana gana-tosita

She stays at Lord Visnu's left side (vamanga-harini visnoh), She is filled
with the auspicious happiness of devotional service (siva-bhakti-
sukhanvita), She is defeated by Lord Krsna (vijita), She is fragrant
(vijitamoda), She is the spiritual sky (gagana), and She is pleased by Her
companions (gana-tosita).

Text 127
hayasya heramba-suta
gana-mata sukhesvari
duhkha-hantri duhkha-hara
sevitepsita-sarvada

She is Lord Hayagriva's beloved (hayasya), Heramba's daughter
(heramba-suta), the demigods' mother (gana-mata), the queen of
happiness (sukhesvari), the destroyer of sufferings (duhkha-hantri and
duhkha-hara), and the goddess who grants everything Her servants wish
(sevitepsita-sarvada).

Text 128
sarvajnatva-vidhatri cha
kula-ksetra-nivasini
lavanga pandava-sakhi
sakhi-madhya-nivasini

She gives omniscience (sarvajnatva-vidhatri). She stays in Her family's place (kula-ksetra-nivasini). She is a lavanga flower (lavanga). She is the Pandavas' friend (pandava-sakhi). She stays with Her friends (sakhi-madhya-nivasini).

Text 129
gramya gita gaya gamya
gamanatita-nirbhara
sarvanga-sundari ganga
ganga-jalamayi tatha

She stays in the village of Vraja (gramya). She is glorified in song (gita). She is the holy city of Gaya (gaya). She is approached by the devotees (gamya). She cannot be approached by non-devotees (gamanatita-nirbhara). All Her limbs are very beautiful (sarvanga-sundari). She is the Ganges (ganga and ganga-jalamayi).

Text 130
gangerita puta-gatra
pavitra-kula-dipika
pavitra-guna-siladhya
pavitrananda-dayini

She is said to be the Ganges (gangerita). Her body is pure and transcendental (puta-gatra). She is a lamp shining in a pure family (pavitra-kula-dipika). She is rich with pure virtues and noble character (pavitra-guna-siladhya). She gives pure transcendental bliss (pavitrananda-dayini).

Text 131
pavitra-guna-simadhya
pavitra-kula-dipani
kampamana kamsa-hara
vindhyachala-nivasini

She is rich with the most exalted pure virtues (pavitra-guna-simadhya). She is a lamp shining in a pure family (pavitra-kula-dipani). She trembles (kampamana). She is the beloved of He who killed Kamsa (kamsa-hara). She has a home in the Vindhya Hills (vindhyachala-nivasini).

Text 132
govardhanesvari govar-
dhana-hasya hayakrtih
minavatara minesi
gaganesi haya gaji

She is the queen of Govardhana Hill (govardhanesvari). She smiles on
Govardhana Hill (govardhana-hasya). She is Lord Haragriva's beloved
(hayakrti and haya) and Lord Matsya's beloved (minavatara and minesi).
She is the queen of the spiritual sky (gaganesi). She is an amorous girl
(gaji).

Text 133
harini harini hara-
dharini kanakakrtih
vidyut-prabha vipra-mata
gopa-mata gayesvari

She is beautiful as a doe (harini). She is captivating (harini). She wears a
beautiful necklace (hara-dharini). Her form is golden (kanakakrti). She is
splendid as lightning (vidyut-prabha). She is the mother of the
brahmanas (vipra-mata), the mother of the gopas (gopa-mata). and the
queen of Gaya (gayesvari).

Text 134
gavesvari gavesi cha
gavisi gavi-vasini
gati-jna gita-kusala
danujendra-nivarini

She is the queen of the surabhi cows (gavesvari, gavesi, and gavisi). She
lives in the cowherd village of Vraja (gavi-vasini). She knows the real
goal of life (gati-jna). Her glories are sung in beautiful songs (gita-
kusala). She stopped the king of the demons (danujendra-nivarini).

Text 135
nirvana-datri nairvani
hetu-yukta gayottara
parvatadhinivasa cha
nivasa-kusala tatha

She gives liberation (nirvana-datri). She is liberated (nairvani). She is an expert logician (hetu-yukta). She is the queen of Gaya (gayottara). She lives on a mountain (parvatadhinivasa). She brings beauty and auspiciousness to Her home (nivasa-kusala).

Text 136

sannyasa-dharma-kusala
sannyasesi saran-mukhi
sarac-chandra-mukhi syama-
hara ksetra-nivasini

She is beautiful with renunciation (sannyasa-dharma-kusala). She is the queen of renunciation (sannyasis (sannyasesi). Her face is like autumn (saran-mukhi). Her face is an autumn moon (sarac-chandra-mukhi). She is a necklace worn by Lord Krsna (syama-hara). She lives in a sacred place (ksetra-nivasini).

Text 137

vasanta-raga-samraga
vasanta-vasanakrtih
chatur-bhuja sad-bhuja
dvi-bhuja gaura-vigraha

The melodies of vasanta-raga fill Her with amorous desires (vasanta-raga-samraga). Her form is filled with the desires of spring (vasanta-vasanakrti). Sometimes She has four arms (chatur-bhuja), and sometimes six arms (sad-bhuja). She has two arms (dvi-bhuja) and Her complexion is fair (gaura-vigraha).

Text 138

sahasrasya vihasya cha
mudrasya mada-dayini
prana-priya prana-rupa
prana-rupiny apavrta

She is the beloved of thousand-headed Lord Ananta Sesa (sahasrasya). She laughs (vihasya). Her face is very expressive (mudrasya). She fills Lord Krsna with amorous passion (mada-dayini). She is more dear to Him than life (prana-priya, prana-rupa, and prana-rupini). She appears before Her devotees (apavrta).

Text 139
krsna-prita krsna-rata
krsna-tosana-tat-para
krsna-prema-rata krsna-
bhakta bhakta-phala-prada

She pleases Lord Krsna (krsna-prita and krsna-rata). She is devoted to pleasing Lord Krsna (krsna-tosana-tat-para). She loves Lord Krsna (krsna-prema-rata and krsna-bhakta). She gives Her devotees the fruits of their service (bhakta-phala-prada).

Text 140
krsna-prema prema-bhakta
hari-bhakti-pradayini
chaitanya-rupa chaitanya-
priya chaitanya-rupini

She loves Krsna (krsna-prema and prema-bhakta). She gives others devotion to Lord Krsna (hari-bhakti-pradayini). She is present in the form of Lord Chaitanya (chaitanya-rupa and chaitanya-rupini). She is dear to Lord Chaitanya (chaitanya-priya).

Text 141
ugra-rupa siva-kroda
krsna-kroda jalodari
mahodari maha-durga-
kantara-sustha-vasini

She manifests the terrible form of Durga-devi (ugra-rupa), where She sits on Lord Siva's lap (siva-kroda). She sits on Lord Krsna's lap (krsna-kroda). She rests on the milk-ocean (jalodari). She descends to the material world (mahodari). She happily lives in a great forest that is like an unapproachable fortress (maha-durga-kantara-sustha-vasini).

Text 142
chandravali chandra-kesi
chandra-prema-tarangini
samudra-mathanodbhuta
samudra-jala-vasini

She is glorious as a host of moons (chandravali and chandra-kesi). She is an ocean the moon of Sri Krsna fills with waves of love (chandra-prema-tarangini). She was born from the churning of the milk-ocean (samudra-mathanodbhuta) and She resides on the ocean of milk (samudra-jala-vasini).

Text 143

samudramrta-rupa cha
samudra-jala-vasika
kesa-pasa-rata nidra
ksudha prema-tarangika

Her form is an ocean of nectar (samudramrta-rupa). She resides on the milk-ocean (samudra-jala-vasika). She carefully braids Her hair (kesa-pasa-rata). She is sleep (nidra), hunger (ksudha), and an ocean filled with waves of love (prema-tarangika).

Text 144

durva-dala-syama-tanur
durva-dala-tanu-ccbavih
nagara nagari-raga
nagarananda-karini

Her form is glorious as a blade of durva grass (durva-dala-syama-tanu and durva-dala-tanu-ccbavi). She is hero Krsna's beloved (nagara). She is His passionate heroine (nagari-raga). She delights the hero Krsna (nagarananda-karini).

Text 145

nagaralingana-para
nagarangana-mangala
uccha-nicha haimavati
priya krsna-taranga-da

She earnestly embraces the hero Krsna (nagaralingana-para). She is happy to embrace the hero Krsna (nagarangana-mangala). She is very humble (uccha-nicha). She is Goddess Parvati (haimavati). She is Lord Krsna's beloved (priya). She is an ocean filled with waves of love for Lord Krsna (krsna-taranga-da).

Text 146

premalingana-siddhangi
siddha sadhya-vilasika

mangalamoda-janani
mekhalamoda-dharini

Her body is expert at lovingly embracing Lord Krsna (premalingana-siddhangi). She is perfect (siddha). She enjoys transcendental pastimes (sadhya-vilasika). She is the mother of auspiciousness and bliss (mangalamoda-janani). She wears a glorious belt and is scented with a sweet fragrance (mekhalamoda-dharini).

Text 147
ratna-manjira-bhusangi
ratna-bhusana-bhusana
jambala-malika krsna-
prana prana-vimochana

Her limbs are decorated with tinkling jewel ornaments (ratna-manjira-bhusangi). She is the ornament that decorates Her jewel ornaments (ratna-bhusana-bhusana). She wears a garland of ketaki flowers (jambala-malika). Lord Krsna is Her life-breath (krsna-prana). She has surrendered Her life to Lord Krsna (prana-vimochana).

Text 148
satya-prada satyavati
sevakananda-dayika
jagad-yonir jagad-bija
vicitra-mani-bhusana

She is truthful (satya-prada and satyavati). She gives the bliss of devotional service (sevakananda-dayika). She is the mother of the universe (jagad-yoni and jagad-bija). She is decorated with wonderful and colorful jewels (vicitra-mani-bhusana).

Text 149
radha-ramana-kanta cha
radhya radhana-rupini
kailasa-vasini krsna-
prana-sarvasva-dayini

She is the beloved of Lord Radharamana (radha-ramana-kanta), the perfect object of worship (radhya), and the personification of devotional service (radhana-rupini). She resides on Kailasa Hill (kailasa-vasini). She has dedicated Her life and everything She has to Lord Krsna (krsna-prana-sarvasva-dayini).

Text 150
krsnavatara-nirata
krsna-bhakta-phalarthini
yachakayachakananda-
karini yachakojjvala

She devotedly serves Lord Krsna's incarnations (krsnavatara-nirata). She gives Lord Krsna's devotees the fruits of their services (krsna-bhakta-phalarthini) and whether they ask for it or not She gives them transcendental bliss (yachakayachakananda-karini). She gloriously appears before they who offer prayers to Her (yachakojjvala).

Text 151
hari-bhusana-bhusadhya-
nanda-yuktardra-pada-ga
hai-hai-tala-dhara thai-thai-
sabda-sakti-prakasini

She is decorated with ornaments that decorate Lord Hari's ornaments (hari-bhusana-bhusadhya). She is blissful (ananda-yukta). She is half of Lord Lord Krsna (ardra-pada-ga). She expertly beats the rhythm hai hai (hai-hai-tala-dhara) and the rhythm thai thai (thai-thai-sabda-sakti-prakasini).

Text 152
he-he-sabda-svarupa cha
hi-hi-vakya-visarada
jagad-ananda-kartri cha
sandrananda-visarada

She expertly sings "Oh! Oh!" (he-he-sabda-svarupa and hi-hi-vakya-visarada). She fills the world with bliss (jagad-ananda-kartri). She is expert at enjoying intense transcendental bliss (sandrananda-visarada).

Text 153
pandita pandita-guna
panditananda-karini
paripalana-kartri cha
tatha sthiti-vinodini

She is wise and learned (pandita). She has the virtues of the wise (pandita-guna). She delights the wise (panditananda-karini). She protects the devotees (paripalana-kartri). She enjoys transcendental pastimes in Her home (sthiti-vinodini).

Text 154

tatha samhara-sabdadhya
vidvaj-jana-manohara
vidusam priti-janani
vidvat-prema-vivardhini

She is eloquent (samhara-sabdadhya). She enchants the wise (vidvaj-jana-manohara). She is the mother of happiness for the wise (vidusam priti-janani). She increases the love the wise feel for Lord Krsna (vidvat-prema-vivardhini).

Text 155

nadesi nada-rupa cha
nada-bindu-vidharini
sunya-sthana-sthita sunya-
rupa-padapa-vasini

She is the queen of words (nadesi). She is eloquent words personified (nada-rupa). She concisely speaks a droplet of words (nada-bindu-vidharini). She stays in a place far beyond the material realm (sunya-sthana-sthita). She stays under a tree far beyond the material realm (sunya- rupa-padapa-vasini).

Text 156

karttika-vrata-kartri cha
vasana-harini tatha
jala-saya jala-tala
sila-tala-nivasini

She performs the vow of Karttika-vrata (karttika-vrata-kartri). She takes away material desires (vasana-harini). She resides on the milk-ocean (jala-saya and jala-tala) and on a hill (sila-tala-nivasini).

Text 157

ksudra-kitanga-samsarga
sanga-dosa-vinasini

koti-kandarpa-lavanya
kandarpa-koti-sundari

She will show Her mercy to the most insignificant creature (ksudra-
kitanga-samsarga). She cures the disease born of contact with the
material energy (sanga-dosa-vinasini). She is more beautiful than many
millions of Kamadevas (koti-kandarpa-lavanya and kandarpa-koti-
sundari).

Text 158
kandarpa-koti-janani
kama-bija-pradayini
kama-sastra-vinoda cha
kama-sastra-prakasini

She is the mother of millions of Kamadevas (kandarpa-koti-janani). She
gives the seed of the desire to attain Lord Krsna (kama-bija-pradayini).
She is expert in the science of amorous pastimes (kama-sastra-vinoda
and kama-sastra-prakasini).

Text 159
kama-prakasika kaminy
animady-asta-siddhi-da
yamini yamini-natha-
vadana yaminisvari

She is an amorous girl (kama-prakasika and kamini). She grants the eight
mystic perfections, beginning with anima (animady-asta-siddhi-da). She
is in control of Her senses (yamini) and She is the leader of all
restrained, self-controlled girls (yamini-natha-vadana and yaminisvari).

Text 160
yaga-yoga-hara bhukti-
mukti-datri hiranya-da
kapala-malini devi
dhama-rupiny apurva-da

She gives the results of Vedic sacrififces (yaga-yoga-hara). She gives
sense gratification and liberation (bhukti-mukti-datri). She gives gold
(hiranya-da). As Durga-devi, She wears a garland of skulls (kapala-
malini). She is a goddess (devi). Her form is splendid and glorious
(dhama-rupini). She gives what has never been given before (apurva-da).

Text 161
krpanvita guna gaunya
gunatita-phala-prada
kusmanda-bhuta-vetala-
nasini saradanvita

She is merciful (krpanvita), virtuous (guna), and the most important
(gaunya). She gives a result that is beyond the three modes of material
nature (gunatita-phala-prada). She kills the kusmandas, bhutas, and
vetalas (kusmanda-bhuta-vetala-nasini). She is glorious like autumn
(saradanvita).

Text 162
sitala savala hela
lila lavanya-mangala
vidyarthini vidyamana
vidya vidya-svarupini

She is pleasingly cool (sitala). She has a great variety of virtues (savala).
She is happiness (hela) and playfulness (lila). She is beautiful and
auspicious (lavanya-mangala). She is an earnest student (vidyarthini).
She is known by the devotees (vidyamana). She is knowledge
personified (vidya and vidya-svarupini).

Text 163
anviksiki sastra-rupa
sastra-siddhanta-karini
nagendra naga-mata cha
krida-kautuka-rupini

She is the science of logic (anviksiki), the Vedas personified (sastra-
rupa), the teacher of the Vedas' final conclusion (sastra-siddhanta-karini,
the beloved of Lord Sesa (nagendra), the mother of the snakes (naga-
mata) and playful and happy (krida-kautuka-rupini).

Text 164
hari-bhavana-sila cha
hari-tosana-tat-para
hari-prana hara-prana
siva-prana sivanvita

She meditates on Lord Hari (hari-bhavana-sila), and is dedicated to pleasing Lord Hari (hari-tosana-tat-para). She is Lord Hari's life and soul (hari-prana), Lord Siva's life and soul (hara-prana and siva-prana), and Lord Siva's companion (sivanvita).

Text 165

narakarnava-samhantri
narakarnava-nasini
naresvari naratita
nara-sevya narangana

She destroys the ocean of hellish sufferings (narakarnava-samhantri and narakarnava-nasini). She is the queen of humans (naresvari), is beyond the world of humans (naratita), should be served by humans (nara-sevya), and is like an ordinary human girl (narangana).

Text 166

yasodanandana-prana-
vallabha hari-vallabha
yasodanandanaramya
yasodanandanesvari

For Yasoda's son She is more dear than life (yasodanandana-prana-vallabha). She is dear to Lord Hari (hari-vallabha). She delights Yasoda's son (yasodanandanaramya). She is the queen of Yasoda's son (yasodanandanesvari).

Text 167

yasodanandanakrida
yasoda-kroda-vasini
yasodanandana-prana
yasodanandanarthada

She enjoys pastimes with Yasoda's son (yasodanandanakrida), sits on the lap of Yasoda's son (yasoda-kroda-vasini), is the life and soul of Yasoda's son (yasodanandana-prana), and fulfills the desires of Yasoda's son (yasodanandanarthada).

Text 168

vatsala kausala kala
karunarnava-rupini
svarga-laksmir bhumi-
laksmir draupadi pandava-priya

She is affectionate (vatsala), expert (kausala), beautiful (kala), and an ocean of mercy (karunarnava-rupini). She is heavenly opulence (svarga-laksmi) and earthly opulence (bhumi-laksmi). She is Draupadi (draupadi), who is dear to the Pandavas (pandava-priya).

Text 169

tatharjuna-sakhi bhaumi
bhaimi bhima-kulodvaha
bhuvana mohana ksina
panasakta-tara tatha

She is Arjuna's friend (arjuna-sakhi), a resident of the earth (bhaumi), very exalted (bhaimi), born in an exalted family (bhima-kulodvaha), a resident of the material worlds (bhuvana), charming (mohana), slender (ksina), and fond of betelnuts (panasakta-tara).

Text 170

panarthini pana-patra
pana-pananda-dayini
dugdha-manthana-karmadhya
dugdha-manthana-tat-para

She begs for betelnuts (panarthini), is Lord Sri Krsna's betelnut cup (pana-patra), and gives the happiness of chewing betelnuts (pana-pananda-dayini). She dutifully churns milk (dugdha-manthana-karmadhya and dugdha-manthana-tat-para).

Text 171

dadhi-bhandarthini krsna-
krodhini nandanangana
ghrta-lipta takra-yukta
yamuna-para-kautuka

Lord Krsna asks for Her jug of yogurt (dadhi-bhandarthini). She becomes angry at Krsna (krsna-krodhini). Sheb is a delightful girl (nandanangana) anointed with ghee (ghrta-lipta), carring buttermilk (takra-yukta), and eager to cross to the Yamuna's other shore (yamuna-para-kautuka).

Text 172

vicitra-kathaka krsna-
hasya-bhasana-tat-para

gopanganavestita cha
krsna-sangarthini tatha

She speaks wonderful and colorful words (vicitra-kathaka). Her words
mock Krsna (krsna-hasya-bhasana-tat-para). She is surrounded by the
gopis (gopanganavestita). She yearns for Lord Krsna's company (krsna-
sangarthini).

Text 173

rasasakta rasa-ratir
asavasakta-vasana
haridra harita hariny
anandarpita-cetana

She is attached to the rasa dance (rasasakta) and She enjoys the rasa
dance (rasa-rati). She is attached to drinking asava nectar (asavasakta-
vasana). Her complexion is fair (haridra and harita) and She is charming
(harini). She brings bliss to the heart (anandarpita-cetana).

Text 174

nischaitanya cha nischeta
tatha daru-haridrika
subalasya svasa krsna-
bharya bhasati-vegini

She faints with love of Krsna (nischaitanya and nisceta) and becomes
like a golden doll made of wood (daru-haridrika). She is Subala's sister
(subalasya svasa), and Krsna's wife (krsna-bharya). She is very eloquent
(bhasati-vegini).

Text 175

sridamasya sakhi dama-
damini dama-dharini
kailasini kesini cha
harid-ambara-dharini

She is Sridama's friend (sridamasya sakhi). She is glorious (dama-damini
and dama-dharini). She is Parvati (kailasini). She has beautiful hair
(kesini). She wears blue garments (harid-ambara-dharini).

Text 176
hari-sannidhya-datri cha
hari-kautuka-mangala
hari-prada hari-dvara
yamuna-jala-vasini

She stays by Lord Krsna's side (hari-sannidhya-datri). She is very happy
to stay with Lord Krsna (hari-kautuka-mangala). She gives Lord Hari
(hari-prada) and She is the door to Lord Hari (hari-dvara). She resides by
the Yamuna (yamuna-jala-vasini).

Text 177
jaitra-prada jitarthi cha
chatura caturi tami
tamisra"tapa-rupa cha
raudra-rupa yaso-'rthini

She gives victory (jaitra-prada). She has conquered Her desires (jitarthi).
She is expert and intelligent (chatura and chaturi). She is darkness (tami
and tamisra). She is austerity (atapa-rupa). She is ferocious (raudra-
rupa). She is famous (yaso-'rthini).

Text 178
krsnarthini krsna-kala
krsnananda-vidhayini
krsnartha-vasana krsna-
ragini bhava-bhavini

She yearns to associate with Lord Krsna (krsnarthini). She is an
expansion of Lord Krsna (krsna-kala). She delights Lord Krsna
(krsnananda-vidhayini). She yearns to associate with Lord Krsna
(krsnartha-vasana), and She passionately loves Lord Krsna (krsna-ragini
and bhava-bhavini).

Text 179
krsnartha-rahita bhakta
bhakta-bhukti-subha-prada
sri-krsna-rahita dina
tatha virahini hareh

She has no desire except to associate with Lord Krsna (krsnartha-rahita).
She is devoted to Lord Krsna (bhakta). She gives happiness and

auspiciousness to the devotees (bhakta-bhukti-subha-prada). Separated
from Lord Krsna (sri-krsna-rahita), She becomes very poor and wretched
(dina). This happens when She is separated from Lord Hari (virahini
hareh).

Text 180
mathura mathura-raja-
geha-bhavana-bhavana
sri-krsna-bhavanamoda
tatho'nmada-vidhayini

She stays in Mathura (mathura). When He stays in the home of
Mathura's king, Lord Krsna always thinks of Her (mathura-raja- geha-
bhavana-bhavana). She is happy when She can think of Lord Krsna (sri-
krsna-bhavanamoda). She is mad with love for Lord Krsna (unmada-
vidhayini).

Text 181
krsnartha-vyakula krsna-
sara-charma-dhara subha
alakesvara-pujya cha
kuveresvara-vallabha

She is agitated with the desire to attain Lord Krsna (krsnartha-vyakula).
She is the beloved of Lord Siva, who wears a deerskin (krsnasara-
charma-dhara). She is beautiful (subha). She is worshiped by Kuvera
(alakesvara-pujya) and She is dear to Kuvera's master, Lord Siva
(kuveresvara-vallabha).

Text 182
dhana-dhanya-vidhatri cha
jaya kaya haya hayi
pranava pranavesi cha
pranavartha-svarupini

She gives great wealth (dhana-dhanya-vidhatri). She is Lord Krsna 's
wife (jaya). Her form is spiritual (kaya). She is the beloved of Lord
Hayagriva (haya and hayi). She is the sacred syllable Om (pranava), the
queen of the sacred syylable Om (pranavesi), and the personification of
the sacred syllable Om (pranavartha-svarupini).

Text 183
brahma-visnu-sivardhanga-
harini saiva-simsapa
raksasi-nasini bhuta-
preta-prana-vinasini

She is the other half of Lord Visnu, Lord Siva, and Lord Brahma
(brahma-visnu-sivardhanga-harini). She is Lord Siva's beloved (saiva-
simsapa). She kills the demonesses (raksasi-nasini). She kills the bhutas
and pretas (bhuta-preta-prana-vinasini).

Text 184
sakalepsita-datri cha
saci sadhvi arundhati
pati-vrata pati-prana
pati-vakya-vinodini
asesa-sadhani kalpa-
vasini kalpa-rupini

She fulfills all desires (sakalepsita-datri). She is Saci (saci). She is
saintly (sadhvi). She is Arundhati (arundhati). She is faithful to Her
husband (pati-vrata). Her husband is Her very life (pati-prana). She
delights in Her husband's words (pati-vakya-vinodini). She has the
power to do anything (asesa-sadhani). All Her desires are automatically
fulfilled (kalpa-vasini and kalpa-rupini).

TEXT NUMBERS OF SRI RADHA'S NAMES

(Herein is the list of names in alphabetical order each followed by the
text number in which it appears.)

Abhayaprada, 84 * Abhistada, 21 * Acyutapriya, 58 * Aharada, 56 *
Akasa-rupa, 121 * Alakesvara-pujya, 181 * Amavasya, 65 * Ambhoda, 56
* Ambika, 73 * Amoha, 29 * Anamsa, 46 * Ananda-yukta, 151 *
Anandaprada, 70 * Anandarpita-cetana, 173 * Ananga-lata, 107 *
Ananga-mohini, 106 * Anda-bahya, 53 * Anda-madhyastha, 53 *
Anda-paripalini, 53 * Anda-rupa, 53 * Anda-samhartri, 53 *
Andhakara-bhaya-dhvasta, 58 * Anga-harini, 100 * Angara-purna, 76 *
Animady-asta-siddhi-da, 159 * Anna-purna, 68 * Anuttama, 19 * Anuttara,
32 * Anviksiki, 163 * Aparajita, 23, 81 * Apavrta, 138 * Apurva, 51 *

46 * Ekanga, 36 * Ela-lavanga-karpura, 92 * Gagana, 126 * Gaganesi, 132 * Gaja-mukta, 105 * Gajendra-gamini, 107 * Gaji, 132 * Gamanagamana-priya, 16 * Gamanatita-nirbhara, 129 * Gamya, 129 * Gana-mata, 127 * Gana-tosita, 126 * Ganadhyaksa, 19 * Ganga, 129 * Ganga-jalamayi, 129 * Gangerita, 130 * Gati, 50 * Gati-jna, 134 * Gati-nistha, 29 * Gati-prada, 16, 29 * Gatimatam-dhatri, 24 * Gati, 19, 21, 24 * Gaunya, 161 * Gaura-candranana, 115 * Gaura-vigraha, 137 * Gaurangi, 53 * Gauri, 53, 56 * Gavadhyaksa, 19 * Gavam, 19 * Gavesi, 134 * Gavesvari, 134 * Gavi-vasini, 134 * Gavisi, 134 * Gaya, 129 * Gayatri, 20 * Gayesvari, 133 * Gayottara, 136 * Geha-bhavana-bhavana, 180 * Ghati, 111 * Ghrta-lipta, 171 * Girbana, 30 * Girbana-gana-sevita, 30 * Girbana-vandya, 30 * Girija, 47 * Gita, 129 * Gita-gamya, 16 * Gita-kusala, 134 * Gokarna, 93 * Gokulananda-dayini, 15 * Gokulananda-kartri, 15 * Gokulantara-geha, 28 * Gokulanvita-deha, 91 * Gokulatva-pradayini, 91 * Gopa, 14 * Gopa-mata, 71, 133 * Gopa-nandinim, 56 * Gopa-patni, 41 * Gopa-rajya-prada, 75 * Gopa-sundari, 71 * Gopa-vanita, 75 * Gopala-palika, 70 * Gopala-vanita, 85 * Gopalasya, 29 * Gopananda-kari, 13 * Gopanganavestita, 172 * Gopaniya, 46 * Gopi, 13 * Gopinatha-manohara, 68 * Gopinathesvari, 69 * Govardhana-hasya, 132 * Govardhanesvari, 132 * Govinda-gana-pujita, 66 * Govinda-priya-karini, 87 * Govinda-raja-grhini, 66 * Gramya, 129 * Guna, 161 * Gunatita-phala-prada, 161 *Hai-hai-tala-dhara, 151 * Haimavati, 50, 145 * Haimi, 99 * Hara, 133, 136 * Hara-kanta, 73 * Hara-patni, 74 * Hara-prana, 164 * Hara-prita, 74 * Hara-rata, 73 * Hara-tosana-tatpara, 74 * Harananda-pradayini, 73 * Harer jaya, 79 * Hares tanuh, 48 * Haresvari, 74 * Hari-bhakti-pradayini, 140 * Hari-bhavana-sila, 164 * Hari-bhusana-bhusadhya, 151 * Hari-dvara, 177 * Hari-kanta, 14 * Hari-kautuka-mangala, 176 * Hari-prada, 177 * Hari-prana, 164 * Hari-priya, 14 * Hari-sannidhya-datri, 176 * Hari-tosana-tat-para, 164 * Hari-vallabha, 166 * Harid-ambara-dharini, 175 * Haridra, 173 * Harini, 57, 133, 184 * Hariny, 173 * Harita, 173 * Hasya-bhasana-tat-para, 172 * Hava-bhavanvita, 111 * Haya, 132, 182 * Hayakrtih, 132 * Hayasya, 127 * Hayi, 182 * He-he-sabda-svarupa, 152 * Hela, 162 * Hema, 116 * Hema-gatri, 19 * Hema-mandana, 116 * Hema-mukhi, 99 * Hema-ragadbya, 113 * Hema-sundari, 25 * Heramba-suta, 127 * Hetu-yukta, 136 * Hi-hi-vakya-visarada, 152 * Himalaya-suta, 47 * Hiranya-da, 160 * Hrdya, 14 *Indranila-mani-nyasta, 65 * Isvari, 46 * Jagad-ambika, 70 * Jagad-ananda-kartri, 152 * Jagad-anvaya, 94 * Jagad-bija, 148 * Jagad-utpatti-karika, 118 * Jagad-yoni, 148 * Jagannatha, 81 * Jagannatha-priya, 25 * Jagannathesvari, 81 * Jagatam-adhisthatri, 73

Vikalotkarsini, 117 * Vikasita-mukhambuja, 15 * Vilasini, 49 * Vilasiny, 23 * Vimala, 32 * Vimalangi, 23 * Vimalodaka, 32 * Vimoha, 29 * Vindhyacala-nivasini, 131 * Vindhyadri-parivasini, 119 * Vindhyalaya, 120 * Vipra-mata, 133 * Viraga-kusala, 116 * Virahini, 179 * Viraja, 78 * Visakha, 30 * Visala-grha-vasa, 123 * Visala-kula-sambhava, 123 * Visala-netra, 123 * Visala-vadari, 123 * Visnor anga-nivasini, 16 * Visnu-bhavana-tatpara, 82 * Visnu-kanta, 16 * Visnu-priya, 16 * Visnu-vaksah-sthala-stha, 82 * Visoka, 20, 30 * Vrksa-rupa, 53 * Vrnda, 48 * Vrndaranya-priya, 48 * Vrndavana-vihari, 15 * Vrndavana-vilasini, 48, 55 * Vrndavanesvari, 12 * Vrsabhanu-suta, 18 * Yacakayacakananda, 150 * Yacakojjvala, 150 * Yadavendra-vadhu, 83 * Yaga-yoga-hara, 160 * Yamalarjuna-bhanjini, 80 * Yamini, 159 * Yamini-natha, 159 * Yaminisvari, 159 * Yamuna, 79 * Yamuna-jala-vasini, 177 * Yamuna-para-kautuka, 171 * Yamuna-tosa-karini, 85 * Yamunangi, 85 * Yasasvini, 13 * Yaso-'rthini, 177 * Yasoda, 56 * Yasoda-kroda-vasini, 167 * Yasodananana-vallabha, 13 * Yasodananda-gehini, 17 * Yasodananda-patni, 17 * Yasodanandana-prana, 166, 167 * Yasodanandanakrida, 167 * Yasodanandanaramya, 166 * Yasodanandanarthada, 167 * Yasodanandanesvari, 166 * Yasogamya, 13 * Yati, 81 * Yauvanananda, 71 * Yoga-gamya, 62 * Yoga-mata, 61 * Yoga-priya, 62 * Yoga-rupini, 88 * Yoga-siddha, 88 * Yogananda-kari, 28 * Yogatita, 61 * Yogesa, 61 * Yogesi, 88 * Yogini, 88 * Yogini-gana-vandita, 62 * Yosid-ananda-karini, 108 * Yosit-sakti-svarupa, 107 * Yuga-priya, 61 * Yuvati, 71, 96

Sruti-phala
The Result of Hearing These Names

Text 1
sri-mahadeva uvacha
ity etat kathitam devi
radha-nama-sahasrakam
yah pathet pathayad vapi
tasya tusyati madhavah

Lord Siva said: Thus I have spoken to you the thousand names of Sri Radha. Lord Madhava is pleased with anyone who reads or has someone else read these names.

Text 2
kim tasya yamunabhir va
nadibhih sarvatah priye
kuruksetradi-tirthais cha
yasya tusto janardanah

When one pleases Lord Janardana what need has he for the sacred rivers
headed by the Yamuna, or the holy places headed by Kuruksetra?

Text 3
stotrasyasya prasadena
kim na sidhyati bhu-tale
brahmano brahma-varchasvi
ksatriyo jagati-patih

What perfection is not attained in this world by the mercy of this prayer?
By its mercy a brahmana becomes powerful as the demigod Brahma and
a ksatriya becomes king of the world.

Texts 4 and 5
vaisyo nidhi-patir bhuyat
sudro mucyeta janmatah
brahma-hatya-sura-pana-
steyader ati-patakat
sadyo mucyeta devesi
satyam satyam na samsayah
radha-nama-sahasrasya
samanam nasti bhu-tale

By its mercy a vaisya becomes the master of great wealth and a Sudra
becomes free from his low birth. By its mercy one becomes free from a
host of sins beginning with killing a brahmana, drinking wine, and
committing theft. O queen of the demigods, it is true. There is no doubt
it is true. In this world there is nothing equal to the thousand names of
Sri Radha.

Text 6
svarge vapy atha patale
girau va jalato 'pi va

natah param subham stotram
tirtham natah param param

In Svargaloka, in Patalaloka, on the mountains, or in the oceans no
prayer is better than this prayer, no holy place is better than this prayer.

Text 7
ekadasyam sucir bhutva
yah pathet susamahitah
tasya sarvartha-siddhih syac
chrinuyad va su-sobhane

A person who becomes clean and attentively reads or hears this prayer
on the ekadasi day attains all his desires, O beautiful one.

Text 8
dvadasyam paurnamasyam va
tulasi-sannidhau sive
yah pathet srinuyad vapi
tasya tat tat phalam srinu

O auspicious one, please hear the result attained by a person who reads
or hears this prayer in the presence of Tulasi-devi on a dvadasi or on the
full-moon day.

Texts 9-14
asvamedham rajasuyam
barhaspatyam tatha trikam
ati-ratram vajapeyam
agnistomam tatha subham

kritva yat phalam apnoti
srutva tat phalam apnuyat
karttike chastamim prapya
pathed va srinuyad api

sahasra-yuga-kalpantam
vaikuntha-vasatim labhet
tatas cha brahma-bhavane
sivasya bhavane punah

suradhinatha-bhavanes
punar yati sa-lokatam
gaiga-tiram samasadya
yah pathet srinuyad api

visnoh sarupyam ayati
satyam satyam suresvari
mama vaktra-girer jata
parvati-vadanasrita

radha-natha-sahasrakhya
nadi trailokya-pavani
pathyate hi maya nityam
bhaktya saktya yathocitam

A person who reads or hears this prayer attains the same result as if he
had performed asvamedha, raajasuya, barhaspatya, trika, atiratra,
vajapeya, and agnistoma yajna. A person who reads or hears this prayer
on the astami day of the month of Karttika lives in Vaikuntha for
thousands of yugas. He goes to Brahma's abode, Siva's abode, and Indra's
abode. A person who on the Ganges shore reads or hears this prayer
attains a spiritual form like that of Lord Visnu. O queen of the demigods,
it is true! It is true! This prayer, called the thousand names of Sri Radha,
is a river born on the mountain of my words that now takes shelter in the
mouth of Sri Parvati, a river that purifies the three worlds. I regularly
read this prayer with devotion, as far as I am able.

Text 15
mama prana-samam hy etat
tava pritya prakasitam
nabhaktaya pradatavyam
pasandaya kadachana
nastikayaviragaya
raga-yuktaya sundari

This prayer is dear to me as life. That is why I have revealed it to you,
my beloved. O beautiful one, this prayer should never be given to one
who is not a devotee, to a blasphemer, to an atheist, to one who is not
austere, or to one filled with material desires.

Text 16
tatha deyam maha-stotram
hari-bhaktaya saìkari
vaisnavesu yatha-sakti
datre punyartha-saline

O auspicious one, this prayer should be given to one who is devoted to
Lord Hari. It should be given to a pious person who will in turn give it to
the Vaisnavas as far as he is able.

Text 17
radha-nama-sudha-vari
mama vaktra-sudhambudheh
uddhritasau tvaya yatnat
yatas tvam vaisnavagranih

You are the best of Vaisnavas because you have carefully taken the
nectar of Sri Radha's names from the nectar ocean of my words.

Texts 18-20
visuddha-sattvaya yathartha-vadine
dvijasya seva-nirataya mantrine
datre yatha-sakti subhakta-manase
radha-pada-dhyana-paraya sobhane

hari-padabja-madhupa-
mano-bhutaya manase
radha-pada-sudhasvada-
saline vaisnavaya cha

dadyat stotram maha-punyam
hari-bhakti-prasadhanam
janmantaram na tasyasti
radha-Krishna-padarthinah

O beautiful one, a person who gives this very sacred prayer, which gives
Krishna-bhakti, to one situated in the mode of pure goodness, to one
who speaks the truth, to one who chants sacred mantras, to one who
gives charity as far as he is able, to one whose heart is devoted to the
Lord, to one who meditates on Sri Radha's feet, to one whose mind is a

bumblebee at the lotus flower of Lord Hari's feet, to one who is
thoughtful, to one who tastes the nectar at Sri Radha's feet, or to one who
is a Vaisnava, attains Sri Sri Radha-Krishna's feet. He does not take birth
again.

Text 21

mama prana vaisnava hi
tesam raksartham eva hi
sulam maya dharyate hi
nanyatha maitra-karanam

The Vaisnavas are my very life. I carry my trident to protect them. There
is no other reason.

Text 22

hari-bhakti-dvisam arthe
sulam sandharyate maya
srinu devi yathartham me
gaditam tvayi su-vrate

I carry my trident to punish they who hate the devotees of Lord Hari.
Hear this, O pious goddess, for to you I speak the truth.

Text 23

bhaktasi me priyasi tvam
adah snehat prakasitam
kadapi nocyate devi
maya nama-sahasrakam

You are my devotee and You are dear to me. Therefore, out of affection
I have revealed this to you. O goddess, I have never before spoken these
thousand names.

CHAPTER NINE

Prayers to Lord Vishnu and Goddess Lakshmi

alam te nirapekshaya
purna-kama namo 'stu te
mahavibhuti-pataye
namah sakala-siddhaye

"My dear Lord, You are full in all opulences, but I do not beg You for opulence. I simply offer my respectful obeisances unto You. You are the husband and master of Lakshmidevi, the goddess of fortune, who has all opulences. Therefore, You are the master of all mystic yoga. I simply offer my obeisances unto You." (*Srimad-Bhagavatam*, 6.19.4)

yatha tvam kripaya bhutya
tejasa mahimaujasa
jushta isa gunaih sarvais
tato 'si bhagavan prabhuhu

"O my Lord, because You are endowed with causeless mercy, all opulences, all prowess and all glories, strength and transcendental qualities, You are the Supreme Personality of Godhead, the master of everyone." (*Bhag.* 6.19.5)

vishnu-patni maha-maye
mahapurusha-lakshane
priyetha me maha-bhage
loka-matar namo 'stu te

"O wife of Lord Vishnu, O internal energy of Lord Vishnu, you are as good as Lord Vishnu Himself, for you have all of His qualities and opulences. O goddess of fortune, please be kind to me. O mother of the entire world, I offer my respectful obeisances unto you." (*Bhag.* 6.19.6)

om namo bhagavate maha-purushaya mahanubhavaya
mahavibhuti-pataye saha maha-vibhutibhir balim upaharamita

"My Lord Vishnu, full in six opulences, You are the best of all enjoyers and the most powerful. O husband of mother Lakshmi, I offer my respectful obeisances unto You, who are accompanied by many associates, such as Vishvaksena. I offer all the paraphernalia for worshiping You." (*Bhag.* 6.19.7)

yuvam tu vishvasya vibhu
jagatah karanam param
iyam hi prakritih suksma
maya-shaktir duratyaya

"My Lord Vishnu and mother Lakshmi, goddess of fortune, you are the proprietors of the entire creation. Indeed, you are the cause of the creation. Mother Lakshmi is extremely difficult to understand because she is so powerful that the jurisdiction of her power is difficult to overcome. Mother Lakshmi is represented in the material world as the external energy, but actually she is always the internal energy of the Lord." (*Bhag.* 6.19.11)

tasya adhishvarah sakshat
tvam eva purushah paraha
tvam sarva-yajna ijyeyam
kriyeyam phala-bhug bhavan

"My Lord, You are the master of energy, and therefore You are the Supreme Person. You are sacrifice [yajna] personified. Lakshmi, the embodiment of spiritual activities, is the original form of worship offered unto You, whereas You are the enjoyer of all sacrifices." (*Bhag.* 6.19.12)

guna-vyaktir iyam devi
vyanjako guna-bhug bhavan
tvam hi sarva-shariry atma
shrih sharirendriyashayaha

"Mother Lakshmi, who is here, is the reservoir of all spiritual qualities, whereas You manifest and enjoy all these qualities. Indeed, You are actually the enjoyer of everything. You live as the Supersoul of all living entities, and the goddess of fortune is the form of their bodies, senses and minds. She also has a holy name and form, whereas You are the support of all such names and forms and the cause for their manifestation." (*Bhag.* 6.19.13)

yatha yuvam tri-lokasya
varadau parameshthinau
tatha ma uttamashloka
santu satya mahashishaha

"You are both the supreme rulers and benedictors of the three worlds. Therefore, my Lord, Uttamashloka, may my ambitions be fulfilled by Your grace." (*Bhag.* 6.19.14)

Om Jaya Jagadish Hare
(The Vishnu Araati)

Om Jaya Jagadish Hare
Swami Jaya Jagadish Hare
Bhakti Jano Ke Sankat
Das Jano Ke Sankat
Shana Mai Dhoora Kare
Om Jaya Jagadish Hare

Oh Lord of the whole Universe
Mighty Lord of the whole Universe
All Your devotees' agonies
All Your devotees' sorrows
Instantly You banish
Oh Lord of the whole Universe

Jo dhyave phal paave
Dhukh vinashe manka
Swami dhukh vinashe manka
Sukha sampati Ghar aave

Sukha sampati Ghar aave
Kashht mite tanka
Om Jaya Jagadish Hare

He who's immersed in devotion
He reaps the fruits of Your love
Lord, he reaps the fruits of Your love
Floating in a cloud of comforts
Floating in a cloud of comforts
Free from all the worldly problems
Oh Lord of the whole Universe

Mata pita tum mere
Sharan padun mai kis ki
Swami sharan padum mai kis ki
Tum bina aur na doojaa
Tum bina aur na doojaa
Asha karun mai kis ki
Om Jaya Jagadish Hare

You art Mother and Father
At Your feet I seek eternal truth
Lord, at Your feet I seek eternal truth
There's none other than You, Lord
There's none other than You, Lord
Guardian of all our hopes
Oh Lord of the whole Universe

Tum pooran Paramatma
Tum Antaryaami
Swami Tum Antaryaami
Para brahma Parameshwara
Para brahma Parameshwara
Tum saba ke Swami
Om Jaya Jagadish Hare

You art Godly perfection
Omnipotent Master of all

Lord, omnipotent Master of all
My destiny's in Your Hand
My destiny's in Your Hand
Supreme Soul of all Creation
Oh Lord of the whole Universe

Tum karuna ke saagar
Tum palan karta
Swami Tum palan karata
Mai murakh phal Khami
Mai sevak tum swaami
Kripa karo bharata
Om Jaya Jagadish Hare

You art an ocean of mercy
Gracious protector of all
Lord, gracious protector of all
I'm Your humble devotee
I'm Your humble devotee
Grant me Your divine grace
Oh Lord of the whole Universe

Tum ho ek agochar
Sab ke prana pati
Swami sab ke prana pati
Kis vidhi miloon dayamaya
Kisi vidhi miloon dayamaya
Tum ko mai kumati
Om Jaya Jagadish Hare

You are beyond all perception
Formless and yet multiform
Lord, formless and yet multiform
Grant me a glimpse of Yourself
Grant me a glimpse of Yourself
Guide me along the path to You
Oh Lord of the whole Universe

Deena bandhu dukh hartaa
Tum rakshak mere
Swami tum rakshak mere
Apane hast uthao
Apane hast uthao
Dwar khada mai tere
Om Jaya Jagadish Hare

Friend of the helpless and feeble
Benevolent saviour of all
Lord, benevolent saviour of all
Offer me Your hand of compassion
Offer me Your hand of compassion
I seek refuge at Your feet
Oh Lord of the whole Universe

Vishaya vikar mithao
Paap haro deva
Swami paap haro deva
Shraddha bhakti badhao
Shraddha bhakti badhao
Santan ki seva
Om Jaya Jagadish Hare

Surmounting the earthly desires
Free from the sins of this life
Lord, free from the sins of this life
Undivided faith and devotion
Undivided faith and devotion
In eternal service unto You
Oh Lord of the whole Universe

Tan man dhan sab kuch hai tera
Swami sab kuch hai tera
Tera tujh ko arpan
Tera tujh ko arpan
Kya laage mera
Om Jaya Jagadish Hare

My body, mind and wealth are all Yours
Lord, everything is Yours
Lord, nothing is mine
It is Yours, I am returning to You
Oh Lord of the whole Universe

Om Jaya Jagadish Hare
Swami Jaya Jagadish Hare
Bhakta janon ke sankat
Bhakta janon ke sankat
Kshan me door kare
Om Jaya Jagadish Hare

Oh Lord of the whole Universe
Mighty Lord of the whole Universe
All Your devotees' agonies
All Your devotees' sorrows
Instantly you banish
Oh Lord of the whole Universe

Narayana Suktam
(Sahasra Sirsham Devam)

om sahasrashirsam devam visvaksham visvashambhuvam,
vishvam narayanam devamaksharam paramam padam.

This universe is the Eternal Being (of Narayana), the imperishable, the
supreme, the goal, multi-headed and multi-eyed (i.e., omnipresent and
omniscient), the resplendent, the source of delight for the whole
universe.

vishvatah paramam nityam vishvam narayanagï harim,
vishvamevedam purushastadvishvamupajivati.

This universe is the Supreme Being (Purusha) alone; hence, it subsists
on That, the Eternal which transcends it (in every way)—the
Omnipresent Absolute which destroys all sins.

patim vishvasyatmeshvaragï shashvatagï shivamachyutam,
narayanam mahajñeyam vishvatmanam parayanam.

The protector of the universe, the Lord of all souls (or Lord over Self),
the perpetual, the auspicious, the indestructible, the Goal of all creation,
the Supreme object worthy of being known, the Soul of all beings, the
Refuge unfailing (is He).

narayanah param brahma tattvam narayanah paraha
narayanah paro jyotiratma narayanah paraha
narayanah paro dhyata dhyanam narayanah paraha

The Lord Narayana is the Supreme Absolute; Narayana is the Supreme
Reality; Narayana is the Supreme Light; Narayana is the Supreme Self;
Narayana is the Supreme Meditator; Narayana is the Supreme
Meditation.

yaccha kiñchijjagatsarvam drishyate shruyate'pi va
antarbahishcha tatsarvam vyapya narayanah sthitaha

Whatever all this universe is, seen or heard of—pervading all this, from
inside and outside alike, stands supreme the Eternal Divine Being
(Narayana).

anantamavyayam kavigï samudre 'ntam vishvashambhuvam
padmakoshapratikashagï hridayam chapyadhomukham.

He is the Limitless, Imperishable, Omniscient, residing in the ocean of
the heart, the Cause of the happiness of the universe, the Supreme End
of all striving, (manifesting Himself) in the ether of the heart which is
comparable to an inverted bud of the lotus flower.

adho nishtaya vitasyante nabhyamupari tishthati,
jvalamalakulam bhati vishvasyayatanam mahat

Below the Adam's apple, at a distance of a span, and above the navel
(i.e., the heart which is the relative seat of the manifestation of Pure
Consciousness in the human being), effulges the Great Abode of the
universe, as if adorned with garlands of flames.

santatagï shilabhistu lambatyakoshasannibham,
tasyante sushiragï sukshmam tasmin sarvam pratishthitam.

Surrounded on all sides by nerve-currents (or arteries), the lotus-bud of
the heart is suspended in an inverted position. In it is a subtle space (a
narrow aperture, the sushumna-nadi), and therein is to be found the
Substratum of all things.

tasya madhye mahanagnirvishvarchirvishvatomukhaha
so'grabhug vibhajan tishthan aharamajarah kavihi

In that space within the heart resides the Great Flaming Fire,
undecaying, all-knowing, with tongues spread out in all directions, with
faces turned everywhere, consuming all food presented before it, and
assimilating it into itself.

tiryagurdhvamadahshayi rashmayastasya santatah
santapayati svam dehamapatatalamastakam
tasya madhye vahnishikha aniyordhva vyavasthitaha

His rays, spreading all round, sideways as well as above and below,
warm up the whole body from head to foot. In the centre of That (Flame)
abides the Tongue of Fire as the topmost among all subtle things.

nilatoyadamadhyasthad vidyullekheva bhasvara
nivarashukavattanvi pita bhasvatyanupama

Brilliant like a streak of lightning set in the midst of the blue
rain-bearing clouds, slender like the awn of a paddy grain, yellow (like
gold) in color, in subtlety comparable to the minute atom, (this Tongue
of Fire) glows splendid.

tasyah shikhaya madhye paramatma vyavasthitaha
sa brahma sa shivah sa harih sendrah so'ksharah paramah svarat

In the middle of that Flame, the Supreme Self dwells. This (Self) is
Brahma (the Creator), Siva (the Destroyer), Hari (the Protector), Indra
(the Ruler), the Imperishable, the Absolute, the Autonomous Being.

ritagï satyam param brahma purusham krishnapingalam
urdhvaretam virupaksham vishvarupaya vai namo namaha

Prostrations again and again to the Omni-formed Being, the Truth, the
Law, the Supreme Absolute, the Purusha of blue-decked yellow hue, the
Centralized-force Power, the All-seeing One.

om narayanaya vidmahe vasudevaya dhimahi,
tanno vishnuh prachodayat.

We commune ourselves with Narayana, and meditate on Vaasudeva;
May that Vishnu direct us (to the Great Goal).

om shantihi shantihi santihi
Om. May there be Peace, Peace, Peace.

CHAPTER TEN

Prayers to Lakshmi, the Goddess of Fortune

These are prayers for protection and for financial facility for more security in both material and spiritual pursuits. These are Prayers to all of the qualities of the Goddess and the blessings that She gives.

Lakshmi-Stuti
(From *Vishnu Purana*, 7.9.116-138)
This Stuti eulogy of Lakshmi, which was spoken by Lord Indra, is the source of all opulence. In this world, poverty never dwells, or dissipates, among those who recite this *stuti* daily.

indra uvacha
namasye sarva-lokanam
jananim abja-sambhavam
Shriyam unnidra-padmaksim
vishnor vakshah-sthala-sthitam

Indra [the demigod king of heaven] said, "I offer my obeisances unto the lotus-born mother of all beings, unto Sri [the Goddess of fortune], having full-blown lotus-like eyes, and reposing in the bosom of Vishnu."

padmalayam padmakaram
padma patra-nibheksanam
vande padma-mukhim devim
padma-nabha-priyam aham

"I offer my obeisances unto the Goddess who is the abode of lotuses, who holds the lotus, whose eyes resemble the petals of a lotus, whose face is a lotus, and who is dear to the Lord who has a lotus navel."

231

tvam siddhis tvam svadha svaha
sudha tvam loka-pavani
sandhya ratrihi prabha bhutir
medha sraddha sarasvati

"You are siddhi, nectar, Svaha and Svadha, O purifier of the worlds. You are twilight, night, effulgence, opulence, intelligence, faith and Sarasvati."

yajna-vidya maha-vidya
guhya-vidya cha shobhane
atma-vidya cha devi tvam
vimukti-phala-dayini

"You are the knowledge of sacrifice, the worship of the universal form, and occult learning, O beauteous one. You are the knowledge of Brahman, O goddess, and the bestower of the fruit of liberation."

anvikshiki trayi varta
danda-nitis tvam eva cha
saumyasaumyair jagad rupais
tvayaitad devi puritam

"You are the science of dialectics, the three Vedas, Varta, the knowledge of chastisement. O goddess, this universe is filled with your gentle and terrifying forms."

ka tv anya tvam rte devi
sarva-yajna-mayam vapuhu
adhyaste deva-devasya
yogi cintyam gada-bhritaha

"O goddess, who except you can dwell in the person of that God of gods, who consists of all forbearance, the bearer of the mace, who is contemplated by the yogis?"

tvayi devi parityaktam
sakalam bhuvana-trayam
vinashta-prayam abhavat
tvaye danim samedhitam

"O goddess, the three worlds, having been abandoned by you, were on the verge of destruction--because of you, they have again recovered their position."

> dara-putras tatha garam
> suhrid-dhanya dhanadikam
> bhavaty etan maha-bhage
> nityam tvad-vikshanam nrinam

"O exalted one, men are endowed with wives, sons, houses, friends, grain and wealth due to your constant glance."

> sharirarogyam aishvaryam
> ari-paksa-ksayam sukham
> devi-tvad-drishti-drishtanam
> purushanam na durlabham

"O goddess, freedom from bodily ailments, riches, destruction of enemies, and happiness are not difficult to attain for persons who view your glances."

> tvam mata sarva-bhutanam
> deva-devo harih pita
> tvayaitad vishnuma chadya
> jagad vyaptam-characharam

"You are the mother of all creatures, as that God of gods, Hari, is their father. And this universe, consisting of moving and nonmoving entities, is presently permeated by you, as well as Vishnu."

> ma nah kosham tatha goshtham
> ma griham ma paricchadam
> ma sariram kalatram cha
> tyajethaha sarva-pavani

"O purifier of all, if you forsake us, neither our treasures, nor our cows, nor our houses, nor our possessions, nor our bodies, nor our wives, are secure."

ma putram ma suhrid-vargam
ma pashun ma vibhushanam
tyajetha mama devasya
vishnor vaksah-sthalalaye

"O you whose abode is the chest of Vishnu, if you forsake me, neither sons, nor friends, nor animals, nor ornaments can be mine."

sattvena satya-shaucabhyam
chatha shiladibhir gunaih
tyajante te narah sadyaha
sansyakto ye tvayamale

"O spotless one, men who are forsaken by you are also forsaken by goodness, truth, purity, good character and other virtues."

tvayavico kitah sadyaha
shiladyair akhilair gunaih
kulaishvaryaish cha muhyante
purusha nirguna api

"And those who are glanced upon by you, although devoid of any good qualities, are infatuated by all good qualities, such as good character, lineage, wealth, etc."

sa shlaghyah sa guni dhanyaha
sa kulinaha sa biddhinam
sa shurah sa cha vikranto
yas tvaya devi vikshitaha

"O goddess, he who is glanced upon by you, is praiseworthy, accomplished, fortunate, intelligent, high-born, heroic and possessed of power."

sadyo vaingunyam ayanti
shiladyah sakala gunaha
paranmukhi jaga-dhatri
yasya tvam vishnu-vallabhe

"O nurse of the universe, O beloved of Vishnu, all virtues, character, etc., immediately abandon him from whom you turn away."

na te varnayitum shakta
gunan jihvapi vedhasaha
prasida devi padmakshi
masmams tyakshih kadachana

"Even the tongue of Brahma is incapable of describing your qualities. O lotus-eyed one, be auspicious unto me. Please do not abandon me."

[Thus ends the Lakshmi-stuti]

Sri [the Goddess of Fortune] said: "I shall never turn my face from one who praises me every morning and evening with this hymn."

Sri Suktam

Sloka 1
Om, Hiranya varnam harinim
Suvarna rajatasrajam
Chandraam hiranmayim
Lakshmim jatavedo ma avaha

O all-knowing fire-god (Agni), would you kindly propitiate Mahalakshmi, the Goddess of prosperity, one whose body has the golden color; one who is decked with gold and silver garlands; one whose sari is yellow colored and one Whose face is like the full moon and whose eyes bless humanity with soothing grace. O Jata Veda, the fire-god, kindly tell Her of our supplications.

Sloka 2
Tamaavaha jatavedo
Lakshmimananpagaminim
Yasyaam hiranyam vindeyam
Gamasvam purushanaham

O, Agni, the great fire-god, with the blessings of Mahalakshmi, wealth and prosperity, gold and cattle, horses and useful animals, family and children and every type of prosperity will come to me. By the arrival of Goddess Lakshmi in my home, the prosperity will be imperishable. Health, friends, knowledge, everlasting peace and finally freedom -- all these types of wealth will be mine by the arrival of the Universal Mother, Lakshmi, into my home.

Sloka 3
Ashwapurvam Rathamadhyam
Hastinada Prabodinim
Sriyam Devimupahvaye
Shrirmadevirjushatam

That Goddess Lakshmi in whose procession the celestial horses and the divine chariots are used, as the elephants roar the OM sound which pleases that Goddess. She being Gajalakshmi or Lakshmi Who is worshiped by the elephants. O Agni, I am invoking that power, the spouse of Vishnu. May I attain Her grace.

Sloka 4
Kamsosmitam Hiranya Prakaramardram
Jvalantim truptam tarpayantim
Padmestitam padmavarnam
Tamihopahvaye sriyam

One Who is sitting on the blossomed thousand-petalled lotus; one whose body has the color of the lotus; may that great Goddess. The compassionate, radiant, ever-smiling, fulfiller of all the desires of Her votaries, hear my prayers. I invoke that Mother, Mahalakshmi of golden color.

Sloka 5
Chandramprabhasam yashasajvalantim
Sriyamloke devajustamudaram
Tam Padminimim Saranamaham
Prapadye Alakshmirme
Nashyatam twam vrune

I invoke Mahalakshmi Who shines like the full moon and like lightening. Her fame is all-pervading. Denizens of heaven constantly worship Her. She is minificent. Her benevolent hands are like lotuses. I take refuge in Her lotus feet. Let Her destroy my poverty forever. O Mother Mahalakshmi, I take shelter at Your lotus feet.

Sloka 6
Aadityavarne Tapasodhijato
Vanaspatistava Vrukshothabilvaha
Tasya phalani Tapasanudantu
Mayantarayascha Bahya Alakshmihi

O Universal Mother, shining like the sun, it is through Your penance that the holiest trees of Bilva and Tulasi are born. They symbolize the tree of life. The fruit of that tree of life removes our poverty from both within and without. In other words, bless us with inner light and outer independence and abundance.

Sloka 7
Upaitumam Devasakhaha
Kirtishcha Maninaa Saha
Praddurbhuto smi rastresmin
Kirthimrudhim dadatume

O Devi, the great Goddess, with Your blessings let Kubera, the treasurer of the gods; his friend, Manibhadra, the protector of wealth, and Keerti, the goddess of fame who was the daughter of Daksha Prajapati.

Sloka 8
Kshutpipasamalam JyesthaAm
Alakshmim nashayamyaham
Abhutimasamruddhim cha
Sarvam Nirnuda me grihat

That goddess of hunger and thirst, one who is reduced to a skeleton; I would like the death of the goddess of poverty. O Mahalakshmi, may You kindly drive away any fear of poverty and inauspiciousness from my home. In other words, bless me always with abundance and joy.

Sloka 9
Gandhadvaram duradharsham
Nitya Pushtam Karishinim
Eshvarim sarvabhutanam
Tamihopahvaye Sriyam

I invoke that supreme Goddess Lakshmi to dwell in my home forever. She
is the supreme power of protection and Goddess of all the universes and
cosmic elements. She is Mother Earth, the bestower of great contentment.
Her blessings are bringing us the fragrance of the sandalwood paste. May
that Ishwari be ever present in me.

Sloka 10
Manasaha-Kamamakutim
Vachasatya mashimahi
Pashunam Rupamanasya mayi
Shrishrayatam yashaha

May Mahalakshmi fulfill all my desires. May I attain perfection. May my
words come true. May I be bestowed with cattle, wealth, food, milk and
honey to share with all. May that Sri Devi come to my home in the form of
undying fame.

Sloka 11
Kardamena Prajabhuta mayi
Sambhava Kardhama
Shriyam Vasayame Kule
Mataram Padma malinim

We are the progeny of our forefather, Sage Kardama, who is one of the
sons of Goddess Lakshmi. We invoke that Sage Kardama to install in his
family the Universal Mother, Mahalakshmi, who is decked with the garland
of lotuses. So be it.

Sloka 12
Apsrujantu Snigdhani Chiklita
Vasa Me Gruhe
Nicha devim Mataram Sriyam
Vasayame kule

We invoke another son of Lakshmi named Chikleeta. May he dwell in our home and may his mother, Mahalakshmi, dwell in our family.

Sloka 13
Ardram pushkarinim Pushtim
Pingalam Padmamalinim
Chandram hiranmayim Lakshmim
Jatavedo Ma avaha

O Agni, may You propitiate Mahalakshmi, the destroyer of demons but merciful to Her devotees, abode of auspiciousness, bestower of total protection, extraordinarily beautiful, bedecked with valuable ornaments, shining like a thousand suns; may that Hiranmayi, the golden colored Goddess, be pleased with us.

Sloka 14
Ardram Yah karinim yastim
Suvarnam hemamalinim
Suryam Hiranmayim Lakshmim
Jatavedo Ma avaha

O Agni, the fire-god, I once again pray unto you to invoke the presence of the Lakshmi Devi with us. The Mother Who is merciful blessings with Her lotus hand. May that yellow-clad, lotus-garlanded, moon-faced Goddess shower Her choicest cup of blessings upon us.

Sloka 15
Tama avaha Jatavedo
Lakshmimanapagaminim
Yasyam Hiranyam Prabhutam gavo
Dasyoshvam Vindeyam Purushanaham

O Agni, please pray to that Lakshmi that we should be blessed with inexhaustible wealth. May that wealth bring that greatest joy and peace along with all material comforts of cows, servants, horses, family and good children, and the highest of all, freedom.

Sloka 16
Om Mahadevyaicha vidmahe Vishnu
Pathnyaicha dhimahi

Tanno Lakshmih prachodayatu
Om Shanti Shanti Shantihi

Let that Mahalakshmi be invoked on Whom I meditate upon, Who is the consort of Lord Vishnu, the Supreme Mother. Let peace prevail everywhere.

108 Names of Goddess Lakshmi
These can be chanted individually by saying Om first, then the name, followed by Namaha. These, like the previous Lakshmi Stutis, can be chanted as part of Lakshmi-puja, or daily for blessings.

Prakruti - Nature
Vikruti - Multi-Faceted Nature
Vidya - Wisdom
Sarvabhootahitaprada - Granter of Universal Niceties
Shraddha - Devoted
Vibhuti - Wealth
Surabhi - Celestial Being
Paramatmika - Omnipresence
Vachi - Nectar-Like Speech
Padmalaya - Residing On The Lotus
Padma – Lotus
Shuchi - Embodiment of Purity
Swaha - Shape of Swahadevi(Auspicious)
Swadha - Shape of Swadhadevi(Inauspicious)
Sudha - Nectar
Dhanya - Personification of Gratitude
Hiranmayi - Golden Appearance
Lakshmi - Goddess of Wealth
NityaPushta - Gaining strength Day By Day
Vibha - Radiant
Aditi - Radiant Like The Sun
Deetya - Answer Of Prayers
Deepta - Flame-Like
Vasudha - Earth
Vasudharini - Bearing the the Burden of Earth
Kamala - Lotus
Kantha - Consort of Vishnu
Kamakshi - One with Attractive Eyes

Kamalasambhava - Emanating from the Lotus
Anugrahaprada - Granter of Good Wishes
Buddhi - Wisdom
Anagha - Sinless
Navadurga - All Nine Forms of Durga
Harivallabhi - Consort of Lord Hari
Ashoka - Dispeller of Sorrows
Amrutha - Nectar
Deepa - Radiant
Lakashokavinashini - Remover of Universal Agonies
Dharmanilaya - Establisher of Eternal Law
Karuna - Compassionate
Lokamatri - Mother of the Universe
Padmapriya - Lover of Lotus
Padmahasta - Having Lotus-Like Hands
Padmakshya - Lotus-eyed
Padmasundari - Beautiful Like the Lotus
Padmodbhava - One Who Emerged Out of the Lotus
Padmamukhi - Lotus-Faced
Padmanabhapriya - Beloved of Padmanabha
Ramaa - Pleaser of the Lord
Padmamaladhara - Wearer of Lotus Garland
Devi - Goddess
Padmini - Lotus
Padmagandhini - Having the Fragrance of Lotus
Punyagandha - Having Divine Perfume
Suprasanna - Ever Cheerful and Beaming
Prasadabhimukhi - Emerging to Grant Boons
Prabha - Radiant Like the Sun
Chandravadana - Moon-Faced
Chanda - Cool Like the moon
Chandrasahodari - Sister of the Moon
Chaturbhuja - with four arms
Chandrarupa - Moon-Faced
Indira - Radiant like the Sun
Indusheetala - Cool like the Moon
Ahladajanani - Source of Happiness
Pushti - Healthy
Shiva - Auspicious
Shivakari - Source of Auspicious Things

Satya - All Truth
Vimala - Pure
Vishwajanani - Mother of the Universe
Pushti - Possessor of All Wealth
Daridriyanashini - Remover of Poverty
Preeta Pushkarini - One with Pleasing Eyes
Shanta - Full with peace or Calm
Shuklamalambara - Wearer of White Garland and Attire
Bhaskari - Radiant like the Sun
Bilvanilaya - Resider Under Bilva Tree
Vararoha - Ready to Offer Boons
Yashaswini - Reputed
Vasundhara - Daughter of the Earth
Udaranga - Endowed with a Beautiful Body
Harini - Deer-Like
Hemamalini - Having Golden Garlands
Dhanadhanyaki - Bestower of Wealth and Foodgrains
Siddhi - Ever Ready to Protect
Straina Soumya - Showering Goodness on Women
Shubhaprada - Granter of Auspicious Things
Nrupaveshvagathananda - Loves to Live in Palaces
Varalakshmi - Granter of Bounty
Vasuprada - Bestower of Wealth
Shubha - Auspicious
Hiranyapraka - Amidst Gold
Samudratanaya - Beloved Daughter of the Ocean of Milk
Jaya - Goddess of Victory
Mangala - Most Auspicious
Devi - The Deity
Vishnuvakshah - Residing in Vishnu's Chect
Vishnupatni - Consort of Vishnu
Prasannakshi - Lively-Eyed
Narayana Samashrita - Sought Refuge in Narayana
Daridriya Dhwamsini - Destroyer of Poverty
Devi - Goddess
Sarvapadravanivarini - Dispeller of all Distresses
Mahakali - A Form of Kali
Brahma-Vishnu-Shivatmika - Trinity of Brahma-Vishnu-Shiva
Trikala-dnyanasampanna - Aware of all 3 -the Past, Present and Future
Bhuvaneshwarya - Supreme Deity

CHAPTER ELEVEN

Prayers of Surrender by Gajendra to Lord Vishnu

These are exceptional prayers from the *Srimad-Bhagavatam* that give to a person advanced spiritual strength and insight.

shri-ganjendra uvacha
om namo bhagavate tasmai
yata etac chid-atmakam
purushayadi-bijaya
pareshayabhidhimahi

Gajendra said: I offer my respectful obeisances unto the Supreme Person, Vasudeva [om namo bhagavate vasudevaya]. Because of Him this material body acts due to the presence of spirit, and He is therefore the root cause of everyone. He is worshipable for such exalted persons as Brahma and Shiva, and He has entered the heart of every living being. Let me meditate upon Him. (*Srimad-Bhagavatam* 8.3.2)

yasminn idam yatash chedam
yenedam ya idam svayam
yo 'smat parasmach cha paras
tam prapadye svayambhuvam

 The Supreme Godhead is the supreme platform on which everything rests, the ingredient by which everything has been produced, and the person who has created and is the only cause of this cosmic manifestation. Nonetheless, He is different from the cause and the result. I surrender unto Him, the Supreme Personality of Godhead, who is self-sufficient in everything. (8.3.3)

yah svatmanidam nija-mayayarpitam
kvachid vibhatam kva cha tat tirohitam
aviddha-drik sakshy ubhayam tad ikshate
sa atma-mula 'vatu mam parat-paraha

The Supreme Personality of Godhead, by expanding His own energy, keeps this cosmic manifestation visible and again sometimes renders it invisible. He is both the supreme cause and the supreme result, the observer and the witness, in all circumstances. Thus He is transcendental to everything. May that Supreme Personality of Godhead give me protection. (8.3.4)

kalena pancatvam iteshu kritsnasho
lokeshu paleshu cha sarva-hetushu
tamas tadasid gahanam gabhiram
yas tasya pare 'bhivirajate vibhuhu

In due course of time, when all the causative and effective manifestations of the universe, including the planets and their directors and maintainers, are annihilated, there is a situation of dense darkness. Above this darkness, however, is the Supreme Personality of Godhead, I take shelter of His lotus feet. (8.3.5)

na yasya deva rishayah padam vidur
jantuh punah ko 'rhati gantum iritum
yatha natasyakritibhir vicheshtato
duratyayanukramanah sa mavatu

An artist onstage, being covered by attractive dresses and dancing with different movements, is not understood by his audience; similarly, the activities and features of the Supreme Artist cannot be understood even by the demigods or great sages, and certainly not by those who are unintelligent like animals. Neither the demigods and sages nor the unintelligent can understand the features of the Lord, nor can they express in words His actual position. May that Supreme Personality of Godhead give me protection. (8.3.6)

didrikshavo yasya padam sumangalam
vimukta-sanga munayah susadhavaha
charanty aloka-vratam avranam vane
bhutatma-bhutah suhridah sa me gatihi

Renunciants and great sages who see all living beings equally, who are friendly to everyone and who flawlessly practice in the forest the vows of brahmacarya [celibate student], vanaprastha [retired] and sannyasa [renunciation] desire to see the all-auspicious lotus feet of the Supreme Personality of Godhead. May that same Supreme Personality of Godhead be my destination. (8.3.7)

> na vidyate yasya cha janma karma va
> na nama-rupe guna-dosha eva va
> tathapi lokapyaya-sambhavaya yaha
> sva-mayaya tany anukalam ricchati

> tasmai namah pareshaya
> brahmane 'nanta-shaktaye
> arupayoru-rupaya
> nama ashcarya-karmane

The Supreme Personality of Godhead has no material birth, activities, name, form, qualities or faults. To fulfill the purpose for which this material world is created and destroyed, He comes in the form of a human being like Lord Rama or Lord Krishna by His original internal potency. He has immense potency, and in various forms, all free from material contamination, He acts wonderfully. He is therefore the Supreme Brahman. I offer my respects to Him. (8.3.8-9)

> nama atma-pradipaya
> sakshine paramatmane
> namo giram viduraya
> manasash chetasam api

I offer my respectful obeisances unto the Supreme Personality of Godhead, the self-effulgent Supersoul, who is the witness in everyone's heart, who enlightens the individual soul and who cannot be reached by exercises of the mind, words or consciousness. (8.3.10)

> sattveno pratilabhyaya
> naishkarmyena vipashcita
> namah kaivalya-nathaya
> nirvana-sukha-samvide

The Supreme Personality of Godhead is realized by pure devotees who act in the transcendental existence of bhakti-yoga. He is the bestower of uncontaminated happiness and is the master of the transcendental world. Therefore I offer my respects unto Him. (8.3.11)

> namah shantaya ghoraya
> mudhaya guna-dharmine
> nirvisheshaya samyaya
> namo jnana-ghanaya cha

I offer my respectful obeisances to Lord Vasudev, who is all-pervading, to the Lord's fierce form as Lord Nrisimhadeva, to the Lord's form as an animal [Lord Varahadeva], to Lord Dattatreya, who preached impersonalism, to Lord Buddha, and to all the other incarnations. I offer my respectful obeisances unto the Lord, who has no material qualities but who accepts the three qualities of goodness, passion and ignorance within this material world. I also offer my respectful obeisances unto the impersonal Brahman effulgence. (8.3.12)

> ksetra-jnaya namas tubhyam
> sarvadhyakshaya sakshine
> purushayatma-mulaya
> mula-prakritaye namaha

I beg to offer my respectful obeisances unto You, who are the Supersoul, the superintendent of everything, and the witness of all that occurs. You are the Supreme Person, the origin of material nature and of the total material energy. You are also the owner of the material body. Therefore, You are the supreme complete. I offer my respectful obeisances unto You. (8.3.13)

> sarvendriya-guna-drashtre
> sarva-pratyaya-hetave
> asata cchayayoktaya
> sad-abhasaya te namaha

My Lord, You are the observer of all the objectives of the senses. Without Your mercy, there is no possibility of solving the problem of doubts. The material world is just like a shadow resembling You. Indeed, one accepts this material world as real because it gives a glimpse of Your existence. (8.3.14)

namo namas te 'khila-karanaya
nishkaranayadbhuta-karanaya
sarvagamamnaya-maharnavaya
namo 'pavargaya parayanaya

My Lord, You are the cause of all causes, but You Yourself have no causes. Therefore You are the wonderful cause of everything. I offer my respectful obeisances unto You, who are the shelter of the Vedic knowledge contained in the shastras like the Pancharatras and Vedanta-sutra, which are Your representations, and who are the source of the parampara system. Because it is You who can give liberation, You are the only shelter for all transcendentalists. Let me offer my respectful obeisances unto You. (8.3.15)

gunarani-cchanna-chid-ushmapaya
tat-kshobha-visphurjita-manasaya
naishkarmya-bhavena vivarjitagama
svayam-prakashaya namas karomi

My Lord, as the fire in arani wood is covered, You and Your unlimited knowledge are covered by the material modes of nature. Your mind, however, is not attentive to the activities of the modes of nature. Those who are advanced in spiritual knowledge are not subject to the regulative principles directed in the Vedic literature. Because such advanced souls are transcendental, You personally appear in their pure minds. Therefore I offer my respectful obeisances unto You. (8.3.16)

madrik prapanna-pashu-pashu-vimokshanaya
muktaya bhuri-karunaya namo 'layaya
svamshena sarva-tanu-bhrin-manasi pratita-
pratyag-drishe bhagavate brihate namaste

Since an animal such as I has surrendered unto You, who are supremely liberated, certainly You will release me from this dangerous position. Indeed, being extremely merciful, You incessantly try to deliver me. By Your partial feature as Paramatma, You are situated in the hearts of all embodied beings. You are celebrated as direct transcendental knowledge, and You are unlimited. I offer my respectful obeisances unto You, the Supreme Personality of Godhead. (8.3.17)

atmatma-japti-griha-vitta-janeshu saktair
dushprapanaya guna-sanga-vivarjitaya
muktatmabhih sva-hridaya paribhavitaya
jnanatmane bhagavate nama ishvaraya

My Lord, those who are completely freed from material contamination
always meditate upon You within the cores of their hearts. You are
extremely difficult to attain for those like me who are too attached to
mental concoction, home, relatives, friends, money, servants and assistants.
You are the Supreme Personality of Godhead, uncontaminated by the
modes of nature. You are the reservoir of all enlightenment, the supreme
controller. I therefore offer my respectful obeisances unto You. (8.3.18)

yam dharma-kamartha-vimukti-kama
bhajanta ishtam gatim apnuvanti
kim chashisho raty api deham avyayam
karotu me 'dabhra-dayo vimokshanam

After worshiping the Supreme Personality of Godhead, those who are
interested in the four principles of religion, economic development, sense
gratification and liberation obtain from Him what they desire. What then
is to be said of other benedictions? Indeed, sometimes the Lord gives a
spiritual body to such ambitious worshipers. May that Supreme Personality
of Godhead, who is unlimitedly merciful, bestow upon me the benediction
of liberation from this present danger and from the materialistic way of life.
(8.3.19)

ekantino yasya na kanchanartham
vanchanti ye vai bhagavat-prapannaha
aty-adbhutam tach-charitam sumangalam
gayanta ananda-samudra-magnaha

tam aksharam brahma param paresham
avyaktam adhyatmika-yoga-gamyam
atindriyam sukshmam ivatiduram
anantam adyam paripurnam ide

Unalloyed devotees, who have no desire other than to serve the Lord,
worship Him in full surrender and always hear and chant about His
activities, which are most wonderful and auspicious. Thus they always

merge in an ocean of transcendental bliss. Such devotees never ask the Lord for any benediction. I, however, am in danger. Thus I pray to the Supreme Personality of Godhead, who is eternally existing, who is invisible, who is the Lord of all great personalities, such as Brahma, and who is available only by transcendental bhakti-yoga. Being extremely subtle, He is beyond the reach of my senses and transcendental to all external realization. He is unlimited, He is the original cause, and He is completely full in everything. I offer my obeisances unto Him. (8.3.20-21)

> yasya bramadayo deva
> veda lokash characharaha
> nama-rupa-vibhedena
> phalgvya cha kalaya kritaha

> yatharchisho 'gneh savitur gabhastayo
> niryanti samyanty asakrit sva-rochishaha
> tatha yato 'yam guna-sampravaho
> buddhir manah khani sharira-sargaha

> sa vai na devasura-martya-tiryan
> na stri na sandho na puman na jantuhu
> nayam gunah karma na san na casan
> nishedha-shesho jayatad ashesaha

The Supreme Personality of Godhead creates His minor parts and parcels, the jiva-tattva, beginning with Lord Brahma, the demigods and the expansions of Vedic knowledge [Sama, Rig, Yajur and Atharva Vedas] and including all other living entities, moving and nonmoving, with their different names and characteristics. As the sparks of a fire or the shining rays of the sun emanate from their source and merge into it again and again, the mind, the intelligence, the senses, the gross and subtle material bodies, and the continuous transformations of the different modes of nature all emanate from the Lord and again merge into Him. He is neither demigod nor demon, neither human nor bird nor beast. He is not woman, man or neuter, nor is He an animal. He is not a material quality, a fruitive activity, a manifestation or nonmanifestation. He is the last word in the discrimination of "not this, or not that," and He is unlimited. All glories to the Supreme Personality of Godhead. (8.3.22-24)

jijivishe naham ihamuya kim
antar bahish chavritayebha-yonya
icchami kalena na yasya viplavas
tasyatma-lokavaranasya moksham

I do not wish to live anymore after I am released from the attack of the
crocodile. What is the use of an elephant's body covered externally and
internally by ignorance? I simply desire eternal liberation from the covering
of ignorance. That covering is not destroyed by the influence of time.
(8.3.25)

so 'ham vishva-srijam vishvam
avishvan vishva-vedasam
vishvatmanam ajam brahma
pranato 'smi param padam

Now, fully desiring release from material life, I offer my respectful
obeisances unto that Supreme Person who is the creator of the universe,
who is Himself the form of the universe and who is nonetheless
transcendental to this cosmic manifestation. He is the supreme knower of
everything in this world, the Supersoul of the universe. He is the unborn,
supremely situated Lord. I offer my respectful obeisances unto Him.
(8.3.26)

yoga-randhita-karmano
hridi yoga-vibhavite
yogino yam prapashyanti
yogesham tam nato 'smy aham

I offer my respectful obeisances unto the Supreme, the Supersoul, the
master of all mystic yoga, who is seen in the core of the heart by perfect
mystics when they are completely purified and freed from the reactions of
fruitive activity by practicing bhakti-yoga. (8.3.27)

namo namas tubhyam asahya-vega-
shakti-trayayakhila-dhi-gunaya
prapanna-palaya duranta-shaktaye
kad-indriyanam anavapya-vartmane

My Lord, You are the controller of formidable strength in three kinds of energy. You appear as the reservoir of all sense pleasure and the protector of the surrendered souls. You possess unlimited energy, but You are unapproachable by those who are unable to control their senses. I offer my respectful obeisances unto You again and again. (8.3.28)

nayam veda svam atmanam
yach-chaktyaham-dhiya hatam
tam duratyaya-mahatmyam
bhagavantam ito 'smy aham

I offer my respectful obeisances unto the Supreme Personality of Godhead, by whose illusory energy the jiva [individual spirit soul], who is part and parcel of God, forgets his real identity because of the bodily concept of life. I take shelter of the Supreme Personality of Godhead, whose glories are difficult to understand. (8.3.29)

[The Lord now replies to Gajendra]
ye mam stuvanty anenanga
pratibudhya nishatyaye
tesham pranatyaye chaham
dadami vipulam gatim

"My dear devotee, unto those who rise from bed at the end of night and offer Me the prayers offered by you, I give an eternal residence in the spiritual world at the end of their lives." (8.4.25)

CHAPTER TWELVE

Shiva's Song

This is a *stotra* or a series of mantras or prayers of Lord Shiva presented to the sons of King Prachinabarhi for teaching the ultimate spiritual perfection. These are from the *Bhagavata Purana*.

It is first described therein (4.24.24-32) that the sons of King Pracinabarhi approached Lord Shiva, who, in return, was very pleased to see them. Lord Shiva first told them, "You are all the sons of King Pracinabarhi, and I wish all good fortune to you. I also know what you are going to do, and therefore I am visible to you just to show you my mercy. Anyone who is surrendered to the Supreme Lord, Krishna, the controller of everything—material nature as well as the living entity—is actually very dear to me. A person who executes his [spiritual] occupational duty properly for one hundred births becomes qualified to occupy the post of Lord Brahma, and if he becomes more qualified he can approach Lord Shiva. Yet, a person who is directly surrendered to Lord Krishna, or Vishnu, in unalloyed devotional service is immediately promoted to the spiritual planets. Lord Shiva and other demigods attain these planets after the destruction of this material world. You are all devotees of the Lord, and as such I appreciate that you are as respectable as the Supreme Person Himself. I know in this way that the devotees also respect me and that I am dear to them. Thus no one can be as dear to the devotees as I am.

"Now I shall chant one mantra which is not only transcendental, pure and auspicious, but is the best prayer for anyone who is aspiring to attain the ultimate goal of life. When I chant this mantra, please hear it carefully and attentively."

Thus, out of his causeless mercy, the exalted personality of Lord Shiva, a great devotee of Lord Narayana [Vishnu, Krishna], continued to speak this sacred set of verses to the King's sons, who were standing with folded hands.

Verse 33
shri-rudra uvacha
jitam ta atma-vid-varya

252

svastya svastir astu me
sarvasma atmane namaha

Lord Shiva addressed the Supreme Personality of Godhead with the
following prayer: O Supreme Personality of Godhead, all glories unto You.
You are the most exalted of all self-realized souls. Since You are always
auspicious for the self-realized, I wish that You be auspicious for me. You
are worshipable by virtue of the all-perfect instructions You give. You are
the Supersoul; therefore I offer my obeisances unto You as the supreme
living being.

Verse 34
namaha pankaja-nabhaya
bhuta-sukshmendriyamane
vasudevaya shantaya
kuta-sthaya sva-rochishe

My Lord, You are the origin of the creation by virtue of the lotus
flower which sprouts from Your navel. You are the supreme controller of
the senses and the sense objects, and You are also the all-pervading
Vasudeva. You are more peaceful, and because of Your self-illuminated
existence, You are not disturbed by the six kinds of transformations.

Verse 35
sankarshanaya sukshmaya
durantayantakaya cha
namo vishva-prabadhaya
pradyumnayantar-atmane

My dear Lord, You are the origin of the subtle material ingredients,
the master of all integration as well as the master of all disintegration, the
predominating Deity named Sankarshana, and the master of all intelligence,
known as the predominating Deity Pradyumna. Therefore, I offer my
respectful obeisances unto You.

Verse 36
namo namo 'niruddhaya
hrishikeshendriyatmane
namah paramahamsaya
purnaya nibhritatmane

My Lord, as the supreme directing Deity known as Aniruddha, You are the master of the senses and the mind. I therefore offer You my obeisances again and again. You are known as Ananta as well as Sankarshana because of Your ability to destroy the whole creation by the blazing fire from Your mouth.

Verse 37

svargapavarga-dvaraya
nityam shuchi-shade namaha
namo hiranya-viryaya
chatur-hotraya tantave

My Lord, O Aniruddha, You are the authority by which the doors of the higher planetary systems and liberation are opened. You are always within the pure heart of the living entity. Therefore I offer my obeisances unto You. You are the possessor of semen which is like gold, and, thus, in the form of fire, You help the Vedic sacrifices, beginning with the chatur-hotra. There fore I offer my obeisances unto You.

Verse 38

nama urja ishe trayyaha
pataye yajna-retase
tripti-daya cha jivanam
namah sarva-rasatmane

My Lord, You are the provider of the pitrilokas (planets of the ancestors) as well as the demigods. You are the predominating deity of the moon and the master of all three Vedas. I offer my respectful obeisances unto You because You are the original source for all living entities.

Verse 39

sarva-sattvatma-dehaya
visheshaya sthaviyase
namas trailokya-palaya
saha ojo-balaya cha

My dear Lord, You are the gigantic universal form which contains all the individual bodies of the living entities. You are the maintainer of the three worlds [three basic planetary systems], and as such You maintain the mind, senses, body and air of life within them. I therefore offer my respectful obeisances unto You.

Verse 40
artha-lingaya nabhase
namo 'ntar-bahir-atmane
namah punyaya lokaya
amushmai bhuri-varchase

My dear Lord, by expanding Your transcendental vibrations, You reveal the actual meaning of everything. You are the all-pervading sky within and without, and You are the ultimate goal of pious activities executed both within this material world and beyond it. I therefore offer my respectful obeisances again and again unto You.

Verse 41
pravrittaya nivrittaya
pitri-devaya karmane
namo 'dharma-vipakaya
mritave duhkha-daya cha

My dear Lord, You are the viewer of the results of pious activities. You are inclination, disinclination and their resultant activities. You are the cause of the miserable conditions of life caused by irreligion, and therefore You are death. I offer You my respectful obeisances.

Verse 42
namas ta ashisham isha
manave karanatmane
namo dharmaya brihate
krishnayakuntha-medhase
purushaya puranaya
sankhya-yogeshvaraya cha

My dear Lord, You are the topmost of all bestowers of all benedictions, the oldest and supreme enjoyer amongst all enjoyers. You are the master of all the world's metaphysical philosophy, for You are the supreme cause of all causes, Lord Krishna. You are the greatest of all religious principles, the supreme mind, and You have a brain which is never checked by any condition. Therefore I repeatedly offer my obeisances unto You.

Verse 43
shakti-traya-sametaya
midhushe 'hankritatmane
cheta-akuti-rupaya
namo vacho vibhutaye

My dear Lord, You are the supreme controller of the worker, sense activities and the results of sense activities [karma]. Therefore, You are the controller of the body, mind and senses. You are also the supreme controller of egotism, known as Rudra. You are the source of knowledge and the activities of the Vedic injunctions.

Verse 44
darshanam no didrikshunam
dehi bhagavatarchitam
rupam priyatamam svanam
sarvendriya-gunanjanam

My dear Lord, I wish to see You exactly in the form that Your very dear devotees worship. You have many other forms, but I wish to see Your form that is especially liked by the devotees. Please be merciful upon me and show me that form, for only that form worshipped by the devotees can perfectly satisfy all the demands of the senses.

Verses 45-46
snigdha-pravrid-ghana-shyamam
sarva-saundarya-sangraham
charv-ayata-chatur-bahu
sujata-rucirananam

padma-kosha-palashaksham
sundara-bhru sunasikam
sudvijam sukapolasyam
sama-karna-vibhushanam

The Lord's beauty resembles a dark cloud during the rainy season. As the rainfall glistens, His bodily features also glisten. Indeed, He is the sum total of all beauty. The Lord has four arms and an exquisitely beautiful face with eyes like lotus petals, a beautiful highly raised nose, a mind-attracting smile, a beautiful forehead, and equally beautiful and fully decorated ears.

Verses 47-48
priti-prahasitapangam
alakai rupa-shobitam
lasat-pankaja-kinjalka
dukulam mrishta-kundalam

sphurat-kirita-valaya-
hara-nupura-makhalam
shankha-chakra-gada-padma-
mala-many-uttamarddhimat

The Lord is superexcellently beautiful on account of His open and merciful smile and His sidelong glance upon His devotees. His black hair is curly, and His garments, waving in the wind, appear like flying saffron pollen from lotus flowers. His glittering earrings, shining helmet, bangles, garland, ankle bells, waist belt, and various other bodily ornaments combine with conchshell, disc, club and lotus flower to increase the natural beauty of the Kaustubha pearl on His chest.

Verse 49
Simha-skandha-tvisho bibhrat
Saubhaga-griva-kaustubham
Shriyanapayinya kshipta
Nikashashmorasollasat

The Lord has shoulders just like a lion's. Upon these shoulders are garlands, necklaces and epaulets, and all of these are always glittering. Besides these, there is the beauty of the Kaustubhamani pearl, and on the dark chest of the Lord there are streaks named Shrivatsa, which are signs of the goddess of fortune. The glittering of these streaks excels the beauty of the golden streaks on a gold-testing stone. Indeed, such beauty defeats the beauty of a gold-testing stone.

Verse 50
pura-rechaka-samvigna-
vali-valgu-dalodaram
pratisankramayad vishvam
nabhyavarta-gabhiraya

The Lord's abdomen is beautiful due to three ripples in the flesh. Being so round, His abdomen resembles the leaf of a banyan tree, and when He exhales and inhales, the movement of the ripples appears very, very beautiful. The coils within the navel of the Lord are so deep that is appears that the entire universe sprouted out of it and yet again wishes to go back.

Verse 51
shyama-shrony-adhi-rochishnu
dukula-svarna-mekhalam
sama-charv-anghri-janghoru-
nimna-janu-sudarshanam

The lower part of the Lord's waist is dark and covered with yellow garments and a belt bedecked with golden embroidery work. His symmetrical lotus feet and the calves, thighs and joints of His legs are extraordinarily beautiful. Indeed, the Lord's entire body appears to be well built.

Verse 52
pada sharat-padma-palasha-rochisha
nakha-dyubhir no 'ntar-agham vidhunvata
pradarshaya sviyam apasta-sadhvasam
padam guro marga-gurus tamo-jusham

My dear Lord, Your two lotus feet are so beautiful that they appear like two blossoming petals of the lotus flower which grows during the autumn season. Indeed, the nails of Your lotus feet emanate such a great effulgence that they immediately dissipate all the darkness in the heart of a conditioned soul. My dear Lord, kindly show me that form of Yours which always dissipates all kinds of darkness in the heart of a devotee. My dear Lord, You are the supreme spiritual master of everyone; therefore all conditioned souls covered with the darkness of ignorance can be enlightened by You as the spiritual master.

Verse 53
etad rupam anudhyeyam
atma-shuddhim abhipsatam
yad-bhakti-yoga 'bhayadaha
sva-dharmam anutishthatam

My dear Lord, those who desire to purify their existence must always engage in meditation upon Your lotus feet, as described above. Those who are serious about executing their occupational duties and who want freedom from fear must take to this process of bhatki-yoga.

Verse 54
bhavan bhaktimata labhya
durlabhah sarva-dehinam
svarajyasyapy abhimata
ekantenatma-vid-gatihi

My dear Lord, the king in charge of the heavenly kingdom is also desirous of obtaining the ultimate goal of life—devotional service. Similarly, You are the ultimate destination of those who identify themselves with You [aham brahmasmi—"I am spiritual"]. However, it is very difficult for them to attain You, whereas a devotee can very easily attain Your Lordship.

Verse 55
tam duraradhyam aradhya
satam api durapaya
ekanta-bhaktya ko vanchet
pada-mulam vina bahih

My dear Lord, pure devotional service is even difficult for liberated persons to discharge, but devotional service alone can satisfy You. Who will take to other processes of self-realization if he is actually serious about the perfection of life?

Verse 56
yatra nirvishtam aranam
kritanto nabhimanyate
vishvam vidhvamsayan virya-
shaurya-visphurjita-bhruva

Simply by expansion of His eyebrows, invincible time personified can immediately vanquish the entire universe. However, formidable time does not approach the devotee who has taken complete shelter at Your lotus feet.

Verse 57
kshanardhenapi tulaye
na svargam napunar-bhavam
bhagavat-sangi-sangasya
martyanam kim utashishaha

If one by chance associates with a devotee, even for a fraction of a moment, he no longer is subject to attraction by the results of karma or jnana [knowledge]. What interest then can he have in the benedictions of the demigods, who are subject to the laws of birth and death?

Verse 58
athanaghanghres tava kirti-tirthayor
antar-bahih-snana-vidhuta-papmanam
bhuteshv anukrosha-susattva-shilinam
syat sangamo 'nugraha eva nas tava

My dear Lord, Your lotus feet are the cause of all auspicious things and the destroyer of all the contamination of sin. I therefore beg Your Lordship to bless me by the association of your devotees, who are completely purified by worshiping Your lotus feet, and who are so merciful upon the conditioned souls. I think that Your real benediction will be to allow me to associate with such devotees.

Verse 59
na yasya chittam bahir-artha-vibhramam
tamo-guhayam cha vishuddham avishat
yad-bhakti-yoganugrihitam anjasa
munir vichaste nanu tatra te gatim

The devotee whose heart has been completely cleansed by the process of devotional service and who is favored by Bhaktidevi does not become bewildered by the external energy, which is just like a dark well. Being completely cleansed of all material contamination in this way, a devotee is able to understand very happily Your name, fame, form, activities, etc.

Verse 60
yatredam vyajyate vishvam
vishvasminn avabhati yat
tat tvam brahma param jyotir
akasham iva vistritam

My dear Lord, the impersonal Brahma spreads everywhere, like the sunshine or the sky. And that impersonal Brahman, which spreads throughout the universe and in which the entire universe is manifested, is You.

Verse 61
yo mayayedam puru-rupayasrijad
bibharti bhuyah kshapayaty avikriyaha
yad-bheda-buddhih sad ivatma-duhsthaya
tvam atma-tantram bhagavan pratimahi

My dear Lord, You have manifold energies, and these energies are manifested in manifold forms. With such energies You have also created this cosmic manifestation, and although You maintain it as if it were permanent, You ultimately annihilate it. Although You are never disturbed by such changes and alterations, the living entities are disturbed by them, and therefore they find the cosmic manifestation to be different or separated from You. My Lord, You are always independent, and I can clearly see this fact.

Verse 62
kriya-kalapair idam eva yoginaha
shraddhanvitah sadhu yajanti siddhaye
bhutendriyantah-karanopalakshitam
vede cha tantre cha ta eva kovidaha

Me dear Lord, Your universal form consists of all five elements, the senses, mind, intelligence, false ego (which is material) and the Paramatma, Your partial expansion, who is the director of everything. Yogis other than devotees—namely the karma-yogi and jnana-yogi—worship You by their respective actions in their respective positions. It is stated both in the Vedas and in the Shastras that are corollaries of the Vedas, and indeed everywhere, that it is only You who are to be worshiped. That is the expert version of all the Vedas.

Verse 63
tvam eka adyah purushah sputa-shaktis
taya rajah-sattva-tamo vibhidyate
mahan aham kham marud agni-var-dharaha
surarshayo bhuta-gana idam yataha

My dear Lord, You are the only Supreme Person, the cause of all causes. Before the creation of this material world, Your material energy remains in a dormant condition. When Your material energy is agitated, the three qualities—namely goodness, passion and ignorance—act, and as a result the total material energy—egotism, ether, air, fire, water, earth, and all the various demigods and saintly persons—becomes manifest. Thus the material world is created.

Verse 64
shrishtam va-shaktyedam anupravishtash
chatur-vidham puram atmamshakena
atho vidus tam purusham santam antar
bhunkte hrishikair madhu saru-gham yaha

My dear Lord, after creating by Your own potencies, You enter within the creation in four kinds of forms. Being within the hearts of the living entities, You know them and know how they are enjoying their senses. The so-called happiness of this material creation is exactly like the bees' enjoyment of honey after it has been collected in the honeycomb [like people who put together a home and then try to enjoy it under great duress].

Verse 65
sa esha lokan atichanda-vego
vikarshasi tvam khalu kala-yanaha
bhutani bhutair anumeya-tattvo
ghanavalir vayur ivavishahyaha

My dear Lord, Your absolute authority cannot be directly experienced, but one can guess by seeing the activities of the world that everything is being destroyed in due course of time. The force of time is very strong, and everything is being destroyed by something else—just as one animal is being eaten by another animal. Time scatters everything, exactly as the wind scatters clouds in the sky.

Verse 66
pramattam uccair iti kriya-chintaya
pravriddha-lobham vishayeshu lalasam
tvam apramattah sahasabhipadyase
kshul-lelihano 'hir ivakhum antakaha

My dear Lord, all living entities within this material world are mad after planning for things, and they are always busy with a desire to do this or that. This is due to uncontrollable greed. The greed for material enjoyment is always existing in the living entity [particularly atheists who do not accept the authority of the Lord], but Your Lordship is always alert, and in due course of time You strike him [in the form of the laws of material existence], just as a snake seizes a mouse and very easily swallows him.

Verse 67
Kas tvat-padabjam vijahati pandito
Yas te 'vamana-vyayamana-ketanaha
Vishankayasmad-gurur archati sma yad
Vinopapattim manavash chaturdasha

My dear Lord, any learned person knows that unless he worships You, his entire life is spoiled. Knowing this, how could he give up worshiping Your lotus feet? Even our father and spiritual master, Lord Brahma, unhesitatingly worshiped You, and the fourteen Manus followed in his footsteps.

Verse 68
atha tvam asi no Brahman
paramatman vipashchitam
vishvam rudra-bhaya-dhvastam
akutashchid-bhaya gatihi

My dear Lord, all actually learned persons know You as the Supreme Brahman and the Supersoul. Although the entire universe is afraid of Lord Rudra, who ultimately annihilates everything, for the learned devotees You are the fearless destination of all.

This ended the sacred mantra and prayer that Lord Shiva taught to the sons of King Pracinabarhi. Thereafter, he gave these princes his final instructions:

"My dear sons of the King, just execute your occupational duty as kings with a pure heart. Just chant this prayer fixing your mind on the lotus feet of the Lord. That will bring you all good fortune, for the Lord will be very much pleased with you. The Supreme Personality of Godhead, Hari, is situated in everyone's heart. He is also within your hearts. Therefore, chant the glories of the Lord and always meditate upon Him.

"In this way, in the form of a prayer, I have delineated the yoga system of chanting the holy name. All of you should take this important stotra within your minds and promise to keep it in order to become great sages. By acting silently like a great sage and by giving attention and reverence, you should practice this method.

"This prayer was first spoken to us by Lord Brahma, the master of all creators. The creators, headed by Bhrigu, were instructed in these prayers because they wanted to create. When all the prajapatis [progenitors] were ordered to create by Lord Brahma, we chanted these prayers in praise of the Supreme Being and became completely free from all ignorance. Thus, we were able to create different types of living beings. A devotee of Lord Krishna whose mind is always absorbed in Him, who with great attention and reverence chants this stotra [prayer], will achieve the greatest perfection of life without delay. Although rendering devotional service to the Supreme Personality and worshiping Him are very difficult, if one vibrates or simply reads this stotra composed and sung by me [Shiva], he will very easily be able to invoke the mercy of the Supreme Lord. The Supreme Being is the dearmost objective of all auspicious benedictions. A human being who sings this song sung by me can please the Supreme Being. Such a devotee, being fixed in the Lord's devotional service, can acquire whatever he wants from the Supreme Lord. A devotee who rises early in the morning and with folded hands chants these prayers sung by me, Lord Shiva, and gives facility to others to hear them certainly becomes free from all bondage to fruitive activities [karma]." (Srimad-Bhagavatam 4.24.69-78)

CHAPTER THIRTEEN

Bhaja Govindam by Sri Adi Shankaracharya

Adi Shankaracharya is widely known for his teachings on Vedanta. Shankaracharya was born in the village of Kaladi, in South India, about 2500 years ago to his Brahmin parents, Sivaguru and Aryamba. He traveled throughout India during his life, preaching and establishing four important maths, or centers, and accepted numerous disciples. He had also composed a number of verses and hymns of his knowledge and insight. However, the Bhaja Govindam is perhaps his greatest. He is still today one of the greatest influences in the present-day understanding of Vedic philosophy, with numerous schools of thought throughout India still expounding his teachings.

He primarily taught the non-dual, or advaita, form of understanding, teaching that everything is ultimately one. Many of the commentaries on the Vedic texts, such as the *Brahma-samhita*, the Upanishads, and others, are written with commentaries by those who follow his advaitic principles. Thus, many such texts have the impersonalistic sway to them, leaving out the idea that everything comes from a personal or Supreme Creator. However, before he left this world, he composed the Bhaja Govindam prayers that evokes the mood of devotion to Lord Govinda, Krishna.

It is in this prayer that he emphasizes above all else the importance for developing devotion for Lord Krishna, which is the principle means for attaining the Grace for the Supreme, and the freedom from further rounds of reincarnating in material existence. It is this prayer that leaves us no doubt that his final instruction was to give up our egotistical differences and surrender to Lord Krishna. It also encapsulates the sum and substance of all Vedantic thought in whatever other works that he had written.

There is a story attached to the composition of this Hymn. It is said that Shankara was walking along a street in Varanasi one day, accompanied by his disciples. He heard an old scholar teaching his grammatical rules. Taking pity on him, he went up and advised him not to waste his time on grammar at his age but to turn his mind to God in worship and adoration. The Hymn to Govinda was composed on this occasion. Besides the refrain of the song beginning with the words "Bhaja Govindam", Shankara is said to have sung twelve verses, hence the hymn bears the title "Dvadasamanjarika-Stotra" (A hymn which is a bunch of twelve verse-blossoms). The fourteen disciples who were with the Master then are believed to have added one verse each. These fourteen verses are together called "Chaturdasa-manjarika-Stotra" (A hymn which is a bunch of fourteen verse-blossoms).

TEXT 1
bhajagovindam bhajagovindam
govindam bhajamuudhamate
sampraapte sannihite kaale
nahi nahi rakshati dukrijnkarane

Worship Govinda, Worship Govinda, Worship Govinda. Oh fool! Rules of Grammar will not save you at the time of your death.

TEXT 2
mudha jahiihi dhanaagamatrishhnaam
kuru sadbuddhim manasi vitrishhnaam
yallabhase nijakarmopaattam
vittam tena vinodaya chittam

Oh fool! Give up your thirst to amass wealth, devote your mind to thoughts to the Real. Be content with what comes through actions already performed in the past.

TEXT 3
naariistanabhara naabhiidesham
drishhtvaa maagaamohaavesham
etanmaamsaavasaadi vikaaram
manasi vichintaya vaaram vaaram

Do not get drowned in delusion by going wild with passions and lust by seeing a woman's navel and chest. Bodies are flesh, fat and blood. Do not fail to remember this again and again in your mind.

TEXT 4
naliniidalagata jalamatitaralam
tadvajjiivitamatishayachapalam
viddhi vyaadhyabhimaanagrastam
lokam shokahatam cha samastam

Uncertain is the life of man as rain drops on a lotus leaf. Know that the whole world remains a prey to disease, ego and grief.

TEXT 5
yaavadvittopaarjana saktah
staavannija parivaaro raktah
pashchaajjiivati jarjara dehe
vaartaam koapi na prichchhati gehe

So long as a man is fit and able to support his family, see the affection all those around him show. But no one at home cares to even have a word with him when his body totters due to old age.

TEXT 6
yaavatpavano nivasati dehe
taavatprichchhati kushalam gehe
gatavati vaayau dehaapaaye
bhaaryaa bibhyati tasminkaaye

When one is alive, his family members enquire kindly about his welfare. But when the soul departs from the body, even his wife runs away in fear of the corpse.

TEXT 7
baalastaavatkriidaasaktah
tarunastaavattaruniisaktah
vriddhastaavachchintaasaktah
pare brahmani koapi na saktah

Childhood is lost in play. Youth is lost by attachment to woman. Old age passes away by thinking over many past things. Alas! Hardly is there anyone who yearns to be lost in Parabrahman.

TEXT 8
kaate kaantaa kaste putrah
samsaaro.ayamatiiva vichitrah
kasya tvam kah kuta aayaatah
tattvam chintaya tadiha bhraatah

Who is your wife? Who is your son? Strange is this samsara. Of whom are you? Where have you come from? Brother, ponder over these truths.

TEXT 9
satsangatve nissngatvam
nissangatve nirmohatvam
nirmohatve nishchalatattvam
nishchalatattve jiivanmuktih

From Satsanga comes non-attachment, from non-attachment comes freedom from delusion, which leads to self-settledness. From self-settledness comes Jivan Mukti (liberation).

TEXT 10
vayasigate kah kaamavikaarah
shushhke niire kah kaasaarah
kshiinevitte kah parivaarah
gyaate tattve kah samsaarah

What good is lust when youth has fled? What use is a lake which has no water? Where are the relatives when wealth is gone? Where is samsara (the continuaiton of birth and death) when the Truth is known?

TEXT 11
maa kuru dhana jana yauvana garvam
harati nimeshhaatkaalah sarvam
maayaamayamidamakhilaM hitvaa
brahmapadaM tvaM pravisha viditvaa

Do not boast of wealth, friends, and youth. Each one of these are destroyed within a minute. Free yourself from the illusion of the world of Maya and attain the timeless Truth.

TEXT 12
dinayaaminyau saayam praatah
shishiravasantau punaraayaatah
kaalah kriidati gachchhatyaayuh
tadapi na mujnchatyaashaavaayuh

Daylight and darkness, dusk and dawn, winter and springtime come and go.
Time plays and life ebbs away. But the storm of desire never leaves.

TEXT 13
dvaadashamajnjarikaabhirasheshhah
kathito vaiyaakaranasyaishhah
upadesho bhuudvidyaanipunaih
shriimachchhankarabhagavachchharanarih

This bouquet of twelve verses was imparted to a grammarian by the
all-knowing Shankara, adored as the bhagavadpada.

TEXT 14
kaate kaantaa dhana gatachintaa
vaatula kim tava naasti niyantaa
trijagati sajjanasam gatiraikaa
bhavati bhavaarnavatarane naukaa

Oh mad man! Why this engrossment in thoughts of wealth? Is there no one
to guide you? There is only one thing in three worlds that can save you
from the ocean of samsara. Get into that boat of satsangha (knowledge of
the Truth) quickly.

TEXT 15
jatilo mundii lujnchhitakeshah
kaashhaayaambarabahukritaveshhah
pashyannapi chana pashyati muudhah
udaranimittam bahukritaveshhah

There are many who go with matted locks, many who have clean shaven
heads, many whose hairs have been plucked out; some are clothed in
saffron, yet others in various colors --- all just for a livelihood. Seeing truth
revealed before them, still the foolish ones see it not.

TEXT 16
angam galitam palitam mundam
dashanavihiinam jatam tundam
vriddho yaati grihiitvaa dandam
tadapi na mujnchatyaashaapindam

Strength has left the old man's body; his head has become bald, his gums toothless and leaning on crutches. Even then the attachment is strong and he clings firmly to fruitless hope.

TEXT 17
agre vahnih prishhthebhaanuh
raatrau chubukasamarpitajaanuh
karatalabhikshastarutalavaasah
tadapi na mujnchatyaashaapaashah

Behold there lies the man who sits warming up his body with the fire in front and the sun at the back; at night he curls up the body to keep out of the cold; he eats his beggar's food from the bowl of his hand and sleeps beneath the tree. Still in his heart, he is a wretched puppet at the hands of passions.

TEXT 18
kurute gangaasaagaragamanam
vrataparipaalanamathavaa daanam
gyaanavihinah sarvamatena
muktim na bhajati janmashatena

One may go to the Ganga, observe fasts, and give away riches in charity! Yet, devoid of jnana, nothing can give mukthi even at the end of a hundred births.

TEXT 19
sura mandira taru muula nivaasah
shayyaa bhuutala majinam vaasah
sarva parigraha bhoga tyaagah
kasya sukham na karoti viraagah

Take your residence in a temple or below a tree, wear the deerskin for the dress, and sleep with mother earth as your bed. Give up all attachments and renounce all comforts. Blessed with such vairagya, could any fail to be content?

TEXT 20
yogarato vaabhogaratovaa
sangarato vaa sangaviihinah
yasya brahmani ramate chittam
nandati nandati nandatyeva

One may take delight in yoga or bhoga, may have attachment or detachment. But only he whose mind steadily delights in Brahman enjoys bliss, no one else.

TEXT 21
bhagavad giitaa kijnchidadhiitaa
gangaa jalalava kanikaapiitaa
sakridapi yena muraari samarchaa
kriyate tasya yamena na charchaa

Let a man read but a little from the Bhagavad-Gita, drink just a drop of water from the Ganga, worship Murari (Krishna) just once. He then will have no altercation with Yama (the lord of death).

TEXT 22
punarapi jananam punarapi maranam
punarapi jananii jathare shayanam
iha samsaare bahudustaare
kripayaa apaare paahi muraare

Born again, death again, birth again to stay in the mother's womb! It is indeed hard to cross this boundless ocean of samsara. Oh Murari! Redeem me through Thy mercy.

TEXT 23
rathyaa charpata virachita kanthah
punyaapunya vivarjita panthah
yogii yoganiyojita chitto
ramate baalonmattavadeva

There is no shortage of clothing for a monk so long as there are rags cast off the road. Freed from vice and virtue, onward he wanders. One who lives in communion with God enjoys bliss, pure and uncontaminated, like a child and as someone intoxicated.

TEXT 24

kastvam ko.aham kuta aayaatah
kaa me jananii ko me taatah
iti paribhaavaya sarvamasaaram
vishvam tyaktvaa svapna vichaaram

Who are you? Who am I? From where do I come? Who is my mother, who is my father? Ponder thus, look at everything as essence-less and give up the world as an idle dream.

TEXT 25

tvayi mayi chaanyatraiko vishhnuh
vyartham kupyasi mayyasahishhnuh
bhava samachittah sarvatra tvam
vaajnchhasyachiraadyadi vishhnutvam

In me, in you and in everything, none but the same Vishnu dwells. Your anger and impatience is meaningless. If you wish to attain the quality of Vishnu soon, have Sama Bhaava always.

TEXT 26

shatrau mitre putre bandhau
maa kuru yatnam vigrahasandhau
sarvasminnapi pashyaatmaanam
sarvatrotsrija bhedaagyaanam

Do not waste your efforts to win the love of or to fight against friend and foe, children and relatives. See yourself in everyone and give up all feelings of duality completely.

TEXT 27

kaamam krodham lobham moham
tyaktvaa atmaanam bhaavaya ko aham
aatmagyaana vihiinaa muudhaah
te pachyante narakaniguudhaah

Give up lust, anger, infatuation, and greed. Ponder over your real nature. Fools are they who are blind to the Self. Cast into hell they suffer there endlessly.

TEXT 28
geyam giitaa naama sahasram
dhyeyam shriipati ruupamajasram
neyam sajjana sange chittam
deyam diinajanaaya cha vittam

Regularly recite from the Bhagavad-Gita, meditate on Vishnu in your heart, and chant His thousand glories. Take delight to be with the noble and the holy. Distribute your wealth in charity to the poor and the needy.

TEXT 29
sukhatah kriyate raamaabhogah
pashchaaddhanta shariire rogah
yadyapi loke maranam sharanam
tadapi na mujnchati paapaacharanam

He who yields to lust for pleasure leaves his body a prey to disease. Though death brings an end to everything, man does not give up the sinful path.

TEXT 30
arthamanartham bhaavaya nityam
naastitatah sukhaleshah satyam
putraadapi dhana bhaajaam bhiitih
sarvatraishhaa vihiaa riitih

Wealth is not welfare, truly there is no joy in it. Reflect thus at all times. A rich man fears even his own son. This is the way of wealth everywhere.

TEXT 31
praanaayaamam pratyaahaaram
nityaanitya vivekavichaaram
jaapyasameta samaadhividhaanam
kurvavadhaanam mahadavadhaanam

Regulate the pranas (life airs within), remain unaffected by external influences and discriminate between the real and the fleeting. Chant the holy name of God and silence the turbulent mind. Perform these with care, with extreme care.

TEXT 32
gurucharanaambuja nirbhara bhakatah
samsaaraadachiraadbhava muktah
sendriyamaanasa niyamaadevam
drakshyasi nija hridayastham devam

Oh devotee of the lotus feet of the Guru! May thou be soon free from Samsara. Through disciplined senses and controlled mind, thou shalt come to experience the indwelling Lord of your heart!

TEXT 33
muudhah kashchana vaiyaakarano
dukrijnkaranaadhyayana dhurinah
shriimachchhamkara bhagavachchhishhyai
bodhita aasichchhodhitakaranah

Thus was a silly grammarian lost in rules cleansed of his narrow vision and shown the Light by Shankara's apostles.

TEXT 34
bhajagovindam bhajagovindam
govindam bhajamuudhamate
naamasmaranaadanyamupaayam
nahi pashyaamo bhavatarane

Worship Govinda, worship Govinda, worship Govinda, Oh fool! Other than chanting the Lord's names, there is no other way to cross the life's ocean.

CHAPTER FOURTEEN

The Purusha Sukta

The Purusha Sukta is a most commonly used Vedic Sanskrit hymn. It is recited in almost all Vedic rituals and ceremonies. It is often used during the worship of the Deity of Vishnu or Narayana in the temple, installation and fire ceremonies, or during the daily recitation of Sanskrit literature or for one's meditation.

The Purusha Sukta is an important part of the *Rig-veda* (10.7.90.1-16). It also appears in the *Taittiriya Aranyaka* (3.12,13), the *Vajasaneyi Samhita* (31.1-6), the *Sama-veda Samhita* (6.4), and the *Atharva-veda Samhita* (19.6). An explanation of parts of it can also be found in the *Shatapatha Brahman*, the *Taittiriya Brahmana*, and the *Shvetashvatara Upanishad*. The *Mudgalopanishad* gives a nice summary of the entire Purusha Sukta. The contents of the Sukta have also been reflected and elaborated in the *Bhagavata Purana* (2.5.35 to 2.6.1-29) and in the *Mahabharata* (Mokshadharma Parva 351 and 352).

The most commonly used portion of the Sukta contains 24 mantras or stanzas. The first 18 mantras are designated as the Purvanarayana, and the rest as the Uttaranarayana. Sometimes 6 more mantras are added. This part is called the Vaishnavanuvaka since it has been taken from another well known hymn called the Vishnusukta, a part of the *Rig-veda Samhita*. Though the mantras of the Uttaranarayana and the Vaishnavanuvaka do not seem to have any coherence with the 16 mantras of the *Rig-veda Samhita*, tradition has somehow tied them together.

The Purusha Sukta is a rather difficult text to explain in a modern way. This is primarily because of the archaic language that cannot always lend itself to interpretations based on the classical Sanskrit, and that many of the words can be taken in several different ways, both literal and symbolic.

Nonetheless, the Purusha Sukta gives us the essence of the philosophy of Vedanta, the Vedic tradition, as well as the *Bhagavad-gita* and *Bhagavata Purana*. It incorporates the principles of meditation (upasana), knowledge (jnana), devotion (bhakti), and rituals and duties (dharma and karma). This is why it is highly regarded and extensively used today as much as thousands of years ago.

The Text

Peace Invocation

Om taccham yoravrini mahe
ghatun yajnaya
ghatun yajnapataye
daivi svastirastu naha
svastir manushebhyaha
urdhvam jigatu bheshajam
sham no astu dvipade
sham chatushpade
Om shantih shantih shantihi

We worship and pray to the Supreme Lord for the welfare of all beings. May all miseries and shortcomings leave us forever so that we may always sing for the Lord during the holy fire ceremonies. May all medicinal herbs grow in potency so that all diseases may be cured. May the gods rain peace on us. May all the two-legged creatures be happy, and may all the four-legged creatures also be happy. May there be peace in the hearts of all beings in all realms.

Text One
Om sahasra shirsha purushaha
sahasrakshas sahasrapat
sa bhumim vishvato vritva
atyatishthad dhashangulam

The Purusha (the Supreme Being) has a thousand heads, a thousand eyes and a thousand feet. He has enveloped this world from all sides and has (even) transcended it by ten angulas or inches.

Text Two
purusha evedagam sarvam
yadbhutam yaccha bhavyam
utamritatva syeshanaha
yadanne natirohati

All this is verily the Purusha. All that which existed in the past or will come into being in the future (is also the Purusha). Also, he is the Lord of immortality. That which grows profusely by food (is also the Purusha).

Text Three
etavanasya mahima
ato jyayagamshcha purushaha
padosya vishva bhutani
tripadasya mritam divi

So much is His greatness. However, the Purusha is greater than this. All the beings form only a quarter (part of) Him. The three-quarter part of His, which is eternal, is established in the spiritual domain.

Text Four
tripadurdhva udaitpurushaha
padosyeha bhavatpunaha
tato vishvajya kramat
sashana ashane abhi

The Purusha with the three-quarters (of His energy) ascended above (the spiritual energy). His one quarter of material energy becomes this creation again (and again). Then He pervades this universe comprising a variety of sentient beings and insentient objects.

Text Five
tasmad viradajayata
virajo adhi purushah
sa jato atyarichyata
pashchad bhumimatho puraha

From Him (the Adipurusha or original Supreme Being) was born the Virat (or Virat Purusha, the immense universal form). Making this Virat as the substratum (another) purusha (or being, Brahma) (was born). As soon as he was born, he multiplied himself. Later, he created this earth and then, the bodies (of the living beings).

Text Six
yatpurushena havisha
deva yajnam atanvata

vasanto asyasidajyam
grishma idhmash sharaddhavihi

When the devas (the demigods or beings of light) performed a yajna (or sacrificial ritual), using the Purusha as the havis (sacrificial material) for the yajna (ritual), the Vasanta (spring) became the ajya (ghee), the Grishma (summer) served as idhma (pieces of wood) and the sharad (autumn) filled the place of havis (oblatory material like the purodasha or rice-cake).

Text Seven
saptasyasan paridhayaha
trissapta samidhah kritaha
deva yadjajnam tanvanaha
abadhnan purusham pashum

For this (yajna or spiritual ceremony) there were seven paridhis (fuel pieces serving as borders). And, twenty-one items were made the samit or sacrificial fuel sticks. When the devas were performing this yajna or ceremony, they tied the purusha (himself) as the pashu (sacrificial animal).

Text Eight
tam yajnam barhishipraukshan
purusham jatamagrataha
tena deva ayajantaha
sadhya rishayashchaye

The devas, the sadhyas and the rishis performed the sacrifice by using that Purusha as the means of yajna, the Purusha who had been born in the beginning, after sprinkling him with water by the barhis (or sacrificial grass).

Text Nine
tasmad yajnat sarvahutaha
sambhritam vrishadajyam
pashugamstya gashchakre
vayavyan aranyan gramashcaye

From that yajna (or sacrificial ritual) wherein the Cosmic Being was Himself the oblation, was produced the prasajya (or curds mixed with ghee). Birds flying in the air, wild animals of the forest as also the domesticated animals of the villages were also produced.

Text Ten
tasmad yajnat sarvahutaha
richassamani jijignire
chandhagamsi jijignire tasmat
yajus tasmad ajayata

From that yajna (or sacrifice) wherein the Cosmic Being was Himself the oblation, were born the riks (the mantras of the Rig-veda) and the samans (the mantras of the Sama-veda). From that (yajna) the metres (like Gayatri) were born. From that (yajna again) the yujas (the Yajur-veda) was born.

Text Eleven
tasmadashva ajayata
ye ke cobhaya dataha
gavo ha jijignire tasmat
tasmad jnata ajavayaha

From that were born the horses, as also animals (like donkeys and mules) which have two rows of teeth. From that were born the cattle. From that (again) were born goats and sheep.

Text Twelve
yatpurusham vyadadhuhu
kadhita vyakalpayan
mukham kimasya kau bahu
kavuru padavuchayate

(Now some questions are raised by the sages:) When the gods decided to (mentally) sacrifice the Viratpurusha (and produce further creation), in how many ways did they do it? What became of his face or mouth? What became of his two arms? What became of His two thighs? What were (the products of) the two feet called?

Text Thirteen
brahmanosya mukhamasit
bahu rajanyah kritaha

uru tadasya yadvaishyaha
padhyagam shudro ajayata

From His face (or the mouth) came the brahmanas. From His two arms came the rajanya (the kshatriyas). From His two thighs came the vaishyas. From His two feet came the shudras.

Text Fourteen
chandrama manaso jataha
chakshoh suryo ajayata
mukhad indrash chagnishcha
pranadvayur ajayata

From His mind was born the moon. From His two eyes was born the sun. From His mouth were born Indra and Agni. From His breath was born the air.

Text Fifteen
nabhya asidanta riksham
shirshno dyauh samavartata
padhyam bhumirdishash shrotrat
tada lokagamm akalpayan

From (His) navel was produced the antariksha (the space between the earth and the heavens). Dyuloka (or heaven) came into existence from His head. The bhumi (the earth) evolved out of His feet, and deek (or spacial directions) from His ears. Similarly (the demigods) produced the worlds (too).

Text Sixteen
vedahametam purusham mahantam
adityavarnam tamasastu pare
sarvani rupani vichitya dhiraha
namani kritva abhivadan yadaste

"I know (through intuitive experience) this great Purusha (the Supreme Being), the wise one, who, having created the various forms and the nomenclatures (for those forms), deals with them by those names, and who is beyond darkness and is brilliant like the sun."

Text Seventeen
dhata purastadya mudajahara
shakrah pravidvan pradishashcha tasraha
tamevam vidvan amrita iha bhavati
nanyah pantha ayanaya vidyate

In the ancient days, Prajapati (Brahma) praised Him. Indra who knows all the four quarters also spoke about Him. Anyone who knows Him thus, will become immortal even in this life. For attaining liberation there is no other path (than knowledge of this Purusha, the Supreme Lord).

Text Eighteen
yajnena yajnam ayajanta devaha
tani dharmani pradhamanyasan
te ha nakam mahimanas sacante
yatra purve sadhyah santi devaha

The (demi)gods worshiped (the Supreme Creator in the form of) yajna through yajna (sacrifical ceremonies). Those very processes became the primary dharmas (laws guiding humanity). Those great ones attain that heaven where the ancient devas (demigods) and sadhyas live.

Text Nineteen
adbhyas sambhutah prithivyai rasacca
vishvakarmanas samavartatadhi
tasya tvashta vidadhad rupameti
tatpurushasya vishvamajanamagre

The Viratpurusha manifested Himself from out of (the all-pervading) water as also the essence of the element of earth. This Viratpurusha was born out of the greatness of the Paramapurusha, the Creator. The (Paramapurusha, known as) Tvashta engaged Himself in the act of creating (the fourteen planetary systems), (which form of the expanded) figure (of the Viratpurusha). (Thus) the entire creation (related to the Viratpurusha) came into existence in the very beginning of creation.

Text Twenty
vcdahametam purusham mahantam
adityavarnam tamasah parastat

tamevam vidvan amrita iha bhavati
nanyah pantha vidyate'yanaya

"I have known that great Purusha (Supreme Being) who is brilliant like the
sun and who is beyond all darkness. One who knows Him thus becomes
immortal (even) here. There is no other path for liberation than this."

Text Twenty-one
prajapatishcharati garbhe antaha
ajayamano bahudha vijayate
tasya dhirah parijananti yonim
marichinam padamicchanti vedhasaha

Prajapati (the Supreme Creator) moves inside the cosmic womb. (Though)
unborn He takes birth in a variety of ways. The wise ones know His (real
nature) as the origin (of the universe). The (secondary) creators desire to
attain the positions of Marichi and others.

Text Twenty-two
yo devebhya atapati
yo devanam purohitaha
purvo yo devebhyo jataha
namo ruchaya brahmaye

Obeisances to Him, the self-luminous Brahman, who shines for the
(demi)gods, who is the leader of the rituals of the gods and who was born
even before the gods.

Text Twenty-three
rucham brahmam janayantaha
deva agre tadabruvan
yastvaivam brahmano vidyat
tasya deva asanvashe

In the beginning of creation, the gods, manifesting the light of Brahman,
addressed Brahman thus: "That brahmana who realizes (You) thus, all the
gods will come under his control."

Twenty-four
hrishcha te lakshmishcha patnyau
ahoratre parshve
nakshatrani rupam
ashvinau vyattam
ishtam manishana
amun manishana
sarvam manishana
Om shanti shanti shantihi

O Purusha! The goddesses Hri (modesty) and Sri (Lakshmi, wealth) are Your consorts. Day and night are Your lateral limbs. The stars are Your form. The Ashvins are your widely opened (mouth). (O Purusha) fulfill our desire for self-knowledge as also our desire for the enjoyments of this world (like longevity, cows, and horses). Give us all that we need. Om, let there be peace, peace, peace.

CHAPTER FIFTEEN

The Sri Isha Upanishad

The *Isha Upanishad* is part of the *White Yajur-veda*. It is short with a total of only 19 mantras or verses. Nonetheless, it contains a concentrated view of the essential Vedic philosophy. It is also considered quite auspicious to recite this *Isha Upanishad*, which produces not only insights into our spiritual position and identity, but also the proper energy from the sound vibrations to invoke purity in the atmosphere as well as realizations in our consciousness. It shows the way the *Upanishads* describe the nonmaterial aspects of the Supreme Being, as when it describes Him as One who walks but does not walk. It is a way of relating how the Lord has no material qualities, but has all spiritual qualities and characteristics. By understanding this, one can begin to perceive the spiritual truths of which the *Upanishads* speak.

The Invocation

om purnam adah purnam idam
purnat purnam udachyate
purnasya purnam adaya
purnam evavashishyate

The Personality of Godhead is perfect and complete. And because He is completely perfect, all emanations from Him, such as this phenomenal world, are perfectly equipped as a complete whole. Whatever is produced of the complete whole is also complete by itself. And because He is the Complete Whole, even though so many complete units emanate from Him, He remains the complete balance.

(1)

ishavasyam idam sarvam
yat kincha jagatyam jagat
tena tyaktena bhunjitha
ma gridhah kasya svid dhanam

Everything animate or inanimate that is within the universe is controlled and owned by the Lord. One should therefore accept only those things necessary for himself, which are set aside as his quota, and one must not accept other things, knowing well to Whom they belong.

(2)
kurvann eveha karmani
jijivisec chatam samaha
evam tvayi nanyatheto 'sti
na karma lipyate nare

One may aspire to live for hundreds of years if he continuously goes on doing work in that way, because that sort of work will not bind him to the law of karma. And there is no alternative to this way for man.

(3)
asurya nama te loka
andhena tamasavritaha
tams te pretyabhigacchanti
ye ke chatma-hano janaha

The killer of the soul, whoever he may be, must enter into the planets known as the worlds of the faithless, full of darkness and ignorance.

(4)
anejad ekam manaso javiyo
nainad deva apnuvan purvan arshat
tad dhavato 'nyan atyeti tishthat
tasminn apo matarishva dadhati

The Personality of Godhead, although fixed in His abode, is more swift then the mind, and can overcome all others running. The powerful demigods cannot approach Him. Although in one place, He has control over those who supply the air and rain. He surpasses all in excellence.

(5)
tad ejati tan naijati
tad dure tad vantike
tad antarasya sarvasya
tad u sarvasyasya bahyataha

The Supreme Lord walks and does not walk. He is far away, but He is very near as well. He is within everything, and again He is outside of everything.

(6)
yas tu sarvani bhutany
atmany evanupashyati
sarva-bhuteshu chatmanam
tato na vijugupsate

A person who sees everything in relation to the supreme Lord, and sees all entities as His parts and parcels, and who sees the Supreme Lord within everything, never hates anything, nor any being.

(7)
yasmin sarvani bhutany
atmaivabhud vijanataha
tatra ko mohah kah shoka
ekatvam anupashyataha

One who always sees all living entities as spiritual sparks, in quality one with the Lord, becomes a true knower of things. What is there as illusion or anxiety for him?

(8)
sa paryagac chukram akayam avranam
asnaviram shuddham apapa-viddham
kavir manishi paribhuh svayambhur
yathatathyato 'rthan vyadadhac chashvatibhyah samabhyaha

Such a person must know in fact the Greatest of all, Who is unembodied, omniscient, beyond reproach, without veins, pure and uncontaminate, the self-sufficient Philosopher who is awarding everyone's desire since time immemorial.

(9)
andham tamah pravishanti
ye 'vidyam upasate
tato bhuya iva te tamo
ya u vidyayam rataha

Those who are engaged in the culture of nescient activities shall enter into the darkest region of ignorance. Worse still are those engaged in the so-called culture of knowledge.

(10)
anyad evahur vidyaya
anyad ahur avidyaya
iti shushruma dhiranam
ye nas tad vichachakshire

The wise have explained to us that one result is derived from the culture of knowledge, and it is said that a different result is obtained from the culture of nescience.

(11)
vidyam chavidyam cha yas
tad vedobhayam saha
avidyaya mrityum tirtva
vidyayamritam ashnute

Only one who can learn the process of nescience and that of transcendental knowledge side by side can transcend the influence of repeated birth and death, and enjoy the full blessings of immortality.

(12)
andham tamah pravishanti
ye 'sambhutim upasate
tato bhuya iva te tamo
ya u sambhutyam rataha

Those who are engaged in the worship of demigods enter into the darkest region of ignorance, and still more so do the worshipers of the impersonal [form of the] Absolute.

(13)
anyad evahuh sambhavad
anyad ahur asambhavat
iti shushruma dhiranam
ye nas tad vichachakshire

It is said that one result is obtained by worshiping the Supreme Cause of all causes, and that another is obtained by worshiping what is not supreme. All this was heard from the undisturbed authorities who clearly explained it.

(14)
sambhutim cha vinasham cha
yas tad vedobhayam saha
vinashena mrityum tirtva
sambhutyamritam ashnute

One should know perfectly well about the Personality of Godhead and His transcendental name, as well as the temporary material creation with its temporary demigods, men and animals. When one knows these, he surpasses death and the ephemeral cosmic manifestation with it, and in the eternal Kingdom of God he enjoys his eternal life of bliss and knowledge.

(15)
hiranmayena patrena
satyasyapihitam mukham
tat tvam pushann apavrinu
satya-dharmaya drishtaye

O my Lord, Sustainer of all that lives, Your real face is covered by Your dazzling effulgence. Kindly remove that covering and exhibit Yourself to Your pure devotee.

(16)
pushann ekarshe yama surya prajapatya
vyuha rashmin samuha tejaha
yat te rupam kalyanatamam tat te pashyami
yo 'sav asau purushah so 'hama smi

O my Lord, O primeval philosopher, maintainer of the universe, O regulating principle, destination of the pure devotees, well-wisher of the progenitors of mankind--please remove the effulgence of Your transcendental rays so that I can see Your form of bliss. You are the eternal Supreme Personality of Godhead, like unto the sun, as am I.

(17)
vayur anilam amritam
athedam bhasmantam shariram
om krato smara kritam smara
krato smara kritam smara

Let this temporary body be burned to ashes, and let the air of life be merged with the totality of air. Now, O my Lord, please remember all my sacrifices, and because You are the ultimate beneficiary, please remember all that I have done for You.

(18)
agne naya supatha raye asman
vishvani deva vayunani vidvan
yuyodhy asmaj juhuranam eno
bhuyistham te nama uktim vidhema

O my Lord, powerful as the fire, omnipotent one, now I do offer You all obeisances and fall at Your feet on the ground. O my Lord, please lead me on the right path to reach You, and since You know all that I have done in the past, please free me from the reactions to my past sins, so that there will be no hindrance to my progress.

CHAPTER SIXTEEN

The Gopala-Sahasra-Nama

This is the Thousand Names of Lord Gopala (Sri Krishna) as explained by Lord Shiva to Parvati, which is most powerful and gives all success to those who chant it. This is especially beneficial to chant on days like Krishna Janmastami, the festival of Lord Krishna's birth.

Introduction

Text 1
sri parvaty uvacha
kailasashikhare ramye
gauri prichchhati shankaram |
brahmandakhilanathastvam
srishtisanharakarakah || 1||

sri-pärvaty uvächa
kailäsa-shikhare ramye
gauri pricchati shaikaram
brahmändäkhila-näthas tvam
srishti-samhära-kärakah

Sri Pärvati said: On the summit of Mount Kailäsa Goddess Gauri asked Lord Shiva: You are the master of the entire universe and its destroyer as well.

Text 2
tvam eva pujyase lokair
brahma-vishnu-surädibhih
nityam pathasi devesha
kasya stotram maheshvara

You are worshiped by Brahmä, Vishnu, all the demigods, and all the worlds. O master of the demigods, O great master, what is this prayer that you recite again and again?

Text 3
äshcaryam idam atyantam
jäyate mama shaìkara
tat pränesha mahä-prajïa
samshayam chindhi shaìkara

O Shiva, a great feeling of wonder and surprise is now born within me. O master of my life, O wise one, O auspicious one, please cut apart my doubt.

Text 4
shri-mahädeva uväca
dhanyäsi krita-puëyäsi
pärvati präna-vallabhe
rahasyäti-rahasyam cha
yat pricchasi varänane

Lord Shiva said: O Pärvati, O beloved more dear than life, You are fortunate and saintly. O girl with the beautiful face, you have asked about the most secret of all secrets.

Text 5
shtri-svabhävän mahä-devi
punas tvam paripricchasi
gopaniyam gopaniyam
gopaniyam prayatnatah

O great goddess, with a woman's curiosity you have asked again and again. What I tell you should be kept secret. It should be kept secret. It should be kept secret with great care.

Text 6
datte ca siddhi-hänih syät
tasmäd yatnena gopayet
idam rahasyam paramam
purushärtha-pradäyakam

Give it to someone and you will lose your spiritual perfections. Therefore
please keep this secret with great care. This is a great secret that brings the
final goal of life.

Text 7
dhana-ratnaugha-mänikya-
turangam gajädikam
dadäti samaranäd eva
mahä-moksha-pradäyakam

Remembering this prayer brings wealth, jewels, rubies, horses, elephants,
and other possessions. It also brings great liberation.

Text 8
tat te 'ham sampravakshyämi
shrinushv avihitä priye
yo 'sau niranjano devash
chit-svarüpi janärdanah

I will tell this to you. O beloved, please listen carefully. Lord Krishna is the
Supreme Personality of Godhead. His form is spiritual. He is never touched
by matter.

Text 9
samsära-sägarottära-
käranäya sadä nrinäm
shri-rangädika-rüpena
trailokyam vyäpya tishöhati

In order to rescue the people from the ocean of repeated birth and death,
again and again He appears in the form of Lord Ranganätha and the forms
of countless other Deities in every corner of the three worlds.

Texts 10 and 11
tato lokä mahä-mudhä
vishnu-bhakti-vivarjitäh
nishcayam nädhigacchanti
punar näräyaëo harih

niranjano niräkäro
bhaktänäm priti-käma-dah
vrindävana-vihäräya
gopälam rüpam udvahan

The great fools of this world have no devotion for Lord Vishnu. They do not understand that He is the Supreme Personality of Godhead. Always untouched by matter, the Supreme Lord, who is known as Näräyana and Hari and who delights His devotees, manifests His form as a cowherd boy to enjoy pastimes in the land of Vrindävana.

Text 12
murali-vadanädhäri
rädhäyai pritim ävahan
amshämshebhyah samunmilya
purna-rüpa-kalä-yutah

Playing on a flute, He brings great happiness to Sri Rädhä. His incarnations, partial incarnations, and the parts of His partial incarnations are all present in that form of a cowherd boy.

Text 13
shri-krishnachandro bhagavän
nanda-gopa-varodyatah
dharini-rüpini mätä
yashodänanda-däyini

That cowherd boy is Sri Krishnachandra, the Supreme Personality of Godhead. He is the son of the cowherd Nanda. His mother is Yashodä, who was the goddess Dharä and who brings great happiness.

Text 14
dväbhyäm prayächito nätho
devakyäm vasudevatah
brähmanäbhyarthito devo
devair api sureshvari

O queen of the demigods, requested by Brahmä, the demigods, and His parents, the Supreme Personality of Godhead became the son of Vasudeva and Devaki.

Text 15
jäto 'vaëyäm mukundo 'pi
murali-veda-recikah
tayä särdhaà vacaù kåtvä
tato jäto mahi-tale

In this way the Supreme Personality of Godhead, the giver of liberation, was born on the earth. He breathed the Vedas into His flute. With His flute He spoke. In this way He was born on the earth.

Text 16
samsära-sära-sarvasvam
shyämalam mahad ujjvalam
etaj jyotir aham vaidya
cintayämi sanätanam

I meditate on Him, the eternal dark splendor that is the treasure of the earth.

Text 17
gaura-tejo vinä yas tu
shyäma-tejah samarchayet
japed vädhyayate väpi
sa bhavet pätaki shive

O auspicious one, a person who worships, glorifies, or studies the dark splendor that is Lord Krishna but does not worship, glorify, or study the fair splendor that is Sri Rädhä finds that he lives in hell.

Text 18
sa brahma-hä suräpi cha
svarna-steyi cha pancamah
etair doshair vilipyeta
tejo bhedän maheshvari

O great goddess, a person who thinks Rädhä and Krishna are different becomes a brähmana-murderer, a wine-drinker, a thief of gold, and an outcaste. He becomes contaminated with all these sins.

Text 19
tasmäj jyotir abhüd dvedhä
rädhä-mädhava-rüpakam
tasmäd idam mahä-devi
gopälenaiva bhäsitam

The splendid Supreme Personality of Godhead is manifest in two forms. He is both Rädhä and Krishna. O great goddess, in this way the Lord is manifest as a cowherd boy.

Text 20
durväsaso muner mohe
kärttikyäm räsa-mandale
tatah prishtavati rädhä
sandeham bhedam ätmanah

When Durväsä Muni was bewildered by the räsa dance in the month of Kärttika, Sri Rädhä asked a question to break his doubt.

Text 21
niranjanät samutpannam
mayädhitam jagan-mayi
shri-krishnena tatah proktam
rädhäyai näradäya cha

O queen of the universe, then Lord Krishna explained the pure spiritual truth to Rädhä, Närada, and me.

Text 22
tato näradatah sarva-
viralä vaishnaväs tatah
kalau jänanti deveshi
gopaniyam prayatnatah

In Kali-yuga all the sincere Vaishnavas learned this truth from Närada. O queen of the demigods, please keep this secret carefully.

Text 23
shathäya kripanäyathä
dambhikäya sureshvari

brahma-hatyäm aväpnoti
tasmäd yatnena gopayet

O queen of the demigods, this truth should not be given to a wicked person,
a miser, or a person filled with pride. One who does so commits the sin of
killing a brähmana. Therefore, please keep this secret carefully.

Text 24

om asya shri-gopäla-sahasra-näma-stotra-mahä-mantrasya. shri-närada
rishih. anushtup chandah. shri-gopälo devatä. käma-bijam. mäyä-shaktih.
candrah kilakam. shri-krishnachandra-bhakti-rüpa-phala-präptaye
shri-gopäla-sahasra-näma-stotra-jape viniyogah. athavä om aim klim
bijam. shrim hrim shaktih. shri-vrindävana-niväsah kilakam.
shri-rädhä-priyam param brahmeti mantrah.
dharmädi-catur-vidha-purushärtha-siddhy-arthe jape viniyogah. om
närada-rishaye namah shirasi. anushtup-chandase namo mukhe.
shri-gopäla-devatäyai namo hridaye. klim kilakäya namo näbhau hrim
shaktaye namo guhye. shrim kilakäya namah padayoh. klim krishnäya
govindäya gopijana-vallabhäya svähä. iti mula-mantrah.

Om. This is the great mantra that is the prayer of the thousand names of
Lord Gopäla. The sage of this prayer is Närada Muni. The meter is
anushtup. The Deity is Lord Gopäla. The bija-syllable is the Käma-bija.
The potency is Yogamäyä. The kilaka is Chandra. The prayer of the
thousand names of Lord Gopäla is chanted to attain the result of devotion
to Lord Krishnachandra.

The alternate bija-syllable is Om aim klim. Then the potency is Srim Hrim.
The kila is Sri Vrindävana-niväsa. This mantra glorifying the Supreme
Personality of Godhead, who is dear to Sri Rädhä, is chanted to attain the
four goals of life, which begin with piety.

On the head is chanted "Om närada-rishaye namah" (Obeisances to Närada
Muni). On the mouth is chanted anushtup-chandase namah (obeisances to
the meter anushthup). Over the heart is chanted "Sri Gopäla-devatäyai
namah" (Obeisances to Lord Gopäladeva). On the navel is chanted "klim
kilakäya namah". Over the private parts is chanted, "hrim shaktaye namah".
Over the feet is chanted, "Srim kilakäya namah". Then is chanted, "klim
krishnaya govindäya gopijana-vallabhäya svähä". That is the müla-mantra.

Text 25

om kläm anugushthäbhyäm namah. om klim tarjanibhyäm namah. om
klum madhyamäbhyäm namah. om klaim anämikäbhyäm namah. om
klaum kanishthikäbhyäm namah. om klah kara-tala-kara-prishöhäbhyäm
namah. om kläm hridayäya namah. om klim shirase svähä. om klum
shikhäyai vashat. om klaim kavachäya hum. om klaum netra-trayäya
vaushat. om klah asträya phat.

Then is chanted, "Om klim anugushthäbhyäh namah (obeisances to the
thumb), "om klim tarjanibhyäm namah" (obeisances to the forefinger), "om
klum madhyamäbhyäm namah" (obeisances to the middle finger), "om
klaim anämikäbhyäm namah" (obeisances to the ring finger), "om klaum
kanishthikäbhyäm namah" (obeisances to the little finger), "om klah
kara-tala-kara-prishthäbhyäm namah" (obeisances to the palms of the
hands), "om kläm hridayäya namah" (obeisances to the heart), "om klim
shirase svähä" (obeisances to the head), "om klum shrikhäyai vashaha"
(obeisances to the shikhä), "om klaim kavachäya hum" (obeisances to the
armor), "om klaum netra-trayäya vaushaha" (obeisances to Lord Shiva. who
has three eyes), and "om klam asträya phaha".

Text 26

atha mula-mantra-nyäsah.
klim aìgushthäbhyäm namah. krishnäya tarjanibhyäm namah. govindäya
madhyamäbhyäm namah. gopijana anämikäbhyäm namah. vallabhäya
kanishthikäbhyäm namah. svähä kara-tala-kara-prishthäbhyäm namah. iti
kara-nyäsah.

Mula-mantra-nyäsa

Klim aìgushthäbhyäm namah (the thumbs). Krishnäya tarjanibhyäm namah
(the forefingers). Govindäya madhyamäbhyäm namah (the middle fingers).
Gopijana anämikäbhyäm namah (the ring fingers). Vallabhäya
kanishthikäbhyäm namah (the little fingers). Svähä
kara-tala-kara-prishthäbhyäm namah (the palms of the hands). These are the
kara-nyäsas.

Text 27
atha hridayädi-nyäsah.
klim hridayäya namah. krishnäya shirase svähä. govindäya shikhäyai
vashat. gopijana kavacäya hum. vallabhäya netra-trayäya vaushat. svähä
asträya phat. iti hridayädi-nyäsah.

Nyäsas Over the Heart and Other Places

Klim hridayäya namah (the heart). Krishnäya shirase svähä (the head).
govindäya shikhäyai vashat (the shikhä). Gopijana kavacäya hum (the
armor). Vallabhäya netra-trayäya vaushat. Svähä asträya phat. These are the
nyäsas over the heart and other places.

Text 28
atha dhyänam.
om. kasturi-tilakam laläta-patale vakshah-sthale kaustubham
näsägre vara-mauktikam kara-tale venum kare kaikanam
sarväige hari-candanam su-lalitam kanthe ca muktävali
gopa-stri-pariveshtito vijayate gopäla-cudä-manih

The Meditation
Om. All glories to the crest jewel of cowherd boys, who has a musk
tilaka-mark on His forehead, a Kaustubha jewel on His chest, a graceful
pearl on the tip of His nose, a flute in His hand, a bracelet on His wrist,
graceful sandal paste on all His limbs, and a necklace of pearls on His neck,
and who is surrounded by a host of gopis.

Text 29
phullendivara-käntim indu-vadanam barhävatämsa-priyam
shrivatsänkam udära-kaustubha-dharam pitämbaram sundaram
gopinäm nayanotpalärcita-tanum go-gopa-sanghävritam
govindam kala-venu-vädana-param divyäiga-bhusham bhaje

I worship Lord Govinda, who is splendid like a blossoming blue lotus,
whose face is like the moon, who is charming with a peacock-feather
crown, who bears the mark of Srivatsa, who wears a great Kaustubha jewel,
who is handsome in yellow garments, whose form is worshiped by the
gopis' lotus eyes, who is surrounded by cows and cowherd boys, who
sweetly plays the flute, and whose limbs are splendid with ornaments.

The Sri Gopala-sahasra-nama
(The Chanting of the Thousands Names of Gopala Starts Here)

Text 1
om klim devah kämadevah
käma-bija-shiromanih
shri-gopälo mahi-pälo
sarva-vedänta-päragah

Om. Klim. The Supreme Personality of Godhead is handsome like Kämadeva. He is the crest jewel of Kämadevas. He is a handsome cowherd boy (sri-gopäla), the protector of the earth (mahi-päla), the learned scholar who has gone to farther shore of all the Vedas (sarva-vedänta-päraga).

Text 2
dharani-pälako dhanyah
pundarikah sanätanah
go-patir bhü-patih shastä
prahartä vishvato-mukhah

He is the protector of the earth (dharani-pälaka), glorious (dhanya), graceful like a blue lotus flower (pundarika), eternal (sanätana), the master of the cows (go-pati), the master of the earth (bhu-pati), the great ruler (shastä), the destroyer (prahartä), and He is all-pervading (visvato-mukha).

Text 3
ädi-kartä mahä-kartä
mahä-kälah pratäpavän
jagaj-jivo jagad-dhätä
jagad-bhartä jagad-vasuh

He is the original creator (ädi-kartä), the great creator (mahä-kartä), great time (mahä-käla), the most powerful (pratäpavän), the life of the universe (jagaj-jiva), the maintainer of the universe (jagad-dhätä and jagad-bhartä), and the wealth of the universe (jagad-vasu).

Text 4
matsyo bhimah kuhu-bhartä
hartä varäha-murtimän

nārāyano hrishikesho
govindo garuda-dhvajah

He is the fish-incarnation (matsya), fearsome (bhima), the master of the
new-moon (kuhu-bhartä), He who takes away everything (hartä), the
boar-incarnation (varäha-murtimän), the resting place of all living entities
(näräyana), the master of the senses (hrishikesa), the Lord who pleases the
cows, land, and senses (govinda), and the Lord whose flag is marked with
the sign of Garuda (garuda-dhvaja).

Text 5
gokulendro mahä-candrah
sharvari priya-kärakah
kamalä-mukha-loläkshah
pundarika-shubhävahah

He is the moon of Gokula (gokulendra), the great moon (mahä-candra), the
night (sarvari), charming (priya-käraka), the Lord whose restless eyes
glance at the goddess of fortune (kamalä-mukha-loläksha), and splendid
like a blue lotus flower (pundarika-subhävaha).

Text 6
durväsäh kapilo bhaumah
sindhu-sägara-sangamah
govindo gopatir gotrah
kälindi-prema-purakah

He is is Durväsä (durväsä), Kapila (kapila), the ruler of the earth (bhauma),
the holy place where the Gangä meets the ocean (sindhu-sägara-sangama),
the Lord who pleases the cows, land, and senses (govinda), the master of
the cows (gopati), the protector of the cows (gotra), and a flood of love
flowing in the Yamunä (kälindi-prema-puraka).

Text 7
gopa-svämi gokulendro
govardhana-vara-pradah
nandädi-gokula-trätä
dätä däridrya-bhaïjanah

He is the master of the cowherds (gopa-svāmi), the king of Gokula (gokulendra), the Lord who granted a boon to Govardhana (govardhana-vara-prada), the protector of Nanda and the other people of Gokula (nandādi-gokula-trātā), the generous philanthropist (dātā), and the Lord who breaks poverty (dāridrya-bhaïjana).

Text 8
sarva-maṅgala-dātā ca
sarva-kāma-pradāyakah
ādi-kartā mahi-bhartā
sarva-sāgara-sindhu-jah

He is the giver of all auspiciousness (sarva-maṅgala-dātā), the fulfiller of all desires (sarva-kāma-pradāyaka), the original creator (ādi-kartā), the maintainer of the earth (maha-bhartā), and the father of all rivers and oceans (sarva-sāgara-sindhu-ja).

Text 9
gaja-sāmi gajoddhāri
kāmi kāma-kalā-nidhih
kalaika-rahitash candro
bimbāsyo bimba-sattamah

He is powerful like an elephant (gaja-sāmi and gajoddhāri), passionate (kāmi), a treasury of amorous arts (kāma-kalā-nidhi), pure (kalaika-rahita), splendid like the moon (candra), with a face splendid like the moon (bimbāsya), and splendid like the moon (bimba-sattama).

Text 10
mālā-kārah kripā-kārah
kokila-svara-bhushanah
rāmo nilāmbaro devo
hali durdama-mardanah

He is expert at making flower garlands (mālā-kāra), merciful (kripā-kāra), decorated with a voice like the cuckoos' singing (kokila-svara-bhushana), Lord Balarāma (rāma), dressed in blue garments (nilāmbara), the Supreme Personality of Godhead (deva), the holder of the plow (hali), and the crusher of the invincible (durdama-mardana).

Text 11
sahasräksha-puri-bhettä
mahä-märici-näshanah
shivah shivatamo bhettä
baläräti-präpujakah

He is the Lord who broke the city of thousand-eyed Indra
(sahasräksha-puri-bhettä), the killer of the great Marici
(mahä-märici-näsana, (auspicious - shiva), most auspicious (shivatama), the
great destroyer (bhettä), and worshiped by powerful enemies
(baläräti-präpujaka).

Text 12
kumäri vara-däyi ca
varenyo mina-ketanah
naro näräyano dhiro
rädhä-patir udära-dhih

He is soft and gentle (kumäri), the giver of boons (vara-däyi), the best
(varenya), handsome like Kämadeva (mina-ketana), the Lord whose form
is like that of a human being (nara), the resting place of all living entities
(näräyana), saintly (dhira), the master of Rädhä (rädhä-pati), and generous
at heart (udära-dhi).

Text 13
sripatih srinidhih srimän
mäpatih pratiräjahä
vrindäpatih kula-grämi
dhämi brahma-sanätanah

He is the master of the goddess of fortune (sripatih), an ocean of
handsomeness, glory, and opulence (srinidhi), handsome and glorious
(srimän), the master of the goddess of fortune (mäpati), the destroyer of
enemy kings (pratiräjahä), the master of Vrindä-devi (vrindäpati), the
leader of the village (kula-grämi), splendid (dhämi), and the eternal
Supreme Personality of Godhead (brahma-sanätana).

Text 14
revati-ramano rämash
cancalash cäru-locanah

rämayana-shariro 'yam
rämi rämah sriyahpatih

He enjoys pastimes with Revati (revati-ramana), and He is Lord Balaräma
(räma). He is restless (cancala), and has handsome eyes (cäru-locana). His
transcendental form is the home of Lord Räma's pastimes
(rämayana-sharira). He is Lord Räma (rämi and räma), and He is the master
of the goddess of fortune (sriyahpati).

Text 15
sharvarah çarvari sharvah
sarvatra-shubha-däyakah
rädhärädhayitärädhi
rädhä-citta-pramodakah

He is night (sarvara and sarvari). He is all-pervading (sarva). He brings
auspiciousness everywhere (sarvatra-shubha-däyaka). He worships Sri
Rädhä (rädhärädhayitä). He is the supreme object of worship (ärädhi). He
delights Rädhä's heart (rädhä-citta-pramodaka).

Text 16
rädhä-rati-sukhopeto
rädhä-mohana-tat-parah
rädhä-vashi-karo rädhä-
hridayämbhoja-shatpadah

He enjoys pastimes with Rädhä (rädhä-rati-sukhopeta). He is enchanted by
Rädhä (rädhä-mohana-tat-para). He has Rädhä under His control
(rädhä-vasi-kara). He is a bee attracted to the lotus of Sri Rädhä's heart
(rädhä- hridayämbhoja-shatpada).

Text 17
rädhälingana-sammoho
rädhä-nartana-kautukah
rädhä-saïjäta-sampriti
rädhä-käma-phala-pradah

He is enchanted by Rädhä's embraces (rädhäliìgana-sammoha). He is eager
to dance with Rädhä (rädhä-nartana-kautuka). He is delighted by Rädhä

(rädhä-saïjäta-sampriti). He fulfills Rädhä's desires
(rädhä-käma-phala-prada).

Text 18
vrindä-patih kosha-nidhih
koka-shoka-vinäshakah
candrä-patish candra-patish
canda-kodanda-bhaïjanah

He is the master of Vrindä-devi (vrindä-pati) and He is a great treasury of
transcendental opulences (kosha-nidhi). He destroys the koka birds' grief
(koka-shoka-vinäshaka). He is the master of Candrävali (candrä-pati), the
master of the moon (candra-pati), and the breaker of the great bow
(canda-kodanda-bhaïjana).

Text 19
rämo däsharathi rämo
bhrigu-vamsa-samudbhavah
ätmärämo jita-krodha-
moho mohändha-bhaïjanah

He is Räma (räma), the son of Dasharatha (däsharathi), and born in the
Bhrigu dynasty (bhrigu-vamsa-samudbhava). He is filled with spiritual bliss
(ätmäräma). He has conquered illusion and anger (jita-krodha-moha). He
has broken the blindness of material illusions (mohändha-bhaïjana).

Text 20
vrishabhänur bhavo bhävih
käshyapih karunä-nidhih
kolähalo hali häli
heli haladhara-priyah

He is a sun rising among the heroic warriors (vrishabhänu). He is the
universal form (bhava) and the father of all existence (bhävi). He is the son
of Kashyapa (käshyapi). He is an ocean of mercy (karunä-nidhi). His voice
is like thunder (kolähala). He is Balaräma, the holder of the plow (hali and
häli). He rebukes His enemies (heli). He is dear to Lord Balaräma
(haladhara-priya).

Text 21
rädhä-mukhäbja-märtando
bhäskaro ravijo vidhuh
vidhir vidhätä varuno
väruno väruni-priyah

He is the sun that makes the lotus of Sri Rädhä's face bloom
(rädhä-mukhäbja-märtanda). He is glorious like the sun (bhäskara and
ravija). He is glorious like the moon (vidhu). He is the creator (vidhi and
vidhätä). He is the controller of Varuna (varuna), the descendent of Varuna
(väruna), and the beloved of Väruni (väruni-priya).

Text 22
rohini-hridayänandi
vasudevätmajo bali
nilämbaro rauhineyo
jaräsandha-vadho 'malah

He is the bliss of Rohini's heart (rohini-hridayänandi), the son of Vasudeva
(vasudevätmaja), powerful (bali), dressed in blue garments (nilämbara), the
son of Rohini (rauhineya), the killer of Jaräsandha (jaräsandha-vadha), and
supremely pure (amala).

Text 23
nägo navämbho virudo
virahä varado bali
go-patho vijayi vidvän
sipivishnah sanätanah

He is the serpent Ananta (näga). He is the cause of new rains (navämbha).
He is a tumultuous sound (viruda), the killer of heroic warriors (virahä), the
giver of benedictions (varada), powerful (bali), the Lord who follows the
path of the cows (go-patha), victorious (vijayi), wise (vidvän), effulgent
(sipivishna), and eternal (sanätana).

Text 24
parashuräma-vaco-grähi
vara-grähi shrigäla-hä
damaghoshopadeshnä cha
ratha-grähi sudarshanah

He is Lord Rämachandra, who followed the orders of Parashuräma (parashuräma-vaco-grähi). He accepted a boon (vara-grähi), killed a jackel (srigäla-hä), taught a lesson to Damaghosha (damaghoshopadeshnä), and rode on a chariot (ratha-grähi). He is handsome (sudarshana).

Text 25
vira-patni yashas-trätä
jarä-vyädhi-vighätakah
dvärikä-väsa-tattva-jïo
hutäshana-vara-pradah

He has a heroic wife (vira-patni), is the protector of fame (yasas-trätä), destroys disease and old age (jarä-vyädhi-vighätaka), and is the wise ruler of Dväräkä (dvärikä-väsa-tattva-jïa). He gives the results of argnihotra-yajïas (hutäshana-vara-prada).

Text 26
yamunä-vega-samhäri
nilämbara-dharah prabhuh
vibhuh sharäsano dhanvi
ganesho gana-näyakah

He stopped the current of the Yamunä (yamunä-vega-samhäri), wears blue garments (nilämbara-dhara), is the all-powerful Supreme Lord (prabhu and vibhu), carries a great quiver (saräsana), is the best of archers (dhanvi), and is the ruler of all (ganesha and gana-näyaka).

Text 27
lakshmano lakshano lakshyo
raksho-vamsha-vinäshanah
vämano vämani bhuto
vamano vamanäruhah

He is Lakshmana (lakshmana). He is virtue (lakshana). He is seen by His devotees (lakshya). He kills the demons' dynasties (raksho-vamsha-vinäshana). He is Lord Vämana (vämana). He became a dwarf (vämani-bhuta). He manifested a gigiantic form (vamana and vamanäruha).

Text 28
yashodä-nandanah kartä
yamalärjuna-mukti-dah
ulukhali mahä-mäni
räma-baddhähvayi shami

He is the joy of Yashodä (yashodä-nandana), the creator (kartä), the giver of liberation to the yamala arjuna trees (yamalärjuna-mukti-da), the boy tied to a ginding mortar (ulukhali), noble-hearted (mahä-mäni), bound with a rope (däma-baddhähvayi), and peaceful (shami).

Text 29
bhaktänukäri bhagavän
keshavo 'cala-dhärakah
keshi-hä madhu-hä mohi
vrishäsura-vighätakah

He becomes the follower of His devotees (bhaktänukäri). He is the supremely opulent Personality of Godhead (bhagavän). He is the master of Brahmä and Shiva (keshava). He lifted Govardhana Hill (acala-dhäraka), killed Keshi (keshi-hä), killed Madhu (madhu-hä), is bewildering to the demons (mohi), and killed Arishtäsura (vrishäsura-vighätaka).

Text 30
aghäsura-vinäshi cha
putanä-moksha-däyakah
kubjä-vinodi bhagavän
kamsa-mrityur mahä-makhi

He killed Aghäsura (aghäsura-vinäshi), liberated Pütanä (pütanä-moksha-däyaka), enjoyed pastimes with Kubjä (kubjä-vinodi), is the Supreme Personality of Godhead (bhagavän), became the death of Kamsa (kamsa-mrityu), and is worshiped in all yajïas (mahä-makhi).

Text 31
ashvamedho väjapeyo
gomedho naramedhavän
kandarpa-koti-lävaëyash
candra-koti-su-shitalah

He is the ashvamedha-yajïa (ashvamedha), väjapeya-yajïa (väjapeya), gomedha-yajïa (gomedha), and naramedha-yajïa (naramedhavän). He is more handsome than many millions of Kämadevas (kandarpa-koti-lävanya), and more pleasingly cool than many millions of moons (candra-koti-su-shitala).

Text 32
ravi-koti-pratikäsho
vayu-koti-mahä-balah
brahmä brahmända-kartä cha
kamalä-vänchita-pradah

He is more splendid than many millions of suns (ravi-koti-pratikäsha), more powerful than many millions of blowing winds (väyu-koti-mahä-bala), the greatest (brahmä), the creator of the universes (brahmända-kartä), and the Lord who fulfills the goddess of fortune's desires (kamalä-vänchita-prada).

Text 33
kamali kamaläkshash cha
kamalä-mukha-lolupah
kamalä-vrata-dhäri cha
kamaläbhah purandarah

He is the master of the goddess of fortune (kamali). His eyes are like lotus flowers (kamaläksha). He yearns to gaze on the goddess of fortune's face (kamalä-mukha-lolupa). He vows to stay by the goddess of fortune (kamalä-vrata-dhäri). He is splendid like a lotus flower (kamaläbha). He is the greatest of kings (purandara).

Text 34
saubhägyädhika-citto 'yam
mahä-mäyi mahotkatah
tärakärih sura-trätä
märica-kshobha-kärakah

His heart is filled with good fortune (saubhägyädhika-citta). He is the master of transcendental potencies (mahä-mäyi). He is the most powerful (mahotkata). He is the enemy of Täraka (tärakäri), the protector of the demigods (sura-trätä), and the source of trouble for Marica (märica-kshobha-käraka).

Text 35
vishvämitra-priyo dänto
rämo räjiva-locanah
laikädhipa-kula-dhvamsi
vibhishana-vara-pradah

He is dear to Vishvämitra (vishvämitra-priya), and He is self-controlled (dänta). He is Lord Rämacandra (räma), whose eyes are lotus flowers (räjiva-locana), who destroyed the dynasty of Laikä's king (laikädhipa-kula-dhvamsi), and who gave a boon to Vibhishana (vibhishana-vara-prada).

Text 36
sitänanda-karo rämo
viro väridhi-bandhanah
khara-dushana-samhäri
säketa-pura-väsanah

He is the delight of Sitä (sitänanda-kara), the supreme enjoyer (räma), the greatest of heroes (vira), the Lord who built a bridge across the ocean (väridhi-bandhana), and the killer of Khara and Dushana (khara-düshana-samhäri). He resides in Ayodhyä (säketa-pura-väsana).

Text 37
chandrävali-patih kulah
keshi-kamsa-vadho 'marah
mädhavo madhu-hä mädhvi
mädhviko mädhavi vibhuh

He is the master of Candrävali (candrävali-pati). He enjoys pastimes on the Yamunä's shore (kula). He killed Keshi and Kamsa (keshi-kamsa-vadha). He never dies (amara). He killed the Madhu demon (mädhava and madhu-hä). He is sweet like nectar (mädhvi, mädhvika, and mädhavi). He is all-powerful (vibhu).

Text 38
muncätavi-gähamäno
dhenukärir dharätmajah
vamshivata-vihäri cha
govardhana-vanäshrayah

He entered the Muncātavi forest (muncātavi-gāhamāna), became the enemy of Dhenukāsura (dhenukāri), is the son of Dharā (dharātmaja), enjoyed pastimes at Vamshivana (vamshivata-vihāri), and entered the forest at Govardhana Hill (govardhana-vanāshraya).

Text 39
tathā tālavanoddeshi
bhāndiravana-saikha-hā
trināvarta-kathā-kāri
vrishabhānusutā-patih

He entered Tālavana (tālavanoddesi), killed Shaikhāsura in Bhandiravana (bhāndiravana-saikha-hā), killed Trināvarta (trināvarta-kathā-kāri), and is the master of King Vrishabhānu's daughter (vrishabhānusutā-pati).

Text 40
rādhā-prāna-samo rādhā-
vadanābja-madhuvratah
gopi-ranjana-daiva-jïo
lilā-kamala-pujitah

He thinks Rādhā as dear as life (rādhā-prāna-sama). He is a bee attracted to Rādhā's lotus face (rādhā-vadanābja-madhuvrata). He delights the gopis (gopi-ra jana-daiva-jïa). He is worshiped with a pastime lotus-flower (lili-kamala-pūjita).

Text 41
kridā-kamala-sandoho
gopikā-priti-ranjanah
ranjako ranjano rango
rangi ranga-mahiruhah

He plays with a pastime lotus-flower (kridā-kamala-sandoha), and He delights the gopis (gopikā-priti-raijana). He is passionate (ranjaka, ranjana, ranga, and rangi). He is a tree of bliss (ranga-mahiruha).

Text 42
kāmah kāmāri-bhakto 'yam
purāna-purushah kavih

narado devalo bhimo
balo bala-mukhambujah

He is handsome like Kämadeva (käma). He is devoted to Kämadeva's enemy, Shiva (kämäri-bhakta). He is the ancient Supreme Personality of Godhead (puräna-purusha), the wisest (kavi). He is the deliverer of the people (närada). He is the Supreme Personality of Godhead (devala). He is ferocious (bhima). He is a child (bäla). His face is a newly blossoming lotus flower (bäla-mukhämbuja).

Text 43
ambujo brahma säkshi cha
yogi datta-varo munih
rishabhah parvato grämo
nadi-pavana-vallabhah

He is graceful like a lotus flower (ambuja). He is the greatest (brahma), the witness (säkshi), the greatest yogi (yogi), the giver of boons (datta-vara), the greatest sage (muni), the best (rishabha), a mountain (parvata), a village (gräma), and dear to the purifier of the rivers (nadi-pavana-vallabha).

Text 44
padma-näbhah sura-jyeshtho
brahmä rudro 'hi-bhushitah
ganänäm-träna-kartä cha
ganesho grahilo grahih

His navel is a lotus flower (padma-näbha). He is the leader of the demigods (sura-jyeshtha). He is Brahmä (brahmä). He is Shiva (rudra). He is decorated with snakes (ahi-bhushita). He is the protector of the living entities (ganänäm-träna-kartä), and the master of the living entities (ganesha). He takes everything away (grahila and grahi).

Text 45
ganäshrayo ganädhyakshah
kridi krita-jagat-trayah
yädavendro dvärakendro
mathurä-vallabho dhuri

He is the shelter of the living entities (ganäshrayoa), the ruler of the living entities (ganädhyaksha), playful (kridi), the creator of the three worlds (krita-jagat-traya), the king of the Yädavas (yädavendra), the king of Dväraka (dvärakendra), the beloved of the people of Mathurä (mathurä-vallabha), and the maintainer of all (dhuri).

Text 46
bhramarah kuntali kunti-
suta-rakshi mahä-makhi
yamunä-vara-dätä cha
kashyapasya-vara-pradah

He is a rake (bhramara). His hair is graceful (kuntali). He is the protector of Kunti's sons (kunti-suta-rakshi). He is worshiped in all yajïas (mahä-makhi). He gave a boon to the Yamunä (yamunä-vara-dätä). He gave a boon to Kashyapa Muni (kashyapasya-vara-prada).

Text 47
shaìkhacuda-vadhoddamo
gopi-rakshana-tat-parah
päncajanya-karo rämi
tri-rämi vanajo jayah

He killed Shaìkhachuda (shaìkhachuda-vadhoddäma). He devotedly protected the gopis (gopi-rakshana-tat-para). He blew the Pänchajanya conchshell (pänchajanya-kara). He is the supreme enjoyer (rämi). He is the enjoyer of the three worlds (tri-rämi). He was born in a forest (vanaja). He is victory (jaya).

Text 48
phälgunah phälguna-sakho
virädha-vadha-kärakah
rukmini-präna-näthash cha
satyabhämä-priyaikarah

He is the friend of Arjuna (phälguna and phälguna-sakha), the killer of Virädha (virädha-vadha-käraka), the life-Lord of Rukmini (rukmini-präna-nätha), and the beloved of Satyabhämä (satyabhämä-priyaikara).

Text 49

kalpa-vriksho mahä-vriksho
däna-vriksho mahä-phalah
aìkusho bhusuro bhämo
bhämako bhrämako harih

He is a kalpa-vriksha tree (kalpa-vriksha, mahä-vriksha, and däna-vriksha),
the greatest result (mahä-phala), an elephant goad (aìkusha), the master of
the earth (bhusura), splendid (bhäma and bhämaka), the greatest cheater
(bhrämaka), and the Lord who takes away everything (hari).

Text 50

saralaù shäshvato viro
yadu-vamsi shivätmakah
pradyumno bala-kartä cha
prahartä daitya-hä prabhuh

He is honest and straightforward (sarala), eternal (shäshvata), heroic (vira),
a descendent of King Yadu (yadu-vamsi), an auspicious son (shivätmaka),
Pradyumna (pradyumna), the most powerful (bala-kartä), the Lord who
takes away everything (prahartä), the killer of the demons (daitya-hä), and
the all-powerful Supreme Personality of Godhead (prabhu).

Text 51

mahä-dhano mahä-viro
vana-mälä-vibhüshanah
tulasi-däma-shobhädhyo
jälandhara-vinäshanah

He is the most wealthy (mahä-dhana), the most heroic (mahä-vira),
decorated with a forest garland (vana-mälä-vibhushana), splendid with a
Tulasi garland (tulasi-däma-shobhädhya), and the killer of Jälandhara
(jälandhara-vinäshana).

Text 52

shurah süryo mrikandash cha
bhäskaro vishva-pujitah
ravis tamo-hä vahnish cha
vädavo vadavänalah

He is the most powerful warrior (shüra), splendid like the sun (sürya, mrikanda, bhäskara, and ravi), worshiped by all the world (vishva-pujita), and the destroyer of darkness (tamo-hä). He is like fire (vahni). He is like a volcano (vädava and vadavänala).

Text 53
daitya-darpa-vinäshi cha
garudo garudägrajah
gopi-nätho mahi-nätho
vrindä-nätho 'varodhakah

He destroys the demons' pride (daitya-darpa-vinäshi). He is Garuda (garuda). He is Garuda's elder brother (garudägraja). He is the master of the gopis (gopi-nätha), the master of the earth (mahi-nätha), and the master of Vrindä-devi (vrindä-nätha). He is the great impediment (avarodhaka).

Text 54
prapanci panca-rüpash cha
latä-gulmash cha go-patih
gangä-cha-yamunä-rüpo
godä-vetravati tathä

He is the creator of the material world (prapanchi), the Lord who assumes five forms (panca-rüpa), the father of the bushes and vines (latä-gulma), the master of the cows (go-pati), the personified Gangä and Yamunä (gangä-cha-yamunä-rüpa), the Godävari river (godä), and the Vetravati river (vetravati).

Text 55
kaveri narmadä täpi
gandaki sarayüs tathä
räjasas tämasah sattvi
sarvängi sarva-locanah

He is the Kaveri river (kaveri), the Narmadä river (narmadä), the Täpi river (täpi), the Gandaki river (gandaki), and the Sarayu river (sarayu). He is the mode of passion (räjasa), the mode of ignorance (tämasa), and the mode of goodness (sattvi). Everything has come from His limbs (sarvängi). His eyes see everywhere (sarva-locana).

Text 56
sudhämayo 'mritamayo
yogini-vallabhah shivah
buddho buddhimatäm-shreshöho
vishnur jishnuh shaci-patih

He is sweet like nectar (sudhämaya and amritamaya). He is dear to the
queen of yoga (yogini-vallabha). He is auspicious (shiva), intelligent
(buddha), the best of the intelligent (buddhimatäm-shreshtha), the all
powerful Supreme Personality of Godhead (vishnu and jishnu), and the
master of Shachi (shaci-pati).

Text 57
vamshi vamsha-dharo loko
viloko moha-näshanah
ravarävi ravo rävo
bälo bäla-balähakah

He plays a flute (vamshi and vamsha-dhara). He is the master of the world
(loka), beyond the world (viloka), the destroyer of illusion (moha-näshana),
the preacher of the Vedas (ravarävi), the Vedas personified (rava and räva),
a child (bäla), and dark like a new cloud (bäla-balähaka).

Text 58
shivo rudro nalo nilo
languli langaläshrayah
päradah pävano hamso
hamsärudho jagat-patih

He is auspicious (shiva), and ferocious (rudra). He was Nala (nala), Nila
(nila), a monkey (languli and langaläshraya), the Lord who made it possible
to cross to the farther shore (pärada), the supreme purifier (pävana), a swan
(hamsa), riding on a swan (hamsärudha), and the master of the universe
(jagat-pati).

Text 59
mohini-mohano mäyi
mahä-mäyo mahä-makhi
vrisho vrishäkapih kälah
käli damana-kärakah

He is the enchanter of Mohini (mohini-mohana), the master of the illusory potency (mäyi and mahä-mäya), the object of worship in all yajnas (mahä-makhi), a bull (vrisha), the Supreme Personality of Godhead (vrishäkapi), time (käla), the master of time (käli), and the conqueror (damana-käraka).

Text 60
kubjä-bhägya-prado viro
rajaka-kshaya-kärakah
komalo väruno räjä
jalajo jaladhärakah

He is the giver of auspiciousness to Kubjä (kubjä-bhägya-prada), a hero (vira), the killer of a washerman (rajaka-kshaya-käraka), soft and gentle (komala), the master of Varuna (väruna), a king (räjä), graceful like a lotus flower (jalaja), and dark like a monsoon cloud (jaladhäraka).

Text 61
härakah sarva-päpa-ghnah
parameshthi pitämahäh
khadga-dhäri kripä-käri
rädhä-ramana-sundarah

He takes away everything (häraka), and destroys all sins (sarva-päpa-ghna). He is the supreme master (parameshthi), and the grandfather of all (pitämahä). He holds a sword (khadga-dhäri). He is merciful (kripä-käri). He is Shri Rädhä's handsome lover (rädhä-ramana-sundara).

Text 62
dvädashäranya-sambhogi
shesha-näga-phanälayah
kämah shyämah sukhah shridah
shripatih shrinidhih kritih

He enjoys pastimes in twelve forests (dvädashäranya-sambhogi), and reclines on the hoods of the serpent Shesha (shesha-näga-phanälaya). He is handsome like Kämadeva (käma), dark (shyäma), blissful (sukha), the giver of opulence (shrida), the master of the goddess of fortune (shripati), a treasury of transcendental opulences (shrinidhi), and the creator of the world (kriti).

Text 63
harir haro naro näro
narottama ishu-priyah
gopäli-chitta-hartä cha
kartä samsära-tärakah

He takes away everything (hari and hara). His form resembles that of a human being (nara). He is the father of all (nära). He is the best of men (narottama), the best of archers (ishu-priya), the lover who steals the gopis' hearts (gopäli-chitta-hartä), the creator (kartä), and the deliverer from the world of repeated birth and death (samsära-täraka).

Text 64
ädi-devo mahä-devo
gauri-gurur anäshrayah
sädhur madhur vidhur dhätä
bhrätäkrura-paräyanah

He is the Supreme Personality of Godhead (ädi-deva and mahä-deva), the master of fair Rädhä (gauri-guru), the Lord who needs no shelter (anäshraya), saintly (sädhu), sweet (madhu), all-powerful (vidhu), generous (dhätä), kind like a brother (bhrätä), and devoted to Akrura (akrura-paräyana).

Text 65
rolambi cha hayagrivo
vänarärir vanäshrayah
vanam vani vanädhyaksho
mahä-vandyo mahä-munih

He is like a bee (rolambi). He is Hayagriva (hayagriva), the enemy of a gorilla (vänaräri), the Lord who stays in a forest (vanäshraya), the Lord who is the forest of Vrindävana (vanam), the Lord who stays in the forest (vani), the ruler of the forest (vanädhyaksha), the supreme object of worship (mahä-vandya), the most wise (mahä-muni).

Text 66
syamantaka-mani-präjno
vijno vighna-vighätakah

govardhano vardhaniyo
vardhäni vardhana-priyah

He is the Lord who knows the powers of the Syamantaka Jewel (syamantaka-mani-präjna), all-knowing (vijna), the destroyer of obstacles (vighna-vighätaka), Govardhana Hill (govardhana), the greatest (vardhaniya, vardhäni, and vardhana-priya).

Text 67
vardhanyo vardhano vardhi
värdhinyah sumukha-priyah
vardhito vriddhako vriddho
vrindäraka-jana-priyah

He is the greatest (vardhanya, vardhana, vardhi, värdhinya, vardhita, vriddhaka, and vriddha), and He loves His devotees (sumukha-priya and vrindäraka-jana-priya)

Text 68
gopäla-ramani-bhartä
sämbakushtha-vinäshanah
rukmini-haranah prema
premi candrävali-patih

He is the husband of the beautiful gopis (gopäla-ramani-bhartä), the killer of Sämbakushtha (sämba-kushtha-vinäshana), the kidnapper of Rukmini (rukmini-harana), love personified (prema), affectionate (premi), and the master of Chandrävali (chandrävali-pati).

Text 69
shri-kartä vishva-bhartä cha
naro näräyano bali
gano gana-patish chaiva
dattätreyo mahä-munih

He is the creator of wealth (shri-kartä), the maintainer of the world (vishva-bhartä), like a human being (nara), the resting place of all living entities (näräyana), powerful (bali), manifest in a great multitude of incarnations (gana), the master of all living entities (gana-pati), Dattätreya (dattätreya), and the greatest sage (mahä-muni).

Text 70
vyäso näräyano divyo
bhavyo bhävuka-dhärakah
shvah sreyäsam shivam bhadram
bhävukam bhävikam shubham

He is Vyäsa (vyäsa), Näräyana (näräyana), splendid (divya), blissful and auspicious (bhavya), the maintainer of the saintly devotees (bhävuka-dhäraka), the spiritual world (shvah), the best (sreyäsa), and auspiciousness (shiva, bhadra, bhävuka, bhävika, and shubha).

Text 71
shubhätmakah shubhah shastä
prashastä megha-näda-hä
brahmanya-devo dinänäm-
uddhära-karana-kshamah

He is auspicious (shubhätmaka and shubha), and the supreme ruler and chastiser (shastä and prashastä). His voice defeats thunder (megha-näda-hä). He is the Deity worshiped by the brähmanas (brahmanya-deva), and He is the deliverer of the fallen (dinänäm-uddhära-karana-kshama).

Text 72
krishnah kamala-paträkshah
krishnah kamala-lochanah
krishnah kämi sadä krishnah
samasta-priya-kärakah

He is all-attractive (krishna). His eyes are lotus petals (kamala-paträksha). He is dark (krishna), His eyes are lotus flowers (kamala-lochana), He is the source of all transcendental bliss (krishna). He is the fulfiller of all desires (kämi). He is Lord Krishna eternally (sadä-krishna). He pleases everyone (samasta-priya-käraka).

Text 73
nando nandi mahänandi
mädi mädanakah kili
mili hili gili goli
golo golälayo guli

He is full of transcendental bliss (nanda, nandi, mahänandi, mädi, and
mädanaka). He enjoys pastimes (kili), meets His devotees (mili), dances
(hili), eats (gili), protects the cows (goli and gola), resides in Goloka
(golälaya), and protects His devotees (guli).

Text 74
gugguli märako shäkhi
vatah pippalakah kriti
mleccha-hä käla-hartä cha
yashodä-yasha eva cha

He is worshiped with offerings of guggula incense (gugguli). He is splendid
like Kämadeva (märaka). He is the master of all the branches of the Vedas
(shäkhi). He is the banyan tree (vata) and the pippala tree (pippalaka). He
is the creator (kriti), the killer of the uncivilized atheists (mleccha-hä), the
Lord who puts and end to time (käla-hartä), and the fame of Yashodä
(yashodä-yasha).

Text 75
acyutah keshavo vishnur
harih satyo janärdanah
hamso näräyano lilo
nilo bhakti-paräyanah

He is infallible (acyuta), the master of Brahmä and Shiva (keshava),
all-pervading (vishnu), the Lord who takes away everything (hari), the
Supreme Truth (satya), the Lord who removes the sufferings of His
devotees (janärdana), a swan (hamsa), the resting place of all living entities
(näräyana), playful (lila), dark (nila), and pleased by devotional service
(bhakti-paräyana).

Text 76
jänaki-vallabho rämo
virämo vighna-näshanah
sahasrämshur mahä-bhänur
vira-bähur mahodadhih

He is dear to Sitä (jänaki-vallabha). He is Lord Rämacandra (räma). He is
the end of obstacles (viräma), the destroyer of obstacles (vighna-näshana),
splendid like the sun with a thousand rays of light (sahasrämshu), splendid

like the sun (mahä-bhänu), with the arms of a hero (vira-bähu), and fathomless like the ocean (mahodadhi).

Text 77
samudro 'bdhir akupärah
päräväraha sarit-patih
gokulänanda-käri cha
pratijnä-paripälakah

He is fathomless like the ocean (samudra and abdhi), Lord Kurma (akupära), the universal form (päravära), the master of the rivers (sarit-pati), the delight of Gokula (gokulänanda-käri), and the Lord who keeps His promise (pratijnä-paripälaka).

Text 78
sadä-rämah kripä-rämo
mahä-rämo dhanur-dharah
parvatah parvatäkäro
gayo geyo dvija-priyah

He is always blissful (sadä-räma), always merciful (kripä-räma), filled with bliss (mahä-räma), the greatest archer (dhanur-dhara), Govardhana Hill (parvata and parvatäkära), the master of transcendental opulence (gaya), the Lord glorified by the devotees' songs (geya), and the Lord dear to the brähmanas (dvija-priya).

Text 79
kambaläshvataro rämo
rämäyana-pravärtakah
dyaur divo divaso divyo
bhavyo bhävi-bhayäpahah

He is glorious (kambaläshvatara), Lord Rämacandra (räma), the origin of the Rämäyana (rämäyana-pravärtaka), and the spiritual world (dyau, diva, divasa, and divya). He is auspiciousness (bhavya). He removes the fears of they who live in the world of repeated birth and death (bhävi-bhayäpaha).

Text 80
pärvati-bhägya-sahito
bhrätä lakshmi-viläsavän

vilāsi sāhasi sarvi
garvi garvita-lochanah

He is the good fortune of Pārvati (pārvati-bhāgya-sahita). He is like a brother (bhrātä). He enjoys pastimes with the goddess of fortune (lakshmi-vilāsavän). He is playful (vilāsi) and tolerant (sāhasi). He is the Lord of all (sarvi). He is confident (garvi). His eyes shine with confidence (garvita-lochana).

Text 81
murārir loka-dharma-jno
jivano jivanāntakah
yamo yamādir yamano
yāmi yāma-vidhāyakah

He is the enemy of Mura (murāri), the knower of the path of religion in this world (loka-dharma-jna), the life of all that lives (jivana), the goal of life (jivanāntaka), and the chastiser of the wicked (yama, yamādi, yamana, yāmi, and yāma-vidhāyaka).

Text 82
vamshuli pamsuli pamsuh
pāndur arjuna-vallabhah
lalitā-chandrikā-māli
māli mālāmbujāshrayah

He plays a flute (vamshuli). He is the master of the gopis (pamsuli and pamsu), splendid (pāndu), the dear friend of Arjuna (arjuna-vallabha), decorated with Lalitā-Chandrikā garlands (lalitā-chandrikā-māli), decorated with a graland (māli), and decorated with a garland of lotus flowers (mālāmbujāshraya).

Text 83
ambujāksho mahā-yaksho
dakshamsh chintāmanih prabhuh
manir dina-manish chaiva
kedāro badari-shrayah

His eyes are lotus flowers (ambujāksha). He is the supreme object of worship (mahā-yaksha). He is expert (daksha). He is a chintāmani jewel (chintämani), the supreme master (prabhu), a jewel (mani), the sun (dina-mani), and Mount Kedära (kedära). He resides in Badarikäshrama (badari-shraya).

Text 84
badari-vana-samprito
vyäsah satyavati-sutah
amaräri-nihantä cha
sudhä-sindhur vidhudayah

He is happy to stay in Badari forest (badari-vana-samprita), Vyäsa (vyäsa), the son of Satyavati (satyavati-suta), the killer of the demigods' enemies (amaräri-nihantä), an ocean of nectar (sudhä-sindhu), and glorious like the rising of the moon (vidhüdaya).

Text 85
chandro ravih shivah shuli
chakri chaiva gadädharah
shri-kartä shripatih shridah
shridevo devaki-sutah

He is the moon (chandra), the sun (ravi), Lord Shiva (shiva), the holder of the trident (shuli), the holder of the chakra (chakri), the holder of the club (gadädhara), the giver of wealth (shri-kartä and shridah), the master of the goddess of fortune (shripatih and shrideva), and the son of Devaki (devaki-suta).

Text 86
shripatih pundarikäkshah
padma-näbho jagat-patih
väsudevo 'prameyätmä
keshavo garuda-dhvajah

He is the master of the goddess of fortune (shripati), lotus-eyed (pundarikäksha), with a lotus navel (padma-näbha), the master of the universes (jagat-pati), all-pervading (väsudeva), limitless (aprameyätmä), the master of Brahmä and Shiva (keshava), and the Lord whose flag is marked with the sign of Garuda (garuda-dhvaja).

Text 87
näräyanah param-dhäma
deva-devo maheshvarah
chakra-pänih kalä-purio
veda-vedyo dayä-nidhih

He is the resting place of all living entities (näräyana), the supreme abode (param-dhäma), the master of the demigods (deva-deva), the supreme master (maheshvara), the Lord who holds the chakra in His hand (chakra-päni), perfect and complete (kalä-purna), to be known by studying the Vedas (veda-vedya), and an ocean of mercy (dayä-nidhi).

Text 88
bhagavän sarva-bhutesho
gopälah sarva-pälakah
ananto nirguno 'nanto
nirvikalpo niranjanah

He is the Supreme Personality of Godhead (bhagavän), the master of all living entities (sarva-bhutesha), the protector of the cows (gopäla), the protector of all (sarva-pälaka), limitless (ananta), untouched by the modes of material nature (nirguna), infallible (nirvikalpa), and untouched by matter (niranjana).

Text 89
nirädhäro nirakäro
niräbhäso niräshrayah
purushah pranavätito
mukundah parameshvarah

He is independent (nirädhära), without a material form (nirakära), infallible (niräbhäsa), independent (niräshraya), the supreme person (purusha), the sacred syllable Om (pranavätita), the giver of liberation (mukunda), and the supreme controller (parameshvara).

Text 90
kshanävanih särvabhaumo
vaikuntho bhakta-vatsalah
vishnur dämodarah krishno
mädhavo mathurä-patiù

He is a festival of happiness for the earth (kshanävani), the master of the earth (särvabhauma), the master of the spiritual world (vaikuntha), affectionate to His devotees (bhakta-vatsala), all-pervading (vishnu), the Lord whose waist was tied with a rope (dämodara), all-attractive (krishna), the husband of the goddess of fortune (mädhava), and the king of Mathurä (mathurä-pati).

Text 91

devaki-garbha-sambhuto
yashodä-vatsalo harih
shivah saìkarshanah shambhur
bhuta-nätho divaspatih

He was born from Devaki's womb (devaki-garbha-sambhuta). He dearly loves Mother Yashodä (yashodä-vatsala). He removes all obstacles (hari and sankarshana), is auspicious (shiva and shambhu), is the master of all living entities (bhuta-nätha), and is the master of the spiritual world (divaspati).

Text 92

avyayah sarva-dharma-jno
nirmalo nirupadravah
nirväna-näyako nityo
nila-jimuta-sannibhah

He is imperishable (avyaya), the knower of all religious principles (sarva-dharma-jna), and supremely pure (nirmala). He is the savior from all calamities (nirupadrava), and the giver of liberation (nirväna-näyaka). He is eternal (nitya). He is splendid like a monsoon cloud (nila-jimuta-sannibha).

Text 93

kaläkshayash cha sarva-jnah
kamalä-rupa-tat-parah
hrishikeshah pita-väsä
vasudeva-priyätmajah

He resides in the spiritual world (kaläkshaya). He knows everything (sarva-jna). He is enchanted by the goddess of fortune's beauty (kamalä-rupa-tat-para). He is the master of the senses (hrishikesha), dressed

in yellow garments (pita-väsä), and the dear son of King Vasudeva
(vasudeva-priyätmaja).

Text 94

nanda-gopa-kumäräryo
navanitäshanah prabhuh
puräna-purushah shreshthah
shaikha-pänih su-vikramah

He is the worthy son of the gopa Nanda (nanda-gopa-kumärärya). He
enjoys pastimes of eating fresh butter (navanitäshana). He is the supreme
master (prabhu), the ancient supreme person (puräna-purusha), the best
(shreshtha), the Lord who holds a conchshell in His hand (shaikha-päni),
and supremely powerful (su-vikrama).

Text 95

aniruddhash chakra-rathah
shärnga-pänish chatur-bhujah
gadädharah surärti-ghno
govindo nandakäyudhah

He is invincible (aniruddha). He is the warrior whose weapon is the
Sudarshana-chakra (chakra-ratha). He holds the Sharnga bow in His hand
(shärnga-päni). He has four arms (chatur-bhuja), holds the club
(gadädhara), kills the demigods' enemies (surärti-ghna), and is the pleasure
of the cows, land, and senses (govinda). His weapon is the Nandaka sword
(nandakäyudha).

Text 96

vrindävana-charah shaurir
venu-vädya-vishäradah
triiävartäntako bhimah
sähaso bähu-vikramah

He walks in Vrindävana forest (vrindävana-chara). He is the descendent of
King Shurasena (shauri). He expertly plays the flute
(venu-vädya-vishärada). He ended Trinävarta's life (trinävartäntaka). He is
ferocious (bhima and sähasa), and very powerful (bähu-vikrama).

Text 97
shakatäsura-samhäri
bakäsura-vinäshanah
dhenukäsura-sanghätah
putanärir nrikesiri

He killed Shakatäsura (shakatäsura-samhäri), killed Bakäsura (bakäsura-vinäshana), and killed Dhenukäsura (dhenukäsura-saìghäta). He is the enemy of Putanä (putanäri). He is Lord Nrisimha (nrikesiri).

Text 98
pitämaho guruh säkshi
pratyag-ätma sadä-shivah
aprameyah prabhuh präjno
'pratarkyah svapna-vardhanah

He is the grandfather (pitämaha), the spiritual master (guru), the witness (säkshi), the all-pervading Supersoul (pratyag-ätmä), always auspicious (sadä-shiva), limitless (aprameya), the supreme master (prabhu), all-knowing (präjna), inconceivable (apratarkya), and the creator of the dream that is the world of birth and death (svapna-vardhana).

Text 99
dhanyo manyo bhavo bhävo
dhirah shänto jagad-guruh
antar-yämishvaro divyo
daivajno devatä-guruh

He is glorious (dhanya), the supreme object of worship (manya), the supreme reality (bhava and bhäva), the wisest (dhira), peaceful (shänta), the master of the universes (jagad-guru), the Supersoul present in everyone's heart (antar-yämi), the supreme controller (ishvara), glorious (divya), all-knowing (daivajna), and the master of the demigods (devatä-guru).

Text 100
kshiräbdhi-shayano dhätä
lakshmiväl lakshmanägrajah
dhätri-patir ameyätmä
chandrashekhara-pujitah

He is Lord Vishnu who resides in the milk-ocean (kshirābdhi-shayana). He is the creator (dhātä), opulent (lakshmivän), the elder brother of Lakshmana (lakshmanägraja), the master of the earth (dhätri-pati), limitless (ameyätmä), and worshiped by Lord Shiva (chandrashekhara-püjita).

Text 101

loka-säkshi jagac-chakshuh
punya-charitra-kirtanah
koti-manmatha-saundaryo
jagan-mohana-vigrahah

He is the witness of all living entities (loka-säkshi), the eye of the universes (jagac-chakshu), the Lord whose transcendental pastimes are glorified by the saintly devotees (punya-charitra-kirtana), more handsome than ten million Kämadevas (koti-manmatha-saundarya), and the Lord whose transcendental form enchants all the worlds (jagan-mohana-vigraha).

Text 102

manda-smita-tamo gopo
gopikä-pariveshtitah
phulläravinda-nayanash
cänurändhra-nishudanah

He has the most graceful gentle smile (manda-smita-tama). He is the protector of the cows (gopa). He is surrounded by the gopis (gopikä-pariveshtita). His eyes are like blossoming lotus flowers (phulläravinda-nayana). He killed the demon Chänura (chänurändhra-nishudana).

Text 103

indivara-dala-shyämo
barhi-barhävatamsakah
murali-ninadählädo
divya-mälyämbaräshrayah

He is dark like a blue-lotus petal (indivara-dala-shyäma). He wears a peacock-feather crown (barhi-barhävatamsaka). He enjoys playing the flute (murali-ninadähläda). He wears a splendid garland (divya-mälyämbaräshraya).

Text 104
su-kapola-yugah su-bhru-
yugalah su-lalätakah
kambu-grivo vishäläksho
lakshmivän shubha-darshanah

His cheeks are graceful (su-kapola-yuga). His eyebrows are graceful (su-bhru-yugala). His forehead is graceful (su-lalätaka). His neck is graceful like a conchshell (kambu-griva). His eyes are large (vishäläksha). He is glorious and opulent (lakshmivän). He is handsome and pleasing to the eyes (shubha-darshana).

Text 105
pina-vakshäsh chatur-bähush
chatur-mürtis tri-vikramah
kalaìka-rahitah shuddho
dushta-shatru-nivarhanah

His chest is broad (pina-vakshä). He has four arms (chatur-bähu). He appears in four forms (chatur-murti). He stepped over the three worlds (tri-vikrama). He is pure (kalaìka-rahita and shuddha). He kills the demons (dushta-shatru-nivarhana).

Text 106
kirita-kundala-dharah
katakängada-manditah
mudrikä-bharanopetah
kati-sutra-viräjitah

He wears earrings and a crown (kirita-kundala-dhara). He is decorated with bracelets and armlets (katakängada-mandita). He wears rings on His fingers (mudrikä-bharanopeta). He wears a splendid belt (kati-sutra-viräjita).

Text 107
manjira-ranjita-padah
sarväbharana-bhushitah
vinyasta-päda-yugalo
divya-mangala-vigrahah

He wears tinkling anklets (manjira-ranjita-pada). He is decorated with all ornaments (sarvābharana-bhushita). He placed His lotus feet on the ground (vinyasta-pāda-yugala). His form is splendid and auspicious (divya-mangala-vigraha).

Text 108
gopikā-nayanānandah
purna-chandra-nibhānanah
samasta-jagad-ānandah
sundaro loka-nandanah

He is the bliss of the gopis' eyes (gopikā-nayanānanda). His face is splendid like a full moon (purna-chandra-nibhānana). He is the bliss of all the worlds (samasta-jagad-ānanda and loka-nandana). He is handsome (sundara).

Text 109
yamunā-tira-sanchāri
rādhā-manmatha-vaibhavah
gopa-nāri-priyo dānto
gopi-vastrāpahārakah

He walks on the Yamunā's shore (yamunā-tira-sanchāré). He is the Kāmadeva that attracts Shri Rādhā (rādhā-manmatha-vaibhava). He loves the gopis (gopa-nāri-priya). He is saintly and self-controlled (dānta). He stole the gopis' garments (gopi-vastrāpahārak).

Text 110
shringāra-murtih shridhāmā
tārako mula-kāranam
srishti-samrakshanopāyah
krurāsura-vibhanjanah

He is conjugal love personified (shringāra-mhrti). He is splendid and glorious (shridhāmā. He is the deliverer (tāraka). He is the root of all existence (mula-kāranam). He is the protector of the worlds (srishti-samrakshanopāya). He cuts apart the cruel demons (krurāsura-vibhanjana).

Text 111
narakäsura-samhäri
murärir vaira-mardanah
äditeya-priyo daitya-
bhi-karash chendu-shekharah

He killed Narakäsura (narakäsura-samhäri). He is the enemy of Mura (muräri). He crushes His enemies (vaira-mardana). He is loved by the demigods (äditeya-priya). He fills the demons with fear (daitya-bhi-kara). The moon is His crown (indu-shekhara).

Text 112
jaräsandha-kula-dhvamsi
kamsärätih su-vikramah
punya-slokah kirtaniyo
yädavendro jagan-nutah

He destroyed Jaräsandha's dynasty (jaräsandha-kula-dhvamsi). He was the enemy of Kamsa (kamsäräti). He is supremely powerful (su-vikrama), praised in graceful verses (punya-sloka), the greatest object of prayers of praise (kirtaniya), the king of the Yädavas (yädavendra), and praised by all the world (jagan-nuta).

Text 113
rukmini-ramanah satya-
bhämä-jämbavati-priyah
mitravindä-nägnajiti-
lakshmanä-samupäsitah

He is the lover of Rukmini (rukmini-ramana), dear to Satyabhämä and Jämbavati (satyabhämä-jämbavati-priya), and worshiped by Mitravindä, Nägnajiti, and Lakshmanä (mitravindä-nägnajiti-lakshmanä-samupäsita).

Text 114
sudhäkära-kule-jäto
'nanta-prabala-vikramah
sarva-saubhägya-sampanno
dvärakäyäm-upasthitah

He was born in the dynasty of the moon-god (sudhäkära-kule-jäta). His power is limitless (ananta-prabala-vikrama). He is all glorious and fortunate (sarva-saubhägya-sampanna), and He resides in Dväraka (dvärakäyäm-upasthita).

Text 115
bhadräsurya-sutä-nätho
lilä-mänusha-vigrahah
sahasra-shodasha-strisho
bhoga-mokshaika-däyakah

He is the master of Shri Rädhä (bhadräsurya-sutä-nätha). He enjoys pastimes as a human being (lilä-mänusha-vigraha). He has 16,108 wives (sahasra-shodasha-strisha). He gives both material enjoyment and liberation (bhoga-mokshaika-däyaka).

Text 116
vedänta-vedyah samvedyo
vedyo brahmända-näyakah
govardhana-dharo näthah
sarva-jiva-dayä-parah

He is known by study of Vedänta (vedänta-vedya). He is the highest object of knowledge (samvedya and vedya). He is the ruler of the universes (brahmända-näyaka). He lifted Govardhana Hill (govardhana-dhara). He is the supreme master (nätha). He is merciful to all living entities (sarva-jiva-dayä-para).

Text 117
murtimän sarva-bhutätmä
ärta-träna-paräyanah
sarva-jnah sarva-sulabhah
sarva-shästra-vishäradah

His form is transcendental (murtimän). He is the Supersoul present in everyone's heart (sarva-bhutätmä). He is the protector from suffering (ärta-träna-paräyana), all-knowing (sarva-jna), easily attainable by all (sarva-sulabha), and learned in all the scriptures (sarva-shästra-vishärada).

Text 118
shad-gunaishvarya-sampannah
purna-kämo dhuran-dharah
mahänubhävah kaivalya-
däyako loka-näyakah

He is the master of six opulences (shad-gunaishvarya-sampanna), and His desires are all fulfilled (purna-käma). He is filled with all virtues and glories (dhuran-dhara and mahänubhäva). He is the giver of liberation (kaivalya-däyaka) and the master of the worlds (loka-näyaka).

Text 119
ädi-madhyänta-rahitah
shuddha-sattvika-vigrahah
asamänah samastätmä
sharanägata-vatsalah

He has neither beginning, middle, nor end (ädi-madhyänta-rahita). His form is situated in pure goodness (shuddha-sattvika-vigraha). He has no equal (asamäna). He is the all-pervading Supersoul (samastätmä). He is affectionate to the surrendered souls (sharanägata-vatsala).

Text 120
utpatti-sthiti-samhära-
käranam sarva-käranam
gambhirah sarva-bhäva-jnah
sac-chid-änanda-vigrahah

He is the cause of creation, maintenance, and destruction (utpatti-sthiti-samhära-käranam). He is the cause of all (sarva-käranam). He is profound (gambhira). He knows everything (sarva-bhäva-jna). His form is eternal and full of knowledge and bliss (sac-chid-änanda-vigraha).

Text 121
vishvaksenah satya-sandhah
satyavän satya-vikramah
satya-vratah satya-samjnah
sarva-dharma-paräyanah

His armies are everywhere (vishvaksena). He is the supreme reality (satya-sandha and satyavän). He is supremely powerful (satya-vikrama), faithful (satya-vrata), wise (satya-samjna), and pious (sarva-dharma-paräyana).

Text 122
apannärti-prasamano
draupadi-mäna-rakshakah
kandarpa-janakah präjno
jagan-nätaka-vaibhavah

He removes all sufferings (apannärti-prasamana). He protected Draupadi's honor (draupadi-mäna-rakshaka). He is the father of Kämadeva (kandarpa-janaka). He is the most wise (präjna). In His pastimes He becomes a dancer in this world (jagan-nätaka-vaibhava).

Text 123
bhakti-vashyo gunätitah
sarvaishvarya-pradäyakah
damaghosha-suta-dveshi
bäna-bähu-vikhandanah

He is conquered by devotion (bhakti-vashya). He is beyond the touch of the modes of material nature (gunätita). He is the giver of all powers and opulences (sarvaishvarya-pradäyaka). He is the enemy of Damaghosha's son (damaghosha-suta-dveshi). He cut Bänäsura's arms (bäna-bähu-vikhandana).

Text 124
bhishma-bhakti-prado divyah
kauravänvaya-näshanah
kaunteya-priya-bandhush cha
pärtha-syandana-särathih

He gave devotional service to Bhishma (bhishma-bhakti-prada). He is glorious (divya). He destroyed the Kaurava dynasty (kauravänvaya-näshana). He is the dear friend of Kunti's sons (kaunteya-priya-bandhu). He drove Arjuna's chariot (pärtha-syandana-särathi).

Text 125
närasimho mahä-virah
stambha-jäto mahä-balah
prahläda-varadah satyo
deva-pujyo 'bhayaikarah

He is Lord Nrisimha (närasimha), a great hero (mahä-vira), born from a pillar (stambha-jäta), very powerful (mahä-bala), the giver of benedictions to Prahläda (prahläda-varada), the supreme reality (satya), worshiped by the demigods (deva-pujya), and the giver of fearlessness (abhayaikara).

Text 126
upendra indrävara-jo
vämano bali-bandhanah
gajendra-varadah svämi
sarva-deva-namaskritah

He is the younger brother of Indra (upendra and indrävara-ja), Vämana (vämana). He bound King Bali (bali-bandhana). He gave a benediction to Gajendra (gajendra-varada). He is the supreme master (svämi). All the demigods bow down before Him (sarva-deva-namaskritah.

Text 127
shesha-paryaika-shayano
vainateya-ratho jayi
avyähata-balaishvarya-
sampannah purna-mänasah

He reclines on the couch of Shesha (shesha-paryaika-shayana). He flies on Garuda (vainateya-ratha). He is victorious (jayi). His power and opulence are limitless and eternal (avyähata-balaishvarya-sampanna). The desires in His heart are always fulfilled (purna-mänasa).

Text 128
yogeshvareshvarah säkshi
kshetra-jno jnana-däyakah
yogi-hrit-pankajäväso
yogamäyä-samanvitah

He is the master of the kings of yoga (yogeshvareshvara). He is the witness (säkshi and kshetra-jna). He is the giver of transcendental knowledge (jnana-däyaka). He resides in the lotus of the yogis' hearts (yogi-hrit-pankajävasa). He is the master of Yogamäyä (yogamäyä-samanvita).

Text 129
näda-bindu-kalätitash
chatur-varga-phala-pradah
sushumnä-märga-sancäri
dehasyäntara-samsthitah

He is the näda-bindu letter (näda-bindu-kalätita). He gives the results of the four vargas (chatur-varga-phala-prada). He travels on the Sushumnä path (sushumnä-märga-sancäri). He is the Supersoul in the body of every conditioned soul (dehasyäntara-samsthita).

Text 130
dehendriya-manah-präna-
säkshi chetah-pradäyakah
sukshmah sarva-gato dehi
jnäna-darpana-gocharah

He is the witness of the body, senses, mind, and life (dehendriya-manah-präna-säkshi). He gives consciousness (cetah-pradäyaka). He is the most subtle (sukshma). He is all-pervading (sarva-gata). His form is transcendental (dehi). He is seen in the mirror of transcendental knowledge (jnäna-darpana-gochara).

Text 131
tattva-trayätmako 'vyakta-
kundali-samupäshritah
brahmanyah sarva-dharma-jnah
shänto dänto gata-klamah

He is the master of the three tattvas (tattva-trayätmaka). He is unmanifested (avyakta). Goddess Käli takes shelter of Him (kundali-samupäshrita). He is worshiped by the brähmanas (brahmanya). He knows all the truths of religion (sarva-dharma-jna). He is peaceful (shänta), self-controlled (dänta), and tireless (gata-klama).

Text 132
shrinivāsah sadānando
vishvamurtir mahā-prabhuh
sahasra-shirshāh purushah
sahasrākshah sahasra-pāt

He is the home of the goddess of fortune (shrinivāsa). His bliss is eternal (sadānanda). He is the universal form (vishvamurti). He is the Supreme Lord (mahā-prabhu). He has a thousand heads (sahasra-shirshā). He is the supreme person (purusha). He has a thousand eyes (sahasrāksha). He has a thousand feet (sahasra-pāt).

Text 133
samasta-bhuvanādhārah
samasta-prāna-rakshakah
samasta-sarva-bhāva-jno
gopikā-prāna-vallabhah

He is the resting place of all the worlds (samasta-bhuvanādhāra). He is the protector of all life (samasta-prāna-rakshaka). He knows everything (samasta-sarva-bhāva-jna). To the gopis He is more dear than life (gopikā-prāna-vallabha).

Text 134
nityotsavo nitya-saukhyo
nitya-shrir nitya-mangalah
vyuhārchito jagan-nāthah
shri-vaikuntha-purādhipah

He is an eternal festival of transcendental bliss (nityotsava and nitya-saukhya). His glory and handsomeness is eternal (nitya-shri). His auspiciousness is eternal (nitya-mangala). He is worshiped by a great host of devotees (vyuhārchita). He is the master of the universes (jagan-nātha). He is the king of the spiritual world (shri-vaikuntha-purādhipa).

Text 135
purnananda-ghani-bhuto
gopa-vesha-dharo harih
kalāpa-kusuma-shyāmah
komalah shānta-vigrahah

He is filled with perfect transcendental bliss (purnananda-ghani-bhuta). He is dressed like a cowherd boy (gopa-vesha-dhara). He takes away what is inauspicious (hari). He is dark like an atasi flower (kaläpa-kusuma-shyäma). He is soft and delicate (komala). He is peaceful (shänta-vigraha).

Text 136
gopäiganävrito 'nanto
vrindävana-samäshrayah
venu-väda-ratah shreshtho
devänäm-hita-kärakah

He is surrounded by a host of gopis (gopäiganävrita). He is limitless (ananta). He stays in Vrindävana (vrindävana-samäshraya). He is fond of playing the flute (venu-väda-rata). He is the best (shreshtha). He brings auspiciousness to the demigods (devänäm-hita-käraka).

Text 137
bäla-kridä-samäsakto
navanitasya-taskarah
gopäla-kämini-järash
chaura-jära-shikhä-manih

He enjoys childhood pastimes (bäla-kridä-samäsakta). He steals butter (navanitasya-taskara). He is the paramour of the passionate gopis (gopäla-kämini-jära). He is the crest jewel of thieves (chaura-jära-shikhä-mani).

Text 138
param-jyotih paräkäshah
paräväsah parisphutah
ashtädasäksharo-mantro
vyäpako loka-pävanah

He is splendid (param-jyoti). He is the great sky (paräkäsha). He is the supreme abode (paräväsa). He appears before His devotees (parisphuta). He is present in the eighteen-syllable mantra (ashtädasäksharo-mantra). He is all-pervading (vyäpaka). He is the purifier of the worlds (loka-pävana).

Text 139
sapta-koti-mahä-mantra-
shekharo deva-shekharah
vijnänam jnäna-sandhänas
tejo-räshir jagat-patih

He is the crown of seventy million great mantras (sapta-koti-mahä-mantra-shekhara). He is the crown of the demigods (deva-shekhara). He is transcendental knowledge (vijnänam and jnäna-sandhäna). He is effulgent (tejo-räshi). He is the master of the worlds (jagat-pati).

Text 140
bhakta-loka-prasannätmä
bhakta-mandära-vigrahah
bhakta-däridrya-damano
bhaktänäm-priti-däyakah

In His heart He is pleased with His devotees (bhakta-loka-prasannätmä). To His devotees He is like a mandära tree (bhakta-mandära-vigraha). He removes His devotees' poverty (bhakta-däridrya-damana). He delights His devotees (bhaktänäm-priti-däyaka).

Text 141
bhaktädhina-manäh pujyo
bhakta-loka-shivaikarah
bhaktäbhishta-pradah sarva-
bhaktäghaugha-nikrintanah

In His heart He is conquered by His devotees (bhaktädhina-manä). He is the supreme object of worship (pujya). He gives auspiciousness to His devotees (bhakta-loka-shivaikara). He fulfills His devotees' desires (bhaktäbhishta-prada). He destroys the great flood of all His devotees' sins (sarva-bhaktäghaugha-nikrintana).

Text 142
apära-karunä-sindhur
bhagavän bhakta-tat-parah

He is a shoreless ocean of mercy (apära-karunä-sindhu). He is the opulent Supreme Personality of Godhead (bhagavän). He loves His devotees (bhakta-tat-para).

TEXT NUMBERS OF THE HOLY NAMES
Each name, arranged in alphabetical order, is followed by the text where it is found.

Abdhi, Text 77 * Abhayankara, Text 125 * Acala-dharaka, Text 29 * Acyuta, 75 * Adi-deva, 64 * Adi-karta, 3, 8 * Adi-madhyanta-rahita, 119 * Aditeya-priya, 111 * Aghasura-vinasi, 30 * Ahi-bhusita, 44 * Akupara, 77 * Amala, 22 * Amara, 37 * Amarari-nihanta, 84 * Ambuja, 43 * Ambujaksa, 83 * Ameyatma, 100 * Amrtamaya, 56 * Ananta, 88, 136 * Ananta-prabala-vikrama, 114 * Anasraya, 64 * Aniruddha, 95 * Ankusa, 49 * Antar-yami, 99 * Apannarti-prasamana, 122 * Apara-karuna-sindhu, 142 * Aprameya-prabhu, 98 * Aprameyatma, 86 * Apratarkya, 98 * Aradhi, 15 * Arjuna-vallabha, 82 * Arta-trana-parayana, 117 * Asamana, 119 * Astadasaksaro-mantra, 138 * Asvamedha, 31 * Atmarama, 19 * Avarodhaka, 53 * Avyahata-balaisvarya-sampanna, 127 * Avyakta-kundali-samupasrita, 131 * Avyaya, 92 * * Badari-sraya, 83 * Badari-vana-samprita, 84 * Bahu-vikrama, 96 * Bakasura-vinasana, 97 * Bala, 42, 57 * Bala-balahaka, 57 * Bala-karta, 50 * Bala-krida-samasakta, 137 * Bala-mukhambuja, 42 * Balarati-prapujaka, 11 * Bali, 22, 69 * Bali-bandhana, 126 * Bana-bahu-vikhandana, 123 * Barhi-barhavatamsaka, 103 * Bhadram, 70 * Bhadrasurya-suta-natha, 115 * Bhagavan, 29, 30, 88, 142 * Bhakta-daridrya-damana, 140 * Bhakta-loka-prasannatma, 140 * Bhakta-loka-sivankara, 141 * Bhakta-mandara-vigraha, 140 * Bhakta-tat-para, 142 * Bhakta-vatsala, 90 * Bhaktabhista-prada, 141 * Bhaktadhina-mana, 141 * Bhaktanam-priti-dayaka, 140 * Bhaktanukari, 29 * Bhakti-parayana, 75 * Bhakti-vasya, 123 * Bhama, 49 * Bhamaka, 49 * Bhandiravana-sankha-ha, 39 * Bhaskara, 21, 52 * Bhauma, 6 * Bhava, 20, 99 * Bhavi, 20 * Bhavi-bhayapaha, 79 * Bhavikam, 70 * Bhavuka-dharaka, 70 * Bhavukam, 70 * Bhavya, 70, 79 * Bhetta, 11 * Bhima, 4, 42 * Bhima-sahasa, 96 * Bhisma-bhakti-prada, 124 * Bhoga-moksaika-dayaka, 115 * Bhramaka, 49 * Bhramara, 46 * Bhrata, 80 * Bhratakrura-parayana, 64 * Bhrgu-vamsa-samudbhava, 19 * Bhu-pati, 2 * Bhusura, 49 * Bhuta, 27, 135 * Bhuta-natha, 91 * Bimba-sattama, 9 * Bimbasya, 9 * Brahma, 32, 43, 44 * Brahma-sanatana, 13 * Brahmanda-karta, 32 * Brahmanya, 131 * Brahmanya-deva, 71 * Buddha, 56 * Buddhimatam-srestha, 56 * * Cakra-pani, 87 * Cakra-ratha, 95 * Cakri, 85 * Cancala, 14 *

Haladhara-priya, 20 * Hali, 10, 20 * Hamsa, 58, 75 * Hamsarudha, 58 *
Hara, 63 * Haraka, 61 * Hari, 49, 63, 75, 91, 135 * Harta, 4 * Hayagriva,
65 * Heli, 20 * Hili, 73 * Hrsikesa, 4, 93 * Hutasana-vara-prada, 25 * *
Indivara-dala-syama, 103 * Indravara-ja, 126 * Isu-priya, 63 * Isvara, 99 *
* Jagac-caksu, 101 * Jagad-bharta, 3 * Jagad-dhata, 3 * Jagad-guru, 99 *
Jagad-vasu, 3 * Jagaj-jiva, 3 * Jagan-mohana-vigraha, 101 *
Jagan-nataka-vaibhava, 122 * Jagan-natha, 134 * Jagan-nuta, 112 *
Jagat-pati, 58, 86, 139 * Jaladharaka, 60 * Jalaja, 60 * Jalandhara-vinasana,
51 * Janaki-vallabha, 76 * Janardana, 75 * Jara-vyadhi-vighataka, 25 *
Jarasandha-kula-dhvamsi, 112 * Jarasandha-vadha, 22 * Jaya, 47 * Jayi,
127 * Jisnu, 56 * Jita-krodha-moha, 19 * Jivana, 81 * Jivanantaka, 81 *
Jnana-darpana-gocara, 130 * Jnana-dayaka, 128 * Jnana-sandhana, 139 *
* Kaivalya-dayaka, 118 * Kala, 59 * Kala-harta, 74 * Kala-purna, 87 *
Kalaksaya, 93 * Kalanka-rahita, 105 * Kalankara-hita, 9 *
Kalapa-kusuma-syama, 135 * Kali, 59 * Kalindi-prema-puraka, 6 *
Kalpa-vrksa, 49 * Kama, 42, 62 * Kama-kala-nidhi, 9 * Kamala-locana, 72
* Kamala-mukha-lolaksa, 5 * Kamala-mukha-lolupa, 33 * Kamala-patraksa,
72 * Kamala-rupa-tat-para, 93 * Kamala-vanchita-prada, 32 *
Kamala-vrata-dhari, 33 * Kamalabha, 33 * Kamalaksa, 33 * Kamali, 33 *
Kamari-bhakta, 42 * Kambalasvatara, 79 * Kambu-griva, 104 * Kami, 9,
72 * Kamsa-mrtyu, 30 * Kamsarati, 112 * Kandarpa-janaka, 122 *
Kandarpa-koti-lavanya, 31 * Kapila, 6 * Karta, 28, 63 * Karuna-nidhi, 20
* Kasyapasya-vara-prada, 46 * Kasyapi, 20 * Katakangada-mandita, 106
* Kati-sutra-virajita, 106 * Kaunteya-priya-bandhu, 124 *
Kauravanvaya-nasana, 124 * Kaveri, 55 * Kavi, 42 * Kedara, 83 * Kesava,
29, 75, 86 * Kesi-ha, 29 * Kesi-kamsa-vadha, 37 * Khadga-dhari, 61 *
Khara-dusana-samhari, 36 * Kili, 73 * Kirita-kundala-dhara, 106 *
Kirtaniya, 112 * Koka-soka-vinasaka, 18 * Kokila-svara-bhusana, 10 *
Kolahala, 20 * Komala, 60, 135 * Kosa-nidhi, 18 *
Koti-manmatha-saundarya, 101 * Krida-kamala-sandoha, 41 * Kridi, 45 *
Krpa-kara, 10 * Krpa-kari, 61 * Krpa-rama, 78 * Krsna, 72, 90 *
Krta-jagat-traya, 45 * Krti, 62, 74 * Krurasura-vibhanjana, 110 *
Ksanavani, 90 * Ksetra-jna, 128 * Ksirabdhi-sayana, 100 *
Kubja-bhagya-prada, 60 * Kubja-vinodi, 30 * Kuhu-bharta, 4 * Kula, 37 *
Kula-grami, 13 * Kumari, 12 * Kuntali, 46 * Kunti-suta-raksi, 46 * *
Laksana, 27 * Laksmana, 27 * Laksmanagraja, 100 * Laksmi-vilasavan, 80
* Laksmivan, 100, 104 * Laksya, 27 * Lalita-candrika-mali, 82 *
Langalasraya, 58 * Languli, 58 * Lankadhipa-kula-dhvamsi, 35 *
Lata-gulma, 54 * Lila, 75 * Lila-kamala-pujita, 40 * Lila-manusa-vigraha,
115 * Loka, 57 * Loka-dharma-jna, 81 * Loka-nandana, 108 *

Vasudevatmaja, 22 * Vata, 74 * Vayu-koti-maha-bala, 32 * Veda-vedya, 87 * Vedanta-vedya, 116 * Vedya-brahmanda-nayaka, 116 * Venu-vada-rata, 136 * Venu-vadya-visarada, 96 * Vibhisana-vara-prada, 35 * Vibhu, 26, 37 * Vidhata, 21 * Vidhi, 21 * Vidhu, 21, 64 * Vidhudaya, 84 * Vidvan, 23 * Vighna-nasana, 76 * Vighna-vighataka, 66 * Vijayi, 23 * Vijna, 66 * Vijnanam, 139 * Vilasi, 80 * Viloka, 57 * Vinyasta-pada-yugala, 107 * Vira, 36, 50, 60 * Vira-bahu, 76 * Vira-patni, 25 * Viradha-vadha-karaka, 48 * Viraha, 23 * Virama, 76 * Viruda, 23 * Visalaksa, 104 * Visnu, 56, 75, 90 * Visva-bharta, 69 * Visva-pujita, 52 * Visvaksena, 121 * Visvamitra-priya, 35 * Visvamurti, 132 * Visvato-mukha, 2 * Vrddha, 67 * Vrddhaka, 67 * Vrnda-natha, 53 * Vrnda-pati, 18 * Vrndapati, 13 * Vrndaraka-jana-priya, 67 * Vrndavana-cara, 96 * Vrndavana-samasraya, 136 * Vrsa, 59 * Vrsabhanu, 20 * Vrsabhanusuta-pati, 39 * Vrsakapi, 59 * Vrsasura-vighataka, 29 * Vyapaka, 138 * Vyasa, 70, 84 * Vyuharcita, 134 * * Yadavendra, 45, 112 * Yadu-vamsi, 50 * Yama, 81 * Yama-vidhayaka, 81 * Yamadi, 81 * Yamalarjuna-mukti-da, 28 * Yamana, 81 * Yami, 81 * Yamuna-tira-sancari, 109 * Yamuna-vara-data, 46 * Yamuna-vega-samhari, 26 * Yasas-trata, 25 * Yasoda-nandana, 28 * Yasoda-vatsala, 91 * Yasoda-yasa, 74 * Yogamaya-samanvita, 128 * Yogesvaresvara, 128 * Yogi, 43 * Yogi-hrt-pankajavasa, 128 * Yogini-vallabha, 56 *

The Glories of the Holy Names

Text 1
atha mähätmyam
iti shri-rädhikä-nätha-
sahasra-näma-kirtanam
smaranät päpa-räshinäm
khandanam mrityu-näshanam

Thus I have spoken the thousand names of Shri Rädhä's master. By remembering these names one breaks into pieces many multitudes of sins. In this way one kills death.

Texts 2-4
vaishnavänäm priya-karam
mahä-roga-niväranam
brahma-hatyä-surä-pänam
para-stri-gamanam tathä

para-dravyapäharanam
para-dvesha-samanvitam
mänasam vächikam käyam
yat-päpam päpa-sambhavam

sahasra-näma-pathanät
sarvam nashyati tat-kshanät
mahä-däridrya-yukto yo
vaishnavo vishnu-bhaktimän

These names delight the Vaishnavas and cure the greatest diseases. When one chants these thousand names his sins of killing brähmanas, drinking wine, adultery, theft, hating others, and all other sins performed with the body, mind, and words, are at once destroyed. By chanting these names one becomes free of great poverty. One becomes a Vaishnava, devoted to Lord Vishnu.

Texts 5 and 6
kärttikyäm sampathed rätrau
shatam ashtottaram kramät
pitämbara-dharo dhimän
sugandhi-pushpa-chandanaih

pustakam pujayitvä tu
naivedyädibhir eva cha
rädhä-dhyänänkito dhiro
vana-mälä-vibhushitah

During an evening in the month of Kärttika a wise devotee of Lord Krishna should chant these names 108 times. With fragrant flowers, sandal paste, foods, and other offerings he should worship the book of these names. He should meditate on Shri Shri Rädhä-Krishna. He should meditate on the Lord decorated with a garland of forest flowers.

Text 7
shatam ashtottaram devi
pathen näma-sahasrakam
chaitra-shukle cha krishne cha
kuhu-sankränti-väsare

On the Kuhü-sankränti day of the bright and dark fortnights of the month of Chaitra (March-April) one should chant these thousand names 108 times.

Text 8
pathitavyam prayatnena
trailokyam mohayet kshanät
tulasi-mälayä yukto
vaishnavo bhakti-tat-parah

With great devotion one should offer Lord Vishnu a tulasi garland and should carefully chant these thousand names. In this way one brings the three worlds under his control.

Texts 9-12
ravi-väre cha shukle cha
dvädashyäm shräddha-väsare
brähmanam pujayitvä cha
bhojayitvä vidhänatah

pathen näma-sahasram cha
tatah siddhih prajäyate
mahä-nishäyäm satatam
vaishnavo yah pathet sadä

deshäntara-gatä lakshmih
samäyäti na samshayah
trailokye cha mahä-devi
sundaryah käma-mohitäh

mugdhäh svayam samäyänti
vaishnavam cha bhajanti tah
rogi rogät pramuchyeta
baddho muchyeta bandhanät

On a Sunday, a bright fortnight, dvädashi, and the shräddha-väsara day one should worship the brähmanas, offer them a feast, and then one should chant these thousand names. In that way one attains perfection. A Vaishnava who regularly chants these names late at night finds that the goddess of fortune comes to his home from far away. Of this there is no doubt. O great goddess, Bewildered with desire, the most beautiful girls in the three worlds voluntarily come and worship him. If he is diseased he becomes free of his disease. If he is imprisoned, he becomes free from prison.

Text 13
gurvini janayet putram
kanyä vindati sat-patim
räjäno vashyatäm yänti
kim punah kshudra-mänaväh

His saintly wife will bear him a son. His daughter will find a good husband. Great kings will become his submissive servants. How much more so will ordinary people serve him?

Text 14
sahasra-näma-shravanät
pathanät pujanät priye
dhäranät sarvam äpnoti
vaishnavo nätra samshayah

O beloved, by hearing, chanting, worshiping, and remembering these thousand holy names a Vaishnava attains everything. Of this there is no doubt.

Texts 15 and 16
vamshivate cänya-vate
tathä pippalake 'thavä
kadamba-päda-patale
gopäla-murti-sannidhau

yah pathed vaishnavo nityam
sa yäti hari-mandiram
krishnenoktam rädhikäyai
mayi proktam purä shive

A Vaishnava who regularly chants these holy names at Vamshivata, under another vata tree, under a pippala tree, under a kadamba tree, or in the presence of the Deity of Lord Gopäla, goes to the transcendental world of Lord Hari. O auspicious one, Lord Krishna spoke these thousand names to Shri Rädhä, and they were also spoken to me.

Text 17
näradäya mayä proktam
näradena prakäshitam
mayä tvayi varärohe
proktam etat su-durlabham

I spoke them to Närada Muni, and then Närada Muni spoke them to others.
O girl with the beautiful thighs, now I have spoken these very rare holy
names to you.

Text 18
gopaniyam prayatnena
na prakäshyam kathanchana
shathäya päpine chaiva
lampatäya visheshatah

Please carefully keep them secret. Never reveal them to a dishonest person,
a sinner, or a rake.

Text 19
na dätavyam na dätavyam
na dätavyam kadächana
deyam shishyäya shäntäya
vishnu-bhakti-ratäya cha

They should never be given to such persons. Never be given. Never be
given. They should be given to a sincere disciple, a peaceful saint, or a
devotee of Lord Vishnu.

Text 20
go-däna-brahma-yajnasya
väjapeya-shatasya cha
ashvamedha-sahasrasya
phalam päthe bhaved dhruvam

A person who chants these holy names attains the result of giving cows in
charity, offering a brahma-yajna, a hundred väjapeya-yajnas, or a thousand
ashvamedha-yajnas.

Text 21
mohanam stambhanam chaiva
maranocchätanädikam
yad yad vänchati chittena
tat tat präpnoti vaishnavah

A Vaishnava who chants these holy names attains the wishes of his heart. If he wishes to bewilder, stun, destroy, ruin, or in another way harm his enemy, he will attain his desire.

Texts 22 and 23
ekädashyäm narah snätvä
sugandhi-dravya-tailakaih
ähäram brähmane dattvä
dakshinäm svarna-bhushanam

tata ärambha-kartäsya
sarvam präpnoti mänavah
shatävrittam sahasram cha
yah pathed vaishnavo janah

A Vaishnava who on ekädashi bathes with fragrant oil, offers a brähmana food and dakshinä of golden ornaments, and then chants these thousand holy names one hundred times attains all his desires.

Text 24
shri-vrindävanachandrasya
prasädät sarvam äpnuyät
yad-grihe pustakam devi
pujitam chaiva tishthati

O goddess, a person who in his home worships the book of these thousand holy names attains everything by the mercy of Lord Vrindävanachandra.

Text 25
na märi na cha durbhiksham
nopasarga-bhayam kvachit
sarpädi-bhuta-yakshädyä
nashyanti nätra samshayah

He does not die. He is not afflicted with poverty. He need not be afraid. Snakes, ghosts, yakshas and others that may try to attack him will perish. Of this there is no doubt.

Text 26
shri-gopälo mahä-devi
vaset tasya grihe sadä
grihe yasya sahasram cha
nämnäm tishthati pujitam

O goddess, Lord Gopäla stays in the home of one who worships these thousand holy names.

CHAPTER SEVENTEEN

The Srimad-Bhagavad-Gita Dhyanam

These are the meditations on Lord Krishna as the source and potency of the *Bhagavad-gita*.

(1)

Om paarthaya pratibodhitaam bhagavata Naaraayanena svayam
Vyaasena grathitaam puraanamuninaa madhye-mahaabhaaratam
Advaitaamritavarshinee bhagavateem ashtaadashaadhyaayineem
Amba tvaamanusandadhami Bhagavad-gita bhavadveshineem

Oh blessed Mother, who showerest (upon us) the nectar of philosophy in the form of (these eighteen) chapters. Thou loving mother, destroyer of rebirth. Bhagavad-gita, upon thee I meditate.

(2)

Namostu te Vyasa vishalabuddhe phullara vindaayata patranetra
Yena tvayaa Bharatataila poornah prajvaalito gyaanamayah pradeepaha

Oh Vyasa, with lotus eyes and mighty intellect, who has lighted the lamp of wisdom filled with the oil of the Mahabharata. Thee we offer our obeisances.

(3)

Prapanna paarijaataaya totravetrai kapaanaye
Gyaanamudraaya Krishnaaya Gitaa-amritduhe namaha

Thou who art the refuge of the (ocean born) Lakshmi. Thou in whose right hand is the shepherd's crook, who art the milker of the divine nectar of the Gita.

(4)
Sarvopanishado gaavo dogdhaa Gopala nandanaha
Paartho vatsah sudheer bhoktaa dugdham gitaamritam mahat

The Upanishads are even as the heard of cows, the son of the cowherd (Krishna) as the milker, Partha (Arjuna) as the sucking calf, and men of purified intellect the drinkers. Of this, the supreme nectar, is the milk of the Gita.

(5)
Vasudevasutam devam kansa chaanoora mardanam
Devaki paramaanandam Krishnam vande jagadgurum

Thou son of Vasudeva (Krishna), destroyer of Kamsa and Chanura, the supreme bliss of (Mother) Devaki, Guru of the worlds, Thee, Oh Krishna, as God, we offer our obeisances.

(6)
Bhishma-drona-tataa jayadrathajalaa gandhaaraneelotpalaa
Shalyagraahavatee kripena vahanee karnena velaakulaa
Ashatthaama-Vikarna-ghora makaraa Duryodhanaa vartinee
Sotteerno khalu Paandavai rananadee Kaivartakah Keshavaha

Of that great river of battle which the Pandavas crossed over, Bhishma and Drona were as the high banks; and Jayadratha as the water of the river; the king of Gandhara the water-lily; Salya as the shark, Kripa as the current; Karna the mighty waves; Asvatthama and Vikarna dread water-monsters; and Duryodhana was the very whirlpool. But thou, Oh Krishna, was the ferryman.

(7)
Paarasharya vachassaroja mamalam Gitaarthagandhotkatam
Naanaakhyaanakakesaram Harikathaa sambhodhanaa bodhitam
Loke sajjana shatpadairaharahah pepeeyamaanam mudaa
Bhooyaada Bhaaratapankajam Kalimalapradhvamsi nah shreyase

This spotless product of words of Vyasa (the compiler of the Mahabharata, of which the Bhagavad-gita is a chapter), this lotus of the Mahabharata, with the Bhagavad-gita, as its strong sweet fragrance, and tales of heroes as its full-blown petals, held ever open. By the talk of Hari, of Him who is the destroyer of the taint of Kali-yuga; this lotus to which come joyously day after day the honey-seeking souls. May this produce in us the highest good!

(8)

Mukam karoti vaachalam pangum langhayate girim
Yatkripaa tamaham vande paramaananda-madhavam

Him whose compassion maketh the dumb man eloquent, and the cripple to cross mountains, Him the all-blissful Madhava, do I offer my obeisances.

(9)

Yam brahmaa-varunendra-rudra-marutah stunvanti divyaih stavaih
Vedaih saangapadakramopanishadair gaayantiyam saamagaaha
Dhyaanaa vasthita tadgatena manasaa pashyanti yam yogino
Yasyaantam na viduh suraasuraganaah devaaya tasmai namaha

To that Supreme One who is bodied forth in Brahma, in Varuna, in Indra, in Rudra and the Maruts; that One whom all Divine beings praise with hymns; Him whom the singers of the Sama Veda tell: Him whose glory the Upanishads and Vedas sing in full choir; Him whom the yogis see, the mind absorbed in perfect meditation; Him of whom all the hosts of Devas and Asuras known not the limitations, to Him the Supreme Good. To Him we offer our obeisances, offer our obeisances, offer our obeisances.

CHAPTER EIGHTEEN

Prayers to Lord Jagannatha, Lord Krishna as Lord of the Universe

Jagannathastaka
(As issued from the mouth of Lord Chaitanya)

kadacit kalindi-tata-vipina-sangitaka-ravo
mudabhiri-nari-vadana-kamalasvada-madhupaha
rama-shambhu-brahmamara-pati-ganesharcita-pado
jagannathah svami nayana-patha-gami bhavatu me

"Sometimes in great happiness Lord Jagannatha, with His flute, makes a loud concert in the groves on the banks of the Yamuna. He is like a bumblebee who tastes the beautiful lotus-like faces of the cowherd damsels of Vraja, and His lotus feet are worshiped by great personalities such as Lakshmi, Shiva, Brahma, Indra and Ganesha. May that Jagannatha Svami be the object of my vision."

bhuje savye venum Shirasi Shikhi-puccham katitate
dukulam netrante sahacara-kataksham vidadhate
sada shrimad-vrindavana-vasati-lila-paricayo
jagannathah svami nayana-patha-gami bhavatu me

"In His left hand Lord Jagannatha holds a flute. On His head He wears the feathers of peacocks and on His hips He wears fine yellow silken cloth. Out of the corners of His eyes He bestows sidelong glances upon His loving devotees and He always reveals Himself through His pastimes in His divine abode of Vrindavana. May that Jagannatha Svami be the object of my vision."

356

mahambhodhes tire kanaka-rucire nila-shikhare
vasan prasadantah sahaja-balabhadrena balina
subhadra-madhya-sthah sakala-sura-sevavasara-do
jagannathah svami nayana-patha-gami bhavatu me

"Residing on the shore of the great ocean, within a large palace situated
upon the crest of the brilliant, golden Nilachala Hill, along with His
powerful brother Balabhadra, and in the middle of Them His sister
Subhadra, Lord Jagannatha bestows the opportunity for devotional service
upon all godly souls. May that Jagannatha Svami be the object of my
vision."

kripa-paravarah sajala-jalada-shreni-ruciro
rama-vani-ramah sphurad-amala-punkeruha-makhaha
surendrair aradhyah shruti-gana-shikha-gita-charito
jagannathah svami nayana-patha-gami bhavatu me

"Lord Jagannatha is an ocean of mercy and He is beautiful like a row of
blackish rain clouds. He is the storehouse of bliss for Lakshmi and
Sarasvati, and His face is like a spotless full-blown lotus. He is worshiped
by the best of demigods and sages, and His glories are sung by the
Upanishads. May that Jagannatha Svami be the object of my vision."

ratharudho gacchan pathi milita-bhudeva-patalaih
stuti-pradurbhavam prati-padam upakarnya sadayaha
daya-sindhur bandhuh sakala-jagatam sindhu-sutaya
jagannathah svami nayana-patha-gami bhavatu me

"When Lord Jagannatha is on His Ratha-yatra cart and is moving along the
road, at every step there is a loud presentation of prayers and songs chanted
by large assemblies of brahmanas. Hearing their hymns Lord Jagannatha is
very favorably disposed towards them. He is the ocean of mercy and the
true friend of all the worlds. May that Jagannatha Svami, along with His
consort Lakshmi, who was born from the ocean of nectar, be the object of
my vision."

para-brahmapidah kuvalaya-dalotphulla-nayano
nivasi niladrau nihita-carano 'nanta-shirasi
rasanando radha-sarasa-vapur-alingana-sukho
jagannathah svami nayana-patha-gami bhavatu me

"He is the ornament of the head of Lord Brahma and His eyes are like the full-blown petals of the lotus. He resides on the Nilachala Hill, and His lotus feet are placed on the heads of Anantadeva. Lord Jagannatha is overwhelmed by the mellows of love and He becomes joyful in the embracing of the body of Srimati Radharani, which is like a cool pond. May that Jagannatha Svami be the object of my vision."

na vai yace rajyam na cha kanaka-manikya-vibhavam
na yace 'ham ramyam sakala-jana-kamyam vara-vadhum
sada kale kale pramatha-patina gita-charito
jagannathah svami nayana-patha-gami bhavatu me

"I do not pray for a kingdom, nor for gold, rubies and wealth. I do not ask for an excellent and beautiful wife as desired by all men. I simply pray that Jagannatha Svami, whose glories are always sung by Lord Shiva, be the constant object of my vision."

hara tvam samsaram drutataram asaram sura-pate
hara tvam papanam vitatim aparam yadava-pate
aho dine 'nathe nihita-charano nishcitam idam
jagannathah svami nayana-patha-gami bhavatu me

"O Lord of the demigods, please quickly remove this useless material existence I am undergoing. O Lord of the Yadus, please destroy this vast ocean of sins which has no shore. Alas, this is certain that Lord Jagannatha's lotus feet are bestowed upon those who feel themselves fallen and have no shelter in this world but Him. May that Jagannatha Svami be the object of my vision."

CHAPTER NINETEEN

Prayers to Lord Chaitanya and Lord Nityananda

This chapter provides beautiful verses to Lord Caitanya, followed by His 108 Names, and then prayers to Lord Nityananda, including the Sri Nityanandastaka (Eight Prayers Glorifying Lord Nityananda), 12 Names of the Moonlike Nityananda Prabhu by Sarvabhauma Bhattacharya, My Most Merciful Nitai, My Lord Nitai is the Jewel of All Transcendental Qualities, The Market Place of the Holy Name, This Holy Name is so Sweet, Sri Nityananda Prabhu Never Gets Angry, My Dear Lord Nitai! Please be Merciful to Me, and The Lotus Feet of Lord Nityananda, Prayers to Nitai.

Prayers to Lord Chaitanya

svardhunyash charu-tire sphuritam ati-brihat-kurma-prishthabha-gatram
ramyaramavritam san-mani-kanaka-mahasadma-sanghaih paritam
nityam pratyalayodyat-pranaya-bhara-lasat-krishna-sankirtanadhyam
shri-vrindatavy-abhinnam tri-jagad-anupamam shri-navadvipam ide

"I praise that holy dham, Navadvipa, which, being entirely nondifferent from Shri Vrindavana, is completely different from the material world consisting of the three planetary systems. It is situated on the gorgeous banks of the Ganges covered by beautiful groves and gardens appearing in form like the back of a gigantic turtle. Situated there are many great palatial houses made of gold bedecked with brilliant jewels, where Krishna-sankirtana is always being performed in the mellow of ecstatic love."

shriman-mauktikadama-baddha-chikuram susmera-chandrananam
shri-khandaguru-charu-chitra-vasanam srag-divya-bhashanchitam
nrityavesha-rasanumoda-madhuram kandarpa-veshojjvalam
caitanyam kanaka-dyutim nija-janaih samsevyamanam bhaje

"I worship Sri Chaitanya Mahaprabhu, who is being served by all His devotees and associates; whose hair is bound with strings of pearls; on whose moonlike face is the nectar of His gentle smile. His beautiful golden body is covered with lovely garments and various shining ornaments. He is so charming, being absorbed as He is in the enjoyment of sweet mellows in dancing, and is more splendid in His dress than even Cupid himself."

yad advaitam brahmopanishadi tad apy asya tanu-bha
ya atmantaryami purusha iti so 'syamsha-vibhavaha
shad-aishvaryaih purno ya iha bhagavan sa svayam ayam
na chaitanyat krishnaj jagati para-tattvam param iha

"What the *Upanishads* describe as the impersonal Brahman is but the effulgence of His body, and the Lord known as the Supersoul is but His localized plenary portion. He is the Supreme Personality of Godhead, Krishna Himself, full with six opulences. He is the Absolute Truth, and no other truth is greater than or equal to Him." (*Caitanya-caritamrita*, Adi-lila 1.3)

anarpita-charim chirat karunayavatirnah kalau
samarpayitum unnatojjvala-rasam sva-bhakti-shriyam
harih purata-sundara-dyuti-kadamba-sandipitaha
sada hridaya-kandare sphuratu vah shacinandanaha

"May that Lord, who is known as the son of Srimati Shacidevi, be transcendentally situated in the innermost chambers of your heart. Resplendent with the radiance of molten gold. He has appeared in the age of Kali by His causeless mercy to bestow what no incarnation ever offered before: the most sublime and radiant spiritual knowledge of the mellow taste of His service." (Cc. Adi, 1.4.)

radha krishna-pranaya-vikritir hladini-shaktir asmad
ekatmanav api bhuvi pura deha-bhedam gatau tau
chaitanyakhyam prakatam adhuna tad-dvayam chaikyam aptam
radha-bhava-dyuti-suvalitam naumi krishna-svarupam

"The loving affairs of Sri Radha and Krishna are transcendental manifestations of the Lord's internal pleasure-giving potency. Although Radha and Krishna are one in Their identity, They have separated Themselves eternally. Now these two transcendental identities have again united in the form of Sri Krishna Chaitanya. I bow down to Him, who has manifested Himself with the sentiment and complexion of Shrimati Radharani although He is Krishna Himself." (Cc.Adi,1.5)

shri-radhayah pranaya-mahima kidrisho vanayaiva-
svadyo yenadbhuta-madhurima kidrisho va madiyaha
saukhyam chasya mad-anubhavatah kidrisham veti lobhat
tad-bhavadhyah samajani shachi-garbha-sindhau harinduhu

"Desiring to understand the glory of Radharani's love, the wonderful qualities in Him that she alone relishes through Her love, and the happiness She feels when She realizes the sweetness of His love, the Supreme Lord Hari, richly endowed with Her emotions, appears from the womb of Srimati Shachidevi, as the moon appears from the ocean." (Cc. Adi. 1.6)

dheyeyam sada paribhava-ghnam abhishta-doham
tirthaspadam shiva-virinchi-mutam sharanyam
bhrilyarti-ham pranata-pala-bhavabdhi-potam
vande mahapurusha te charanaravindam

"O Supreme Personality of Godhead, O protector of the surrendered souls, You are now playing the role of Your own devotee, and Your lotus feet are the only object of perpetual meditation for the pure living entities. They destroy the material existence of the living entity. They are the fulfiller of all desires, the abode of all holy places, worshipable even by Lord Brahma and Lord Shiva, the shelter of all that exists, the destroyer of the troubles of Your devotees and the only boat for crossing over the ocean of material existence. Therefore I offer my obeisances unto Your lotus feet." (*Bhagavatam* 11.5.33)

tyaktva-sudustyaja-surepsita-rajya-laksmim
dharmishtha arya-vachasa yadagad aranyam
maya-mrigam dayitayepsitam anvadhavad
vande mahapurusha te charanaravindam

"O Mahaprabhu, You have given up the goddess of fortune (Lakshmi, Your wife), whose glance is desired by the great demigods, and who is the most difficult attachment to renounce. In order to keep the word of some brahmana's curse, You have gone to the forest. Thus to show Your great mercy to the helpless living entities who are following maya--the illusory energy--You have chased after them to give them Your own devotional service. Therefore I offer my humble obeisances unto Your lotus feet." (*Bhagavatam* 11.5.34)

pancha-tattvatmakam krishnam
bhakta-rupa-svarupakam
bhaktavataram bhaktakhyam
namami bhakta-shaktikam

"I bow down to Lord Krishna, who appears as a devotee (Lord Chaitanya), as His personal expansion (Sri Nityananda), His incarnation (Sri Advaita), His devotee (Sri Srivasa), and His energy (Sri Gadadhara), and who is the source of strength for the devotees." (Cc.Adi.1.14)

ananda-lilamaya-vigrahaya
hemabha-divyach-chavi-sundaraya
tasmai maha-prema-rasa-pradaya
caitanya-chandraya namo namas te

"Obeisances unto Him, Sri Chaitanya-chandra, the giver of the mellow of the highest love of Godhead, who is the embodiment of blissful pastimes, and who is so beautiful, having a dazzling luster, like gold." (*Chaitanya-chandramrita*)

namo maha-vadanyaya
krishna-prema-pradaya te
krishnaya krishna-chaitanya-
namne gaura-tvise namaha

"O most munificent incarnation! You are Krishna Himself appearing as Sri Krishna Caitanya Mahaprabhu. You have assumed the golden color of Srimati Radharani, and You are widely distributing pure love of Krishna. We offer our respectful obeisances unto You." (Cc.Madhya. 19.53)

Sri Gauranga-Ashtottara-Shata-Nama-Stotram
108 Names of Lord Chaitanya
by Sarvabhauma Bhattacharya

1) namaskritya pravaksyami deva-devam jagad-gurum
namnam-ashtotara-shatam caitanyasya mahatmanaha

After offering my respectful obeisances unto the Lord of Lords, Who is the
spiritual master of the entire universe, I will now narrate 108 holy names
of Lord Chaitanya, the great soul.

2) vishvambharo jita-krodho maya-manusha-vigrahaha
amayi mayinam shreshto vara-desho dvijottamaha

Vishvambhara--He sustains the universe
Jita-krodha--He is victorious over the influence of mundane anger
Maya-manusha-vigraha--He assumes the illusory form of a human
Amayi--He is bereft of fraudulent behavior
Mayinam Shresta--He is the foremost of (transcendental) cheaters
Vara-desha--He appears in the best of lands
Dvijottama--He is the ultimate brahmana

3) jagannatha-priya-sutah pitri-bhakto maha-manaha
lakshmi-kantah shachi-putrah premado bhakta-vatsalah

Jagannatha-priya-suta--He is the dearest son of Jagannatha Mishra
Pitri-bhakta–He is the devotee of His father
Maha-mana--He has great mental power
Lakshmi-kanta--He is the beloved husband of the Goddess of Fortune
Shachi-putra--He is the son of mother Shachi
Premada--He is the bestower of ecstatic loving devotion
Bhakta-vatsala--He is very affectionate to His devotees

4) dvija-priyo dvija-varo vaishnava-prana-nayakaha
dvi-jati-pujakah shantah shrivasa-priya ishvaraha

Dvija-priya--He is dear to the twice-initiated brahmanas
Dvija-vara--He is the best amongst the brahmanas
Vaishnava-prana-nayaka--He is the hero of the devotees' life & soul
Dvi-jati-pujaka--He is the worshiper of the brahmanas

Shanta--He is peaceful and saintly
Shrivasa-priya--He is very dear to Srivasa Pandita
Ishvara--He is the supreme controller

5) tapta-kanchana-gaurangah simha-grivo maha-bhujaha
pita-vasa rakta-pattah sad-bhujo 'tha chatur-bhujaha

Tapta-kanchana-gauranga--His complexion is like molten gold
Simha-griva--His neck is like the lion's
Maha-bhuja--His arms are very muscular
Pita-vasa--He wears yellow cloth (when a householder)
Rakta-patta--He wears red cloth (when a sannyasi)
Sad-bhuja--He exhibits a six-armed form [atha--and furthermore]
Chatur-bhuja--He exhibits a four-armed form

6) dvi-bhujash cha gada-panih chakri padma-dharo 'malaha
pancha-janya-dharah sharngi venu-panih surottamaha

Dvi-bhuja--He exhibits a two armed form [ca--and]
Gada-pani--He holds the mace
Chakri--He holds the discus
Padma-dhara--He holds the lotus
Amala--He is sinless
Pancha-janya-dhara--He holds the Panca-janya conchshell
Sharngi--He holds the bow
Venu-pani--He holds the flute
Surottama--He is the foremost of the demigods

7) kamalaksheshvara prito gopa-liladhara yuva
nila-ratna-dharo rupya-hari kaustubha-bhushanaha

Kamalaksheshvara--He is the Lord of the lotus-eyed Lakshmi
Prita--He is beloved to all living beings
Gopa-liladhara--He is the abode of cowherding pastimes
Yuva--He is supremely youthful
Nila-ratna-dhara--He likes to wear sapphires
Rupya-hari--He likes to wear silver necklaces
Kaustubha-bhushana--He is adorned with the Kaustubha gem

8) shrivatsa-lanchano bhasvan-mani-dhrik kanja-lochanaha
tatanka-nila-shrih rudra-lila-kari guru-priyaha

Shrivatsa-lanchana--He is decorated with the mark of Shrivatsa
Bhasvan-mani-dhrik--His form is embellished with many beautiful jewels
Kanja-lochana--He has lotus petal-shaped eyes
Tatanka-nila-shri--His majesty is enhanced by sapphire earrings
Rudra-lila-kari--He sometimes enacts the pastimes of Lord Shiva
Guru-priya--He is very dear to His spiritual master

9) sva-nama-guna-vakta-cha namopadesha-dayakaha
achandala-priyah shuddhah sarva-prani-hite rataha

Sva-nama-guna-vakta--He is aware of the attributes of His own holy name
Namopadesha-dayaka--He imparts teachings about the holy names
Achandala-priya--He is dear even to the lowest outcastes
Shuddha--His character is totally immaculate
Sarva-prani-hite-rata--He is engaged in the welfare of all living beings

10) vishvarupanujah sandhyavatarah shitalashayaha
nihsima-karuno gupta atma-bhakti-pravartakaha

Vishvarupanuja--He is the younger brother of Vishvarupa
Sandhyavatara--He incarnated during the time of dusk
Shitalashaya--He is desirous of cooling the burning sufferings of living
            beings
Nihsima-karuna--His compassion is limitless
Gupta--He is very secretive
Atma-bhakti-pravartaka--He preaches devotion unto the true Self

11) mahanando nato nritya-gita-nama-priyah kavihi
arti-priyah shuchih shuddho bhavado bhagavat-priyaha

Mahananda--He is absorbed in the greatest bliss
Nata--He behaves as a dramatic actor
Nritya-gita-nama-priya--He is fond of dancing, singing & chanting the holy
            names
Kavi--He is a learned scholar and poet
Arti-priya--He is dear to those who are suffering
Shuchi--He is meticulously clean

Shuddha--He is spotlessly pure
Bhavada--He confers ecstatic loving emotions
Bhagavat-priya--He is intimate with the great devotees

12) indradi-sarva-lokesha-vandita-shri-padambujaha
nyasi-chudamanih krishnah sannyasashrama-pavanaha

Indradi-sarva-lokesha-vandita-shri-padambuja--His divine lotus feet are
worshiped by Lord Indra and all the rulers of various heavenly planets
Nyasi-chudamani--He is the crest jewel of renunciates
Krishna--He is the all attractive Supreme Personality of Godhead
Sannyasashrama-pavana--He is the purifier of the renounced order

13) chaitanya krishna-chaitanya danda-dhrig nyasta-dandakaha
avadhuta-priyo nityananda-shad-bhuja-darshakaha

Chaitanya--He is the living force of all creation
Krishna-Chaitanya--He is the all-attractive living force
Danda-dhrik--He carries the staff of the renounced order
Nyasta-dandaka--He abandons the staff of the renounced order
Avadhuta-priya--He is dear to the divine madman (Srila Nityananda
        Prabhu)
Nityananda-sad-bhuja-darshaka--He shows His six-armed form to
        Nityananda

14) mukunda-siddhi-do dino vasudevamrita-pradaha
gadadhara-prana-natha arti-ha sharana-pradaha

Mukunda-siddhi-da--He gives perfection to His devotee Mukunda
Dina--He behaves with meek and humble mannerisms
Vasudevamrita-prada--He gives nectar to this devotee Vasudeva (the leper)
Gadadhara-prana-natha--He is the Lord of the life of Gadadhara Pandita
Arti-ha--He removes the distress of His devotees
Sharana-prada--He bestows ultimate shelter to His devotees

15) akinchana-priyah prano guna-grahi jitendriyaha
adosha-darshi sumukho madhurah priya-darshanaha

Akinchana-priya--He is dear to those who possess nothing
Prana--He is the life and soul of all creation

Guna-grahi--He accepts only the good qualities of others
Jitendriya--He is victorious over the influence of the material senses
Adosha-darshi--He is blind to the faults of others
Sumukha--He has a pleasant face
Madhura--He is supremely sweet
Priya-darshana--He is very precious to behold

16) pratapa-rudra-samtrata ramananda-priyo guruhu
ananta-guna-sampannah sarva-tirthaika-pavanaha

Pratapa-rudra-samtrata--He delivers Maharaja Pratapa Rudra from
        obstacles
Ramananda-priya--He is the beloved of Ramananda Raya
Guru--He is the spiritual master of every living being
Ananta-guna-sampannah--He is endowed with limitless good qualities
Sarva-tirthaika-pavana--He is the sole purifier of all places of pilgrimage

17) vaikuntha-natho lokesho bhaktabhimata-rupa-dhrik
narayano maha-yogi jnana-bhakti-pradah prabhuhu

Vaikuntha-natha--He is the Lord of the spiritual world of no anxiety
Lokesha--He is the Lord of all the material planets
Bhaktabhimata-rupa-dhrik--He assumes different forms according to the
        desires of His devotees
Narayana--He is the supreme shelter for all living beings
Maha-yogi--He is the greatest performer of yoga
Jnana-bhakti-pradah--He imparts intellectual knowledge of devotion
Prabhu--He is the Lord and Master of all

18) piyusha-vachanah prithvi-pavanah satya-vak sahaha
oda-desha-jananandi sandohamrita-rupa-dhrik

Piyusha-vachana--His words emit showers of pure nectar
Prithvi-pavana--He is the savior of the earth
Satya-vak--He speaks truthfully
Saha--He can endure all forms of misery
Oda-desha-jananandi--He delights the people of Orissa
Sandohamrita-rupa-dhrik--He embodies the form of all universal nectar

19) yah pathed pratar utthaya chaitanyasya mahatmanaha
shraddhaya parayopetah stotram sarvagha-nashanam
prema-bhaktir harau tasya jayate natra samshayaha

It is recommended that upon rising in the morning, one faithfully approach and recite this transcendental sin-destroying prayer to Sri Chaitanya Mahaprabhu, the great soul. One who does will feel the awakening of ecstatic loving devotion unto Lord Hari; of this there is no doubt.

20) asadhya-roga-yukto 'pi muchyate roga-sankatat
sarvaparadha-yukto 'pi so 'paradhat pramucyate

Even if one is afflicted with an incurable disease, one becomes freed from all danger of the ailment. Even if one has committed all types of offenses, one becomes freed from their effects.

21) phalguni-paurnamasyan tu chaitanya-janma-vasare
shraddhaya paraya bhaktya maha-stotram japan purch
yad yat prakurute kamam tat tad evachiral labhet

If one chants this great prayer with faith and transcendental devotion on Lord Chaitanya's appearance day (the full moon day in the month of Phalguna), then one perpetually attains the fulfillment of their each and every pure desire.

22) aputro vaishnavam putram labhate natra-samshayaha
ante chaitanya-devasya smritir bhavati shashvati

If a devotee couple wishes to have a child but are unable, then they will obtain a Vaishnava child without a doubt. And at the time of death, they will attain remembrance of Sri Chaitanya-deva and enter His eternal pastimes.

Prayers to Lord Nityananda

nityanandam aham naumi
sarvananda-karam param
hari-nama-pradam devam
avadhuta-shiromanim

"I bow down to the Supreme Lord Nityananda Prabhu, who is the awarder of the highest joy to all, the bestower of the holy name and the crest jewel of all paramahamsa mendicants."

> sankarsanah karana-toya-shayi
> garbhoda-shayi cha payobdhi-shayi
> sheshash cha yasyamsha-kalah sa nitya-
> nandakhya-ramah sharanam mamastu

"May Sri Nityananda Rama be the object of my constant remembrance. Sankarshana, Shesha Naga and the Vishnus who lie on the Karana Ocean [Maha-Vishnu], Garbha Ocean [Garbodakashayi Vishnu] and ocean of milk [Kshirodakashayi Vishnu] are His plenary portions and the portion of His plenary portions." (Cc.Adi.1.7)

> mayatite vyapi-vaikuntha-loke
> purnaishvarye shri-chatur-vyuha-madhyc
> rupam yasyodbhati sankarshanakhyam
> tam shri-nityananda-ramam prapadye

"I surrender unto the lotus feet of Sri Nityananda Rama, who is known as Sankarshana in the midst of the chatur-vyuha (consisting of Vasudeva, Sankarshana, Pradyumna and Aniruddha). He possesses full opulences and resides in Vaikunthaloka, far beyond the material creation." (Cc.Adi.1.8)

> maya-bhartajanda-sanghashrayangaha
> shete sakshat karanambhodhi-madhye
> yasyaikamshah shri-puman adi-devas
> tam shri-nityananda-ramam prapadye

"I offer my full obeisances unto the feet of Sri Nityananda Rama, whose partial representation called Karanodakashayi Vishnu, lying on the Karana Ocean, is the original purusha, the master of the illusory energy, and the shelter of all the universes." (Cc.Adi.1.9)

> yasyamshamsha shrila-garbhoda-shayi
> yan-nabhy-abjam loka-sanghata-nalam
> loka-srashtuh sutika-dhama dhatus
> tam shri-nityananda-ramam prapadye

"I offer my full obeisances unto the feet of Sri Nityananda Rama, a partial part of whom is Garbhodakashayi Vishnu. From the navel of Garbhodakashayi Vishnu sprouts the lotus that is the birthplace of Brahma, the engineer of the universe. The stem of that lotus is the resting place of the multitude of planets." (Cc.Adi.1.10)

> yasyamshamshamshah paratmakhilanam
> poshta vishnur bhati dugdhabdhi-shayi
> kshauni-bharta yat-kala so 'py anantas
> tam shri-nityananda-ramam prapadye

"I offer my respectful obeisances unto the feet of Sri Nityananda Rama, whose secondary part is the Vishnu lying in the ocean of milk. That Kshirodakashayi Vishnu is the Supersoul of all living entities and the maintainer of all the universes. Shesha Naga is His further sub-part." (Cc.Adi.1.11)

> vande shri-krishna-chaitanya-
> nityanandau sahoditau
> gaudodaye pushpavantau
> chitra shandau tamo-nudau

"I offer my respectful obeisances unto Sri Krishna Caitanya and Lord Nityananda, who are like the sun and moon. They have arisen simultaneously on the horizon of Gauda to dissipate the darkness of ignorance and thus wonderfully bestow benediction upon all." (Cc.Adi.1.2.)

> shri-krishna-chaitanya prabhu nityananda
> shri-adwaita gadadhara shrivasadi-gaura-bhakta-vrinda

> Hare Krishna, Hare Krishna, Krishna Krishna, Hare Hare
> Hare Rama, Hare Rama, Rama Rama, Hare Hare

Sri-Nityanandastaka
Eight Prayers Glorifying Lord Nityananda
by Srila Vrndavana dasa Thakura
(Translations by Srila Gour Govinda Svami)

TEXT 1
sarac-candra-bhrdntim sphurad-amala-kantim gaja-gatim
hari-premonmattam dhrta-parama-sattvam smita-mukham
sadaghurnan-netram kara-kalita-vetram kali-bhidam
bhaje nityanandam bhajana-taru-kandam niravadhi

Sri Nityananda Prabhu's face is more beautiful and cooling than the autumnal moon. The effulgence coming out from His body is supremely beautiful. He always moves like a mad elephant, since He is always intoxicated with krsna-prema (love of God). He is always mad after krsna-prema. His body is completely pure spiritual energy. He always has a smiling face. His eyes are very fickle, moving to and fro. His lotus hand always holds a glowing staff. Yes, that is Sri Nityananda, who by the beating of that staff, destroys all our reactions of Kali-yuga. We should take shelter of Sri Nityananda and cry for the mercy of Sri Nityananda! He is the root of krsna-prema bhakti-kalpa-taru, the root of the tree of loving devotion unto Krsna. I do my bhajana of Lord Nityananda, the very root of the krsna-bhakti-vrksa.

TEXT 2
rasanam agaram svajana-gana-sarvasvam atulam
tadiyaika-prana-pramita-vasudha-jahnava-patim
sada-premonmadam param aviditam manda-manasam
bhaje nityanandam bhajana-taru-kandam niravadhi

Sri Nityananda Prabhu is the reservoir of all transcendental mel-lows. He is the life and soul of all the devotees. Nobody can compare to Him in all the three planetary systems. He is very dear to one and all. He is the beloved husband of Sri Vasudha and Sri Jahnava. He is always in an ecstatic mood of love! Always maddened and intoxicat-ed with that mellow of love, krsna-prema. He is unknown to crooked and evil-minded persons. I do my bhajana of Lord Nityananda, the very root of the krsna-bhakti-vrksa.

TEXT 3

sacl-sunu-prestham nikhila-jagad-istam sukha-mayam
kalau majjaj-jivoddharana-karanodddma-karunam
harer dkhydndd vd bhava-jaladhi-garvonnati-haram
bhaje nitydnandam bhajana-taru-kandam niravadhi

Lord Nityananda is very dear to Sriman Gaurahga Mahaprabhu. He always does good to the whole universe. He is always supremely bliss-ful. He is the embodiment of supreme happiness and blissfulness. He comes to this material world in this Kali-yuga to deliver the sinful persons. There is no limit to His mercy. He constantly does nama-sankirtana, (congregational chanting of the Lord's holy names) destroying the pride of this dreadful ocean of material existence. I do my bhajana of Lord Nityananda, the very root of the krsna-bhakti-vrksa.

TEXT 4

aye bhratar ninam kali-kalusinam kim nu bhuvita
tatha prayascittam racaya yad-anayasata ime
vrajanti tvam ittham saha bhagavata mantrayati yo
bhaje nityanandam bhajana-taru-kandam niravadhi

Lord Nityananda tells Sriman Gauranga Mahaprabhu, "0 brother, what will happen to those most distressed and fallen jivas of Kali-yuga? What will happen to them unless You shower Your mercy on them? Please show them a way for their deliverance by which they can approach and get Your lotus feet." He always talks to Sriman Mahaprabhu like this. I do my bhajana of Lord Nityananda, the very root of the krsna-bhakti-vrksa.

TEXT 5

yathestham re bhratah kuru hari-hari-dhvanam anisam
tato vah samsarambudhi-tarana-dayo mayi laget
idam bahu-sphotair atati ratayan yah pratigrham
bhaje nityanandam bhajana-taru-kandam niravadhi

Lord Nityananda goes to every doorstep and requests everyone with folded hands, "0 my dear brothers, all of you engage yourselves in the chanting of hari-nama (chanting the holy names of Hari). If you do this and follow My instruction, I promise that you will very easily cross over this dreadful ocean of material existence." I do my bhajana of Lord Nityananda, the very root of the krsna-bhakti-vrksa.

TEXT 6

balat samsarambhonidhi-harana-kumhhodbhavam aho
satam sreyah-sindhunnati-kumuda-bandhum samuditam
khala-sreni-sphurjit-timira-hara-surya-prabham aham
bhaje nityanandam bhajana-taru-kandam niravadhi

Like Agastya Muni, who by drinking a handful of water made all
the oceans dry up, He forcibly swallows the ocean of repeated birth and
death. He arose like a moon to swell up the ocean of mercy for the welfare
of the jivas. He very easily destroys the sinful reactions of the most sinful
degraded persons. He is very dear to the devotees. He is always busy doing
good to the devotees. He is like the sun that dis-pels the darkness of the
ignorant fools which descended by their sin-ful activities. I do my bhajana
of Lord Nityananda, the very root of the krsna-bhakti-vrksa.

TEXT 7

natantam gayantam harim anuvadantam pathi pathi
vrajantam pasyantam svam api na dayantam janu-ganam
prakurvantam santam sa-karuna-drg-antam prakalanad
bhaje nityanandam bhajana-turu-kandam niravadhi

He is always dancing and chanting, "Haribol! Haribol!" Uttering
the name of Hari. He always engages in hari-nama-sankirtana. He always
wanders on the streets of every city, town, and village casting His merciful
glance over His dear devotees. I do my bhajana of Lord Nityananda, the
very root of the krsna-hhakti-vrksa.

TEXT 8

su-bibhranam bhratuh kara-sarasijam komalataram
mitho vaktralokocchalitu-paramananda-hridayam
bhramantam madhuryair ahaha madayantam pura-janan
bhaje nityanandam bhajana-taru-kandam niravadhi

He moves with Sri Gauranga Mahaprabhu holding His very soft
lotus-like palm. He always looks at the moon-like beautiful face of Sri
Gauracandra and becomes ecstatic and blissful! And Sriman Gauranga
Mahaprabhu also looks at the moon-like, beautiful face of Sri Nitai. In this
way, the two of Them are completely filled with blissfulness. He always
makes all the inhabitants of the towns and cities wherever He goes mad

with the intoxication of His beauty. I do my bhajana of Lord Nityananda, the very root of the krsna-bhakti-vrksa.

TEXT 9
rasanam adharam rasika-vara-sad-vaisnava-dhanam
rasagaram saram patita-tati-taram smaranataha
param nityanandastakam idum apurvam pathati yah
tad-anghri-dvandvabjam sphuratu nitaram tasya hridaye

Srila Vrindavana dasa Thakura says, "Whoever reads and recites with firm faith this Sri Nityanandastakam, will have the lotus feet of Sri Nityananda Prabhu soon revealed to him. These eight verses are the essence of bhakti-rasa. They are the life and soul of all rasika-bhaktas and the reservoir of all mellows. Lord Nityananda is the essence of the universe, the three planetary systems, and by His remembrance, the sinful reactions of all sinful persons are destroyed."

12 Names of the Moonlike Nityananda Prabhu
by Sarvabhauma Bhattacharya

One who recites these 12 auspicious holy names of the moonlike Nityananda-chandra everyday between 6 - 8.30 a.m. will become free from all difficulties, and attain all his most cherished desires. Very soon he will receive the mercy of Shri Chaitanya-deva.

nityanando 'vadhutendur, vasudha-prana-vallabhah
jahnavi-jivita-patih, krishna-prema-pradah prabhu

Shri Nityananda Prabhu is the embodiment of eternal bliss. He is the moon of all avadhutas, and the beloved of the life-breath of Vasudha (his wife). Lord Nityananda is the husband enthusing Jahnavi with life. Nityananda Rama bestows ecstatic love for Krishna, and He is the Lord and Master of the devotees.

padmavati-sutah shriman, shaci-nandana-purvajah
bhavonmatto jagat-trata, rakta-gaura-kalevarah

Shri Nityananda is the dear son of Padmavati, and He is full of splendrous transcendental majesty. Nitai is the older brother of Shacimata's son Nimai. Nityananda Avadhuta is maddened in overwhelming ecstatic emotions. Shri Nityananda Prabhu is the savior of the universe. His complexion is golden tinged with red.

Nitai Amardayar Avadhi
My Most Merciful Nitai
By Srila Vrndavana dasa Thakura

are bhai! nitai amar doyara avadhi!
jivere karuna kori,' dese dese phiri' phiri'
prema-dhana jache nirabadhi
adwaitera sange ranga, dharane na jaya anga,
gora-preme gada tanu khani
dhuliya dhuliya chale, bahu tuli' hari bole,
du-nayane bahe nitaiera pani

kapale tilaka sobhe, kutila-kuntala-lole
gunjara antuni chuda taya

kesarijiniya kati, kati tate niladhati
bajana nupura ranga paya

bhubana-mohana besa! majaila sava desa!
rasd bese atta atta hasa!
prabhu mora nityananda kevala ananda-kanda
guna gaya vrindavana dasa

TRANSLATION
1. 0 Brothers! My Nitai's mercy is limitless. He wanders village to village giving prema-dhana (the mood of love of God) to one and all.

2. He always cuts jokes with Sri Advaita Acarya. His whole body is made of love for Gauranga Mahaprabhu. He is always intoxicated with prema-rasa. An intoxicated person is unable to walk properly. How does He walk? Like that: dhuliya dhuliya chale. Raising His arms and saying, "Haribol! Haribol! Haribol!" and shedding tears from His two lotus eyes.

3. Nice tilaka and curly locks beautifully decorate His forehead. His hair is bound up with red gunja. A blue belt encircles His lion-like waist. His feet look red. He wears nupura on his reddish feet always making a tinkling, tinkling sound.

4. His beauty enchants the whole world. Always absorbed in prema-rasa, He smiles and laughs! —Atta atta hasa! Vrindavana dasa sings, "Lord Nityananda Prabhu is my Prabhu (master). He's full of nothing but pleasure."

Nitai Guna-Mani Amara
My Lord Nitai is the Jewel of all Transcendental Qualities
By Srila Locana dasa Thakura

nitai guna-mani amara, nitai guna-mani
aniya premera banya bhasailo avani

premera banya loiya nitai aila gauda-dese
dubilo bhakata-gana dina hina bhase

dina hina patita pamara nahi bachhe
brahmara durlabha prema sabakare jache

abaddha karuna-sindhu katiya muhana
ghare ghare bule prema-amiyara bana

lochan bole hena nitai jeba na bhajilo
janiya suniya sei atma-ghati hoilo

TRANSLATION
It is said that Srila Nityananda Prabhu is more merciful, more magnanimous, more munificent than Sriman Gauranga (Sri Caitanya) Mahaprabhu.

1. My Nitai is the jewel of transcendental qualities, the jewel of transcendental qualities. Bringing the flood of prema, He inundated the earth.

2. Sri Nitai came to Gauda-desa with a flood of krishna-prema. dubilo bhakata-gana dina hind bhase, those who are bhaktas drowned in that flood, premera banya. But the dina hina, the fallen souls and unfortunate, floated on the surface!

3. Lord Nityananda Prabhu offers this pure love of Godhead, pure love of Krishna indiscriminately. He distributes this prema with two hands! He never discriminates whether one is patita or pamara: most degraded, most fallen or most elevated, qualified or not qualified. He never

discriminates. Even it is very difficult for Brahma to get such prema. But Sri Nitai gives indiscriminately.

4. That prema is karuna-sindhu—like an ocean of mercy. Nitai broke down the strong embankment of the ocean of love. Completely devastated that dam! That ocean of love is an unlimited ocean of love. So then there was a heavy rush flowing, heavy rush! Such a flood came. A flood in every home. That flood came to every home. It inundated the whole world!

5. Locana says, "He is an unfortunate fellow who does not take shelter of Nitai and does not do the bhajana of Sri Nityananda Prabhu, begging for the mercy of Sri Nitai. He willingly commits suicide.

Sri Nagar Kirtana
The Market Place of the Holy Name
By Srila Bhaktivinoda Thakura

nadiya-godrume nityananda mahajana
patiyache nam-hatta jivera karana

(sraddhavan jana he, sraddhavan jana he)
prabhura ajnay, bhai, magi ei bhiksha
bolo krsna, bhajo krsna, koro krsna-shiksa

aparadha-shunya ho 'ye leha krsna-nama
krsna mata, krsna pita, krsna dhana-prana

krsnera samsara koro chadi anacara
jive doya, krsna-nama-sarva-dharma-ssra

TRANSLATION

1. Nityananda Mahajana so mercifully opened a marketplace in Nadiya-Godruma for the welfare of the suffering souls. In that market place only the Holy Name is traded.

2. What is the price? sraddhavana jana he! sraddhavana jana he! Those who have faith in the Holy Name and faith in the words of sadhu, sastra, guru. This is the price! Faith! Only those persons are allowed to enter that marketplace. They can buy and sell the Holy Name. Sri Nityananda Prabhu requests the faithful persons, those who have developed faith in the Holy Name, to come and take it! Sri Nityananda Prabhu says,

'This is the order of My Lord! My Prabhu! My Master! Therefore I have come to your doorstep, 0 brother! I am a beggar! I beg for these alms. 'Utter the name of Krsna! Do krsna-bhajana! Accept what Krsna has taught us!' These are the alms I am begging from you.

3. Chant this Holy Name without offense. Chant the pure Name of Sri Krishna. Sri Krishna is Mother, Sri Krishna is Father, Sri Krishna is wealth and asset. Sri Krishna is the Lord of my heart, Sri Krishna is life and soul, Krishna is everything.

4. Give up all your bad dealings, habits, and behavior and enter into krsna-samsara. The only relationship is with Sri Krishna, establish yourself in that relationship. Shower mercy on all the jivas seeing them as Sri Krishna's and completely surrender unto the Holy Name of Sri Krishna. This is the essence of all dharma.

Madhura E Harinama
This Holy Name is So Sweet
By Srila Bhaktivinoda Thakura

hare krsna hare
nitai ki nam eneche re
(nitai) nam eneche, namer hate
sraddha-mulye nam diteche re
hare krsna hare krsna krsna krsna hare hare re
hare rama hare rama rama rama hare hare re
(nitai) jiver dasa malina dekhe',
nam eneche braja theke re

e nam siva jape pancha-mukhe re
(madhur e harinam)

e nam brahma jape catur-mukhe re
(madhur e harindm)

e nam narada jape bina-jantre re
(madhur e harindm)

e nama base ajamilo vaikunthe gelo re
e nam bolte bolte braje calo re
(bhaktivinoda bole)

TRANSLATION

Sri Sri Gaura-Nitai (Lord Chaitanya and Lord Nityananda) are so wonderfully merciful. They brought this harinama from Goloka-Vrndavana. Golokera prema-dhana hari-nama sankirtana. It doesn't belong to this material world. Sri Sri Gaura-Nitai brought it here because they are so wonderfully merciful. Who is the custodian of nam-hatta? Sri Nitai! Nama-hatta means market-place. A market-place where the (holy) name is sold and purchased. What is the price? The price is unflinching faith. He who has strong faith, unflinching faith in the Holy Name and faith in the words of sadhu, sastra, Sri Guru and Sri Krishna, only he can purchase it. The market is always eternally open.

hare krsna hare krsna krsna krsna hare hare re
hare rama hare rama rama rama hare hare re

Sri Nitai is more merciful than Sriman Gauranga Mahaprabhu. Sri Gaurasundara (Lord Chaitanya) is wonderfully merciful. Sri Nitai is more merciful than Sri Gaurasundara. Sri Nitai is so merciful. He saw that the jivas have been suffering here, drowning in this ocean of materialistic existence from time immemorial. His heart bleeds, so Sri Nitai felt love, affection and compassion for them. He became sympathetic for the suffering souls, so He brought the Holy Name from Sri Vrajabhumi for those Kali-yuga people.

Lord Sivaji with His five faces is chanting this madhura e harinama; this is so sweet this harinama! Lord Brahma chants this Sri-nama with His four faces, because it is so sweet!

Sri Narada Muni sings this Holy Name with his stringed instrument,

hare krsna hare krsna krsna krsna hare hare
hare rama hare rama rama rama hare hare

All are chanting because it is so sweet!

Srila Bhaktivinoda Thakura says, "By only obtaining the namabhasa stage (offenseless chanting), Ajamila, a greatly sinful person was delivered. All his sinful reactions were destroyed, then at last he went to Vaikuntha!" So Srila Bhaktivinoda Thakura says, "Just chant this Name, utter this Holy Name and go to Sri Vrajabhumi."

Akrodha Paramananda Nityananda Raya
Sri Nityananda Prabhu Never Gets Angry
By Srila Locana dasa Thakura

akrodha paramananda nityananda raya
abhimana shunya nitai nagare bedaya

adhama patita jivera dware dware giya
harinama maha mantra dena bilaiya

jare dekhe tare kahe dante trina dhori'
amare kiniya laha bhaja gaurahari

eta boli' nityananda bhume gadi jaya
sonara parvata jena dhulate lotaya

hena avatare jara rati na janmilo
locana bole sei papi elo ara gelo

TRANSLATION
1. Lord Nityananda Raya never gets angry. He is always in ecstasy, supreme bliss. He has no false ego. He wanders to every town and village in Nadia chanting Hare Krishna, dancing, and offering krishna-prema (love of Krishna) to everyone indiscriminately.

2. Sri Nitai goes to every doorstep and knocks on the door, 'Tap! Tap! Tap!' He goes to those who are very much distressed, degraded, and fallen. He goes to them and gives them krishna-prema. He says, "Please Chant! Please Chant! ": Hare Krishna, Hare Krishna, Krishna Krishna, Hare Hare / Hare Rama, Hare Rama, Rama Rama, Hare Hare. If they do not chant and shut the door, then He rolls there on the ground and cries!

3. Whomever He meets, catching a straw between His teeth, He begs, "0 Brothers! Please do the bhajana of Sri Gaurahari and purchase Me, purchase Me, purchase Me."

4. Saying this, Lord Nityananda rolls on the ground in the dust, cries, and sheds tears, looking like a mountain of gold rolling on the ground.

5. Such a merciful incarnation is Lord Nityananda. If someone doesn't develop love for such an incarnation as Sri Nityananda-Rama, Lochana says, "Such a sinful person wastes his life, remaining in the cycle of birth and death. He cannot be delivered."

Doya Koro More Nitai
My Dear Lord Nitai! Please Be Merciful To Me
By Srila Kanu Ramadasa Thakura

Doya koro more nitai, doya koro more
agatira gati nitai sadhu loke bole

jaya prema bhakti data-pataka tomara
uttama adhama kichhu na kaila bichara

prema dane jagajanera mana kaila sukhi
tumi hena doyara thakura ami kene dukhi

kanu rama dasa bole ki boliba ami
e bada bharasa more kulera thakura tumi

TRANSLATION
1. 0 my Nitai, please shower your mercy on me. All sadhus say, "You are so merciful. You give the right destination to the fallen souls."

2. Lord Nityananda has a flag. That flag gives prema-bhakti. He never discriminates whether one is uttama or adhama, most elevated or most degraded. He gives prema-bhakti to one and all.

3. Sri Nityananda Prabhu gives prema to one and all and makes the whole world happy. You are such a merciful Thakura, why am I so unhappy?

4. Kanu Ramadasa says, "What more shall I say? 0 Lord Nityananda, You are the Lord of our parampara; so this is a great hope for me, that You are such a merciful Lord."

Nitai-Pada-Kamala
The Lotus Feet of Lord Nityananda
By Srila Narottama dasa Thakura

nitai-pada-kamala, koti-chandra-susitala,
je chayay jagatu juray
heno nitai bine bhai, radha-krsna paite nai,
dridha kori' dharo nitair pay

se sambandha nahi ja'r, britha janma gelo ta'r,
se pashu bodo durachara
nitai na bolilo mukhe, majilo samsara-sukhe,
vidya-kule ki koribe tara

ahankare matta hoiya, nitai-pada pasariya,
asatyere satya kori mani
nitaiyer karuna habe, braje radha-krsna pabe,
dharo nitai-charana du'khani

nitaiyer carana satya, tanhara sevaka nitya,
nitai-pada sada koro asha
narottama bodo dukhi, nitai more koro sukhi,
rakho ranga-charanera pasha

Translation

1. The lotus feet of Sri Nityananda are as cool as millions of moons. The whole universe gets peace by the shade of those lotus feet. Without the mercy of Sri Nityananda, nobody can get Radha and Krishna, the aim of human life. Therefore, catch hold of the two lotus feet of Sri Nityananda Prabhu very tightly.

2. One who has not established a relationship with Sri Nityananda is a two-legged animal. A great beast! His whole life is finished. He cannot be called a human being. He never utters the name of Sri Nityananda. He is always immersed in enjoying material happiness and has forgotten Sri Nitai. He may have acquired all material scholarship and learning, but what is the value of such education? This will never help.

3. They are so puffed up with their mundane education and scholarship. They are never humble at all. They have forgotten the lotus feet of Sri Nitai because of their false ego and pride. They are completely under the clutches of Maya. They accept the untruth as truth. If Sri Nityananda showers His mercy upon someone, he will get Sri Sri Radha Krishna in Vrajabhumi. So catch hold of the two lotus feet of Lord Nityananda very tightly.

4. The lotus feet of Sri Nityananda are eternally true. And those followers or servants of those lotus feet of Sri Nityananda are also eternal. Always aspire for the lotus feet of Sri Nityananda. Srila Narottama dasa Thakura says, "I am very distressed, and an unhappy person. I am drowning in this dreadful ocean of material existence. O Sri Nityananda Prabhu, please make me very happy! Please keep me at Your lotus feet."

Prayers to Nitai

isad-arunya-svarnabham nanalankara-bhusitam
hainam malinam divyopavitam prema-varshinam
aghurnita-locanam cha nilambara-dharam prabhum
prema-dam paramanandam nityanandam smaramy aham

I meditate on Lord Nityananda Prabhu, supreme bliss personified. For bestowing pure love of God, he has created a shower of that love. His body, shining with the luster of red-tinged gold, is decorated with various ornaments and a necklace. Donned in blue garments, he wears a flower garland and divine sacred thread.

suddha-svarna-vidambi-sundara-tanum ratnadi-bhushañchitam
premonmatta-gajendra-vikrama-lasat-premasru-dharakulam
suklam sukshma-navambaradi-dadhatam sankirtanaika-priyam
nityanandam aham bhaje sa-karunam premarnavam sundaram

I worship Lord Nityananda, who is the beautiful ocean of prema endowed with compassion and the sole lover of sankitana. His handsome bright form, dressed in fresh fine clothes and decorated with ornaments like precious jewels, derides the glow of pure gold. Possessing the prowess of an intoxicated regal elephant and mad in pure love of God, Lord Nityananda is filled with the streams of tears shed out of that love.

vidyud-dama-madabhimardana-rucim vistirna-vakshah-sthalam
premodghurnita-locanachala-lasat-smerabhiramyananam
nana-bhushana-bhushitam su-madhuram bibhrad-ghanabhambaram
sarvananda-karam param pravara-nityananda-chandram bhaje

I worship the transcendental moon of the foremost Lord Nityananda, who, being exquisitely sweet, makes everyone blissful. His effulgence defeats the pride of a string-like lightning. His chest is broad and his face extremely pleasing with its shining smile, and its eyes, restless out of pure love of God, making sidelong glances. He wears garments resembling a rain cloud and is adorned with various ornaments. ?

— Translated by Nityananda Das from Sri Manohara Bhajana Dipika, published by Sri Sudhasindhu Das. Govardhan.

CHAPTER TWENTY

The Thousand Names of Lord Balarama

This includes chapters 13, and 9 - 12 from the *Garga-samhita*, which are *Sri Balabhadra Sahasra-nama* (The Thousand Names of Lord Balarama), *Sri Rama-rasa-krida* (Lord Balarama's Rasa Dance), *Sri Balarama-paddhati-patala* (The Paddhati and Patala of Lord Balarama), *Sri Balabhadra-stava-raja* (The King of Prayers to Lord Balarama), and *Sri Balabhadra-stotra-kavaca* (The Prayer and Armor of Lord Balarama).

Sri Balabhadra-sahasra-näma
A Thousand Names of Lord Balaräma
The Balarama Pranams

namas te halagraha
namas te musalayudha
namas te revati-kanta
namas te bhakta-vatsala

namas te dharani-dhara
namas te balanam srestha
pralambare namas te 'stu
ehi mam krsna-purvaja

From *Garga-samhita* Canto 8: Chapter Thirteen

Text 1
duryodhana uvaca
balabhadrasya devasya
pradvipaka maha-mune
namnam sahasram me bruhi
guhyam deva-ganair api

384

Duryodhana said: O great sage Pradvipaka, please tell me the thousand names of Lord Balarama, names kept secret from even the demigods.

Text 2
sri-pradvipaka uvaca
sadhu sadhu maha-raja
sadhu te vimalam yasah
yat prcchase param idam
gargoktam deva-durlabham

Sri Pradvipaka said: Well done! Well done! Well done! O king, your fame is spotless. Your question has been answered by Garga Muni in words rarely heard by even the demigods.

Text 3
namnam saharsam divyanam
vaksyami tava cagratah
gargacaryena gopibhyo
dattam krsna-tate subhe

I will tell you Lord Balarama's thousand transcendental names, names that Garga Muni gave to the gopis on the beautiful bank of the Yamuna.

Text 4
om asya sri-balabhadra-sahasra-nama-stotra-mantrasya gargacarya rsih
anustup
chandah sankarsanah paramatma devata balabhadra iti bijam revatiti
saktih
ananta iti kilakam balabhadra-prity-arthe jape viniyogah.

Om. Of the mantra-prayer of the thousand names of Lord Balarama the sage is Garga Muni, the meter is anustup, the Deity is Lord Balarama, the Supreme Personality of Godhead, the bija is Balabhadra, the sakti is Revati, the kilaka is Ananta, and the purpose of chanting the names is the pleasure of Lord Balarama.

Text 4 (b)
atha dhyanam
sphurad-amala-kiritam kinkini-kankanarham
calad-alaka-kapolam kundala-sri-mukhabjam

tuhina-giri-manojnam nila-meghambaradhyam
hala-musala-visalam kama-palam samide

Meditation
I glorify Lord Balarama, decorated with a glittering crown, bracelets, tinkling ornaments, moving locks of hair on His cheeks, splendid earrings on His handsome lotus face, and garments dark like monsoon clouds, holding a great club and plow, fulfilling all desires, and handsome like a mountain of ice and snow.

Text 5
om balabhadro ramabhadro
ramah sankarsano 'cyutah
revati-ramano devah
kama-palo halayudhah

Om. Lord Balarama is supremely powerful and happy (balabhadra), the supreme enjoyer (ramabhadra and (rama), all-attractive (sankarsana), infallible (acyuta), the lover of Revati (revati-ramana), the splendid Supreme Personality of Godhead (deva), the Lord who fulfills desires (kama-pala), and He who carries a plow-weapon (halayudha).

Text 6
nilambarah sveta-varno
baladevo 'cyutagrajah
pralambaghno maha-viro
rauhineyah pratapavan

He is dressed in blue garments (nilambara), fair-complexioned (sveta-varna), splendid and powerful (baladeva), the elder brother of the infallible Supreme Personality of Godhead (acyutagraja), the killer of Pralamba (pralambaghna), a great hero (maha-vira), the son of Rohini (rauhineya), and very powerful (pratapavan).

Text 7
talanko musali hali
harir yadu-varo bali
sira-panih padma-panir
lagudi venu-vadanah

He bears the insignia of a palm tree (talanka), holds a club (musali), holds a plow (hali), takes away all that is inauspicious (hari), is the best of the Yadus (yadu-vara), is powerful (bali), holds a plow in His hand (sira-pani), has lotus hands (padma-pani), holds a club (lagudi), and plays the flute (venu-vadana).

Text 8
kalindi-bhedano viro
balah prabalah urdhvagah
vasudeva-kalanantah
sahasra-vadanah svarat

He divided the Yamuna (kalindi-bhedana). He is a heroic (vira), powerful (bala, and prabala), exalted (urdhvaga), a plenary expansion of Lord Krsna (vasudeva- Skala), and limitless (ananta), has a thousand heads (sahasra-vadana), and is independent (svarat).

Text 9
vasur vasumati-bharta
vasudevo vasuttamah
yaduttamo yadavendro
madhavo vrsni-vallabhah

He is opulent (vasu), the goddess of fortune's husband (vasumati-bharta), the son of Vasudeva (vasudeva), the best of the Vasus (vasuttama), the best of the Yadavas (yaduttama), the king of the Yadavas (yadavendra), the goddess of fortune's husband (madhava), and dear to the Vrsnis (vrsni-vallabha).

Text 10
dvarakeso mathureso
dani mani maha-manah
purnah puranah purusah
paresah paramesvarah

He is the king of Dvaraka (dvarakesa), the king of Mathura (mathuresa), generous (dani), noble (mani), noble-hearted (maha-mana), perfect (purna), the ancient Supreme Personality of Godhead (purana), the Supreme Person (purusa), the Supreme Master (paresa), and the Supreme Controller (paramesvara).

Text 11
paripurnatamah saksat
paramah purusottamah
anantah sasvatah seso
bhagavan prakrteh parah

He is the perfect Supreme Personality of Godhead (paripurnatama), the Supreme Personality of Godhead directly (saksat-parama), the Supreme Person (purusottama), limitless (ananta), eternal (sasvata), Lord Sesa (sesa), the supremely opulent Lord (bhagavan), and beyond the world of matter (prakrteh para).

Text 12
jivatma paramatma ca
hy antaratma dhruvo 'vyayah
catur-vyuhas catur-vedas
catur-murtis catus-padah

He is the father of all living entities (jivatma), the Supersoul present in everyone's heart (paramatma and antaratma), eternal (dhruva), imperishable (avyaya), the origin of the catur-vyuha expansions (catur-vyuha), the author of the four Vedas (catur-veda), the origin of the catur-vyuha (catur-murti), and the master of the four worlds (catus-pada).

Text 13
pradhanam prakrtih saksi
sanghatah sanghavan sakhi
maha-mana buddhi-sakhas
ceto 'hankara avrtah

He is pradhana (pradhana), prakrti (prakrti), the witness (saksi), accompanied by His associates (sanghata, sanghavan, and sakhi), noble-hearted (maha-mana), and the best counselor (buddhi-sakha). He is consciousness (ceta), and ego (ahankara). He is accompanied by His associates (avrta).

Text 14
indriyeso devatatma
jnanam karma ca sarma ca
advitiyo dvitiyas ca
nirakaro niranjanah

He is the master of the senses (indriyesa), the Supreme Personality of Godhead (devata), the Supersoul (atma), knowledge (jnana), action (karma), auspiciousness (sarma), one without a second (advitiya), different from the individual living entities (dvitiya), a person whose form is not material (nirakara), and not touched by matter (niranjana).

Text 15
virat samrat mahaughas ca
dharah sthasnus carisnuman
phanindrah phani-rajas ca
sahasra-phana-manditah

He is the entire universe (virat), the supreme monarch (samrat), a great flood (mahaugha), the maintainer of all (dhara), unmoving (sthasnu), going everywhere (carisnuman), the king of serpents (phanindra, and phani-raja), and the serpent with a thousand hoods (sahasra-phana-mandita).

Text 16
phanisvarah phani sphurtih
phutkari citkarah prabhuh
mani-haro mani-dharo
vitali sutali tali

He is the king of serpents (phanisvara, and phani), the Supreme Personality of Godhead who has appeared in the material world (sphurti), a hissing serpent (phutkari, and citkara), the supreme master (prabhu), and decorated with a jewel necklace (mani-hara, and mani-dhara). He resides in Vitalaloka (vitali), Sutalaloka (sutali), and Talaloka (tali).

Text 17
atali sutalesas ca
patalas ca talatalah
rasatalo bhogitalah
sphurad-danto mahatalah

He resides in Atalaloka (atali), and is the king of Sutalaloka (sutalesa). He resides in Patalaloka (patala), Talatalaloka (talatala), and Rasatalaloka (rasatala). He has great hoods (bhogitala), and glittering fangs (sphurad-danta). He resides on Mahatalaloka (mahatala).

Text 18
vasukih sankhacudabho
devadatto dhananjayah
kambalasvo vegataro
dhrtarasto maha-bhujah

He is Vasuki (vasuki). He is splendid like a conch-jewel (sankhacudabha), is the benefactor of the demigods (devadatta), and is the winner of wealth (dhananjaya). He is Kambalasva (kambalasva). He is the fastest (vegatara), the king (dhrtarasta), and the hero of mighty arms (maha-bhuja).

Text 19
varuni-mada-mattango
mada-ghurnita-locanah
padmaksah padma-mali ca
vanamali madhusravah

He is intoxicated by drinking varuni (varuni-mada-mattanga), His eyes roll in intoxication (mada-ghurnita-locana), His eyes are lotus flowers (padmaksa), He wears a lotus garland (padma-mali), and a forest garland (vanamali), and His fame is sweet (madhusrava).

Text 20
koti-kandarpa-lavanyo
naga-kanya-samarcitah
nupuri katisutri ca
kataki kanakangadi

He is more handsome than millions of Kamadevas (koti-kandarpa-lavanya), and He is worshiped by the naga-kanyas (naga-kanya-samarcita). He wears tinkling anklets (nupuri), a belt (katisutri), golden bracelets (kataki), and golden armlets (kanakangadi).

Text 21
Smukuti kundali dandi
sikhandi khanda-mandali
kalih kali-priyah kalo
nivata-kavacesvarah

He wears a crown (mukuti) and earrings (kundali). He carries a staff (dandi). He wears a peacock feather (sikhandi), and a khanda-mandala (khanda-mandali). He likes to fight (kali and kali-priya), He is time (kala), and He is fitted with armor (nivata-kavacesvara).

Text 22

samhara-krd rudra-vapuh
kalagnih pralayo layah
mahahih paninih sastra-
bhasya-karah patanjalih

He destroys the universe (samhara-krt). He is the forms of the Rudras (rudra-vapu), the fire of time (kalagni), the destruction of the universe (pralaya and laya), a great serpent (mahahi), Panini (panini), the author of commentaries (sastra-bhasya-kara), and Patanjali (patanjali).

Text 23

katyayanah pakvimabhah
sphotayana urangamah
vaikuntho yajniko yajno
vamano harino harih

He is Katyayana (katyayana), and He is glorious (pakvimabhah and sphotayana). He is the serpent Ananta (urangama). He is the master of the spiritual world (vaikuntha), the performer of yajnas (yajnika) yajna itself (yajna), Vamana (vamana), fair-complexioned (harina), and Lord Hari (hari).

Text 24

krsno visnur maha-visnuh
prabhavisnur visesa-vit
hamso yogesvaro kurmo
varaho narado munih

He is Krsna (krsna), Visnu (visnu), Maha-visnu (maha-visnu), all-powerful (prabhavisnu), all-knowing (visesa-vit), like a swan (hamsa), the master of yoga (yogesvara), Kurma (kurma), Varaha (varaha), Narada (narada), and a great sage (muni).

Text 25
sanakah kapilo matsyah
kamatho deva-mangalah
Sdattatreyah prthur vrddha
rsabho bhargavottamah

He is Sanaka (sanaka), Kapila (kapila), Matsya (matsya and kamatha), the auspiciousness of the demigods (deva-mangala), Dattatreya (dattatreya), Prthu (prthu), Vrddha (vrddha), Rsabha (rsabha), and the best of the Bhrgu dynasty (bhargavottama).

Text 26
dhanvantarir nrsimhas ca
kalkir narayano narah
ramacandro raghavendrah
kosalendro raghudvahah

He is Dhanvantari (dhanvantari), Nrsimha (nrsimha), Kalki (kalki), Narayana (narayana), Nara (nara), and Ramacandra (ramacandra, raghavendra, kosalendra, and raghudvaha).

Text 27
kakutsthah karuna-sindhu
rajendrah sarva-laksanah
suro dasarathis trata
kausalyananda-vardhanah

He is the most exalted (kakutstha), and ocean of mercy (karuna-sindhu), the king of kings (rajendra), all glorious (sarva-laksana), heroic (sura), the son of Dasaratha (dasarathi), the great protector (trata), and the bliss of Kausalya (kausalyananda-vardhana).

Text 28
saumitrir bharato dhanvi
satrughnah satru-tapanah
nisangi kavaci khadgi
sari jyahata-kosthakah

He is the son of Sumitra (saumitri), Bharata (bharata), a great bowman (dhanvi), Satrughna (satrughna and satru-tapana), a great bowman (nisangi), a warrior wearing armor (kavaci), a warrior carrying a sword (khadgi), and a great bowman (sari and jyahata-kosthaka).

Text 29
baddha-godhanguli-tranah
sambhu-kodanda-bhanjanah
yajna-trata yajna-bharta
marica-vadha-karakah

He wears the shoulder and finger armor of a bowman (baddha-godhanguli-trana). He broke Lord Siva's bow (sambhu-kodanda-bhanjana). He protected the yajna (yajna- Strata and yajna-bharta). He killed Marica (marica-vadha-karaka).

Text 30
asuraris tatakarir
vibhisana-sahaya-krt
pitr-vakya-karo harsi
viradharir vanecarah

He is the enemy of the demons (asurari), the enemy of Tataka (tatakari), the ally of Vibhisana (vibhisana-sahaya-krt), a son who followed His father's order (pitr-vakya-kara), (harsi), happy (viradhari), and the Lord who wandered in the forest (vanecara).

Text 31
munir muni-priyas citra-
kutaranya-nivasa-krt
kabandhaha dandakeso
ramo rajiva-locanah

He is a sage (muni), dear to the sages (muni-priya), a resident of Citrakuta forest (citrakutaranya-nivasa-krt), the killer of Kabandha (kabandhaha), the master of Dandaka forest (dandakesa), Lord Rama (rama), and lotus-eyed (rajiva-locana).

Text 32
matanga-vana-sancari
neta pancavati-patih
sugrivah sugriva-sakho
hanumat-prita-manasah

He wandered in Matanga forest (matanga-vana-sancari). He is supreme
leader (neta). He is the master of Pancavati forest (pancavati-pati). He has
a graceful neck (sugriva), and is the friend of Sugriva (sugriva-sakha). In
His heart He loves Hanuman (hanumat-prita-manasa).

Text 33
setubandho ravanarir
lanka-dahana-tat-parah
ravanyarih puspakastho
janaki-virahaturah

He built the bridge at Setubandha (setubandha), is the enemy of Ravana
(ravanari), burned Lanka to the ground (lanka-dahana-tat-para), is the
enemy of Ravana (ravanyari), traveled in a flower-chariot (puspakastha),
and was distressed in separation from Sita (janaki-virahatura).

Text 34
ayodhyadhipatih srimal
lavanarih surarcitah
surya-vamsi candra-vamsi
vamsi-vadya-visaradah

He was the king of Ayodhya (ayodhyadhipati), handsome and glorious
(srimal), the enemy of Lavanasura (lavanari), worshiped by the devas
(surarcita), born in the Surya dynasty (surya-vamsi), born in the Candra
dynasty (candra-vamsi), and expert at playful the flute
(vamsi-vadya-visarada).

Text 35
gopatir gopa-vrndeso
gopo gopisatavrtah
gokuleso gopa-putro
gopalo go-ganasrayah

He is the master of the surabhi cows (gopati), the master of the gopas
(gopa-vrndesa), a gopa (gopa), surrounded by hundred of gopis
(gopisatavrta), the master of Gokula (gokulesa), the son of a gopa
(gopa-putra), the protector of the cows (gopala), and the shelter of the cows
(go-ganasraya).

Text 36

putanarir bakaris ca
trnavarta-nipatakah
agharir dhenukaris ca
pralambarir vrajesvarah

He is the enemy of Putana (putanari), the enemy of Baka (bakari), the killer
of Trnavarta (trnavarta-nipataka), the enemy of Aghasura (aghari), the
enemy of Dhenuka (dhenukari), the enemy of Pralamba (pralambari), and
the king of Vraja (vrajesvara).

Text 37

arista-ha kesi-satrur
vyomasura-vinasa-krt
agni-pano dugdha-pano
vrndavana-latasritah

He is the killer of Arista (arista-ha), the enemy of Kesi (kesi-satru), the
killer of Vyomasura (vyomasura-vinasa-krt), the swallower of a forest-fire
(agni-pana), a child who drinks milk (dugdha-pana), and a boy who stays
among the flowering vines of Vrndavana forest (vrndavana-latasrita).

Text 38

yasomati-suto bhavyo
rohini-lalitah sisuh
rasa-mandala-madhya-stho
rasa-mandala-mandanah

He is the son of Yasoda (yasomati-suta), glorious, charming, handsome,
and auspicious (bhavya), a child who plays with Rohini (rohini-lalita), a
child (sisu), the dancer in the middle of the rasa-dance circle
(rasa-mandala-madhya-stha), and the ornament of the rasa-dance circle
(rasa-mandala-mandana).

Text 39
gopika-sata-yutharthi
sankhacuda-vadhodyatah
govardhana-samuddharta
sakra-jid vraja-raksakah

He yearns to enjoy pastimes with hundreds of gopis (gopika-sata-yutharthi).
He is the killer of Sankhacuda (sankhacuda-vadhodyata), the lifter of
Givardhana Hill (govardhana-samuddharta), the warrior who defeated Indra
(sakra-jid), and the protector of Vraja (vraja-raksaka).

Text 40
vrsabhanu-varo nanda
anando nanda-vardhanah
nanda-raja-sutah srisah
kamsarih kaliyantakah

He is the groom King Vrsabhanu chose for his daughter (vrsabhanu-vara).
He is bliss personified (nanda and ananda), delightful (nanda-vardhana), the
son of King Nanda (nanda-raja-suta), the master of the goddess of fortune
(srisa), the enemy of Kamsa (kamsari), and the subduer of Kaliya
(kaliyantaka).

Text 41
rajakarir mustikarih
kamsa-kodanda-bhanjanah
canurarih kuta-hanta
salaris tosalantakah

He is the enemy of a washerman (rajakari), the enemy of Mustika
(mustikari), the breaker of Kamsa's bow (kamsa-kodanda-bhanjana), the
enemy of Canura (canurari), the killer of Kuta (kuta-hanta), the enemy of
Sala (salari), and the killer of Tosala (tosalantaka).

Text 42
kamsa-bhratr-nihanta ca
malla-yuddha-pravartakah
gaja-hanta kamsa-hanta
kala-hanta kalanka-ha

He is the killer of Kamsa's brothers (kamsa-bhratr-nihanta), San expert wrestler (malla-yuddha-pravartaka), the killer of an elephant (gaja-hanta), the killer of Kamsa (kamsa-hanta), the killer of Kala (kala-hanta), and the killer of Kalanka (kalanka-ha).

Text 43

magadharir yavana-ha
pandu-putra-sahaya-krt
catur-bhujah syamalangah
saumyas caupagavi-priyah

He is the enemy of Jarasandha (magadhari), the killer of Kalayavana (yavana-ha), the ally of the Pandavas (pandu-putra-sahaya-krt), four-armed Lord Narayana (catur-bhuja), dark-complexioned Lord Krsna (syamalanga), gentle (saumya), and dear to Aupagavi (aupagavi-priya).

Text 44

yuddha-bhrd uddhava-sakha
mantri mantra-visaradah
vira-ha vira-mathanah
sankha-cakra-gada-dharah

He is a warrior (yuddha-bhrd), the friend of Uddhava (uddhava-sakha), a counselor (mantri), expert at giving counsel (mantra-visarada), a killer of great warriors (vira-ha and vira-mathana), and the holder of a conch, disc, and club (sankha-cakra-gada-dhara).

Text 45

revati-citta-harta ca
raivati-harsa-vardhanah
revati-prana-nathas ca
revati-priya-karakah

He charmed Revati's heart (revati-citta-harta), delighted Revati (raivati-harsa-vardhana), is the Lord of Revati's life (revati-prana-natha), and is the delight of Revati (revati-priya-karaka).

Text 46

jyotir jyotismati-bharta
revatadri-vihara-krt

dhrta-natho dhanadhyakso
danadhyakso dhanesvarah

He is splendor (jyoti), the master of Jyotismati (jyotismati-bharta), the
enjoyer of pastimes on Mount Revata (revatadri-vihara-krt), the master of
patience and tolerance (dhrta-natha), the final judge (dhanadhyaksa),
(danadhyaksa), and the master of wealth (dhanesvara).

Text 47
maithilarcita-padabjo
manado bhakta-vatsalah
duryodhana-gurur gurvi
gada-siksa-karah ksami

His lotus feet were worshiped by the people of Mithila
(maithilarcita-padabja), He gives honor to others (manada), He loves His
devotees (bhakta-vatsala), He is the guru of Duryodhana
(duryodhana-guru), He is devoted to His guru (gurvi), He taught the art of
fighting with a club (gada-siksa-kara), and He is tolerant and forgiving
(ksami).

Text 48
murarir madano mando
'niruddho dhanvinam varah
kalpa-vrksah kalpa-vrksi
kalpa-vrksa-vana-prabhuh

He is the enemy of Mura (murari), handsome like Kamadeva (madana),
gentle (manda), invincible (aniruddha), the best of bowmen (dhanvinam
vara), a kalpa-vrksa tree (kalpa-vrksa and kalpa-vrksi), and the master of a
forest of (kalpa-vrksa trees (kalpa-vrksa-vana-prabhu).

Text 49
symantaka-manir manyo
gandivi kairavesvarah
kumbhanda-khandana-karah
kupakarna-prahara-krt

He is the owner of the Syamantaka jewel (symantaka-mani), glorious
(manya), the friend of Arjuna (gandivi), the king of the Kauravas

(kauravesvara), the killer of Kumbandha (kumbhanda-khandana-kara), and the killer of Kupakarna (kupakarna-prahara-krt).

Text 50
sevyo raivata-jamata
madhu-madhava-sevitah
balistha-pusta-sarvango
hrstah pustah praharsitah

He is the final object of devotional service (sevya), the son-in-law of King Revata (raivata-jamata), served by Lord Krsna and the residents of Mathura (madhu-madhava-sevita), most powerful in every limb (balistha-pusta-sarvanga), happy (hrsta and praharsita), and stout and strong (pusta).

Text 51
varanasi-gatah kruddhah
sarvah paundraka-ghatakah
sunandi sikhari silpi
dvividanga-nisudanah

He traveled to Varanasi (varanasi-gata). He may become angry (kruddha). He is everything (sarva). He killed Paundraka (paundraka-ghataka). He carries the sword Sunanda (sunandi), wears a crown (sikhari), is artistic (silpi), and killed Dvivida (dvividanga-nisudana).

Note: Sunanda is the name of Lord Krsna's sword.

Text 52
hastinapura-sankarsi
rathi kaurava-pujitah
visva-karma visva-dharma
deva-sarma daya-nidhih

He dragged the city of Hastinapura (hastinapura-sankarsi), is a great chariot-warrior (rathi), is worshiped by the Kauravas (kaurava-pujita), created the universes (visva-karma), is the giver of religion to the universes (visva-dharma), is the happiness of the demigods (deva-sarma), and is an ocean of mercy (daya-nidhi).

Text 53
maha-raja-cchatra-dharo
maha-rajopalaksanah
siddha-gitah siddha-kathah
sukla-camara-vijitah

He holds the royal parasol (maha-raja-cchatra-dhara), has all the qualities of a great king (maha-rajopalaksana), is glorified by the siddhas (siddha-gita and siddha-katha), and is fanned with white camaras (sukla-camara-vijita).

Text 54
taraksah kiranasas ca
bimbosthah su-smita-cchavih
karindra-kara-kodandah
pracando megha-mandalah

His eyes are glittering stars (taraksa), His nose is graceful like a parrot's beak (kiranasa), His lips are bimba fruits (bimbostha), His gentle smile is splendid and glorious (su-smita-cchavi), His arms are elephants' trunks (karindra-kara-kodanda), He is ferocious (pracanda), and He is splendid like a host of monsoon clouds (megha-mandala).

Text 55
kapata-vaksah pinamsah
padma-pada-sphurad-dyutih
maha-vibhutir bhuteso
bandha-moksi samiksanah

His chest is a great door (kapata-vaksa), His shoulders are broad (pinamsa), His feet are splendid lotus flowers (padma-pada-sphurad-dyuti), He is very powerful and glorious (maha-vibhuti), He is the master of all living entities (bhutesa), He is the liberator from material bondage (bandha-moksi), and He is the most wise and intelligent (samiksana).

Text 56
caidya-satruh satru-sandho
dantavakra-nisudakah
ajata-satruh papa-ghno
hari-dasa-sahaya-krt

He is the enemy of Sisupala (caidya-satru), the end of His enemies (satru-sandha), the killer of Dantavakra (dantavakra-nisudaka), a person who has no enemy (ajata-satru), the destroyer of sins (papa-ghna), and the ally of Lord Krsna's servants (hari-dasa-sahaya-krt).

Text 57

sala-bahuh salva-hanta
tirtha-yayi janesvarah
naimisaranya-yatrarthi
gomati-tira-vasa-krt

His arms are like palm trees (sala-bahu). He is the killer of Salva (salva-hanta), a pilgrim (tirtha-yayi), the master of all living entities (janesvara), a pilgrim to Naimisaranya (naimisaranya-yatrarthi), and He who lived by the Gomati river (gomati-tira-vasa-krt).

Text 58

gandaki-snana-van sragvi
vaijayanti-virajitah
amlana-pankaja-dharo
vipasi sona-samplutah

He bathed in the Gandaki river (gandaki-snana-van), wears a garland (sragvi), is splendid with a Vaijayanti garland (vaijayanti-virajita), holds an unfading lotus (amlana-pankaja-dhara), visited the Vipasa river (vipasi), and bathed in the Sona river (sona-sampluta).

Text 59

prayaga-tirtha-rajas ca
sarayuh setu-bandhanah
gaya-siras ca dhanadah
paulastyah pulahasramah

He visited Prayaga, the king of holy places (prayaga-tirtha-raja), and He also visited the Sarayu river (sarayu), and Setubandha (setu-bandhana). He touched His head to the holy city of Gaya (gaya-sira). He gives wealth in charity (dhanada). He visited the sage Pulastya (paulastya), and He visited the asrama of the sage Pulaha (pulahasrama).

Text 60
ganga-sagara-sangarthi
sapta-godavari-patih
veni bhimarthi goda
tamraparni vatodaka

He visited Ganga-sagara (ganga-sagara-sangarthi). He is the master of the seven Godavaris (sapta-godavari-pati). He is the Veni (veni), Bhimarathi (bhimarathi), Goda (goda), Tamraparni (tamraparni), and Vatodaka rivers (vatodaka).

Text 61
krtamala maha-punya
kaveri ca payasvini
pratici suprabha veni
triveni sarayupama

He is the Krtamala) (krtamala), Maha-punya (maha-punya), Kaveri (kaveri), Payasvini (payasvini), Pratici (pratici), Suprabha (suprabha), Veni (veni), Triveni (triveni), and and Sarayupama rivers (sarayupama).

Text 62
krsna pampa narmada ca
ganga bhagirathi nadi
siddhasramah prabhasas ca
bindur bindu-sarovarah

He is the Krsna (krsna), Pampa (pampa), Narmada (narmada), Ganga (ganga), and Bhagirathi rivers (bhagirathi). He is all sacred rivers (nadi). He is Siddhasrama (siddhasrama), Prabhasa (prabhasa), Bindu (bindu), and Bindu-sarovara (bindu-sarovara).

Text 63
puskarah saindhavo jambu
nara-narayanasramah
kuruksetra-pati ramo
jamadagnyo maha-munih

He is Puskara (puskara), Saindhava (saindhava), Jambu (jambu), and Nara-narayanasrama (nara-narayanasrama). He is the master of Kuruksetra

(kuruksetra-pati). He is Lord Rama (rama). He is Parasurama (jamadagnya). He is a great sage (maha-muni).

Text 64
ilvalatmaja-hanta ca
sudama-saukhya-dayakah
visva-jid visva-nathas ca
triloka-vijayi jayi

He killed Narakasura (ilvalatmaja-hanta), delighted Sudhama (sudama-saukhya-dayaka), conquered the universe (visva-jid), is the master of the universe (visva-natha), is the master of the three worlds (triloka-vijayi), and is victorious (jayi).

Text 65
vasanta-malati-karsi
gado gadyo gadagrajah
gunarnavo guna-nidhir
guna-patro gunakarah

He is glorious with vasanta and malati flowers (vasanta-malati-karsi). He is strong like a great mace (gada). He is expert at fighting with a mace (gadya). He is the elder brother of Gada (gadagraja). He is an ocean of virtues (gunarnava and guna-nidhi), and a reservoir of virtues (guna-patra and gunakara).

Text 66
rangavalli-jalakaro
nirgunah saguno brhat
drstah sruto bhavad bhuto
bhavisyac calpa-vigrahah

He is decorated with vine-flowers (rangavalli), enjoys water-pastimes (jalakara), is beyond the modes of material nature (nirguna), is filled with transcendental qualities (saguna), is the greatest (brhat), is seen by the great devotees (drsta), is heard by the great devotees (sruta), and is the present (bhavad), the past (bhuta), and the future (bhavisyat). He is the Supersoul, whose form is so small He stays in every atom (alpa-vigraha).

Text 67
anadir adir anandah
pratyag-dhama nirantarah
gunatitah samah samyah
sama-drn nirvikalpakah

He is without beginning (anadi), is the beginning of everything (adi), is bliss personified (ananda), is the Supersoul who stays in everyone's heart (pratyag-dhama), is eternal S(nirantara), is beyond the modes of nature (gunatita), is equal to all (sama, samya and nirvikalpaka), and sees everyone with equal vision (sama-drk).

Text 68
gudha-vyudho guno gauno
gunabhaso gunavrtah
nityo 'ksaro nirvikaro
'ksaro 'jasra-sukho 'mrtah

He is concealed (gudha) and He is openly manifested (vyudha). He is filled with transcendental virtues (guna, gauna, gunabhasa, and gunavrta). He eternal (nitya), imperishable (aksara), unchanging (nirvikara), undying (aksara), always happy (ajasra-sukha), and like nectar (amrta).

Text 69
sarvagah sarvavit sarthah
sama-buddhih sama-prabhah
akledyo 'cchedya apurno
'sosyo 'dahyo nivartakah

He is all-pervading (sarvaga), all-knowing (sarvavit), the most valuable (sartha), equal to all (sama-buddhi and sama-prabha), untouched by water (akledya), unbreakable (acchedya), perfect and complete (apurna), never dried or withered (asosya), and never to be burned by fire (adahya). He is the destroyer of the worlds (nivartaka).

Text 70
brahma brahma-dharo brahma
jnapako vyapakah kavih
adhyatmako 'dhibhutas ca-
dhidaivah svasrayasrayah

He is Brahman (brahma), the origin of Brahman (brahma-dhara), the origin of demigod Brahma (brahma), the supreme teacher (jnapaka), all-pervading (vyapaka), and the greatest philosopher (kavi). He is present in the hearts of all living entities (adhyatmaka). He is present in the material elements (adhibhuta). He is present among the demigods (adhidaiva). He is the shelter of all shelters (svasrayasraya).

Text 71

maha-vayur maha-viras
cesta-rupa-tanu-sthitah
prerako bodhako bodhi
trayo-vimsatiko ganah

He is the great wind (maha-vayu). He is a great hero (maha-vira). As the power of action He stays in every body (cesta- Srupa-tanu-sthita). He inspires the living entities (preraka), and enlightens them (bodhaka). He is the mist wise (bodhi). He is the master of the demigods (trayo-vimsatika-gana).

Text 72

amsamsas ca naraveso
'vataro bhupari-sthitah
mahar janas tapah satyam
bhur bhuvah svar iti tridha

He expands in many incarnations (amsamsa). He appears as a sakty-avesa incarnation (naravesa). He descends to the material world (avatara and bhupari-sthita). He is Maharloka (mahah), Janaloka (jana), Tapoloka (tapah), and Satyaloka (satyam). He is the three planetary systems: Bhuloka (bhu), Bhuvarloka (bhuvah), Svarloka (svah).

Text 73

naimittikah prakrtika
atyantika-mayo layah
sargo visargah sargadir
nirodho rodha utiman

Although He appears in the material world (naimittika and prakrtika), He is eternal (atyantika-maya). He is cosmic devastation (laya), cosmic creation (sarga), the secondary stage of cosmic creation (visarga), and the beginning of creation (sargadi). He is the greatest obstacle (nirodha and rodha), and the greatest protector (utiman).

Text 74
manvantaravataras ca
manur manu-suto 'naghah
svayambhuh sambhavah sankuh
svayambhuva-sahaya-krt

He appears as the Manvantaravataras (manvantaravatara). He is Manu (manu) and the sons of Manu (manu-suta). He is sinless (anagha), self-born (svayambhu), and a friend of Lord Siva (sambhava). He is like a great lance (sanku). He is the ally of Svayambhuva Manu (svayambhuva-sahaya-krt).

Text 75
suralayo deva-girir
merur hemarcito girih
giriso gana-nathas ca
gairiso giri-gahvarah

He is the home of the demigods (suralaya), the mountain of the demigods (deva-giri), Mount Meru (meru), splendid like gold (hemarcita), and a great ountain (giri). He stays on a mountain (girisa). He is the master of the devotees (gana-natha) and a friend of Lord Siva (gairisa). He stays in a mountain cave (giri-gahvara).

Text 76
vindhyas trikuto mainakah
subalah paribhadrakah
patangah sisirah kanko
jarudhih saila-sattamah

He is the Vindhya mountains (vindhya), Mount Trikuta (trikuta), and Mount Mainaka (mainaka). He is very powerful (subala). He is the paribhadraka tree (paribhadraka), the sun (patanga), the winter season (sisira), Yama (kanka), Jarudhi (jarudhi), and the best of mountains (saila-sattama).

Text 77
kalanjaro brhat-sanur
dari-bhrn nandikesvarah
santanas taru-rajas ca
mandarah parijatakah

He is Kalanjara (kalanjara) and Brhat-sanu (brhat-sanu). He stays in a mountain cave (dari-bhrt). He is Nandikesvara (nandikesvara), the santana tree (santana), the king of trees (taru-raja), the mandara tree (mandara), and the parijata tree (parijataka).

Text 78
jayanta-krj jayantango
jayanti-dig jayakulah
vrtra-ha devalokas ca
sasi kumuda-bandhavah

He is victorious (jayanta-krt jayantanga, jayanti-dig, and jayakula). He is the killer of Vrtra (vrtra-ha). He is the planets of the demigods (devaloka), and the moon (sasi and kumuda-bandhava).

Text 79
naksatresah sudha-sindhur
mrgah pusyah punarvasuh
hasto 'bhijic ca sravano
vaidhrtir bhaskarodayah

He is the moon (naksatresa), an ocean of nectar (sudha-sindhu), the star Mrgasirsa (mrga), the star Pusya (pusya), the star Punarvasu (punarvasu), the star Hasta (hasta), the star Abhijit (abhijit), and the star Sravana (sravana). He is the vaidhrti formation of the stars (vaidhrti), and He is the sunrise (bhaskarodaya).

Text 80
aindrah sadhyah subhah suklo
vyatipato dhruvah sitah
sisumaro devamayo
brahmaloko vilaksanah

He is the star Aindra (aindra). He is Sadhyaloka (sadhya). He is the
auspicious conjunction of stars (subha). He is the bright fortnight (sukla).
He is the astrological condition known as vyatipata (vyatipata). He is
Dhruvaloka (dhruva). He is the bright fortnight (sita), the Sisumara-cakra
(sisumara), the planets of the demigods (devamaya), and Brahmaloka
(brahmaloka). He is beyond the material world (vilaksana).

Text 81

ramo vaikuntha-nathas ca
vyapi vaikuntha-nayakah
svetadvipo jita-pado
lokalokacalasritah

He is Lord Rama (rama). He is the master of Vaikuntha (vaikuntha-natha
and vaikuntha-nayaka). He is all-pervading (vyapi), the master of
Svetadvipa (svetadvipa), the Lord who has conquered everything
(jita-pada), and the Lord who stays on Mount Lokaloka (lokalokacalasrita).

Text 82

bhumi-vaikuntha-devas ca
koti-brahmanda-karakah
asankhya-brahmanda-patir
golokeso gavam-patih

He is the master of Bhumi-vaikuntha (bhumi-vaikuntha-deva), the creator
of millions of universes (koti-brahmanda-karaka), the master of countless
universes (asankhya-brahmanda-pati), the master of Goloka (golokesa), and
the master of the cows (gavam-pati).

Text 83

goloka-dhama-dhisano
gopika-kantha-bhusanah
sridharah sridharo lila-
dharo giri-dharo dhuri

He resides in Goloka (goloka-dhama-dhisana). The gopis' embraces have
become His necklace (gopika-kantha-bhusana). He is the master of the
goddess of fortune (sridhara). He is the master of all handsomeness, glory,
and opulence (sridhara). He is playful (lila-dhara). He lifted Govardhana
Hill (giri-dhara). He is the maintainer of the world (dhuri).

Text 84
kunta-dhari trisuli ca
bibhatsi gharghara-svanah
sula-sucy-arpita-gajo
gaja-carma-dharo gaji

He is Lord Siva who carries a trident (kunta-dhari and trisuli), who is terrifying (bibhatsi), who roars ferociously (gharghara-svana), who with His trident attacked an elephant (sula-sucy-arpita-gaja), who wears an elephant-skin garemnt (gaja-carma-dhara), and who rides on an elephant (gaji).

Text 85
antra-mali munda-mali
vyali dandaka-mandaluh
vetala-bhrd bhuta-sanghah
kusmanda-gana-samvrtah

He is Lord Nrsimha who wears a garland of entrails (antra-mali). He is Lord Siva who wears a necklace of skulls (munda-mali), who is ferocious (vyali), who carries a club (dandaka-mandalu), who is accompanied by Vetalas (vetala-bhrd), who is accompanied by ghosts (bhuta-sangha), and who is accompanied by Kusmandas (kusmanda-gana-samvrta).

Text 86
pramathesah pasu-patir
mrdaniso mrdo vrsah
krtanta-kala-sangharih
kutah kalpanta-bhairavah

He is Lord Siva who is the master of the Pramathas (pramathesa), the master of the Pasus (pasu-pati), the husband of Parvati (mrdanisa), gentle (mrda), powerful (vrsa), the killer of His enemies (krtanta-kala-sanghari), most exalted (kuta), and who appears as Bhairava at the end of time (kalpanta-bhairava).

Text 87
sad-anano vira-bhadro
daksa-yajna-vighatakah
kharparasi visasi ca
sakti-hastah sivarthadah

He is Karttikeya, who has six heads (sad-anana). He is Virabhadra (vira-bhadra). He destroyed the Daksa-yajna (daksa-yajna-vighataka). He eats from a bowl that is a skull (kharparasi). He drinks poison (visasi), holds a sakti weapon in His hand (sakti-hasta), and grants auspiciousness (sivarthada).

Text 88

pinaka-tankara-karas
cala-jhankara-nupurah
panditas tarka-vidvan vai
veda-pathi srutisvarah

When He releases arrows from His bow it makes a great twanging sound (pinaka-tankara-kara). He wears tinkling anklets (cala-jhankara-nupura). He is wise (pandita), a master logician (tarka-vidvan), learned in the Vedas (veda-pathi), and the master of the Vedas (srutisvara).

Text 89

vedanta-krt sankhya-sastri
mimamsi kana-nama-bhak
kanadir gautamo vadi
vado naiyayiko nayah

He is the author of Vedanta (vedanta-krt), learned in Sankhya (sankhya-sastri), learned in Mimamsa (mimamsi), known by the name Kanada (kana-nama-bhak and kanadi), known as Gautama (gautama), and expert in philosophical debate (vadi, vada, naiyayika, and naya).

Text 90

vaisesiko dharma-sastri
sarva-sastrartha-tattva-gah
vaiyakarana-krc chando
vaiyyasah prakrtir vacah

He is learned in the Vaisesa philosophy (vaisesika), learned in the dharma-sastras (dharma-sastri), learned in all the scriptures (sarva-sastrartha-tattva-ga), the author of grammar (vaiyakarana-krt), learned in the meters of poetry (chanda), the Vyasa's son (vaiyyasa), nature (prakrti), and speech (vacah).

Text 91

parasari-samhita-vit
kavya-krn nataka-pradah
pauranikah smrti-karo
vaidyo vidya-visaradah

He is learned in the Parasara-sastra (parasari-samhita-vit), the author of poetry (kavya-krt), the giver of dramas (nataka-prada), learned in the Puranas (pauranika), the author of the Vedas (smrti-kara), the first physician (vaidya), and very learned (vidya-visarada).

Text 92

Salankaro laksanartho
vyangya-viddhanavad-dhvanih
vakya-sphotah pada-sphotah
sphota-vrttis ca sartha-vit

He is the ornaments of poetry (alankara), the secondary meanings of words (laksanartha), the hinted meanings of words (vyangya-viddhanavad-dhvani), and the meaning that first comes to mind when one hears a statement (vakya-sphota, pada-sphota, and (sphota-vrtti). He knows the meanings of words (sartha-vit).

Text 93

srngara ujjvalah svaccho
'dbhuto hasyo bhayanakah
asvattho yava-bhoji ca
yava-krito yavasanah

He is decoration (srngara), splendor (ujjvala and svaccha), wonder (adbhuta), joking (hasya), fear (bhayanaka), the banyan tree (asvattha), and the philosopher Kanada (yava-bhoji, yava-krita, and yavasana).

Text 94

prahlada-raksakah snigdha
aila-vamsa-vivardhanah
gatadhir ambarisango
vigadhir gadhinam varah

He is the protector of Prahlada (prahlada-raksaka), affectionate (snigdha), the glory of the Aila dynasty (aila-vamsa-vivardhana), free of anxiety (gatadhi), Ambarisa (ambarisanga), Gadhi (vigadhi), the best of Gadhi's descendents (gadhinam vara).

Text 95
nana-mani-samakirno
nana-ratna-vibhusanah
nana-puspa-dharah puspi
puspa-dhanva su-puspitah

He is decorated with many jewels (nana-mani-samakirna and nana-ratna-vibhusana) and decorated with many flowers (nana-puspa-dhara, puspi, and su-puspita). He is Kamadeva who holds a bow of flowers (puspa-dhanva).

Text 96
nana-candana-gandhadhyo
nana-puspa-rasarcitah
nana-varna-mayo varno
nana-vastra-dharah sada

He is fragrant with sandal paste (nana-candana-gandhadhya), Sanointed with the fragrant juices of many flowers (nana-puspa-rasarcita), decorated with garments and ornaments of many colors (nana-varna-maya), glorious (varna), always dressed in opulent and elaborate garments (nana-vastra-dhara sada).

Text 97
nana-padma-karah kausi
nana-kauseya-vesa-dhrk
ratna-kambala-dhari ca
dhauta-vastra-samavrtah

He holds many lotus flowers in His hand (nana-padma-kara), is dressed in silk garments (kausi nana-kauseya-vesa-dhrk), wears a jewel cloak (ratna-kambala-dhari), and is dressed in splendid clean garments (dhauta-vastra-samavrta).

Text 98
uttariya-dharah purno
ghana-kancuka-sanghavan
pitosnisah sitosniso
raktosniso dig-ambarah

He wears an upper garment (uttariya-dhara). He is perfect (purna). He wears strong armor (ghana-kancuka-sanghavan), a yellow turban (pitosnisa), a white turban (sitosnisa), or a red turban (raktosnisa). Sometimes He wears the four directions as His garment (dig-ambara).

Text 99
divyango divya-racano
divya-loka-vilokitah
sarvopamo nirupamo
golokanki-krtanganah

His limbs are splendid (divyanga), He is decorated with great splendor (divya-racana), the residents of Devaloka gaze on Him (divya-loka-vilokita), He is the best of all (sarvopama), He is without peer (nirupama), and He stays with His associates in the realm of Goloka (golokanki-krtangana).

Text 100
krta-svotsanga-go lokah
kundali-bhuta asthitah
mathuro mathura-darsi
calat-khanjana-locanah

He stays in Goloka (krta-svotsanga-goloka), He is Lord Ananta (kundali-bhuta), He is all-pervading (asthita), He stays in Mathura (mathura), He gazes at the sights of Mathura (mathura-darsi), and His eyes are like restless khanjana birds (calat-khanjana-locana).

Text 101
dadhi-harta dugdha-haro
navanita-sitasanah
takra-bhuk takra-hari ca
dadhi-caurya-krta-sramah

As a child He is a yogurt thief (dadhi-harta), a milk thief (dugdha-hara), an eater of butter (navanita-sitasana), a drinker of buttermilk (takra-bhuk), a thief of buttermilk (takra-hari), and exhausted by stealing yogurt (dadhi-caurya-krta-srama).

Text 102
prabhavati-baddha-karo
dami damodaro dami
sikata-bhumi-cari ca
bala-kelir vrajarbhakah

As a child His hands were tied by His powerful mother (prabhavati-baddha-kara), He was tied up (dami), He was tied at the waist (damodara), He was tied up (dami), He crawled on the ground (sikata-bhumi-cari), and He enjoyed the pastimes of a child (bala-keli). He was a child in Vraja (vrajarbhaka).

Text 103
dhuli-dhusara-sarvangah
kaka-paksa-dharah sudhih
mukta-keso vatsa-vrndah
kalindi-kula-viksanah

As a child all His limbs were sometimes covered with dust (dhuli-dhusara-sarvanga), He was decorated with crow's feathers (kaka-paksa-dhara), He was intelligent (sudhi), His hair was sometimes dishevelled (mukta-kesa), He stayed with the calves (vatsa-vrnda), and He gazed at the Yamuna's shore (kalindi-kula-viksana).

Text 104
jala-kolahali kuli
panka-prangana-lepakah
sri-vrndavana-sancari
vamsivata-tata-sthitah

He played in the Yamuna's waves (jala-kolahali), and on its shore (kuli), As He crawled in the courtyard He became anointed with mud (panka-prangana-lepaka), He wandered in Vrndavana forest (sri-vrndavana-sancari), and He rested at Vamsivata (vamsivata-tata-sthita).

Text 105
Smahavana-nivasi ca
lohargala-vanadhipah
sadhuh priyatamah sadhyah
sadhv-iso gata-sadhvasah

He resided in Mahavana (mahavana-nivasi), He was the king of Lohargalavana (lohargala-vanadhipa), He was a great saint (sadhu), the most dear (priyatama), attainable by the devotees (sadhya), the Lord of the devotees (sadhv-isa), and fearless (gata-sadhvasa).

Text 106
ranga-natho vittaleso
mukti-natho 'gha-nasakah
su-kirtih su-yasah sphito
yasasvi ranga-ranjanah

He is the Lord of Rangaksetra (ranga-natha), the Lord of Vittala (vittalesa), the Lord of liberation (mukti-natha), the destroyer of sins (agha-nasaka), glorious (su-kirti, su-yasa, sphita), and yasasvi), and the delight of the devotees (ranga-ranjana).

Text 107
raga-satko raga-putro
ragini-ramanotsukah
dipako megha-mallarah
sri-rago mala-kosakah

He is the six kinds of ragas (raga-satka). He is the ragas Raga-putra (raga-putra), Ragini-ramanotsuka (ragini-ramanotsuka), Dipaka (dipaka), Megha-mallara (megha-mallara), Sri-raga (sri-raga), and Mala-kosaka (mala-kosaka).

Text 108
hindolo bhairavakhyas ca
svara-jati-smaro mrduh
talo mana-pramanas ca
svara-gamyah kalaksarah

He is the raas Hindola (hindola) and Bhairava (bhairavakhya). He is love born by hearing beautiful melodies (svara-jati-smara). He is gentle (mrdu). He is graceful musical rhythms (tala and mana-pramana). He is melody (svara-gamya), and He is graceful singing (kalaksara).

Text 109
sami syami satanandah
sata-yamah sata-kratuh
jagarah supta asuptah
susuptah svapna urvarah

He self-controlled (sami). He is dark-complexioned Lord Krsna (syami). He has a hundred blisses (satananda), He forgives a hundred offenses (sata-yama), He performed a hundred yaj{.sy 241}as (sata-kratu), He is awake and alert (jagara), He sleeps (supta, asupta, susupta, svapna). He is great (urvara).

Text 110
urjah sphurjo nirjaras ca
vijvaro jvara-varjitah
jvara-jij jvara-karta ca
jvara-yuk tri-jvaro jvarah

He is power (urja), and glory (sphurja). He is free from the fever of anxiety (nirjara, vijvara, jvara-varjita, and jvara-jit), He lights the fever of anxiety in the demons (jvara-karta), He is passionate (jvara-yuk), He is the three passions (tri-jvara), and He is passion (jvara).

Text 111
jambavan jambukasanki
jambudvipo dvipari-ha
salmalih salmali-dvipah
plaksah plaksavanesvarah

He is Jambavan (jambavan), He does not trust the demons (jambukasanki), He resides in Jambudvipa (jambudvipa), He killed an elephant that attacked Him (dvipari-ha), He is Salmali (salmali), He resides in Salmalidvipa (salmali-dvipa), He is Plaksa (plaksa), and He is the master of Plaksavana forest (plaksavanesvara).

Text 112
kusa-dhari kusah kausi
kausikah kusa-vigrahah
kusasthali-patih kasi-
natho bhairava-sasanah

He holds a blade of kusa grass (kusa-dhari, kusa, kausi, kausika, and kusa-vigraha). He is the king of Dvaraka (kusasthali-pati), the king of Varanasi (kasi-natha), and the master of Bhairava (bhairava-sasana).

Text 113
dasarhah satvato vrsnir
bhojo 'ndhaka-nivasa-krt
andhako dundubhir dyotah
pradyotah satvatam-patih

He is the great descendent of King Dasarha (dasarha), and a great king of the Satvata dynasty (satvata), the Vrsni dynasty S(vrsni), and the Bhoja dynasty (bhoja). He stays among the kings of the Andhaka dynasty (andhaka-nivasa-krt and andhaka). He is glorified by the sounding of Dundubhi drums (dundubhi). He is glorious (dyota and pradyota). He is the master of the Satvatas (satvatam-pati).

Text 114
suraseno 'nuvisayo
bhoja-vrsny-andhakesvarah
ahukah sarva-niti-jna
ugraseno mahogra-vak

He is Surasena (surasena), He is Anuvisaya (anuvisaya), He is the king of the Bhoja, Vrsni, and Andhaka dynasties (bhoja-vrsny-andhakesvara), He is Ahuka (ahuka), He knows what is right (sarva-niti-jna), He is Ugrasena (ugrasena), and He can speak very fiercely (mahogra-vak).

Text 115
ugrasena-priyah prarthyah
paryo yadu-sabha-patih
sudharmadhipatih sattvam
vrsni-cakravrto bhisak

He is dear to King Ugrasena (ugrasena-priya), the devotees offer prayers to Him (prarthya), He is the Pandavas (partha), He is the leader of the assembled Yadavas (yadu-sabha-pati), He is the leader of the Sudharma assembly (sudharmadhipati), He is existence (sattvam), He is surrounded by the Vrsnis (vrsni-cakravrta), and He is the supreme physician (bhisak).

Text 116
sabha-silah sabha-dipah
sabhagnis ca sabha-ravih
sabha-candrah sabha-bhasah
sabha-devah sabha-patih

He is an exalted member of the assembly (sabha-sila), He is a lamp shining in the assembly (sabha-dipa), the fire of the assembly (sabhagni), the sun of the assembly (sabha-ravi), the moon of the assembly (sabha-candra), the splendor of the assembly (sabha-bhasa), the Deity of the assembly (sabha-deva), and the master of the assembly (sabha-pati).

Text 117
prajarthadah praja-bharta
praja-palana-tat-parah
dvaraka-durga-sancari
dvaraka-graha-vigrahah

He fulfills the desires of the citizens (prajarthada), maintains the citizens (praja-bharta), protects the citizens (praja-palana-tat-para), guards the Dvaraka fort (dvaraka-durga-sancari), and stays in Dvaraka (dvaraka-graha-vigraha).

Text 118
dvaraka-duhkha-samharta
dvaraka-jana-mangalah
jagan-mata jagat-trata
jagad-bharta jagat-pita

He removes all sufferings from Dvaraka (dvaraka-duhkha-samharta). He is the auspiciousness of Dvaraka's citizens (dvaraka-jana-mangala), the mother of the universes (jagan-mata), the protector of the universes (jagat-trata), the maintainer of the universes (jagad-bharta), and the father of the universes (jagat-pita).

Text 119

jagad-bandhur jagad-bhrata
jagan-mitro jagat-sakhah
brahmanya-devo brahmanyo
brahma-pada-rajo-dadhat

He is the friend of the universes (jagad-bandhu, jagan-mitra, and jagat-sakha), the creator of the universes (jagad-dhata), and the Deity worshiped by the brahmanas (brahmanya-deva and brahmanya). He respectfully touches the dust of the brahmanas' feet (brahma-pada-rajo-dadhat).

Text 120

brahma-pada-rajah-sparsi
brahma-pada-nisevakah
vipranghri-jala-putango
vipra-seva-parayanah

He respectfully touches the dust of the brahmanas' feet (brahma-pada-rajah-sparsi), He serves the brahmanas' feet (brahma-pada-nisevaka), He purifies Himself by sprinkling on His head the water that has washed the brahmanas' feet (vipranghri-jala-putanga), and He devotedly serves the brahmanas (vipra-seva-parayana).

Text 121

vipra-mukhyo vipra-hito
vipra-gita-maha-kathah
vipra-pada-jalardrango
vipra-padodaka-priyah

He is the best of the brahmanas (vipra-mukhya), the auspiciousness of the brahmanas (vipra-hita), the supreme master whose glories are sung by the brahmanas (vipra-gita-maha-katha), Sand the supreme master who sprinkles on Himself the water that has washed the brahmanas' feet (vipra-pada-jalardranga and vipra-padodaka-priya).

Text 122

vipra-bhakto vipra-gurur
vipro vipra-padanugah
aksauhini-vrto yoddha
pratima-panca-samyutah

He is devoted to the brahmanas (vipra-bhakta), the guru of the brahmanas (vipra-guru), a brahmana (vipra), a follower of the brahmanas (vipra-padanuga), accompanied by an aksauhini military division (aksauhini-vrta), a great warrior (yoddha), and manifested as five Deities (pratima-panca-samyuta).

Text 123
catur angirah padma-varti
samantoddhrta-padukah
gaja-koti-prayayi ca
ratha-koti-jaya-dhvajah

He is Catu (catu), Angira (angira), and Padmavarti (padma-varti). Samanta Muni worships His feet (samantoddhrta-paduka). He is powerful like ten million elephants (gaja-koti-prayayi). His flag of victory flies over the defeat of ten million chariot-warriors (ratha-koti-jaya-dhvaja).

Text 124
maharathas catiratho
jaitram syandanam asthitah
narayanastri brahmastri
rana-slaghi ranodbhatah

He is a great chariot warrior (maharatha and atiratha). He rides a victory-chariot jaitram-syandanam-asthita). He wields the narayanastra weapon (narayanastri) and the brahmastra weapon (brahmastri). He is a famous warrior (rana-slaghi and ranodbhata).

Text 125
madotkato yuddha-viro
devasura-bhayankarah
kari-karna-marut-prejat-
kuntala-vyapta-kundalah

He is a ferocious warrior (madotkata), a hero in battle (yuddha-vira), and frightening even to the demigods and demons (devasura-bhayankara). Moving in the wind, His long hair and earrings are like a great elephant's ear (kari-karna-marut-prejat-kuntala-vyapta-kundala).

Text 126

agrago vira-sammardo
mardalo rana-durmadah
bhatah pratibhatah procyo
bana-varsisutoyadah

He is the first before all others (agraga). He crushes the enemy warriors in battle (vira-sammarda, mardala, rana-durmada, bhata, and pratibhata). He is glorious (procya). He rains a shower of arrows on the enemy (bana-varsi and isu-toyada).

Text 127

khadga-khandita-sarvangah
sodasabdah sad-aksarah
vira-ghosah klista-vapur
vajrango vajra-bhedanah

With His sword He cuts the enemy to pieces (khadga-khandita-sarvanga). He is a sixteen-year-old youth eternally (sodasabda). He does not suffer the six material distresses (sad-aksara). He makes a heroic roar (vira-ghosa). He brings distress to His enemies (klista-vapu). His limbs are powerful like a series of thunderbolts (vajranga). He breaks apart the thunderbolt weapons of His enemies (vajra-bhedana).

Text 128

rugna-vajro bhagna-dantah
satru-nirbhartsanodyatah
atta-hasah patta-dharah
patta-rajni-patih patuh

He breaks apart the thunderbolt weapons of His enemies (rugna-vajra). He breaks His enemies' teeth (bhagna-danta). He rebukes His enemies (satru-nirbhartsanodyata). He laughs loudly (atta-hasa). He wears silk garments (patta-dhara). He is the husband of a noble queen (patta-rajni-pati). He is very intelligent (patu).

Text 129

kalah pataha-vaditro
hunkaro garjita-svanah
sadhur bhakta-paradhinah
svatantrah sadhu-bhusanah

He is time (kala). Pataha drums are sounded to celebrate His victory (pataha-vaditra). He roars ferociously (hunkara and garjita-svana). He is saintly (sadhu), submissive to His devotees (bhakta-paradhina), independent (svatantra), and decorated with the ornaments of saintly qualities (sadhu-bhusana).

Text 130
asvatantrah sadhumayah
sadhu-grasta-mana manak
sadhu-priyah sadhu-dhanah
sadhu-jnatih sudha-ghanah

He is not independent (asvatantra). He is dependent on His devotees (sadhumaya). His heart is rapt in thinking of His devotees (sadhu-grasta-mana). He loves His devotees and they love Him (sadhu-priya). He is charitable to His devotees (sadhu-dhana). He is His devotees' kinsman (sadhu-jnati). He is a monsoon cloud of nectar (sudha-ghana).

Text 131
sadhu-cari sadhu-cittah
sadhu-vasi subhaspadah
iti namnam sahasram tu
balabhadrasya kirtitam

He stays among His devotees (sadhu-cari and sadhu-vasi). His devotees stay in His heart (sadhu-citta). He is the abode of auspiciousness. These are the thousand names of Lord Balarama.

Text 132
sarva-siddhi-pradam nrnam
catur-varga-phala-pradam
sata-varam pathed yas tu
sa vidyavan bhaved iha

He becomes wise who a hundred times recites these names, which give the four goals of life and all perfection.

Text 133
indiram ca vimurtim ca-
bhijanam rupam eva ca

bala-bhojas ca pathanat
sarvam prapnoti manavah

One who recites these names pleases Lord Balarama and thus sustains all wealth, glory, good descendants, and handsomeness.

Text 134
ganga-kule 'tha kalindi-
kule devalaye tatha
sahasravarta-pathena
balat siddhih prajayate

By reciting these names a thousand times on the Ganga's shore, on the Yamuna's shore, or in the Lord's temple, by Lord Balarama's mercy one attains perfection.

Text 135
putrarthi labhate putram
dhanartho labhate dhanam
bandhat pramucyate baddho
rogi rogan nivartate

One who desires a son attains a good son. One who desires wealth attains wealth. One who is imprisoned becomes free from prison. One who is diseased becomes cured of his disease.

Text 136-7
ayutavarta-pathe ca
purascarya-vidhanatah
homa-tarpana-godana-
viprarcana-krtodyamat

patalam paddhatim stotram
kavacam tu vidhaya ca
maha-mandala-bharta syan
mandito mandalesvaraih

One who performs purascarya, recites the patala, paddhati, stotra, and kavaca, recites these names ten thousand times, offers homa and tarpana, gives cows in charity, and worships the brahmanas becomes a great king decorated with a great host of vassal-kings.

Text 138
mattebha-karna-prahita
mada-gandhena vihvala
alankaroti tad-dvaram
bhramad-bhrngavali bhrsam

Pushed by an elephant's ear, and maddened by the sweet fragrance they find there, a host of bees decorates his door.

Text 139
nishkäranah pathed yas tu
prity-artham revati-pateh
nämnäm sahasram räjendra
sa jivan-mukta ucyate

O great king, one who without any personal motive, only to please Lord Balaräma, recites these thousand names, is said to be liberated in this life.

Text 140
sadä vaset tasya grihe
balabhadro 'cyutägrajah
mahä-patäky api janah
pathen näma-sahasrakam

Lord Balaräma, the elder brother of Lord Krishna, eternally resides in the home of even a great sinner who recites these thousand names.

Text 141
chittvä meru-samam päpam
bhuktvä sarva-sukham tn iha
parät param mahä-räja
golokam dhäma yäti hi

O great king, that person destroys a host of sins equal to Mount Meru. He enjoys great happiness, and then He goes to the realm of Goloka, which is above the highest place in the spiritual world.

Text 142
shri-närada uväca iti shrutvacyutägrajasya baladevasya
panängam-dhritimän dhärtaräshtrah saparyayä sahitayä parayä bhaktyä
prädvipäkam- püjayäm äsa tam anujnäpyäshisham-dattvä prädvipäko
munindro gajähvayät sväshramam-jagäma

Shri Närada said: After hearing these five procedures for worshiping Lord
Balaräma, the saintly son of Dhritarashttra worshiped Pradvipka Muni with
great devotion. After giving his blessings, Pradvipka, the king of sages, left
Hastinäpura and returned to his own äshrama.

Text 143
bhagavato 'nantasya balabhadrasya para-brahmanah kathäm-yah shrinute
shrävayate tayänanda-mayo bhavati

One who hears or repeats these descriptions of limitless Lord Balaräma. the
Supreme Personality of Godhead, becomes filled with bliss.

Text 144
idam mayä te kathitam nripendra
sarvärthadam sri-balabhadra-khandam
shrinoti yo dhäma hareh sa yäti
vishokam änandam akhanda-rupam

O great king, thus I have recited for you the Balaräma-khanda, which
fulfills all desires. Anyone who hears it goes to Lord Krishna's
transcendental abode, which is eternal, full of bliss, and free of any
suffering.

TEXT NUMBERS OF LORD BALARAMA'S THOUSAND NAMES
(The name is placed first and the Text Number follows.)
Abhijit, 79; Acchedya, 69; Acyuta, 5; Acyutagraja, 6; Adahya, 69;
Adbhuta, 93; Adhibhuta, 70; Adhidaiva, 70; Adhyatmaka, 70; Adi, 67;
Advitiya, 14; Agha-nasaka, 106; Aghari, 36; Agni-pana, 37; Agraga, 126;
Ahankara, 13; Ahuka, 114; Aila-vamsa-vivardhana, 94; Aindra, 80;
Ajasra-sukha, 68; Ajata-satru, 56; Akledya, 69; Aksara, 68; Aksauhini-vrta,
122; Alankara, 92; Alpa-vigraha, 66; Ambarisanga, 94;
Amlana-pankaja-dhara, 58; Amrta, 68; Amsamsa, 72; Anadi, 67; Anagha,
74; Ananda, 40, 67; Ananta, 11; Andhaka, 113; Andhaka-nivasa-krt, 113;
Angira, 123; Aniruddha, 48; Antaratma, 12; Antra-mali, 85; Anuvisaya,

Sri Rama-rasa-krida
Lord Balaräma's Räsa Dance

Text 1
duryodhana uvächa muni-shärdula bhagavän balabhadro näga-kanyäbhir
gopibhih kadä kälindi-kule vijahära.

Duryodhana said: O tiger of sages, when did Lord Balaräma enjoy the räsa dance on the Yamuna's shore with gopis that had been snake-girls in their previous birth?

Text 2
shri-prädvipäka uvächa ekadä dväräkä-nägaräd dhi tälänkam ratham
ästhäpya surän didrikshuh param utkantho
nanda-räja-gokula-go-gopäla-gopi-gana-sankulah sankarshana ägatash
chirotkanthäbhyäm nandaräja-yashodäbhyäm parishvakto
gopi-gopäla-gobhir militvä tatra dvau masau vasantikau cävatsit.

Shri Prädvipäka Muni said: One day, eager to see His devotees, Lord Balaräma mounted His chariot bearing a palm-tree flag, left Dväraka, and, yearning to see the gopas, gopis, and cows, went to Gokula. Yashoda and King Nanda embraced Him when He arrived. Later He met with the gopas and gopis. He stayed there for two months.

Text 3
atha cha yä näga-kanyäh purvoktäs tä gopa-kanyä bhutvä
balabhadra-präpty-artham- gargäcäryäd balabhadrapancängam- grihitvä
tenaiva siddhä babhuvuh. täbhir baladeva ekadä prasannah kälindi-kule
räsa-mandalam- samärebhe. tadaiva caitra-purnimäyäm- pürna-candro
'runa-varnah sampurnam-vanam-ranjayan vireje.

The previously described snake-girls became gopis and, in order to attain Lord Balaräma's association, on Garga Muni's advice followed the five methods of worshiping Lord Balaräma. In this way they became perfect. Pleased with them, Lord Balaräma enjoyed a räsa-dance with them on the full-moon night of the month of Caitra (March-April), a night when the red moon reddened the whole of Vrindavana forest.

Text 4
shritalä manda-yänäh kamala-makaranda-renu-vrinda-samvritäh sarvato
väyavah parivavuh kalinda-giri-nandini-cala-laharnibhir änanda-däyini
pulinam-vimalam-hy acitam-chakära. tathä cha
kunja-prängana-nikunja-punjaih sphural-lalita-pallava-pushpa-parägair
mayura-kokila-pumskokila-kujitair madhupa-madhura-dhvanibhir
vraja-bhumir vibhräjamänä babhuva.

Cooling, gentle, delightful, lotus-pollen filled breezes pushed the Yamuna's waves and blew to the splendid shore. Then the land of Vraja became very splendid, its many forest groves and courtyards filled with the fragrant pollen of playfully and gracefully blossoming flowers, with the cooing of cuckoos and peacocks, and with the sweet humming of bees.

Text 5
tatra kvanad-ghantikä-nupurah
sphuran-mani-maya-kataka-kati-sutra-keyura-hära-kirita-kundalayor
upari kamala-patrair nilämbaro vimala-kamala-paträksho yakshibhir
yaksha-räd iva gopibhir gopa-räd, räsa-mandale reje.

Decorated with tinkling ankle-bells, glittering gold and jewel necklace, armlets, belt, crown, and earrings, and with many lotus petals, dressed in blue garments, and His eyes like glittering lotus petals, Lord Balaräma was splendid with the gopis in the räsa-dance circle. He was like Kuvera surrounded by a host of beautiful yakshis.

Text 6

atha varuna-preshitä väruëi devi
pushpa-bhara-gandhi-lobhi-milinda-nädita-vriksha-kotarebhyah patanti
sarvato vanam-surabhi-cakära. tat-päna-mada-vihvalah
kamala-vishäla-tämräksho makaradhväjävesha-calad-dhuryänga-bhango
vihära-kheda-prasvedämbu-kanair galad-ganda-sthala-patra-bhango
gajendra-gatir gajendra-shundädaëda-sama-dordanda-mandito gajibhir
gaja-räjendra ivonmattah simhäsane nyasta-halo musala-pänih
kotindu-purna-mandala-sankäshah
prodgamad-ratna-manjira-pracala-nupura-prakvanat-kanaka-kinkinibhih
kaìkana-sphurat-tätanka-purata-hära-shri-kanthänguliya-shiromanibhih
pravidambini-krita-sarpini-shyäma-veni-kuntala-lalita-ganda-sthala-paträ
valibhih sundaribhir bhagavän bhuvaneshvaro vibhräjamäno viraräja
atha cha reme

Then, sent by the demigod Varuna, Goddess Varuni, in the form of honey oozing from the hollows of trees filled with the humming of bees made greedy by the sweet scent of the flowers, made the entire forest very fragrant. Eager to drink that honey, His eyes now red lotus flowers, His limbs weakened by enjoying amorous pastimes, perspiration born from the fatigue of His pastimes now streaming down His cheeks and washing away the pictures and designs drawn there, walking like an elephant king, decorated with mighty arms like the trunks of elephant kings, as if intoxicated, sitting on a throne, relinquishing His plow, His club still in His hand, splendid like ten million full moons, His jewel anklets, bracelets, and other ornaments tinkling, His gold earrings, necklaces, finger-rings, and jewel crown glittering, and surrounded by beautiful gopis, their cheeks decorated with graceful pictures and designs and their black braids mocking the beautiful snake girls, Lord Balaräma, the Supreme Personality of Godhead, the master of the worlds, shone with great splendor, and enjoyed transcendental pastimes.

Text 7
atha ha väva
kälindi-kula-käntära-paryatana-vihära-parishramodyat-sveda-bindu-vyäpt
a-mukhäravindah snänärtham jala-kridärtham yamunäm dürät sa
äjuhäva. tatas tö anägatam tatinim halägrena kupito vicakarsha iti hoväca
cha

His lotus face covered with perspiration born from the fatigue of wandering
along the Yamuna's shore and enjoying many pastimes, Lord Balaräma
called for the Yamuna to come to Him so He could bathe and enjoy
water-pastimes. When the Yamuna did not come, Lord Balaräma became
angry and began to drag it to Him, scratching its shore with the tip of His
plow. Lord Balaräma said:

Text 8
adya mäm avajnäya nayasi mayähutäpi musalena tvam käma-cärinim
çatadhä neshya eva nirbhartsitä sa bhuri-bhita yamunä cakitä tat-pädayoh
patitoväca

"Today you have no respect for Me. Even though I call, you ignore My
order and go your own way as you wish. Now I will divide you into a
hundred tiny streams." Rebuked with these words and now very afraid, the
Yamuna came before Lord Balaräma, fell at His feet, and said:

Text 9
räma räma sankarshana balabhadra mahä-bäho tava param vikramam na
jäne. yasyaikasmin murdhni sarshapavat sarvam bhu-khanda-mandalam-
drishyate. tasya tava param anubhävam ajänantim prapannäm mäm
moktum yogyo 'si. tvam bhakta-vatsalo 'si

"Räma! Räma! Sankarshana! Balabhadra! O mighty-armed one! I did not
know Your great power. The entire earth is seen resting like a single tiny
mustard-seed on one of Your many heads. It is proper for You to release
me, who have now surrendered to You and who did not know Your true
glories. You should release me because You are always affectionate to
Your devotees.

Text 10
ity evam yäcito balabhadro yamunäm tato vyamunchat punah karenubhih
kariva gopibhir gopa-räd jale vijagäha. punar jaläd vinirgatya tata-sthäya

balabhadräya sahasä yamunä copäyanam nilämbaräni
hema-ratna-maya-bhushanäni divyäni cha dadau ha väva täni
gopi-yuthäya prithak prithak vibhajya svayam nilämbare vasitvä
känchanim mäläm nava-ratna-mayim dhritvä mahendro väranendra iva
balabhadro vireje

Begged in this way, Lord Balaräma released the Yamunä. Then He enjoyed in the Yamunä's waters, as an elephant enjoys with its many wives. When He returned to the shore the Yamuna approached and gave Him gifts of many blue garments and many ornaments of gold and jewels. Lord Balaräma divided the gifts among the girls, giving some to each gopi. Then He dressed in one of the blue garments and decorated Himself with a necklace of gold and nine kinds of jewels. Then He enjoyed with the gopis as the king of elephants enjoys with its many wives.

Text 11
ittham kauravendra yädavendrasya rämatah sarvä väsantikir nishä vyatitä babhuvuh. bhagavato balabhadrasya hastinäpuram iva viryam sucayativa hy adyäpi cha krishna-vartmanä yamunä vahati. imam rämasya räsa-kathäm yah shrinoti shrävayati cha sa sarva-päpa-patalam chittvä tasya parasparam änanda-padam pratiyäti. kim bhuyah shrotum icchasi

O king of the Kauravas, in this way Lord Balaräma, the king of the Yädavas, spent that springtime night with the gopis. Even today the Yamuna' flows in many divided streams at that place, a testimony to the great strength, equal to that of a host of elephants, of Lord Balaräma, the Supreme Personality of Godhead. A person who hears or recounts these pastimes of Lord Balaräma destroys the entirety of a great host of sins and attains transcendental bliss. What more do you wish to hear?

Sri Balaräma-paddhati-patala
The Paddhati and Patala of Lord Balaräma
Text 1
duryodhana uvächa bhagavan gargäcäryena gopi-yuthäya kathäm dattam balabhadra-pancängam tat-krpayä vadatät. tvam sarvajno 'si.

Duryodhana said: O master, you know everything. Please kindly repeat to me what Garga Muni spoke to the gopis to tell them of the five-part worship of Lord Balaräma.

Text 2
shri prädvipäka uvächa kauravendra ekadä gargäcäryah
kalinda-nandinim snätum gargäcaläd vraja-mandalam cäjagäma.
tatraikänte
marul-liläijal-lalita-latä-taru-pallava-pushpa-gandha-matta-milinda-punje
kälindi-kula-kalita-nikunje shri-räma-krishna-dhyäna-tat-param
gargäcäryam pranamya nagendra-kanyäh sma iti jäti-smarä gopa-kanyäh
shrimad-balabhadra-präpty-artham sevanam papracchus täsäm paramäm
bhaktim vikshya paddhati-patala-stotra-kavacha-sahasra-nämäni
gopi-yuthäya sa pradadau. kim bhuyas tvam tad-grahanam kartum
icchasi vadatät.

Shri Prädvipäka Muni said: O king of the Kauravas, one day Garga Muni
left Mount Garga and went to Vraja to bathe in the Yamunä. In a certain
forest grove by the Yamuna's shore, where gentle breezes moved the
graceful trees, flowering vines, and new sprouts, and where the bees were
maddened by the sweet scent of the flowers, some gopis bowed down
before Garga Muni, who was rapt in meditation on Lord Krishna and Lord
Balaräma. Remembering their previous birth as snake-princesses, the gopis
asked him what kind of devotional service they should perform to attain the
company of Lord Balaräma. Seeing their great devotion, Garga Muni gave
these gopis the paddhati, patala, stotra, kavaca, and sahasra-näma of Lord
Balaräma. What more do you wish to hear? You may ask.

Text 3
duryodhana uväca
rämasya paddhatim bruhi
yayä siddhim vrajämy aham
tvam bhakta-vatsalo brahman
guru-deva namo 'stu te

Duryodhana said: Please describe the paddhati of Lord Balaräma, reciting
which I may attain perfection. O brähmana, you are affectionate to the
devotees. O gurudeva, I bow down before you.

Text 4
shri-prädvipäka uväca
räma-märgasya niyamam
shrinu pärthiva-sattama
yena prasanno bhavati

balabhadro mahä-prabhuh

Shri Prädvipäka Muni said: O best of kings, please hear the regulative principles of the path to Lord Balaräma. When one follows these principles Lord Balaräma, the Supreme Personality of Godhead, becomes pleased with him.

Text 5
sahasra-vadano devo
bhagavän bhuvaneshvarah
na dänair na ca tirthaish cha
bhaktyä labhyas tan ananyayä

Lord Balaräma, who is the Supreme Personality of Godhead, the master of the worlds, and who is also thousand-headed Lord Ananta, is not attained by giving charity or going on pilgrimage. He is attained only by devotional service.

Text 6
sat-saìgam etyäshu shikshed
bhaktim vai shri-harer guroh
sa siddhah kathito jätam
yasya vai prema-lakshanam

By associating with the devotees, one quickly learns the truth of devotion to Lord Krishna and to one's guru. A person who learns this is said to have attained perfection. He has attained love for Lord Krishna.

Text 7
brähme muhurte cotthäya
räma-krishneti cha bruvan
natvä gurum bhuvam caiva
tato bhumyäm padam nyaset

One should rise at brähma-muhurta, chant the holy names of Lord Krishna and Lord Balaräma, and bow down before one's guru. Only then should one place his feet on the ground.

Text 8
väry upasparshya rahasi
sthito bhutvä kushäsane

hastäv utsanga ädhäya
sva-näsägra-nirnkshanah

In a secluded place one should touch water, sit on a kusha-grass mat, place
his hands on his lap, and gaze at the tip of his nose.

Text 9
dhyäyet param harim devam
balabhadram sanätanam
gauram nilämbaram hy ädyam
vana-mälä-vibhushitam

Then one should meditate on Lord Balaräma, the eternal Supreme
Personality of Godhead, whose complexion is fair, and who is dressed in
blue garments and decorated with a forest garland.

Texts 10 and 11
evam dhyäna-paro nityam
prity-artham halinah prabhoh
tri-käla-sandhyä-krich chuddho
mauni krodha-vivarjitah
akämi gata-lobhaç cha
nirmohah satya-väg bhavet
dvi-väram jala-pänärthi
eka-bhukto jitendriyah

Pure, silent, free from anger, lust, greed, and illusion, speaking truthfully,
controlling the senses, drinking water twice in a day and eating only once,
to please Lord Balaräma one should thus meditate on Him at sunrise, noon,
and sunset.

Text 12
kshaumämbaro bhumi-shäyi
bhutvä päyasa-bhojanah
evam nirjita-shad-vargo
bhaved ekägra-mänasah

Wearing simple cotton clothing, sleeping on the ground, and fasting from
all but milk, one may conquer the material tendencies and meditate with
single-pointed concentration.

Text 13
tasya prasanno bhavati
sadä sankarshano harih
paripurnatamah säkshät
sarva-kärana-käranah

With such a person Lord Balaräma, the perfect and complete Supreme
Personality of Godhead, the cause of all causes, becomes pleased.

Text 14
ittham shri-balabhadrasya
kathitä paddhatir mayä
kauravendra mahä-bäho
kim bhuyah shrotum icchasi

O mighty-armed Kaurava king, now I have described to you the paddhati
of Lord Balaräma. What more do you wish to hear.

Text 15
duryodhana uväca
munindra deva-devasya
patalam bruhi me prabhoh
yena seväm karisyämi
tat-padämbujayoh sadä

Duryodhana said: O king of sages, O master of the demigods, please
describe to me the patala of Lord Balaräma, following which I will always
serve Lord Balaräma's lotus feet.

Text 16
shri-prädvipäka uvächa
balasya patalam guhyam
viddhi siddhi-pradäyakam
ekänte brahmanä dattam
näradäya mahätmane

Shri Prädvipäka Muni said: Now please understand Lord Balaräma's patala,
which brings perfection, and which the demigod Brahma' gave to Närada
Muni.

Text 17
pranavam purvam uddhritya
käma-bijam tatah param
kälindi-bhedana-padam
sankarshanam atah param

First, speak the syllable Om. Then, speak the Käma-bija syllable (klim).
Then recite the names Kalindi-bhedana (the breaker of the Yamuna, and
Sankarshana.

Text 18
caturthyam tam dvayam kritva
svähäm pashcad vidhäya cha
mantra-räjam imam räjan
brahmoktam shodashäkshäram

After speaking these two names, then recite the word svähä. O king, this
sixteen-syllable king of mantras was spoken by the demigod Brahmä.
Note: The mantra then is Om-klim-kälindi-bhedanäya sankarshanaya svähä.

Text 19
japel laksham vrati bhutvä
sahasräni ca shodasha
ihämutra paräm siddhim
sampräpnoti na samshayah
Following this vow one should chant this mantra 116,000 times. Thus
one will attain the supreme perfection in this life and the next. Of this there
is no doubt.

Texts 20 and 21
atha japtasya mantrasya
mahä-pujäm samäcaret
dvatrimshat-patra-samyuktam
karnikä-kesharojjvalam
bhavyam kanjam panca-varnam
likhitvä sthandile shubhe
tasyopari nyased räjan
hema-simhäsanam shubham
tasmin shri-baladevasya
paräm arcäm prapujayet

Then the person who has chanted the mantra this number of times should perform the great worship of Lord Balaräma. On auspicious ground he should draw a thirty-two petal lotus of five colors and with a splendid whorl. O king, he should place there a beautiful golden throne, and on that throne He should place Lord Balaräma. Then he should perform the great worship of Lord Balaräma.

Text 22

om-namo bhagavate purushottamäya väsudeväya sankarshanäya sahasra-vadanäya mahänantäya svähä. anena mantrena shikhä-bandhanam- kritvä sarvatas tam-pranamya tat-sammukho bhutvä svayam-nato bhavet. om-jaya jayänanta balabhadra käma-päla tälänka kälindi-bhanjana ävirävirbhüya mama sammukho bhaveti. anena mantrenävähanam-kuryät. om-namas te 'stu sira-päne hala-musala-dhara rauhineya nilämbara räma revati-ramana namo 'stu te. anena mantrenäsana-padyärghya-snäna-madhuparka-dhupa-dipa-yajnopavita-na ivedya-vastra-bhushana-gandha-pushpäkshata-pushpänjali-niräjanädin upacärän prakalpayet. om-vishnave madhusudanäya vämanäya trivikramäya shridharäya hrishikeshäya padmanäbhäya dämodaräya sankarshanäya väsudeväya pradyumnäyäniruddhäyädhokshajäya purushottamäya shri-krishnäya namah. iti päda-gulpha-jänuru-katy-udara-pärshva-prishthi-bhuja-kandhara-netra-sh irämsi prithak prithak pujayämiti mantrena sarvänga-pujäm- kuryät. atha shankha-chakra-gadä-padmäsi-dhanur-bäna-hala-musala-kaustubha-vana mälä-shrivatsa-pitämbara-nilämbara-vamshi-vetra-gadänka-tälänka-ratha -däruka-sumati-kumuda-kumudäksha-shridämädin pranava-purvena cäturthyam-tena namah samyuktena näma-mantrena prithak prithak sampujya. tathä vishvaksena-vedavyäsa-durgä-vinäyaka-dikpäla-grahädin kamale sarvatah sve sve sthäne sampujayet. punah parisamuhanädi-sthäli-päka-vidhänena vaishvänaram-sampujya purvoktena mula-mantrena panca-vimshati-sahasräny ähutir juhuyät. tathäshtau sahasräni dvädasäkshärena tathäshtau sahasräni catur-vyüha-mantrenähutir juhuyät. tato 'gnim-pradäkshini-kritya namaskrityächäryam-mahärha-vastra-suvarnäbharana-tämra-patra-savats a-go-suvarna-dakshinäbhih sampujya tathä brahmanän bhojanädyaih sampujya nagara-janebhyo bhojanam-dattväcäryän pranamet. ittham-balas

ya patalänusärena yo 'nusmarati ihämutra siddhi-samriddhibhih samvrito
bhavati. shri-räma-patalam-guhyam-mayä te hy anuvarnitam.
sarva-siddhi-pradam- räjan kim-bhuyah shrotum icchasi.

Chanting the mantra "om-namo bhagavate purushottamäya väsudeväya
sankarshanäya sahasra-vadanäya mahänantäya svähä" (Obeisances to the
Supreme Personality of Godhead, Lord Saikarñana, who is
thousand-headed Lord Ananta, and who is the son of Vasudeva), one
should tie his shikha. Then one should bow down before the deity and in
all directions.

Then, chanting the mantra "om-jaya jayänanta balabhadra
käma-päla tälänka kälindi-bhanjana ävirävirbhuya mama sammukho bhava"
(Om. O Lord Balaräma, O Lord Ananta, O fulfiller of desires, O Lord who
carries a palm-tree flag, O Lord who broke the Yamunä, all glories to You!
O Lord, please appear before me.), one should request Lord Balaräma to
appear.

Then, chanting the mantra "om-namas te 'stu sira-päne
hala-musala-dhara rauhineya nilämbara räma revati-ramana namo 'stu te"
(O Lord who holds a plow in Your hand, O Lord who holds a plow and
club, O son of Rohini, O Lord dressed in blue garments, O Balaräma, O
husband of Revati, obeisances to You!), one should offer a throne, padya,
arghya, bath, madhuparka, incense, lamp, sacred thread, food, garments,
ornaments, fragrant flowers, unbroken grains of rice, handsful of flowers,
ärati, and other services.

Then, chanting the mantra, "om-vishnave madhusudanäya
vämanäya trivikramäya shridharäya hrishikeshäya padmanäbhäya
dämodaräya sankarshanäya väsudeväya
pradyumnäyäniruddhäyädhokshajäya purushottamäya shri-krishnäya
namah. (Om. Obeisances to Lord Vishnu, the killer of Madhu, the Lord
who is the Vämana incarnation, the Lord who covered the universe in three
steps, the Lord who maintains the goddess of fortune, the master of the
senses, the Lord whose navel is a lotus flower, the Lord whose waist was
bound by a rope, the Lord who was carried from Devaki's womb, the Lord
who is the son of Vasudeva, the Lord who is Pradyumna, the Lord who is
Aniruddha, the Lord who is beyond the material senses, the Supreme
Personality of Godhead, who is all-attractive Shri Krishna!, and also the
mantra "päda-gulpha-jänuru-katy-udara-pärshva-prishthi-bhuja-kandhara-
netra-shirämsi prithak prithak pujayämi" (I worship the Lord's feet, ankles,
knees, thighs, hips, belly, sides, back, arms, shoulders, eyes, and head.), one
should worship all the limbs of Lord Balaräma.

Then, chanting the word namah before each one, and putting each word in the dative case, one should worship Lord Balaräma's conchshell (with the mantra shankhäya namah), dish (cakräya namah), club (gadäyai namah), lotus (padmäya namah), sword (asaye namah), bow (dhanushe namah), arrows (bänebhyah namah), plow (haläya namah), club (musaläya namah), Kaustubha jewel (kaustubhäya namah), forest garland (vanamäläyai namah), Shrivatsa mark (shrivatsäya namah), yellow garments (pitämbaräya namah), blue garments (nilämbaräya namah), flute (vamshyai namah), stick (veträya namah), chariot marked with the flag of Garuda (garudänka-rathäya namah), chariot marked with the flag of a palm tree (tälänka-rathäya namah), and His associates Däruka (darukäya namah), Sumati (sumataye namah), Kumuda (kumudäya namah), Kumudäksha (kumudäkshäya namah), and Shridäma' (shridämäya namah).

Then one should place Vishvaksena, Vedavyäsa, Durgä, Ganesha, the planets, and the protectors of the directions in their respective places in the lotus and then one should worship them. Then, sprinkling water and offering food cooked in an earthen pot, one should worship the sacred fire.

Then, chanting the previously described mula-mantra (om- klim-kälindi-bhedanäya sankarshanäya svähä, one should offer 25,000 oblations. Then, chanting the twelve-syllable mantra (om-namo bhagavate väsudeväya), one should offer 8,000 oblations. Then, chanting the chatur-vyüha mantra (om-namo bhagavate tubhyam-väsudeväya säkshine, pradyumnäyäniruddhäya namah sankarshanäya cha), one should again offer 8,000 oblations.

Then one should circumambulate the sacred fire, bow down before the guru, worship him with dakshina' of valuable garments, gold ornaments, copper vessels, cows with their newborn calves, and much gold, worship the brähmanas by offering them food and gifts, feed the people of the city, and bow down before the gurus. Meditating on Lord Balaräma by following this paddhati, one attains perfection in this life and the next. In this way I have described to you Lord Balaräma's confidential paddhati, which gives all perfection. O king, what more do you wish to hear?

Sri Balabhadra-stava-räja
The King of Prayers to Lord Balaräma

Text 1
duryodhana uväca
stotram shri-baladevasya
prädvipäka mahä-mune

vada mäm kripayä säkshät
sarva-siddhi-pradäyakam

Duryodhana said: O Prädvipäka, O great sage, please kindly tell me the
prayer of Lord Balaräma, which grants all perfection.

Text 2
shri-prädvipäka uväca
stava-räjam tu rämasya
vedavyäsa-kritam shubham
sarva-siddhi-pradam räjan
chrinu kaivalyadam nrinäm

Shri Prädvipäka Muni said: O king, please hear the regal and beautiful
prayer of Lord Balaräma, a prayer that brings liberation and all perfection.

Text 3
devädi-deva bhagavan
käma-päla namo 'stu te
namo 'nantäya sheshäya
säkshäd-rämäya te namah

O master of the demigods, O Supreme Personality of Godhead, O
fulfiller of desires, obeisances to You! O Lord Ananta Shesha, obeisances
to You! O Lord Balaräma, obeisances to You!

Text 4
dharä-dharäya purnäya
sva-dhämne sira-pänaye
sahasra-shirase nityam
namah sankarshanäya te

O Lord who maintains the earth, O glorious Lord, O perfect and complete
Lord, O Lord who holds a plow in Your hand, O Lord who has a thousand
heads, O Lord Sankarshana, eternal obeisances to You!

Text 5
revati-ramana tvam vai
baladeväcyutägraja

haläyudha pralamba-ghna
pähi mäm purushottama

O husband of Revati, O Lord Balaräma, O elder brother of Lord Krishna, O Lord who holds a plow-weapon, O killer of Pralambäsura, O Supreme Personality of Godhead, please protect me!

Text 6
baläya balabhadräya
tälänkäya namo namah
nilämbaräya gauräya
rauhineyäya te namah

O Lord Balaräma, who carries a palm-tree flag, obeisances to You! O son of Rohini, O fair-complexioned Lord dressed in blue garments, obeisances to You!

Text 7
dhenukärir mushtikärih
kutärir balvaläntakah
rukmy-arih kupakarnärih
kumbhandäris tvam eva hi

You are the enemy of Dhenuka, the enemy of Mushtika, the enemy of Kuta, the killer of Balvala, the enemy of Rukmi, the enemy of Kupakarna, and the enemy of Kumbhanda.

Text 8
kälindi-bhedano 'si tvam
hastinäpura-karshakah
dvividärir yädavendro
vraja-mandala-mandanah

You are the Lord who broke the Yamuna' and dragged Hastinäpura. You are the enemy of Dvivida. You are the king of the Yädavas. You are the ornament of Vraja's circle.

Text 9
kamsa-bhrätri-prahantäsi
tirtha-yäträ-karah prabhuh

duryodhana-guruh säkshät
pähi pähi prabho tö atah

You are the killer of Kamsa's brothers. You are the supreme master, the
Lord who went on pilgrimage, and Duryodhana's guru. O master, please
protect me! Please protect me!

Text 10
jaya jayäcyuta-deva parät para
svayam ananta-dig-anta-gata-shruta
sura-munindra-phanindra-caräya te
musaline baline haline namah

O infallible Lord, greater than the greatest, O Lord whose glories are heard
in all directions without limit, glory to You! Glory to You! O Lord served
by the demigods, the kings of the sages, and the kings of the serpents, O
powerful Lord who holds a plow and a club, obeisances to You!

Text 11
yah pathet satatam stavanam narah
sa tu hareh paramam padam ävrajet
jagati sarva-balam to ari-mardanam
bhavati tasya dhanam sva-janam dhanam

A person who regularly recites this prayer attains Lord Hari's
transcendental abode. All the strength in the universe is his. He crushes his
enemies. He attains great wealth and a great dynasty.

Sri Balabhadra-stotra-kavacha
The Prayer and Armor of Lord Balaräma

Text 1
duryodhana uväca
gopibhyäm kavacam dattam
gargäcäryena dhimatä
sarva-rakshä-karam divyam
dehi mahyam mahä-mune

Duryodhana said: O great sage, please give me the transcendental Balaräma-kavacha, which wise Garga Muni gave to the gopis, and which gives all protection.

Text 2
shri-prädvipäka uväca
snätvä jale kshauma-dharah kushäsanah
pavitra-päniù krita-mantra-marjanah
smritvätha natvä balam acyutägrajam
sandhärayed dharma-samähito bhavet

Shri Prädvipäka Muni said: After bathing and dressing in clean cotton garments, a person should sit on a kusha-grass mat, purify his hands with mantras, bow down, and with fixed intelligence meditate on Lord Krishna's elder brother, Lord Balaräma.

Text 3
goloka-dhämädhipatih pareshvarah
pareshu mäm pätu pavitra-kirtanahbhu-
mandalam sarshapavad vilakshyate
yan-murdhni mäm pätu sa bhumi-mandale

May Lord Balaräma, who is the master of Goloka, who is the supreme controller of all controllers, and whose fame is spotless, protect me. May Lord Balaräma, who on His head holds the earth as if it were a single mustard seed, protect me in this world.

Text 4
senäsu mäm rakshatu sira-pänir
yuddhe sadä rakshatu mäm hali cha
durgeshu chävyän musali sadä mäm
vaneshu sankarshana ädi-devah

May Lord Balaräma protect me when I am surrounded by many armies. May Lord Balaräma, who holds a plow, always protect me in battle. May Lord Balaräma, who holds a club, always protect me in many fortresses. May Lord Balaräma, the Supreme Personality of Godhead protect me in the forest.

Text 5
kalindajä-vega-haro jaleshu
nilämbaro rakshatu mäm sadägnau
väyau cha rämo 'vatu khe balash cha
mahärnave 'nanta-vapuh sadä mäm

May Lord Balaräma, who wears blue garments and who stopped the
Yamunä, always protect me in fire. May Lord Balaräma protect me in the
wind. May Lord Balaräma protect me in the sky. May Lord Balaräma, who
is Lord Ananta Himself, always protect me in the great ocean.

Text 6
shri-väsudevo 'vatu parvateshu
sahasra-shirshä cha mahä-viväde
rogeshu mäm rakshatu rauhineyo
mäm käma-pälo 'vatu va vipatsu

May Lord Balaräma, who is Vasudeva's son, protect me on mountains. May
Lord Balaräma, who has a thousand heads, protect me in great disputes.
May Lord Balaräma, who is Rohini's son, protect me from diseases. May
Lord Balaräma, who fulfills desires, protect me from catastrophes.

Text 7
kämät sadä rakshatu dhenukärih
krodhät sadä mäm dvivida-prahäri
lobhät sadä rakshatu balvalärir
mohät sadä mäm kila mägadhärih

May Lord Balaräma, who is the enemy of Dhenukäsura, always protect me
from lust. May Lord Balaräma, who killed Dvivida, always protect me from
anger. May Lord Balaräma, who is the enemy of Balvala, always protect me
from greed. May Lord Balaräma, who is the enemy of Jaräsandha, always
protect me from illusion.

Text 8
prätah sadä rakshatu vrishni-dhuryah
prähne sadä mäm mathurä-purendrah
madhyandine gopa-sakhah prapätu
svarät parähne 'vatu mäm sadaiva

May Lord Balaräma, who is the best of the Vrishnis, always protect me at sunrise. May Lord Balaräma, who is the king of Mathura' City, always protect me in the morning. May Lord Balaräma, who is the friend of the gopas, always protect me at midday. May Lord Balaräma, who is supremely independent, always protect me in the afternoon.

Text 9
säyam phanindro 'vatu mäm sadaiva
parät paro rakshatu mäm pradoshe
purne nishithe cha duranta-viryah
pratyusha-käle 'vatu mäm sadaiva

May Lord Balaräma, who is the king of serpents, always protect me at sunset. May Lord Balaräma, who is greater than the greatest, always protect me in the evening. May Lord Balaräma, whose power is invincible, always protect me in the middle of the night. May Lord Balaräma always protect me at every sunrise.

Text 10
vidikshu mäm rakshatu revati-patir
dikshu pralambärir adho yadüdvahah
urdhvam sadä mäm balabhadra ärät
tathä samantäd baladeva eva hi

May Lord Balaräma, who is the master of Revati, protect me from every direction. May Lord Balaräma, who is the enemy of Pralamba, protect me from every direction. May Lord Balaräma, who is the best of the Yädavas, protect me from below. May Lord Balaräma always protect me from above. May Lord Balaräma protect me from near and far. May Lord Balaräma protect me everywhere.

Text 11
antah sadävyät purushottamo bahir
nägendra-lilo 'vatu mäm mahä-balah
sadäntarätmä cha vasan harih svayam
prapätu purnah parameshvaro mahän

May Lord Balaräma, who is the Supreme Personality of Godhead, always protect me from within. May powerful Lord Balaräma, who enjoys pastimes as the king of serpents, protect me from without. May Lord

Balarāma, who is the Supreme Personality of Godhead, the Supersoul residing in everyone's heart, always protect me.

Text 12
devāsurānām bhaya-nāshanam cha
hutāshanam pāpa-chayendhanānām
vināshanam vighna-ghatasya viddhi
siddhāsanam varma-varam balasya

Please know that this kavacha of Lord Balarāma is the best of armors. It destroys the fears of the demigods and demons. It is a blazing fire that burns up the fuel of a host of sins. It is the death of a host of obstacles. It is the abode of spiritual perfection.

CHAPTER TWENTY-ONE

The Narayana-Kavacha
The Protective Mantric Shield
From Lord Narayana

This is found in the *Srimad-Bhagavatam* 6.8.1-42.

TEXTS 1-2

sri-rajovacha
yaya guptah sahasrakshaha
savahan ripu-sainikan
tri-lokya bubhuje shriyam

bhagavams tan mamakhyahi
varma narayanatmakam
yathatatayinah shatrun
yena gupto 'jayan mridhe

King Pariksit inquired from Sukadeva Gosvami: My lord, kindly explain the Visnu mantra armor that protected King Indra and enabled him to conquer his enemies, along with their carriers, and enjoy the opulence of the three worlds. Please explain to me that Narayana armor, by which King Indra achieved success in battle, conquering the enemies who were endeavoring to kill him.

TEXT 3

shri-badarayanir uvacha
vritah purohitas tvashtro
mahendrayanuprecchate
narayanakhyam varmaha
tad ihaika-manah shrinu

Sri Sukadeva Gosvami said: King Indra, the leader of the demigods, inquired about the armor known as Narayana-kavaca from Visvarupa, who was engaged by the demigods as their priest. Please hear Visvarupa's reply with great attention.

TEXTS 4–6

shri-vishvarüpa uvächa
dhautanghri-panir achamya
sapavitra udan-mukhah
krita-svanga-kara-nyaso
manträbhyäm vag-yatah shuchihi

narayana-param varma
sannahyed bhaya agate
padayor janunor ürvor
udare hridy athorasi

mukhe shirasy änupürvyäd
omkaradini vinyaset
om namo näräyanäyeti
viparyayam athäpi vä

TRANSLATION

Visvarupa said: If some form of fear arrives, one should first wash his hands and legs clean and then perform acamana by chanting this mantra: om apavitrah pavitro va sarvavastham gato 'pi va. yah smaret pundarikaksam sa bahyabhyantarah suchihi. sri-visnu sri-visnu sri-visnu. Then one should touch kusa grass and sit gravely and silently, facing north. When completely purified, one should touch the mantra composed of eight syllables to the eight parts of his body and touch the mantra composed of twelve syllables to his hands. Thus, in the following manner, he should bind himself with the Narayana coat of armor. First, while chanting the mantra composed of eight syllables [om namo narayanaya], beginning with the pranava, the syllable om, one should touch his hands to eight parts of his body, starting with the two feet and progressing systematically to the knees, thighs, abdomen, heart, chest, mouth and head. Then one should chant the mantra in reverse, beginning from the last syllable [ya], while touching the parts of his body in the reverse order. These two processes are known as utpatti-nyasa and samhara-nyasa respectively.

TEXT 7

kara-nyäsam tatah kuryäd
dvädashäkshara-vidyayä
pranavädi-ya-käräntam
anguly-angushtha-parvasu

TRANSLATION

Then one should chant the mantra composed of twelve syllables [om namo bhagavate vasudevaya]. Preceding each syllable by the omkara, one should place the syllables of the mantra on the tips of his fingers, beginning with the index finger of the right hand and concluding with the index finger of the left. The four remaining syllables should be placed on the joints of the thumbs.

TEXTS 8–10

nyased dhridaya omkaram
vi-karam anu murdhani
sha-karam tu bhruvor madhye
na-karam shikhaya nyaset

ve-käram netrayor yunjyan
na-käram sarva-sandhishu
ma-karam astram uddishya
mantra-murtir bhaved budhah

savisargam phad-antam tat
sarva-dikshu vinirdishet
om vishnave nama iti

TRANSLATION

One must then chant the mantra of six syllables [om visnave namah]. One should place the syllable "om" on his heart, the syllable "vi" on the top of his head, the syllable "sa" between his eyebrows, the syllable "na" on his tuft of hair [sikha], and the syllable "ve" between his eyes. The chanter of the mantra should then place the syllable "na" on all the joints of his body and meditate on the syllable "ma" as being a weapon. He should thus become the perfect personification of the mantra. Thereafter, adding visarga to the final syllable "ma," he should chant the mantra "mah astraya phat" in all directions, beginning from the east. In this way, all directions will be bound by the protective armor of the mantra.

TEXT 11

ätmänam paramam dhyäyed
dhyeyam shat-shaktibhir yutam
vidyä-tejas-tapo-mürtim
imam mantram udäharet

TRANSLATION

After finishing this chanting, one should think himself qualitatively one with the Supreme Personality of Godhead, who is full in six opulences and is worthy to be meditated upon. Then one should chant the following protective prayer to Lord Narayana, the Narayana-kavaca.

TEXT 12

om harir vidadhyän mama sarva-rakshäm
nyastänghri-padmah patagendra-prishthe
darari-carmasi-gadeshu-cäpa-
päshän dadhäno 'shta-guno 'sta-bähuh

TRANSLATION

The Supreme Lord, who sits on the back of the bird Garuda, touching him with His lotus feet, holds eight weapons--the conchshell, disc, shield, sword, club, arrows, bow and ropes. May that Supreme Personality of Godhead protect me at all times with His eight arms. He is all-powerful because He fully possesses the eight mystic powers [anima, laghima, etc.].

TEXT 13

jaleshu mäm rakshatu matsya-mürtir
yädo-ganebhyo varunasya päshät
sthaleshu mäyävatu-vämano 'vyät
trivikramah khe 'vatu vishvarüpah

TRANSLATION

May the Lord, who assumes the body of a great fish, protect me in the water from the fierce animals that are associates of the demigod Varuna. By expanding His illusory energy, the Lord assumed the form of the dwarf Vamana. May Vamana protect me on the land. Since the gigantic form of the Lord, Visvarupa, conquers the three worlds, may He protect me in the sky.

TEXT 14

durgeshv atavy-äji-mukhädishu prabhuh
päyän nrishimho 'sura-yüthapärih
vimunchato yasya mahätta-häsam
disho vinedur nyapatamsh cha garbhäha

TRANSLATION

May Lord Nrsimhadeva, who appeared as the enemy of Hiranyakasipu, protect me in all directions. His loud laughing vibrated in all directions and caused the pregnant wives of the asuras to have miscarriages. May that Lord be kind enough to protect me in difficult places like the forest and battlefront.

TEXT 15

rakshatv asau mädhvani yajna-kalpah
sva-damshtrayonnita-dharo varähah
rämo 'dri-küteshv atha vipraväse
salakshmano 'vyäd bharatägrajo 'smän

TRANSLATION

The Supreme indestructible Lord is ascertained through the performance of ritualistic sacrifices and is therefore known as Yajnesvara. In His incarnation as Lord Boar, He raised the planet earth from the water at the bottom of the universe and kept it on His pointed tusks. May that Lord protect me from rogues on the street. May Parasurama protect me on the tops of mountains, and may the elder brother of Bharata, Lord Ramacandra, along with His brother Laksmana, protect me in foreign countries.

TEXT 16

mäm ugra-dharmäd akhilät pramädän
näräyanah pätu narash cha häsät
dattas tv ayogäd atha yoga-näthah
päyäd guneshah kapilah karma-bandhät

TRANSLATION

May Lord Narayana protect me from unnecessarily following false religious systems and falling from my duties due to madness. May the Lord in His appearance as Nara protect me from unnecessary pride. May Lord Dattatreya, the master of all mystic power, protect me from falling while performing bhakti-yoga, and may Lord Kapila, the master of all good qualities, protect me from the material bondage of fruitive activities.

TEXT 17
sanat-kumäro 'vatu kämadeväd
dhayashirshä mäm pathi deva-helanät
devarshi-varyah purushärchanäntarät
kürmo harir mäm nirayäd asheshät

TRANSLATION
May Sanat-kumara protect me from lusty desires. As I begin some auspicious activity, may Lord Hayagriva protect me from being an offender by neglecting to offer respectful obeisances to the Supreme Lord. May Devarsi Narada protect me from committing offenses in worshiping the Deity, and may Lord Kurma, the tortoise, protect me from falling to the unlimited hellish planets.

TEXT 18
dhanvantarir bhagavän pätv apathyäd
dvandväd bhayäd rshabho nirjitätmä
yajnash cha lokäd avatäj janäntäd
balo ganät krodha-vashäd ahindrah

TRANSLATION
May the Supreme Personality of Godhead in His incarnation as Dhanvantari relieve me from undesirable eatables and protect me from physical illness. May Lord Rsabhadeva, who conquered His inner and outer senses, protect me from fear produced by the duality of heat and cold. May Yajna protect me from defamation and harm from the populace, and may Lord Balarama as Sesa protect me from envious serpents.

TEXT 19
dvaipäyano bhagavän aprabodhäd
buddhas tu päshanda-gana-pramädät
kalkih kaleh käla-malät prapätu
dharmävanäyoru-kritävatäraha

TRANSLATION
May the Personality of Godhead in His incarnation as Vyasadeva protect me from all kinds of ignorance resulting from the absence of Vedic

knowledge. May Lord Buddhadeva protect me from activities opposed to Vedic principles and from laziness that causes one to madly forget the Vedic principles of knowledge and ritualistic action. May Kalkideva, the Supreme Personality of Godhead, who appeared as an incarnation to protect religious principles, protect me from the dirt of the age of Kali.

TEXT 20
mäm keshavo gadayä prätar avyäd
govinda äsangavam ätta-venuh
näräyaëah prähna udätta-shaktir
madhyan-dine vishnur arindra-pänihi

TRANSLATION
May Lord Kesava protect me with His club in the first portion of the day, and may Govinda, who is always engaged in playing His flute, protect me in the second portion of the day. May Lord Narayana, who is equipped with all potencies, protect me in the third part of the day, and may Lord Visnu, who carries a disc to kill His enemies, protect me in the fourth part of the day.

TEXT 21
devo 'parähne madhu-hogradhanvä
säyam tri-dhämävatu mädhavo mäm
doshe hrishikesha utärdha-rätre
nishitha eko 'vatu padmanäbhah

TRANSLATION
May Lord Madhusudana, who carries a bow very fearful for the demons, protect me during the fifth part of the day. In the evening, may Lord Madhava, appearing as Brahma, Visnu and Mahesvara, protect me, and in the beginning of night may Lord Hrsikesa protect me. At the dead of night [in the second and third parts of night] may Lord Padmanabha alone protect me.

TEXT 22
shrivatsa-dhämäpara-rätra ishah
pratyüsha isho 'si-dharo janärdanah
dämodaro 'vyäd anusandhyam prabhäte
vishveshvaro bhagavän käla-mürtihi

TRANSLATION

May the Supreme Personality of Godhead, who bears the Srivatsa on His chest, protect me after midnight until the sky becomes pinkish. May Lord Janardana, who carries a sword in His hand, protect me at the end of night [during the last four ghatikas of night]. May Lord Damodara protect me in the early morning, and may Lord Visvesvara protect me during the junctions of day and night.

TEXT 23

cakram yugäntänala-tigma-nemi
bhramat samantäd bhagavat-prayuktam
dandagdhi dandagdhy ari-sainyam äshu
kaksam yathä väta-sakho hutäshaha

TRANSLATION

Set into motion by the Supreme Personality of Godhead and wandering in all the four directions, the disc of the Supreme Lord has sharp edges as destructive as the fire of devastation at the end of the millennium. As a blazing fire burns dry grass to ashes with the assistance of the breeze, may that Sudarsana cakra burn our enemies to ashes.

TEXT 24

gade 'shani-sparshana-visphulinge
nishpindhi nishpindhy ajita-priyäsi
kushmända-vainäyaka-yaksha-raksho-
bhüta-grahämsh cürmaya cürmayärin

TRANSLATION

O club in the hand of the Supreme Personality of Godhead, you produce sparks of fire as powerful as thunderbolts, and you are extremely dear to the Lord. I am also His servant. Therefore kindly help me pound to pieces the evil living beings known as Kusmandas, Vainayakas, Yaksas, Raksasas, Bhutas and Grahas. Please pulverize them.

TEXT 25

tvam yätudhäna-pramatha-preta-mätri-
pishächa-vipragraha-ghora-drishtin
darendra vidrävaya krishna-pürito
bhima-svano 'rer hridayäni kampayan

TRANSLATION

O best of conchshells, O Pancajanya in the hands of the Lord, you are always filled with the breath of Lord Krsna. Therefore you create a fearful sound vibration that causes trembling in the hearts of enemies like the Rakshasas, pramatha ghosts, Pretas, Matas, Pisacas and brahmana ghosts with fearful eyes.

TEXT 26

tvam tigma-dhäräsi-varäri-sainyam
isha-prayukto mama chindhi chindhi
chakshumshi charman chata-chandra chädaya
dvishäm aghonäm hara päpa-cakshushäm

TRANSLATION

O king of sharp-edged swords, you are engaged by the Supreme Personality of Godhead. Please cut the soldiers of my enemies to pieces. Please cut them to pieces! O shield marked with a hundred brilliant moonlike circles, please cover the eyes of the sinful enemies. Pluck out their sinful eyes.

TEXTS 27–28

yan no bhayam grahebhyo 'bhüt
ketubhyo nribhya eva cha
sarishpebhyo damshtribhyo
bhütebhyo 'mhobhya eva cha

sarväny etäni bhagavan-
näma-rüpänukirtanät
prayäntu sankshayam sadyo
ye nah shreyah-pratipakäh

TRANSLATION

May the glorification of the transcendental name, form, qualities and paraphernalia of the Supreme Personality of Godhead protect us from the influence of bad planets, meteors, envious human beings, serpents, scorpions, and animals like tigers and wolves. May it protect us from ghosts and the material elements like earth, water, fire and air, and may it also protect us from lightning and our past sins. We are always afraid of these hindrances to our auspicious life. Therefore, may they all be completely destroyed by the chanting of the Hare Krsna maha-mantra.

TEXT 29
garudo bhagavän stotra-
stobhash chandomayah prabhuù
rakshatv ashesha-kricchrebhyo
vishvaksenah sva-nämabhih

TRANSLATION

Lord Garuda, the carrier of Lord Visnu, is the most worshipable lord, for he is as powerful as the Supreme Lord Himself. He is the personified Vedas and is worshiped by selected verses. May he protect us from all dangerous conditions, and may Lord Visvaksena, the Personality of Godhead, also protect us from all dangers by His holy names.

TEXT 30
sarväpadbhyo harer näma-
rüpa-yänäyudhäni nah
buddhindriya-manah-pränän
päntu pärshada-bhüshanäha

TRANSLATION

May the Supreme Personality of Godhead's holy names, His transcendental forms, His carriers and all the weapons decorating Him as personal associates protect our intelligence, senses, mind and life air from all dangers.

TEXT 31
yathä hi bhagavän eva
vastutah sad asac cha yat
satyenänena nah sarve
yäntu näsham upadraväha

TRANSLATION

The subtle and gross cosmic manifestation is material, but nevertheless it is nondifferent from the Supreme Personality of Godhead because He is ultimately the cause of all causes. Cause and effect are factually one because the cause is present in the effect. Therefore the Absolute Truth, the Supreme Personality of Godhead, can destroy all our dangers by any of His potent parts.

TEXTS 32–33
yathaikātmyānubhāvānām
vikalpa-rahitah svayam
bhūshanāyudha-lingākhyā
dhatte shaktih sva-māyayā

tenaiva satya-mānena
sarva-jno bhagavān harih
pātu sarvaih svarūpair nah
sadā sarvatra sarva-gah

TRANSLATION

The Supreme Personality of Godhead, the living entities, the material energy, the spiritual energy and the entire creation are all individual substances. In the ultimate analysis, however, together they constitute the supreme one, the Personality of Godhead. Therefore those who are advanced in spiritual knowledge see unity in diversity. For such advanced persons, the Lord's bodily decorations, His name, His fame, His attributes and forms and the weapons in His hand are manifestations of the strength of His potency. According to their elevated spiritual understanding, the omniscient Lord, who manifests various forms, is present everywhere. May He always protect us everywhere from all calamities.

TEXT 34
vidikshu dikshūrdhvam adhah samantād
antar bahir bhagavān nārasimhah
prahāpayal loka-bhayam svanena
sva-tejasā grasta-samasta-tejāh

TRANSLATION

Prahlada Maharaja loudly chanted the holy name of Lord Nrsimhadeva. May Lord Nrsimhadeva, roaring for His devotee Prahlada Maharaja, protect us from all fear of dangers created by stalwart leaders in all directions through poison, weapons, water, fire, air and so on. May the Lord cover their influence by His own transcendental influence. May Nrsimhadeva protect us in all directions and in all corners, above, below, within and without.

TEXT 35

maghavann idam äkhyätam
varma näräyanätmakam
vijeshyase 'njasä yena
damshito 'sura-yüthapän

TRANSLATION

Visvarupa continued: O Indra, this mystic armor related to Lord Narayana
has been described by me to you. By putting on this protective covering,
you will certainly be able to conquer the leaders of the demons.

TEXT 36

etad dhärayamänas tu
yam yam pashyati chakshushä
padä vä samsprishet sadyah
sädhvasät sa vimucyate

TRANSLATION

If one employs this armor, whomever he sees with his eyes or touches with
his feet is immediately freed from all the above-mentioned dangers.

TEXT 37

na kutashcid bhayam tasya
vidyäm dhärayato bhavet
räja-dasyu-grahädibhyo
vyädhy-ädibhyash cha karhicit

TRANSLATION

This prayer, Narayana-kavaca, constitutes subtle knowledge
transcendentally connected with Narayana. One who employs this prayer
is never disturbed or put in danger by the government, by plunderers, by
evil demons or by any type of disease.

TEXT 38

imäm vidyäm purä kashcit
kaushiko dhärayan dvijah
yoga-dhäranayä svängam
jahau sa maru-dhanvani

TRANSLATION

O King of heaven, a brahmana named Kausika formerly used this armor when he purposely gave up his body in the desert by mystic power.

TEXT 39

tasyopari vimänena
gandharva-patir ekadä
yayau citrarathah stribhir
vrito yatra dvija-kshayah

TRANSLATION

Surrounded by many beautiful women, Citraratha, the King of Gandharvaloka, was once passing in his airplane over the brahmana's body at the spot where the brahmana had died.

TEXT 40

gaganän nyapatat sadyah
savimäno hy aväk-shiräh
sa välikhilya-vacanäd
asthiny ädäya vismitah
präsya präci-sarasvatyäm
snätvä dhäma svam anvagät

TRANSLATION

Suddenly Citraratha was forced to fall from the sky headfirst with his airplane. Struck with wonder, he was ordered by the great sages named the Valikhilyas to throw the brahmana's bones in the nearby River Sarasvati. He had to do this and bathe in the river before returning to his own abode.

TEXT 41

shri-shuka uvächa
ya idam shrinuyät käle
yo dhärayati chädritah
tam namasyanti bhütäni
muchyate sarvato bhayät

TRANSLATION

Sri Sukadeva Gosvami said: My dear Maharaja Pariksit, one who employs this armor or hears about it with faith and veneration when afraid because of any conditions in the material world is immediately freed from all dangers and is worshiped by all living entities.

TEXT 42
etäm vidyäm adhigato
vishvarüpäc chatakratuh
trailokya-lakshmim bubhuje
vinirjitya mridhe 'surän

TRANSLATION
King Indra, who performed one hundred sacrifices, received this prayer of protection from Visvarupa. After conquering the demons, he enjoyed all the opulences of the three worlds.

CHAPTER TWENTY-TWO

Powerful Prayers for Protection to Lord Narasimhadeva

These are powerful mantras for protection to the Lord's half-lion incarnation and His weapons. These are for protection from such things as malevolent spirits, ghosts, enemies, negative forces, and for blessings for the reduction of material desires, as well as for increased spiritual progress and a peaceful world.

This chapter contains an assortment of powerful mantras, including prayers to the Lord's weapons, the *Sudarshana Nrisimha Mantra*, *Ugra-Nrisimha Dhyana* (Meditation on the angry form of Lord Nrisimhadave), *Nrisimha Gayatris, Sri Nrisimha Pranama, Nrisimha Maha-mantra*, and two editions of the *Sri Nrisimha Kavacha*, Five Prayers by Bhaktivinoda Thakur, *Sri Ahovalam Stotram, Sri Nakha Stuti, Sri Narasimha Stuti*, The 108 Names of Lord Narasimahadev, Names of Sri Narasimha Yajna, the *Sri Lakshmi-Narasimha karuna-rasa-stotra* by Adi Shankaracharya, Lord Ramacandra's *Nrisimha Pancamrita, Rina-mochana Nrisimha Stotra, Sri Nrisimhashtakam, Sri Nrisimha Ashtakam*, the *Sri Shanischara-krta Sri Narasimha Stuti*, and the Thousand Names of Lord Narasimha, The *Manyu Shutka* of the *Rig Veda*, and the *Sri Nrisimha Astottara Nama Stotram*.

Prayers to the Lord's Weapons

To the Chakra

chakram yugantanala-tigma-nemi
bhramat samantad bhagavat-prayuktam
dandagdhi dandagdhy ari-sainyam ashu
kaksham yatha vata-sakho hutashaha

Set into motion by the Supreme Personality of Godhead and wandering in all the four directions, the disc of the Supreme Lord has sharp edges as destructive as the fire of devastation at the end of the millennium. As a blazing fire burns dry grass to ashes with the assistance of the breeze, may the Sudarshana chakra burn our enemies to ashes.

To the Club

gade 'shani-sparshana-visphulinge
nishpindhi nishpindhy ajita-priyasi
kushmanda-vainayaka-yaksha-raksho
bhuta-grahamsh churnaya churnayarin

O club in the hand of the Supreme Personality of Godhead, you produce sparks of fire as powerful as thunderbolts, and you are extremely dear to the Lord. I am also His servant. Therefore kindly help me pound to pieces the evil living beings known as Kushmandas, Vainayakas, Yakshas, Rakshasas, Bhutas and Grahas. Please pulverize them.

To the Conchshell

tvam yatudhana-pramatha-preta-matri
pishacha-vipragraha-ghora-drishtin
darendra vidravaya krishna-purito
bhima-svano 'rer hridayani kampayan

O best of the conchshells, O Panchajanya in the hands of the Lord, you are always filled with the breath of Lord Krishna. Therefore you create a fearful sound vibration that causes trembling in the hearts of enemies like the Rakshasas, Pramatha ghosts, Pretas, Matas, Pishachas and brahmana ghosts with fearful eyes.

Sudarshana Nrisimha Mantra

Om Sahasrara Jivalavartine
Ksaum Ham Ham Hum Phat Swaha
Om Shri Nrisinghaye namaha
Om Jaya Jaya Sri Nrisimhaye namaha
Om Nrim Nrim Nrim Nrisimhaye namaha

To Lord Narasimhadeva

vag-isha yasya vadane
laksmir yasya cha vakshasi
yasyate hridaye samvit
tam nrisimham aham bhaje

"Lord Nrisimhadeva is always assisted by Sarasvati, the goddess of learning and He is always embracing to His chest the goddess of fortune. The Lord is always complete in knowledge within Himself. Let us offer obeisances unto Nrisimhadeva." (By Sridhara Swami in his commentary on *Srimad-Bhagavatam* 10.87.1)

vidikshu dikshurdhvam adhah samantad
antar bahir bhagavan narasimhah
prahapayal loka-bhayam svanena
sva-tejasa grasta-samasta-tejaha

"Prahlada Maharaja loudly chanted the holy name of Lord Nrisimha. May Lord Nrisimhadeva, roaring for His devotee, Prahlada Maharaja, protect us from all fear of dangers created by stalwart leaders in all directions through poison, weapons, water, fire, air, and so on. May the Lord cover their influence by His own transcendental influence. May Nrisimhadeva protect us from all directions and in all corners, above, below, within and without." (*Bhag.*6.8.34)

ko nv atra te 'khila-guro bhagavan prayasa
uttarane shva bhava-sambhava-lopa-hetoho
mudheshu vai mahad-anugraha arta-bandho
kim tena te priya-janan anusevatam naha

"O my Lord, O Supreme Personality of Godhead, original spiritual master of the entire world, what is the difficulty for You, who manages the affairs of the universe, in delivering the fallen souls engaged in Your devotional service? You are the friend of all suffering humanity, and for great personalities it is necessary to show mercy to the foolish. Therefore, I think that you will show your causeless mercy to persons like us who engage in Your service." (*Bhag.*7.9.42)

om kraum narasimhaya namaha
om ksaum namo bhagavate narasimhaya
jvala-maline dipta-damstrayagni-netraya
sarva-raksho-ghnaya sarva-bhuta vinashaya
sarva-jvara-vinashaya daha daha pacha pacha
raksha raksha hum phat

"Obeisances to the Lord Nrisimhaya, burning with His own scorching effulgence which are ablaze and whose eyes pour forth torrents of living fire, matched only by the glow of His glowing teeth. Obeisances to the destroyer of all demons, to the slayer of all ghosts, to the destroyer of all sorts of fever. Burn and burn, cook and cook, preserve and preserve."

shri nrisimha, jaya nrisimha, jaya jaya nrisimha
prahladesha jaya padma-mukha-padma bringa

"All glories to Nrisimhadeva, who is the Lord of Prahlada Maharaja and, like the honey bee, is always engaged in beholding the lotus-like face of the goddess of fortune."

prahlada-hridayahladam
bhaktavidya-vidaram
sharad-indu-ruchim vande
parindra-vandanam harim

"Let me offer my obeisances unto Lord Nrisimhadeva who is always enlightening Prahlada Maharaja within his heart and who always kills the nescience that attacks the devotees. His mercy is distributed like the moonshine, and His face is like that of a lion. Let me offer my obeisances unto Him again and again."

om namo bhagavate narasimhaya
namas tejas-tejase avir-avirbhava
vajra-nakha vajra-damshtra karmashayan
randhaya randhaya tamo grasa grasa om svaha.
Abhayam abhayam atmani bhuyishtha om ksraum

"I offer my respectful obeisances unto Lord Nrisimhadeva, the source of all power. O my Lord who possesses nails and teeth just like thunderbolts, kindly vanquish our demon-like desires for fruitive activity in this material world. Please appear in our hearts and drive away our ignorance so that by Your mercy we may become fearless in the struggle for existence in this material world." (*Srimad-Bhagavatam*, 5.18.8)

> svasty astu vishvasya khalah prasidatam
> dhyayantu bhutani shivam mitho dhiya
> namash cha bhadram bhajatad adhokshaje
> aveshyatam no matir apy ahaituki

"May there be good fortune throughout the universe, and may all envious persons be pacified. May all living entities become calm by practicing bhakti-yoga, for by accepting devotional service they will think of each other's welfare. Therefore, let us all engage in the service of the supreme transcendence, Lord Sri Krishna, and always remain absorbed in thought of Him." (*Srimad-Bhagavatam*, 5.18.9)

> ugro 'py anugra evayam
> sva-bhaktanam nri-keshari
> kesarivo sva-potanam
> anyesham ugra-vikramaha

"Although very ferocious, the lioness is very kind to her cubs. Similarly, although very ferocious to non-devotees like Hiranyakashipu, Lord Nrisimhadeva is very, very soft and kind to devotees like Prahlada Maharaja."

> durgesv atavy-aji-mukhadishu prabhuh
> payan nrisimha shura-yuthaparihi
> vimunchato yasya mahatta-hasam
> disho vinedur hyapatamsh cha garbhaha

"May Lord Nrisimhadeva, who appeared as the enemy of Hiranyakashipu, protect me in all directions. His loud laughing vibrated in all directions and caused the pregnant wives of the asuras (the demoniac) to have miscarriages. May that Lord be kind enough to protect me in difficult places like the forest and battlefront." (*Srimad-Bhagavatam*, 6.8.14)

Ugra-Nrisimha Dhyana
(Meditation on the angry form of Lord Nrisimhadave)

mimamsamanasya samutthito 'grato
nrisimha-rupas tad alam bhayanakam

pratapa-chamikara-chanda-lochanam
sphurat sata-keshara-jrimbhitananam
karala-damstram karavala-chanchala
kshuranta-jihvam bhrukuti-mukholbanam

stabdhordhva-karnam giri-kandaradbhuta
vyattasya-nasam hanu-bheda-bhishanam
divi-sprishat kayam adirgha-pivara
grivoru-vakshah-sthalam alpa-madhyamam

chandramshu-gauraish churitam tanuruhair
vishvag bhujanika-shatam nakhayudham
durasadam sarva-nijetarayudha-
praveka-vidravita-daitya-danavam

"Hiranyakashipu studied the form of the Lord, trying to decide who the form of Nrisimhadeva standing before him was. The Lord's form was extremely fearsome because of His angry eyes, which resembled molten gold; His shining mane, which expanded the dimensions of His fearful face; His deadly teeth; and His razor-sharp tongue, which moved about like a dueling sword. His ears were erect and motionless, and His nostrils and gaping mouth appeared like caves of a mountain. His jaws parted fearfully, and His entire body touched the sky. His neck was very short and thick, His chest broad, His waist thin, and the hairs on His body as white as the rays of the moon. His arms, which resembled flanks of soldiers, spread in all directions as He killed the demons, rogues and atheists with His conchshell, disc, club, lotus and other natural weapons." (*Bhag.*7.8.19-22)

Sri Nrisimha Pranama
(from the *Nrisimha Purana*, offered by Sri Caitanya Mahaprabhu to Lord Jagannatha in Jagannatha Puri)

namas te narasimhaya
prahladahlada-dayine

hiranyakashipor vakshaha
shila-tanka-nakhalaye

"I offer my respectful obeisances unto You, Lord Nrisimhadeva. You are
the giver of pleasure to Prahlada Maharaja, and your nails cut the chest of
Hiranyakashipu like a chisel cutting stone."

ito nrisimhah parato nrisimho
yato yato yami tato nrisimhah
bahir nrisimho hridaye nrisimho
nrisimham adim sharanam prapadye

"Lord Nrisimha is here and also there. Wherever I go Lord Nrisimha is
there. He is in the heart and is outside as well. I surrender to Lord
Nrisimha, the origin of all things and the supreme refuge."

The Nrisimha Gayatris

Om Nrisimhaye vidmahe
vajranakhaya dhimahi
tan nah simhah pracodayat

"Om. Let us think well aware of Nrisimha, the lightning-nailed. May the
Lion promote our thought."

vajra nakhaya vidmahe
tikshna damstraya dhimahi
tan no narasimhah prachodayat

"Let us meditate on He who is known as the possessor of nails as hard as
thunderbolts and sharp teeth. Let us be enthused by Lord Narasimhadeva."

Sri Nrisimha Maha-mantra

ugram viram maha-vishnum
jvalantam sarvato mukham
nrisimham bhishanam bhadram
mrityur mrityum namamy aham

"I bow down to Lord Narasimha who is ferocious and heroic like Lord Vishnu. He is burning from every side. He is terrific, auspicious and the death of death personified."

It is stated in Shastra that this mantra is the essence of all kavacha mantras, or mantras meant for wearing in a kavacha (capsule). The mantra is often written on a small piece of bark, such as from the botch tree. Then it is sealed in the capsule with a tulasi leaf or even flower petals that have been offered to the deity of Lord Narasimha. After worshipping the deity of Lord Narasimha with sixteen upacharas or items of worship, the pujari or priest performs a ritual called prana-pratistha: he calls the Lord to reside in the kavacha. He then worships the kavacha. Then it has full protective power. Men wear the kavacha around the neck or on the upper right arm, while women wear it around the neck or on the upper left arm. The Kavacha may be worn in all circumstances, at any time, or in any place.

Sri Nrisimha Kavacha
From the Trailokya Vijaya in the Samhita of Brahma

> 1. Sri Narada-uvaca
> indr-adi deva vrndesa
> pateshvara jagat-pate
> maha vishnor nrisimhasya
> kavacho bruhi me prabho
> yasya prana thanad vidvan
> trilokya vijayi bhavet

Sri Narad Muni said: "My dear father and lord, master of the Universe, lord of the multitude of demigods headed by Indra, kindly tell me the kavaca mantra of Lord Nrsimha, the incarnation of Visnu. O master, reading this kavaca aloud, a learned man will become victorious throughout the three worlds."

> 2. sri brahmovaca
> srinu narada vaksyami
> putra shrestha tapodhana
> kavacham narasimhasya
> trailokya vijaya bhavet

"Lord Brahma said: My dear Narada, please hear me. O best of my sons, who are rich in austerity, I shall speak this kavacha of Lord Narasimha, which gives victory over the three worlds."

> 3. yasya prapathanad vayami
> trailokya vijayi bhavet
> shresthaham jagatam vatsa
> pathanat dharanat yataha

"My dear boy, by recitation of this kavaca an eloquent person will become victorious throughout the three worlds. It is by reciting this and meditating deeply on it that I (lord Brahma) am the creator of all these planetary systems."

> 4. laksmir jagat-trayam pati
> samharta cha maheshvaraha
> pathanad dharanad deva
> babhuvush cha digishvaraha

"It is by reciting and meditating upon this that Laksmi maintains the three worlds, and Lord Siva destroys them. Also the demigods in this way became controllers of the different directions."

> 5. brahma mantra nayam vakshye
> bhutadi vinvakaram
> yasya prasadad durvasa
> trailokya vijayi munih
> pathanad dharanad yasya
> shasta cha krodha bhairavaha

"I shall speak this essence of all Vedic mantras, which wards off all kinds of ghosts and hobgoblins. By its grace the sage Durvasa became victorious throughout the three worlds, commanding respect and most fearful in his anger."

> 6. trailokya-vijayasyasa
> kavachasya prajapatih
> rshish chandash cha gayatri
> nrisimho devata vibhuhu

"For this kavacha, which is directly perceived as giving victory over the three worlds, I (Brahma) am the Rsi, Gayatri is the metre, and the all powerful Nrsimhadev is the Deity."

> 7+ 8 ksraum bijam me shirah pati
> chandra-varno maha-manuhu
> "ugram viram maha-visnum
> jvalantam sarvatomukham
> nrisimham bhishanam bhadram
> mrtyu-mrtyum namamy aham"
> dva-trimshad aksharo mantro
> mantra-rajah sura drumaha

"One should place Lord Nrsimha's mantra bija, ksraum, on one's head, thinking, 'May my head be protected by the moon-colored one, who is the greatest among humans. My obeisances unto the ferocious and powerful, the great Visnu, the fiery one, who's faces are on all sides, the fearful one, Nrsimha, who causes the death of even death personified, or the one who can overcome death.' One should place this mantra, composed of thirty two syllables upon his head. It is the king of all mantras. It is like a wish fulfilling tree for the demigods and devotees."

> 9. kantham patu dhruvam ksraum hrid
> bhagavato chakshusha mama
> narasimhaya cha jvala
> maline patu mastakam

"One should also place ksraum firmly upon his neck for protection. Placing the word bhagavate upon his heart, narasimhaya upon his two eyes, and jvala maline on the top of his head, one meditates upon the different parts of this narasimha mantra protecting the different parts of his body."

> 10. dipta-damshtraya cha tatha
> agni netraya cha nasikam
> sarva-raksho-ghnaya sarva
> bhuta-vinashanaya cha

"One should place on his nose the syllables dipta damstraya agni netraya sarva rakso ghnaya sarva bhuta vinasanaya. (Obeisances unto Him, whose teeth are blazing, whose eyes are fire, and who destroys all ghosts and raksasas.)"

> 11. sarva-jvara-vinashaya
> daha daha pacha dvayam
> raksha raksha sarva-mantra
> svaha patu mukham mama

"Meditating on the protection of one's face, one should place there the syllables 'sarva jvara vinasaya daha daha paca paca raksa raksa. ksraum ugram viram maha visnum jvalanatam sarvatomukham nrsimham bhisanam bhadram mrtyu mrtyum namamy aham. ksraum bhagavate narasimhya jvalamaline dipta damstrayagni netraya sarva rakso ghnaya sarva bhuta vinasanaya svaha'. (This means: Unto He who vanquishes all fevers, oblations. Burn and burn, cook and cook, protect protect. My obeisances unto the ferocious and powerful, the great Visnu, the fiery one whose faces are on all sides, the fearful one, Nrsimha, who causes the death of even death personified, or who can overcome even death. Unto the Personality of Godhead Narasimha, garlanded with blazing energy, whose teeth are glowing and whose eyes are fiery, who kills all raksasas and demons and annihilates the ghosts, to You my oblations)"

> 12. taradi ramachandraya
> namah payad gudam mama
> klim payat pani-yugmam cha
> taram namah padam tataha
> narayanaya parshvam cha
> am hrim kraum kshraum cha hum phat

"Meditating on the protection of one's rectum, one should first sip water for purification and chant om Ramacandra namah. Sipping water again one should place the bija mantra klim on both of his hands together. Thereafter one should place om namah on his feet and narayanaya on his side, as well as the bija mantras am hrim kraum ksraum hum phat."

> 13. varaksarah katim patu
> om namah bhagavate padam
> vasudevaya cha prishtham
> klim krishnaya uru-dvayam

"Praying for the protection of one's waist, one should place there the varaksara Om. One should place the syllables om namo bhagavate upon his feet, vasudevaya on his back, and klim krsnaya upon his two thighs."

14. klim krishnaya sada patu
januni cha manuttamaha
klim glaum klim syamalangaya
namah payat pada dvayam

"Upon his knees, one should place the mantra klim krsnaya, thinking that the Lord may always protect me in His form as the best of human beings. Then one should sip water for purification and place the mantra klim glaum klim syamalangaya namah upon his feet."

15. kshraum narasimhaya kshraum cha
sarvangam me sadavatu

"One should meditate upon the constant protection of the body, placing the mantra kshraum narasimhaya kshraum upon all his limbs."

16. iti te kathitam vatsa
sarva-mantraugha-vigraham
tava snehan mayakhyatam
pravaktavyam na kasyachit

"Lord Brahma continued: My dear boy, thus I have told you the embodiment of the potencies of all mantras. Because of your great affection I have explained it to you, although it is not to be spoken to just anyone."

17. guru-pujam vidhayatha
grihniyat kavacham tataha
sarva-punya-yuto bhutva
sarva-siddhi-yuto bhavet

"Having performed worship of the spiritual master, one may accept this kavaca. Having become enriched in his pious activities he will attain all perfections."

18. shatam ashtottaram chaiva
purashcharya vidhih smritaha
havanadin dashamshena
kritva sadhaka-sattamaha

"Performing the ritualistic ceremonies of purification (purascarya) one hundred and eight times is equal to one tenth the effect received by that best of devotees who chants this kavacha."

19. tatas tu siddha-kavacaha
punyatma madanopaman
sparddham uddhuya bhavana
lakshmir vani vaset tataha

"Laksmi, the Goddess of fortune, and Sarasvati, the Goddess of speech and learning, reside in the home of that fortunate soul who has become perfected by this kavaca, giving up the intoxication of competing with others for supremacy."

20. pushpanjalyashtakam dattva
mulenaiva pathet sakrit
api varsa sahasranam
pujayah phalam apnuyat

"Simply offering eight times puspajali and reading only once the original version, one attains the result of even a thousand years of worship."

21. bhurje vilikhya gutikam
svarnastham dharayed yadi
kanthe va dakshine bahau
narasimho bhavet svayam

"If one write this down on a leaf or bark of a tree and keeps it within a golden capsule on his neck or right arm, Lord Nrsimhadeva will be personally present."

22. yoshid vama-bhuje chaiva
purusho dakshine kare
vibhryat kavacham punyam
sarva-siddhi-yuto bhavet

"A woman may keep it on her left arm, a man on the right hand. Certainly this most auspicious kavaca brings all perfection to the bearer."

23. kaka-vandhya cha ya nari
mrita-vatsa cha ya bhavet
janma-vandhya nashta putra
bahu-putravati bhavet

"A woman who is totally barren, or who bears only one child, or whose sons are lost or dead may become possessed of many sons."

24. kavachasya prasadena
jivan mukta bhaven-naraha
trilokyam kshobhayasyeva
trailokya vijayi bhavet

"By the grace of this kavaca, a man becomes jivan mukta, liberated soul even within this life time. He is able to move the whole universe, and certainly becomes victorious throughout the three worlds."

25. bhuta-preta-pishachash cha
rakshasa danavash cha ye
tam drishtva prapalayante
deshad deshantaram dhruvam

"Certainly bhutas, pretas, pisacas, raksasas, and danavas all immediately flee from the country and go to another upon seeing it."

26. yasmin gehe cha kavacham
grame va yadi tishthati
tam deshantu parityajya
prayanti chatidurantaha

"In the home or even the same village where this kavaca exists, all such demoniac creatures, once having understood its presence, give up that place and go far away."

Thus ends the Sri Nrsimha Kavaca, of the Trailokya Vijaya in the Samhita of Brahma.

Sri Nrisimha Kavacha of Prahlad
from the *Brahmanda Purana.*

shri nrisimha kavacha-stotram

nrisimha-kavacham vakshye
prahladenoditam puraa
sarva-raksha-karam punyam
sarvopadrava-naashanam

1. I shall now recite the Narasimha-kavacha, formerly spoken by Prahlada Maharaja. It is most pious, vanquishes all kinds of impediments, and provides one all protection.

sarva-sampat-karam chaiva
svarga-moksha-pradaayakam
dhyaatva nrisimham devesham
hema-sinhaasana sthitamah

2. It bestows upon one all opulences and can give one elevation to the heavenly planets or liberation. One should meditate on Lord Narasimha, Lord of the universe, seated upon a golden throne.

vivritasyam tri-nayanam
sharad-indu-sama-prabham
lakshmyaalingita-vaamaangam
vibhuutibhi rupaashritam

3. His mouth is wide open, He has three eyes, and He is as radiant as the autumn moon. He is embraced by Lakshmi devi on his left side, and His form is the shelter of all opulences, both material and spiritual.

chatur-bhujam komalaangam
svarna-kundala-shobhitam
saroja-shobitoraskam
ratna-keyuura-mudritam

4. The Lord has four arms, and His limbs are very soft. He is decorated with golden earrings. His chest is resplendent like the lotus flower, and His arms are decorated with jewel-studded ornaments.

tapta-kaanchana-sankasham
pita-nirmala-vasasam
indradi-sura-maulishthaha
sphuran manikya-diptibhih

5. He is dressed in a spotless yellow garment, which exactly resembles molten gold. He is the original cause of existence, beyond the mundane sphere, for the great demigods headed by Indra. He appears bedecked with rubies which are blazingly effulgent.

virajita-pada-dvandvam
shankha-chakradi-hetibhihi
garutmata cha vinayat
stuyamanam mudanvitam

6. His two feet are very attractive, and He is armed with various weapons such as the conch, disc, etc. Garuda joyfully offers prayers with great reverence.

sva-hrit-kamalasamvaasam
kritvaa tu kavacham pathet
nrisimho me shirah patu
loka-rakshartha-sambhavaha

7. Having seated Lord Narasimhadeva upon the lotus of one's heart, one should recite the following mantra: "May Lord Nrisimha, who protects all the planetary systems, protect my head."

sarvago 'pi stambha vasaha
phalam me rakshatu dhvanim
nrisimho me drishau paatu
soma-suryagni-lochanaha

8. Although the Lord is all-pervading, He hid Himself within a pillar. May He protect my speech and the results of my activities. May Lord Narasimha, whose eyes are the sun, and fire, protect my eyes.

smritam me patu nriharih
muni-vaarya-stuti-priyaha

nasam me simha-nasas tu
mukham lakshmi-mukha-priyaha

9. May Lord Nrihari, who is pleased by the prayers offered by the best of sages, protect my memory. May He who has the nose of a lion protect my nose, and may He whose face is very dear to the goddess of fortune protect my mouth.

sarva-vidyadhipaha patu
nrisimho rasanam mama
vaktram patv indu-vadanam
sada prahlaada-vanditaha

10. May Lord Narasimha, who is the knower of all sciences, protect my sense of taste. May He whose face is beautiful as the full moon and who is offered prayers by Prahlada Maharaja protect my face.

Nrisimha patu me kantham
skandhau bhu-bhrid ananta krit
divyastra-shobhita-bhujaha
nrisimhah patu me bhujaha

11. May Lord Narasimha protect my throat. He is the sustainer of the earth and the performer of unlimitedly wonderful activities. May He protect my shoulders. His arms are resplendent with transcendental weapons. May He protect my shoulders.

karau me deva-varado
nrisimhah patu sarvataha
hridayam yogi-sadhyash cha
nivasam patu me harih

12. May the Lord, who bestows benedictions upon the demigods, protect my hands, and may He protect me from all sides. May He who is achieved by the perfect yogis protect my heart, and may Lord Hari protect my dwelling place.

madhyam patu hiranyaksha
vaksha-kukshi-vidaranaha
nabhim me patu nriharihi
' sva-nabhi-brahma-samstutaha

13. May He who ripped apart the chest and abdomen of the great demon HiraNyaaksha protect my waist, and may Lord Nrihari protect my navel. He is offered prayers by Lord Brahmaa, who has sprung from his own navel.

> brahmanda-kotayah katyam
> yasyasau patu me katim
> guhyam me patu guhyanam
> mantranam guhya-rupa-drik

14. May He on whose hips rest all the universes protect my hips. May the Lord protect my private parts. He is the knower of all mantras and all mysteries, but He Himself is not visible.

> uru manobhavah patu
> januni nara-ruupa-drik
> janghe patu dhara-dhara
> harta yo 'sau nri-keshari

15. May He who is the original Cupid protect my thighs. May He who exhibits a human-like form protect my knees. May the remover of the burden of the earth, who appears in a form which is half-man and half-lion, protect my calves.

> sura-rajya-pradah patu
> padau me nriharishvarah
> sahasra-shirsha-purushaha
> patu me sarvashas tanum

16. May the bestower of heavenly opulence protect my feet. He is the Supreme Controller in the form of a man and lion combined. May the thousand-headed Supreme enjoyer protect my body from all sides and in all respects.

> mahograh purvatah patu
> maha-viragrajo 'ghnitaha
> maha-vishnur dakshine tu
> maha-jvalas tu nairritaha

17. May that most ferocious personality protect me from the east. May He who is superior to the greatest heroes protect me from the southeast, which

is presided over by Agni. May the Supreme Vishnu protect me from the south, and may that person of blazing luster protect me from the southwest.

> pashchime patu sarvesho
> dishi me sarvatomukhaha
> nrisimhah patu vayavyam
> saumyam bhushana-vigrahaha

18. May the Lord of everything protect me from the west. His faces are everywhere, so please may He protect me from this direction. May Lord Narasimha protect me from the northwest, which is predominated by Vaayu, and may He whose form is in itself the supreme ornament protect me from the north, where Soma resides.

> ishanyam patu bhadro me
> sarva-mangala-dayakaha
> samsara-bhayatah patu
> mrityor mrityur nrikeshari

19. May the all-auspicious Lord, who Himself bestows all-auspiciousness, protect from the northeast, the direction of the sun-god, and may He who is death personified protect me from fear of the rotation of birth and death in this material world.

> idam nrisimha-kavacham
> prahlada-mukha-manditam
> bhaktiman yah pathenaityam
> sarva-papaih pramuchyate

20. This Narasimha-kavacha has been ornamented by issuing from the mouth of Prahlada Maharaja. A devotee who reads this becomes freed from all sins.

> putravan dhanavan loke
> dirghayur upajayate
> kamayate yam yam kamam
> tam tam prapnoty asamshayam

21. Whatever one desires in this world he can attain without doubt. One can have wealth, many sons, and a long life.

sarvatra jayam apnoti
sarvatra vijayii bhavet
bhumyantariksha-divyanam
grahanam vini varanam

22. He becomes victorious who desires victory, and indeed becomes a
conqueror. He wards off the influence of all planets, earthly, heavenly, and
everything in between.

vrishchikoraga-sambhuta
vishhapaharanam param
brahma-rakshasa-yakshanam
durotsarana-karanam

23. This is the supreme remedy for the poisonous effects of serpents and
scorpions, and Brahma-raakshasa ghosts and Yakshas are driven far away.

bhuje va tala-patre va
kavacham likhitam shubham
kara-mule dhritam yena
sidhyeyuh karma-siddhayaha

24. One may write this most auspicious prayer on his arm, or inscribe it on
a palm-leaf and attach it to his wrist, and all his activities will become
perfect.

devasura-manushyeshhu
svam svam eva jayam labhet
eka-sandhyam tri-sandhyam va
yah pathen niyato naraha

25. One who regularly chants this prayer, whether once or thrice (daily), he
becomes victorious whether among demigods, demons, or human beings.

sarva-mangala-mangalyam
bhuktim muktim cha vindati
dva-trimshati-sahasrani
pathet shuddhatmanam nrinam

26. One who with purified heart recites this prayer 32,000 times attains the most auspicious of all auspicious things, and material enjoyment and liberation are already understood to be available to such a person.

> kavachasyasya mantrasya
> mantra-siddhih-prajayate
> anena mantra-rajena
> kritva bhasmabhir mantranam

27. This Kavacha-mantra is the king of all mantras. One attains by it what would be attained by anointing oneself with ashes and chanting all other mantras.

> tilakam vinyased yas tu
> tasya graha-bhayam haret
> tri-varam japamanas tu
> dattam varyabhimantrya cha

28. Having marked ones body with tilaka, taking achamana with water, and reciting this mantra three times, one will find that the fear of all inauspicious planets is removed.

> prasayed yo naro mantram
> nrisimha-dhyanam acharet
> tasya rogah pranashyanti
> ye cha syuh kukshi-sambhavaha

29. That person who recites this mantra, meditating upon Lord Narasimhadeva, has all of his diseases vanquished, including those of the abdomen.

> garjantam garjayantam nija-bhuja-patalam sphotayantam hatantam
> rupyantam tapayantam divi bhuvi ditiyam kshepayantam kshipantam
> krandantam roshayantam dishi dishi satantam samharantam bharantam
> vikshantam purnayantam kara-nikara-shatair divya-simham namami

30. Lord Narasimha roars loudly and causes others to roar. With His multitudes of arms He tears the demons asunder and kills them in this way. He is always seeking out and tormenting the demonic descendants of Diti, both on this earth planet and in the higher planets, and He throws them

down and scatters them. He cries with great anger as He destroys the demons in all directions, yet with His unlimited hands He sustains, protects, and nourishes the cosmic manifestation. I offer my respectful obeisances to the Lord, who has assumed the form of a transcendental lion.

iti shri brahmanda-purane prahladoktam
shri nrisimha-kavacham sampurnam

Thus ends the Narasimha-kavacha as it is described by Prahlada Maharaja in the *Brahmanda Purana*.

Five Prayers to Lord Narasimha
by Bhaktivinoda Thakura

Srila Bhaktivinoda Thakura has written five beautiful prayers in "Sri Navadvipa Bhava Taranga" for receiving the mercy of Lord Narasimha. These prayers are certainly assurance to all sincere devotees that the worship of Lord Narasimha is purely in the line of aspiring love and devotion to Sri Sri Radha and Krishna. Those prayers are as follows.

e dusta hrdaye kama adi ripu chaya
kutinati pratisthasa sathya sada raya
hrdaya-sodhana ara krsnera vasana
nrsimha-carane mora ei to' kamana

Within my sinful heart the six enemies headed by lust perpetually reside, as well as duplicity, the desire for fame, plus sheer cunning. At the lotus feet of Lord Narasimha, I hope that He will mercifully purify my heart and give me the desire to serve Lord Krsna.

kandiya nrsimha-pade magibo kakhana
nirapade navadvipe jugala-bhajana
bhaya bhaya paya yan'ra darsane se hari
prasanna hoibo kabe more daya kari

Weeping, I will beg at the lotus-feet of Lord Narasimha for the benediction of worshipping Radha and Krsna in Navadvipa, perfectly safe and free from all difficulties. When will this Lord Hari, Whose terrible form strikes fear into fear itself, ever become pleased and show me His mercy?

yadyapi bhisana murti dusta-jiva-prati
prahladadi krsna-bhakta-jane bhadra ati
kabe va prasanna ho'ye sa krpa-vacane
nirbhaya karibe ei mudha akincane

Even though Lord Narasimha is terrifying toward the sinful souls, He offers great auspiciousness unto the devotees of Lord Krishna headed by Prahlada Maharaja. When will He be pleased to speak words of compassion unto me, a worthless fool, and thereby make me fearless?

svacchande baiso he vatsa sri-gauranga-dhame
jugala-bhajana hau rati hau name
mama bhakta-krpa-bale vighna jabe dura
suddha cite bhajo radha-krsna-rasa-pura

He will say, "Dear child! Sit sown freely and live happily here in Sri Gauranga-dhama. May you nicely worship the Divine Couple, and may you develop loving attachment for Their Holy Names. By the mercy of My devotees, all obstacles are cast far away. With a purified heart, just perform the worship of Radha and Krishna, for such worship overflows with sweet nectar."

ei boli' kabe mora mastaka-upara
sviya sri-carana harse dharibe isvara
amani jugala-preme sattvika vikare
dharaya lutibo ami sri-nrsimha-dvare

Saying this, will that Lord delightedly place His own divine lotus-feet upon my head? I will experience sublime love for the Divine Couple Radha-Krsna and undergo the ecstatic transformations called sattvika. Falling on the ground, I will roll about at the door of Sri Narasimha's temple.

(Srila Bhaktivinoda Thakura, - "Sri Navadvipa Bhava Taranga", 36-40)

Sri Ahovalam Stotram

(Obeisances to Ahovalam Narasimha)
(Use the same meter as the *Brahma-samhita*. These were written in glorification of all the Deities in the holy place of Lord Nrisimha at Ahobalam)

lakshmi-kataksha-sarasi-ruha-raja-hamsam
pakshindra-shaila-bhavanam bhava-nasham isham
gokshira-sara-ghana-sara-patira-varnam
vande kripa-nidhim ahobala-narasimham

"I offer my obeisances to that ocean of mercy, Ahobala Nrisimha. He is a great swan swimming amongst the lotuses of Lakshmi's furtive glances. He is the Supreme Lord, who puts an end to material imprisonment and who appeared from the stone of the Garuda pillar. His body has lines of color: both a creamy color and the color of rain clouds."

adyanta-shunyam ajam avyayam aprameyam
aditya-candra-shikhi-locanam adi-devam
abja-mukabja-mada-lolupa-matta-bhringam
vande kripa-nidhim ahobala-narasimham

"I offer my obeisances to that ocean of mercy, Ahobala Nrisimha. He has no beginning or end. He is unborn, everlasting, and immeasurable. He is the original God who gives brightness to the sun, moon, and to fire. He is like a honey bee intoxicated by his passionate desire for the lotus face of Lakshmi."

kotira-koti-ghatitojjvala-kanti-kantam
keyura-hara-mani-kundala manditangam
cudagra-ranjita-sudhakara-purna-bimbam
vande kripa-nidhim ahobala-narasimham

"I offer my obeisances to that ocean of mercy, Ahobala Nrisimha. He looks splendid with his thick shiny mane tied back and with his body decorated with armlets, necklaces, and jewelled ear rings. His face is like the disc of the full moon, adorned with his crown."

varaha-vamana-nrisimha-subhagyam isham
krida-vilola-hridayam vibhudendra-vandyam
hamsatmakam paramahamsa-mano-viharam
vande kripa-nidhim ahobala-narasimham

"I offer my obeisances to that ocean of mercy, Ahobala Nrisimha. He is the all-fortunate supreme Lord: Varaha, Vamana, and Nrisimha. His heart is

frolicking with his own playful pastimes. The most intelligent persons pray
to him, the Supreme soul, who fascinates the great sages."

mandakini-janana-hetu-padaravindam
vrndarakalaya-vinodanam ujjvalangam
mandara-pushpa-tulasi-racitanghri-padmam
vande kripa-nidhim ahobala-narasimham

"I offer my obeisances to that ocean of mercy, Ahobala Nrisimha. His lotus
feet are the source of the Ganges. His body is resplendent as he enjoys
himself in his superexcellent abode, and his lotus feet are bedecked with
Tulasi leaves and the flowers from the heavenly coral tree."

tarunya-krishna-tulasi-dala-dhama-rabhyam
dhatri ramabhi ramanam mahaniya-rupam
mantradhi-raja-matha-danava-mana-bhangam
vande kripa-nidhim ahobala-narasimham

"I offer my obeisances to that ocean of mercy, Ahobala Nrisimha. His most
favorite thing is fresh dark Tulasi leaves. He exhibits a magnificent form
as he enjoys with his female assistants, the goddesses of fortune. He breaks
the pride of the demons by destroying Ravana, that master of magic spells."

<h3 style="text-align:center">Sri Nakha Stuti</h3>
(offered to Madhvacharya)

paantvasmaam puruuhutavairi balavanmaatanga maadyadghataa
kumbhocchaadri vipaatanaadhi kapatu pratyekavajraayitaah
Shrimat kanthiravaasya pratatasunakharaa daaritaaraatiduura
pradhvasta dhvaatashaanta pravitata manasaa bhaavitaa nakivrnda

"May the wide-spread and auspicious nails of the lion-faced God,
Narasimha, Who is in the company of His consort Laxmi, protect us. His
nails are like thunderbolts and are highly skilled in tearing asunder the lofty
mountain-like heads of the herds of strong and intoxicated elephants in the
form of demons; the foes of Indradev. His nails are also meditated upon by
the groups of devas with their broad minds which are concentrated upon
Him and from which the darkness of ignorance is driven away to a great
distance and the internal enemies of lust, anger, etc., are torn in twain."

lakshmikaanta samantato vikalayannai veshituste saman
pashyaamyuttama vastu duurataarato paastam rasoyo stumah
yadrosotkara daksanetra kutila prantotthitogni sphurat
khadyotopamavisphylinya bhasitaa brhmeshushakrot karaan

"Oh consort of Laxmi! Although I've made an all round study of the
shastras, I don't find anything equal to You, Who are my master! The thing
thought superior to You is therefore flung far and is similar to the 8th tuste
(it does not exist). Brahma, Shiva, Indra and their hosts are reduced to
ashes by the sparks of fire resembling sparking glowworms and issuing
from the curved edge of Your right eye which is filled with masses of
wrath."

(From the Introduction of Sri Hari Vayuh Stuti of Trivikram Panditacharya)

Sri Narasimha Stuti

This is a powerful prayer to Lord Narasimha for one's protection
from the dark elements and demons within this material world. It was
written by Pandit Trivikramacharya, a leading disciple of Sri
Madhvacharya.

1. udaya ravi sahasra-dhyotitam ruksa-viksam
pralaya jaladhi-nadam kalpa-krid vahni-vaktram
sura-pati-ripu-vakshah-kshoda-rakta-kshitangam
pranata-bhaya-haram tam narasimham namami

The radiance of a thousand rising suns is the glow on the Lord's face. His
eyes are fiery and His voice roars like the turbulent ocean of devastation.
His body is wet with the blood of Indra's foe, Hiranyakashipu. Lord
Narasimha, the redeemer of the fear ridden, I bow down to Your feet.

2. pralaya-ravi-karalakara-ruk chakra-valam
virala-yaduru-rocirocitashanta-ralam
prati-bhaya-tama-kopatyutkatoccatta-hasin
daha daha narasimasahya-viryahitam me

Your effulgence is dazzling like that of the destructive sun, pralayaravi. It
glows and glitters, makes the wicked tremble with fear. You laugh in a

piercing high tone at the fear, ignorance and anger of the demons. Burn Narasimha, burn my adversaries with Your unbearable power.

> 3. sara-sa rabha-sapadapata-bharabhirava
> pracakita-chala-sapta-dvandva-loka-stutas tvam
> ripu-rudhira-nishekenaiva shonamghri-shalin
> daha daha narasimasahya-viryahitam me

Your lotus feet are reddened by the blood of the enemy. Fourteen lokas are scared by the stamping of Your feet. Demigods assemble, fear and tremble and pray for Your mercy. Burn Narasimha, burn my adversaries with Your unbearable power.

> 4. tava ghanaghana-ghosho ghoram aghraya jamgha
> parigham alaghum uru-vyaja-tejo-girim cha
> ghana vighatitam aga-daitya-jamghala-samgho
> daha daha narasimasahya-viryahitam me

You take great pleasure in slaughtering the armies of the demons. You wield Your heavy mace in a most cunning manner with the force of a great mountain. As You chop demons into pieces others immediately flee for their lives. Burn Narasimha, burn my adversaries with Your unbearable power.

> 5. kataki-kata-karala-dhatakagrya-stha-labha
> prakata-pata-tadit te sat-katishthati-patvi
> katuka katuka dushtatopadrishti-pramushtau
> daha daha narasimhasahya viryahitam me

The mountains of Your hips are nicely decorated with yellow garments, which appear just like lightning in its intense brilliance. Attacking fiercely he who had the foremost position (the seat of King Indra), You removed the threat of that exceedingly wicked one. O ferocious one! Burn Narasimha, burn my adversaries with Your unbearable power.

> 6. prakhara-nakhara-vajrotkhata-rukshari-vakshaha
> shikhari-shikhara raktai rakta nandoha-deha
> suvalibha-shubha-kukshe bhadra gambhira-nabhe
> daha daha narasimasahya viryahitam me

As Your nails, sharp like thunderbolts, tore the abdomen of the enemy, blood surged from the body of the demon and bathed You. Your lotus-like navel is deep and Your abdomen is decorated with the auspicious three lines. Burn Narasimha, burn my adversaries with Your unbearable power.

> 7. sphurayati tava sakshat saiva nakshatra-mala
> kshapita-ditija-vaksho-vyapta-nakshatra-marga
> ari-dara-dhara-janvasakta-hasta-dvayaho
> daha daha narasimasahya viryahitam me

Your two hands, as they directly burst open the chest of the son of Diti, appear just like a necklace of stars. Supporting him on Your knees, You tore his chest apart which blocked the path of the stars. Burn Narasimha, burn my adversaries with Your unbearable power.

> 8. katu-vikata-sataudho-dhattanad bhrashta-bhuyo
> ghana-patala-vishalakasha-labdhavakasham
> kara-parigha-vimarda-prodyamam dhyayatas te
> daha daha narasimasahya viryahitam me

Your mane is burning and monstrous, and You cause the enemy to fall from his position by tearing apart his chest. Once attaining the opportunity, under the broad roof of the clouds and sky, You raise Your hand, powerful as a mace, to strike. I meditate upon You in this form. Burn Narasimha, burn my adversaries with Your unbearable power.

> 9. hata-lutada-laghisthotkantha-dashto 'sta-vidyut
> sata-shata-katianorah-pitha-bhit sushtu nistham
> patati nu tava kanthadhishtha-ghorantramala
> daha daha narasimasahya viryahitam me

Appearing brilliantly illuminated, Your neck, with hundreds of mane-hairs, is raised lightly and appears to be bitten by eight bolts of lightning. You divide the chest and very strong position of Hiranyakashipu. You are garlanded with his ghastly entrails. Burn Narasimha, burn my adversaries with Your unbearable power.

> 10. hata-bahu-mihirabhasa hy asamhara-ramho
> huta-vaha-bahu-hetir hrepikananta-hetihi

ahata-yihita-mohan samvihansai ham asyam
daha daha narasimhasahya viryahitam me

The effulgence of many suns is destroyed by Your uncheckable potency.
The many weapons sent against You are like sacrificial offerings, and You
reply with unlimited weaponry. Put down, strike and slay my illusion. Burn
Narasimha, burn my adversaries with Your unbearable power.

11. guru-guru-giri-rajat-kandarantargad eva
dina-mani-mani-shringevanta-vahni-pradipte
daddhad ati-kau-damstre bhishanojjihva-vaktram
daha daha narasimhasahya viryahitam me

My Lord, Your fearful countenance, with tongue extended and sharp teeth
blazing as if illuminated from within, appears as the peak of a huge
mountain of gems lit by the sunrise and by fire coming from within its
caves. Burn Narasimha, burn my adversaries with Your unbearable power.

12. adharita-vibudhadhi-dhyana-dhairya vididhyad
vividha-vibudhadhi shraddha-pitendrari-nasham
vidadhad ati-katahoddhatanoddhatta-hasam
daha daha narasimhasahya viryahitam me

The enemy of Indra (Hiranyakashipu) made waves in the ocean of
demigods and took the shraddha offerings meant for the forefathers.
Confounding the intelligence of the demigods, he minimized their austerity
and position in various ways. But You, O Narasimha, melted him in the pot
of Your shrill laughter. Burn Narasimha, burn my adversaries with Your
unbearable power.

13. tri-bhuvana-trina-matra-trana-trishardra
netra-trayam ati-laghitarchir vishtapavishtapadam
navatara-ravi-tamram dharayan ruksha-viksham
daha daha narasimhasahya viryahitam me

Every living being in the three worlds, down to the blade of grass, was
scorched by the flame of Hiranyakashipu. But You, with Your three eyes,
have annihilated this flame. Your appearance is threatening to the
miscreants, and Your color is coppery like the newly risen sun. Burn
Narasimha, burn my adversaries with Your unbearable power.

14. bhramad abhi-bhava-bhubhrid bhuri-bhubhara-sad
bhidbhida-nava-vibhava-bhru-vibhramadabhra-shubhra
ripu-bhava-bhayam etar bhasi bho bho vibho 'bhir
daha daha narasimhasahya viryahitam me

You wander about without resistance, for You are the supreme power and
the maintainer of the earth. Hail to You, O Lord; You are effulgent and
fearful to Your enemies, although You fear no one. You divided into nine
parts the burden of the earth (Hiranyakashipu) simply by the effulgence
produced by the movement of Your eyebrows. Burn Narasimha, burn my
adversaries with Your unbearable power.

15. shravana-khachita-canchat-kundaloccanda-ganda
bhrukuti katu lalata-shreshtha-nasarunoshta
varada surada rajat-kesarotsaritare
daha daha narasimhasahya viryahitam me

Your ears are prominent, Your earrings swing to and fro and Your face
appears ferocious. Your eyebrows give Your forehead a threatening aspect,
and You are most beautiful with Your high nose and reddish lips. O giver
of benedictions, well-wisher of the demigods and devotees, the enemy is
scattered by the effulgence the hair of Your mane. Burn Narasimha, burn
my adversaries with Your unbearable power.

16. pravikavacha-kacha-rajad-ratna kotira-shalin
gala-gata galad-usradara-ratnangadadhya
kanaka-kataka-kanchi sinjini sudrikavan
daha daha narasimhasahya viryahitam me

You wear no armor, yet You are decorated by beautiful locks of shining
hair and many ornaments made of jewels. Your bodily effulgence appears
as if You had swallowed the newly-risen sun. Your hands exhibit various
mudras, and Your waist is decorated with a gold chain, making a tinkling
noise. Burn Narasimha, burn my adversaries with Your unbearable power.

17. ari-daram asi hetau chapa-banau gadam
san-mushalam api kapolam cankusham pasha-shulam
dadhad api vidhutantra-sragvi-bhinnari-vaksho
daha daha narasimhasahya viryahitam me

You are equipped with bow and arrow, as well as various astras or missiles, club, mace, rod for controlling elephants, noose, and trident. Placing the enemy upon Your lap and tearing open his abdomen, he is thus purified of all contamination, and therefore You take his intestines and wear them as a victory garland. Burn Narasimha, burn my adversaries with Your unbearable power.

> 18. cata cata cata duram mohayan bhramayarin
> kada kada kada kayam jvalaya sphotayasva
> jahi jahi jahi vegam shatravah sanubandham
> daha daha narasimhasahya viryahitam me

Fall upon my foes, fall upon them, fall upon them. Bewilder them and drive them far away. Consume, consume, consume the bodies of the enemies; incinerate and burst them asunder. Conquer, conquer, conquer forcefully my foes and their followers. Burn Narasimha, burn my adversaries with Your unbearable power.

> 19. vidhi-bhava-vibudhesha-bhramakagni-sphulinga
> prasavi-vikata-damshtrojjihva-vaktra trinetra
> kala kala kala kalam pahi mam te subhaktam
> daha daha narasimhasahya viryahitam me

Even Lord Brahma, Lord Shiva and King Indra are bewildered to see Your tongue, like a firebrand, pressed between Your gigantic teeth. O three-eyed one, Your face appears most fearful, like time personified. Sound out the fate of the demons and kindly protect me, Your surrendered servant. Burn Narasimha, burn my adversaries with Your unbearable power.

> 20. kuru kuru karunam tvam sankuram daitya-pote
> disha disha vishadam me shashvatim deva-drishtim
> jaya jaya jaya murte 'narta jetavya-paksha
> daha daha narasimhasahya viryahitam me

O supreme form, Have mercy, have mercy upon me. Dispel, dispel my ignorance just as You uprooted the child of Diti. You are never subjected to the sufferings of material existence. Neither are You defeated; indeed, whoever You favor will always triumph. Be victorious. Bestow upon me the divine vision to see You always. Burn Narasimha, burn my adversaries with Your unbearable power.

21. stutir iyam ahita-ghnisevita narasimhi
tanur iva parishanta-malini sabhitolam
tad akhila-gurum agrya-shrida-rupa-mahadbhihi
daha daha narasimhasahya viryahitam me

This prayer, offered in devotional service to Lord Narasimhadeva, destroys all inauspicious things. That Lord of the universe, the universal teacher, appearing as if garlanded by the destroyed body of Hiranyakashipu, bestows all good fortune and opulence upon His worshipers. Burn Narasimha, burn my adversaries with Your unbearable power.

22. likucha-tilaka-sunuh sad-dhitartanusari
narahari-nitim etam shatru-samhara-hetum
akrita-sakala-papa-dhvamsanim yah pathet tam
daha daha narasimhasahya viryahitam me

The Lord appears in a seemingly bitter form to act for the protection of His devotee Prahlada. Anyone who reads this description of the character of Lord Narahari causes his enemies to retreat, and his sins are undone and vanquished. Burn Narasimha, burn my adversaries with Your unbearable power.

108 Names of Lord Narasimhadeva

1. Om narasimhaya namah
    Obeisances unto the half-man half-lion Lord
2. Om mahasimhaya namah
    Obeisances to the great lion
3. Om diyva-simhaya namah
    Obeisances to the Divine lion
4. Om mahabalaya namah
    Obeisances to the greatly powerful
5. Om ugra-simhaya namah
    Obeisances to the angry terrifying lion
6. Om mahadevaya namah
    Obeisances to the Lord of lords
7. Om stambha-ja-aya namah
    Obeisances to One who appeared from the pillar
8. Om ugra-locanaya namah
    Obeisances to one who possesses terrifying eyes

9. Om raudraya namah
     Obeisances to the angry one
10. Om sarvadbhutaya namah
     Obeisances to one who is wonderful in every way
11. Om srimanaya namah
     Obeisances to the most beautiful
12. Om yoganandaya namah
     Obeisances to the source of yogic bliss
13. Om trivikramaya namah
     Obeisances to Lord Vamana (Who took three great steps)
14. Om harine namah
     Obeisances to Sri Hari Who takes our troubles away
15. Om kolahalaya namah
     Obeisances to the roaring (Varahadeva - Varaha-nrisimha)
16. Om cakrine namah
     Obeisances to Him Who carries the disk
17. Om vijayaya namah
     Obeisances to Him Who is always victorious
18. Om jaya-vardhanaya namah
     Obeisances unto Him Who has ever increasing glories
19. Om panchananaya namah
     Obeisances unto Him Who is five-headed
20. Om param-brahma-aya namah
     Obeisances unto Supreme Absolute Truth
21. Om aghoraya namah
     Obeisances to Him Who for His devotees is not horrible
22. Om ghora-vikramaya namah
     Obeisances to Him Who has terrifying activities
23. Om jvalan-mukhaya namah
     Obeisances to One Who has an effulgent face
24. Om jvala-maline namah
     Obeisances to Him with effulgent garland of flames
25. Om mahajvalaya namah
     Obeisances to He Who is most effulgent
26. Om maha-prabhuhaya namah
     Obeisances to the Supreme Master
27. Om niti-laksaya namah
     Obeisances to Him Who possesses all good (moral) qualities
28. Om sahasraksaya namah
     Obeisances to the thousand-eyed One

29. Om durniriksyaya namah
     Obeisances to Him Who is difficult to see (difficult to look at)
30. Om pratapanaya namah
     Obeisances to Him Who oppresses His enemies with great heat
31. Om mahadamstraya namah
     Obeisances to Him Who possesses huge teeth
32. Om yudha-prajnaya namah
     Obeisances to the Supremely intelligent in battle (ready to fight)
33. Om canda-kopine namah
     Obeisances to Him Who is likened to an angry moon
34. Om sada-sivaya namah
     Obeisances to the All auspicious Lord
35. Om hiranyakasipu-dhvamsine namah
     Obeisance to Him Who destroys Hiranyakasipu
36. Om daitya-danava-bhanjanaya namah
      Obeisances to He Who destroys the masses of the race of demons
      and giants
37. Om guna-bhadraya namah
     Obeisances unto Narasimha Who is full of wonderful qualities
38. Om mahabhadraya namah
     Obeisances to Him Who is very auspicious
39. Om bala-bhadraya namah
     Obeisances to Him Who is auspiciously powerful
40. Om subhadrakaya namah
     Obeisances to the extremely auspicious One
41. Om karalaya namah
     Obeisances to He Who possesses a wide open mouth
42. Om vikaralaya namah
     Obeisances to Him with very wide open mouth
43. Om vikartaya namah
     Obeisances to the Lord Who performs wonderful activities
44. Om sarva-kartrikaya namah
     Obeisances to the Lord Who performs ALL activities
45. Om sisumaraya namah
     Obeisances to Him Who also appears as Matsya
46. Om trilokatmaya namah
     Obeisances to the Soul of the three worlds
47. Om isaya namah
     Obeisances to the Lord known as the controller

48. Om sarvesvaraya namah
      Obeisances to that supreme controller
49. Om vibhuaya namah
      Obeisances to Narasimha Who is the BEST
50. Om bhaivaradambaraya namah
      Obeisances to Him Who causes terror by roaring in the sky
51. Om divyaya namah
      Obeisances to That Divine Person Narasimha
52. Om acyutaya namah
      Obeisances to our infallible Lord Nara-simha
53. Om kavine namah
      Obeisances to the Supreme intelligent (poet)
54. Om madhavaya namah
      Obeisances to the husband of Srimati Laksmi devi
55. Om adhoksajaya namah
      Obeisances to Him Who is beyond understanding (or beyond
      explaining)
56. Om aksaraya namah
      Obeisances to the infallible One
57. Om sarvaya namah
      Obeisances to He Who is the origin of everything
58. Om vanamaline namah
      Obeisances to Him Who wears garland of forest flowers (or
      adorned by His loving devotees)
59. Om varapradaya namah
      Obeisances to the Merciful Lord Who grants boons to the
      deserving like Prahlada
60. Om visvambaraya namah
      Obeisances to Narasimha Who maintains the universe
61. Om adbhutaya namah
      Obeisances to Him Who is wonderful
62. Om bhavyaya namah
      Obeisances to He Who determines the future (Who is the future for
      His devotees)
63. Om sri-visnave namah
      Obeisances to that Narasimha Who is the all pervading Lord
      Vishnu
64. Om purusottamaya namah
      Obeisances to Narasimha Who is the Supreme Enjoyer

65. Om anaghastra namah
    Obeisances to Him Who can never be wounded by weapons
66. Om nakhastraya namah
    Obeisances to Him Who has sharp nails for weapons
67. Om surya-jyotine namah
    Obeisances to Narasimha the source of Suns rays
68. Om suresvaraya namah
    Obeisances to Narasimhadev, Lord of devatas
69. Om sahasra-bahu-aya namah
    Obeisances to Nara-hari the thousand-armed Lord
70. Om sarva-jnaya namah
    Obeisances to Him Who is the all-knowing
71. Om sarva-siddhi-pradayakaya namah
    Obeisances to Him Who awards all perfections to the sadhakas
    (devotees)
72. Om vajra-damstraya namah
    Obeisances to Narasimha Who has teeth like lightning bolts
73. Om vajra-nakhaya namah
    Obeisances to Narasimha Who possesses nails like piercing
    lightning bolts
74. Om mahanandaya namah
    Obeisances to the source of supreme bliss - Atmananda -
    Narasimha
75. Om param-tapaya namah
    Obeisances to the source of All austerities, spiritual energy (and
    taptah - heat)
76. Om sarva-mantraika-rupa namah
    Obeisances to that Divine Personality Who although one, he
    appears as the many mantrika formulas
77. Om sarva-yantra-vidaramaya namah
    Obeisances to Him Who destroys all machines (demoniac
    plans/arrangements/vehicles for demoniac works)
78. Om sarva-tantratmakaya namah
    Obeisances to Narasimha the essence of, and proprioter of all
    tantras (ritual rites - pujas)
79. Om avyaktaya namah
    Obeisances to the Lord Who appears unmanifest
80. Om suvyaktaya namah
    Obeisances unto Nara-simha Who for His devotees becomes
    wonderfully manifest from the pillar (or when needed)

81. Om bhakta-vatsala namah
    Obeisances to the Lord Who always has the well-being of His
    devotee at heart
82. Om vaisakha-sukla-bhototthaya namah
    Obeisances to That Narasimhadeva Who appeared during waxing
    moon of the month of Visakha (April-May)
83. Om saranagata-vatsalaya namah
    Obeisances to the Lord Who is kind to those surrendered to Him
    (like the mother lioness who is kind to her cubs)
84. Om udara-kirtine namah
    Obeisances to Nara-simha Who is universally famous
85. Om punyatmaya namah
    Obeisances to Him Who is the essence of piety
86. Om mahatmaya namah
    Obeisances to That great personality, Nara-simha
87. Om candra-vikramaya namah
    Obeisances to Him Who is the performer of moonlike or great
    deeds, or who performs deeds that eclipse all others.
88. Om vedatrayaya namah
    Obeisances to the Lord of the three original Vedas (Rg, Yajur,
    Sama)
89. Om prapujyaya namah
    Obeisances to Narasimha Who is supremely worshipable
90. Om bhagavanaya namah
    Obeisances to Narasimha the Supreme Personality of Godhead
91. Om paramesvaraya namah
    Obeisances to He Who is the Supreme Controller
    (Nara-simha-deva)
92. Om srivatsamkaya namah
    Obeisances to the Lord Who is just like Krishna, being marked
    with symbol of Laksmi
93. Om jagat-vyapine namah
    Obeisances to Narasimha Who pervades the entire universe
94. Om jagan-mayaya namah
    Obeisances to the Supreme Mystic Who makes the material world
    seem real
95. Om jagat-palaya namah
    Obeisances to the protector of the universe (Nara-simha)
96. Om jagannathaya namah
    Obeisances to the Lord of Universe

97. Om mahakhagaya namah
    Obeisances to Him Who moves in the air or with the movement of
    the air (is everywhere)
98. Om dvi-rupa-bhrtaya namah
    Obeisances to Him Who has double form (man-lion)
99. Om paramatmaya namah
    Obeisances to Him Who is the Supersoul of All beings
100. Om param-jyotine namah
    Obeisances to Him (Nara-simha) Whose effulgence is the source
    of Brahman
101. Om nirgunaya namah
    Obeisances to Narasimha Who possesses transcendental qualities
    (not those of the material nature)
102. Om nrkesarine namah
    Obeisances unto Him man-lion (or having a lion's mane while
    appearing part human)
103. Om para-tattvaya namah
    Obeisances to the Supreme Absolute Truth (One Who is of the
    Supreme nature)
104. Om param-dhamaya namah
    Obeisances to He Who comes from the Supreme Abode
105. Om sac-cid-ananda-vigrahaya namah
    Obeisances to Narasimha Whose Form is made of eternal
    knowledge and bliss
106. Om laksmi-nrsimhaya namah
    Obeisances unto the Man-Lion Form together with the Supreme
    Goddess of Fortune Srimati Laksmi-devi
107. Om sarvatmaya namah
    Obeisances unto the universal, primeval soul (the Supreme
    Personality of Godhead - Narasimhadeva)
108. Om dhiraya namah
    Obeisances unto Narasimha who is always sober (being never
    bewildered)
Om prahlada-palakaya namah
    Obeisances unto Narasimha Who is the protector of Prahlada
    Maharaja, and those of that nature - surrendered unto Him.

Names of Sri Narasimha Yajna
(Narasimha name mantras to be chanted during the Narasimha rite, especially on the appearance day festival of Lord Narasimha.)

1. Om narasimhaya swaha-aa idam narasimhaya idan na mama
2. Om mahasimhaya swaha-aa idam narasimhaya idan na mama
3. Om diyva-simhaya swaha-aa idam narasimhaya idan na mama
4. Om mahabalaya swaha-aa idam narasimhaya idan na mama
5. Om ugra-simhaya swaha-aa idam narasimhaya idan na mama
6. Om mahadevaya swaha-aa idam narasimhaya idan na mama
7. Om stambha-ja-aya swaha-aa idam narasimhaya idan na mama
8. Om ugra-locanaya swaha-aa idam narasimhaya idan na mama
9. Om raudraya swaha-aa idam narasimhaya idan na mama
10. Om sarvadbhutaya swaha-aa idam narasimhaya idan na mama
11. Om srimanaya swaha-aa idam narasimhaya idan na mama
12. Om yoganandaya swaha-aa idam narasimhaya idan na mama
13. Om trivikramaya swaha-aa idam narasimhaya idan na mama
14. Om harine swaha-aa idam narasimhaya idan na mama
15. Om kolahalaya swaha-aa idam narasimhaya idan na mama
16. Om cakrine swaha-aa idam narasimhaya idan na mama
17. Om vijayaya swaha-aa idam narasimhaya idan na mama
18. Om jaya-vardhanaya swaha-aa idam narasimhaya idan na mama
19. Om panchananaya swaha-aa idam narasimhaya idan na mama
20. Om param-brahma-aya swaha-aa idam narasimhaya idan na mama
21. Om aghoraya swaha-aa idam narasimhaya idan na mama
22. Om ghora-vikramaya swaha-aa idam narasimhaya idan na mama
23. Om jvalan-mukhaya swaha-aa idam narasimhaya idan na mama
24. Om jvala-maline swaha-aa idam narasimhaya idan na mama
25. Om mahajvalaya swaha-aa idam narasimhaya idan na mama
26. Om maha-prabhuhaya swaha-aa idam narasimhaya idan na mama
27. Om niti-laksaya swaha-aa idam narasimhaya idan na mama
28. Om sahasraksaya swaha-aa idam narasimhaya idan na mama
29. Om durniriksyaya swaha-aa idam narasimhaya idan na mama
30. Om pratapanaya swaha-aa idam narasimhaya idan na mama
31. Om mahadamstraya swaha-aa idam narasimhaya idan na mama
32. Om yudha-prajnaya swaha-aa idam narasimhaya idan na mama
33. Om canda-kopine swaha-aa idam narasimhaya idan na mama
34. Om sada-sivaya swaha-aa idam narasimhaya idan na mama
35. Om hiranyakasipu-dhvamsine swaha-aa idam narasimhaya idan na mama

36. Om daitya-danava-bhanjanaya swaha-aa idam narasimhaya idan na mama

37. Om guna-bhadraya swaha-aa idam narasimhaya idan na mama

38. Om mahabhadraya swaha-aa idam narasimhaya idan na mama

39. Om bala-bhadraya swaha-aa idam narasimhaya idan na mama

40. Om subhadrakaya swaha-aa idam narasimhaya idan na mama

41. Om karalaya swaha-aa idam narasimhaya idan na mama

42. Om vikaralaya swaha-aa idam narasimhaya idan na mama

43. Om vikartaya swaha-aa idam narasimhaya idan na mama

44. Om sarva-kartrikaya swaha-aa idam narasimhaya idan na mama

45. Om sisumaraya swaha-aa idam narasimhaya idan na mama

46. Om trilokatmaya swaha-aa idam narasimhaya idan na mama

47. Om isaya swaha-aa idam narasimhaya idan na mama

48. Om sarvesvaraya swaha-aa idam narasimhaya idan na mama

49. Om vibhuaya swaha-aa idam narasimhaya idan na mama

50. Om bhaivaradambaraya swaha-aa idam narasimhaya idan na mama

51. Om divyaya swaha-aa idam narasimhaya idan na mama

52. Om acyutaya swaha-aa idam narasimhaya idan na mama

53. Om kavine swaha-aa idam narasimhaya idan na mama

54. Om madhavaya swaha-aa idam narasimhaya idan na mama

55. Om adhoksajaya swaha-aa idam narasimhaya idan na mama

56. Om aksaraya swaha-aa idam narasimhaya idan na mama

57. Om sarvaya swaha-aa idam narasimhaya idan na mama

58. Om vanamaline swaha-aa idam narasimhaya idan na mama

59. Om varapradaya swaha-aa idam narasimhaya idan na mama

60. Om visvambaraya swaha-aa idam narasimhaya idan na mama

61. Om adbhutaya swaha-aa idam narasimhaya idan na mama

62. Om bhavyaya swaha-aa idam narasimhaya idan na mama

63. Om sri-visnave swaha-aa idam narasimhaya idan na mama

64. Om purusottamaya swaha-aa idam narasimhaya idan na mama

65. Om anaghastra swaha-aa idam narasimhaya idan na mama

66. Om nakhastraya swaha-aa idam narasimhaya idan na mama

67. Om surya-jyotine swaha-aa idam narasimhaya idan na mama

68. Om suresvaraya swaha-aa idam narasimhaya idan na mama

69. Om sahasra-bahu-aya swaha-aa idam narasimhaya idan na mama

70. Om sarva-jnaya swaha-aa idam narasimhaya idan na mama

71. Om sarva-siddhi-pradayakaya swaha-aa idam narasimhaya idan na mama

72. Om vajra-damstraya swaha-aa idam narasimhaya idan na mama

73. Om vajra-nakhaya swaha-aa idam narasimhaya idan na mama

74. Om mahanandaya swaha-aa idam narasimhaya idan na mama
75. Om param-tapaya swaha-aa idam narasimhaya idan na mama
76. Om sarva-mantraika-rupa swaha-aa idam narasimhaya idan na mama
77. Om sarva-yantra-vidaramaya swaha-aa idam narasimhaya idan na mama
78. Om sarva-tantratmakaya swaha-aa idam narasimhaya idan na mama
79. Om avyaktaya swaha-aa idam narasimhaya idan na mama
80. Om suvyaktaya swaha-aa idam narasimhaya idan na mama
81. Om bhakta-vatsala swaha-aa idam narasimhaya idan na mama
82. Om vaisakha-sukla-bhototthaya swaha-aa idam narasimhaya idan na mama
83. Om saranagata-vatsalaya swaha-aa idam narasimhaya idan na mama
84. Om udara-kirtine swaha-aa idam narasimhaya idan na mama
85. Om punyatmaya swaha-aa idam narasimhaya idan na mama
86. Om mahatmaya swaha-aa idam narasimhaya idan na mama
87. Om candra-vikramaya swaha-aa idam narasimhaya idan na mama
88. Om vedatrayaya swaha-aa idam narasimhaya idan na mama
89. Om prapujyaya swaha-aa idam narasimhaya idan na mama
90. Om bhagavanaya swaha-aa idam narasimhaya idan na mama
91. Om paramesvaraya swaha-aa idam narasimhaya idan na mama
92. Om srivatsamkaya swaha-aa idam narasimhaya idan na mama
93. Om jagat-vyapine swaha-aa idam narasimhaya idan na mama
94. Om jagan-mayaya swaha-aa idam narasimhaya idan na mama
95. Om jagat-palaya swaha-aa idam narasimhaya idan na mama
96. Om jagannathaya swaha-aa idam narasimhaya idan na mama
97. Om mahakhagaya swaha-aa idam narasimhaya idan na mama
98. Om dvi-rupa-bhrtaya swaha-aa idam narasimhaya idan na mama
99. Om paramatmaya swaha-aa idam narasimhaya idan na mama
100. Om param-jyotine swaha-aa idam narasimhaya idan na mama
101. Om nirgunaya swaha-aa idam narasimhaya idan na mama
102. Om nrkesarine swaha-aa idam narasimhaya idan na mama
103. Om para-tattvaya swaha-aa idam narasimhaya idan na mama
104. Om param-dhamaya swaha-aa idam narasimhaya idan na mama
105. Om sac-cid-ananda-vigrahaya swaha-aa idam narasimhaya idan na mama
106. Om laksmi-nrsimhaya swaha-aa idam narasimhaya idan na mama
107. Om sarvatmaya swaha-aa idam narasimhaya idan na mama
108. Om dhiraya swaha-aa idam narasimhaya idan na mama

Sri Lakshmi-Narasimha karuna-rasa-stotra

This was written by Adi Shankaracharya for the mercy of Sri Sri Lakshmi-Narasimha. It reflects the same devotional mood as his *Govindashtakam* and *Prabhodashudhakara*, and does not hold any of his impersonalistic teachings.

> 1. Shrimat-pavo-nidhi-niketana chakra-pane
> bhogindra-bhoga-mani-rajita punya-murte
> yogisha shashvata sharanya bhavabdhi-pota
> lakshmi-nrisimha mama dehi karavalambam

Lord, Your form is all beautiful because you are the master of the goddess of fortune. You reside in the ocean of milk, and You carry the Sudarshana disc in Your hand. Your all-auspicious form is made even more resplendent by the jewel-like body of Anantadeva, the king of serpents upon whom You rest. You are the eternal deliverer from the ocean of birth and death for all those who seek Your shelter and You are the master of all mystics. O Lakshmi-Nrisimha, please bless me with the touch of Your lotus hands.

> 2. Brahmendra rudra-marud arka-kirita-koti
> sanghattitangri-kamalamala-kanti-kanta
> lakshmi lasat-kucha saroruha-raja-hamsa
> lakshmi-nrisimha mama dehi karavalambam

Lord Brahma, Lord Indra, Lord Shiva, the Maruts and the sun-god all fall down with their tens and millions of helmets at Your lotus feet, which are most dear to the goddess of fortune, Lakshmi, who appears as beautiful as a royal swan enjoying the lotus flower of Your chest. O Lakshmi-Nrisimha, please bless me with the touch of Your lotus hands.

> 3. Samsara-dava dahanakula bhishanoru
> jvalavalibhih ati-daghda tanuru-hasya
> tvat pada-padmasarasim sharanagatasya
> lakshmi-nrisimha mama dehi karavalambam

The conditioned soul suffers on the path of repeated birth and death exactly like one caught in a forest fire. Being fearful, his body burnt by the licking flames, he cries most pitiably. Just as one tormented by a forest fire may take shelter in a pond. Your lotus feet are just like a pond giving refuge to the surrendered soul from the forest fire of samsara. O Lakshmi-Nrisimha, please bless me with the touch of Your lotus hands.

> 4. Samsara-jala-patitasya jagan-nivasa
> sarvendriyarta-badishagra-jhashopamasya
> protkampita-prachurataluka-mastakasya
> lakshmi-nrisimha mama dehi karavalambam

O abode of the universe, I have fallen into the net of repeated birth and death. Just like an aquatic animal, I eagerly accept the hook baited with the sense objects. And just as the fish is caught trembling, and his head is cut off, so my real consciousness is lost as I am punished by the material nature. O Lakshmi-Nrisimha, please bless me with the touch of Your lotus hands.

> 5. Samsara-kupam ati-ghoram agadha-mulam
> samprapya dukha-shata-sarpa-samakulasya
> dinasya deva kripaya padam agatasya
> lakshmi-nrisimha mama dehi karavalambam

Having fallen into the horrible and bottomless well of repeated birth and death, I am tormented by the serpent of hundred fold miseries. In this fallen condition, O Lord, by Your mercy I am surrendered to Your lotus feet. O Lakshmi-Nrisimha, please bless me with the touch of Your lotus hands.

> 6. Samsara-bhikara-karindra-karabhighata
> nishpidyamana-vapushah sakalarti-nasa
> prana-prayana bhava-bhiti-samakulasya
> lakshmi-nrisimha mama dehi karavalambam

You slay the king of the demons, Hiranyakashipu, whose body is as strong as an elephant by squeezing him with your hands. In this way You destroy all miseries by breaking the fearful cycle of birth and death. You are the ultimate goal of life for those who are disturbed by fear of material existence. O Lakshmi-Nrisimha, please bless me with the touch of Your lotus hands.

> 7. Samsara-sarpa-visha-digdha mahogra-tivra
> damstragra-koti-paridashta vinashta-murte

nagari-vahana sudhabdhi-nivasa shaure
lakshmi-nrisimha mama dehi karavalambam

I have been bitten by the tens of millions of terrible sharp fangs of the snake of material existence. Having been injected with its powerful poison, I have lost my consciousness as the eternal servant of Krishna. The best remedy for snakebite is nectar, therefore O Lord Shauri, You reside in the ocean of nectar and Your carrier is Garuda the great enemy of snakes. O Lakshmi-Nrisimha, please bless me with the touch of Your lotus hands.

8. Samsara-vriksha agha-bijam ananta-karma
shakha-yutam karana-patram ananga-pushpam
aruhya dukha-phalinam patitam dayalo
lakshmi-nrisimha mama dehi karavalambam

The tree of samsara, or material existence, is sprouted from the seed of sinful desire. The unlimited reactions to fruitive activities are its branches, the senses are its leaves and its flowers is Cupid's attraction of sex desire. O merciful one, I climbed up this tree but I have only obtained the fruit of misery and am now fallen. O Lakshmi-Nrisimha, please bless me with the touch of Your lotus hands.

9. Samsara-sagara-vishala-karala-kala
nakra-graha-grasita-nigraha-vigrahasya
vyadhasya raga-nichayormini piditasya
lakshmi-nrisimha mama dehi karavalambam

In the broad ocean of material existence I am broken and smashed again and again by the powerful waves of my accumulated attachments. Grasped in the jaws of the fearful crocodile of the external time factor, I am pierced, ripped apart, and swallowed. O Lakshmi-Nrisimha, please bless me with the touch of Your lotus hands.

10. Samsara-sagara-nimajjana-muhyamanam
dinam vilokaya vibho karuna-nidhe mam
prahlada-kheda-parihara-kritavatara
lakshmi-nrisimha mama dehi karavalambam

O all-powerful, ocean of mercy, cast Your glance upon me. I am bewildered, helplessly sinking in the sea of samsara. You descended to remove the distress of your devotee Prahlada Maharaja. O Lakshmi-Nrisimha, please bless me with the touch of Your lotus hands.

> 11. Samsara-ghora-gahane charato murare
> marogra vbhikara mriga prachurarditasya
> artasya matsara-nidagdha-suduhkhitasya
> lakshmi-nrisimha mama dehi karavalambam

O Murari, I have fallen into the pit of material existence and I am wandering just like an animal greatly tormented by fear of horrible death that awaits him. Distressed and miserable, I am burnt by envy. O Lakshmi-Nrisimha, please bless me with the touch of Your lotus hands.

> 12. Baddhva gale yama-bhata bahu taryajantaha
> karshanti yatra bhava-pasha-shatair yutam mam
> ekakinam para-vasha chakitam dayalo
> lakshmi-nrisimha mama dehi karavalambam

Binding me with ropes, the servants of Yamaraja drag me to his abode, beating me severely along the path. Bound by material existence in hundreds of ways, I stand alone, helpless and trembling, under the influence of the superior force of daiva maya. O Lakshmi-Nrisimha, please bless me with the touch of Your lotus hands.

> 13. Lakshmi-pate kamala-nabha suresha vishno
> yajnesha yajna madhusudana vishvarupa
> brahmanya keshava janardana vasudeva
> lakshmi-nrisimha mama dehi karavalambam

You are the Lord of Lakshmi and the master of the demigods. O Vishnu, Your navel is just like a lotus. You are the Lord of sacrifice and the embodiment of sacrificial performance. O Madhusudana, Vishvarupa, You are always favorably disposed to the brahmanas. O Keshava, Janardana, Vasudeva, O Lakshmi-Nrisimha, please bless me with the touch of Your lotus hands.

> 14. Ekena chakram aparena karena shankham
> anyena sindhu-tanayam avalambya tishthan
> vametarena varadabhaya-padma-chihnam
> lakshmi-nrisimha mama dehi karavalambam

In one of Your four hands You hold the Sudarshana disc and in another a
conch. With another You embrace Lakshmi, who was born from the milk
ocean, and with another on the left You bestow fearlessness. The palm of
that hand which is raised to give the benediction is marked with the lotus
symbol. O Lakshmi-Nrisimha, please bless me with the touch of Your lotus
hands.

15. Andhasya me hrita-viveka-maha-dhanasya
corair mahabalibhir indriya-namadheyaiha
mohandhakara-kuhare vinipatitasya
lakshmi-nrisimha mama dehi karavalambam

Although I was very wealthy, I am blind and without discrimination. I have
been robbed of my great treasure (Krishna consciousness) by the thieves
known as the senses. Despite all my attempts to appease them with
different types of offerings, they have thrown me into the pit of illusion and
darkness. O Lakshmi-Nrisimha, please bless me with the touch of Your
lotus hands.

16. Prahlada-narada-parasara-pundarika
vyasadi-bhagavata-pungava-hrin-nivasa
bhaktanurakta-paripalana-parijata
lakshmi-nrisimha mama dehi karavalambam

You reside in the hearts of the best devotees such as Prahlada Maharaja,
Narada Muni, Parashara Muni, Pundarika, Vyasadeva and others. You are
very fond of Your devotees and You are their parijata tree of protection. O
Lakshmi-Nrisimha, please bless me with the touch of Your lotus hands.

17. Lakshmi-nrisimha-charanabja-madhu-vratena
stotram kritam shubha-karam bhuvi shankarena
ye tatpathanti manuja hari-bhakti-yuktaha
lakshmi-nrisimha mama dehi karavalambam

This prayer, bestowing auspiciousness in this world, has been composed by
Shankaracharya, who is a honeybee in the lotus flower of the feet of Sri-Sri
Lakshmi-Nrisimha. Those who read this prayer with devotion to Lord
Krishna attain the shelter of Sri Sri Lakshmi-Nrisimha's lotus feet and also
attain their eternal spiritual form, which is never annihilated.

Lord Ramachandra's Nrisimha-Panchamrita

(These prayers are from the 47th chapter of the *Harivamsa Purana* which narrates the story of Lord Ramachandra's visit to the holy place of Ahobalam to see the Deity of Nrisimha, where it is said that Lord Nrisimha appeared and saved His devotee Prahlada.)

ahobalam narasimham gatva ramah pratapavan
namaskutya sri nrisimham astaushit kamala patim

The glorious Rama once visited Ahobala where He saw the Deity of Lord Nrisimha. He offered His obeisances to Lord Kamalapati (husband of the Goddess of Fortune) and prayed as follows.

1. Govinda keshava janardana vasudeva
vishvesha-vishva madhusudana vishvarupa
shri padmanabha purushottama pushkaraksha
narayanachyuta nrisimho namo namaste

O Govinda, Keshava, Janardana, Vasudeva, Vishvesha (the controller of the universe), Vishva, Madhusudana, Vishvarupa, Sri Padmanabha, Purushottama, Pushkaraksha, Narayana, Achyuta. O Lord Narasimha I offer my respectful obeisances unto You again and again.

2. Devah samastah khalu gopi mukhyaha
gandharva vidyadhara kinnarash cha
yat pada-mulam satatam namanti
tam narasimham sharanam gato shmi

I have taken shelter of Lord Nrisimha unto whose lotus feet demigods, prominent yogis, gandharvas, vidyadharas and kinnaras are constantly offering their obeisances.

3. Vedan samastan khalu shastragarbhan
vidyam balam kirtimatim cha lakshmim
yasya prasadat purusha labhante
tam narasimham sharanam gato shmi

I have taken shelter of Lord Nrisimha by whose mercy people receive all the Vedas, the essence of all scriptures, knowledge, strength, reputation and wealth.

4. Brahma shivas tvam purushottamash cha
narayano 'shau marutam patish cha
chandrarka vayvagni marud-ganash cha
tvam eva tam tvam shatatam nato'shmi

You are Lord Brahma, Lord Shiva and the best person Lord Narayana. You are the master of the Marutas and You are the sun, the moon, air and the fire as well as the Marut-ganas. I offer my obeisances unto You.

5. Snapne'pi nitya jagatam ashesam
srashta cha hanta vibhura prabheyaha
trata tvam eka strividho vibinnaha
tam tvam nrisimham satatam nato'smi

I offer my obeisances unto Lord Nrisimha who is the creator, the maintainer and the destroyer of the entire universe. Although You perform all of these three acts simultaneously, You are completely beyond these activities. You are the all-pervading, unlimited supreme spirit.

Iti stutva raghushreshthaha
pujayamasa tam harim
pushpa vrishtih papatashu
tasya devasya murdhani

Praying this way, the best of the Raghus, Lord Ramacandra worshipped Lord Hari. At that time the demigods showered a rain of flowers on the head of Lord Nrisimhadeva.

Raghavena kutam stotram
panchamrita manuktamam
pathanti ye dvijavaraha
tesham svargastu shashvataha

This is the best of prayers, called panchamrita or five nectars compiled by Lord Rama Himself. One who reads this will be liberated eternally.

Rina-mochana Narasimha Stotra
This is a stotram from the *Narasimha Purana* is a prayer to Lord Narasimha for the release of all kinds of worldly obligations.

> 1. Devata-karya-siddhyartam
> sabha-stambha-samudbhavam
> sri nrisimham maha-viram
> namami rina-muktaye

Lord Narasimha is to be worshipped if perfection is desired. Unto the all-powerful Sri Narasimha, who appeared from the pillar of the assembly hall, I offer my obeisances so that I may become released from mundane obligations.

> 2. Lakshmyalingita vamangam
> bhaktanam vara-dayakam
> sri nrisimham maha-viram
> namami rina-muktaye

Embraced on His left side by Lakshmidevi, Lord Narasimha gives benedictions to His devotees. My obeisances to the all-powerful Lord Narasimha, so that I may be released from all other obligations.

> 3. Antra-mala-dharam shankha
> chakrabjayudha-dharinam
> sri nrisimham maha-viram
> namami rina-muktaye

Wearing a garland of intestines, He carries the conch, disc, lotus, club and other weapons. Unto Lord Narasimha, the all-powerful, I offer my obeisances to become free from worldly debts.

> 4. Samaranat sarva-papa-ghnam
> kadruja-visha-nashanam
> sri nrisimham maha-viram
> namami rina-muktaye

By remembrance of Lord Narasimha all sins are destroyed and the poisonous effect of the descendants of Kadru (serpents) are nullified. My obeisances unto Him the all-powerful, so that I may become free from all other debts.

> 5. Simha-nadena mahata
> dig-danti bhaya-nashanam

sri nrisimha maha-viram
namami rina-muktaye

By His greatly ferocious roar and His fearful teeth, which encompass all ten directions, He destroys all fear. Unto the all-powerful Lord Narasimha my obeisances, so that I may become free from worldly obligations.

6. Prahlada-varadam shrisham
daityeshvara-vidaranam
sri nrisimham maha-viram
namami rina-muktaye

Lord Narasimha is the Lord of Lakshmi and the giver of benedictions to Prahlada Maharaja, yet He ripped apart the king of demons, Hiranyakashipu. May I become free from debts by offering obeisances unto the all-powerful Lord Narasimha.

7. Krura-grahaih piditanam
bhaktanan abhaya-pradam
sri nrisimham maha-viram
namami rina-muktaye

When His devotees are oppressed by inauspicious planets, Lord Narasimha gives them fearlessness. I offer my obeisances unto the all-powerful Lord Narasimha so that I may be released from worldly obligations.

8. Veda-vedanta-yajnesham
brahma-rudradi-vanditam
sri nrisimham maha-viram
namami rina-muktaye

Lord Narasimha is the master of all the Vedas, Vedanta and the process of sacrifice. He is offered prayers by Lord Brahma, Lord Shiva and the other demigods. I offer my obeisances unto the all-powerful Lord Narasimha so that I may be freed from all other debts.

9. Ya idam pathate nityam
rina-mochana-samjnitam
anrini jayate sadyo
dhanam shighram avapnuyat

Whoever reads this regularly, consciously desiring freedom from debts, immediately becomes freed from all obligations and very soon attains opulence.

Sri Nrisimhashtakam
By Paramahamsat Yati Jiyar, a Sri Vaishnava Acharya

1. Shrimad akalanka paripurna shashikoti
shridhara manohara satapatakanta
palaya kupalaya bhavambudhi nimagnam
daityavarakala narasimha narasimha

O Lord Narasimha, O Lord Narasimha, You are the husband of Sri, the goddess of fortune. You are the death of the greatest demon, Hiranyakashipu. I am sinking into the ocean of birth and death, O Kripalaya, the treasure house of mercy, please protect me.

2. Pada kamalavanata pataki jananam
pataka davanala patatri varaketo
bhavana parayana bhavarti haraya mam
pahi kripayaiva narasimha narasimha

O Lord Narasimha, You are the forest fire of sins of the sinful people who bow down to Your lotus feet. You are known as Garuda-dvaja, whose chariot flag is adorned by Garuda. O Lord Narasimha, You are the cause of creation and the best shelter. Please protect me and bestow your mercy upon me which alone can remove the distress of birth and death.

3. Tunga nakha-pankti-dalitasuravarasrik
panka nava kunkuma vipankila mahoraha
pandita nidhana kamlalaya namaste
pankaja nishnna narasimha narasimha

O Lord Narasimha, Your raised nails have ripped apart the great demon, Hiranyakashipu. The blood that squirted out made Your chest wet and made it look like that fresh kumkum was applied on You. O Lord Narasimha, You are the shelter of the best persons including Kamala, the goddess of fortune. You always dwell in Your abode which resembles a lotus flower. I offer my obeisances unto You.

4. Maulishu vibhushanam iva maravaranam
yogihridayeshu cha shirassu nigamanam
rajad aravinda ruchiram padayugam te
dehi mama murdhni narasimha narasimha

O Lord Narasimha, O Lord Narasimha, please keep Your illuminating lotus feet on my head which are placed as ornaments on the helmets of the demigods, in the hearts of the yogis and on the nigamas, the Vedic scriptures.

5. Varija vilochana mad antima dashayam
klesha vivashikrita samasta karanayam
ehi ramaya saha sharanya vihaganam
natham adhiruhya narasimha narasimha

O Lord Narasimha, O Lord Narasimha, O lotus eyed one, please give me Your audience along with Rama, Your consort riding on the back of Garuda, the king of birds, when all my senses will be suffering in distress and I will be in my last difficulty at the time of giving up my body.

6. Hataka kiritavara hara vanamala
tararashana makara kundala manindraih
bhushitam-ashesha-nilayam tava vapurme
chotasi chakasta narasimha narasimha

O Lord Narasimha, O Lord Narasimha, Your transcendental body, which is the ultimate shelter of everything. Is decorated with a beautiful golden crown, a forest garland, shark-like earrings, various excellent jewels and an out projecting wide tongue.

7. Indu ravi pavaku vilochana ramayaha
mandira mahabhuja lasadvara rathanga
sundara chiraya ramatam tvayi mano me
nandita suresha narasimha narasimha

O Lord Narasimha, O beautiful one, let me mind always be engaged in enjoying Your form. The sun, the moon and the fire are Your eyes and Your strong arm is beautified by a huge wheel. O Lord Narasimha, You are the only shelter of goddess Ramaa (Lakshmi) and You are honored even by Lord Indra.

8. Madhava mukunda madhusudana murare
vamana nrisimha sharanam bhava natanam
kamada ghrinin nikhila karana nayeyam
kalam amaresha narasimha narasimha

O Lord Narasimha, O Mukunda, Madhusudana, Murari, Vamana, You are the shelter of the surrendered souls. O Lord of the demigods, cause of all causes, please do not neglect me. Kindly fulfill my desire of passing my whole life chanting Your holy names.

9. Ashtakam idam sakala pataka bhayaghnam
kamadam ashesha duritamaya ripughnam
yah pathati santatam ashesha nilayam te
gacchati padam sa narasimha narasimha

O Lord Narasimha, one who reads these eight prayers daily becomes free from all the fear of sinful reactions. All desires become fulfilled, kills all his enemies and destroys all kinds of diseases. He will attain the abode of Lord Narasimha, the Lord reclining on Shesha.

Sri Narasimha Ashtakam
(Prayers for the protection of Lord Narasimha)

1. Dhyayami narasimhakyam
brahma vedanta-gocharam
bhavabdhi taran opayam
shankha chakra dharam param

I am meditating on the Supreme Person known as Narasimha who is attainable through Vedanta philosophy. He is the carrier of the conch and the Sudarshana disc, and He is the only means for crossing the ocean of birth and death.

2. Nilam ramam cha paribhuya kripa rasena
stambhe sva-shakti-managham vinidhaya deva
prahlada rakshana vidhavi yati kripa te
shri narasimha paripalaya mam cha bhaktam

You mercifully protect Nila and Rama with Your chaste, spiritual internal potency. You also extend Your protective energy over Prahlada Maharaja. O Narasimha please protect me too, for I am also trying to be Your devotee.

3. Indra-adi deva nikarasya kirita koti
pratyupta ratna prati-bimbita pada-padma
kalpa-anta kala ghana garjana tulya-nada
shri narasimha paripalaya mam cha bhaktam

Your lotus feet are comparable in effulgence to the brilliance of the sum total of the jewelry possessed by all the demigods. Your roaring is like that of the thundering clouds at the universal dissolution. O Narasimha please protect me too, for I am also trying to be Your devotee.

4. Prahlada posha pralayarka samana vaktra
hum-kara nirjita nishachara vrinda nada
sri-narada muni sangha sugiyamana
sri narasimha paripalaya mam cha bhaktam

You are the maintainer of Prahlada Maharaja and Your open mouth is exactly as the sun which causes the destruction of the universe. O Lord, Your grunts frighten all the roaming predators of the night. You are always beautifully glorified by sages such as Narada Muni. O Narasimha please protect me too, for I am also trying to be Your devotee.

5. Ratrin charadri jatarat parisramsya-mana raktam
nipiya pari-kalpita sa-antara-mala
vidravita-akhila surogra nrisimha rupam
sri narasimha paripalaya mam cha bhaktam

O Narasimha, Your divine form is horrifying. You are tearing apart all the wild animals descending from the caves of the mountains to terrify and to drink the blood of everyone. O Narasimha please protect me too, for I am also trying to be Your devotee.

6. Yogi-indra yoga pari-rakshaka deva deva
dina-arthi-hari vibhava-agama giyamana
mam vikshya dinam asaranyam aganya-shilam
sri narasimha paripalaya mam cha bhaktam

O King of the yogis, Lord of Lords and the protector of the process of yoga. You are the remover of the sufferings of those who are dear to You. Your wonderful form is described in the agamas. Please glance upon me who is without shelter and possesses no good qualities. O Narasimha please protect me too, for I am trying to be Your devotee.

> 7. Prahlada shoka vinivarana bhadra-simha
> naktan-charendra mada khandana vira-simha
> indra-adi deva-jana sangnuta pada-padma
> sri narasimha paripalaya mam cha bhaktam

You are the auspicious lion that dispersed the grief of Prahlada Maharaja. O Powerful Lion, who tears everything apart in an intoxicated mood, You are the Lord of the ferocious predators of the dark night. Your lotus feet are surrounded by all divine and pious personalities beginning with Lord Indra. O Narasimha please protect me too, for I am also trying to be Your devotee.

> 8. Gyanena kechid avalambya padambhujam te
> kechit sukarma nikarena pare ch bhaktya
> muktim gatah khalu janah kripaya murare
> sri narasimha paripalaya mam cha bhaktam

Some people try to embrace Your lotus feet through the process of knowledge. Others try by performing pious activities and yet others by the path of devotion. O Murari by Your mercy all of them attain liberation. O Narasimha please protect me too, for I am also trying to be Your devotee.

> Iti sri nrisimha ashtakam sampurnam
> Thus ends the Narasimha ashtakam.

Sri Shanishchara-krita Sri Narasimha Stuti

Everyone is afraid of the malefic planet Shani (Saturn) because generally he is associated with extreme sorrow and suffering. However, Shanideva himself has devised a way of solving this problem by obtaining the blessings of Lord Narasimha.

Shani made an agreement with the Lord that he would never trouble those who recite his Narasimha Stuti when they are facing troubles related to dvädasa-añstama-païcama (a situation where Sani-käta lasts for 7 1/2 births)

If one recites with devotion Sani's Sri Narasimha Stuti, especially on Sanivära (Saturdays) and when Sani graha comes to 12-8-5 Janma Rsi, one will please the Lord who is the Supersoul of Shanaishchara and the Lord will remove all obstacles and suffering and bless His devotee.

sulabho bhakti yuktänämà durdarso dusta cetasäm |
ananya gatikänäm ca prabhu bhaktaika-vatsalah
Sanaishcara tatra nrsimha-deva cakärämala-citta-vrtih |
pranamya sastangam asesa-loka kirita niräjita päda-padmam || 1 |

Lord Narasimàhadeva is easily accessible to the devotees and punishes those who are evil-minded. He is the saviour for those who are helpless who desire to seek refuge in Him. When the demigods of innumerable planets bow down to His lotus feet, the bright jewels from their crowns are reflected on His toenails which gives the impression that lamps are being waved in front of them. Unto His lotus feet, Sanideva prostrated and prayed (in the court of Brahmä).

Sri Sanir-uväca -
yat päda-pankaja-raja paramädharena
samsevitam sakala kalmashs räsi-näsam |
kalyäna kärakam asesanijänugänam |
sa tvam nrsimha mayi dehi krpä-valokam ||2||

Sri Sani said -
By the mercy of the dust of Your lotus feet which destroy a multitude of sins, grant infinite auspiciousness to Your devotee who always worships Your lotus feet with devotion. O Lord Narasimha, please bestow upon me Your merciful side-long glance.

sarvatra cancalatayä sthitayäpi laksmyäh |
brahmädi-vandya-padayä stirayänya sevi ||
pädäravinda-yugalam paramä-dharena |
sa tvam nrsimha mayi dehi krpä valokam ||3||

Your lotus feet are worshipped by Goddess Lakshmi, even though She is fickle by nature (chanchala [meaning that She, or wealth, easily moves from one place to another, though She is ever-steady in Her devotion to the

Lord]) and by Lord Brahmä and Lord Siva whose feet are worthy of worship with devotion. O Lord Narasimha, please bestow upon me Your merciful side-long glance.

> yad rüpam ägama-Sirah pratipädhyamädhya |
> ädhyätmikädi paritäpa haram vicintyam ||
> yogésvarair apathagäkhila dosa sanghaih |
> sa tvam nrsimha mayi dehi krpä-valokam ||4||

By contemplating or meditating upon Your appearance, which is expounded in the Vedas extensively, the best of the saints are liberated from the three-fold miseries and from all misfortunes. O Lord Narasimha, please bestow upon me Your merciful side-long glance.

> prahläda bhakta vacasä harir äviräsa |
> stambhe hiraëyakasipum ya udhärabhävah ||
> urvau nidhäya udharam nakhärai dadhära |
> sa tvam nrsimha mayi dehi krpä-valokam ||5||

By the word of His devotee named Prahläda, Lord Hari, who is generous and kind, appeared from a pillar and by placing Hiranyakasipu on His thighs split open his stomach with His nails. O Lord Narasimha, please bestow upon me Your merciful side-long glance.

> yo naija bhaktam analämbudhi bhüdharogra |
> sringa-prapäta visa dhamti sarisupebhyah |
> sarvätmakaù parama-käruniko raraksa |
> sa tvam nrsimha mayi dehi krpä-valokam ||6||

You protected your own devotee Prahläda from a raging fire, the deep ocean, from falling from a tall mountain peak, poison, a mad elephant and the fangs of poisonous serpents. You are omnipresent and supremely generous. O Lord Narasimha, please bestow upon me Your merciful side-long glance.

> yannirvikära para-rüpa vicintanena |
> yogisvarä visaya sägara vita rägäh ||
> visrämtim äpura-vinäsa vatim paräkhyäm |
> sa tvam nrsimha mayi dehi krpä-valokam ||7||

By meditating upon He whose great form is devoid of imperfections, the best of the saints attained liberation from the ocean of materialistic attachments and obtained unmitigated salvation. O Lord Narasimha, please bestow upon me Your merciful side-long glance.

yad rüpam-ugra parimardana bhäva säli |
samcintanena sakalägha vinäsa käri |
bhüta jvara graha samudbhava bhiti näsam |
sa tvam nrsimha mayi dehi krpä-valokam ||8||

By meditating upon He whose form is fearsome, all peace, happiness and prosperity can be obtained, all sins can be obliterated, the fear arising from evil spirits, fevers and unfavorable planetary positions can be removed, O Lord Narasimha, please bestow upon me Your merciful side-long glance.

yasyottamam yasa umä-patim padma-janma |
sakrädi daivata sabhäsu samasta-gitam ||
saktaiva sarvasa-mala prasamaika daksam |
sa tvam nrsimha mayi dehi krpä-valokam ||9||

Your transcendental fame is sung gloriously in all the divine assemblies of Shiva, Brahmä and Indra, etc. and whose power is steadfast in wiping out all impurities, O Lord Narasimha, please bestow upon me Your merciful side-long glance.

evam srutvä stutim devah
saninäm kalpitämà harih |
uväca brahma vrndasta
sanim tam bhakta-vatsalah ||10||

On listening to the heartfelt prayer composed by Sanideva in the assembly of Lord Brahmä, Lord Hari who is ever compassionate to His devotees, spoke to Sanideva as follows.

Sri narasimha uväca -
prasannoham sane tubhyam |
varam varaya sobhanam ||
yam vänchasi tameva tvam |
sarva-loka hitävaham ||11||

Sri Narasimha said – O Sani, I am pleased with your devotion. What ever you desire that will benefit the world, ask for that kind of boon and I will grant it.

Sri Sanir uväca -
nrsimha tvam mayi krpäm
kuru deva dayä-nidhe |
mad väsaras tava priti-
kara syat devatä-pate ||12||

mat krtam tvat param stotram
srnvanti ca patanti ca |
sarvän käman pürayetäs
tesäm tvam loka-bhävanah ||13||

SrI Sanideva replied – O Lord Narasimha, O reservoir of compassion, please be kind to me. O Lord of all gods, let my week-day (Saturday) be Your favorite day. O Purifier of all the worlds, may You fulfill the desires of all those who listen to or read this great prayer to You composed by me."

Sri narasimha uväca -
tataivästu saneham vai
rakso-bhuvana samsthitah |
bhakta kämän pürayisye
tvam mamaika vacah srinu ||
tvat kritam mat param stotram
yah patecchrinu yäccha yah |
dvädasastama janmastäd
bhayam mästu tasya vai ||14||

Sri Narasimha said – O Sani, let it be so! By virtue of My being the universal protector (raksobhuvana), I fulfill the desires of all My devotees. Please listen to My words - let there be no fear of the twelfth and eighth birth positions (and implicitly any unfavorable birth positions) and consequent troubles from you for any one who reads or listens to this prayer to Me composed by you.

Sani naraharim devam
tateti pratyuväca ha

tatah parama-samtusto
jayeti munayovadan ||15||

Then Sanideva replied to Lord Narahari that he would follow the Lord's instructions. Then the joyful saints and sages present there (in Brahma's assembly) responded with cries of, 'jaya, jaya!'".

Sri krsna uvächa -
itam sanaiscarasyäta nrsimha deva |
samvädam etat stavanam cha mänavah ||
srinoti yahù srävayate cha bhaktyä
sarvänyäbhistäni cha vindate dhruvam ||16||

Sri Krishna told Dharmaräja, "Whoever listens to or recites this conversation between Sanideva and Lord Narasimha in the form of this prayer of devotion will definitely have all desires fulfilled and will always rejoice."
iti Sri bhavisyottara puräne raksobhuvana mahätme sri
Sanaiscara krta Sri nrsimha stuti sampürnam

Thus ends the prayers offered from the Bhavisyoattara Purana to the universal protector Sri Narasimha by the great soul Sani.

Sri Nrisimha-sahasra-nama
(The Thousand Names of Lord Narasimha)

Text 1
om namo narasimhäya
vajra-damshträya vajrine
vajra-dehäya vajräya
namo vajra-nakhäya cha

Obeisances to Lord Nrisimha, whose teeth are thunderbolts (vajra-damshtra), who holds a thunderbolt (vajri), whose body is a thunderbolt (vajra-deha), who is a thunderbolt (vajra), whose claws are thunderbolts (vajra-nakha), . . .

Text 2
väsudeväya vandyäya
varadäya varätmane

varadäbhaya-hastäya
varäya vara-rüpine

. . . who is the son of Vasudeva (väsudeva), to whom all should bow down (vandya), who is the giver of boons (varada), who is most glorious (varätmä), whose hand gives the blessing of fearlessness (varadäbhaya-hasta), and who is the greatest (vara), whose transcendental form is glorious (vara-rüpi.

Text 3
varenyäya varishthäya
sri-varäya namo namah
prahläda-varadäyaiva
pratyaksha-varadäya cha

Obeisances to Lord Narasimha, who is the greatest (vareëya and variñöha), and who is the goddess of fortune's husband (sri- vara). Obeisances to Lord Narasimha, who is the giver of benedictions to Prahläda (prahläda-varada), who is the giver of benedictions to they who approach Him (pratyakña-varada), . . .

Text 4
parät-para-pareshäya
paviträya pinäkine
pävanäya prasannäya
päshine päpa-härine

. . . who is the supreme master, greater than the greatest (parät-para-paresha), who is the most pure (pavitra), who carries a bow (pinäki), who is the most pure (pävana), who is filled with transcendental bliss (prasanna), who carries a rope (päshi), and who removes sins (päpa-häri).

Text 5
purustutäya punyäya
puruhutäya te namah
tat-purushäya tathyäya
puräna-purushäya cha

O Lord Nrisimha, glorified with many prayers (puru-stuta), who is the most pure (punya), whose holy names are chanted by the devotees (puru-huta), who are the Supreme Person (tat-purusha), the Supreme Truth (tathya), the ancient Supreme Personality of Godhead (puräna-purusha), obeisances unto You!

Text 6
purodhase pürvajäya
pushkaräkshäya te namah
pushpa-häsäya häsäya
mahä-häsäya shärngine

O Lord Nrisimha, who are the supreme priest (purodha), the oldest (pürvaja), lotus-eyed (pushkaräksha), lotus-smiled (pushpa- häsa), fond of joking (mahä-häsa), and who hold the Shärnga Bow (shärngi), obeisances unto You!

Text 7
simhäya simha-räjäya
jagad-väsyäya te namah
atta-häsäya roshäya
jala-väsäya te namah

O Lord who are a lion (simha), the king of lions (simha- räja), and the master of the universe (jagad-vashya), obeisances unto You! O Lord who laugh loudly (atta-häsa), are angry (rosha), and reside on the water (jala-väsa), obeisances unto You!

Text 8
bhüta-väsäya bhäsäya
shri-niväsäya khadgine
khadga-jihväya simhäya
khadga-väsäya te namah

O Lord Nrisimha, who reside in everyone's heart (bhüta-väsa), who are effulgent (bhäsa), who are the resting-place of Goddess Lakshmi (shri-niväsa), who hold a sword (khadgi), whose tongue is a sword (khadga-jihva), who are a lion (simha), and who hold a sword (khadga-väsa), obeisances unto You!

Text 9
namo müladi-väsäya
dharma-väsäya dhanvine
dhanaïjayäya dhanyäya
namo mrityunjayäya cha

Obeisances to Lord Nrisimha, who is the root of all (müladi- väsa), the home of religion (dharma-väsa), the great archer (dhanvi), the winner of wealth (dhanaïjaya), and the most glorious (dhanya). Obeisances to He who is the conqueror of death (mrityunjaya).

Text 10
shubhänjayäya süträya
namah satrunjayäya cha
niranjanäya niräya
nirgunäya gunäya cha

Obeisances to Lord Nrisimha, who is the conqueror of handsomeness (shubhänjaya), the thread upon which all is strung (sütra), the conqueror of foes (satrunjaya), untouched by matter (niranjana), who lies down on the Kärana Ocean (nira), who is free from the modes of material nature (nirguna), who is glorious with transcendental qualities (guna), . . .

Text 11
nishpräpanchäya nirväna-
pradäya nividya cha
nirälambäya niläya
nishkaläya kaläya cha

. . . who is aloof from the material world (nishpräpaca), who is the giver of liberation (nirväna-prada), who is all-pervading (nivida), who is independent (nirälamba), whose complexion is dark (nila), who is perfect and complete (nishkala), who appears in many incarnations (kala), . . .

Text 12
nimeshäya nibandhäya
nimesha-gamanäya cha
nirdvandväya niräshäya
nishcayäya niräya cha

. . . who is the blinking of an eye (nimesha), who is the bondage of material existence (nibandha), who appears in the blinking of an eye (nimesha-gamana), who is free of duality (nirdvandva), who is all-pervading (nirāsha), who is the Absolute Truth (nishcaya), . . .

Text 13
nirmalāya nibandhāya
nirmohāya nirākrite
namo nityāya satyāya
sat-karma-niratāya cha

. . . who is free from all material impurity (nirmala), who is self-control (nibandha), who is free from illusion (nirmoha), whose form is not material (nirākriti), who is eternal (nitya), who is spiritual (satya), and whose activities are all spiritual (sat-karma-nirata).

Text 14
satya-dhvajāya munjāya
munjā-keshāya keshine
harishāya cha shoshāya
gudākeshāya vai namah

Obeisances to Lord Nrisimha, who carries truth as His flag (satya-dhvaja), who is the sacred munja grass (munja), whose hair is the sacred munja grass (munjā-kesha), whose hair is graceful (keshi), who is the master of Brahmā and Shiva (harisha), who makes all that is inauspicious wither away (shosha), who is the conqueror of sleep (gudakesha), . . .

Text 15
sukeshāyordhva-keshāya
keshi-simha-rakāya cha
jaleshāya sthaleshāya
padmeshāyogra-rūpine

. . . whose mane is glorious (sukesha and ürdhva-kesha), who is the süryamani jewel of great-maned lions (keshi-simha-raka) who is the master of the waters (jalesha), who is the master of all places (sthalesha), who is the husband of the goddess of fortune (padmesha), and who is ferocious (ügra-rüpi).

Text 16
kusheshayäya kuläya
keshaväya namo namah
sükti-karnäya süktäya
rakta-jihväya rägine

Obeisances to Lord Nrisimha, who is graceful like a lotus flower
(kusheshaya), who is the greatest (küla), who has a glorious mane
(keshava), whose ears delight in hearing His devotees' prayers
(sükti-karna), who is the Vedic prayers personified (sükta), whose tongue
is red (rakta-jihva), and who loves His devotees (rägi).

Text 17
dipta-rüpäya diptäya
pradiptäya pralobhine
pracchinnäya prabodhäya
prabhave vibhave namah

Obeisances to Lord Nrisimha, whose form is splendid (dipta- rüpa,
dipta, and pradipta), who is all-attractive (pralobhi), who is the destroys of
all that is inauspicious (pracchinna), who gives spiritual enlightenment
(prabodha), who is the supreme master (prabhu), who has all powers
(vibhu), . . .

Text 18
prabhanjanäya pänthäya
pramäyäpramitäya cha
prakäshäya pratäpäya
prajvaläyojjvaläya cha

. . . who destroys all that is inauspicious (prabhajana), who is glorious like
the sun (päntha), who is the Absolute Truth (prama), who is limitless
(apramita), who is splendid (prakasha, pratäpa, prajvala, and ujjvala), . . .

Text 19
jvälä-mälä-svarüpäya
jvälä-jihväya jväline
maho-jväläya käläya
käla-mürti-dharäya cha

. . . whose effulgent form seems to be garlanded with flames (jvälä-mälä-svarüpa), whose tongue is a flame (jvälä-jihva), who is splendid like a host of flames (jväli and maho-jväla), who is time personified (käla and käla-mürti-dhara), . . .

Text 20
käläntakäya kalpäya
kalanäya krite namah
käla-chakräya shakräya
vashat-chakräya chakrine

. . . who puts an end to time (käläntaka), who is all-powerful (kalpa, kalana, and krit), who is the wheel of time (käla-chakra), who is the most expert (shakra), who is the word vashat in the Vedic mantras (vashat-chakra), who holds the Sudarshana cakra (chakri), . . .

Text 21
akrüräya kritäntäya
vikramäya kramäya cha
kritine kritiväsäya
kritaghnäya kritätmane

. . . who is gentle to the devotees (akrüra), who is death to the demons (kritänta), who is all-powerful (vikrama, krama, kriti, and kritiväsa), who kills the demons (kritaghna), who is the all- pervading Supersoul (kritätmä), . . .

Text 22
sankramäya cha kruddhäya
kränta-loka-trayäya cha
arüpäya svarüpäya
haraye paramätmane

. . . who descends to this world (sankrama), who is angry with the demons (kruddha), who steps over the three worlds (kränta- loka-traya), whose form is not material (arüpa), whose form is transcendental (svarüpa), who removes all that is inauspicious (hari), who is the Supersoul (paramätmä),

Text 23
ajayäyädi-deväya
akshayäya kshayäya cha
aghoräya su-ghoräya
ghoräghora-taräya cha

. . . who is never defeated (ajaya), who is the Supreme Personality of
Godhead (ädi-deva), who is immortal (akshaya), who kills the demons
(kshaya), who is gentle (aghora), who is ferocious (su-ghora), and who
rescues the gentle devotees from the fearsome demons (ghoräghora-tara).

Text 24
namo 'stv aghora-viryäya
lasad-ghoräya te namah
ghorädhyakshäya dakshäya
dakshinäryäya sambhave

Obeisances to Lord Nrisimha, who is both gentle and powerful
(aghora-virya). O Lord Nrisimha, who are splendid with ferocious power
(lasad- ghora), who are the most ferocious (ghorädhyaksha), the most
expert (daksha), the most saintly (dakshinärya), and the most auspicious
(sambhave), . . .

Text 25
amoghäya gunaughäya
anaghäyägha-härine
megha-nädäya nädäya
tubhyam meghätmane namah

. . . who are infallible (amogha), a flood of transcendental virtues
(gunaugha), pure (anagha), and the remover of sins (agha- häri), who roar
like thunder (megha-näda), and who roar ferociously (näda). Obeisances
to You, Lord Nrisimha, who are like a monsoon cloud (meghätmä).

Text 26
mogha-vahana-rüpäya
megha-shyämäya mäline
vyäla-yajïopaviträya
vyaghra-dehäya vai namah

Obeisances to Lord Nrisimha, who is like a host of monsoon clouds (mogha-vahana-rüpa), who is dark like a monsoon cloud (megha-shyäma), who wear a garland (mäli), whose sacred-thread is a snake (vyäla-yajnopavitra), and who has the form of a lion (vyaghra-deha).

Text 27

vyaghra-pädäya cha vyaghra-
karmine vyäpakäya cha
vikatäsyäya viräya
vistara-shravase namah

Obeisances to Lord Nrisimha, who has the paws of a lion (vyaghra-päda), and the ferocious deeds of a lion (vyaghra-karmi), who is all-pervading (vyäpaka), whose face is fearsome (vikatäsya), who is very powerful and heroic (vira), and who is all-famous (vistara-shraväh).

Text 28

vikirna-nakha-damshträya
nakha-damshträyudhäya cha
vishvaksenäya senäya
vihvaläya baläya cha

Obeisances to Lord Nrisimha, who has sharp claws and teeth (vikirna-nakha-damshtra), whose weapons are His claws and teeth (nakha-damshträyudha), whose armies are everywhere (vishvaksena), who has a great army (sena), who is ferocious (vihvala), who is powerful (bala), . . .

Text 29

virupäkshäya viräya
visheshäkshäya säkshine
vita-shokäya vistirna-
vadanäya namo namah

Obeisances to Lord Nrisimha, whose eyes are fearsome (virüpäksha), who is powerful and heroic (vira), whose eyes are handsome (visheshäksha), who is the witness of all (säkshi), who never grieves (vita-shoka), and whose mouth is wide (vistirna-vadana).

Text 30
vidhānāya vidheyāya
vijayāya jayāya cha
vibudhāya vibhāvāya
namo vishvambharāya cha

Obeisances to Lord Nrisimha, who is the author of the rules of
scriptures (vidhāna), who is the goal to be attained by following the rules
of scripture (vidheya), who is victory (vijaya and jaya), who knows
everything (vibudha), who is the only friend (vibhāva), and who is the
maintainer of the universe (vishvambhara).

Text 31
vita-ragāya viprāya
vitanika-nayanāya cha
vipulāya vinitāya
vishva-yonaye namo namah

Obeisances to Lord Nrisimha, who is not affected by the mode of
passion (vita-raga), who is the first of brāhmanas (vipra), whose eyes are
glorious (vitanka-nayana), who form is large (vipula), who is humble
(vinita), and who is the creator of the universe (vishva-yoni), . . .

Text 32
chid-ambarāya vittāya
vishrutāya viyonaye
vihvalāya vikalpāya
kalpātitāya shilpine

. . . , who is the master of the spiritual sky (chid-ambara), the wealth of the
devotees (vitta), all-famous (vishruta), unborn (viyoni), ferocious
(vihvala), most expert (vikalpa, kalpātita, and shilpi), . . .

Text 33
kalpanāya svarūpāya
phani-talpāya vai namah
tadit-prabhāya taryāya
tarunāya tarasvine

. . . who is the creator (kalpana), whose form is transcendental (svarūpa), whose couch is a serpent (phani-talpa), who is splendid like lightning (tadit-prabha), who is the final goal (tarya), who is eternally youthful (taruna), who is all-powerful (tarasvi), . . .

Text 34

tapanāya tapaskāya
tāpa-traya-harāya cha
tārakāya tamo-ghnāya
tattvāya cha tapasvine

. . . who is effulgent (tapana and tapaska), who removes the three-fold miseries of material life (tāpa-traya-hara), who is the deliverer (tāraka), who destroys the darkness of ignorance (tamo-ghna), who is the Absolute Truth (tattva), and who is glorious (tapasvi).

Text 35

takshakāya tanu-trāya
tatine taralāya cha
shata-rūpāya shāntāya
shata-dhārāya te namah

Obeisances to You, O Lord Nrisimha, who are the architect of the worlds (takshaka), who protect Your devotees (tanu-tra), who stay on the farther shore of the ocean of repeated birth and death (tati), who are splendid (tarala), who manifest a hundred forms (shata-rūpa), who are peaceful (shānta), and who hold a thunderbolt (shata-dhāra).

Text 36

shata-patrāya tarkshyāya
sthitaye shata-mūrtaye
shata-kratu-svarūpāya
shāshvatāya shatātmane

Obeisances to Lord Nrisimha, who is graceful like a hundred-petal lotus (shata-patra), who is carried by Garuda (tarkshya), who is the maintainer (sthiti), who manifests a hundred forms (shata-mūrti), who is a hundred yajnas personified (shata-kratu-svarūpa), who is eternal (shāshvata), who manifests a hundred forms (shatātmā), . . .

Text 37
namah sahasra-shirase
sahasra-vadanäya cha
sahasräkshäya deväya
disha-shroträya te namah

. . . who has a thousand heads (sahasra-shiräh and sahasra-vadana), who
has a thousand eyes (sahasräksha), and who is the Supreme Personality of
Godhead (deva). Obeisances unto You, O Lord Nrisimha, whose ears are
the different directions (disha-shrotra).

Text 38
namah sahasra-jihväya
mahä-jihväya te namah
sahasra-nämadheyäya
sahasräkshi-dhäräya cha

Obeisances unto You, O Lord Nrisimha, who have a thousand tongues
(sahasra-jihva), a great tongue (mahä-jihva), a thousand names
(sahasra-nämadheya), and a thousand eyes (sahasräkshi- dhära).

Text 39
sahasra-bähave tubhyam
sahasra-caranäya cha
sahasrärka-prakäshäya
sahasräyudha-dhäriëe

O Lord Nrisimha, who have a thousand arms (sahasra-bähu), and a
thousand feet (sahasra-carana), who are splendid like a thousand suns
(sahasrärka-prakäshäya), who hold a thousand weapons
(sahasräyudha-dhäri), . .

Text 40
namah sthüläya sükshmäya
susükshmäya namo namah
sükshunyäya subhikshäya
surädhyakshäya shaurine

. . . who are larger than the largest (sthüla), smaller than the smallest
(sükshma and susükshma), ferocious (sükshunya), the   maintainer

(subhiksha), and the ruler of the demigods (surädhyaksha), heroic (shauri), obeisances unto You.

Text 41
dharmädhyakshäya dharmäya
lokädhyakshäya vai namah
prajädhyakshäya shikshäya
vipaksha-kshaya-mürtaye

Obeisances to You, O Lord Nrisimha, who are the ruler of religious principles (dharmädhyaksha), religion personified (dharma), the ruler of the worlds (lokädhyaksha), the ruler of the living entities (prajädhyaksha), the teaching of the Vedas (shiksha), the destroyer of the demons (vipaksha-kshaya-mürti), . . .

Text 42
kälädhyakshäya tikshnäya
mülädhyakshäya te namah
adhokshajäya miträya
sumitra-varunäya cha

. . . the controller of time (kälädhyaksha), ferocious (tikshna), the ruler of the root of matter (mülädhyaksha), beyond the perception of the material senses (adhokshaja), the true friend (mitra), and the Deity worshiped by Mitra and Varuna (sumitra- varuna).

Text 43
shatrughnäya avighnäya
vighna-koti-haräya cha
rakshoghnäya tamoghnäya
bhütaghnäya namo namah

Obeisances to Lord Nrisimha, who is the killer of enemies (shatrughna), free to do whatever He wishes (avighna), the Lord who removes millions of obstacles (vighna-koti-hara), the killer of demons (rakshoghna), the destroyer of ignorance (tamoghna), and the killer of ghosts (bhütaghna).

Text 44
bhüta-päläya bhütäya
bhüta-väsäya bhütine

bhüta-vetäla-ghätäya
bhütädhipataye namah

Obeisances to Lord Nrisimha, who is the protector of the people (bhüta-päla), the Lord who appears before His devotee (bhüta), the Lord who descends to the material world (bhüta- väsa), the master of the material world (bhüti), the destroyer of ghosts and evil spirits (bhüta-vetäla-ghäta), and the controller of the material world (bhütädhipati).

Text 45
bhüta-graha-vinäshäya
bhüta-samyamate namah
mahä-bhütäya bhrigave
sarva-bhütätmane namah

Obeisances to Lord Nrisimha, who is the killer of ghosts and evil spirits (bhüta-graha-vinäsha), the controller of the material world (bhüta-samyamän), the greatest (mahä-bhüta), a descendent of Maharshi Bhrigu (bhrigave), and the all-pervading Supersoul (sarva-bhütätmä).

Text 46
sarvärishta-vinäshäya
sarva-sampatkaräya cha
sarvädhäräya sarväya
sarvärti-haraye namah

Obeisances to Lord Nrisimha, who is the destroyer of all calamities (sarvärishta-vinäsha), the bringer of all good fortune (sarva-sampatkara), the resting place of all the worlds (sarvädhära), everything (sarva), and the remover of all sufferings (sarvärti-hari).

Text 47
sarva-duhkha-prashäntäya
sarva-saubhägya-däyine
sarvadäyäpy anantäya
sarva-shakti-dharäya cha

Obeisances to You, O Lord Nrisimha, who are the remover of all sufferings (sarva-duhkha-prashänta), the giver of all good fortune (sarva-saubhägya-däyi), the giver of everything (sarvada), limitless (ananta), the master of all potencies (sarva-shakti-dhara), . . .

Text 48

sarvaishvarya-pradätre cha
sarva-kärya-vidhäyine
sarva-jvara-vinäshäya
sarva-rogäpahärine

. . . the giver of all powers and opulences (sarvaishvarya- pradätä), the giver of all duties (sarva-kärya-vidhäyi), the destroyer of all fevers (sarva-jvara-vinäsha), the physician who cures all diseases (sarva-rogäpahäri), . . .

Text 49

sarväbhicära-hantre cha
sarvaishvarya-vidhäyine
pingäkshäyaika-shringäya
dvi-shringäya marichaye

. . . the destroyer of all magic spells (sarväbhichära-hantä), and the giver of all powers and opulences (sarvaishvarya- vidhäyi), red-eyed (pingäksha), who have one horn (eka-shringa), who have two horns (dvi-shringa), who are splendid like the sun (marichi), . . .

Text 50

bahu-shringäya lingäya
mahä-shringäya te namah
mangalyäya manojnäya
mantavyäya mahätmane

. . . who have many horns (bahu-shringa), who are not different from Your Deity form (linga), who have a great horn (mahä-shringa), who are the supreme auspiciousness (mangalya), who are supremely handsome and charming (manojna), who are the proper object of meditation (mantavya), who are the Supreme Personality of Godhead (mahätmä), . . .

Text 51

mahä-deväya deväya
mätulinga-dharäya cha

mahä-mäyä-prasütäya
prastutäya cha mäyine

. . . who are the Supreme Personality of Godhead (mahä-deva and deva), who hold a mätulinga (mätulinga-dhara), who are the origin of the mahä-mäyä potency (mahä-mäyä-prasüta), who are glorified by the sages (prastuta), who are the master of the illusory potency mäyä (mäyi), . . .

Text 52
anantänanta-rüpäya
mäyine jala-shäyine
mahodaräya mandäya
madadäya madäya cha

. . . who manifested limitless forms (anantänanta-rüpa), who are the master of the illusory potency mäyä (mäyi), who rest on the waters (jala-shäyi), whose belly is gigantic (mahodara), who are gentle (manda), who give bliss to the devotees (madada), who are transcendental bliss personified (mada), . . .

Text 53
madhu-kaitabha-hantre cha
mädhaväya muräraye
mahä-viryäya dhairyäya
chitra-viryäya te namah

. . . who killed Madhu and Kaitabha (madhu-kaitabha-hantä), who are the goddess of fortune's husband (mädhava), who are the enemy of the Mura demon (muräri), who are all-powerful (mahä-virya), who are all-patient (dhairya), and who are wonderfully powerful (chitra-virya).

Text 54
chitra-kürmäya citräya
namas te chitra-bhänave
mäyätitäya mäyäya
mahä-viräya te namah

O Lord Nrisimha, obeisances to You, who are a wonderful tortoise (chitra-kürma), wonderful (chitra), splendid like a   wonderful sun (chitra-bhänu), beyond the illusory potency mäyä (mäyätita), the master of the illusory potency mäyä (mäya), and all-powerful (mahä-vira).

Text 55
mahä-tejäya bijäya
tejo-dhämne cha bijine
tejomäya nrisimhäya
namas te chitra-bhänave

Obeisances to You, O Lord Nrisimha, who are splendid and powerful (mahä-teja), the seed of all existence (bija), the Lord who resides in the splendid spiritual world (tejo-dhämä), the seed of all existence (biji), effulgent (tejoma), half-man and half-lion (nrisimha), and splendid like a wonderful sun (chitra- bhänu).

Text 56
mahä-damshträya tushtäya
namah pushti-karäya cha
shipivishtäya hrishtäya
pushtäya parameshtine

Obeisances to Lord Nrisimha, who has large and fearsome teeth (mahä-damshtra), who is filled with happiness (tushta), who maintains and protects His devotees (pushti-kara), effulgent (shipivishta), happy (hrishta), powerful (pushta), and the supreme controller (parameshti).

Text 57
vishishtäya cha shishtäya
garishthäyeshta-däyine
namo jyeshthäya shreshthäya
tushtäyämita-tejase

Obeisances to Lord Nrisimha, who is the greatest (vishishta, shishta, and garishtha), who fulfills His devotees' desires (ishta- däyi), the oldest (jyeshtha), the best (shreshtha), happy (tushta), and unlimitedly powerful (amita-tejäh).

Text 58
säshtänga-nyasta-rüpäya
sarva-dushtäntakäya cha

vaikunöhäya vikunöhäya
keshi-kanthäya te namah

Obeisances to You, O Lord Nrisimha, to whom the devotees offer dandavat obeisances (säshtänga-nyasta-rüpa), who are the killer of all the demons (sarva-dushtäntaka), the master of the spiritual world (vaikuntha and vikuntha), and who have a lion's neck (keshi-kantha).

Text 59
kanthiraväya lunthäya
nishathäya hathäya cha
sattvodriktäya rudräya
rig-yajuh-sama-gäya cha

Obeisances to Lord Nrisimha, whose throat is filled with a roar (kanthi-rava), who robs the devotees of their entrapment in the world of birth and death (luntha), who is supremely honest (nishatha), who is ferocious (hatha), who is situated in transcendental goodness (sattvodrikta), who is angry (rudra), who is the hymns of the Rig, Yajur, and Säma Vedas (rig-yajuh-sama-ga), . . .

Text 60
ritu-dhvajäya vajräya
mantra-rajäya mantrine
tri-neträya tri-vargäya
tri-dhämne cha tri-shüline

. . . who is the flage of the seasons (ritu-dhvaja), a thunderbolt (vajra), the king of mantras (mantra-raja), and the best advisor (mantri), who has three eyes (tri-netra), three classes of followers (tri-varga), three abodes (tri-dhämä), a trident (tri-shüli), . . .

Text 61
tri-käla-jnäna-rüpäya
tri-dehäya tridhätmane
namas tri-mürti-vidyäya
tri-tattva-jnänine namah

. . . who knows everything of the three phases of time (tri-käla-jnäna-rüpa), who has three forms (tri-deha), and three expansions (tridhätmä). Obeisances to Lord Nrisimha, who knows the three truths (tri-mürti-vidya and tri-tattva-jäni).

Text 62
akshobhyäyäniruddhäya
aprameyäya mänave
amritäya anantäya
amitäyämitaujase

Obeisances to Lord Nrisimha, who is peaceful (akshobhya), who cannot be thwarted (aniruddha), who is immeasurable (aprameya), the goddess of fortune's husband (mänu), immortal (amrita), limitless (ananta and amita), unlimitledly powerful (amitaujäh), . .

Text 63
apamrityu-vinäshäya
apasmara-vighätine
ana-däyäna-rüpäya
anäyäna-bhuje namah

. . . the destroyer of untimely death (apamrityu-vinäsha), the destroyer of forgetfulness (apasmara-vighäti), the giver of life (anada), the form of life (ana-rüpa), life (ana), and the enjoyer of life (ana-bhuk).

Text 64
nädyäya niravadyäya
vidyäyädbhuta-karmane
sadyo-jätäya sanghäya
vaidyutäya namo namah

Obeisances to Lord Nrisimha, who is glorified with many prayers (nädya), who is supremely pure (niravadya), who is filled with transcendental knowledge (vidya), whose activities are wonderful (adbhuta-karmä), who suddenly appears before His devotee (sadyo-jäta), who is accompanied by His devotees (sangha), and who is splendid like lightning (vaidyuta).

Text 65
adhvätitäya sattväya
väg-ätitäya vägmine

vāg-ishvarāya go-pāya
go-hitāya gavām-pate

Obeisances to Lord Nrisimha, who stays far from the path of the materialists (adhvātita), who is the Absolute Truth (sattva), who is beyond the descriptive power of material words (vāg- ātita), who is most eloquent (vāgmi and vāg-ishvara), who is the protector of the cows (gopa), the auspiciousness of the cows (go-hita), and the master of the cows (gavām-pati), . . .

Text 66
gandharvāya gabhirāya
garjitāyorjitāya cha
parjanyāya prabuddhāya
pradhāna-purushāya cha

. . . whose voice is melodious (gandharva), who is profound (gabhira), who roars ferociously (garjita), who is very powerful (ürjita), who roars like thunder (parjanya), who is the most wise (prabuddha), who is the Supreme Personality of Godhead, the controller of the material world (pradhāna-purusha), . . .

Text 67
padmābhāya sunābhāya
padma-nābhāya mānine
padma-netrāya padmāya
padmāyāh-pataye namah

. . . who is splendid like a lotus flower (padmābha), whose navel is graceful (sunābha), whose navel is a lotus flower (padma-nābha), who is glorious (māni), whose eyes are lotus flowers (padma-netra), who is graceful like a lotus flower (padma), and who is the goddess of fortune's husband (padmāyāh-pati).

Text 68
padmodarāya pütāya
padma-kalpodbhavāya cha
namo hrit-padma-vāsāya
bhü-padmoddharanāya cha

Obeisances to Lord Nrisimha, whose abdomen is a lotus flower (padmodara), who is supremely pure (püta), who appeared in the Padma-kalpa (padma-kalpodbhava), who stays on the lotus of His devotee's heart (hrit-padma-väsa), and who picked up the earth as if it were a lotus flower (bhü-padmoddharana).

Text 69

shabda-brahma-svarüpäya
brahma-rüpa-dharäya cha
brahmaëe brahma-rüpäya
padma-neträya te namah

Obeisances to You, O Lord Nrisimha, who are the Vedas personified (shabda-brahma-svarüpa and brahma-rüpa-dhara), the Supreme Personality of Godhead (brahma), and the Lord whose form is spiritual (brahma-rüpa), and whose eyes are lotus flowers (padma-netra).

Text 70

brahma-däya brahmanäya
brahma-brahmätmane namah
subrahmanyäya deväya
brahmanyäya tri-vedine

Obeisances to Lord Nrisimha, who gives the most valuable gift (brahma-da), who is worshiped by Brahmä (brähmana), who is the Supersoul who guides the brähmanas (brahma-brahmätmä), who is worshiped by the brähmanas (subrahmanya), who is the glorious Supreme Personality of Godhead (deva), who is worshiped by the brähmanas (brahmanya), and who is the author of the three Vedas (tri-vedi).

Text 71

para-brahma-svarüpäya
panca-brahmätmane namah
namas te brahma-shirase
tadäshva-shirase namah

Obeisances to Lord Nrisimha, whose form is spiritual (para-brahma-svarüpa), who is the panca-brahma (panca-brahmätmä), who is the head of the Vedas (brahma-shiräh), and who appears in a form with a horse's head (tadäshva-shiräh).

Text 72
atharva-shirase nityam
ashani-pramitäya cha
namas te tikshna-damshträya
laläya lalitäya cha

Obeisances to You, O Lord Nrisimha, who are the head of the Atharva
Veda (atharva-shiräh), who hurl a thunderbolt (ashani-pramita), whose
teeth are sharp (tikshna-damshtra), and who are graceful and playful (lala
and lalita).

Text 73
lavanyäya laviträya
namas te bhäsakäya cha
lakshana-jnäya lakshäya
lakshanäya namo namah

Obeisances to You, O Lord Nrisimha, who are handsome (lavanya),
who are a scythe for mowing down the demons (lavitra), who are effulgent
(bhäsaka), who know everything (lakshana-jna), and who are filled with
transcendental qualities (laksha and lakshana).

Text 74
lasad-ripräya lipräya
vishnave prabhavishnave
vrishni-müläya krishnäya
shri-mahä-vishnave namah

Obeisances to You, O Lord Nrisimha, who purify sins (lasad- ripra),
who are glorious (lipra), all-pervading (vishnu), all-powerful
(prabhavishnu), the root of the Vrishni dynasty (vrishni-müla), Lord
Krishna (krishna), and Lord Mahä-Vishnu (shri-mahä-vishnu).

Text 75
pashyämi tväa mahä-simham
harinam vana-mälinam
kiritinam kundalinam
sarvängam sarvato-mukham

I gaze on You, O Lord Nrisimha, who are a great lion (mahä-simha), who take away all that is inauspicious (hari), who wear a forest garland (vana-mäli), a helmet (kiriti), earrings (kundali), who are all-pervading (sarvänga), whose faces are everywhere (sarvato-mukha), . . .

Text 76
sarvatah-päni-padoram
sarvato-'kshi-shiro-mukham
sarveshvaram sada-tushtam
samartham samara-priyam

. . . whose hands, feet, and thighs are everywhere (sarvatah- päni-padora), whose eyes, heads, and faces are everywhere (sarvato-'kshi-shiro-mukha), who are the controller of all (sarveshvara), who are always blissful (sadä-tushta), who are all- powerful (samartha), who are fond of a fight (samara-priya), . . .

Text 77
bahu-yojana-vistirnam
bahu-yojana-mäyatam
bahu-yojana-hastänghrim
bahu-yojana-näsikam

. . . who are many yojanas in size (bahu-yojana-vistirna and bahu-yojana-mäyata), whose hands and feet are many yojanas (bahu-yojana-hastänghri), whose nose is many yojanas (bahu-yojana-näsika), . . .

Text 78
mahä-rüpam mahä-vaktram
mahä-damshtram mahä-bhujam
mahä-nädam mahä-raudram
mahä-käyam mahä-balam

. . . whose form is gigantic (mahä-rüpa), whose mouth is gigantic (mahä-vaktra), whose teeth are gigantic (mahä-damshtra), whose arms are gigantic (mahä-bhuja), whose roar is gigantic (mahä-näda), who are very ferocious (mahä-raudra), whose body is gigantic (mahä-käya), who has all power (mahä-bala), . . .

Text 79
änäbher-brahmano-rüpam
ägaläd-vaishëavam tathä
äshirsäd-randhram ishänam
tad-agre-sarvatah-shivam

. . . who are Brahmä from the beginning of Your navel
(änäbher-brahmano-rüpa), Who are Lord Vishnu from the beginning of
Your neck (ägaläd-vaishnava), who are Lord Rudra from the beginning of
Your head (äshirsäd-randhra), who are the supreme controller (ishäna), and
who are all-auspicious everywhere (tad-agre-sarvatah-shiva).

Text 80
namo 'stu näräyana narasimha
namo 'stu näräyana vira-simha
namo 'stu näräyana krüra-simha
namo 'stu näräyana divya-simha

O Näräyana, O Narasimha, obeisances unto You! O Näräyana, O heroic
lion (vira-simha), obeisances unto You! O Näräyana, O ferocious lion
(krüra-simha), obeisances unto You! O Näräyana, O splendid
transcendental lion (divya-simha), obeisances unto You!

Text 81
namo 'stu näräyana vyaghra-simha
namo 'stu näräyana puccha-simha
namo 'stu näräyana pürna-simha
namo 'stu näräyana raudra-simha

O Näräyana, O ferocious lion (vyaghra-simha), obeisances unto You!
O Näräyana, O transcendental lion (puccha-simha), obeisances unto You!
O Näräyana, O perfect lion (pürna-simha), obeisances unto You! O
Näräyana, O angry lion (raudra-simha), obeisances unto You!

Text 82
namo namo bhishana-bhadra-simha
namo namo vihvala-netra-simha
namo namo briahita-bhüta-simha
namo namo nirmala-chitra-simha

O fearsome lion (bhishana-bhadra-simha), obeisances unto You! O lion with angry eyes (vihvala-netra-simha), obeisances unto You! O gigantic lion (briahita-bhüta-simha), obeisances unto You! O splendid, pure, and wonderful lion (nirmala-chitra-simha), obeisances unto You!

Text 83
namo namo nirjita-käla-simha
namo namo kalpita-kalpa-simha
namo namo kämada-käma-simha
namo namas te bhuvanaika-simha

O lion who defeat time (nirjita-käla-simha), obeisances unto You! O all-powerful lion (kalpita-kalpa-simha), obeisances unto You! O lion who fulfills all desires (kämada-käma-simha), obeisances unto You! O lion who rules the world (bhuvanaika-simha), obeisances unto You!

Text 84
dyävä-pritivyor idam antaram hi
vyäptam tvayaikena dishash cha sarväh
drishtvädbhutam rüpam ugram tavedam
loka-trayam pravyathitam mahätman

Although You are one, You are spread throughout the sky and the planets and all space between. O great one, as I behold this terrible form, I see that all the planetary systems are perplexed.*

Text 85
ami hitvä sura-sanghä vishanti
kechid bhitäh pranjalayo grinanti
svastity uktvä munayah siddha-sanghäh
stuvanti tväa stutibhih pushkaläbhih

All the demigods are surrendering and entering into You. They are very much afraid, and with folded hands they are singing the Vedic hymns.*

Text 86
rudrädityä väsavo ye cha sädhyä
vishvedevä marutash cosmapäsh cha
gandharva-yakshäh sura-siddha-sanghä
vikshanti tväa vismitäsh chaiva sarve

The different manifestations of Lord Shiva, the Adityas, the Vasus, the Sädhyas, the Vishvadevas, the two Ashvins, the Maruts, the forefathers, and the Gandharvas, the Yakshas, Asuras, and all perfected demigods are beholding You in wonder.*

Text 87
leliyase grasamän asamantäl
lokän samagrän vadanair jvaladbhih
tejobhir äpürya jagat samagram
bhäsäs tavogräh pratapanti vishnoh

O Vishnu, I see You devouring all people in Your flaming mouths and covering the universe with Your immeasurable rays. Scorching the worlds, You are manifest.

Text 88
bhävishnus tvam sahishnus tvam
bhrajishnur jishnur eva cha
prithivim antariksham tvam
parvatäranyam eva cha

O Lord Nrisimha, You are the future (bhävishnu). You are the most patient and tolerant (sahishnu). You are the most glorious (bhrajishnu). You are always victorious (jishnu). You are the earth (prithivi), the sky (antariksha), and the mountains and forests (parvatäranya).

Text 89
kalä-käshthä viliptatvam
muhürta-praharädikam
aho-rätram tri-sandhyä cha
paksha-mäsartu-vatsarah

You are the differing units of time, such as the kalä, käshthä, vilipta, muhürta, and prahara. You are day and night (aho-rätram), You are the three junctions known as sunrise, noon, and sunset (tri-sandhyä). You are the two fortnights (paksha), the months (mäsa), the seasons (ritu), and the year (vatsara).

Text 90
yugädir yuga-bhedas tvam
samyuge yuga-sandhäyäh
nityam naimittikam dainam
mahä-pralayam eva cha

You are the beginning of the yuga (yugädi), the various yugas (yuga-bheda), the junctions of the yugas (samyuge yuga-sandhäyäh), and the four kinds of cosmic annihilations called nitya, naimittika, daina, and mahä-pralaya.

Text 91
käranam karanam kartä
bhartä hartä tvam ishvarah
sat-kartä sat-kritir goptä
sac-chid-änanda-vigrahah

You are the cause (kärana), the instrument (karana), the creator (kartä), the maintainer (bhartä), the remover (hartä), the controller (ishvara), the doer of good (sat-kartä and sat- kriti), the protector (goptä), and the Lord whose form is eternal and full of knowledge and bliss (sac-cid-änanda-vigraha).

Text 92
pränas tvam präninam pratyag
ätmä tvam sarva-dehinäm
su-jyotis tvam param-jyotir
ätma-jyotih sanätanah

You are the life of all that live (pränah präninam), You are the Supersoul (pratyag-ätmä). You are the splendor of all embodied souls (sarva-dehinäm su-jyotih). You are the supreme effulgence (param-jyotih and ätma-jyotih). You are eternal (sanätana).

Text 93
jyotir loka-svarüpas tvam
tvam jyotir jyotishäa patih
svähä-karah svadhä-käro
vashat-kärah kripä-karah

You are the spiritual effulgence (jyotih), the personification of all the worlds (loka-svarüpa), the light of all lights (jyotir jyotishäm), the supreme master (pati), the sacred word sväha (svähä-kära), the sacred word svadhä (svadhä-kära), the sacred word vashat (vashat- kära), merciful (kripä-kara),

Text 94
hanta-käro niräkäro
vega-kärash cha shankarah
akärädi-hakäränta
omkäro loka-kärakah

... the sacred word hanta (hanta-kära), without a material form (niräkära), the fastest and most powerful (vega-kära), auspicious (shankara), the entire alphabet, beginning with a and concluding with ha (akärädi-hakäränta), the sacred syllable om (omkära), and the creator of the worlds (loka-käraka).

Text 95
ekätmä tvam anekätmä
chatur-ätmä chatur-bhujah
chatur-mürtish chatur-damshtrash
chatur-veda-mayottamah

You are the one Supreme Personality of Godhead (ekätmä), who appears in many forms (anekätmä), who manifests as the chatur-vyüha (chatur-ätmä), who has four arms (chatur-bhuja), who appears in four forms (chatur-mürti), who has four teeth (chatur-damshtra), and who is the Vedas personified (chatur-veda-mayottama).

Text 96
loka-priyo loka-gurur
lokesho loka-näyakah
loka-säkshi loka-patir
lokätmä loka-locanah

You are dear to the worlds (loka-priya), the master of the worlds (loka-guru, lokesha, and loka-näyaka), the witness of the worlds (loka-säkshi), the master of the worlds (loka-pati), the Supersoul omnipresent in the worlds (lokätmä), the eye of the worlds (loka-lochana),
. . .

Text 97
loka-dhäro brihal-loko
lokäloka-mayo vibhuh
loka-kartä vishva-kartä
kritävartäh kritägamah

. . . the maintainer of the worlds (loka-dhära), the universal   form
(brihal-loka and lokäloka-maya), all-powerful (vibhu), and the creator of
the worlds (loka-kartä and vishva-kartä, kritävarta and kritägama).

Text 98
anädis tvam anantas tvam
abhüto bhüta-vigrahah
stutih stutyah stava-pritah
stotä netä niyämakah

You have no beginning (anädi). You have no end (ananta). You were
never created (abhüta). You are the form of all that exists (bhüta-vigraha),
You are the prayers offered to You (stuti). You are the object of Your
devotees' prayers (stutya). You are pleased by Your devotees' prayers
(stava-prita). You glorify   Your devotees (stotä). You are the supreme
leader (netä). You are the supreme controller (niyämaka).

Text 99
tvam gatis tvam matir mahyam
pitä mätä guruh sakhä
suhridash chätma-rüpas tvam
tvam vinä nästi me gatih

You are my goal (gati). I meditate on You (mati). You are my father
(pitä), mother (mätä), spiritual master (guru), friend (sakhä), well-wisher
(suhrit), and Supersoul (ätma-rüpa). Without You I have no goal and no
auspicious future.

Text 100
namas te mantra-rüpäya
astra-rüpäya te namah
bahu-rüpäya rüpäya
pancha-rüpa-dharäya cha

Obeisances to You, who are sacred mantras personified (mantra-rüpa), who are weapons personified (astra-rüpa), who appear in many forms (bahu-rüpa), whose form is transcendental (rüpa), who appear in five forms (panca-rüpa-dhara), . . .

Text 101
bhadra-rüpäya rütäya
yoga-rüpäya yogine
sama-rüpäya yogäya
yoga-pitha-sthitäya cha

. . . whose form is auspicious (bhadra-rüpa), who are the Vedic mantras personified (ruta), who are yoga personified (yoga-rüpa), the master of yoga (yogi), whose form is graceful (sama-rüpa), who are yoga personified (yoga), who stay in the most sacred of sacred places (yoga-pitha-sthita), . . .

Text 102
yoga-gamyäya saumyäya
dhyäna-gamyäya dhyäyine
dhyeya-gamyäya dhämne cha
dhämädhipataye namah

. . . who are attained by yoga practice (yoga-gamya), who are handsome and gentle (saumya), who are attained by meditation (dhyäna-gamya), who are the object of meditation (dhyäyi and dhyeya-gamya), who are the spiritual world (dhäma), and the ruler of the spiritual world (dhämädhipati).

Text 103
dharädharägha-dharmäya
dhäranäbhiratäya cha
namo dhätre cha sandhätre
vidhätre cha dharäya cha

Obeisances to Lord Nrisimha, who removes the sins of the world (dharädharägha-dharma), who is attained by meditation (dhäranäbhirata), who is the creator (dhätä, sandhätä, vidhätä, and dhara), . . .

Text 104
dämodaräya däntäya
dänavänta-karäya cha
namah samsära-vaidyäya
bheshajäya namo namah

... whose waist was bound with a rope (dämodara), who is peaceful and self-controlled (dänta), who kills the demons (dänavänta-kara), who is a physician expert in curing the disease of repeated birth and death (samsära-vaidya and bheshaja).

Text 105
sira-dhvajäya shitäya
vätäyäpramitäya cha
särasvatäya samsära-
näshanäyäksha-mäline

Obeisances to Lord Nrisimha, whose flag is marked with a plough (sira-dhvaja), who is the cold season (shita), who is the wind (väta), who is immeasurable (apramita), who is scholarship (särasvata), who puts an end to the cycle of birth and death (samsära-näshana), who wears a necklace of aksha beads (aksha-mäli), ...

Text 106
asi-charma-dharäyaiva
shat-karma-niratäya cha
vikarmäya sukarmäya
para-karma-vidhäyine

... who holds a sword and shield (asi-charma-dhara), who is expert in the six pious deeds (shat-karma-nirata), who is free from karma (vikarmä), whose deeds are glorious (sukarmä), whose deeds are transcendental (para-karma-vidhäyi), ...

Text 107
susharmane manmathäya
namo varmäya varmine
kari-charma-vasänäya
karäla-vadanäya cha

. . . who is most auspicious (susharmä), who is Kämadeva (manmatha), who is armor (varma), who wears armor (varmi and kari-carma-vasäna), whose face is fearsome (karäla-vadana), . . .

Text 108
kavaye padma-garbhäya
bhüta-garbha-ghrinä-nidhe
brahma-garbhäya garbhäya
brihad-garbhäya dhürjite

. . . who is the best of philosophers (kavi), who gave birth to Brahmä in a lotus flower (padma-garbha), who gave birth to all living beings (bhüta-garbha-ghrinä-nidhi), who gave birth to Brahmä (brahma-garbha), who gave birth to all that exists (garbha and brihad-garbha, and dhürjit), . . .

Text 109
namas te vishva-garbhäya
shri-garbhäya jitäraye
namo hiranyagarbhäya
hiranya-kavachäya cha

O Lord Nrisimha, obeisances unto You, the creator of the universes (vishva-garbha), the creator of beauty and opulence (shri-garbha), the warrior who defeats His enemies (jitäri), the universal form (hiranyagarbha), the Lord covered with golden armor (hiranya-kavacha),

Text 110
hiranya-varna-dehäya
hiranyäksha-vinäshine
hiranyakasipor-hantre
hiranya-nayanäya cha

. . . whose form is the color of gold (hiranya-varna-deha), who killed Hiranyäksha (hiranyäksha-vinäshi), who killed Hiranyakasipu (hiranyakasipor-hantä), whose eyes are golden (hiranya-nayana), . . .

Text 111
hiranya-retase tubhyam
hiranya-vadanäya cha

namo hiranya-shringäya
nisha-shringäya shringine

. . . whose seed is golden (hiranya-retäh), whose face is   golden
(hiranya-vadana), whose horn is golden (hiranya-shringa), whose horn is
night (nisha-shringa), who has a great horn (shringi), . . .

Text 112
bhairaväya sukeshäya
bhishanäyäntri-mäline
chandäya runda-mäläya
namo danda-dharäya cha

. . . who are fearsome (bhairava), whose mane is graceful (sukesha), who
is fearsome (bhishana), who wear a garland of intestines (antri-mäli), who
are ferocious (chanda), who wear a necklace of skulls (runda-mäla), who
hold a staff (danda-dhara), . . .

Text 113
akhanda-tattva-rüpäya
kamandalu-dharäya cha
namas te khanda-simhäya
satya-simhäya te namah

. . . who are the Absolute Truth (akhanda-tattva-rüpa), who hold a
kamandalu (kamandalu-dhara), who are a great lion (khanda-simha), and
who are a transcendental lion (satya-simha).

Text 114
namas te shveta-simhäya
pita-simhäya te namah
nila-simhäya niläya
rakta-simhäya te namah

O Lord Nrisimha, obeisances unto You, who are a white lion
(shveta-simha), a yellow lion (pita-simha), a black lion (nila-simha), black
(nila), and a red lion (rakta-simha).

Text 115
namo häridra-simhäya
dhümra-simhäya te namah
müla-simhäya müläya
brihat-simhäya te namah

O Lord Nrisimha, obeisances unto You, who are a yellow lion (häridra-simha), a smoke-colored lion (dhümra-simha), the root of all lions (müla-simha), the root of all that exists (müla),   and a great lion (brihat-simha).

Text 116
pätäla-sthita-simhäya
namo parvata-väsine
namo jala-stha-simhäya
antariksha-sthitäya cha

Obeisances to Lord Nrisimha, who is the lion in Pätälaloka (pätäla-sthita-simha), the lion in the mountains (parvata-väsi), the lion in the waters (jala-stha-simha), and the lion in the sky (antariksha-sthita).

Text 117
kälägni-rudra-simhäya
chanda-simhäya te namah
ananta-simha-simhäya
ananta-gataye namah

Obeisances to You, O Lord Nrisimha, who are the angry lion of the fire of time (kälägni-rudra-simha), who are a ferocious lion (chanda-simha), who are the limitless lion of lions (ananta-simha-simha), and who are the goal that has no limit (ananta-gati).

Text 118
namo vichitra-simhäya
bahu-simha-svarüpine
abhayankara-simhäya
narasimhäya te namah

Obeisances to You, O Lord Nrisimha, who are a wonderful lion (vichitra-simha), the form of many lions (bahu-simha-svarüpi), the lion that gives fearlessness (abhayankara-simha), and half-man half-lion (narasimha).

Text 119
namo 'stu simha-räjäya
narasimhäya te namah
säptäbdhi-mekhaläyaiva
satya-satya-svarüpine

Obeisances to Lord Nrisimha, who is the king of lions (simha-räja), half-man half-lion (narasimha), the earth, which wears the seven oceans like a belt (säptäbdhi-mekhala), the Lord whose form is transcendental (satya-satya- svarüpi), . . .

Text 120
sapta-lokäntara-sthäya
sapta-svara-mayäya cha
saptärchih-rüpa-damshträya
saptäshva-ratha-rüpine

. . . who stays in the seven worlds (sapta-lokäntara-stha), who is glorified with songs in the seven notes (sapta-svara-maya), whose teeth are splendid like seven suns (saptärchih-rüpa-damshtra), and who is gigantic like seven horse-drawn chariots (saptäshva-ratha-rüpi).

Text 121
sapta-väyu-svarüpäya
sapta-cchando-mayäya cha
svacchäya svaccha-rüpäya
svacchandäya cha te namah

Obeisances to You, O Lord Nrisimha, who are like seven strong winds (sapta-väyu-svarüpa), who are glorified by prayers in the seven meters (sapta-cchando-maya), who are pure (svaccha and svaccha-rüpa), and who are supremely independent (svacchanda).

Text 122
shrivatsäya suvedhäya
shrutaye shruti-mürtaye

shuchi-shravāya shūrāya
su-prabhāya su-dhanvine

Obeisances to Lord Nrisimha, who bears the mark of Shrivatsa
(shrivatsa), who is decorated with earrings (suvedha), who is the Vedas
personified (shruti and shruti-mūrti), whose fame is spotless
(shuchi-shrava), who is heroic (shūra), who is effulgent (su-prabha), who
carries a great bow (su-dhanvi), . . .

Text 123
shubhrāya sura-nāthāya
su-prabhāya shubhāya cha
sudarshanāya sūkshmāya
niruktāya namo namah

. . . who is glorious (shubhra), the master of the demigods (sura-nātha),
effulgent (su-prabha), auspicious (shubha), handsome (sudarshana), subtle
(sūkshma), and eloquent (nirukta).

Text 124
su-prabhāya svabhāvāya
bhāvāya vibhavāya cha
sushākhāya vishākhāya
sumukhāya mukhāya cha

Obeisances to Lord Nrisimha, who is effulgent (su-prabha), spiritual
(svabhāva), eternally existing (bhāva), the cause of spiritual love (vibhava),
handsome (sushākha), perfect and complete (vishākha), with a handsome
face (sumukha), the first of all (mukha), . . .

Text 125
su-nakhāya su-damshtrāya
surathāya sudhāya cha
sankhyāya sura-mukhyāya
prakhyātāya prabhāya cha

. . . whose claws are glorious (su-nakha), whose teeth are glorious
(su-damshtra), who is like a great chariot (suratha), who is like nectar
(sudha), who is described by the sankhya philosophy (sankhya), who is the

leader of the demigods (sura-mukhya), who is all-famous (prakhyäta), who is effulgent (prabha), . . .

Text 126
namah khatvanga-hastäya
kheta-mudgara-pänaye
khagendräya mrigendräya
nägendräya dridhäya cha

. . . who holds a khatvänga staff in His hand (khatvanga-hasta), who holds a kheta-mudgara club in His hand (kheta-mudgara-päni), who is carried by Garuda (khagendra), who is a great lion (mrigendra), who is the king of the nägas (nägendra), who is firm and resolute (dridha), . . .

Text 127
näga-keyüra-häräya
nägendräyägha-mardine
nadn-väsäya nägäya
nänä-rüpa-dharäya cha

. . . who wears a necklace and armlets of snakes (näga-keyüra-hära), who is worshiped by the king of snakes (nägendra), who   crushes sins (agha-mardi), who stays in the sacred rivers (nadi-väsa), who is powerful and swift (näga), who assumes many forms (nänä-rüpa-dhara), . . .

Text 128
nägeshvaräya nägäya
namitäya naräya cha
nägänta-karathäyaiva
nara-näräyanäya cha

. . . who is the ruler of the nägas (nägeshvara and näga), who is the Lord worshiped and honored by the devotees (namita), who   appears in a humanlike form (nara), who rides on garuda (nägänta-karatha), and who is Nara-Näräyana Rishis (nara-näräyana).

Text 129
namo matsya-svarüpäya
kacchapäya namo namah

namo yajna-varahäya
narasimhäya te namah

Obeisances to He who assumes the form of Matsya (matsya-svarüpa)!
Obeisances to He who assumes the form of Kürma (kacchapa)! Obeisances
to He who assumes the form of Yajna-Varäha (yajna-varäha)! O Lord
Nrisimha, obeisances to You!

Text 130
vikramäkranta-lokäya
vämanäya mahaujase
namo bhärgava-rämäya
rävanänta-karäya cha

Obeisances to Lord Nrisimha, who crosses over all the worlds
(vikramäkranta-loka), who is Vämana (vämana), who is all-powerful
(mahaujäh), who is Parashuräma (bhärgava-räma), and who is the Räma
that ended Rävana's life (rävanänta-kara).

Text 131
namas te balarämäya
kamsa-prädhvamsa-kärine
buddhäya buddha-rüpäya
tikshna-rüpäya kalkine

Obeisances to You, O Lord Nrisimha, who appear as Balaräma
(balaräma), who kill Kamsa (kamsa-prädhvamsa-käri), who are Buddha
(buddha and buddha-rüpa), who are ferocious (tikshna-rüpa), and who are
Kalki (kalki).

Text 132
ätreyäyägni-neträya
kapiläya dvijäya cha
ksheträya pashu-päläya
pashu-vakträya te namah

Obeisances to You, O Lord Nrisimha, who appear as Dattätreya (ätreya),
whose eyes are fire (agni-netra), who appear Kapila (kapila), who are the
leader of the brähmanas (dvija), who are the universal form (kshetra), who

are the protector of the cows (pashu-päla), and who have a lion's face
(pashu-vaktra).

Text 133
grihasthäya vanasthäya
yataye brahmachärine
svargäpavarga-dätre cha
tad-bhoktre cha mumukshave

Obeisances to You, O Lord Nrisimha, who are worshiped by the
grihasthas (grihastha), who are worshiped by the vänaprasthas (vanastha),
who are worshiped by the sannyäsis (yati), who are worshiped by the
brahmachhäris (brahmachäri), who give liberation   and residence in
Svargaloka (svargäpavarga-dätä), who are the   supreme enjoyer
(tad-bhoktä), who yearn to give liberation to the living entities
(mumukshu), . . .

Text 134
shälagräma-niväsäya
kshiräbdhi-shayanäya cha
shri-shailädri-niväsäya
shilä-väsäya te namah

. . . who appear as the Shälagräma-shilä (shälagräma-niväsa), who recline
on the milk-ocean (kshiräbdhi-shayana), who   reside in Shri Shaila
(shri-shailädri-niväsa), and who appear as a stone (shilä-väsa).

Text 135
yogi-hrit-padma-väsäya
mahä-häsäya te namah
guhä-väsäya guhyäya
guptäya gurave namah

. . . who stay in the lotus of the yogis' hearts (yogi-hrit-padma-väsa), and
who smile and laugh (mahä-häsa). Obeisances to Lord Nrisimha, who stays
in the cave of the heart (guhä-väsa, guhya, and gupta), and who is the
supreme spiritual master (guru).

Text 136
namo mülädhiväsäya
nila-vastra-dharäya cha
pita-vasträya shasträya
rakta-vastra-dharäya cha

Obeisances to Lord Nrisimha, who is the root of all existence (mülädhiväsa), who wears blue garments (nila-vastra-dhara), who wears yellow garments (pita-vastra), who is armed with many weapons (shastra), who wears red garments (rakta-vastra-dhara), . . .

Text 137
rakta-mälä-vibhüshäya
rakta-gandhänulepine
dhurandharäya dhürtäya
durdharäya dharäya cha

. . . who wears a red garland (rakta-mälä-vibhüsha), who is anointed with red scents (rakta-gandhänulepi), who is the maintainer of all (dhurandhara), who is cunning (dhürta), who is invincible (durdhara), who is the maintainer of all (dhara), . . .

Text 138
durmadäya duräntäya
durdharäya namo namah
durnirikshyäya nishthäya
durdanäya drumäya cha

. . . who is ferocious (durmada), infinite (duranta), invincible (durdhara), who is difficult to see (durnirikshya), who is faithful (nishtha), who is difficult to attain (durdana), who is like a tree (druma), . . .

Text 139
durbhedäya duräshäya
durlabhäya namo namah
driptäya dripta-vakträya
adripta-nayanäya cha

. . . who cannot be defeated (durbheda), who destroys the demons' hopes (duräsha), who is difficult to attain (durlabha), who is ferocious (dripta), whose face is ferocious (dripta-vaktra), who is the leader of the gentle and humble (adripta-nayana), . . .

Text 140
unmattäya pramattäya
namo daityäraye namah
rasajnäya raseshäya
ärakta-rasanäya cha

. . . who is wild (unmatta and pramatta), who is the demons' enemy (daityäri), who is expert at relishing the transcendental mellows (rasajïa), who is the king of transcendental mellows (rasesha), and whose tongue is red (ärakta-rasana).

Text 141
patyäya paritoshäya
rathyäya rasikäya cha
ürdhva-keshordhva-rüpäya
namas te chordhva-retase

O Lord Nrisimha, obeisances to You, who are the master of all (patya), who are filled with bliss (paritosha), who ride on a chariot (rathya), who relish transcendental mellows (rasika), who have a great mane (ürdhva-kesha), whose form is tall and massive (ürdhva-rüpa), and who are the best of the celibates (ürdhva-retäh).

Text 142
ürdhva-simhäya simhäya
namas te chordhva-bähave
para-pradhvamsakäyaiva
shankha-chakra-dharäya cha

O Lord Nrisimha, obeisances to You, who are a gigantic lion (ürdhva-simha and simha), who have mighty arms (ürdhva-bähu), who kill the demons (para-pradhvamsaka), who hold a conch and chakra (shankha-chakra-dhara), . . .

Text 143
gadä-padma-dharäyaiva
panca-bäna-dharäya cha

kämeshvaräya kämäya
käma-päläya kämine

. . . who hold a club and lotus (gadä-padma-dhara), who hold five arrows
(panca-bäna-dhara), who are the controller of Kämadeva (kämeshvara),
who are Kämadeva (käma), who protect Kämadeva (käma-päla), and who
control Kämadeva (kämi).

Text 144
namah käma-vihäräya
käma-rüpa-dharäya cha
soma-süryägni-neträya
somapäya namo namah

Obeisances to Lord Nrisimha, who enjoys amorous pastimes
(käma-vihära), who has the power to assume any form at will
(käma-rüpa-dhara), whose three eyes are the sun, moon, and fire
(soma-süryägni-netra), and who protects the moon (somapa).

Text 145
namah somäya vämäya
vämadeväya te namah
säma-svanäya saumyäya
bhakti-gamyäya vai namah

Obeisances to You, O Lord Nrisimha, who are Soma (soma), Väma
(väma), Vämadeva (vämadeva), the hymns of the Säma Veda
(säma-svana), handsome (saumya), and attainable by devotional service
(bhakti-gamya).

Text 146
kushanda-gana-näthäya
sarva-shreyas-karäya cha
bhishmäya bhisha-däyaiva
bhima-vikramanäya cha

Obeisances to You, O Lord Nrisimha, who are the master of the
kushandas (kushanda-gana-nätha), the benefactor of all
(sarva-shreyas-kara), ferocious (bhishma and bhisha-däya), all-powerful
(bhima-vikramana), . . .

Text 147
mriga-grivaya jivaya
jitayajita-karine
jatine jamadagnaya
namas te jata-vedase

. . . with a lion's neck (mriga-griva), the life of all that live (jiva), the conqueror of the demons (jita), invincible (ajita-kari), whose hair is matted (jati), who are Parashurama (jamadagna), and who are the master of all opulences (jata-vedah).

Text 148
japa-kusuma-varnaya
japyaya japitaya cha
jarayujayanda-jaya
sveda-jayodbhijaya cha

Obeisances to You, O Lord Nrisimha, whose complexion is the color of a rose (japa-kusuma-varna), who are glorified with japa-mantras (japya and japita), who are the creator of all living entities born from wombs (jarayuja), who are the creator of the living entities born from eggs (anda-ja), who are the creator of living entities born from perspiration (sveda-ja), who are the creator of living entities sprouted from seeds (udbhija), . . .

Text 149
janardanaya ramaya
jahnavi-janakaya cha
jara-janmadi-duraya
pradyumnaya pramodine

. . . who remove Your devotees' sufferings (janardana), who are the supreme enjoyer (rama), who are the father of the Ganges (jahnavi-janaka), who rescue the living entities from birth, old-age, and a host of troubles (jara-janmadi-dura), who are Pradyumna (pradyumna), who are blissful (pramodi), . .

Text 150
jihva-raudraya rudraya
virabhadraya te namah

chid-rüpäya samudräya
kad-rudräya pracetase

. . . whose tongue shows Your anger (jihvä-raudra), who are ferocious (rudra), who are heroic (virabhadra), whose form is transcendental (chid-rüpa), who are the ocean (samudra), whose are ferocious (kad-rudra), and who are most intelligent (pracetäh).

Text 151
indriyäyendriya-jnäya
namo 'stv indränujäya cha
atindriyäya säräya
indirä-pataye namah

Obeisances to Lord Nrisimha, who is the master of the senses (indriya), knowable by spiritual senses (indriya-jna), the younger brother of Indra (indränuja), beyond the reach of material senses (atindriya), the best (sära), the husband of the goddess of fortune (indirä-pati), . . .

Text 152
ishänäya cha idyäya
ishitäya inäya cha
vyomätmane cha vyomne cha
namas te vyoma-keshine

Obeisances to You, O Lord Nrisimha, who are the supreme master (ishäna), the supreme object of worship (idya), the supreme controller (ishita), all-glorious (ina), and the master of the spiritual sky (vyomätmä and vyoma), and whose mane touches the sky (vyoma-keshi).

Text 153
vyoma-dhäräya cha vyoma-
vakträyäsura-ghätine
namas te vyoma-damshträya
vyoma-väsäya te namah

Obeisances to You, O Lord Nrisimha, who hold up the sky (vyoma-dhära), whose wide-open mouth is like the sky (vyoma- vaktra), who kill the demons (asura-ghäti), whose teeth are like the sky (vyoma-damshtra), and whose home is in the spiritual sky (vyoma-väsa).

Text 154
sukumäräya rämäya
shubhäcäräya te namah
vishväya vishva-rüpäya
namo vishvätmakäya cha

Obeisances to You, O Lord Nrisimha, who are gentle and soft (sukumära), the supreme enjoyer (räma), auspicious (shubhächära), and the universal form (vishva, vishva-rüpa, and vishvätmaka).

Text 155
jnänätmakäya jnänäya
vishveshäya parätmane
ekätmane namas tubhyam
namas te dvädashätmane

Obeisances to You, O Lord Nrisimha, who are the object of transcendental knowledge (jnänätmaka and jnäna), the master of the universe (vishvesha), the Supersoul (parätmä), the Supreme Personality of Godhead, who has no rival (ekätmä), and the Supreme Lord who appears in twelve forms (dvädashätmä).

Text 156
chatur-vimshati-rüpäya
panca-vimshati-mürtaye
shad-vimshakätmane nityah
sapta-vimshatikätmane

... who appear in twenty-four forms (chatur-vimshati-rüpa), who appear in twenty-five forms (pancha-vimshati-mürti), who appear in twenty-six forms (shad-vimshakätmä), and who appear in twenty-seven forms (sapta-vimshatikätmä).

Text 157
dharmärtha-käma-mokshäya
viraktäya namo namah
bhäva-shuddhäya siddhäya
sädhyäya sharabhäya cha

Obeisances to Lord Nrisimha, who gives religion, economic development, sense-gratification, and liberation (dharmärtha-käma-moksha), who is always aloof from matter (virakta), who is the most pure (bhäva-shuddha), who is perfect (siddha), who is the goal of spiritual life (sädhya), who is ferocious like a sharabha monster (sharabha), . . .

Text 158
prabodhäya subodhäya
namo budhi-priyäya cha
snigdhäya cha vidagdhäya
mugdhäya munaye namah

. . . who is transcendental knowledge personified (prabodha and subodha), and who is dear to the wise (budhi-priya). Obeisances to Lord Nrisimha, who loves His devotees (snigdha), who is most intelligent (vidagdha), who is charming (mugdha), and who is wise (muni).

Text 159
priyam-vadäya shravyäya
shruk-shruväya shritäya cha
griheshäya maheshäya
brahmeshäya namo namah

Obeisances to Lord Nrisimha, who speaks sweetly (priyam-vada), whose glories should be heard (shravya), for whose pleasure yajnas are offered (shruk-shruva), the shelter of the devotees (shrita), the Lord of every home (grihesha), the Supreme Personality of Godhead (mahesha), and the Lord of the brähmanas (brahmesha).

Text 160
shridharäya sutirthäya
hayagriväya te namah
ügräya ügra-vegäya
ügra-karma-ratäya cha

O Lord Nrisimha, obeisances to You, who are the husband of the goddess of fortune (shridhara), the best of holy saints (sutirtha), the Hayagriva incarnation (hayagriva), fearsome (ügra), powerful (ügra-vega), and ferocious (ügra-karma-rata).

Text 161
ügra-neträya vyaghräya
samagra-guna-shäline
bala-graha-vinäshäya
pishäca-graha-ghätine

O Lord Nrisimha, obeisances to You, whose eyes are fearsome
(ügra-netra), who are ferocious (vyaghra), who have all virtues
(samagra-guna-chäli), who destroy the demons and evil spirits
(bala-graha-vinäsha), who destroy witches (pishächa-graha-ghäti), . . .

Text 162
dushta-graha-nihantre cha
nigrahänugrahäya cha
vrisha-dhvajäya vrishnyäya
vrishäya vrishabhäya cha

. . . who kill evil spirits (dushta-graha-nihantä), who are most merciful
(nigrahänugraha), who carry a flag marked with a bull (vrisha-dhvaja),
who are the best (vrishnya, vrisha, and vrishabha), . . .

Text 163
ügra-shraväya shäntäya
namah shruti-dharäya cha
namas te deva-devesha
namas te madhusüdana

. . . who are most famous (ügra-shrava), who are peaceful (shänta), who
remember everything (shruti-dhara), and who are the ruler of the demigods
(deva-devesha). Obeisances to You, the killer of the Madhu demon
(madhusüdana).

Text 164
namas 'te pundarikäksha
namas 'te durita-kshaya
namas 'te karunä-sindho
namas 'te samitinjäya

O lotus-eyed Lord (pundarikäksha), obeisances to You! O Lord who
rescue Your devotees from a host of troubles (durita-kshaya), obeisances

to You! O ocean of mercy (karunä-sindhu), obeisances to You! O Lord
victorious in battle (samitijäya), obeisances to You!

Text 165
namas 'te narasimhäya
namas 'te garuda-dhvaja
yajna-netra namas te 'stu
käla-dhvaja jaya-dhvaja

O Lord Nrisimha, obeisances to You! O Lord whose flag is marked
with Garuda (garuda-dhvaja), obeisances to You! Obeisances to You, O
Lord whose eyes are the Vedic yajnas (yajna-netra), whose flag is time
(käla-dhvaja), who hold a victory-flag (jaya-dhvaja)!

Text 166
agni-netra namas te 'stu
namas te hy amara-priya
mahä-netra namas te 'stu
namas te bhakta-vatsala

O Lord whose eyes are fires (agni-netra), obeisances to You! O Lord
dear to the demigods (amara-priya), obeisances to You! O Lord whose
eyes are great (mahä-netra), obeisances to You! O Lord who love Your
devotees (bhakta-vatsala), obeisances to You!

Text 167
dharma-netra namas te 'stu
namas te karunä-kara
punya-netra namas te 'stu
namas te 'bhishta-däyaka

O eye of religion (dharma-netra), obeisances to You! O merciful one
(karunä-kara), obeisances to You! O Lord whose eyes are most sacred
(punya-netra), obeisances to You! O Lord who fulfills Your devotees'
desires (abhishta-däyaka), obeisances to You!

Text 168
namo namas te daya-simha-rüpa
namo namas te narasimha-rüpa

namo namas te rana-simha-rüpa
namo namas te narasimha-rüpa

O merciful lion (daya-simha-rüpa), obeisances to You! O Lord
Nrisimha, obeisances to You! O warrior-lion (rana-simha-rüpa), obeisances
to You! O Lord Nrisimha, obeisances to You!

Text 169
uddhatya garvitam daityam
nihatyäjau sura-dvisham
deva-käryam mahat kritvä
garjase vätma-tejase

O Lord, You have killed the proud demon who hated Your devotee, and
have fulfilled Your mission of saving Your devotee. Now You roar loudly.

Text 170
ati-rudram idam rüpam
duhsaham duratikramam
drishtvä tu shankitä sarvä
devatäs tväm upägatäh

Gazing at this ferocious, powerful, and invincible form, the frightened
demigods approach You.

Texts 171 and 172
etän pashyan maheshänam
brahmänam mäm shaci-patim
dik-pälän dvädashädityän
rudrän uraga-räkshasän
sarvän rishi-ganän saptam
atrim gaurim sarasvatim
lakshmim nadish cha tirthäni
ratim bhüta-ganäny api

Please look at them, at Shiva, at me, who am Brahmä, at Indra, at the
dik-pälas, at the twelve Adityas, at the Rudras, at the Uragas and
Rakshasas, at all the sages, at the seven sages, at Atri, Gauri, Sarasvati,
Lakshmi, the sacred rivers personified, the holy places personified, Rati,
and the Bhütas.

Text 173
prasida tvam mahä-simha
ügra-bhävam imam tyaja
prakriti-stho bhava tvam hi
shänta-bhävam cha dhäraya

O great lion, please be merciful to us. Please give up Your anger. Please become Your self. Please be pacified.

Text 174
ity uktvä dandavad bhümau
papäta sa pitämahah
prasida tvam prasida tvam
prasideti punah punah

After speaking these words, Grandfather Brahmä fell to the ground like a stick. Again and again he said: Please be merciful! Please be merciful! Please be merciful!

TEXT NUMBERS OF THE NAMES
Each name is followed by it's text number.

Abhayankara-simha 118 * Abhista-dayaka 167 * Abhuta 98 * Adbhuta-karma 64 * Adhoksaja 42 * Adhvatita 65 * Adi-deva 23 * Adrpta-nayana 139 * Agalad-vaisnava 79 * Agha-hari 25 * Agha-mardi 127 * Aghora 23 * Aghora-virya 24 * Agni-netra 132 166 * Aho-ratram 89 * Ajaya 23 * Ajita-kari 147 * Akaradi-hakaranta 94 * Akhanda-tattva-rupa 113 * Akrura 21 * Aksa-mali 105 * Aksaya 23 * Aksobhya 62 * Amara-priya 166 * Amita 62 * Amita-tejah 57 * Amitaujah 62 * Amogha 25 * Amrta 62 * Ana 63 * Ana-bhuk 63 * Ana-rupa 63 * Anabher-brahmano-rupa 79 * Anada 63 * Anadi 98 * Anagha 25 * Ananta 47 62 98 * Ananta-gati 117 * Ananta-simha-simha 117 * Anantananta-rupa 52 * Anda-ja 148 * Anekatma 95 * Aniruddha 62 * Antariksa 88 * Antariksa-sthita 116 * Antri-mali 112 * Apamrtyu-vinasa 63 * Apasmara-vighati 63 * Aprameya 62 * Apramita 18 105 * Arakta-rasana 140 * Arupa 22 * Asani-pramita 72 * Asi-carma-dhara 106 * Asirsad-randhra 79 * Astra-rupa 100 * Asura-ghati 153 * Atharva-sirah 72 * Atindriya 151 * Atma-jyotih 92 * Atma-rupa 99 * Atreya 132 * Atta-hasa 7 * Avighna 43 * * Bahu-rupa 100 * Bahu-simha-svarupi 118 * Bahu-srnga 50 * Bahu-yojana-hastanghri 77 * Bahu-yojana-mayata 77 *

Manda 52 * Mangalya 50 * Mani 67 * Manmatha 107 * Manojna 50 * Mantavya 50 * Mantra-raja 60 * Mantra-rupa 100 * Mantri 60 * Manu 62 * Marici 49 * Masa 89 * Mata 99 * Mati 99 * Matsya-svarupa 129 * Matulinga-dhara 51 * Maya 54 * Mayatita 54 * Mayi 51 52 * Megha-nada 25 * Megha-syama 26 * Meghatma 25 * Mitra 42 * Mogha-vahana-rupa 26 * Mrga-griva 147 * Mrgendra 126 * Mrtyunjaya 9 * Mugdha 158 * Mukha 124 * Mula 115 * Mula-simha 115 * Muladhivasa 136 * Muladhyaksa 42 * Muladi-vasa 9 * Mumuksu 133 * Muni 158 * Munja 14 * Munja-kesa 14 * Murari 53 * * Nada 25 * Nadi-vasa 127 * Nadya 64 * Naga 127 128 * Naga-keyura-hara 127 * Naganta-karatha 128 * Nagendra 126 127 * Nagesvara 128 * Nakha-damstrayudha 28 * Namita 128 * Nana-rupa-dhara 127 * Nara 128 * Nara-narayana 128 * Narasimha 118 119 * Neta 98 * Nibandha 12 13 * Nigrahanugraha 162 * Nila 11 114 * Nila-simha 114 * Nila-vastra-dhara 136 * Nimesa 12 * Nimesa-gamana 12 * Nira 10 * Nirakara 94 * Nirakrti 13 * Niralamba 11 * Niranjana 10 * Nirasa 12 * Niravadya 64 * Nirdvandva 12 * Nirguna 10 * Nirjita-kala-simha 83 * Nirmala 13 * Nirmala-citra-simha 82 * Nirmoha 13 * Nirukta 123 * Nirvana-prada 11 * Nisa-srnga 111 * Nisatha 59 * Niscaya 12 * Niskala 11 * Nisprapanca 11 * Nistha 138 * Nitya 13 * Nivida 11 * Niyamaka 98 * Nrsimha 55 * * Omkara 94 * * Padma 67 * Padma-garbha 108 * Padma-kalpodbhava 68 * Padma-nabha 67 * Padma-netra 67 69 * Padmabha 67 * Padmayah-pati 67 * Padmesa 15 * Padmodara 68 * Paksa 89 * Panca-bana-dhara 143 * Panca-brahmatma 71 * Panca-rupa-dhara 100 * Panca-vimsati-murti 156 * Pantha 18 * Papa-hari 4 * Para-brahma-svarupa 71 * Para-karma-vidhayi 106 * Para-pradhvamsaka 142 * Param-jyotih 92 * Paramatma 22 * Paramesti 56 * Parat-para-paresa 4 * Paratma 155 * Paritosa 141 * Parjanya 66 * Parvata-vasi 116 * Parvataranya 88 * Pasi 4 * Pasu-pala 132 * Pasu-vaktra 132 * Patala-sthita-simha 116 * Pati 93 * Patya 141 * Pavana 4 * Pavitra 4 * Phani-talpa 33 * Pinaki 4 * Pingaksa 49 * Pisaca-graha-ghati 161 * Pita 99 * Pita-simha 114 * Pita-vastra 136 * Prabha 125 * Prabhanjana 18 * Prabhavisnu 74 * Prabhu 17 * Prabodha 17 158 * Prabuddha 66 * Pracchinna 17 * Pracetah 150 * Pradhana-purusa 66 * Pradipta 17 * Pradyumna 149 * Prahlada-varada 3 * Prajadhyaksa 41 * Prajvala 18 * Prakasa 18 * Prakhyata 125 * Pralobhi 17 * Prama 18 * Pramatta 140 * Pramodi 149 * Pranah 92 * Praninam 92 * Prasanna 4 * Prastuta 51 * Pratapa 18 * Pratyag-atma 92 * Pratyaksa-varada 3 * Priyam-vada 159 * Prthivi 88 * Puccha-simha 81 * Pundarikaksa 164 * Punya 5 * Punya-netra 167 * Purana-purusa 5 * Purna-simha 81 * Purodha 6 * Puru-huta 5 * Puru-stuta 5 * Purvaja 6 * Puskaraksa 6 * Puspa-hasa 6 * Pusta 56 *

* Stota 98 * Stuti 98 * Stutya 98 * Su-damstra 125 * Su-dhanvi 122 *
Su-ghora 23 * Su-jyotih 92 * Su-nakha 125 * Su-prabha 122 123 124 *
Subha 123 * Subhacara 154 * Subhanjaya 10 * Subhiksa 40 * Subhra 123
* Subodha 158 * Subrahmanya 70 * Suci-srava 122 * Sudarsana 123 *
Sudha 125 * Suhrt 99 * Sukarma 106 * Sukesa 15 112 * Suksma 40 123 *
Suksunya 40 * Sukta 16 * Sukti-karna 16 * Sukumara 154 *
Sumitra-varuna 42 * Sumukha 124 * Sunabha 67 * Sura 122 *
Sura-mukhya 125 * Sura-natha 123 * Suradhyaksa 40 * Suratha 125 *
Susakha 124 * Susarma 107 * Susuksma 40 * Sutirtha 160 * Sutra 10 *
Suvedha 122 * Svabhava 124 * Svaccha 121 * Svaccha-rupa 121 *
Svacchanda 121 * Svadha-kara 93 * Svaha-kara 93 * Svargapavarga-data
133 * Svarupa 22 33 * Sveda-ja 148 * Sveta-simha 114 * *
Tad-agre-sarvatah-siva 79 * Tad-bhokta 133 * Tadasva-sirah 71 *
Tadit-prabha 33 * Taksaka 35 * Tamo-ghna 34 * Tamoghna 43 * Tanu-tra
35 * Tapa-traya-hara 34 * Tapana 34 * Tapaska 34 * Tapasvi 34 * Taraka
34 * Tarala 35 * Tarasvi 33 * Tarksya 36 * Taruna 33 * Tarya 33 *
Tat-purusa 5 * Tathya 5 * Tati 35 * Tattva 34 * Tejo-dhama 55 * Tejoma
55 * Tiksna 42 * Tiksna-damstra 72 * Tiksna-rupa 131 * Tri-deha 61 *
Tri-dhama 60 * Tri-kala-jnana-rupa 61 * Tri-murti-vidya 61 * Tri-netra 60
* Tri-sandhya 89 * Tri-suli 60 * Tri-tattva-jnani 61 * Tri-varga 60 *
Tri-vedi 70 * Tridhatma 61 * Tusta 56 57 * * Udbhija 148 * Ugra 160 *
Ugra-karma-rata 160 * Ugra-netra 161 * Ugra-rupi 15 * Ugra-srava 163 *
Ugra-vega 160 * Ujjvala 18 * Unmatta 140 * Urdhva-bahu 142 *
Urdhva-kesa 15 141 * Urdhva-retah 141 * Urdhva-rupa 141 *
Urdhva-simha 142 * Urjita 66 * * Vag-atita 65 * Vag-isvara 65 * Vagmi
65 * Vaidyuta 64 * Vaikuntha 58 * Vajra 1 60 * Vajra-damstra 1 *
Vajra-deha 1 * Vajra-nakha 1 * Vajri 1 * Vama 145 * Vamadeva 145 *
Vamana 130 * Vana-mali 75 * Vanastha 133 * Vandya 2 * Vara 2 *
Vara-rupi 2 * Varada 2 * Varadabhaya-hasta 2 * Varatma 2 * Varenya 3 *
Varistha 3 * Varma 107 * Varmi 107 * Vasat-cakra 20 * Vasat-kara 93 *
Vasudeva 2 * Vata 105 * Vatsara 89 * Vega-kara 94 * Vibhava 30 124 *
Vibhu 17 97 * Vibudha 30 * Vicitra-simha 118 * Vidagdha 158 * Vidhana
30 * Vidhata 103 * Vidheya 30 * Vidya 64 * Vighna-koti-hara 43 *
Vihvala 28 32 * Vihvala-netra-simha 82 * Vijaya 30 * Vikalpa 32 *
Vikarma 106 * Vikatasya 27 * Vikirna-nakha-damstra 28 * Vikrama 21 *
Vikramakranta-loka 130 * Vikuntha 58 * Vinita 31 * Vipaksa-ksaya-murti
41 * Vipra 31 * Vipula 31 * Vira 27 29 * Vira-simha 80 * Virabhadra 150
* Virakta 157 * Virupaksa 29 * Visakha 124 * Visesaksa 29 * Visista 57
* Visnu 74 * Visruta 32 * Vistara-sravah 27 * Vistirna-vadana 29 * Visva
154 * Visva-garbha 109 * Visva-karta 97 * Visva-rupa 154 * Visva-yoni

31 * Visvaksena 28 * Visvambhara 30 * Visvatmaka 154 * Visvesa 155 * Vita-raga 31 * Vita-soka 29 * Vitanka-nayana 31 * Vitta 32 * Viyoni 32 * Vrsa 162 * Vrsa-dhvaja 162 * Vrsabha 162 * Vrsni-mula 74 * Vrsnya 162 * Vyaghra 161 * Vyaghra-deha 26 * Vyaghra-karmi 27 * Vyaghra-pada 27 * Vyaghra-simha 81 * Vyala-yajnopavitra 26 * Vyapaka 27 * Vyoma 152 * Vyoma-damstra 153 * Vyoma-dhara 153 * Vyoma-kesi 152 * Vyoma-vaktra 153 * Vyoma-vasa 153 * Vyomatma 152 * * Yajna-netra 165 * Yajna-varaha 129 * Yati 133 * Yoga 101 * Yoga-gamya 102 * Yoga-pitha-sthita 101 * Yoga-rupa 101 * Yogi 101 * Yogi-hrt-padma-vasa 135 * Yuga-bheda 90 * Yuga-sandhayah 90 * Yugadi 90

The Manyu Shutka of the Rig Veda

(Manyu, the personification and presiding Deity of anger, is a form of Narasimhadeva. This Shukta very much follows the tendency of the *Rig Veda* and is chanted during the fire rituals for the destruction of enemies. Thus, it is very powerful.)

Rig Veda 10.6.15

Text 1
harih om
yaste manyo 'vidhadujra jayaka jaha ojah pushyati vishvamanupak
sahyama dasamaryam tvaya yuja sahaskritena sahasa sahasvata

"O Manyu, the persons who worship You, who is like a thunderbolt, the destroyer of enemies, enjoys all power and strength combined, may we overcome our enemies with You as our friend, invigorating and strong."

Text 2
manyurindro manyurevasa devo manyurhota varuno jatavedaha
manyum visa ilate manusiryaha pahi no manyo tapasa sajoshaha

"Manyu is Indra, He is Varuna and Agni. Those of human descent praise Manyu. Protect us Manyu, be pleased with our austerities."

Text 3
abhihi manyo tapasastaviyan tapasa yuja vi jahi satrun
amitraha vritraha dasyuha cha vishva vasunya bhara tvam naha

"Come to us Manyu, You who are the strongest of the strong. With austerity as your companion, overthrow our enemies. Give us spiritual wealth, O slayer of enemies, adversaries and foes."

Text 4
tvam hi manyo abhi bhutyojah svayam bhurbhamau abhimatishahah
vishva charshanih sahurih sahava-nasmasvoja pritanasu dhehi

"Give us strength in battle, Manyu, O you who posses overpowering strength. You are self-existent, furious, the overthrower of enemies, the beholder of all, enduring, and vigorous."

Text5
abhagah sannapa pareto asmi tava kratva tavishasya pracetaha
tam tva manyo akraturjihila-ham sva tanur-baladeyaya mahi

"O Lord Manyu, not taking part in Your worship (not offering oblations at the ritual) I was forced to retreat before my enemies. I avoided and neglected your worship. Yet please be kind and give me strength."

Text 6
ayam te asmyupa mehyarvan praticinah sahure vishvadhayaha
manyo vajrin-nabhi mama vavritsva hanava dasyugm ruta bodhyapehe

"I am yours! Come to me, turn Your face towards me! O resister of the foes, sustainer of all, Manyu, the holder of a thunderbolt, come to me. Let us slay the demons, and help Your devotees."

Text 7
abhi prehi dakshinato bhava me 'dha vritrani janghanava muri
juhomi te dharunam madhvo agra mubha upamshu prathama pibava

"Approach me by my right side and let us slay a multitude of foes. I offer you the best part of the Soma juice, let us drink it together in privacy."

Rig Veda 10.6.16

Text 1
tvaya manyo sarathamarujanto harshamanaso dhrishita marutvaha
tigmeshava ayudha samsishana abhi prayantu naro agnirupaha

"May the priests, who resemble Agni, ascend the same chariot as You. O Manyu, who is accompanied by the Maruts. May You proceed in battle, advancing, exulting, indignant, armed with sharp arrows, whetting Your weapons."

Text 2
Agniriva manyo tvishitah sahasva senanirnah sahure huta edhi
Hatvaya shatrun vi bhajasva veda aujo mimano vi mridho nudasva

"Blazing like fire, O Manyu, overcome our foes, come as our general, when invoked by us in battle. Having slain the enemies, divide their wealth. Granting us strength, scatter our foes."

Text 3
Sahasva manyo abhimatimasme rujan mrinan pramrinan prehi shatrun
Ugram te pajo nanva rurudhre vasi vasham nayasa ekaja tvam

"O Manyu, overthrow our enemies. Advance against our foes, wounding, killing, annihilating them. O You who depend on no-one, who can resist Your fierce might?"

Text 4
eko bahunamasi manyavilito vishamvisham yudhaye sam shishadhi
ekrittaruk tvaya yuja vayam dyumantam ghosham vijayaya krinmahe

"You are praised, O Manyu, as the conqueror of all. Help us contend with all men. With You as our friend, O radiant one, we cry out in victory."

Text 5
vijeshakridindra ivanavabravo 'smakam manyo adhipa bhaveha
priyam te nama sahure grinimasi vidma tamutsam yata ababhutha

"O Manyu, giver of victory, You are irreproachable like Lord Indra. Please protect this ritual. O Enduring One, we sing to you appropriate praises. We know this to be the source where You have come from."

Text 6
abhutya sahaja vajra sayaka saho bibharsya-bhibhuta uttaram
kratva no manyo saha medhyedi maha-dhanarya puruhuta samsriji

"O Manyu, You are like a destructive thunderbolt, the overpowerer of foes, the twin brother of victory, and have extreme strength. Be favorable to us, Manyu, in our deeds, O You who are invoked by many in the shock of battle."

Text 7
Samsristam dhanam ubhayam samakrita
Masmabhayam dattam varunashcha manyuh
Bhiyam dadhana hridayesu shatravaha
Parajitaso apa ni layantam

"May Manyu and Varuana bestow upon us undivided spiritual and material wealth; may our enemies, fear within their hearts, be overcome and utterly destroyed."

Sri Narasimha Astottara Nama Stotram
This is made of 108 names of Lord Narahari, Narasimhadeva. This is often chanted by the pujaris or priests in the temple when they are offering flowers dipped in sandalwood to the feet of the deities.

Text 1
narasimho mahasimho
divya simho mahabala
ugra simho maha deva
stambajash chogra lacana

Half man half lion. Great lion. Transcendental lion. Greatly strong. Terrible lion. Greatest of demigods. Born of a pillar. Possessor of terrible eyes.

Text 2
raudra sarvadbhuta shriman
yoganandas trivikramah
harim kolahalash chakri
vijaya jaya vardhana

Angry One. The all wonderful. Who is accompanied by Lakshmi. The one blissful in yoga. The tallest. Lord Hari. One who roars. The holder of the Sudarshana. Ever glorious. Always victorious.

Text 3
panchananah param brahma
chaghoro ghoravikramaha
jvalan mukho jvalamaha
maha jvalo maha prabhuh

One with five mouths. Supreme Brahman. Horrible One. Whose activites are terrible. Possessor of flaming mouth. Possessor of fiery garland. Greatly fiery. Great master.

Text 4
nitilaksha sahasrakso
dumirikshyah parantapaha
maha damstra yudhah prajnas
chandakopi sadashivaha

Whose eyes resemble sesame seeds. Thousand eyed One. Who is difficult to see. Chastiser of enemies. Possessor of great teeth. Expert in war. Who is angry at Chanda (a demon, brother of Prachanda). Always auspicious.

Text 5
hiranyaka-nisudana
daitya danava bhanjanaha
guna bhadro maha bhadro
bala-bhadrah subhadrakaha

The killer of Hiranyakasipu. The threatener of the daityas and the danavas. One with auspicious qualities. Greatly auspicious. Possesor of auspicious strength. The very auspicious one.

Text 6
karalo vikaratals cha
vikarta sarva-katrika
shishumaras trilokatma
ishah sarveshvara-vibhuh

Fearful One. Very fearful. Non-doer. The doer behind everything. The killer of the killer (Hiranyakashipu). The soul of the three worlds. The controller. The controller of everything. Master.

Text 7
bhairava-dambharo divyas
chachyutah kavi madhavaha
adhokshajo 'ksharah sarvo
vana-mali vara-pradaha

Whose activities are fearful. Transcendental. Infallible. Poet. The husband of the goddess of fortune. Beyond material conception. Indestructible. All in all. Adorned by a garland of forest flowers. Giver of benedictions.

Text 8
vishvambaro 'dbhuto bhavyaha
shri-vishnuh purushottamaha
anangastro nakshatras cha
suryo jyotir sureshvaraha

The maintainer of the universe. The wonderful one. Ever existing. The all pervading. The best person. The holder of Cupid's weapon. Star. The effulgent sun. Lord of all demigods.

Text 9
sahasra bahuh sarvagyaha
sarva-siddhi pradayakaha
vajra-dhamstro vajra-nakho
mahananda param-tapaha

Thousand handed on. Knower of the everything. Bestower of all mystic poers. Whose teeth are like thunderbolts. Whose nails are like thunderbolts. Greatly blissful. The highest of ascetics.

Text 10
sarva-mantraikarupash cha
sarva-yantra vidaranaha
sarva tantra mahavyaktaha
suvyakto bhakta-vatsalaha

The form of all mantras. The destroyer of all obstacles in the path of progress. The goal of all rituals. The unmanifested One. Whose manifestation is auspicious. The protector of the devotees.

Text 11
vaishaka-shukla bhutoltha
sharanagata-vatsalaha
udara-kirtih punyatma
mahatma chanda-vikramaha

Who is born in the month of Vaishakha in shukla paksha. The up holder of the earth planet. Affectionate to those surrendered unto Him. Whose fame is spread all over. Pure soul. Great soul. Glorified in the Vedas.

Text 12
vatatrayo prapujash cha
bhagavan parameshvaraha
shri-vatsamkah shri-nivaso
jagad-vyapi jaganmayaha

Who is worshipped by the three deities (Brahma, Vishnu, Shiva). The Supreme Personality of Godhead. The Supreme controller. Who is marked by the Sri Vatsa. The shelter of Sri (Lakshmi). Who pervades through the universe. Whose body is the universe.

Text 13
jagat palo jagannatho
mahakyo dvirupabrit
paramatma param-jyoti
nirgunash cha nri-keshari

The protector of the universe. The Lord of the universe. Who is known as the Great One. Who has two features (man and lion). The supersoul.

Supreme Effulgence. Who is devoid of material qualities. Half man half
lion.

Text 14

para-tattvam param-dhama
sat-chid-ananda-vigraha
lakshmi nrisimha sarvatma
dhira prahlada-palakaha

The highest truth. The highest abode. Whose form is sat-chid-ananda.
Lakshmi-Nrisimha, the soul of all living beings. The protector of the sober
Prahlada.

CHAPTER TWENTY-THREE

Additional Prayers for Protection

These are from the *Srimad-Bhagavatam* (10th Canto, 6th Chapter, verses 22-29), wherein Sukadeva Gosvami explained to Maharaja Pariksit how the cowherd women of Vrindavana chanted these mantras to protect child Krishna at the time. These same prayers are very powerful and can also protect us in a similar way. They are as follows:

Texts 22-23
avyad ajo 'nghri manimams tava janv athoru
yagyo 'cyutah kati-tatam jatharam hayasyaha
hrit keshavas tvad-ura isha inas tu kantham
vishnur bhujam mukham urukrama ishvarah kam

chakry agratah saha-gado harir astu pashchat
tvat-parshvayor dhanur-asi madhu-hajanash cha
koneshu shankha urugaya upary upendras
tarkshyah kshitau haladharah purusha samantat

May Aja protect Your legs, may Maniman protect Your knees, Yajna Your thighs, Acyuta the upper parts of your waist, and Hayagriva Your abdomen. May Keshava protect Your heart, Isha Your chest, the sun-god Your neck, Vishnu Your arms, Urukrama Your face, and Ishvara your head. May Chakri protect You from the front; may Sri Hari, Gadadhari, the carrier of the club, protect You from the back; and may the carrier of the bow, who is known as the enemy of Madhu, and Lord Ajana, the carrier of the sword, protect Your two sides. May Lord Urugaya, the carrier of the conchshell, protect You from all corners; may Upendra protect You from above; may Garuda protect You on the ground; and may Lord Haladhara, the Supreme Person, protect You on all sides.

Text 24
indriyani hrishikeshaha
pranan narayano 'vatu
shvetadvipa-patish chittam
mano yogeshvaro 'vatu

May Hrishikesh protect Your senses, and Narayana Your life air.
May the master of Shvetadvipa protect the core of Your heart, and may
Lord Yogeshvara protect Your mind.

Text 25-26
prishnigarbhas tu te buddhim
atmanam bhagavan paraha
kridantam patu govindaha
shayanam patu madhavaha

vrajantam avyad vaikuntha
asinam tvam shriyah patihi
bhunjanam yagyabhuk patu
sarva-graha-bhayankaraha

May Lord Prishnigarbha protect Your intelligence, and the
Supreme Personality of Godhead Your soul. While You are playing, may
Govinda protect You, and while You are sleeping may Madhava protect
You. May Lord Vaikuntha protect You while You are walking, and May
Lord Narayana, the husband of the goddess of fortune, protect You while
You are sitting. Similarly, may Lord Yajnabhuk, the fearful enemy of all
evil planets, always protect you while you enjoy life.

Test 27-29
dakinyo yatudhanyash cha
kushmanda ye 'rbhaka-grahaha
bhuta-preta-pishachash cha
yaksha-raksho-vinayakaha

kotara revati jyeshtha
putana matrikadayaha
unmade ye hy apasmara
deha-pranendriya-druhaha

svapna-drishta mahotpata
vriddha bala-grahash cha ye
sarve nashyantu te vishnor
nama-grahana-bhiravaha

The evil witches known as Dakinis, Yatudhanis and Kushmandas are the greatest enemies of children, and the evil spirits like Bhutas, Pretas, Pishachas, Yakshas, Rakshasas and Vinayakas, as well as witches like Kotara, Revati, Jyeshtha, Putana and Matrika, are always ready to give trouble to the body, the life air and the senses, causing loss of memory, madness and bad dreams. Like the most experienced evil stars, they all create great disturbances, especially for children, but one can vanquish them simply by uttering Lord Vishnu's names, for when Lord Vishnu's name resounds, all of them become afraid and go away.

CHAPTER TWENTY-FOUR

Gayatri Mantras to God, His Avatars, the Vedic Divinities, and the Planets for Assistance

This includes prayers and gayatri mantras to Vishnu, Lakshmi, Narayana, Narasimha, Ganesh, Shiva, Durga, Brahma, Sarasvati, Kuvera, and others, the Maha Mrityunjaya Mantra, mantras for the well-being of society, mantras to the planets, and for each day of the week for benefits and welfare.

Gayatris to Lord Sri Krishna, for spiritual success:
Aum Devkinandanaye Vidmahe
Vasudavaye Dhi-mahi
Tanno Krishnah Prachodayat

Translation: "Om. Let us meditate on Sri Krishna, beloved son of Devaki and Vasudeva. May that Lord Krishna of dark complexion, who steals the heart, inspire and illumine our mind and understanding."

Om Dhamodharaya Vidhmahe
Rukmani Vallabhay Dheemahe
Tanno Krishna Prachodayath

Translation: Om, Let me meditate on the God whose belly was tied by a rope, Oh, consort of Rukhmani, give me higher intellect, and let God Krishna illuminate my mind.

Om Govindaya Vidhmahe
Gopi Vallabhaya Dheemahe
Tanno Krishna Prachodayath

Also this one to offer obeisances to Lord Vasudeva, the Supreme Person, for requesting that He reveal the supreme spiritual truth to us:

Om namo bhagavate vasudeya

Translation: Om, Let me meditate on the god who takes care of all beings, Oh, darling of all gopis, give me higher intellect, and let God Krishna illuminate my mind.

To Radha, for increasing our devotion and divine love:
Aum Vrashbhanujaye Vidmahe
Krishnapriyaye Dhi-Mahi
Tanno Radha Prachodayat

Translation: "Om. Let us meditate on Sri Radha, the beloved of Sri Krishna, the daughter of Vrishabhanu. May that Radha Devi inspire and illumine our mind and understanding."

To Vishnu, for welfare:
Aum Narayanaye Vidmahe
Vasudavaye Dhimahi
Tanno Vishnu Prachodayat

Translation: "Om. Let us meditate on Sri Narayana, the Lord who dwells in all beings, and is known as the Sovereign of the world. May that Sri Vishnu inspire and illumine our mind and understanding."

To Goddess Lakshmi, for increasing wealth, luxuries, promotion, status:
Aum Mahalakshmaye Vidmahe
Vishnupriyaye Dhimahi
Tanno Lakshmih Prachodayat

Similar Gayatris for Lakshmi are:
Om Mahalakshmyai cha vidmahe
Vishnu patnyai cha dhimahi
Tanno Lakshmihi prachodayat

Translation: "Om. Let us meditate on the Great Goddess Sri Lakshmi, the consort of Sri Maha Vishnu. May that effulgent Maha Lakshmi Devi inspire and illumine our mind and understanding."

Om Mahadevyaicha Vidhmahe
Vishnu Pathniyaicha Dheemahe
Thanno Lakshmi Prachodayath

Translation: "Om, Let me meditate on the greatest goddess, Oh, wife of Lord Vishnu, give me higher intellect, And let Goddess Lakshmi illuminate my mind."

Another to Goddess Lakshmi. This mantra is said to get *siddha* or perfection after chanting it 108 times a day for 11 days. This mantra is never failing for one who seeks success in business and financial prosperity, or who faces barriers in business growth, or other obstacles to prosperity. This mantra is very dear to Goddess Lakshmi, who told Vasistha that, "I am very pleased by this mantra and if any person recites this mantra even once, I will establish myself in his home." It is:

Om Shreem Hreem Kleem Shreem
Laxmirachagachha
Mama Mandire Tishtha-Tishtha Swaha

Another mantra to Lakshmi. Shring is the seed. Japa is 100,000 times after which one gets the blessings of peace and prosperity:
Aum Shring Hring Kleeng Maha Lakshmaye Namaha, Aum.

The Shri *Rig Veda* Maha Lakshmi Devi Mantra is:
Om Shrim Hrim Shrim
Kamale Kamalalaye
Praseedha Praseedha
Shrim Hrim Shrim Om
Shri Mahalakshmi Devyai namaha

The Shri Soubagya Mahalakshmi Mantra is:
Om Shrim Hrim Klim Aim
Kamala Vasinyai Swaha

Another to Lakshmi is:
Sarva mangala mangalye
sive sarvardha sadhike
saranye trayambake devi
narayani namostute

Another traditional mantra to Lakshmi is:
Om sreem hreem kleem
kamale kamalalaye
prasida prasida
sreem hreem kleem
sri maha lakshmyi namaha

Translation: Underlying vibration of all creation, abundance please, cherishing your lotus feet, be pleased Great Lakshmi Goddess, I bow to You.

The Sri Mahalakshmi Mula Mantra:
Om srim hrim klim hrim srim
mahalakshmayai namaha

To Lord Rama, for security and status:
Aum Dasharathaye Vidmahe
Sita Ballabhaye Dhimahi
Tanno Ramah Prachodayat

Translation: "Om. Let us meditate on the divine son of King Dasharatha. May that Sri Rama, beloved husband of Sita Devi, inspire and illumine our mind and understanding."

To Srimati Sita, for increasing power to work on oneself, penance, and tolerance:
Aum Janaknandiniye Vidmahe
Bhumijayai Dhimahi
Tanno Sita Prachodayat

To Lord Narayana, to increase administrative power:
Aum Narayanaya Vidmahe
Vasudevaya Dhimahi
Tanno Narayanah Prachodayat

Translation: "Om. Let us meditate on the Great Lord Narayana who pervades all creation. May that glorious Maha Vishnu, who appeared on Earth as the adorable Sri Krishna, son of Vasudeva, inspire and illumine our mind and understanding."

Venkateswara Gayatri Mantra:
Nirnajanaya Vidmahe
Nirapasaya Dheemahe
Thanno Srinivasa Prachodayath

Translation: Om, Let me meditate on the god who is eternal truth, Oh, God who does not have attachments, give me higher intellect, and let God Srinivasa illuminate my mind.

To Lord Narasimha, to increase our ability to help others:
Aum Ugranarsinghaye Vidmahe
Vajranakhaye Dhi-Mahi
Tanno Narsingha Prachodayat

Translation: "Om. Let us meditate on the fierce and terrible form of Lord Narasimha, the half-man and half-lion form. May that great God, with nails hard and strong as diamonds, inspire and illumine our mind and understanding."

A similar Narasimha Gayatri is:
Om Narasimhaya vidmahe
Vajra nakhaya dhimahi
Tanno Narasimha prachodayat

Translation: "Om. Let us meditate on Sri Narasimha, who incarnated as half-man and half-lion. May that Lord with adamantine claws inspire and illumine our mind and understanding."

To Hamsa, for increasing power of discrimination:
Aum Paramhamsaye Vidmahe
Mahahamsaye Dhimahi
Tanno Hamsah Prachodayat

Translation: "Om. Let us meditate on Sri Hamsa Deva, the glorious, pure white divine swan of supreme discrimination. May that great Lord in the form of a swan, who exemplifies paramahamsas, blissful self-realized souls, inspire and illumine our mind and understanding."

To Hayagriva, to increase courage and remove fear:
Aum Vanishwaraye Vidmahe
Hayagrivaye Dhimahi
Tanno Hayagrivah Prachodayat

Translation: "Om. Let us meditate on the glorious Lord Hayagriva, who is the embodiment of Sri Maha Vishnu. May that great Vagishwara, the Lord of Speech, and consort of Vagishwari, Sarasvati Devi, the Goddess of Knowledge and Speech, inspire and illumine our mind and understanding."

To Lord Shiva, for easing problems, and giving peace & prosperity:
Aum Panchvaktraye Vidmahe
Mahadevaye Dhimahi
Tanno Rudra Prachodayat

Translation: "Om. Let us meditate on the great Lord with five faces. May that fierce Rudra inspire and illumine our mind and understanding."

Om Tat Purushaya Vidhmahe
Mahadevaya Dheemahe
Thanno Rudra Prachodayath

"Om. Let me meditate on the great Purusha, Oh, greatest God, give me higher intellect, and let God Rudra illuminate my mind."

To Goddess Durga, for victory over obstacles, pains & enemies:
Aum Girijaye cha Vidmahe
Shiva Priyaye cha Dhimahi
Tanno Durga Prachodayat

Translation: "Om. Let us meditate on Girija Devi, Daughter of the Mountain. May that beloved of Lord Shiva inspire and illumine our mind and understanding."

Om Kathyayanaya Vidhmahe
Kanya Kumari cha Dheemahe
Thanno Durgaya Prachodayat

"Om. Let me meditate on the goddess who is daughter of Kathyayana, Oh, maiden Goddess, give me higher intellect, and let Goddess Durga illuminate my mind."

To Ganesh, for removing obstacles:
Aum Eikdantaya vidmahe
Vakratunaye Dhimahi
Tanno Buddhih Pracodayat

Another Ganesh Gayatri similar to this is:
Aum Eka dantaya vidmahe
Vakra tundaya dhimahi
Tanno dantih prachodayat

Translation: "Om. Let us meditate on Sri Ganesh, the lord with one tusk. May that great lord with curved elephant trunk inspire and illumine our mind and understanding."

To Brahma, for increasing productivity:
Aum Parmeshwaraye Vidmahe
Paratattvaye Dhimahi
Tanno Brahma Prachodayat

Another similar Gayatri for Brahma is:
Aum chatur mukhaya vidmahe
Hamsarudhaya dhimahi
Tanno brahma prachodayat

Translation: "Let us meditate on the glorious lord with four divine faces, who is seated on a pure white swan. May that great Brahma, Creator of the Universe, inspire and illumine our mind and understanding."

Also to Brahma is:
Om Vedathmanaya vidmahe,
Hiranya Garbhaya Dheemahi,
Thanno Brahma prachodayath

"Om, Let me meditate on the God who is the soul of Vedas, Oh God, who holds the entire world within you, give me higher intellect, and let the Lord Brahma illuminate my mind."

To Goddess Saraswati, for memory, wisdom, knowledge, and creativity:
Aum Saraswateye cha Vidmahe
Brahmaputriye cha Dhimahi
Tanno Saraswati Prachodayat

Translation: "Om. Let us meditate on Sri Saraswati Devi. May that glorious consort of Lord Brahma inspire and illumine our mind and understanding."

Om Vakdeviyai cha Vidhmahe
Virinji Pathniyai cha Dheemahe
Tanno Vani Prachodayath

"Om, Let me meditate on the goddess of speech, Oh, wife of Lord Brahma, give me higher intellect, and let Goddess Vani illuminate my mind."

To Indra, for security in aggression or war:
Aum Sahasra-Netraye Vidmahe
Vajra hastraye Dhimahi
Tanno Indrah Prachodayat

Translation: "Om. Let us meditate on Indira, the Lord with a thousand eyes. May that great God who holds the invincible thunderbolt in his hand inspire and illumine our mind and understanding."

The Devendra (Indra) Gayatri:
Om Sahasra nethrayeVidhmahe
Vajra hasthaya Dheemahe
Tanno Indra Prachodayath

"Om, Let me meditate on the thousand eyed one, Oh, Lord with Vajra as weapon, give me higher intellect, And let Indra illuminate my mind."

To Hanuman, for love of selfless service
Aum Anjaneyaye Vidmahe
Mahabalaye Dhimahi
Tanno Hanuman Prachodayat

Another similar Gayatri for Hanuman is:
Aum anjani sutaya cha vidmahe
Vayu putraya cha dhimahi
Tanno marutih prachodayat

Translation: "Om. Let us meditate on Sri Hanuman, whose mother is
Anjani Devi. May that supremely brave and strong Maruti, son of the Wind
god, inspire and illumine our mind and understanding."

To Yama the lord of death, for freedom from the fear of death:
Aum Surya-Putraye Vidmahe
Mahakalaye Dhimahi
Tanno Yamah Prachodayat

Translation: "Om. Let us meditate on the great son of the sun god. May that
Yama Deva, the lord of time, inspire and illumine our mind and
understanding."

To Varuna, for increase of love between man & woman:
Aum Jalbimbaye Vidmahe
Nila Purushaye Dhimahi
Tanno Varunah Prachodayat

Translation: "Om. Let us meditate on the great Lord Varuana. All the
waters in the world are His reflection. May that glorious Varuna Deva,
whose form is a beautiful luminous blue, inspire and illumine our mind and
understanding."

To Agni the fire deity, to provide vitality and ojas to the body & mind:
Aum Mahajwalaye Vidmahe
Agnidevaye Dhimahi
Tanno Agnih Prachodayat

Translation: "Om. Let us meditate on the great God of fire in the form of
blazing flames. May that radiant Agni Deva inspire and illumine our mind
and understanding."

Two additional mantras to Agni:
Om angimile purohitamyyajnasya devamritvijam
Hotaram ratnadhatamam harih om harih om

"I glorify Agni, the high priest of the (agnihotra) sacrifice, the divine, the ministering priest, who offers oblations (to the gods), and is the possessor of great wealth. Om, glories to Hari."

Agna ayahi vitaye
Grinano havyadataye
Nohota satsi barhishi
Harih om harih om

"Please come oh Agni, the luminous, pervading and giver of enjoyable objects. Thou art worthy of adoration, present in the world and our self, like a Hota (priest) in the ritual. Om, glories to Hari."

The Subrahamanya Gayatri Mantra:
Om Tat Purushaya Vidhmahe
Maha Senaya Dheemahe
Tanno Shanmuga Prachodayath

"Om. Let me meditate on that great male, Oh, commander in chief, give me higher intellect, And let the six faced one illuminate my mind."

To Prithvi, for stability, patience, cooperation:
Aum Prithvidevaye cha Vidmahe
Sahasramoortaye cha Dhimahi
Tanno Prithvi Prachodayat

Translation: "Om. Let us meditate on Prithvi Devi, Mother Earth. May that Mother Prithvi of a thousand forms inspire and illumine our mind and understanding."

To Kam, for increase in stamina, vitality, & sexual power:
Aum Kamdevaye Vidmahe
Pushpvanaye Dhimahi
Tanno Kamah Prachodayat

The Sri Tulasi Gayatri for clarity in our devotion and spirituality:
Aum tulasi devyai cha vidmahe
Vishnu priyayai cha dhimahi
Tanno brindah Prachodayat

Translation: "Om. Let us meditate on Sri Tulasi Devi, who is very dear to the heart of Lord Maha Vishnu. May that glorious Devi, the divine embodiment of the sacred tulasi plant also known by the sweet name of Vrinda, inspire and illumine our mind and understanding."

The Devi Varahi Mantra:
(Mantra to the consort of Lord Varaha for ridding oneself of negativity)
Om shreem hreem kleem dhum
jwaalaa jwaalaa
shulini asya yajamaanasya
sarva shatroon samhara samhara
kshema laabham kuru kuru
dushta graham
hum phat svaha

The Garuda Gayatri Mantra:
Om Thathpurushaya Vidhmahe
Suvarna Pakshaya Dheemahe
Tanno Garuda Prachodayath

"Om. Let me meditate on that great living being, Oh, Bird with golden wings, give me higher intellect, And let the God Garuda illuminate my mind"

The Sudharshana Chakra Gayatri Mantra:
Om Sudharshanaya Vidmahe
Maha Jwalaya Dheemahe
Tanno Chakra Prachodayath

"Om. Let me meditate on the holy wheel of Sudharshana, Oh, Wheel which has great brilliance, give me higher intellect, And let the wheel illuminate my mind."

The Gayatri Mantra for Nandi, Shiva's Bull Carrier:
Om Thathpurushaya Vidhmahe
Chakrathundaya Dheemahe
Tanno Nandi Prachodayath

"Om. Let me meditate on that great living being, Oh, Lord of devas, give me higher intellect, And let the God Nandi illuminate my mind."

The Famous Sri Gayatri Mantra

Om bhur bhuvaha svah
tat savitur varenyam
bhargo devasya dhimahi
dhiyo yo nah prachodayat
(*Rig-veda* 3.62.10)

This Sri Gayatri is a very important and well known Gayatri mantra, chanted silently in the mind, three times a day. It translates as: "Om, Let us meditate on that worshipable effulgence of the divine sun, Savitri, Creator of the Earth, Heaven and ether, and who enthuses our meditation."

Word for word meaning of this mantra is:

Om or aum - It is the chief and the most appropriate name for God. This word is made of the combination of 'a', 'u', and 'm': 'a' means creator of the universe, 'u' means sustainer of the universe, 'm' means annihilation of the universe. Thus the word 'aum' imbibes in itself all the chief qualities of God.

Bhur - The substratum of life; dearer than even life; the Giver and Sustainer of all life.

Bhuvah - The destroyer of all kinds of miseries; the Remover of all sorrows.

Svah - The form of pleasure and the bestower of pleasure/bliss.

Tat - That God

Savitur - The progenitor of the entire world; The Creator of the Universe; One who always inspires us.

Varenayam - Worth acquiring, the superior most; You alone are worthy of worship.

Bhargo - Of the pure form; You are the light that illuminates us, the Fire which burns away all our evil desires.

Devasya - Of God; You are the Supreme Being.

Dhimahi - Let us meditate upon.

Dhiyo - intellect so we move forward, may be able to tell right from wrong and follow the right path.

Yo - Who, i.e. the God referred to; You who have all these qualities.

Nah - Of ours

Prachodayat - May inspire (for good deeds).

Additional Mantras for Blessings

Invocation to Ganesh:
Gajananam Bhutganadisevitam
Kapittha Jamboo Phalcharu Bhakshanam
Umasutam Shokvinashkarakam
Namami Vighneshwar Padpankajam
Translation: "Oh Elephant-faced, worshiped by the existing beings, of all living beings, tasting the elephant apple (kaith) and jambolana (jamun), the Son of Uma, destroyer of grief, I bow to the lotus feet of Ganesh who is lord of all."

Ganesh Gayatri Mantras for increasing intellect:
Om Lambhodaraya vidmahe
Mahodaraya deemahi
Tanno danthi prachodayath

Om. Let me meditate on that god with broad paunch Oh, God with a big belly, give me higher intellect, And let the elephant faced one illuminate my mind.

Om Thatpurashaya vidhmahe
Vakrathundaya dheemahi
Tanno danthi prachodayath

"Om. Let me meditate on that great male, Oh, God with broken tusk, give me higher intellect, And let the elephant faced one illuminate my mind."

To Ganesh for removing obstacles, a good way to start any projects, studies or rituals:
Ganapati Bappa Morya
Pudhachya Varshi Lovkar Yaa

Use this to Ganesh prayer before beginning any new project so impediments may be removed and your endeavor may be crowned with success: Om gam ganapataye namaha.

The Ganesh Maha-mantra:
Om gam ganapataye namaha

The Ganesh Mula Mantra:
Om srim hrim klim glaum gam ganapataye svaha
Om shanti shanti shantihi

Also:
Om gam-gau-ganapataye
Bighna-binashi ne-svaha

For one who wants wealth and prosperity, meditate on the golden color
of Ganesh and say this prayer:
Om Lakshmi Ganapataye namaha

Another to Ganesh, Japa is 5,000 times a day for 25 days:
Om Gum Ganapataye Namaha, Om

Also to Ganesh:
Om gam ganeshaya namaha
Om klim gam gam gam mahaganapataye namaha

To Ganesh for blessings for spiritual success:
Om gananam tva ganapatigm havamahe kavim
kavinamupamashravastamam
Jyeshtharajam brahmanam brahmanaspata snah shrinvanutibhissida
sadanam
Mahaganapataye namaha

Translation: Om. Oh lord of speech, we worship you, the lord of the gods,
the wisest among the wise, the one having incomparable fame, the best
among the praiseworthy, and the lord of the Vedic hymns. While listening
to our praises, come with your protecting powers and be rested in our
yajnashala (temple). Obeisances to Mahaganapati.

Agajananapadmarkam gajananamaharnisham
Anekadantam bhaktanamekadantamupasmahe

Translation: We meditate, day and night, on the one-tusked one (Ganesh)
who is the sun for the lotus in the form of the face of Parvati, the one with
the elephant face and the one who is the giver of plenty to his devotees.

Shanmukha Gayatri Mantra to Murugan:
Om Thatpurushaya Vidhmahe
Maha Senaya Dhimahi
Thannah Shanmukha Prachodhayath

Translation: Om, let us meditate that Supreme lord who is the Supreme General of the great Deva Army, Lord Shanmukha or Muruga. May He enlighten us and lead us to be one with him.

The following mantra is to Lord Kuvera, the treasurer of the demigods. The ancient books refer to this as the supreme mantra. Lord Shankara revealed its secret to the powerful Ravana. Through its use he could create his golden capital and could attain supreme financial accomplishments. This mantra has been found to be powerful enough to yield beneficial results very quickly. It becomes siddha after chanting it 108 times each day for 11 days. It is good for financial progress, removal of obstacles, material happiness, home ownership, reputation, victory, longevity, etc.

Om Yakshaya Kuberaya Vaishravanaya Dhana-Dhanyadi
Pataye Dhana Dhanyadi Samruddhim Me
Dehi Dapaya Swaha

Another to lord Kubera, the treasurer of the demigods, for financial assistance:
Om rajadhirajaya prasahyasahine
Namo vayan vaishravanaya kurmahe
Sa me kaman kamakamaya mahyam
Kameshvaro vaishravano dadatu
Kuberaya vaishravanaya maharajaya namaha

"We offer salutations unto Vaisravana (the son of Visrava, Kubera), the king of kings, whose nature is to help without any purpose of his own. May Vaisravana, the lord of deities, give me, the seeker of desires, what I desire. Salutations unto the great lord Kubera, the son of Visrava."

To Goddess Sarasvati, it is said that after japa of 500,000 times, one becomes enlightened and all knowledge is revealed. Aing is seed of this Sarasvati mantra:
Om Aim Saraswatye Namaha, Om.

Another to Sarasvati for clarity:
Om Aim Shreem Hreem
Saraswathi Devyai Namaha

A Sarasvati Bhija Mantra:
Om aim klim sarasvatyai namaha

The Shiva Panchakshari Mantra:
Om namah shivaya

Shiva Shakti Panchakshari Mantra:
Om hrim namah shivaya

To Shiva as Dakshinamurti:
Nidhaye sarvavidyanam bhishale bhavaroginam
Gurave sarvalokanam dkashinamurtaye namaha

Translation: "Salutations to Dakshinamurti, the storehouse of all learning, the healer of all those who suffer the diseases of samsara (cycles of birth and death), and the teacher of the whole world."

Another popular mantra to Durga, japa is 500,000 times:
Om Aim Hrim Kleem Chamundaye Vichchey, Om.

Also: Om dum Durgaye Namaha, Om.

The Shri Durga Mantra is:
Om Hrim Dhum Durga Devyai namaha

A Durga Gayatri:
Om girijayai vidmahe
shiva priyayai dhimahi
tanno durga prachodayat

A mantra for Kali, Kring is the seed of the Kali mantra. Japa is 500,000 for mantra siddha:
Om Kring Kalikaye Namaha, Om.

Sri Mahakali Mantra:
Om hrim srim krim
paramesvari kalike
hrim srim krim svaha

The Shri Annapurna Mantra is:
Om Annapurnayai namaha
Om Sadapurnayai namaha

The Shri Chakra Mantra is:
Om Shri Chakravasinyai namaha
Om Shri Lalithambikayai namaha

The Maha Mrityunjaya Mantra to Lord Shiva for removing ailments, ill health and fear:

Om Triyambakam Yajamahe
Sugandhim Pushti Vardhanam
Urvarukamiva Bandhanat
Mrityor Mukshiya Mamritat

Translation: "We worship the Three-eyed One (Lord Shiva) who is fragrant and who nourishes well all beings, and grants liberation just as the cucumber is severed from bondage to the creeper."

A mantra to Lord Rama for invoking the healing energy:
Om apadamapa hataram
dataram sarva sampadam
loka bhi ramam shri ramam
bhuyo bhuyo namamyaham

Translation: Om. O most compassionate Lord Rama. Please send You healing energy here to the Earth, to the Earth. Obeisances to You."

To Lord Dhanvanatari, the great avatara of Vishnu and physician of the gods, for healing any ailments:
Om shri dhanvatari namaha

"Om. Obeisances to Lord Dhanvantari."

Prayers / Mantras for the welfare of everyone:

Om Sarvesham Svasti Bhavatu
Sarvesham Santir Bhavatu
Sarvesham Purnam Bhavatu
Sarvesham Mangalam Bhavatu

"May everybody have prosperity. May everybody have peace. May everybody have perfection. May everybody have auspiciousness."

Sarve Bhavantu Sukinah
Sarve Santu Nirmayaah
Sarve Bhadrani Pasyantu
Ma kaschid-Dukha-Bhag-Bhavet

"May all be happy. May all be free from disabilities. May all look for the good in others. May none suffer from sorrows."

Om Asato Ma Sat Gamaya
Tamaso Ma Jyotir-Gamaya
Mrityor-Ma Maritam Gamaya

"Lead us from the unreal to the real. Lead us from darkness (ignorance) to light. Lead us from death to everlasting immortality."

Mantras for the Planets
(Used when certain planets need to be strengthened in our astrological chart, or for benedictions.)

To the Sun:
Japa kusuma-sankarsham kashyapeyam maha-dyutim
tamo-rim sarva-papa-ghnam pranato 'smi divakaram

"Let us chant the glories of the Sun god, whose beauty rivals that of a flower. I bow to him, the greatly effulgence son of Kashyapa, who is the enemy of darkness and destroyer of all sins."

To Surya the sun deity, for freedom from disease:
Aum Bhaskaraye Vidmahe
Divakraraye Dhimahi
Tanno Suryah Prachodayat

Translation: "Om. Let us meditate on the shining Sun god who gives light to the whole world. May that Divakara, the radiant lord who is the cause of day, inspire and illumine our mind and understanding."

Also these following mantras:
Om Suryaye Namah
Aum Bhaskaraye Vidmahe
Divakraraye Dheemahi
Tanno Suryah Prachodayat

Om Aswadwajaya Vidhmahe
Pasa Hasthaya Dheemahe
Thanno Surya Prachodayath

"Om, Let me meditate on the god who has a horse flag, Oh, God who holds the rope, give me higher intellect, and let Sun God illuminate my mind."

To the Moon:
dadhi-shankha-tusharabham kshirodarnava-sambhavam
namami shashinam somam sambhor mukuta-bhushanam

"I offer my obeisances to the Moon god, whose complexion resembles curds, the whiteness of conch shells, and snow. He is the ruling deity of the soma-rasa born from the Ocean of Milk, and he serves as the ornament on top of the head of Lord Shambhu."

To Chandra, the moon deity, for subduing anxiety and worries:
Aum Kshirputraye Vidmahe
Amrittattvaye Dhimahi
Tanno Chandrah Prachodayat

Translation: "Om. Let us meditate on the glorious son of milk, the glowing Moon. May that Chandra, the essence of nectar, inspire and illumine our mind and understanding."

Om Padmadwajaya Vidhmahe
Hema roopaya Dheemahe
Thanno Chandra Prachodayath

"Om. Let me meditate on God who has lotus in his flag, Oh, God of golden color, give me higher intellect, And let moon God illuminate my mind."

To Venus (Shukra) for creativity and success in such things as trading in the markets:
hima-kunda-mrnalabham
daityanam paramam gurum
sarva-shastra-pravaktaram
bhargavam pranamamy aham

"I offer my obeisances to the descendant of Bhrigu Muni (Venus), whose complexion is white like a pond covered with ice. He is the supreme spiritual master of the demoniac enemies of the demigods, and has spoken to them all the revered scriptures."

Om aswadhwajaaya vidmahae
dhanur hastaaya dheemahi
tanno shukra prachodayaat

"Om. Let me meditate on him who has horse in his flag, Oh, He who has a bow in his hand, give me higher intellect, And let Shukra illuminate my mind."

To Mars (Angaaraka):
dharani-garbha-sambhutim vidyut-kanti-samaprabha
kumaram shakti-hastam cha mangalam pranamamy aham

"I offer my obeisances to Sri Mangala, god of the planet Mars, who was born from the womb of the earth goddess. His brilliant effulgence is like that of lightening, and he appears as a youth carrying a spear in his hand."

Om veeradhwajaaya vidmahae
vighna hastaaya dheemahi
tanno bhouma prachodayaat

"Om. Let me meditate on him who has hero in his flag, Oh, He who has power to solve problems, give me higher intellect, And let the son of earth God illuminate my mind."

To Mercury (Budha):
priyangava-gulikashyam rupena pratimambadam
saumyam saumya-gunopetam tam budham pranamamy aham

"I bow down to Buddha, god of the planet Mercury, whose face is like a fragrant globe of the priyangu herb and whose beauty matches that of a lotus flower. He is most gentle, possessing all attractive qualities."

Om gajadhwajaaya vidmahae
sukha hastaaya dheemahi
tanno budha prachodayaat

"Om. Let me meditate on him who has elephant in his flag, Oh, He who has power to grant pleasure, give me higher intellect, And let Budha illuminate my mind."

To Jupiter (Guru):
devanam cha rishinam cha gurum kanchana-sannibham
buddhi-bhutam tri-lokesham tam namami brihaspatim

"I bow down to Brihaspati, god of the planet Jupiter. He is the spiritual master of all the demigods and sages. His complexion is golden, and he is full of intelligence. He is the controlling lord of all three worlds."

Om vrishabadhwajaaya vidmahae
kruni hastaaya dheemahi
tanno guru prachodayaat

Om, Let me meditate on him who has bull in his flag, Oh, He who has power to get things done, give me higher intellect, And let Guru illuminate my mind.

To Saturn or Shani:
nilanjana-samabhasam ravi-putram yamagrajam
chaya-martanda-sambhutam tam namami shanaishcharan

"I bow down to slow moving Saturn, whose complexion is dark blue like nilanjana ointment. The elder brother of Lord Yamaraja, he is born from the Sun-god and his wife Chaya."

The Shani Gayatri Mantra:
Om Sanaischaraya vidhmahe
Sooryaputraya dhimahi
tanno manda prachodayat

Sanishwara (Saturn) Gayatri Mantra:
Om kaakadhwajaaya vidmahae
khadga hastaaya dheemahi
tanno mandah prachodayaat

"Om, Let me meditate on him who has crow in his flag, Oh, He who has a sword in his hand, give me higher intellect, And let Saneeswara illuminate my mind."

Shani Dhyan Mantra:
Nilanjana samabhasam raviputram yamagrajam
chaya martanda sambhutam tam namami shaishcharam

"I bow to Lord Shani, who is black in colour and son of Sun and born to Chaya and brother of Yama , who moves very slowly."

To Rahu:
ardha-kayam mahim-viryam chandraditya-vimardanam
simhika-garbha-sambhutam tam rahum pranamamy aham

"I offer my obeisances to Rahu, born from the womb of Simhika, who was only half a body yet possesses great power, being able to subdue the Sun and Moon."

Rahu Gayatri Mantra:
Om Sookdantaya Vidmahe,
Ugraroopaya Dhimahi,
Tanno Rahu Prachodayat

om naakadhwajaaya vidmahae
padma hastaaya dheemahi
tanno raahu prachodayaat

Om, Let me meditate on him who has snake in his flag, Oh, He who has a lotus in his hand, give me higher intellect, And let Rahu illuminate my mind.

To Ketu:
palasa-puspa-sankasam
taraka-graha-mastakam
raudram raudratmakam ghoram
tam ketum pranamamy aham

"I offer my obeisances to the violent and fearsome Ketu, who is endowed with the potency of Lord Shiva. Resembling in his complexion the flower of a palasa plant, he serves as the head of the stars and planets."

om aswadhwajaaya vidmahae
soola hastaaya dheemahi
tanno ketu prachodayaat

Om, Let me meditate on him who has horse in his flag, Oh, He who has a trident in his hand, give me higher intellect, And let Kethu illuminate my mind.

The Navagraha Stotram
(One mantra for counteracting all ill effects from any of the planets and improve the positive energy by favorable planetary positions.)

Aarogyam pradadathuno Dinakara / Chandro yasho nirmalam
Bhoomim Bhoomisutha Sudhaamshu Thanaya / Prajyam Gurur gourava
Kavya komala Vagvila samathulam / Mandho mudam sarvada
Rahur bahu balam virodha shamanam / Kethur kulasonnayathim

After chanting this sloka for 1 Or 8 /16/64/108 times chant the following for 8 times:

Om Navagrahaya Namaha

Mantras for Each Day of the Week

For Sunday:
Om namo Narayanaya
Reverence to Narayana (Vishnu) brings love, prosperity, power, and
glory.

For Monday:
Om namah Shivaya
Reverence to Shiva, destroys negative tendencies and effects. Gives
freedom from attachments that bind one to material consciousness.

For Tuesday:
Om Sri Subramunyaya Namah
Reverence to Subramunya, Shiva's son, gives success, drives away evil
influences, gives spiritual victory and in battle.

For Wednesday:
Om namo Bhagavate Vasudevaya
Reverence to Lord Krishna, the all-pervading Divine Lord. Gives
success in all activities and offers divine love, and eases a troubled mind.

For Thursday:
Om namo Bhagavate Shivanandaya
Reverence to the guru who can give great power and bliss of
enlightenment to you.

For Friday:
Om Sri Maha Lakshmiyai Namah
Reverence to Lakshmi, bestows prosperity, truthfulness, nonviolence,
humility, spiritual understanding, and spiritual wisdom.

For Saturday:
Om Sri Hanumate Namah
Reverence to Hanuman, invokes unbounded love for Lord Rama, gives
strength, success in devotional activities, reveals the power of the soul
that can triumph over adversities for attaining highest realizations.

CHAPTER TWENTY-FIVE

The 108 Names of Lord Sri Rama

This contains a selection of the names of Lord Rama for chanting on special occasions, such as on Ram Navami or His appearance day celebration. There is also the *Sri Ram Stuti*, and *Raghupati Raghava*.

OM SHRI RAMAYA NAMAHA
Obeisances to Sri Rama, the Giver of happiness

OM RAMABHADRAYA NAMAHA
Obeisances to Sri Rama, the Auspicious One

OM RAMACHANDRAYA NAMAHA
Obeisances to Sri Rama, who is as lustrous as the moon

OM SHASHVATAYA NAMAHA
Obeisances to Sri Rama, to the ever-lasting one

OM RAJIVALOCHANAYA NAMAHA
Obeisances to Sri Rama, the Lotus-eyed

OM SHRIMATE NAMAHA
Obeisances to Sri Rama, the Abode of Lakshmi

OM RAJENDRAYA NAMAHA
Obeisances to Sri Rama, the King of kings

OM RAGHUPUNGAVAYA NAMAHA
Obeisances to Sri Rama, the Most Exalted of the Raghu dynasty

OM JANAKI VALLABHAYA NAMAHA
Obeisances to Sri Rama, the Beloved of Janaki

OM JAITRAYA NAMAHA
Obeisances to Sri Rama, the Triumphant

OM JITAMITRAYA NAMAHA
Obeisances to Sri Rama, the Conqueror of His enemies

OM JANARDHANAYA NAMAHA
Obeisances to Sri Rama, the Refuge of the people

OM VISHVAMITRA PRIYAYA NAMAHA
Obeisances to Sri Rama, the Beloved of Sage Vishvamitra

OM DANTAYA NAMAHA
Obeisances to Sri Rama, the well-controlled One

OM SHARANATRANA TATPARAYA NAMAHA
Obeisances to Sri Rama, the One who is keen to protect those who take
refuge in Him

OM BALI PRAMATHANAYA NAMAHA
Obeisances to Sri Rama, the Vanquisher of Bali

OM VAGMINE NAMAHA
Obeisances to Sri Rama, the Eloquent

OM SATYAVACHE NAMAHA
Obeisances to Sri Rama, the One of truthful speech

OM SATYAVIKRAMAYA NAMAHA
Obeisances to Sri Rama, the One who is valiant in defending Truth

OM SATYAVRATAYA NAMAHA
Obeisances to Sri Rama, the One of truthful vows

OM VRATADHARAYA NAMAHA
Obeisances to Sri Rama, the One who faithfully keeps His vows

OM SADA HANUMADASHRITAYA NAMAHA
Obeisances to Sri Rama, the One who is always served by Hanuman

OM KAUSALEYAYA NAMAHA
Obeisances to Sri Rama, the Son of Kausalya

OM KHARADHVAMSINE NAMAHA
Obeisances to Sri Rama, the Annihilator of the demon Khara

OM VIRADHA VANAPANDITAYA NAMAHA
Obeisances to Sri Rama, the Expert in destroying the demon Viradha

OM VIBHISHANA PARITRATRE NAMAHA
Obeisances to Sri Rama, the Protector of Vibhishan

OM KODANDA KHANDANAYA NAMAHA
Obeisances to Sri Rama, the One who broke the mighty bow

OM SAPTATALA PRABHEDRE NAMAHA
Obeisances to Sri Rama, the One who permeates the seven planes of existence

OM DASHAGRIVA SHIROHARAYA NAMAHA
Obeisances to Sri Rama, the One who cut off Ravana's heads

OM JAMADAGNYA MAHADARPPA DALANAYA NAMAHA
Obeisances to Sri Rama, the One who shattered the pride of Parasurama

OM TATAKANTAKAYA NAMAHA
Obeisances to Sri Rama, the Slayer of Tataka

OM VEDANTA SARAYA NAMAHA
Obeisances to Sri Rama, the Essence of Vedanta

OM VEDATMANE NAMAHA
Obeisances to Sri Rama, the Self of the Vedas

OM BHAVAROGASYA BHESHAJAYA NAMAHA
Obeisances to Sri Rama, the Healer of the disease of Becoming

OM DUSHANATRI SHIROHANTRE NAMAHA
Obeisances to Sri Rama, the One who cut off the head of Dushana

OM TRIMURTAYE NAMAHA
Obeisances to Sri Rama, the Embodiment of the Three Gods

OM TRIGUNATMAKAYA NAMAHA
Obeisances to Sri Rama, the Source of the three gunas

OM TRIVIKRAMAYA NAMAHA
Obeisances to Sri Rama, the Lord as Vamana

OM TRILOKATMANE NAMAHA
Obeisances to Sri Rama, the source of the three planetary systems

OM PUNYACHARITRA KIRTANAYA NAMAH
Obeisances to Sri Rama, the One whose story is a source of merit to
those who sing it

OM TRILOKA RAKSHAKAYA NAMAHA
Obeisances to Sri Rama, the Protector of the three world systems

OM DHANVINE NAMAHA
Obeisances to Sri Rama, the wielder of the bow

OM DANDAKARANYA KARTANAYA NAMAHA
Obeisances to Sri Rama, the Dweller in the Dandaka forest

OM AHALYA SHAPASHAMANAYA NAMAHA
Obeisances to Sri Rama, the Remover of Ahalya's curse

OM PITRU BHAKTAYA NAMAHA
Obeisances to Sri Rama, the Worshipper of His father Dasaratha

OM VARA PRADAYA NAMAHA
Obeisances to Sri Rama, the giver of boons

OM JITENDRIYAYA NAMAHA
Obeisances to Sri Rama, THE Conqueror of the senses

OM JITAKRODHAYA NAMAHA
Obeisances to Sri Rama, the Conqueror of anger

OM JITAMITRAYA NAMAHA
Obeisances to Sri Rama, the One who wins over friends

OM JAGAD GURAVE NAMAHA
Obeisances to Sri Rama, the Guru of the world

OM RIKSHA VANARA SANGHATINE NAMAHA
Obeisances to Sri Rama, the Lord who organized the hordes of monkeys

OM CHITRAKUTA SAMASHRAYAYA NAMAHA
Obeisances to Sri Rama, the Lord who took refuge at Chitrakuta Hill

OM JAYANTA TRANA VARADAYA NAMAHA
Obeisances to Sri Rama, the Lord who blessed Jayanta

OM SUMITRA PUTRA SEVITAYA NAMAHA
Obeisances to Sri Rama, the Lord who is served by Sumitra's son
(Lakshmana)

OM SARVA DEVADHI DEVAYA NAMAHA
Obeisances to Sri Rama, the Lord of all the gods

OM MRITAVANARA JIVANAYA NAMAHA
Obeisances to Sri Rama, the Lord who revived the dead monkeys (after
the war)

OM MAYAMARICHA HANTRE NAMAHA
Obeisances to Sri Rama, the Destroyer of the demon Maricha who
practiced illusion

OM MAHADEVAYA NAMAHA
Obeisances to Sri Rama, the Great Lord

OM MAHABHUJAYA NAMAHA
Obeisances to Sri Rama, the Lord of mighty arms

OM SARVADEVA STUTAYA NAMAHA
Obeisances to Sri Rama, the Lord who is praised by all the gods

OM SAUMYAYA NAMAHA
Obeisances to Sri Rama, the Calm One

OM BRAHMANYAYA NAMAHA
Obeisances to Sri Rama, the Absolute Reality

OM MUNI SAMSTUTAYA NAMAHA
Obeisances to Sri Rama, the Lord who is praised by sages

OM MAHAYOGINE NAMAHA
Obeisances to Sri Rama, the Great Yogin

OM MAHADARAYA NAMAHA
Obeisances to Sri Rama, the Noble One

OM SUGRIVEPSITA RAJYADAYE NAMAHA
Obeisances to Sri Rama, the Lord who returned the kingdom to Sugriva

OM SARVA PUNYADHI KAPHALAYA NAMAHA
Obeisances to Sri Rama, the Giver of fruits of pious work, good karmas

OM SMRITA SARVAGHA NASHANAYA NAMAHA
Obeisances to Sri Rama, the Remover of all afflictions

OM ADIPURUSHAYA NAMAHA
Obeisances to Sri Rama, the Primal Being

OM PARAMAPURUSHAYA NAMAHA
Obeisances to Sri Rama, the Supreme Being

OM MAHAPURUSHAYA NAMAHA
Obeisances to Sri Rama, the Great Being

OM PUNYODAYAYA NAMAHA
Obeisances to Sri Rama, the Source of all blessings

OM DAYASARAYA NAMAHA
Obeisances to Sri Rama, the Embodiment of compassion

OM PURANA PURUSHOTTAMAYA NAMAHA
Obeisances to Sri Rama, the Most Ancient Person

OM SMITA VAKTRAYA NAMAHA
Obeisances to Sri Rama, the One who smiling speaks

OM MITA BHASHINE NAMAHA
Obeisances to Sri Rama, the One of moderate speech

OM PURVA BHASHINE NAMAHA
Obeisances to Sri Rama, the One who rarely speaks

OM RAGHAVAYA NAMAHA
Obeisances to Sri Rama, the scion of the Raghu dynasty

OM ANANTA GUNAGAMBHIRAYA NAMAHA
Obeisances to Sri Rama, the Lord of infinite majestic qualities

OM DHIRODATTA GUNOTTAMAYA NAMAHA
Obeisances to Sri Rama, the Lord of Valorous qualities

OM MAYA MANUSHA CHARITRAYA NAMAHA
Obeisances to Sri Rama, the Lord who incarnated as a man through His
maya

OM MAHADEVADI PUJITAYA NAMAHA
Obeisances to Sri Rama, the Lord who is worshiped by Lord Shiva

OM SETUKRITE NAMAHA
Obeisances to Sri Rama, The builder of the bridge (at Setubandha to Sri
Lanka)

OM JITA VARASHAYE NAMAHA
Obeisances to Sri Rama, the Conqueror of desires

OM SARVA TIRTHAMAYAYA NAMAHA
Obeisances to Sri Rama, the Lord who is the sum of all holy places

OM HARAYE NAMAHA
Obeisances to Sri Rama, the Destroyer

OM SHYAMANGAYA NAMAHA
Obeisances to Sri Rama, the Dark-complexioned One

OM SUNDARAYA NAMAHA
Obeisances to Sri Rama, the Beautiful One

OM SURAYA NAMAHA
Obeisances to Sri Rama, the Lord

OM PITAVASASE NAMAHA
Obeisances to Sri Rama, the Lord clad in yellow raiment

OM DHANURDHARAYA NAMAHA
Obeisances to Sri Rama, the Bearer of the bow

OM SARVA YAJNADHIPAYA NAMAHA
Obeisances to Sri Rama, the Lord of sacrifice

OM YAJVINE NAMAHA
Obeisances to Sri Rama, the Sacrificer

OM JARAMARANA VARJITAYA NAMAHA
Obeisances to Sri Rama, the Conqueror of birth and death

OM VIBHISHANA PRATISHTHATRE NAMAHA
Obeisances to Sri Rama, the Lord who established Vibhishana on the
throne

OM SARVABHARANA VARJITAYA NAMAHA
Obeisances to Sri Rama, the Lord who relinquished all adornment

OM PARAMATMANE NAMAHA
Obeisances to Sri Rama, the Supreme Self

OM PARABRAHMANE NAMAHA
Obeisances to Sri Rama, the Supreme Absolute

OM SACHIDANANDA VIGRAHAYA NAMAHA
Obeisances to Sri Rama, the Embodiment of Existence, Awareness and
Bliss

OM PARASMAI JYOTISHE NAMAHA
Obeisances to Sri Rama, the Supreme Light

OM PARASMAI DHAMNE NAMAHA
Obeisances to Sri Rama, the Supreme Abode

OM PARAKASHAYA NAMAHA
Obeisances to Sri Rama, the Supreme Space

OM PARATPARAYA NAMAHA
Obeisances to Sri Rama, the Supreme beyond the highest

OM PARESHAYA NAMAHA
Obeisances to Sri Rama, the Supreme Lord

OM PARAKAYA NAMAHA
Obeisances to Sri Rama, the Lord who takes His devotees across (the
ocean of samsara--birth and death)

OM PARAYA NAMAHA
Obeisances to Sri Rama, the Supreme Being

OM SARVA DEVATMAKAYA NAMAHA
Obeisances to Sri Rama, the Lord who is the Source of all gods

OM PARASMAI NAMAHA
Obeisances to Sri Rama, the Supreme Lord

The Sri Ram Stuti

(1) sri ramacandra krpalu bhaju mana harana bhavabhaya darunam I
navakamja-locana, kamja-mukha, kara-kamja, pada-kamjarunam II

O mind, remember Rama, the Lord of compassion, who will eradicate even the most terrible dread of life; his eyes are like newly-blown lutuses set in his lotus-face; lotus-like are his hands and like ruddy lotuses his feet.

(2) kamdarpa aganita amita chabi, navanila-nirada sundaram I
pata pital manahu tarita ruci suci naumi janaka sutavaram II

With utmost humility I do obeisance to Sita's consort, Ramacandra, whose boundless beauty excels that of myriads of Cupids (taken together). He is as winsome as the rain-laden clouds. The yellow attire on his body, beautifully and sanctified, looks as charming as the flashes of lighting.

(3) bhaju dinabamdhu dinesa danava-daitya-vamsa-nikamdanam I
raghunamda anamdakamda kosalacamda dasaratha namdanam II

Meditate on Rama, the delight of the house of of Raghu, root of all bliss, soothing as the moon to the Kosalas, Dasaratha's son, compassionate to the destitute, the scion of the solar race and the extirpator of the demons and diabolical daityas (giants).

(4) sri mukuta kundala tilaka chaaru udaaru anga vibhusanana
ajaanubhuja shara chaap-dhara, sangraama-jit-kharadushanam

He has a (resplendent) crown on his head, a pair of pendants in his ears, a lovely caste-mark on his forehead and ornaments on his lustrous body. The arms that reach the knees are holding the bow and arrows of the conqueror of Khara and Dusana (two of demonic adversaries).

(5) iti vadati tulasida samkara-sesa-muni-mana-ramjanam I
mama hrdaya-kamj-nivasa kuru, kamadi khala-dala-gamjanam II

Tulasi Das says, "Sri Rama who brings about happiness and joy to the hearts of Lord Shiva and all others, may He reside in the depths of my heart and destroy all the evil thoughts such as desires, temptations, etc."

Raghupati Raghava

Raghupati Rahgava raja Ram, pati tapavana Sita Ram,
Raghupati Rahgava raja Ram, pati tapavana Sita Ram,

Sita Ram, Sita Ram, Bhaj Pyaare tu Sita Ram,
Shankar Shakti tero naam, sab ko samati de Bhagawan, (x2)
Raghupati Rahgava raja Ram, pati tapavana Sita Ram,
Ratre nindra, diwase kaam, Kya-re bhajso Sita Ram (x2)
Raghupati Rahgava raja Ram, pati tapavana Sita Ram,
Haathe karjo ghar na kaam, Mukh-se bolo Sita Ram, (x2)
Raghupati Rahgava raja Ram, pati tapavana Sita Ram,
Ram, Laxman, Jaanki... Jai bolo Hanuman ki (x2)
Raghupati Rahgava raja Ram, pati tapavana Sita Ram,
Raghupati Rahgava raja Ram, pati tapavana Sita Ram,
Sita Ram, Sita Ram, Bhaj Pyaare tu Sita Ram.

OR

Raghupathi Raaghava Raajaa Raam Patita Paavana Sitaa Raam
Raghupathi Raaghava Raajaa Raam Patita Paavana Sitaa Raam
Raghupathi Raaghava Raajaa Raam Patita Paavana Sitaa Raam
Sitaa Raam Sitaa Raam Bhaja Pyare Tu Sitaa Raam
Raghupathi Raaghava Raajaa Raam Patita Paavana Sitaa Raam
Ishvara Alla Tera Naam Sabako Sanmati De Bhagavan
Raghupathi Raaghava Raajaa Raam Patita Paavana Sitaa Raam
Rama Lakshmana Janaki Jai Bola Hanuman Ki
Raghupathi Raaghava Raajaa Raam Patita Paavana Sitaa Raam

CHAPTER TWENTY-SIX

The 108 Names of Lord Shiva

This is a selection of names and the translations that can be chanted on special occasions, such as Shivaratri, etc. This also contains the *Shivastakam* by Lord Chaitanya and the *Shiva Chalisa*.

OM SHIVAYA NAMAHA
Obeisances to the Auspicious One

OM MAHESHVARAYA NAMAHA
Obeisances to the Great God Shiva

OM SHAMBHAVE NAMAHA
Obeisances to the God who exists for our happiness alone

OM PINAKINE NAMAHA
Obeisances to Shiva, who guards the path of dharma

OM SHASHISHEKHARAYA NAMAHA
Obeisances to the God who wears the crescent moon in his hair

OM VAMADEVAYA NAMAHA
Obeisances to the God who is pleasing and auspicious in every way

OM VIRUPAKSHAYA NAMAHA
Obeisances to the God of spotless form

OM KAPARDINE NAMAHA
Obeisances to the Lord with thickly matted hair

OM NILALOHITAYA NAMAHA
Obeisances to the God splendid as the red sun at daybreak

OM SHANKARAYA NAMAHA
Obeisances to the source of all prosperity

OM SHULAPANAYE NAMAHA
Obeisances to the God who carries a spear

OM KHATVANGINE NAMAHA
Obeisances to the God who carries a knurled club

OM VISHNUVALLABHAYA NAMAHA
Obeisances to Shiva, who is dear to Lord Vishnu

OM SHIPIVISHTAYA NAMAHA
Obeisances to the Lord whose form emits great rays of light

OM AMBIKANATHAYA NAMAHA
Obeisances to Ambika's Lord

OM SHRIKANTAYA NAMAHA
Obeisances to he whose throat is shining blue

OM BHAKTAVATSALAYA NAMAHA
Obeisances to the Lord who loves His devotees like new born calves

OM BHAVAYA NAMAHA
Obeisances to the God who is existence itself

OM SARVAYA NAMAHA
Obeisances to Shiva who is all

OM TRILOKESHAYA NAMAHA
Obeisances to Shiva who is the Lord of all the three worlds

OM SHITAKANTHAYA NAMAHA
Obeisances to the primal soul whose throat is deep blue

OM SHIVAPRIYAYA NAMAHA
Obeisances to the god who is dear to Shakti

OM UGRAYA NAMAHA
Obeisances to Shiva whose presence is awesome and overwhelming

OM KAPALINE NAMAHA
Obeisances to the God whose begging bowl is a human skull

OM KAMARAYE NAMAHA
Obeisances to Shiva who conquers all passions

OM ANDHAKASURA SUDANAYA NAMAHA
Obeisances to the Lord who killed the asura Andhaka

OM GANGADHARAYA NAMAHA
Obeisances to the God who holds the Ganges River in his hair

OM LALATAKSHAYA NAMAHA
Obeisances to the Lord whose sport is creation

OM KALAKALAYA NAMAHA
Obeisances to Shiva who is the death of death

OM KRIPANIDHAYE NAMAHA
Obeisances to the God who is the treasure of compassion

OM BHIMAYA NAMAHA
Obeisances to Shiva whose strength is awesome

OM PARASHU HASTAYA NAMAHA
Obeisances to the God who wields an axe in his hands

OM MRIGAPANAYAE NAMAHA
Obeisances to the Lord who looks after the soul in the wilderness

OM JATADHARAYA NAMAHA
Obeisances to Shiva who bears a mass of matted hair

OM KAILASAVASINE NAMAHA
Obeisances to the God who abides on Mount Kailas

OM KAVACHINE NAMAHA
Obeisances to the Lord who is wrapped in armor

OM KATHORAYA NAMAHA
Obeisances to Shiva who causes all growth

OM TRIPURANTAKAYA NAMAHA
Obeisances to the Lord who destroyed the three demonic cities

OM VRISHANKAYA NAMAHA
Obeisances to the God whose emblem is a bull (Nandi)

OM VRISHABHARUDHAYA NAMAHA
Obeisances to Shiva who rides a bull

OM BHASMODDHULITA VIGRAHAYA NAMAHA
Obeisances to the Lord covered with holy ash

OM SAMAPRIYAYA NAMAHA
Obeisances to the God exceedingly fond of hymns from the Sama Veda

OM SVARAMAYAYA NAMAHA
Obeisances to Shiva who creates through sound

OM TRAYIMURTAYE NAMAHA
Obeisances to the Lord who is worshiped in three forms

OM ANISHVARAYA NAMAHA
Obeisances to the undisputed Lord

OM SARVAGYAYA NAMAHA
Obeisances to the God who knows all things

OM PARAMATMANE NAMAHA
Obeisances to the Supreme Self

OM SOMASURAGNI LOCHANAYA NAMAHA
Obeisances to the light of the eyes of Soma, Surya and Agni

OM HAVISHE NAMAHA
Obeisances to Shiva who receives oblations of ghee

OM YAGYAMAYAYA NAMAHA
Obeisances to the architect of all sacrificial rites

OM SOMAYA NAMAHA
Obeisances to the Moon-glow of the mystic's vision

OM PANCHAVAKTRAYA NAMAHA
Obeisances to the God of the five activities

OM SADASHIVAYA NAMAHA
Obeisances to the eternally auspicious benevolent Shiva

OM VISHVESHVARAYA NAMAHA
Obeisances to the all-pervading ruler of the cosmos

OM VIRABHADRAYA NAMAHA
Obeisances to Shiva the foremost of heroes

OM GANANATHAYA NAMAHA
Obeisances to the God of the Ganas

OM PRAJAPATAYE NAMAHA
Obeisances to the Creator

OM HIRANYARETASE NAMAHA
Obeisances to the God who emanates golden souls

OM DURDHARSHAYA NAMAHA
Obeisances to the unconquerable being

OM GIRISHAYA NAMAHA
Obeisances to the monarch of the holy mountain Kailas

OM GIRISHAYA NAMAHA
Obeisances to the Lord of the Himalayas

OM ANAGHAYA NAMAHA
Obeisances to Shiva who can inspire no fear

OM BUJANGABHUSHANAYA NAMAHA
Obeisances to the Lord adorned with golden snakes

OM BHARGAYA NAMAHA
Obeisances to the foremost of rishis

OM GIRIDHANVANE NAMAHA
Obeisances to the God whose weapon is a mountain

OM GIRIPRIYAYA NAMAHA
Obeisances to the Lord who is fond of mountains

OM KRITTIVASASE NAMAHA
Obeisances to the God who wears clothes of hide

OM PURARATAYE NAMAHA
Obeisances to the Lord who is thoroughly at home in the wilderness

OM BHAGAVATE NAMAHA
Obeisances to the Lord of prosperity

OM PRAMATHADHIPAYA NAMAHA
Obeisances to the God who is served by goblins

OM MRITUNJAYAYA NAMAHA
Obeisances to the conqueror of death

OM SUKSHMATANAVE NAMAHA
Obeisances to the subtlest of the subtle

OM JAGADVYAPINE NAMAHA
Obeisances to Shiva who fills the whole world

OM JAGADGURAVE NAMAHA
Obeisances to the guru of all the worlds

OM VYOMAKESHAYA NAMAHA
Obeisances to the God whose hair is the spreading sky above

OM MAHASENAJANAKAYA NAMAHA
Obeisances to the origin of Mahasena

OM CHARUVIKRAMAYA NAMAHA
Obeisances to Shiva, the guardian of wandering pilgrims

OM RUDRAYA NAMAHA
Obeisances to the Lord who is fit to be praised

OM BHUTAPATAYE NAMAHA
Obeisances to the source of living creatures, including the Bhutas, or
ghostly creatures

OM STHANAVE NAMAHA
Obeisances to the firm and immovable deity

OM AHIRBUDHNYAYA NAMAHA
Obeisances to the Lord who waits for the sleeping kundalini

OM DIGAMBARAYA NAMAHA
Obeisances to Shiva whose robes is the cosmos

OM ASHTAMURTAYE NAMAHA
Obeisances to the Lord who has eight forms

OM ANEKATMANE NAMAHA
Obeisances to the God who is the one soul

OM SATVIKAYA NAMAHA
Obeisances to the Lord of boundless energy

OM SHUDDHA VIGRAHAYA NAMAHA
Obeisances to him who is free of all doubt and dissension

OM SHASHVATAYA NAMAHA
Obeisances to Shiva, endless and eternal

OM KHANDAPARASHAVE NAMAHA
Obeisances to the God who cuts through the mind's despair

OM AJAYA NAMAHA
Obeisances to the instigator of all that occurs

OM PAPAVIMOCHAKAYA NAMAHA
Obeisances to the Lord who releases all fetters

OM MRIDAYA NAMAHA
Obeisances to the Lord who shows only mercy

OM PASHUPATAYE NAMAHA
Obeisances to the ruler of all evolving souls, the animals

OM DEVAYA NAMAHA
Obeisances to the foremost of devas, demigods

OM MAHADEVAYA NAMAHA
Obeisances to the greatest of the gods

OM AVYAYAYA NAMAHA
Obeisances to the one never subject to change

OM HARAYE NAMAHA
Obeisances to Shiva who dissolves all bondage

OM PASHUDANTABHIDE NAMAHA
Obeisances to the one who punished Pushan

OM AVYAGRAYA NAMAHA
Obeisances to the Lord who is steady and unwavering

OM DAKSHADHVARAHARAYA NAMAHA
Obeisances to the destroyer of Daksha's conceited sacrifice

OM HARAYA NAMAHA
Obeisances to the Lord who withdraws the cosmos

OM BHAGANETRABHIDE NAMAHA
Obeisances to Shiva who taught Bhaga to see more clearly

OM AVYAKTAYA NAMAHA
Obeisances to Shiva who is subtle and unseen

OM SAHASRAKSHAYA NAMAHA
Obeisances to the Lord of limitless forms

OM SAHASRAPADE NAMAHA
Obeisances to the God who is standing and walking everywhere

OM APAVARGAPRADAYA NAMAHA
Obeisances to the Lord who gives and takes all things

OM ANANTAYA NAMAHA
Obeisances to the God who is unending

OM TARAKAYA NAMAHA
Obeisances to the great liberator of mankind

OM PARAMESHVARAYA NAMAHA
Obeisances to the great God

Sri Sivastakam

(Eight prayers glorifying Lord Shiva, spoken by Sriman Chaitanya
Mahaprabhu. Recorded in Murari Gupta's "Sri Caitanya Carita
Mahakavya.")

1) namo namaste tri-dasheshvaraya
bhutadi nathaya mridaya nityam
gagga-taraggotthita-bala-chandra-
chudaya gauri-nayanotsavaya

"I repeatedly offer my obeisances unto you, the controller of the thirty
primal demigods; unto you, the original father of all created beings; unto
you, whose character is gracious; unto you, whose head is crested by the
sickle moon arisen from the waves of the Ganga and unto you, who are a
festival for the eyes of the fair goddess Gauri."

2) sutapta chamikara-chandra-nila-
padma-pravalambuda-kanti-vastraih
sa nritya-raggesta-vara-pradaya
kaivalya-nathaya vrisa-dhvajaya

"I offer my obeisances unto you, who are dressed in garments resembling molten gold, the moon, blue lotuses, coral, and dark rain clouds; unto you, who bestow the most desirable boons on your devotees by means of your delightful dancing; unto you, who are the master of the impersonalists and unto you, whose flag bears the image of the bull."

3) sudhamzu-suryagni-vilochanena
tamo-bhide te jagatah shivaya
sahasra-shubhramshu-sahasra-rashmi-
sahasra-sajjit-tvara-tejase'stu

"I offer my obeisances unto you, who dispells darkness with your three eyes --the moon, the sun and fire; unto you, who causes auspiciousness for all the living entities of the universe and unto you, whose potency easily defeats that of thousands of moons and suns."

4) nageza-ratnojjvala-vigrahaya
shardula-charmamzuka-divya-tejase
sahasra-patropari samsthitaya
varaggada-mukta-bhuja-dvayaya

"I offer my obeisances unto you, whose form is brilliantly illuminated by the jewels of Ananta, the king of snakes; unto you, who are clothed by a tiger-skin and thus radiate divine effulgence; unto you, who sits upon a thousand-petalled lotus and unto you, whose two arms are adorned by lusterous bangles."

5) su-nupura-ragjita-pada-padma
ksarat-sudha-bhritya-sukha-pradaya
vichitra-ratnaugha-vibhusitaya
premanam evadya harau videhi

"I offer my obeisances unto you, who brings happiness to your servitors, as you pour on them the liquid nectar from your two reddish lotus feet, which ring with charming ankle bells. Obeisances unto you, who is adorned with an abundance of gems - please endow me with pure love for Lord Hari."

6) sri rama govinda mukunda shaure
sri krishna narayana vasudeva
ity-adi namamririta-pana-matta-
bhriggadhi-payakhila-dukha-hantre

"O Shri Rama, O Govinda, O Mukunda, O Shauri, O Shri krsna, O Narayana, O Vaasudeva!' I offer my obeisances unto you, Lord Shiva, the monarch of intoxicated bee-like devotees, maddened by drinking the nectar of these and other holy names of the Lord. Obeisances unto you, the destroyer of all grief."

7) sri naradadyaih satatam sugopya-
jijjasita-yashu vara-pradaya
tebhyo harer bhakti-sukha-pradaya
shivaya sarva-gurave namo namaha

"I offer my respectful obeisances again and again unto you, who is forever enquired of confidentially by Shri Narada and other sages; unto you, who also grants favors to them very quickly; unto you, who bestows the happiness of Hari-bhakti; unto you, who creates auspiciousness and unto you, who is the guru of everyone."

8) sri gaura-netrosava-maggalaya
tat-prana-nathaya rasa-pradaya
sada samutkantha-govinda-lila-
gana-pravinaya namo'stu tubhyam

"I offer my obeisances unto you, who are a festival of auspiciousness for the eyes of Goddess Gauri; unto you, who is the monarch of her life-breath; unto you, who is capable of bestowing transcendental rasa and unto you, who is expert in forever singing songs of the pastimes of Lord Govinda with great longing."

9) etat shivasyastakam adbhutam mahat
shrinvan hari-prema labheta shighram
jjanam ca vijjanam apurva-vaibhavam
yo bhava-purnah paramam samadaram

"A person, filled with loving feelings, who hears with rapt attention this wonderful eight-fold prayer to Lord Shiva, can quickly gain Sri Hari-prema as well as transcendental knowledge, the realization of that knowledge, and unprecedented powers."

Shiva Chalisa

Shiva Chalisa is a "forty verse" prayer. Verses are recited or chanted by groups. The acts and deeds of Shiva are recalled in these verses to aid the devotee to meditate on virtuous and noble qualities.

ll Doha ll
Jai Ganesh Girija Suvan, Mangal Mool Sujaan l l
Kahat Ayodhyadas Tum, Dehu Abhaya Vardan l

Glory to Lord Ganesh, the Divine Son of Goddess Girija, the cause of all auspiciousness and intelligence. Ayodha Dass (the composer of these verses) humbly requests that every one be blessed with the boon of being fearless.

ll Chaupai ll
Jai Girijapati Deen Dayala, Sada Karat Santan Pratipala
Bhal Chandrama Sohati Neeke, Kanan Kundal Nag Phani Ke

O Glorious Lord, consort of Parvati You are most merciful. You always bless the poor and pious devotees. Your beautiful form is adorned with the moon on Your forehead and on your ears are earrings of snakes' hood.

Ang Gaur Shiv Ganga Bahaye, Mundamal Tan Kshar Lagaye
Vastra Khaal Baghambar Sohe, Chhavi Ko Dekh Nag Muni Mohe

The holy Ganges flows from your matted hair. The saints and sages are attracted by Your splendid appearance. Around Your neck is a garland of skulls. White ash beautifies Your Divine form and clothing of lion's skin adorns Your body.

Maina Matu Ki Priya Dulari, Bam Ang Sohat Chhavi Pyari
Kar Trishul Sohat Chhavi Bhari, Karat Sada Shatrun Shaykari

O Lord, the beloved daughter of Maina on Your left adds to Your splendid appearance. O Wearer of the lion's skin, the trishul in Your hand destroys all enemies.

Nandi Ganesh Sohe Tanha Kaise, Sagar Madhya Kamal Hain Jaise
Kartik Shyam Aur Gana Raau, Ya Chhavi Ko Kahi Jaat Na Kaau

Nandi and Shri Ganesh along with Lord Shiva appear as beautiful as two lotuses in the middle of an ocean. Poets and philosophers cannot describe the wonderful appearance of Lord Kartikeya and the dark complexioned Ganas (attendants).

Devan Jabhee Jaaye Pukara,Tabahin Dukh Prabhu Ap Nivaara
Keen Upadrava Taarak Bhari, Devan Sab Mili Tumhee Pukari

O Lord, whenever the Deities humbly sought Your assistance, You kindly and graciously uprooted all their problems. You blessed the Deities with Your generous help when the demon Tarak outraged them and You destroyed him.

Turat Shadanan Ap Pathayo, Luv Nimesh Mahi Mar Girayo
Ap Jallandhar Asur Sanhara, Suyash Tumhar Vidit Sansara

O Lord, You sent Shadanan without delay and thus destroyed the evil ones Lava and Nimesh. You also destroyed the demon Jalandhara. Your renown is known throughout the world.

Tripurasur Sang Yuddha Machayi, Sabahin Kripa Kari Leen Bachayi
Keeya Taphin Bhagirath Bhari, Purahi Pratigya Tasu Purari

O Lord, Purari, You saved all Deities and mankind by defeating and destroying the demons Tripurasura. You blessed Your devotee Bhagirath and he was able to accomplish his vow after rigorous penance.

Danin Mahan Tum Sama Kou Nahin, Sevak Astuti Karat Sadahin
Veda Nam Mahima Tab Gayaee, Akatha Anandi Bhed Nahin Payee

O Gracious One, devotees always sings Your glory. Even the Vedas are unable to describe Your greatness. No one is as generous as You are.

Pragati Udadhi Manthan Mein Jwala, Jare Surasur Bhaye Vihaala
Mahadeva Tab Kari Sahayee, Neelkantha Tav Nam Dharayee

Lord, when the ocean was churned and the deadly poison emerged, out of
Your deep compassion for all, You drank the poison and saved the world
from destruction. Your throat became blue, thus You are known as
Nilakantha.

Poojan Ramchandra Jab Keenha, Lanka Jeet Vibhishan Deenha
Sahas Kamal me ho rahe dhaari, Keenha Pareeksha Tabahi Purari

When Lord Rama worshipped You, He became victorious over the king of
demons, Ravana. When Lord Rama wished to worship Thee with one
thousand lotus flowers, the Divine Mother, to test the devotion of Shri
Ram, hid all the flowers at Your request.

Ek Kamal Prabhu Rakheu johee, Kamal Nayan Poojan Chahin Soyee
Kathin Bhakti Dekhi Prabhu Shankar, Bhaye Prasanna Deya Icchhit Var

O Lord, You kept on looking at Shri Ram, who wished to offer His
lotus-like eyes to worship Thee. When You observed such intense devotion,
You were delighted and blessed Him. You granted His heart's desire.

Jai Jai Jai Ananta Avinasi, Karat Kripa Sab Ke Ghatvasi
Dushta Sakal Mohi Nitya Sataven, Bhramita Rahe Mohe Chain Na Aave

Glory be unto You O Gracious, Infinite, Immortal, All-pervading Lord. Evil
thought torture me and I keep on travelling aimlessly in this world of
mundane existence. No relief seems to be coming my way.

Trahi Trahi Main Nath Pukaro, Yeh Avasar Mohi Ani Ubaro
Lai Trishool Shatrun Ko Maro, Sankat Se Mohi Ani Ubaro

O Lord! I beseech Your help and seek your divine blessing at this very
moment. Save and protect me. Destroy my enemies with Your Trishul.
Release me from the torture of evil thoughts.

Mata Pita Bhrata Sab Hoi, Sankat Mein Poochat Nahi Koi
Swami Ek Hai Aas Tumhari, Aaye Harahu Mam Sankat Bhaari

O Lord, when I am in distress, neither my parents, brothers, sisters nor loved ones can relieve my suffering. I depend only on You. You are my hope. Eliminate the cause of this tremendous torture and bless me with Your compassion.

Dhan Nirdhan Kon Det Sadaee, Arat Jan Ki Peer Mitaee
Astuti Kehi Vidhi Karahu Tumhari, Shamhu Naath Ab Chook Hamari

O Lord, You bless the downtrodden with prosperity and grant wisdom to the ignorant. Lord, due to my limited knowledge, I omitted to worship Thee. Please forgive me and shower Your grace upon me.

Shanker Ho Sankat Ke Nashan, Vighna Vinashan Mangal Kaaran
Yogi Yati Muni Dhyan Lagave, Sharad Narad Sheesh Navave

O Lord Sankar, You are the destroyer of all miseries. You remove the cause of all obstacles and grant Your devotees eternal bliss. The saints and sages meditate upon Thy most beautiful form. Even celestial beings like Sharad and Narad bow in reverence to You.

Namo Namo Jai Namah Shivaye, Sur Brahmadik Par Na Paaye
Jo Yeh Path Kare Man Layee, Tapar Hot Hain Shambu Sahayee

O Lord, prostration to You. Even Brahma is unable to describe Thy greatness. Whosoever recites these verses with faith and devotion receives Your infinite blessings.

Riniya Jo Koi Ho Adhikaari, Paath Kare So Paavanhaari
Putra Heen Ichha Kar Koi, Nishchaya Shiv Prasad Tehi Hoi

Devotees who chant these verses with intense love become prosperous by the grace of Lord Shiva. Even the childless wishing to have children, have their desires fulfilled after partaking of Shiva-prasad with faith and devotion.

Pandit Triyodashi Ko Lave, Dhyan Poorvak Hom Karave
Triyodashi Vrata Kare Hamesha, Tan Nahi Take Rahe Kalesha

On Trayodashi (13th day of the dark and bright fortnights) one should invite a pandit and devotedly make offerings to Lord Shiva. Those who fast and pray to Lord Shiva on Trayodashi are always healthy and prosperous.

Dhoop Deep Naivedya Chadhavai, Shanker Sanmukha Path Karavahi
Janam Janam Ki Pap Nasave, Anta Vaas Shivpur Men Paave

Whosoever offers incense, prasad and performs arti to Lord Shiva, with love and devotion, enjoys material happiness and spiritual bliss in this world and hereafter ascends to the abode of Lord Shiva. The poet prays that Lord Shiva removed the suffering of all and grants them eternal bliss.

Hey Shankar Hai Aas Tumhari, Dukh Peera Ab Harahu Hamari

ll Doha ll
Nit Nem Kar Praatha Hee ,Paath Karo Chaalis l
Tum Meri Manokaamna, Puran Karo Jagdeesh ll
Magsar Chhati Hemant Ritu, Sanvat Chausadh Jaan l
Astuti Chaalisa Shivhi, Puran Keen Kalyaan ll

O Universal Lord, every morning as a rule I recite this Chalisa with devotion. Please bless me so that I may be able to accomplish my material and spiritual desires.

CHAPTER TWENTY-SEVEN

The 108 Names of Goddess Devi

This is especially for devotees of the Divine Mother, and includes the Dhyanam of the *Sri Lalita Sahasranam Stotram* followed by a selection of 108 names with translations from the *Lalita Sahasranam* and the *Bhavaanyashtakam* (Prayers to Devi).

Dhyanam of the
Shri Lalita Sahasranam Stotram
(This is a meditation on Devi chanted at the beginning of the Sri Lalita Sahasranam, the Thousand Names of Devi)

sindhur aruna vigraham trinayanam
manikya mauli spurat
tara nayaka shekharam
smita mukhim apina vakshoruham
panibhyam alipurna ratna chashakam
raktotpalam bibhratim
saumyam ratna ghatastha rakta
charanam dhyayet param ambikam

dhyayet padmasanastham
vikasita vadanam padma patraya takshim
hemabham pita vastram karakali talasat
hemapadmam varangim

sarvalankara yuktam satatam abhayatam
bhaktanamram bhavanim
shri vidyam shanta murtim sakala suranutam
sarva sampat pradatrim

sakumkuma vilepana
mallika chumbi kasturikam

samanda hasitekshanam
sashara chapa pashamkusham

asesha jana mohinim
aruna malya bhushojvalam
japa kusuma bhasuram
japavidhau smaretambikam

arunam karunam
tarangi takshim
dhrita pasham
kusha pushpa bana chapam
animadibhi ravratam mayukhai
rahamityeva vibhavayet mahesim

TRANSLATION

She has three eyes; Her hue is like that of red sindhura; the diadem of precious stones She wears has a crescent on it shining wonderfully.

That She is easily accessible is indicated by Her benign smile; Her children have an inexhaustible store of the milk of life in Her full breasts; the vessel of honey in one hand and the red lotus in the other symbolize joy and wisdom of which She alone in the source; and Her feet placed on the precious pot full of valuable gems indicate that these are not difficult for those who surrender to Her feet and take refuge in Her.

I meditate on Sri Bhavani who is seated in the lotus of expansive countenance, Whose eyes are like lotus petals, who is golden-hued, who wears a yellow raiment, who has in her hand lotus flowers of gold, who always dispels fear, whose devotees bow before her, who is the embodiment of peace, who is Sri Vidya Herself who is praised by the gods, and who gives every wealth that is sought...

I meditate on the Mother whose eyes are smiling a little, who has in Her hands the arrow, the bow, the noose and goad, who bewitches everybody, who is glittering with red garlands and ornaments, who is painted with vermillion, whose forehead is kissed with the mark of musk and who is red and tender like the japa flower...

I mediate on the great Empress who is light red in color, whose eyes are full of compassion, who has in Her hands the noose, the goad, the bow and the flowery arrow and who is surrounded on all sides by powers, such as 'anima,' like rays, as if She is the Self within me...

108 Names of Devi, the Divine Mother

(This is a selection of names from the *Shri Lalita Sahasranam*,
the Thousand Names of Devi that can easily be chanted by the devotee.)

OM SHRI LALITAMBIKAYAI NAMAHA
Salutations to the great goddess Shri Lalitambika

OM SHRI MATRE NAMAHA
Salutations to the sacred Mother

OM SHRI MAHA RAGNYAI NAMAHA
Salutations to the great Empress

OM BHAVANYAI NAMAHA
Salutations to the consort of Shiva

OM BHAVANA GAMYAYAI NAMAHA
Salutations to the Mother who is reached through constant reflection on
Truth

OM BHADRA PRIYAYAI NAMAHA
Salutations to the Mother who loves to be benevolent

OM BHADRA MURTYAI NAMAHA
Salutations to the Mother who is the embodiment of benevolence

OM BHAKTI PRIYAYAI NAMAHA
Salutations to the Mother who is pleased by Her devotees' loving
worship

OM BHAKTI GAMYAYAI NAMAHA
Salutations to the Mother who is reached by yearning service and
meditation

OM BHAKTI VASYAYAI NAMAHA
Salutations to the Mother who is made one's own by loving acts of
devotion

OM BHAYA PAHAYAI NAMAHA
Salutations to the Mother who dispels all fear

OM SHAMBHAVYAI NAMAHA
Salutations to the Mother who worships Shambhu

OM SHARADARADHYAYAI NAMAHA
Salutations to the Mother who is worshiped as the Goddess of learning
in the autumn

OM SHARVANYAI NAMAHA
Salutations to the Mother who is the consort of Sarva

OM SHARMADAYINYAI NAMAHA
Salutations to the Mother who is always the giver of happiness

OM SHANKARYAI NAMAHA
Salutations to the Mother who is inseparable from Parama Shiva

OM SHRIKARYAI NAMAHA
Salutations to the Mother who is Vishnu's consort, Lakshmi

OM SHATODARYAI NAMAHA
Salutations to the Mother who has a slender waist

OM SHANTIMATYAI NAMAHA
Salutations to the Mother who is ever at peace with Her devotees

OM NIRADHARAYAI NAMAHA
Salutations to the Mother who has no other support

OM NIRANJANAYAI NAMAHA
Salutations to the Mother who is unstained

OM NIRLEPAYAI NAMAHA
Salutations to the Mother who is untouched

OM NIRMALAYAI NAMAHA
Salutations to the Mother who is ever pure

OM NITYAYAI NAMAHA
Salutations to the Mother who is eternal

OM NIRAKARAYAI NAMAHA
Salutations to the Mother who is without form

OM NIRAKULAYAI NAMAHA
Salutations to the Mother who is never perturbed

OM NIRGUNAYAI NAMAHA
Salutations to the Mother who is attributeless

OM NISHKALAYAI NAMAHA
Salutations to the Mother who is indivisible

OM SHANTAYAI NAMAHA
Salutations to the Mother who is perfectly serene

OM NISHKAMAYAI NAMAHA
Salutations to the Mother who is free from all desires

OM NITYAMUKTAYAI NAMAHA
Salutations to the Mother who is eternally free from illusion

OM NIRVIKARAYAI NAMAHA
Salutations to the Mother who is the unchanging basis for all change

OM NISHPRAPANCHAYAI NAMAHA
Salutations to the Mother who is beyond all phenomena of the world

OM NIRASHRAYAYAI NAMAHA
Salutations to the Mother who depends on none

OM NITYA SHUDDHAYAI NAMAHA
Salutations to the Mother who is eternally taintless

OM NITYA BUDDHAYAI NAMAHA
Salutations to the Mother who is perpetual abode of knowledge

OM NIRAVADYAYAI NAMAHA
Salutations to the Mother who is entirely free from flaw

OM NIRANTARAYAI NAMAHA
Salutations to the Mother who is without end

OM NISHKARANAYAI NAMAHA
Salutations to the Mother who is without beginning

OM NISHKALANKAYAI NAMAHA
Salutations to the Mother who has no lapse whatsoever

OM NIRUPADHAYE NAMAHA
Salutations to the Mother who is limitless

OM NIRISHVARAYAI NAMAHA
Salutations to the Motherwho is supreme

OM NIRAGAYAI NAMAHA
Salutations to the Mother who has no passions

OM RAGA MATHANYAI NAMAHA
Salutations to the Mother who destroys all attachments

OM NIRMADAYAI NAMAHA
Salutations to the Mother who has no pride

OM MADANASHINYAI NAMAHA
Salutations to the Mother who wipes out arrogance

OM NISHCHINTAYAI NAMAHA
Salutations to the Mother who is free from all anxiety

OM NIRAHANKARAYAI NAMAHA
Salutations to the Mother who is completely free from ego

OM NIRMOHAYAI NAMAHA
Salutations to the Mother who is completely free of delusion

OM MOHA NASHINYAI NAMAHA
Salutations to the Mother who cures the delusions of Her devotees

OM NIRMAMAYAI NAMAHA
Salutations to the Mother who has no ego or "my"-ness

OM MAMATA HANTRYAI NAMAHA
Salutations to the Mother who destroys conceit and selfishness in Her
devotees

OM NISHPAPAYAI NAMAHA
Salutations to the Mother who is the negation of sin

OM PAPA NASHINYAI NAMAHA
Salutations to the Mother who completely destroys sin by the mere
repetition of Her name

OM NISHKRODHAYAI NAMAHA
Salutations to the Mother who has no enemy or anger

OM KRODHA SHAMANYAI NAMAHA
Salutations to the Mother who extinguishes anger rising in the minds of
Her devotees

OM NIRLOBHAYAI NAMAHA
Salutations to the Mother who is completely free from greed

OM LOBHA NASHINYAI NAMAHA
Salutations to the Mother who removes greed from the minds of Her
devotees

OM NIHSAMSHAYAYAI NAMAHA
Salutations to the Mother who is free from doubt

OM NIRBHAVAYAI NAMAHA
Salutations to the Mother who has no origin

OM BHAVA NASHINYAI NAMAHA
Salutations to the Mother who puts an end to the rounds of birth and
death

OM NIRVIKALPAYAI NAMAHA
Salutations to the Mother who is the eternal pure intelligence

OM NIRABADHAYAI NAMAHA
Salutations to the Mother who remains ever untroubled

OM NIRBHEDAYAI NAMAHA
Salutations to the Mother in whom all are one

OM BHEDA NASHINYAI NAMAHA
Salutations to the Mother who destroys the distinctions made by the
mind

OM NIRNASHAYAI NAMAHA
Salutations to the Mother who is immortal

OM MRITYU MATHANYAI NAMAHA
Salutations to the Mother who uproots the cause of death in Her
devotees

OM NISHKRIYAYAI NAMAHA
Salutations to the Mother who is beyond all action

OM NISHPARIGRAHAYAI NAMAHA
Salutations to the Mother who takes nothing

OM NISTULAYAI NAMAHA
Salutations to the Mother who is unequaled

OM NILA CHIKURAYAI NAMAHA
Salutations to the Mother who has locks of shining black hair

OM NIRAPAYAYAI NAMAHA
Salutations to the Mother who never departs

OM NIRATYAYAYAI NAMAHA
Salutations to the Mother who is beyond all danger

OM DURLABHAYAI NAMAHA
Salutations to the Mother who is attained through long-sustained and
necessary efforts

OM DURGAMAYAI NAMAHA
Salutations to the Mother who is not reached without painstaking
continued exertion

OM DURGAYAI NAMAHA
Salutations to the Mother who is Goddess Durga

OM DUKHA HANTRYAI NAMAHA
Salutations to the Mother who destroys sorrow

OM SUKHA PRADAYAI NAMAHA
Salutations to the Mother who confers the bliss of liberation

OM SARVAGNAYAI NAMAHA
Salutations to the Mother who is omniscient

OM SANDRA KARUNAYAI NAMAHA
Salutations to the Mother who is intensely compassionate

OM SARVA SHAKTI MAYYAI NAMAHA
Salutations to the Mother who is the source of all power

OM SARVA MANGALAYAI NAMAHA
Salutations to the Mother who possesses all that is auspicious

OM SAD GATI PRADAYAI NAMAHA
Salutations to the Mother who takes the seeker to the supreme goal

OM SARVESHVARYAI NAMAHA
Salutations to the Mother who is the queen of the universe

OM SARVAMAYYAI NAMAHA
Salutations to the Mother who is immanent in all

OM MAHESHVARYAI NAMAHA
Salutations to the Mother who transcends nature and is the source of all

OM MAHA KALYAI NAMAHA
Salutations to the Mother who is the great goddess Kali who destroys
even death

OM MAHA DEVYAI NAMAHA
Salutations to the Mother who is the great goddess

OM MAHA LAKSHMYAI NAMAHA
Salutations to the Mother who is the great goddess Lakshmi who is the
source of life's bounty

OM MAHA RUPAYAI NAMAHA
Salutations to the Mother who is the supreme form

OM MAHA PUJYAYAI NAMAHA
Salutations to the Mother who is worthy of worship

OM MAHA MAYAYAI NAMAHA
Salutations to the Mother who is the great creator of the illusory energy

OM MAHA SATTVAYAI NAMAHA
Salutations to the Mother who is the supreme existence

OM MAHA SHAKTYAI NAMAHA
Salutations to the Mother who is the supreme energy

OM MAHA RATYAI NAMAHA
Salutations to the Mother who is boundless bliss

OM MAHA BHOGAYAI NAMAHA
Salutations to the Mother who is the supreme enjoyment and luxury

OM MAHAISHVARYAYAI NAMAHA
Salutations to the Mother who has supreme dominion

OM MAHA VIRYAYAI NAMAHA
Salutations to the Mother of supreme prowess and strength

OM MAHA BALAYAI NAMAHA
Salutations to the Mother who is of great strength

OM MAHA BUDDHYAI NAMAHA
Salutations to the Mother who is supreme intelligence

OM MAHA SIDDHYAI NAMAHA
Salutations to the Mother whose attainments are supreme

OM MAHA TANTRAYAI NAMAHA
Salutations to the Mother who is the subject of the great Tantras

OM MAHA MANTRAYAI NAMAHA
Salutations to the Mother who is the great mantra

OM MAHA YANTRAYAI NAMAHA
Salutations to the Mother who is worshiped in the symbols of yantras

OM MAHASANAYAI NAMAHA
Salutations to the Mother whose seat is worthy of great worship

OM PARAM JYOTYAI NAMAHA
Salutations to the Mother who is the supreme radiance

OM PARAM DHAMNE NAMAHA
Salutations to the Mother who is the supreme abode

OM PARAMANAVE NAMAHA
Salutations to the Mother who is the most subtle

OM PARAT PARAYAI NAMAHA
Salutations to the Mother who is the greatest

OM PARA SHAKTYAI NAMAHA
Salutations to the Mother who is the supreme energy

OM SHRI SHIVAYAI NAMAHA
Salutations to the Mother who is with the worshipful Shiva

OM SHIVA SHAKTAIKYA RUPINYAI NAMAHA
Salutations to the Mother who is the form of energy or potency united
with Lord Shiva

OM VISHNU SHAKTYAIKYA RUPINYAI NAMAHA
Salutations to the Mother who is a form of the potency (shakti) united
with Lord Vishnu

OM BRAHMA SHAKTYAIKYA RUPINYAI NAMAHA
Salutations to the Mother who is a form of the potency (shakti) united
with Brahma

OM SHRI LALITAMBIKAYAI NAMAHA
Salutations to the Mother who is the goddess Shri Lalitambika

OM SHRI MATA AMRITANANDAMAYE NAMAHA
Salutations to the Mother who is called Amritanandamayi

OM SHRI MAHA TRIPURA SUNDARYAI NAMAHA
Salutations to the Mother whose name is also the divine Mother
Tripurasundari

Bhavaanyashtakam (Prayers to Devi)

(1)
Na taato na maataa na bandhur na daataa
Na putro na putree na bhrityo na bhartaa
Na jaayaa na vidyaa na vrittir mamaiva
Gatistvam gatistvam tvamekaa Bhavaani

Oh Bhavani, I have not father, no mother, no relatives, no giver, no son, no
daughter, no servant, no master, no wife, no knowledge, no occupation. Oh,
Bhavaani! You are the only One Recourse.

(2)
Bhavaabdhaavapare Mahaadukh Bhiruh
Prapaata Prakaami pralobhi pramattaha
Kusamsaarpaashah prabaddhah sadaaham
Gatistvam Gatistvam tvamekaa Bhavaani

In this endless ocean of worldly life in which I have fallen, I am fearful of
the vast misery, I am lustful, greedy and careless. I am always tied up with
the chain of wicked worldliness. Oh, Bhavaani! You are the only One
Recourse.

(3)

Na Jaanaami Daanam na cha dhyaanayogam
Na jaanaami tantram na cha stotramantram
Na jaanaami poojaam na cha nyasayogam
Gatistvam gatistvam tvamekaa Bhavaani

I do not know how to offer charity or meditate. I do not know Tantras, of praise (of God), I do not know how to worship or have the knowledge of Yoga. Oh, Bhavaani! You are the only One Recourse.

(4)

Na jaanaami punyam na jaanaami teertham
Na jaanaami muktim layam vaa kadaachit
Na jaanaami bhaktim vratam vaapi maataha
Gatistvam gatistvam tvamekaa Bhavaani

I do not know what are good deeds or what are Holy places. I do not know what is liberation or meditation (on the Supreme Lord); I do not know what is devotion or what is religious observance. Oh, Bhavaani! You are the only One Recourse.

(5)

Kukarmi kusangi kubudhihi kudaasaha
Kulaachaaraheenah kadaacharaleenaha
Kudrishtih kuvaakya prabandhah sadaaham
Gatistvam gatistvam tvamekaa Bhavaani

I am engrossed in evil actions, bad company, have poor discrimination (lack of moral qualities), am a disobedient servant; devoid of noble conduct and am absorbed in immoral behavior. I am always visualizing and perceiving bad things and use bad speech. Oh, Bhavaani! You are the only One Recourse.

(6)

Prajesham ramesham mahesham suresham
Dinesham nisheethe shvaram vaa kadaachit
Na jaanaami chaanyat sadaaham sharanye
Gatistvam gatistvam tvamekaa Bhavaani

I do not know Brahma, Vishnu, Shiva, India, Sun, or Moon. You are the one who protects everyone! I do not know anyone else (except You). Oh, Bhavaani! You are the only One Recourse.

(7)

Vivaade vishaade pramaade pravaase
Jale chaanale parvate shatru madhye
Aranye sharanye sadaa maam prapaahi
Gatistvam gatistvam tvamekaa Bhavaani

You who protects everyone! Please protect me always in the midst of disputes, sorrow, danger, foreign travels, in the waters, fire, mountains, or while among the enemies or in the forest. Oh, Bhavaani! You are the only One Recourse.

(8)

Anaatho daridro jaraaroga yukto
Mahaaksheena deenah sadaa jaanya vaktraha
Vipatto Pravishtah pranashtah sadaaham
Gatistvam gatistvam tvamekaa Bhavaani

I am an orphan, poor, accompanied with disease and old age, am very weak, unfortunate, sunk in sorrow and my face always has a dull and sluggish look. Having fallen in distress, I am lost. Oh, Bhavaani! You are the only One Recourse.

CHAPTER TWENTY-EIGHT

108 Names of Lord Ganesh

This is a selection of names with translations that can be especially used and chanted on holidays like Holi, Ganesh Chaturthi, etc. When chanting these names, you can start each name with Om and after each name with *namaha*, such as "Om Akhurath Namaha."

1. Akhurath--One who has Mouse as His Charioteer
2. Alampata--Ever Eternal Lord
3. Amit--Incomparable Lord
4. Anantachidrupamayam--Infinite and Consciousness Personified
5. Avaneesh--Lord of the whole World
6. Avighna-- Remover of Obstacles
7. Balaganapati--Beloved and Lovable Child
8. Bhalchandra--Moon-Crested Lord
9. Bheema--Huge and Gigantic
10. Bhupati--Lord of the Gods
11. Bhuvanpati--God of the Gods
12. Buddhinath--God of Wisdom
13. Buddhipriya--Knowledge Bestower
14. Buddhividhata--God of Knowledge
15. Chaturbhuj--One who has Four Arms
16. Devadeva--Lord of All Lords
17. Devantakanashakarin--Destroyer of Evils and Asuras
18. Devavrata--One who accepts all Penances
19. Devendrashika--Protector of All Gods
20. Dharmik--One who gives Charity
21. Dhoomravarna--Smoke-Hued Lord
22. Durja--Invincible Lord
23. Dvaimatura--One who has two Mothers
24. Ekaakshara--He of the Single Syllable
25. Ekadanta--Single-Tusked Lord
26. Ekadrishta--Single-Tusked Lord

27. Eshanputra--Lord Shiva's Son
28. Gadadhara--One who has The Mace as His Weapon
29. Gajakarna--One who has Eyes like an Elephant
30. Gajanana--Elephant-Faced Lord
31. Gajananeti--Elephant-Faced Lord
32. Gajavakra--Trunk of The Elephant
33. Gajavaktra--One who has Mouth like an Elephant
34. Ganadhakshya--Lord of All Ganas
35. Ganadhyakshina--Leader of All The Celestial Bodies
36. Ganapati--Lord of All Ganas
37. Gaurisuta--The Son of Gauri (Parvati)
38. Gunina--One who is The Master of All Virtues
39. Haridra--One who is Golden Colored
40. Heramba--Mother's Beloved Son
41. Kapila--Yellowish-Brown Colored
42. Kaveesha--Master of Poets
43. Kriti--Lord of Music
44. Kripalu--Merciful Lord
45. Krishapingaksha--Yellowish-Brown Eyed
46. Kshamakaram--Place of Forgiveness
47. Kshipra--One who is easy to Appease
48. Lambakarna--Large-Eared Lord
49. Lambodara--The Huge Bellied Lord
50. Mahabala--Enormously Strong Lord
51. Mahaganapati--Omnipotent and Supreme Lord
52. Maheshwaram--Lord of The Universe
53. Mangalamurti--All Auspicious Lord
54. Manomay--Winner of Hearts
55. Mrityuanjaya--Conqueror of Death
56. Mundakarama--Abode of Happiness
57. Muktidaya--Bestower of Eternal Bliss
58. Musikvahana--One who has Mouse as Charioteer
59. Nadapratithishta--One who Appreciates and Loves Music
60. Namasthetu--Vanquisher of All Evils and Vices and Sins
61. Nandana--Lord Shiva's Son
62. Nideeshwaram--Giver of Wealth and Treasures
63. Omkara--One who has the Form of OM
64. Pitambara--One who has Yellow-Colored Body
65. Pramoda--Lord of All Abodes
66. Prathameshwara--First Among All

67. Purush–The Omnipotent Personality

68. Rakta--One who has Red-Colored Body

69. Rudrapriya--Beloved of Lord Shiva

70. Sarvadevatman--Acceptor of All Celestial offerings

71. Sarvasiddhanta--Bestower of Skills and Wisdom

72. Sarvatman--Protector of The Universe

73. Hambhavi--The Son of Parvati

74. Shashivarnam--One who has a Moon like Complexion

75. Shoorpakarna--Large-Eared Lord

76. Shuban--All Auspicious Lord

77. Shubhagunakanan--One who is The Master of All Virtues

78. Shweta--One who is as Pure as the White Color

79. Siddhidhata--Bestower of Success and Accomplishments

80. Siddhipriya--Bestower of Wishes and Boons

81. Siddhivinayaka--Bestower of Success

82. Skandapurvaja--Elder Brother of Skanda (Lord Kartikeya)

83. Sumukha--Auspicious Face

84. Sureshwaram--Lord of All Lords

85. Swaroop--Lover of Beauty

86. Tarun--Ageless

87. Uddanda--Nemesis of Evils and Vices

88. Umaputra--The Son of Goddess Uma (Parvati)

89. Vakratunda--Curved Trunk Lord

90. Varaganapati--Bestower of Boons

91. Varaprada--Granter of Wishes and Boons

92. Varadavinayaka--Bestower of Success

93. Veeraganapati--Heroic Lord

94. Vidyavaridhi--God of Wisdom

95. Vighnahara--Remover of Obstacles

96. Vignaharta--Demolisher of Obstacles

97. Vighnaraja--Lord of All Hindrances

98. Vighnarajendra--Lord of All Obstacles

99. Vighnavinashanaya–Destroyer of All Obstacles and Impediments

100. Vigneshwara--Lord of All Obstacles

101. Vikat--Huge and Gigantic

102. Vinayaka--Lord of All

103. Vishwamukha--Master of The Universe

104. Vishwaraja--King of the World

105. Yagnakaya--Acceptor of All Sacred and Sacrificial Offerings

106. Yashaskaram--Bestower of Fame and Fortune

107. Yashvasin--Beloved and Ever Popular Lord
108. Yogadhipa--The Lord of Meditation

CHAPTER TWENTY-NINE

The Hanuman Chalisa

This includes the prayers to the great devotee of Lord Rama, Hanuman, and a list of names of Hanuman and their meanings.

> sri guru carana saroj raja nija mana mukura sudhar,
> varanaun raghuvara vimala yasa, yo dayaka phala chara

"Having cleaned the mirror of my mind with the dust from the lotus feet of my Guru, I sing the pure glories of Lord Ramachandra, who bestows the four fruits of life: religion, wealth, pleasure and liberation."

> buddhina tanu janike sumiraun pavana kumara,
> bala buddhi vidya dehu mohin, harau klesa vikara

"As I know I am an ignorant fool, I meditate on the Son of Wind, Hanuman, and pray him to give me strength, wisdom and knowledge, purifying me from all defects and bad things."

> siyavara ramachandra ki jaya,
> pavanasuta hanumana ki jaya,
> umapati mahadeva ki jaya

"All glories to Mother Sita, all glories to Lord Ramachandra, all glories to the Son of the Wind, Hanuman, all glories to Lord Shiva, consort of Parvati."

> jaya hanumana jnana guna sagara, jaya kapisa tihun loka ujagara,
> rama duta atulita bala dhama, anjani putra pavana suta nama

"Glory to Hanuman, ocean of knowledge and good qualities. Glory to the lord of the Vanaras. His fame echoes through the three worlds. Glory to the divine messenger and servant of Sri Rama! He is known as Pavana Suta, son of the Wind and Mother Anjana, and his prowess is invincible."

mahavira vikrama bajarangi kumati nivara sumati ke sangi,
kanchana varana viraja suvesa, kanana kundala kunchita kesa

"O Hanuman, you have unlimited courage and strength, you destroy ignorance and grant wisdom. Your complexion is golden, your hair is curly and you wear ear-rings."

hatha bajur aru dhvaja virajai, kandhe munja janeu sajai,
sankara suvana kesari nandana, tej pratapa maha jaga vandana

"In one hand you hold the divine Vajra weapon, in the other you have the flag with your emblem. Your shoulder is decorated with the holy thread. You are the [11th Rudra] avatara of Lord Shiva and son of Sri Keshari. Your great prowess is famous all over the world."

vidyavan guni ati chatur, rama kaja karive ko atur,
prabhu charitra sunive ko rasiya, rama lakshmana sita mana basiya

"You have the greatest wealth of divine knowledge. You are virtuous and intelligent, always ready to serve Lord Rama, and your greatest pleasure is listening to His glories. Rama, Laksmana and Sita always reside in your heart."

suksma rupa dhari siyahin dikhava, vikata rupa dhari lanka jarava,
bhima rupa dhari asura sanhare, ramachandra ke kaja sanvare

"You appeared before Sita in a very small form, but you burned Lanka with a terrifying form and a killed the demons with a gigantic form. In this way you always serve Lord Rama."

lae sanjivana lakhan jiyaye sri raghuvira harshi ura laye,
raghupati kinhi bahuta badai, tum mama priya bharatai sama bhai

"You brought the medicinal herb to revive Lakshmana, and overcome with joy Rama embraced you and glorified you, saying that He loves you as much as He loves His own brother Bharata."

sahasa vadana tumharo yasa gaven, asa kahi sripati kantha lagaven,
sanakadika brahmadi munisa narada sarada sahita ahisa

"Seshanaga with his thousands mouths is singing your glories: with these words, Rama embraced you. Even the Kumaras, Narada, Sarasvati cannot complete describe your glories."

yama kuvera digapala jahante kavi kovida kahi saken kahante,
tuma upakara sugrivahin kinha rama milaya raja pada dinha

"Even Yama, Kuvera, the lords of the directions, poets and sages are incapable of fully describing your glories. You introduced Rama to Sugriva, causing him to become the king of the Vanaras."

tumharo mantra vibhisana mana lankesvara bhae saba jaga jana,
yuga sahasra yojana para bhanu, lilyo tahi madhura phala janun

"By following your advice, Vibhisana became the king of Lanka: everyone knows this. You grabbed the sun, millions of kilometers away in the sky, taking it for a ripe fruit."

prabhu mudrika meli mukha mahin jaldi landi gaye acaraja nahin,
durgama kaja jagata ke jete, sugama anugraha tumhare te te

"You crossed the ocean keeping Rama's ring in your mouth as a token for Sita. You could perform such a miraculous task because with your grace even impossible tasks become possible and even easy."

rama duare tuma rakhavere hot na ajna vinu paisare,
saba sukha lahai tumhari sarana, tuma raksaka kahu ko darana

"You always guard the door of Sri Rama, and without your permission no one can enter. By taking shelter in you, all the joys of life are obtained, and one under your protection has nothing to fear."

apana teja samharo ape tinon loka hankate kanpe,
bhuta pisacha nikata nahin ave, mahavira japa nama sunave

"Your radiance is supreme, and the three worlds tremble when you move. You are the supreme brahmachari, conserving your energy. By repeating the name of Hanuman, all the ghosts and demons are chased away."

nashai roga harai saba pira, japata nirantara hanumata vira,
sankata se hanumana churavai, mana rama vachana dhyana jo lavai

"All diseases and sufferings are destroyed by the constant repetition of the name of Hanuman. One who meditates on him with his mind, heart and activities is saved from all difficulties."

saba para rama tapasvi raja tina ke kaja sakala tuma saja,
aur manoratha jo koi lavai soy amita jivana phala pavain

"Rama is the Lord of yoga, and all your actions are dedicated to Him. By your grace, all desires are granted."

charon yuga paratapa tumhara, hai parasiddhi jagata uyjiara,
sadhu santa ke tum rakhavare, asura nikandana rama dulare

"In all times, you are famous for your prowess and talents, your glories are spread all over the universe. You protect the devotees and the sages, you destroy the demons, and you are Rama's beloved."

asta siddhi nava nidhi ke data, asa vara dina janaki mata,
rama rasayana tumhare pasa, sada raho raghupati ke dasa

"Mother Sita blessed you with the power to grant the eight spiritual perfections and the nine material prosperities, and Sri Rama gave you the power to heal. You are always His humble servant."

tumhare bhajana rama ko pavai janma janma ke dukha visravai,
anta kale raghupati pura jay, jahan janmen hari bhakta kahai

"By meditating on you, one reaches Lord Rama, and eliminates the sufferings of many lifetimes. After death, your devotee will reach the abode of Rama, where he will always be a devotee of the Lord."

aur devata chitta na dharai, hanumata sei sarva sukha karai,
sankata harai mitai saba pira, jo sumire hanumata balavira

"The other Devas do not care for the sufferings of the human beings: only Hanuman is the source of all joys, and by remembering him all sufferings disappear."

jaya jaya jaya hanumana gosain, kripa karau gurudeva ki nain,
yah satavara patha kara jaya chhutahin band maha sukha hoy

"Victory and glory to lord Hanuman! O divine Guru, bless us with your grace. By repeating this mantra one hundred times, one is liberated by all problems and obtains unlimited happiness."

jo yaha parhai hanumana chalisa haya siddhi sakhi gaurisha,
tulasidasa sada harichera kije natha hridaya mahana dera

"One who repeats this song with the glories of lord Hanuman obtains all the spiritual perfections. Tulasidasa, the eternal servant of the Lord, gives this promise in the name of Mahadeva, the lord of Gauri. O lord, may you always reside in my heart."

pavanatanaya sankata harana mangala murti rupa,
rama laskmana sita sahita hridaya basahu sura bhupa

"O Son of the Wind, you destroy all difficulties. Your form is all auspicious, and you always reside in my heart together with Rama, Laksmana and Sita."

siyavara ramachandra ki jaya,
pavana suta hanumana ki jaya,
umapati mahadeva ki jaya

"Glories to Sita Rama, glories to lord Hanuman, son of the wind, and glory to Shiva Mahadeva, husband of Uma!"

Om Sri Hanumate Namah

Yatra yatra raghunatha kirtanam;
Tatra tatra kritha masthakanjalim;
Bhaspavaari paripurna lochanam;
Maarutim namata raakshasanthakam

MEANING: "We bow to Maruti, Sri Hanuman, who stands with his palms folded above his forehead, with a torrent of tears flowing down his eyes wherever the Names of Lord Rama are sung".

The Names of Hanuman

When chanting these names, you can chant "Om" before each name followed by "Namaha." This is especially nice for days like Hanuman Jayanthi, his appearance day, or special days connected with Sita-Rama.

1. Anjaneya--Son of Anjana
2. Anjanagarbhasambhoota--Born of Anjani
3. Ashokavanikachhetre--Destroyer of Ashoka Orchard
4. Akshahantre--Slayer of Aksha
5. Balarka--Sadrushanana Like the Rising Sun
6. Bheemasenasahayakrute--Helper of Bheema
7. Batnasiddhikara--Granter of Strength
8. Bhakthavatsala--Protector of Devotees
9. Bajrangbali--With strength of daamod
10. Bhavishya--Chaturanana Aware of Future Happenings
11. Chanchaladwala --Glittering Tail Suspended Above The Head.
12. Chiranjeevini--Immortal
13. Chaturbahave--Four-Armed
14. Dashabahave--Ten-Armed
15. Danta--Peaceful
16. Dheera--Courageous
17. Deenabandhave--Defender of the Oppressed
18. Daithyakulantaka--Destroyer of Demons
19. Daityakarya--Vidhyataka Destroyer of All Demons' Activities
20. Dhruddavrata--Determined Meditator
21. Dashagreevakulantaka--Slayer of the Ten-Headed Ravana Race
22. Gandharvavidya--Tatvangna Exponent in the Art of Celestials
23. Gandhamadhana--Shailastha Resident of Gandhamadhana
24. Hanumanta--One with Puffy Cheeks
25. Indrajit--Prahitamoghabrahmastra Vinivaraka Remover of the Effect of Indrajit's Brahmastra
26. Jambavatpreeti--Vardhana Winner of Jambavan's Love
27. JaiKapeesh--Hailing Monkey
28. Kapeeshwara--Lord of Monkeys
29. Kabalikruta--One who swallowed the Sun
30. Kapisenanayaka--Head of the Monkey Army
31. Kumarabrahmacharine--Youthful Bachelor
32. Kesarinandan--Son of Kesari
33. Kesarisuta--Son of Kesari
34. Kalanemi--Pramathana Slayer of Kalanemi

35. Harimarkatamarkata--Lord of the Monkeys
36. Karagrahavimoktre--One who Frees from Imprisonment
37. Kalanabha--Organizer of Time
38. Kanchanabha--Golden-Hued Body
39. Kamaroopine--Altering Form at Will
40. Lankineebhanjana--Slayer of Lankini
41. Lakshmanapranadatre--Reviver of Lakshmana's Life
42. Lankapuravidahaka--The One Who Burnt Lanka
43. Lokapujya--Worshipped by the Universe
44. Maruti--Son of Marut (wind god)
45. Mahadhyuta--Most Radiant
46. Mahakaya--One with colossal body
47. Manojavaya--Swiftness like Wind
48. Mahatmane--Supreme Being
49. Mahavira--Most Courageous
50. Marutatmaja--Adored Like Gems
51. Mahabala--Parakrama Of Great Strength
52. Mahatejase--Most Radiant
53. Maharavanamardana--Slayer of the Famous Ravana
54. Mahatapase--Great Meditator
55. Navavyakruti--Pandita Skilful Scholar
56. Parthadhwajagrasamvasine--Having Principal Place on Arjuna's Flag
57. Pragnya--Scholar
58. Prasannatmane--Cheerful
59. Pratapavate--Known for Valour
60. Paravidhyaparihara--Destroyer of Enemies Wisdom
61. Parashaurya--Vinashana Destroyer of Enemy's Valour
62. Parijata--Tarumoolastha Dweller under the Parijata Tree
63. Prabhave--Popular Lord
64. Paramantra--Nirakartre Acceptor of Rama's Mantra Only
65. Pingalaksha--Pink-Eyed
66. Pavanputra--Son of Wind god
67. Panchavaktra--Five-Faced
68. Parayantra--Prabhedaka Destroyer of Enemies' Missions
69. Ramasugreeva--Sandhatre Mediator between Rama and Sugreeva
70. Ramakathalolaya--Crazy of listening Rama's Story
71. Ratnakundala--Deeptimate Wearing Gem-Studded Earrings
72. Rudraveerya--Samudbhava Born of Shiva
73. Ramachudamaniprada--Deliverer of Rama's Ring
74. Ramabhakta--Devoted to Rama

Prayers, Mantras and Gayatris

75. Ramadhuta--Ambassador of Rama
76. Rakshovidhwansakaraka--Slayer of Demons
77. Sankatamochanan--Reliever of sorrows
78. Sitadevi--Mudrapradayaka Deliverer of the Ring of Sita
79. Sarvamayavibhanjana--Destroyer of All Illusions
80. Sarvabandha--Vimoktre Detacher of all Relationship
81. Sarvagraha--Nivashinay Killer of all Evil Effects of Planets
82. Sarvaduhkhahara--Reliever of all Agonies
83. Sarvalolkacharine--Wanderer of all Places
84. Sarvamantra--Swaroopavate Possessor of all Hymns
85. Sarvatantra--Sawaroopine Shape of all Hymns
86. Sarvayantratmaka--Dweller in all Yantras
87. Sarvarogahara--Reliever of all Ailments
88. Sarvavidhyasampath--Pradayaka Granter of Knowledge and Wisdom
89. Shrunkalabandhamochaka--Reliever from a Chain of Distresses
90. Sitashoka--Nivarana Destroyer of Sita's Sorrow
91. Shrimate--Honored
92. Simhikaprana--Bhanjana Slayer of Simhika
93. Sugreeva--Sachiva Minister of Sugreeva
94. Shoora--Gallant
95. Surarchita--Worshipped by Celestials
96. Sphatikabha--Spotless, Crystal-Clear
97. Sanjeevananagahatre--Carrier of Sanjeevi Mount
98. Shuchaye--Pure, Chaste
99. Shanta--Very Composed and Calm
100. Shatakanttamadapahate--Destroyer of Shatakantta's Arrogance
101. Sitanveshana--Pandita Skilful in finding Sita's Whereabouts
102. Sharapanjarabhedaka--Destroyer of the Nest made of Arrows
103. Sitaramapadaseva--Always engaged in Rama's Service
104. Sagarotharaka--Leapt Across the Ocean
105. Tatvagyanaprada--Granter of Wisdom
106. Vanara--Monkey
107. Vibheeshanapriyakara--Beloved of Vibheeshana
108. Vajrakaya--Hard Like Metal
109. Vardhimainakapujita--Worshipped by Mynaka
110. Vagmine--Spokesman
111. Vijitendriya--Controller of the Senses
112. Vajranakha--Strong-Nailed
113. Vagadheeksha--Lord of Spokesmen
114. Yogine--Yogi (Saint)

CHAPTER THIRTY

The Vishnu Sahasranama

The Sri Vishnu Sahasranam, or the Thousand Names of Vishnu, is an important Stotram that is chanted in many temples of Vishnu throughout the world. It is used at important times or occasions, or even simply for personal meditation. It is extremely powerful and offers numerous spiritual benefits. The chanting of the Vishnu Sahasranama is said by *shastras* to create a most spiritual atmosphere for all, destroys negative influences and elements, wards off troubles that arise from the ill position of stars and planets, or the anger of rulers, ruthless enemies, and incurable diseases. Moreover this also purifies the mind by letting one gain more inner poise for meditation, allows us greater understanding of the characteristics of the Supreme, invokes His energy into our life and consciousness, and produces a high vibration for peace and positivity.

The 1000 names of Lord Vishnu are meant to invoke a sense of bonding with the Lord, who is the most intimate one. The meanings of the names given here will help in understanding the magnitude and depth of the Supreme Being. There are exactly 1031 names of Lord Vishnu in the 'Sahasranama' but we also find some repetitions.

The Sri Vishnu Sahasranama is found in the *Mahabharata*, Anusasana Parva, Section 149, verses 14 to 120, and authored by Srila Vyasadeva. The edition of the *Mahabharata* by Kisari Mohan Ganguli offers an easy translation of the text in English. However, copies of the Vishnu Sahasranama are available in books that concentrate on the Stotram alone, with texts, translations, explanations, etc., depending on which one you get.

Many devotees chant this everyday. If that is not convenient, they perform this at least on their birthdays, or on eclipse days, festival days, or on the day which the sun moves from one zodiac sign to another.

The full Vishnu Sahasranam Stotram consists of a Prolog, which gives the background on why the Stotram was imparted to the great and just Yudhishthira by Bhishma. Then there is the Dhyanam or meditation on its importance. This is followed by the essential verses with the thousand names of Vishnu, organized in a poetic format in 107 stanzas, in the anushtup chandas (a meter with eight syllables in a quarter), with two quarters per line, and two lines per stanza. This is then followed by the conclusion, called Phala Sruti, or a recounting of the benefits that can accrue by chanting this Stotram.

What follows herein is the introductory Dhyanam or meditation for those who wish to chant it, and then the essential Sahasranama verses with the thousand names of Lord Vishnu, followed by a list of the names and their translated meanings.

Sri Vishnu-Sahasranama Dhyanam

kshiirodhan.vatpradeshe shuchimani.vilasatsaikate mauktikaanaam
maalaakliptaasanasthaha sphatikamani-nibhair-mauktikair-
manditaangah||

shubhrai-rabhrairadabhrai-ruparivirachitairmuktapiiyuushha varshhaih
aanandii nah puniiyaadarinalinagadaa shankhapaanirmukundah ||

bhooh paadaoo yasya naabhirviyadasuranilashchandra sooryau cha netre
karnaavaashaah shiro dyaurmukhamapi dahano yasya vaasteyamabdhih |

antahstham yasya vishvam suranarakhagagobhogigandharvadaityaih
chitram ramramyate tam tribhuvana vapushham vishhnumiisham
namaami ||

shaantaakaaram bhujaga-shayanam padmanaabham suresham
vishvaakhaaram gagana-sadrisham meghavarnam shubha-angam |

lakshmee-kaantam kamala-nayanam yogibhir-dhyaana-gamyam
vande vishhnum bhava-bhaya-haram sarva-lokaika-naatham ||

meghashyaamam peethakausheya-vaasam srivata-saangam
kausthubhodh-bhaasithaangam |
punyopeytham pundareekayathaksham vande vishnum
sarva-lokaika-naatham ||

sashankha chakram sakireeda kundalam sapeetha vastram
saraseeruhekshanam |
sahaaravakshah sthalakausthubhasriyam namaami vishnum
shirsachaturbhujam ||

chaayaayaam paarijaathasya hemasimhasanopari
aasinamambuda shyama maaya thakshamalankritham |

chandrananan chaturbaahum srivatsangitavakshasam
rukmani satyabhaamaabhyam sahitam krishnam asrayei ||

The Vishnu-Sahasranama Verses

Harih OM
1)
vishvam vishnur-vashatkaaro
bhoota-bhavya-bhavat-prabhuh
bhoota-krit bhoota-bhrit bhaavo
bhootaatmaa bhoota-bhaavanah
2)
pootaatmaa paramaatmaa cha
muktaanaam paramaa gatih
avyayah purushah saakshee
kshetrajno 'kshara eva cha
3)
yogo yoga-vidaam netaa
pradhaana-purusheshvarah
naarasimha-vapuh shreemaan
keshavah purushottamah
4)
sarvas-sharvas-shivah sthaanur
bhootaadir nidhir-avyayah
sambhavo bhaavano bhartaa
prabhavah prabhur-eeshvarah
5)
svayambhooh shambhur aadityah
pushkaraaksho mahaasvanah
anaadi-nidhano dhaataa
vidhaataa dhaaturuttamah
6)
aprameyo hrisheekeshah
padmanaabho-a-maraprabhuh
vishvakarmaa manustvashtaa
sthavishtah sthaviro dhruvah

7)
agraahyah shaashvatah krishno
lohitaakshah pratardanah
prabhootas trikakub-dhaama
pavitram mangalam param
8)
eeshanah praanadah praano
jyeshthah shreshthah prajaapatih
hiranya-garbho bhoo-garbho
maadhavo madhu-soodanah
9)
eeshvaro vikramee dhanvee
medhaavee vikramah kramah
anuttamo duraadharshah
kritajnah kritir-aatmavaan
10)
sureshah sharanam sharma
visva-retaah prajaa-bhavah
ahah samvatsaro vyaalah
pratyayah sarvadarshanah
11)
ajah sarveshvarah siddhah
siddhih sarvaadir achyutah
vrishaakapir ameyaatmaa
sarva-yoga-vinissritah
12)
vasur-vasumanaah satyah
samaatmaa sammitah samah
amoghah pundareekaaksho
vrishakarmaa vrishaakritih
13)
rudro bahu-shiraa babhrur
visvayonis-shuchi-shravaah
amritah shaashvatah-sthaanur-
varaaroho mahaatapaah
14)
sarvagah sarvavid-bhaanuh-
vishvak-seno janaardanah
vedo vedavid-avyango
vedaango vedavit kavih

15)
lokaadhyakshah suraadhyaksho
dharmaadhyakshah krita-akritah
chaturaatmaa chaturvyoohas-
chatur-damstras-chatur-bhujah
16)
bhraajishnur-bhojanam bhoktaa
sahishnur-jagadaadijah
anagho vijayo jetaa
vishvayonih punarvasuh
17)
upendro vaamanah praamsur-
amoghah shuchir-oorjitah
ateendrah samgrahah sargo
dhritaatmaa niyamo yamah
18)
vedyo vaidyah sadaa-yogee
veerahaa maadhavo madhuh
ati-indriyo mahaamayo
mahotsaaho mahaabalah
19)
mahaabuddhir-mahaa-veeryo
mahaa-shaktir mahaa-dyutih
anirdeshya-vapuh shreemaan
ameyaatmaa mahaadri-dhrik
20)
maheshvaaso maheebhartaa
shreenivaasah sataam gatih
aniruddhah suraanando
govindo govidaam-patih
21)
mareechir-damano hamsah
suparno bhujagottamah
hiranyanaabhah sutapaah
padmanaabhah prajaapatih
22)
amrityus-sarva-drik simhah
san-dhaataa sandhiman sthirah
ajo durmarshanah shaastaa
visrutaatmaa suraarihaa

23)
gurur-gurutamo dhaama
satyas-satya-paraakramah
nimisho-a-nimishah sragvee
vaachaspatir-udaara-dheeh

24)
agraneer-graamaneeh shreemaan
nyaayo netaa sameeranah
sahasra-moordhaa vishvaatmaa
sahasraakshas-sahasrapaat

25)
aavartano nivritaatmaa
samvritah sam-pramardanah
ahassamvartako vahnir
anilo dharaneedharah

26)
suprasaadah prasanaatmaa
vishva-dhrik-vishvabhuk vibhuh
satkartaa satkritah saadhur
jahnur-naaraayano narah

27)
asankhyeyo 'prameyaatmaa
vishishtah shishta-krit-shuchih
siddhaarthah siddhasankalpah
siddhidah siddhisaadhanah

28)
vrishaahee vrishabho vishnur-
vrishaparvaa vrishodarah
vardhano vardhamaanash cha
viviktah shruti-saagarah

29)
subhujo durdharo vaagmee
mahendro vasudo vasuh
naika-roopo brihad-roopah
shipivishtah prakaashanah

30)
ojas-tejo-dyutidharah
prakaashaatmaa prataapanah
riddhah spashtaaksharo mantras-
chandraamsur-bhaaskara-dyutih

31)
amritaamsoodbhavo bhaanuh
shashabindhuh sureshvarah
aushadham jagatas-setuh
satya-dharma-paraakramah
32)
bhoota-bhavya-bhavan-naathah
pavanah paavano 'nalah
kaamahaa kaamakrit-kaantah
kaamah kaamapradah prabhuh
33)
yugaadi-krit yugaavarto
naikamaayo mahaashanah
adrishyo vyaktaroopash cha
sahasrajit anantajit
34)
ishto visishtah sishteshtah
shikhandee nahusho vrishah
krodhahaa krodhakrit kartaa
visvabaahur maheedharah
35)
achyutah prathitah praanah
praanado vaasavaanujah
apaam nidhir-adhishthaanam
apramattah pratishthitah
36)
skandah skanda-dharo dhuryo
varado vaayuvaahanah
vasudevo brihat bhaanur
aadidevah purandarah
37)
ashokas-taaranas-taarah
shoorah shaurih-janeshvarah
anukoolah sataavarttah
padmee padmanibhekshanah
38)
padmanaabho 'ravindaakshah
padmagarbhah shareerabhrit
maharddhi-riddhah uriddhaatmaa
mahaaksho garudadhvajah

39)
atulah sharabho bheemah
samayajno havirharih
sarva-lakshana-lakshanyo
lakshmeevaan samitinjayah
40)
viksharo rohito maargo
hetur daamodarah sahah
maheedharo mahaabhaago
vegavaan-amitaashanah
41)
udbhavah kshobhano devah
shreegarbhah parameshvarah
karanam kaaranam kartaa
vikartaa gahano guhah
42)
vyavasaayo vyavasthaanah
samsthaanah sthaanado-dhruvah
pararddhih paramaspashtah-
tushtah pushtah shubhekshanah
43)
raamo viraamo virajo
maargo neyo nayo 'nayah
veerah shaktimataam-shrestho
dharmo dharmaviduttamah
44)
vaikunthah purushah praanah
praanadah pranavah prituh
hiranyagarbhah shatrughno
vyaapto vaayur-adhokshajah
45)
rituh sudarshanah kaalah
parameshthee parigrahah
ugrah samvatsaro daksho
vishraamo vishva-dakshinah
46)
vistaarah sthaavarah sthaanuh
pramaanam beejamavyayam
artho 'nartho mahaakosho
mahaabhogo mahaadhanah

47)
anirvinnah sthavishtho 'bhoor-
dharma-yoopo mahaa-makhah
nakshatranemir nakshatree
kshamah kshaamah sameehanah
48)
yajnah ijyo mahejyash cha
kratuh satram sataam gatih
sarvadarshee vimuktaatmaa
sarvajno jnaanamuttamam
49)
suvratah sumukhah sookshmah
sughoshah sukhadah suhrit
manoharo jita-krodho
veerabaahur-vidaaranah
50)
svaapanah svavasho vyaapee
naikaatmaa naikakarmakrit
vatsaro vatsalo vatsee
ratnagarbho dhaneshvarah
51)
dharmagub dharmakrit dharmee
sadasatksharam-aksharam
avijnaataa sahasraamshur
vidhaataa kritalakshanah
52)
gabhastinemih sattvasthah
simho bhoota-maheshvarah
aadidevo mahaadevo
devesho devabhrit guruh
53)
uttaro gopatir-goptaa
jnaanagamyah puraatanah
shareera bhootabhritbhoktaa
kapeendro bhooridakshinah
54)
somapomritapah somah
purujit purusattamah
vinayo jayah satyasandho
daashaarhah saatvataam patih

55)
jeevo vinayitaa-saakshee
mukundo 'mitavikramah
ambho-nidhir-anantaatmaa
mahodadhishayo 'ntakah
56)
ajo mahaarhah svaabhaavyo
jitaamitrah pramodanah
aanando nandano nandah
satyadharmaa trivikramah
57)
maharshih kapilaachaaryah
kritajno medineepatih
tripadas-tridashaadhyaksho
mahaashringah kritaantakrit
58)
mahaavaraaho govindah
sushenah kanakaangadee
guhyo gabheero gahano
guptas chakra-gadaadharah
59)
vedhaah svaangojitah krishno
dridhah sankarshanochyutah
varuno vaaruno vrikshah
pushkaraaksho mahaamanaah
60)
bhagavaan bhagahaa 'nandee
vanamaalee halaayudhah
aadityo jyotiraadityah
sahishnur-gatisattamah
61)
sudhanvaa khanda-parashur-
daaruno dravinapradah
divah-sprik sarvadrik vyaaso
vaachaspatir-ayonijah
62)
trisaamaa saamagah saama
nirvaanam bheshajam bhishak
samnyaasa-krit-samah shaanto
nishthaa shaantih paraayanam

63)
shubhaangah shaantidah shrashtaa
kumudah kuvaleshayah
gohito gopatir goptaa
vrishabhaaksho vrishapriyah
64)
anivartee nivrittaatmaa
samksheptaa kshemakrit-shivah
shreevatsa-vakshaah shrevaasah
shreepatih shreemataam varah
65)
shreedah shreeshah shreenivaasah
shreenidhih shreevibhaavanah
shreedharah shreekarah shreyah
shreemaan-loka-trayaashrayah
66)
svakshah svangah shataanando
nandir-jyotir-ganeshvarah
vijitaatmaa vidheyaatmaa
sat-keertis-chinnasamshayah
67)
udeernah sarvatash-chakshur-
aneeshah shaashvata-sthirah
bhooshayo bhooshano bhootir
vishokah shoka-naashanah
68)
archishmaan-architah kumbho
vishuddhaatmaa vishodhanah
anniruddho 'pratirathah
pradyumno 'mitavikramah
69)
kaalanemi-nihaa veerah
shauri shoora-janeshvarah
trilokaatmaa trilokeshah
keshavah keshihaa harih
70)
kaamadevah kaamapaalah
kaamee kaantah kritaagamah
anirdeshya-vapur-vishnur
veero 'nanto dhananjayah

71)
brahmanyo brahmakrit brahmaa
brahma brahma-vivardhanah
brahmavid braahmano brahmee
brahmajno braahmana-priyah
72)
mahaakramo mahaakarmaa
mahaatejaah mahoragah
mahaakratur-mahaayajvaa
mahaayajno mahaahavih
73)
stavyah stavapriyah stotram
stutih stotaa ranapriyah
poornah poorayitaa punyah
punya-keertir-anaamayah
74)
manojavas-teerthakaro
vasuretaah vasupradah
vasuprado vaasudevo
vasur-vasumanaah havih
75)
sadgatih satkritih satta
sadbhootih satparaayanah
shooraseno yadu-shresthah
sannivaasah suyaamunah
76)
bhootaavaaso vaasudevah
sarvaasunilayo 'nalah
darpahaa darpado dripto
durdharo 'thaaparaajitah
77)
vishvamoortir-mahaamortir
deeptamoortir-a-moortirmaan
anekamoortir-avyaktah
shatamoortih shataananah
78)
eko naikah savah kah kim
yat-tat-padam-anuttamam
lokabandhur-lokanaatho
maadhavo-bhaktavatsalah

79)
suvarna-varno hemaango
varaangash-chandanaangadee
veerahaa vishama shoonyo
ghritaaseer-acalas-chalah
80)
amaanee maanado maanyo
lokasvaamee trilokadhrik
sumedhaa medhajo dhanyah
satyamedhah dharaadharah
81)
tejovrisho dyutidharah
sarva-shastra-bhritaam-varah
pragraho nigraho vyagro
naikashringo gadaagrajah
82)
chaturmoortis-chaturbaahus
chaturvyoohas-chaturgatih
chaturaatmaa chaturbhaavas
chatur-vedavid-ekapaat
83)
samaavarto 'nivrittaatmaa
durjayo duratikramah
durlabho durgamo durgo
duraavaaso duraarihaa
84)
shubhaango lokasaarangah
sutantus-tantu-vardhanah
indrakarmaa mahaakarmaa
kritakarmaa kritaagamah
85)
udbhavah sundarah sundo
ratna-naabhah sulochanah
arko vaajasanah shringee
jayantah sarvavij-jayee
86)
suvarna-bindur-akshobhyah
sarva-vaageeshvareshvarah
mahaahrado mahaagarto
mahaabhooto mahaanidhih

87)
kumudah kundarah kundah
parjanyah paavano 'nilah
amritaasho 'mritavapuh
sarvajna sarvato-mukhah
88)
sulabhah suvratah siddhah
shatrujit shatrutaapanah
nyagrodhodumbaro 'shvattas
chaanooraandhra-nishoodanah
89)
sahasraarchih saptajihvah
saptaidhaah saptavaahanah
amoortiranagho 'cintyo
bhayakrit bhayanaashanah
90)
anurbrihat krishah sthoolo
gunabhrin-nirguno mahaan
adhritah svadhritah svaasyah
praagvamsho vamshavardhanah
91)
bhaarabhrit-kathito yogee
yogeeshah sarvakaamadah
aashramah shramanah kshaamah
suparno vaayuvaahanah
92)
dhanurdharo dhanurvedo
dando damayitaa damah
aparaajitah sarvasaho
niyantaa niyamo yamah
93)
sattvavaan saattvikah satyah
satya-dharma-paraayanah
abhipraayah priyaarho 'rhah
priyakrit-preetivardhanah
94)
vihaayasa-gatir-jyotih
suruchir-hutabhug vibhuh
ravir-virochanah sooryah
savitaa ravilochanah

95)
ananto hutabhug-bhoktaa
sukhado naikajo 'grajah
anirvinnah sadaamarshee
lokaadhishthaanam-adbhutah
96)
sanaat sanaatanatamah
kapilah kapir-apyayah
svastidah svastikrit svasti
svastibhuk svastidakshinah
97)
araudrah kundalee chakree
vikramy oorjita-shaasanah
shabdaatigah shabdasahah
shishirah sharvaree-karah
98)
akroorah peshalo daksho
dakshinah kshaminaam varah
vidvattamo veetabhayah
punya-shravana-keertanah
99)
uttaarano dushkritihaa
punyo duh-svapna-naashanah
veerahaa rakshanah santo
jeevanah paryavasthitah
100)
anantaroopo 'nantashreer
jitamanyur bhayapahah
chaturashro gabheeraatmaa
vidisho vyaadisho dishah
101)
anaadir-bhoor-bhuvo lakshmeeh
suveero ruchiraangadah
janano jana-janmaadir
bheemo bheema-paraakramah
102)
aadhaaranilayo `dhaataa
pushpahaasah prajaagarah
oordhvaga satpathaachaarah
praanadah pranavah panah

103)
pramaanam praananilayah
praanibhrit praanajeevanah
tattvam tattvavid-ekaatmaa
janma-mrityu-jaraatigah
104)
bhoor-bhuvah svas-tarus-taarah
savitaa prapitaamahah
yajno yajnapatir-yajvaa
yajnaango yajnavaahanah
105)
yajnabhrid-yajnakrid-yajnee
yajnabhug-yajnasaadhanah
yajnaantakrid-yajnaguhyam
annam-annaada eva cha
106)
aatmayonih-svayamjaato
vaikhaanah saamagaayanah
devakee-nandanah srashtaa
kshiteeshah paapa-naashanah
107)
samkha-bhrin-nandakee chakree
shaarnga-dhanvaa-gadaadharah
rathaanga-paanir-akshobhyah
sarva-praharanaayudhah

SREE SARVA-PRAHARANAAYUDHAH OM NAMAH ITI

THE ONE THOUSAND NAMES OF LORD VISHNU
TRANSLATIONS AND MEANINGS

1) vishvam: He who is the universe, the virat-purusha
2) vishnuh: He who pervades everywhere
3) vashatkaarah: He who is invoked for oblations
4) bhoota-bhavya-bhavat-prabhuh: The Lord of past, present and future
5) bhoota-krit: The creator of all creatures
6) bhoota-bhrit: He who nourishes all creatures
7) bhaavo: He who becomes all moving and nonmoving things

8) bhootaatmaa: The aatman of all beings
9) bhoota-bhaavanah: The cause of the growth and birth of all creatures
10) pootaatmaa: He with an extremely pure essence
11) paramaatmaa: The Supersoul
12) muktaanaam paramaa gatih: The final goal, reached by liberated souls
13) avyayah: Without destruction
14) purushah: He who dwells in the city of nine gates
15) saakshee: The witness
16) kshetrajnah: The knower of the field
17) akshara: Indestructible
18) yogah: He who is realized through yoga
19) yoga-vidaam netaa: The guide of those who know yoga
20) pradhaana-purusheshvarah: Lord of pradhaana and purusha
21) naarasimha-vapuh: He whose form is man-lion
22) shreemaan: He who is always with shree
23) keshavah: He who has beautiful locks of hair
24) purushottamah: The Supreme Controller
25) sarvah: He who is everything
26) sharvas: The auspicious
27) shivah: He who is eternally pure
28) sthaanuh: The pillar, the immovable truth
29) bhootaadih: The cause of the five great elements
30) nidhir-avyayah: The imperishable treasure
31) sambhavah: He who descends of His own free will
32) bhaavanah: He who gives everything to his devotees
33) bhartaa: He who governs the entire living world
34) prabhavah: The womb of the five great elements
35) prabhuh: The Almighty Lord
36) eeshvarah: He who can do anything without any help
37) svayambhooh: He who manifests from Himself
38) shambhuh: He who brings auspiciousness
39) aadityah: The son of Aditi (Vaamana)
40) pushkaraakshah: He who has eyes like the lotus
41) mahaasvanah: He who has a thundering voice
42) anaadi-nidhanah: He without origin or end
43) dhaataa: He who supports all fields of experience
44) vidhaataa: The dispenser of fruits of action
45) dhaaturuttamah: The subtlest atom
46) aprameyah: He who cannot be perceived
47) hrisheekeshah: The Lord of the senses

48) padmanaabhah: He from whose navel comes the lotus
49) amaraprabhuh: The Lord of the devas
50) vishvakarmaa: The creator of the universe
51) manuh: He who has manifested as the Vedic mantras
52) tvashtaa: He who makes huge things small
53) sthavishtah: The supremely gross
54) sthaviro dhruvah: The ancient, motionless one
55) agraahyah: He who is not perceived sensually
56) shaashvatah: He who always remains the same
57) krishno: He whose complexion is dark
58) lohitaakshah: Red-eyed
59) pratardanah: The Supreme destruction
60) prabhootas: Ever-full
61) trikakub-dhaama: The support of the three quarters
62) pavitram: He who gives purity to the heart
63) mangalam param: The Supreme auspiciousness
64) eeshanah: The controller of the five great elements
65) praanadah: He who gives life
66) praano: He who ever lives
67) jyeshthah: Older than all
68) shreshthah: The most glorious
69) prajaapatih: The Lord of all creatures
70) hiranyagarbhah: He who dwells in the womb of the world
71) bhoogarbhah: He who is the womb of the world
72) maadhavah: Husband of Lakshmi
73) madhusoodanah: Destroyer of the Madhu demon
74) eeshvarah: The contoller
75) vikramee: He who is full of prowess
76) dhanvee: He who always has a divine bow
77) medhaavee: Supremely intelligent
78) vikramah: He who stepped (Vaamana)
79) kramah: All-pervading
80) anuttamah: Incomparably great
81) duraadharshah: He who cannot be attacked successfully
82) kritajnah: He who knows all that is
83) kritih: He who rewards all our actions
84) aatmavaan: The self in all beings
85) sureshah: The Lord of the demigods
86) sharanam: The refuge
87) sharma: He who is Himself infinite bliss

88) visva-retaah: The seed of the universe

89) prajaa-bhavah: He from whom all praja comes

90) ahah: He who is the nature of time

91) samvatsarah: He from whom the concept of time comes

92) vyaalah: The serpent (vyaalah) to athiests

93) pratyayah: He whose nature is knowledge

94) sarvadarshanah: All-seeing

95) ajah: Unborn

96) sarveshvarah: Controller of all

97) siddhah: The most famous

98) siddhih: He who gives moksha

99) sarvaadih: The beginning of all

100) achyutah: Infallible

101) vrishaakapih: He who lifts the world to dharma

102) ameyaatmaa: He who manifests in infinite varieties

103) sarva-yoga-vinissritah: He who is free from all attachments

104) vasuh: The support of all elements

105) vasumanaah: He whose mind is supremely pure

106) satyah: The truth

107) samaatmaa: He who is the same in all

108) sammitah: He who has been accepted by authorities

109) samah: Equal

110) amoghah: Ever useful

111) pundareekaakshah: He who dwells in the heart

112) vrishakarmaa: He whose every act is righteous

113) vrishaakritih: The form of dharma

114) rudrah: He who makes all people weep

115) bahu-shiraah: He who has many heads

116) babhrur: He who rules over all the worlds

117) vishvayonih: The womb of the universe

118) shuchi-shravaah: He who has beautiful, sacred names

119) amritah: Immortal

120) shaashvatah-sthaanur: Permanent and immovable

121) varaaroho: The most glorious destination

122) mahaatapaah: He of great tapas

123) sarvagah: All-pervading

124) sarvavid-bhaanuh: All-knowing and effulgent

125) vishvaksenah: He against whom no army can stand

126) janaardanah: He who gives joy to good people

127) vedah: He who is the Vedas

128) vedavid: The knower of the Vedas

129) avyangah: Without imperfections

130) vedaangah: He whose limbs are the Vedas

131) vedavit: He who contemplates upon the Vedas

132) kavih: The seer

133) lokaadhyakshah: He who presides over all lokas

134) suraadhyaksho: He who presides over all devas

135) dharmaadhyakshah: He who presides over dharma

136) krita-akritah: All that is created and not created

137) chaturaatmaa: The four-fold self

138) chaturvyoohah: Vasudeva, Sankarshan etc

139) chaturdamstrah: He who has four canines (Nrsimha)

140) chaturbhujah: Four-handed

141) bhraajishnur: Self-effulgent consciousness

142) bhojanam: He who is the sense-objects

143) bhoktaa: The enjoyer

144) sahishnuh: He who can suffer patiently

145) jagadaadijah: Born at the beginning of the world

146) anaghah: Sinless

147) vijayah: Victorious

148) jetaa: Ever-successful

149) vishvayonih: He who incarnates because of the world

150) punarvasuh: He who lives repeatedly in different bodies

151) upendrah: The younger brother of Indra (vaamana)

152) vaamanah: He with a dwarf body

153) praamshuh: He with a huge body

154) amoghah: He whose acts are for a great purpose

155) shuchih: He who is spotlessly clean

156) oorjitah: He who has infinite vitality

157) ateendrah: He who surpasses Indra

158) samgrahah: He who holds everything together

159) sargah: He who creates the world from Himself

160) dhritaatmaa: Established in Himself

161) niyamo: The appointing authority

162) yamah: The administrator

163) vedyah: That which is to be known

164) vaidyah: The Supreme doctor

165) sadaa-yogee: Always in yoga

166) veerahaa: He who destroys the mighty heroes

167) maadhavo: The Lord of all knowledge

168) madhuh: Sweet

169) ateendriyo: Beyond the sense organs

170) mahaamayo: The Supreme Master of all Maayaa

171) mahotsaaho: The great enthusiast

172) mahaabalah: He who has supreme strength

173) mahaabuddhir: He who has supreme intelligence

174) mahaa-veeryah: The supreme essence

175) mahaa-shaktih: All-powerful

176) mahaa-dyutih: Greatly luminous

177) anirdeshya-vapuh: He whose form is indescribable

178) shreemaan: He who is always courted by glories

179) ameyaatmaa: He whose essence is immeasurable

180) mahaadri-dhrik: He who supports the great mountain

181) maheshvaasah: He who wields shaarnga

182) maheebhartaa: The husband of mother earth

183) shreenivaasah: The permanent abode of Shree

184) sataam gatih: The goal for all virtuous people

185) aniruddhah: He who cannot be obstructed

186) suraanando: He who gives out happiness

187) govindah: The protector of the cows

188) govidaam-patih: The Lord of all men of wisdom

189) mareechih: Effulgence

190) damanah: He who controls rakshasas

191) hamsah: The swan

192) suparnah: Beautiful-winged (Two birds analogy)

193) bhujagottamah: The serpent Ananta

194) hiranyanaabhah: He who has a golden navel

195) sutapaah: He who has glorious tapas

196) padmanaabhah: He whose navel is like a lotus

197) prajaapatih: He from whom all creatures emerge

198) amrityuh: He who knows no death

199) sarva-drik: The seer of everything

200) simhah: He who destroys

201) sandhaataa: The regulator

202) sandhimaan: He who seems to be conditioned

203) sthirah: Steady

204) ajah: He who takes the form of Aja, Brahma

205) durmarshanah: He who cannot be vanquished

206) shaastaa: He who rules over the universe

207) visrutaatmaa: He who is called atma in the Vedas

208) suraarihaa: Destroyer of the enemies of the devas

209) guruh: The teacher

210) gurutamah: The greatest teacher

211) dhaama: The goal

212) satyah: He who is Himself the truth

213) satya-paraakramah: Dynamic Truth

214) nimishah: He who has closed eyes in contemplation

215) animishah: He who remains unwinking; ever knowing

216) sragvee: He who always wears a garland of undecaying flowers

217) vaachaspatir-udaara-dheeh: He who is eloquent in championing the Supreme law of life; He with a large-hearted intelligence

218) agraneeh: He who guides us to the peak

219) graamaneeh: He who leads the flock

220) shreemaan: The possessor of light, effulgence, glory

221) nyaayah: Justice

222) netaa: The leader

223) sameeranah: He who sufficiently administers all movements of all living creatures

224) sahasra-moordhaa: He who has endless heads

225) vishvaatmaa: The soul of the universe

226) sahasraakshah: Thousands of eyes

227) sahasrapaat: Thousand-footed

228) aavartanah: The unseen dynamism

229) nivritaatmaa: The soul retreated from matter

230) samvritah: He who is vieled from the jiva

231) sam-pramardanah: He who persecutes evil men

232) ahassamvartakah: He who thrills the day and makes it function vigorously

233) vahnih: Fire

234) anilah: Air

235) dharaneedharah: He who supports the earth

236) suprasaadah: Fully satisfied

237) prasanaatmaa: Ever pure and all-blissful self

238) vishva-dhrik: Supporter of the world

239) vishvabhuk: He who enjoys all experiences

240) vibhuh: He who manifests in endless forms

241) satkartaa: He who adores good and wise people

242) satkritah: He who is adored by all good people

243) saadhur: He who lives by the righteous codes

244) jahnuh: Leader of men

245) naaraayanah: He who resides on the waters

246) narah: The guide

247) asankhyeyah: He who has numberless names and forms

248) aprameyaatmaa: A soul not known through the pramanas

249) vishishtah: He who transcends all in His glory

250) shishta-krit: The law-maker

251) shuchih: He who is pure

252) siddhaarthah: He who has all arthas

253) siddhasankalpah: He who gets all He wishes for

254) siddhidah: The giver of benedictions

255) siddhisaadhanah: The power behind our sadhana

256) vrishaahee: Controller of all actions

257) vrishabhah: He who showers all dharmas

258) vishnuh: Long-striding

259) vrishaparvaa: The ladder leading to dharma (As well as dharma itself)

260) vrishodarah: He from whose belly life showers forth

261) vardhanah: The nurturer and nourisher

262) vardhamaanah: He who can grow into any dimension

263) viviktah: Separate

264) shruti-saagarah: The ocean for all scripture

265) subhujah: He who has graceful arms

266) durdurdharah: He who cannot be known by great yogis

267) vaagmee: He who is eloquent in speech

268) mahendrah: The lord of Indra

269) vasudah: He who gives all wealth

270) vasuh: He who is Wealth

271) naika-roopo: He who has unlimited forms

272) brihad-roopah: Vast, of infinite dimensions

273) shipivishtah: The presiding deity of the sun

274) prakaashanah: He who illuminates

275) ojas-tejo-dyutidharah: The possessor of vitality, effulgence and beauty

276) prakaashaatmaa: The effulgent self

277) prataapanah: Thermal energy; one who heats

278) riddhah: Full of prosperity

279) spashtaaksharo: One who is indicated by OM

280) mantrah: The nature of the Vedic mantras

281) chandraamshuh: The rays of the moon

282) bhaaskara-dyutih: The effulgence of the sun

283) amritaamsoodbhavo: The moon who gives flavor to vegetables

284) bhaanuh: Self-effulgent

285) shashabindhuh: The moon who has a rabbit-like spot
286) sureshvarah: A person of extreme charity
287) aushadham: Medicine
288) jagatas-setuh: A bridge across the material energy
289) satya-dharma-paraakramah: One who champions heroically for truth
      and righteousness
290) bhoota-bhavya-bhavan-naathah: The Lord of past, present and future
291) pavanah: The air that fills the universe
292) paavanah: He who gives life-sustaining power to air
293) analah: Fire
294) kaamahaa: He who destroys all desires
295) kaamakrit: He who fulfills all desires
296) kaantah: He who is of enchanting form
297) kaamah: The beloved
298) kaamapradah: He who supplies desired objects
299) prabhuh: The Lord
300) yugaadi-krit: The creator of the yugas
301) yugaavartah The law behind time
302) naikamaayah: He whose forms are endless and varied
303) mahaashanah: He who eats up everything
304) adrishyah: Imperceptible
305) vyaktaroopah: He who is perceptible to the yogi
306) sahasrajit: He who vanquishes thousands
307) anantajit: Ever-victorious
308) ishtah: He who is invoked through Vedic rituals
309) visishtah: The noblest and most sacred
310) sishteshtah: The greatest beloved
311) shikhandee: He who wears a peacock feather
312) nahushah: He who binds all with maya
313) vrishah: He who is dharma
314) krodhahaa: He who destroys anger
315) krodhakrit-kartaa: He who generates anger against the lower tendency
316) visvabaahuh: He whose hand is in everything
317) maheedharah: The support of the earth
318) achyutah: He who undergoes no changes
319) prathitah: He who exists pervading all
320) praanah: The prana in all living creatures
321) praanadah: He who gives prana
322) vaasavaanujah: The brother of Indra
323) apaam-nidhih: Treasure of waters (the ocean)

324) adhishthaanam: The substratum of the entire universe

325) apramattah: He who never makes a wrong judgement

326) pratishthitah: He who has no cause

327) skandah: He whose glory is expressed through Subrahmanya

328) skanda-dharah: Upholder of withering righteousness

329) dhuryah: Who carries out creation etc without hitch

330) varadah: He who fulfills boons

331) vaayuvaahanah: Controller of winds

332) vaasudevah: Dwelling in all creatures although not affected by that condition

333) brihat-bhaanuh: He who illumines the world with the rays of the sun and moon

334) aadidevah: The primary source of everything

335) purandarah: Destroyer of cities

336) ashokah: He who has no sorrow

337) taaranah: He who enables others to cross

338) taarah: He who saves

339) shoorah: The valiant

340) shaurih: He who incarnated in the dynasty of Shoora

341) janeshvarah: The Lord of the people

342) anukoolah: Well-wisher of everyone

343) sataavarttah: He who takes infinite forms

344) padmee: He who holds a lotus

345) padmanibhekshanah: Lotus-eyed

346) padmanaabhah: He who has a lotus-navel

347) aravindaakshah: He who has eyes as beautiful as the lotus

348) padmagarbhah: He who is being meditated upon in the lotus of the heart

349) shareerabhrit: He who sustains all bodies

350) maharddhi: One who has great prosperity

351) riddhah: He who has expanded Himself as the universe

352) Vriddhaatmaa: The ancient self

353) mahaakshah: The great-eyed

354) garudadhvajah: One who has Garuda on His flag

355) atulah: Incomparable

356) sharabhah: One who dwells and shines forth through the bodies

357) bheemah: The terrible

358) samayajnah: One whose worship is nothing more than keeping an equal vision of the mind by the devotee

359) havirharih: The receiver of all oblation

360) sarva-lakshana-lakshanyah: Known through all proofs

361) lakshmeevaan: The consort of Laksmi

362) samitinjayah: Ever-victorious

363) viksharah: Imperishable

364) rohitah: The fish incarnation

365) maargah: The path

366) hetuh: The cause

367) daamodarah: Whose stomach is marked with three lines

368) sahah: All-enduring

369) maheedharah: The bearer of the earth

370) mahaabhaago: He who gets the greates share in every Yajna

371) vegavaan: He who is swift

372) amitaashanah: Of endless appetite

373) udbhavah: The originator

374) kshobhanah: The agitator

375) devah: He who revels

376) shreegarbhah: He in whom are all glories

377) parameshvarah: The Supreme Lord

378) karanam: The instrument

379) kaaranam: The cause

380) kartaa: The doer

381) vikartaa: Creator of the endless varieties that make up the universe

382) gahanah: The unknowable

383) guhah: He who dwells in the cave of the heart

384) vyavasaayah: Resolute

385) vyavasthaanah: The substratum

386) samsthaanah: The ultimate authority

387) sthaanadah: He who confers the right abode

388) dhruvah: The changeless in the midst of changes

389) pararddhih: He who has supreme manifestations

390) paramaspashtah: The extremely vivid

391) tushtah: One who is contented with a very simple offering

392) pushtah: One who is ever-full

393) shubhekshanah: All-auspicious gaze

394) raamah: One who is most handsome

395) viraamah: The abode of perfect-rest

396) virajo: Passionless

397) maargah: The path

398) neyah: The guide

399) nayah: One who leads

400) anayah: One who has no leader

401) veerah: The valiant

402) shaktimataam-shresthah: The best among the powerful

403) dharmah: The law of being

404) dharmaviduttamah: The highest among men of realization

405) vaikunthah: One who prevents men from straying on wrong paths

406) purushah: One who dwells in all bodies

407) praanah: Life

408) praanadah: Giver of life

409) pranavah: He who is praised by the gods

410) prituh: The expanded

411) hiranyagarbhah: The creator

412) shatrughnah: The destroyer of enemies

413) vyaaptah: The pervader

414) vaayuh: The air

415) adhokshajah: One whose vitality never flows downwards

416) rituh: The seasons

417) sudarshanah: He whose meeting is auspicious

418) kaalah: He who judges and punishes beings

419) parameshthee: One who is readily available for experience within the heart

420) parigrahah: The receiver

421) ugrah: The terrible

422) samvatsarah: The year

423) dakshah: The smart

424) vishraamah: The resting place

425) vishva-dakshinah: The most skilful and efficient

426) vistaarah: The extension

427) sthaavarah-sthaanuh: The firm and motionless

428) pramaanam: The proof

429) beejamavyayam: The Immutable Seed

430) arthah: He who is worshiped by all

431) anarthah: One to whom there is nothing yet to be fulfilled

432) mahaakoshah: He who has got around him great sheaths

433) mahaabhogah: He who is of the nature of enjoyment

434) mahaadhanah: He who is supremely rich

435) anirvinnah: He who has no discontent

436) sthavishthah: One who is supremely huge

437) a-bhooh: One who has no birth

438) dharma-yoopah: The post to which all dharma is tied

439) mahaa-makhah: The great sacrificer
440) nakshatranemir: The nave of the stars
441) nakshatree: The Lord of the stars (the moon)
442) kshamah: He who is supremely efficient in all undertakings
443) kshaamah: He who ever remains without any scarcity
444) sameehanah: One whose desires are auspicious
445) yajnah: One who is of the nature of yajna
446) ijyah: He who is fit to be invoked through yajna
447) mahejyah: One who is to be most worshiped
448) kratuh: The animal-sacrifice
449) satram: Protector of the good
450) sataam-gatih: Refuge of the good
451) sarvadarshee: All-knower
452) vimuktaatmaa: The ever-liberated self
453) sarvajno: Omniscient
454) jnaanamuttamam: The Supreme Knowledge
455) suvratah: He who ever-perfoeming the pure vow
456) sumukhah: One who has a charming face
457) sookshmah: The subtlest
458) sughoshah: Of auspicious sound
459) sukhadah: Giver of happiness
460) suhrit: Friend of all creatures
461) manoharah: The stealer of the mind
462) jita-krodhah: One who has conquered anger
463) veerabaahur: Having mighty arms
464) vidaaranah: One who splits asunder
465) svaapanah: One who puts people to sleep
466) svavashah: He who has everything under His control
467) vyaapee: All-pervading
468) naikaatmaa: Many souled
469) naikakarmakrit: One who does many actions
470) vatsarah: The abode
471) vatsalah: The supremely affectionate
472) vatsee: The father
473) ratnagarbhah: The jewel-wombed
474) dhaneshvarah: The Lord of wealth
475) dharmagub: One who protects dharma
476) dharmakrit: One who acts according to dharma
477) dharmee: The supporter of dharma
478) sat: existence

479) asat: illusion

480) ksharam: He who appears to perish

481) aksharam: Imperishable

482) avijnaataa: The non-knower (The knower being the conditioned soul within the body)

483) sahasraamshur: The thousand-rayed

484) vidhaataa: All supporter

485) kritalakshanah: One who is famous for His qualities

486) gabhastinemih: The hub of the universal wheel

487) sattvasthah: Situated in sattva

488) simhah: The lion

489) bhoota-maheshvarah: The great lord of beings

490) aadidevah: The first deity

491) mahaadevah: The great deity

492) deveshah: The Lord of all devas

493) devabhrit-guruh: Advisor of Indra

494) uttarah: He who lifts us from the ocean of samsara

495) gopatih: The shepherd

496) goptaa: The protector

497) jnaanagamyah: One who is experienced through pure knowledge

498) puraatanah: He who was even before time

499) shareera-bhootabhrit: One who nourishes the nature from which the bodies came

500) bhoktaa: The enjoyer

501) kapeendrah: Lord of the monkeys (Rama)

502) bhooridakshinah: He who gives away large gifts

503) somapah: One who takes Soma in the yajnas

504) amritapah: One who drinks the nectar

505) somah: One who as the moon nourishes plants

506) purujit: One who has conquered numerous enemies

507) purusattamah: The greatest of the great

508) vinayah: He who humiliates those who are unrighteous

509) jayah: The victorious

510) satyasandhah: Of truthful resolution

511) daashaarhah: One who was born in the Dasarha race

512) saatvataam-patih: The Lord of the Satvatas

513) jeevah: One who functions as the ksetrajna

514) vinayitaa-saakshee: The witness of modesty

515) mukundah: The giver of liberation

516) amitavikramah: Of immeasurable prowess

517) ambho-nidhir: The substratum of the four types of beings

518) anantaatmaa: The infinite self

519) mahodadhishayah: One who rests on the great ocean

520) antakah: The death

521) ajah: Unborn

522) mahaarhah: One who deserves the highest worship

523) svaabhaavyah: Ever rooted in the nature of His own self

524) jitaamitrah: One who has conquered all enemies

525) pramodanah: Ever-blissful

526) aanandah: A mass of pure bliss

527) nandanah: One who makes others blissful

528) nandah: Free from all worldly pleasures

529) satyadharmaa: One who has in Himself all true dharmas

530) trivikramah: One who took three steps

531) maharshih kapilaachaaryah: He who incarnated as Kapila, the great
      sage

532) kritajnah: The knower of the creation

533) medineepatih: The Lord of the earth

534) tripadah: One who has taken three steps

535) tridashaadhyaksho: The Lord of the three states of consciousness

536) mahaashringah: Great-horned (Matsya)

537) kritaantakrit: Destroyer of the creation

538) mahaavaraaho: The great boar

539) govindah: One who is known through Vedanta

540) sushenah: He who has a charming army

541) kanakaangadee: Wearer of bright-as-gold armlets

542) guhyo: The mysterious

543) gabheerah: The unfathomable

544) gahano: Impenetrable

545) guptah: The well-concealed

546) chakra-gadaadharah: Bearer of the disc and mace

547) vedhaah: Creator of the universe

548) svaangah: One with well-proportioned limbs

549) ajitah: Vanquished by none

550) krishnah: Dark-complexioned

551) dridhah: The firm

552) sankarshanochyutah: He who absorbs the whole creation into His
      nature and never falls away from that nature

553) varunah: One who sets on the horizon (Sun)

554) vaarunah: The son of Varuna (Vasistha or Agastya)

555) vrikshah: The tree
556) pushkaraakshah: Lotus eyed
557) mahaamanaah: Great-minded
558) bhagavaan: One who possesses six opulences
559) bhagahaa: One who destroys the six opulences during pralaya
560) aanandee: One who gives delight
561) vanamaalee: One who wears a garland of forest flowers
562) halaayudhah: One who has a plough as His weapon
563) aadityah: Son of Aditi
564) jyotiraadityah: The resplendence of the sun
565) sahishnuh: One who calmly endures duality
566) gatisattamah: The ultimate refuge for all devotees
567) sudhanvaa: One who has Shaarnga
568) khanda-parashur: One who holds an axe
569) daarunah: Merciless towards the unrighteous
570) dravinapradah: One who lavishly gives wealth
571) divah-sprik: Sky-reaching
572) sarvadrik-vyaaso: One who creates many men of wisdom
573) vaachaspatir-ayonijah: One who is the master of all vidyas and who is unborn through a womb
574) trisaamaa: One who is glorified by Devas, Vratas and Saamans
575) saamagah: The singer of the sama songs
576) saama: The Sama Veda
577) nirvaanam: All-bliss
578) bheshajam: Medicine
579) bhishak: Physician
580) samnyaasa-krit: Institutor of sannyasa
581) samah: Calm
582) shaantah: Peaceful within
583) nishthaa: Abode of all beings
584) shaantih: One whose very nature is peace
585) paraayanam: The way to liberation
586) shubhaangah: One who has the most beautiful form
587) shaantidah: Giver of peace
588) shrashtaa: Creator of all beings
589) kumudah: He who delights in the earth
590) kuvaleshayah: He who reclines in the waters
591) gohitah: One who does welfare for cows
592) gopatih: Husband of the earth
593) goptaa: Protector of the universe

594) vrishabhaaksho: One whose eyes rain fulfilment of desires

595) vrishapriyah: One who delights in dharma

596) anivartee: One who never retreats

597) nivrittaatmaa: One who is fully restrained from all sense indulgences

598) samksheptaa: The involver

599) kshemakrit: Doer of good

600) shivah: Auspiciousness

601) shreevatsa-vakshaah: One who has sreevatsa on His chest

602) shrevaasah: Abode of Sree

603) shreepatih: Lord of Laksmi

604) shreemataam varah: The best among glorious

605) shreedah: Giver of opulence

606) shreeshah: The Lord of Sree

607) shreenivaasah: One who dwells in the good people

608) shreenidhih: The treasure of Sree

609) shreevibhaavanah: Distributor of Sree

610) shreedharah: Holder of Sree

611) shreekarah: One who gives Sree

612) shreyah: Liberation

613) shreemaan: Possessor of Sree

614) loka-trayaashrayah: Shelter of the three worlds

615) svakshah: Beautiful-eyed

616) svangah: Beautiful-limbed

617) shataanandah: Of infinite varieties and joys

618) nandih: Infinite bliss

619) jyotir-ganeshvarah: Lord of the luminaries in the cosmos

620) vijitaatmaa: One who has conquered the sense organs

621) vidheyaatmaa: One who is ever available for the devotees to command in love

622) sat-keertih: One of pure fame

623) chinnasamshayah: One whose doubts are ever at rest

624) udeernah: The great transcendent

625) sarvatah-chakshuh: One who has eyes everywhere

626) aneeshah: One who has none to Lord over Him

627) shaashvata-sthirah: One who is eternal and stable

628) bhooshayah: One who rested on the ocean shore (Rama)

629) bhooshanah: One who adorns the world

630) bhootih: One who is pure existence

631) vishokah: Sorrowless

632) shoka-naashanah: Destroyer of sorrows

633) archishmaan: The effulgent

634) architah: One who is constantly worshipped by His devotees

635) kumbhah: The pot within whom everything is contained

636) vishuddhaatmaa: One who has the purest soul

637) vishodhanah: The great purifier

638) anniruddhah: He who is invincible by any enemy

639) apratirathah: One who has no enemies to threaten Him

640) pradyumnah: Very rich

641) amitavikramah: Of immeasurable prowess

642) kaalanemi-nihaa: Slayer of Kalanemi

643) veerah: The heroic victor

644) shauri: One who always has invincible prowess

645) shoora-janeshvarah: Lord of the valiant

646) trilokaatmaa: The self of the three worlds

647) trilokeshah: The Lord of the three worlds

648) keshavah: One whose rays illumine the cosmos

649) keshihaa: Killer of Kesi

650) harih: The destroyer

651) kaamadevah: The beloved Lord

652) kaamapaalah: The fulfiller of desires

653) kaamee: One who has fulfilled all His desires

654) kaantah: Of enchanting form

655) kritaagamah: The author of the agama scriptures

656) anirdeshya-vapuh: Of Indescribable form

657) vishnuh: All-pervading

658) veerah: The courageous

659) anantah: Endless

660) dhananjayah: One who gained wealth through conquest

661) brahmanyah: Protector of Brahman (anything related to Narayana)

662) brahmakrit: One who acts in Brahman

663) brahmaa: Creator

664) brahma: Biggest

665) brahma-vivardhanah: One who increases the Brahman

666) brahmavid: One who knows Brahman

667) braahmanah: One who has realized Brahman

668) brahmee: One who is with Brahma

669) brahmajno: One who knows the nature of Brahman

670) braahmana-priyah: Dear to the brahmanas

671) mahaakramo: Of great step

672) mahaakarmaa: One who performs great deeds

673) mahaatejaah: One of great resplendence

674) mahoragah: The great serpent

675) mahaakratuh: The great sacrifice

676) mahaayajvaa: One who performed great yajnas

677) mahaayajnah: The great yajna

678) mahaahavih: The great offering

679) stavyah: One who is the object of all praise

680) stavapriyah: One who is invoked through prayer

681) stotram: The hymn

682) stutih: The act of praise

683) stotaa: One who adores or praises

684) ranapriyah: Lover of battles

685) poornah: The complete

686) poorayitaa: The fulfiller

687) punyah: The truly holy

688) punya-keertir: Of Holy fame

689) anaamayah: One who has no diseases

690) manojavah: Swift as the mind

691) teerthakaro: The teacher of the tirthas

692) vasuretaah: He whose essence is golden

693) vasupradah: The free-giver of wealth

694) vasupradah: The giver of salvation, the greatest wealth

695) vaasudevo: The son of Vasudeva

696) vasuh: The refuge for all

697) vasumanaah: One who is attentive to everything

698) havih: The oblation

699) sadgatih: The goal of good people

700) satkritih: One who is full of Good actions

701) satta: One without a second

702) sadbhootih: One who has rich glories

703) satparaayanah: The Supreme goal for the good

704) shoorasenah: One who has heroic and valiant armies

705) yadu-shresthah: The best among the Yadava clan

706) sannivaasah: The abode of the good

707) suyaamunah: One who attended by the people who dwell on the banks
        of Yamuna

708) bhootaavaaso: The dwelling place of the elements

709) vaasudevah: One who envelops the world with Maya

710) sarvaasunilayah: The abode of all life energies

711) analah: One of unlimited wealth, power and glory

712) darpahaa: The destroyer of pride in evil-minded people
713) darpadah: One who creates pride, or an urge to be the best, among the righteous
714) driptah: One whio is drunk with Infinite bliss
715) durdharah: The object of contemplation
716) athaaparaajitah: The unvanquished
717) vishvamoortih: Of the form of the entire Universe
718) mahaamortir: The great form
719) deeptamoortir: Of resplendent form
720) a-moortirmaan: Having no form
721) anekamoortih: Multi-formed
722) avyaktah: Unmanifeset
723) shatamoortih: Of many forms
724) shataananah: Many-faced
725) ekah: The one
726) naikah: The many
727) savah: The nature of the sacrifice
728) kah: One who is of the nature of bliss
729) kim: What (the one to be inquired into)
730) yat: Which
731) tat: That
732) padam-anuttamam: The unequalled state of perfection
733) lokabandhur: Friend of the world
734) lokanaathah: Lord of the world
735) maadhavah: Born in the family of Madhu
736) bhaktavatsalah: One who loves His devotees
737) suvarna-varnah: Golden-colored
738) hemaangah: One who has limbs of gold
739) varaangah: With beautiful limbs
740) chandanaangadee: One who has attractive armlets
741) veerahaa: Destroyer of valiant heroes
742) vishama: Unequalled
743) shoonyah: The void
744) ghritaaseeh: One who has no need for good wishes
745) acalah: Non-moving
746) chalah: Moving
747) amaanee: Without false vanity
748) maanadah: One who causes, by His maya, false identification with the body
749) maanyah: One who is to be honored

750) lokasvaamee: Lord of the universe

751) trilokadhrik: One who is the support of all the three worlds

752) sumedhaa: One who has pure intelligence

753) medhajah: Born out of sacrifices

754) dhanyah: Fortunate

755) satyamedhah: One whose intelligence never fails

756) dharaadharah: The sole support of the earth

757) tejovrisho: One who showers radiance

758) dyutidharah: One who bears an effulgent form

759) sarva-shastra-bhritaam-varah: The best among those who wield weapons

760) pragrahah: Receiver of worship

761) nigrahah: The killer

762) vyagrah: One who is ever engaged in fulfilling the devotee's desires

763) naikashringah: One who has many horns

764) gadaagrajah: One who is invoked through mantra

765) chaturmoortih: Four-formed

766) chaturbaahuh: Four-handed

767) chaturvyoohah: One who expresses Himself as the dynamic center in the four vyoohas

768) chaturgatih: The ultimate goal of all four varnas and asramas

769) chaturaatmaa: Clear-minded

770) chaturbhaavas: The source of the four

771) chatur-vedavid: Knower of all four vedas

772) ekapaat: One-footed (BG 10.42)

773) samaavartah: The efficient turner

774) nivrittaatmaa: One whose mind is turned away from sense indulgence

775) durjayah: The invincible

776) duratikramah: One who is difficult to be disobeyed

777) durlabhah: One who obtained with effort

778) durgamah: One who is realized with great effort

779) durgah: Not easy to storm into

780) duraavaasah: Not easy to lodge

781) duraarihaa: Slayer of the asuras

782) shubhaangah: One with enchanting limbs

783) lokasaarangah: One who understands the universe

784) sutantuh: Beautifully expanded

785) tantu-vardhanah: One who sustains the continuity of the drive for the family

786) indrakarmaa: One who always performs gloriously auspicious actions

787) mahaakarmaa: One who accomplishes great acts

788) kritakarmaa: One who has fulfilled his acts

789) kritaagamah: Author of the Vedas

790) udbhavah: The ultimate source

791) sundarah: Of unrivalled beauty

792) sundah: Of great mercy

793) ratna-naabhah: Of beautiful navel

794) sulochanah: One who has the most enchanting eyes

795) arkah: One who is in the form of the sun

796) vaajasanah: The giver of food

797) shringee: The horned one

798) jayantah: The conquerer of all enemies

799) sarvavij-jayee: One who is at once omniscient and victorious

800) suvarna-binduh: With limbs radiant like gold

801) akshobhyah: One who is ever unruffled

802) sarva-vaageeshvareshvarah: Lord of the Lord of speech

803) mahaahradah: One who is like a great refreshing swimming pool

804) mahaagartah: The great chasm

805) mahaabhootah: The great being

806) mahaanidhih: The great abode

807) kumudah: One who gladdens the earth

808) kundarah: The one who lifted the earth

809) kundah: One who is as attractive as Kunda flowers

810) parjanyah: He who is similar to rain-bearing clouds

811) paavanah: One who ever purifies

812) anilah: One who never slips

813) amritaashah: One whose desires are never fruitless

814) amritavapuh: He whose form is immortal

815) sarvajna: Omniscient

816) sarvato-mukhah: One who has His face turned everywhere

817) sulabhah: One who is readily available

818) suvratah: One who has taken the most auspicious forms

819) siddhah: One who is perfection

820) shatrujit: One who is ever victorious over His hosts of enemies

821) shatrutaapanah: The scorcher of enemies

822) nyagrodhah: The one who veils Himself with Maya

823) udumbarah: Nourishment of all living creatures

824) ashvattas: Tree of life

825) chaanooraandhra-nishoodanah: The slayer of Canura

826) sahasraarchih: He who has thousands of rays

827) saptajihvah: He who expresses himself as the seven tongues of fire
    (Or types of agni)
828) saptaidhaah: The seven effulgences in the flames
829) saptavaahanah: One who has a vehicle of seven horses (sun)
830) amoortih: Formless
831) anaghah: Sinless
832) acintyo: Inconceivable
833) bhayakrit: Giver of fear
834) bhayanaashanah: Destroyer of fear
835) anuh: The subtlest
836) brihat: The greatest
837) krishah: Delicate, lean
838) sthoolah: One who is the fattest
839) gunabhrit: One who supports
840) nirgunah: Without any properties
841) mahaan: The mighty
842) adhritah: Without support
843) svadhritah: Self-supported
844) svaasyah: One who has an effulgent face
845) praagvamshah: One who has the most ancient ancestry
846) vamshavardhanah: He who multiplies His family of descendents
847) bhaarabhrit: One who carries the load of the universe
848) kathitah: One who is glorified in all scriptures
849) yogee: One who can be realized through yoga
850) yogeeshah: The king of yogis
851) sarvakaamadah: One who fulfils all desires of true devotees
852) aashramah: Haven
853) shramanah: One who persecutes the worldly people
854) kshaamah: One who destroys everything
855) suparnah: The golden leaf (Vedas) BG 15.1
856) vaayuvaahanah: The mover of the winds
857) dhanurdharah: The wielder of the bow
858) dhanurvedah: One who declared the science of archery
859) dandah: One who punishes the wicked
860) damayitaa: The controller
861) damah: Beautitude in the self
862) aparaajitah: One who cannot be defeated
863) sarvasahah: One who carries the entire Universe
864) aniyantaa: One who has no controller
865) niyamah: One who is not under anyone's laws

866) ayamah: One who knows no death

867) sattvavaan: One who is full of exploits and courage

868) saattvikah: One who is full of sattvic qualities

869) satyah: Truth

870) satya-dharma-paraayanah: One who is the very abode of truth and dharma

871) abhipraayah: One who is faced by all seekers marching to the infinite

872) priyaarhah: One who deserves all our love

873) arhah: One who deserves to be worshiped

874) priyakrit: One who is ever-obliging in fulfilling our wishes

875) preetivardhanah: One who increases joy in the devotee's heart

876) vihaayasa-gatih: One who travels in space

877) jyotih: Self-effulgent

878) suruchih: Whose desire manifests as the universe

879) hutabhuk: One who enjoys all that is offered in yajna

880) vibhuh: All-pervading

881) ravih: One who dries up everything

882) virochanah: One who shines in different forms

883) sooryah: The one source from where everything is born

884) savitaa: The one who brings forth the Universe from Himself

885) ravilochanah: One whose eye is the sun

886) anantah: Endless

887) hutabhuk: One who accepts oblations

888) bhoktaaA: One who enjoys

889) sukhadah: Giver of bliss to those who are liberated

890) naikajah: One who is born many times

891) agrajah: The first-born

892) anirvinnah: One who feels no disappointment

893) sadaamarshee: One who forgives the trespasses of His devotees

894) lokaadhishthaanam: The substratum of the universe

895) adbhutah: Wonderful

896) sanaat: The beginningless and endless factor

897) sanaatanatamah: The most ancient

898) kapilah: The great sage Kapila

899) kapih: One who drinks water

900) apyayah: The one in whom the universe merges

901) svastidah: Giver of Svasti

902) svastikrit: One who robs all auspiciousness

903) svasti: One who is the source of all auspiciousness

904) svastibhuk: One who constantly enjoys auspiciousness

905) svastidakshinah: Distributor of auspiciousness

906) araudrah: One who has no negative emotions or urges

907) kundalee: One who wears shark earrings

908) chakree: Holder of the chakra

909) vikramee: The most daring

910) oorjita-shaasanah: One who commands with His hand

911) shabdaatigah: One who transcends all words

912) shabdasahah: One who allows Himself to be invoked by Vedic declarations

913) shishirah: The cold season, winter

914) sharvaree-karah: Creator of darkness

915) akroorah: Never cruel

916) peshalah: One who is supremely soft

917) dakshah: Prompt

918) dakshinah: The most liberal

919) kshaminaam-varah: One who has the greatest amount of patience with sinners

920) vidvattamah: One who has the greatest wisdom

921) veetabhayah: One with no fear

922) punya-shravana-keertanah: The hearing of whose glory causes holiness to grow

923) uttaaranah: One who lifts us out of the ocean of change

924) dushkritihaa: Destroyer of bad actions

925) punyah: Supremely pure

926) duh-svapna-naashanah: One who destroys all bad dreams

927) veerahaa: One who ends the passage from womb to womb

928) rakshanah: Protector of the universe

929) santah: One who is expressed through saintly men

930) jeevanah: The life spark in all creatures

931) paryavasthitah: One who dwells everywhere

932) anantaroopah: One of infinite forms

933) anantashreeh: Full of infinite glories

934) jitamanyuh: One who has no anger

935) bhayapahah: One who destroys all fears

936) chaturashrah: One who deals squarely

937) gabheeraatmaa: Too deep to be fathomed

938) vidishah: One who is unique in His giving

939) vyaadishah: One who is unique in His commanding power

940) dishah: One who advises and gives knowledge

941) anaadih: One who is the first cause

942) bhoor-bhuvo: The substratum of the earth

943) lakshmeeh: The glory of the universe

944) suveerah: One who moves through various ways

945) ruchiraangadah: One who wears resplendent shoulder caps

946) jananah: He who delivers all living creatures

947) jana-janmaadir: The cause of the birth of all creatures

948) bheemah: Terrible form

949) bheema-paraakramah: One whose prowess is fearful to His enemies

950) aadhaaranilayah: The fundamental sustainer

951) adhaataa: Above whom there is no other to command

952) pushpahaasah: He who shines like an opening flower

953) prajaagarah: Ever-awakened

954) oordhvagah: One who is on top of everything

955) satpathaachaarah: One who walks the path of truth

956) praanadah: Giver of life

957) pranavah: Omkara

958) panah: The supreme universal manager

959) pramaanam: He whose form is the Vedas

960) praananilayah: He in whom all prana is established

961) praanibhrit: He who rules over all pranas

962) praanajeevanah: He who maintains the life-breath in all living creatures

963) tattvam: The reality

964) tattvavit: One who has realized the reality

965) ekaatmaa: The one self

966) janma-mrityu-jaraatigah: One who knows no birth, death or old age in Himself

967) bhoor-bhuvah svas-taruh: The tree of bhur, bhuvah and svah

968) taarah: One who helps all to cross over

969) savitaa: The father of all

970) prapitaamahah: The father of the father of beings (Brahma)

971) yajnah: One whose very nature is yajna

972) yajnapatih: The Lord of all yajnas

973) yajvaa: The one who performs yajna

974) yajnaangah: One whose limbs are the things employed in yajna

975) yajnavaahanah: One who fulfils yajnas in complete

976) yajnabhrid: The ruler of the yajanas

977) yajnakrit: One who performs yajna

978) yajnee: Enjoyer of yajnas

979) yajnabhuk: Receiver of all that is offered

980) yajnasaadhanah: One who fulfils all yajnas

981) yajnaantakrit: One who performs the concluding act of the yajna

982) yajnaguhyam: The person to be realized by yajna

983) annam: One who is food

984) annaadah: One who eats the food

985) aatmayonih: The uncaused cause

986) svayamjaatah: Self-born

987) vaikhaanah: The one who cut through the earth

988) saamagaayanah: One who sings the sama songs

989) devakee-nandanah: Son of Devaki

990) srashtaa: Creator

991) kshiteeshah: The Lord of the earth

992) paapa-naashanah: Destroyer of sin

993) samkha-bhrit: One who has the divine Pancajanya

994) nandakee: One who holds the Nandaka sword

995) chakree: Carrier of Sudarsana

996) shaarnga-dhanvaa: One who aims His shaarnga bow

997) gadaadharah: Carrier of Kaumodakee club

998) rathaanga-paanih: One who has the wheel of a chariot as His weapon

999) akshobhyah: One who cannot be annoyed by anyone

1000) sarva-praharanaayudhah: He who has all implements for all kinds of
            assault and fight

CONCLUSION

Connecting to the Mantra

After going through the mantras and *stotras* and utilizing the ones you like, you may want to get mote out of your practice. That means you need to go deeper.

Connecting deeply to the sound vibrations within the mantras, prayers, or *stotras* that have been provided in this book, a person can effectively and positively change his or her consciousness and spiritual awareness. However, whenever you feel you have not or cannot connect to the mantra, or to yourself, or to the Supreme, then you must go deeper. That is the most common difficulty, and the most common solution. You must allow the sound and vibration of the mantra to take over all of your concentration, absorption and awareness.

There is a whole new world within the mantra, a whole universe, an unlimited realm waiting to be revealed. The mantra is the doorway, the mantra is the path that can reveal this, and finally you will see that the mantra is the vibration, the frequency within which is the Divine Himself (or Herself, depending on the object of the mantra). By going deep within the mantra, you can go deep into this perception, and into the unlimited, and the experience of the unfathomable bliss.

How deep you go is up to you. But as it is with any relationship, the key to closeness, to intimacy is the depth of communication that exists between the subjects, such as between man and wife. Similarly, the deeper you go into the vibration of the mantra, and the mood of the prayer or stotra, the deeper is the communication you develop between you and the Divine. Thus, the deeper becomes the reciprocation between you and the Supreme, until the Supreme reveals all you can perceive, depending on your qualification, which depends on your sincerity, and eagerness to know and get closer to the Supreme.

For example, Krishna is known as the God of love. Thus, the more you want to love, the more you have to reach the Source of all love, and the more He will love you back. But you must go deep within, free of all mental and bodily interpretations of love. It must be purely spiritual, and you will then know a love, a happiness, a bliss which is beyond measure. It is waiting for you.

The mantra is the doorway, the guide, the path, the means, and a vehicle to the goal, but is also the Divine Light itself, which will be revealed to you if you enter into it deeply enough, as in a complete meditation reaching *dhyana* or *samadhi*. Our ultimate rest, our ultimate completion is to reach the shelter of the soothing warmth of Krishna's love. This is far beyond mere self-realization, but the way to directly enter into those loving pastimes.

In summary, the mantra opens our mind and hearts to perceive higher levels of existence, the higher dimension, leading us all the way into the spiritual realm. The mantra, when chanted with pure intent, takes you beyond the mind and senses. It reaches and opens the soul itself and then connects it with the Supreme, the Divine. When our devotion reaches the Divine, it becomes amplified and is sent back to you in the form of Supreme love, in which the soul explodes in Divine bliss wherein it is aware of nothing else. This is the goal of *samadhi*. The secret to reaching this is to be sincere, follow the instructions or your guru or guide who knows this path, go deeper within you and within the mantra, and never give up. This, of course, is the highest aspect and purpose of chanting mantras.

GLOSSARY

Acarya--the spiritual master who sets the proper standard by his own example.

Advaita--nondual, meaning that the Absolute Truth is one, and that there is no individuality between the Supreme Being and the individual souls which merge into oneness, the Brahman, when released from material existence. The philosophy taught by Sankaracharya.

Agni--fire, or Agni the demigod of fire.

Agnihotra--the Vedic sacrifice in which offerings were made to the fire, such as ghee, milk, sesame seeds, grains, etc. The demigod Agni would deliver the offerings to the demigods that are referred to in the ritual.

Ahankara--false ego, identification with matter.

Ahimsa--nonviolence.

Airavateshvara--Shiva as Lord of the heavenly elephant.

Akarma--actions which cause no *karmic* reactions.

Akasha--the ether, or etheric plane; a subtle material element in which sound travels.

Amba, Ambika--name of Mother Durga.

Amrita--the nectar of immortality derived from churning the ocean of milk.

Amriteshvara--Shiva as Lord of Ambrosia.

Ananda--spiritual bliss.

Ananta--unlimited.

Annapurna--Parvati, a name meaning Filled with Food.

Aranyaka--sacred writings that are supposed to frame the essence of the *Upanishads.*

Arati--the ceremony of worship when incense and ghee lamps are offered to the Deities.

Arca-vigraha--the worshipable Deity form of the Lord made of stone, wood, etc.

Ardhanarishvara--Shiva as half Shiva and half Parvati.

Aryan--a noble person, one who is on the Vedic path of spiritual advancement.

Asana--postures for meditation, or exercises for developing the body into a fit instrument for spiritual advancement.

Asat--that which is temporary.

Ashrama--one of the four orders of spiritual life, such as *brahmacari* (celibate student), *grihastha* (married householder), *vanaprastha* (retired stage), and *sannyasa* (renunciate); or the abode of a spiritual teacher or *sadhu.*

Ashvamedha--a Vedic ritual involving offerings to God made by brahmana priests.

Astanga-yoga--the eightfold path of mystic yoga.

Asura--one who is ungodly or a demon.

Atma--the self or soul. Sometimes means the body, mind, and senses.

Atman--usually referred to as the Supreme Self.

Avatara--an incarnation of the Lord who descends from the spiritual world.

711

Avidya--ignorance or nescience.

Aum--*om* or *pranava*

Ayodhya--the birthplace of Lord Rama in East India.

Ayurveda--the original wholistic form of medicine as described in the Vedic literature.

Babaji--wandering mendicant holy man.

Bhagavan--one who possesses all opulences, God.

Bhairava--Shiva as the terrifying destroyer.

Bhajan--song of worship.

Bhajan kutir--a small dwelling used for one's worship and meditation.

Bhakta--a devotee of the Lord who is engaged in *bhakti-yoga*.

Bhakti--love and devotion for God.

Bhakti-yoga--the path of offering pure devotional service to the Supreme.

Bhava--preliminary stage of love of God.

Bhavani--name of Parvati.

Bhikshatanamurti--Shiva as a wandering beggar.

Bhu, Bhumidevi--Earth, a goddess associated with Vishnu.

Bhutanatha--Shiva as Lord of the *bhutas*, ghosts.

Bhuvaneshvari--Parvati as Ruler of the World.

Brahma--the demigod of creation who was born from Lord Vishnu, the first created living being and the engineer of the secondary stage of creation of the universe when all the living entities were manifested.

Brahmacari--a celebate student, usually five to twenty-five years of age, who is trained by the spiritual master. One of the four divisions or *ashramas* of spiritual life.

Brahmajyoti--the great white light or effulgence which emanates from the body of the Lord.

Brahmaloka--the highest planet or plane of existence in the universe; the planet where Lord Brahma lives.

Brahman--the spiritual energy; the all-pervading impersonal aspect of the Lord; or the Supreme Lord Himself.

Brahmana or brahmin--one of the four orders of society; the intellectual class of men who have been trained in the knowledge of the *Vedas* and initiated by a spiritual master.

Brahmana--the supplemental books of the four primary *Vedas*. They usually contained instructions for performing Vedic *agnihotras*, chanting the *mantras*, the purpose of the rituals, etc. The *Aitareya* and *Kaushitaki Brahmanas* belong to the *Rig-veda*, the *Satapatha Brahmana* belongs to the *White Yajur-veda*, and the *Taittiriya Brahmana* belongs to the *Black Yajur-veda*. The *Praudha* and *Shadvinsa Brahmanas* are two of the eight *Brahmanas* belonging to the *Atharva-veda*.

Buddha--Lord Buddha or a learned man.

Caitanya-caritamrta--the scripture by Krishnadasa Kaviraja which explains the teachings and pastimes of Lord Chaitanya Mahaprabhu.

Candala--a person in the lowest class, or dog-eater.

Chaitanya Mahaprabhu--the most recent incarnation of the Lord who appeared in
    the 15th century in Bengal and who originally started the *sankirtana*
    movement, based on congregational chanting of the holy names.

Chakra--a wheel, disk, or psychic energy center situated along the spinal column
    in the subtle body of the physical shell.

Chandra--the moon.

Chandrashekara--Shiva as Moon Crested.

Chhandas--sacred hymns of the *Atharva-veda*.

Chaturbhuja--Shiva as Four-armed.

Chitragupta--name of Surya, the demigod of the sun.

Chit--eternal knowledge.

Darshan--the devotional act of seeing and being seen by the Deity in the temple.

Dakshinamurti--Shiva as teacher of yoga and universal knowledge.

Dasara--the ten-day festival in September-October when Durga is worshiped and
    the victory of Lord Rama over the demon Ravana is celebrated.

Dashavatara--the ten incarnations of Lord Vishnu: Matsya, Kurma, Varaha,
    Narasimha, Vamana, Parashurama, Rama, Krishna, Buddha, and Kalki.

Deity--the *arca-vigraha*, or worshipful form of the Divinity in the temple.

Deva--a demigod, or higher being.

Devaloka--the higher planets or planes of existence of the devas.

Devaki--the devotee who acted as Lord Krishna's mother.

Devas--demigods or heavenly beings from higher levels of material existence, or
    a godly person.

Dham--a holy place.

Dharma--the essential nature or duty of the living being.

Diksha--spiritual initiation.

Dualism--as related in this book, it refers to the Supreme as both an impersonal
    force (Brahman) as well as the Supreme Person.

Durga--the form of Parvati, Shiva's wife, as a warrior goddess known by many
    names according to her deeds, such as Simhavahini when riding her
    lion, Mahishasuramardini for killing the demon Mahishasura,
    Jagaddhatri as the mother of the universe, Kali when she killed the
    demon Raktavija, Tara when killing Shumba, etc. She assumes or
    incarnates in as many as 64 different forms, depending on her activities.
    Dvapara-yuga--the third age which lasts 864,000 years.

Dwaita--dualism, the principle that the Absolute Truth consists of the infinite
    Supreme Being along with the infinitesimal, individual souls.

Gana--Shiva's dwarf attendants.

Ganapati--Ganesh as Lord of the *ganas*.

Gandharvas--the celestial angel-like beings who have beautiful forms and
    voices, and are expert in dance and music, capable of becoming
    invisible and can help souls on the earthly plane.

Ganesh--a son of Shiva, said to destroy obstacles (as Vinayaka) and offer good
    luck to those who petition him. It is generally accepted that the way
    Ganesh got the head of an elephant is that one time Parvati asked him to

guard her residence. When Shiva wanted to enter, Ganesh stopped him, which made Shiva very angry. Not recognizing Ganesh, Shiva chopped off his head, which was then destroyed by one of Shiva's goblin associates. Parvati was so upset when she learned what had happened, Shiva, not being able to find Ganesh's original head, took the head of the first creature he saw, which was an elephant, and put it on the body of Ganesh and brought him back to life. The large mouse carrier of Ganesh symbolizes Ganesh's ability to destroy all obstacles, as rodents can gradually gnaw their way through most anything.

Ganges--the sacred and spiritual river which, according to the *Vedas*, runs throughout the universe, a portion of which is seen in India. The reason the river is considered holy is that it is said to be a drop of the Karana Ocean outside of the universe that leaked in when Lord Vishnu, in His incarnation as Vamanadeva, kicked a small hole in the universal shell with His toe. Thus, the water is spiritual as well as being purified by the touch of Lord Vishnu.

Garbhodakasayi Vishnu--the expansion of Lord Vishnu who enters into each universe.

Garuda--Lord Vishnu's bird carrier.

Gaudiya--a part of India sometimes called Aryavarta or land of the Aryans, located south of the Himalayas and north of the Vindhya Hills.

Gaudiya *sampradaya*--the school of Vaishnavism founded by Sri Caitanya.

Gauri--name of Parvati meaning Fair One.

Gaurishankara--Shiva and Parvati together.

Gayatri--the spiritual vibration or *mantra* from which the other *Vedas* were expanded and which is chanted by those who are initiated as *brahmanas* and given the spiritual understanding of Vedic philosophy.

Goloka Vrindavana--the name of Lord Krishna's spiritual planet.

Gopuram--the tall ornate towers that mark the gates to the temples, often found in south India.

Gosvami--one who is master of the senses.

Govardhana-shila--a sacred stone from Govardhana Hill, considered as a direct form or expansion of Lord Krishna.

Govinda--a name of Krishna which means one who gives pleasure to the cows and senses.

Govindaraja--Krishna as Lord of the Cowherds.

Grihastha--the householder order of life. One of the four *ashramas* in spiritual life.

Gunas--the modes of material nature of which there is *sattva* (goodness), *rajas* (passion), and *tamas* (ignorance).

Guru--a spiritual master.

Hanuman--the popular monkey servant of Lord Rama.

Hare--the Lord's pleasure potency, Radharani, who is approached for accessibility to the Lord.

Hari--a name of Krishna as the one who takes away one's obstacles on the
    spiritual path.

Haribol--a word that means to chant the name of the Lord, Hari.

Harinam--refers to the name of the Lord, Hari.

Har Ki Pauri--the holy bathing *ghats* in Hardwar where the Ganges leaves the
    mountains and enters the plains. It is at this spot where the Kumbha
    Mela is held every twelve years.

Hatha-yoga--a part of the yoga system which stresses various sitting postures
    and exercises.

Hayagriva--Lord Vishnu as the giver of knowledge.

Hiranyagarbha--another name of Brahma who was born of Vishnu in the
    primordial waters within the egg of the universe.

Hiranyakashipu--the demon king who was killed by Lord Vishnu in His
    incarnation as Narasimha.

Hrishikesa--a name for Krishna which means the master of the senses.

Impersonalism--the view that God has no personality or form, but is only an
    impersonal force (Brahman) which the individual souls merge back into
    when released from material existence.

Impersonalist--those who believe God has no personality or form.

Incarnation--the taking on of a body or form.

Indra--the King of heaven and controller of rain, who by his great power
    conquers the forces of darkness.

Jagadambi--Parvati as Mother of the World.

Jagannatha----Krishna as Lord of the Universe, especially as worshipped in
    Jagannatha Puri.

Jagat Kishora--name of Krishna.

Jai or *Jaya*--a term meaning victory, all glories.

Japa--the chanting one performs, usually softly, for one's own meditation.

Japa-mala--the string of beads one uses for chanting.

Jiva--the individual soul or living being.

Jivanmukta--a liberated soul, though still in the material body and universe.

Jiva-shakti--the living force.

Jnana--knowledge which may be material or spiritual.

Kailash--Shiva's mountain home.

Kala--eternal time, Yama.

Kali--the demigoddess who is the fierce form of the wife of Lord Shiva. The
    word *kali* comes from *kala*, the Sanskrit word for time: the power that
    dissolves or destroys everything.

Kali-yuga--the fourth and present age, the age of quarrel and confusion, which
    lasts 432,000 years and began 5,000 years ago.

Kalki--future incarnation of Lord Vishnu who appears at the end of Kali-yuga.

Kalpa--a day in the life of Lord Brahma which lasts a thousand cycles of the four
    yugas.

Kama--lust or inordinate desire.

Kapila--an incarnation of Lord Krishna who propagated the Sankhya philosophy.

Karanodakasayi Vishnu (Maha-Vishnu)--the expansion of Lord Krishna who
    created all the material universes.
Karma--material actions performed in regard to developing one's position or for
    future results which produce *karmic* reactions. It is also the reactions
    one endures from such fruitive activities.
Karma-kanda--the portion of the *Vedas* which primarily deals with
    recommended fruitive activities for various results.
Karma-yoga--system of yoga for using one's activities for spiritual advancement.
Karmi--the fruitive worker, one who accumulates more *karma*.
Karttikeya--son of Shiva and Parvati, also known as Skanda, Subramanya,
    Kumara, or son of the Pleiades (Krittika constellation).
Keshava--Krishna with long hair.
Kirtana--chanting or singing the glories of the Lord.
Krishna--the name of the original Supreme Personality of Godhead which means
    the most attractive and greatest pleasure. He is the source of all other
    incarnations, such as Vishnu, Rama, Narasimha, Narayana, Buddha,
    Parashurama, Vamanadeva, Kalki at the end of Kali-yuga, etc.
Krishnaloka--the spiritual planet where Lord Krishna resides.
Kshatriya--the second class of *varna* of society, or occupation of administrative
    or protective service, such as warrior or military personnel.
Ksirodakasayi Vishnu--the Supersoul expansion of the Lord who enters into each
    atom and the heart of each individual.
Kuvera--the pot bellied chief of the *yakshas*, and keeper of earth's treasures.
Kurma--incarnation of Vishnu as a tortoise.
Lakshmi--the goddess of fortune and wife of Lord Vishnu.
Lila--pastimes.
Lilavataras--the many incarnations of God who appear to display various
    spiritual pastimes to attract the conditioned souls in the material world.
Linga--the formless symbol of Lord Shiva, often represents universal space.
Madana-mohana--name of Krishna as one who fills the mind with love.
Madhava--Krishna.
Mahabhagavata--a great devotee of the Lord.
Mahabharata--the great epic of the Pandavas, which includes the *Bhagavad-
    gita*, by Vyasadeva.
Maha-mantra--the best *mantra* for self-realization in this age, called the Hare
    Krishna *mantra*.
Mahatma--a great soul or devotee.
Mahat-tattva--the total material energy.
Maha-Vishnu or Karanodakasayi Vishnu--the Vishnu expansion of Lord Krishna
    from whom all the material universes emanate.
Mahishamardini--Durga as the slayer of the buffalo demon.
Mandakini--another name of River Ganga.
Mandapa or *Mandapam*–the front hallway of a Vedic temple.
Mandir--a temple.
Mantra--a sound vibration which prepares the mind for spiritual realization and

delivers the mind from material inclinations. In some cases a *mantra* is chanted for specific material benefits.

Matsya--Lord Vishnu as the fish incarnation.

Maya--illusion, or anything that appears to not be connected with the eternal Absolute Truth.

Mayavadi--the impersonalist or voidist who believes that the Supreme has no form, or that any form of God is but a product of *maya*.

Moksha--liberation from material existence.

Mukteshvara--Shiva as the giver of liberation.

Mukunda--Krishna as the giver of spiritual liberation.

Murti--a Deity of the Lord or an image of a demigod or spiritual master that is worshiped.

Murugan--means the divine child, the Tamil name for Subramaniya, one of the sons of Shiva and Parvati, especially worshiped in South India. It is said that he was born to destroy the demon Tarakasura. He was born in a forest of arrow-like grass and raised by the six divine mothers of the Krittika constellation (Pleiades). Thus, he is also called Kartikeya and Sanmatura, and he assumed six faces (and twelve arms) to suckle the milk of the six mothers. Being young and virile, he is also called Kumara or Sanatkumara. He is also called Skanda for being very forceful in war. His two consorts are Velli, the daughter of a humble chieftan of an agricultural tribe, and Devasena, the daughter of the demigod Indra.

Nanda--the foster father of Krishna.

Nandi--Shiva's bull carrier.

Narasimha--Lord Vishnu's incarnation as the half-man half-lion who killed the demon Hiranyakashipu.

Narayana--the four-handed form of the Supreme Lord.

Nataraja--King of Dance, usually referring to Shiva, but also Krishna.

Nirguna--without material qualities.

Nityananda--the brother of Sri Chaitanya, and *avatara* of Lord Balarama.

Om or *Omkara*--*pranava*, the transcendental *om mantra*, generally referring to the attributeless or impersonal aspects of the Absolute.

Paramatma--the Supersoul, or localized expansion of the Lord.

Parampara--the system of disciplic succession through which transcendental knowledge descends.

Parashurama--incarnation of Vishnu with an axe who cleansed the world of the deviant *kshatriya* warriors.

Parthasarathi--Krishna as Arjuna's chariot driver.

Parvati--Lord Shiva's spouse, daughter of Parvata. Parvata is the personification of the Himalayas. She is also called Gauri for her golden complexion, Candi, Bhairavi (as the wife of Bhairava, Shiva), Durga, Ambika, and Shakti.

Pashupati--Shiva as Lord of the animals.

Prana--the life air or cosmic energy.

Pranayama--control of the breathing process as in *astanga* or *raja-yoga*.

Pranava--same as *omkara*.

Prasada--food or other articles that have been offered to the Deity in the temple and then distributed amongst people as the blessings or mercy of the Deity.

Prema--matured love for Krishna.

Puja--the worship offered to the Deity.

Pujari--the priest who performs worship, *puja*, to the Deity.

Purusha or *Purusham*--the supreme enjoyer.

Radha--Krishna's favorite devotee and the personification of His bliss potency.

Rahu--deity representation of the planetary node that causes solar eclipses.

Rajarsi--a Raja or great *rishi* or sage.

Raja-yoga--the eightfold yoga system.

Rajo-guna--the material mode of passion.

Ramachandra--an incarnation of Krishna as He appeared as the greatest of kings.

Ramanuja--Vaishnava philosopher.

Ramayana--the great epic of the incarnation of Lord Ramachandra.

Rasa--an enjoyable taste or feeling, a relationship with God.

Ravana--demon king of the *Ramayana*.

Rishi--saintly person who knows the Vedic knowledge.

Sacrifice--in this book it in no way pertains to human sacrifice, as many people tend to think when this word is used. But it means to engage in an austerity of some kind for a higher, spiritual purpose.

Sati--Shiva's wife who killed herself by immolation in fire.

Sac-chid-ananda-vigraha--the transcendental form of the Lord or of the living entity which is eternal, full of knowledge and bliss.

Sadhana--a specific practice or discipline for attaining God realization.

Sadhu--Indian holy man or devotee.

Saguna Brahman--the aspect of the Absolute with form and qualities.

Samadhi--trance, the perfection of being absorbed in the Absolute.

Samsara--rounds of life; cycles of birth and death; reincarnation.

Sanatana-dharma--the eternal nature of the living being, to love and render service to the supreme lovable object, the Lord.

Sankirtana-yajna--the prescribed sacrifice for this age: congregational chanting of the holy names of God.

Sannyasa--the renounced order of life, the highest of the four *ashramas* on the spiritual path.

Sarasvati--the goddess of knowledge and intelligence.

Sattva-guna--the material mode of goodness.

Sati--the name of Durga after she sacrificed herself.

Satya-yuga--the first of the four ages which lasts 1,728,000 years.

Shabda-brahma--the original spiritual vibration or energy of which the *Vedas* are composed.

Shaivites--worshipers of Lord Shiva.

Shakti--energy, potency or power, the active principle in creation. Also the active power or wife of a deity, such as Shiva/Shakti.

Shastra--the authentic revealed Vedic scripture.

Shiva--the benevolent one, the demigod who is in charge of the material mode of
  ignorance and the destruction of the universe. Part of the triad of
  Brahma, Vishnu, and Shiva who continually create, maintain, and
  destroy the universe. He is known as Rudra when displaying his
  destructive aspect.

Sikha--a tuft of hair on the back of the head signifying that one is a Vaishnava.

Skanda--son of Shiva and Parvati, leader of the army of the gods; also known as
  Karttikeya and Subramanya or Murugan.

Smaranam--remembering the Lord.

Smriti--the traditional Vedic knowledge "that is remembered" from what was
  directly heard by or revealed to the *rishis*.

Sravanam--hearing about the Lord.

Sri, Sridevi--Lakshmi, the goddess who embodies beauty and prosperity, wife of
  Lord Vishnu.

Sridhara--Lord Vishnu.

Srimad-Bhagavatam--the most ripened fruit of the tree of Vedic knowledge
  compiled by Vyasadeva.

Sruti--scriptures that were received directly from God and transmitted orally by
  brahmanas or *rishis* down through succeeding generations.
  Traditionally, it is considered the four primary *Vedas*.

Sudra--the working class of society, the fourth of the *varnas*.

Surya--Sun or solar deity.

Svami--one who can control his mind and senses.

Svetambara--one of the two main Jain sects, white robed.

Swayambhu or *svayambhu*–a deity or image that is self-manifested, without
  being carved or produced by man.

Tamo-guna--the material mode of ignorance.

Tilok--the clay markings that signify a person's body as a temple, and the sect or
  school of thought of the person.

Tirtha--a holy place of pilgrimage.

Treta-yuga--the second of the four ages which lasts 1,296,000 years.

Trilochana--Three-eyed Shiva.

Trilokanatha--Shiva as Lord of the Three Worlds.

Trimurti--triad of Vishnu, Brahma, and Shiva.

Trivikrama--Lord Vishnu as Vamadeva, the *brahmana* dwarf who covered the
  entire universe in three steps.

Tulasi--the small tree that grows where worship to Krishna is found. It is called
  the embodiment of devotion, and the incarnation of Vrinda-devi.

Uma--Parvati

Upanishads--the portions of the *Vedas* which primarily explain philosophically
  the Absolute Truth. It is knowledge of Brahman which releases one
  from the world and allows one to attain self-realization when received
  from a qualified teacher. Except for the *Isa Upanishad*, which is the

40th chapter of the *Vajasaneyi Samhita* of the *Sukla* (*White*) *Yajur-veda*, the *Upanishads* are connected to the four primary *Vedas*, generally found in the *Brahmanas*.

Vaikunthas--the planets located in the spiritual sky.

Vaishnava--a worshiper of the Supreme Lord Vishnu or Krishna and His expansions or incarnations.

Vaisya--the third class of society engaged in business or farming.

Vamana--dwarf incarnation of Vishnu who covered the universe in three steps.

Vanaprastha--the third of the four *ashramas* of spiritual life in which one retires from family life in preparation for the renounced order.

Varaha--Lord Vishnu's boar incarnation.

Varna--sometimes referred to as caste, a division of society, such as *brahmana* (a priestly intellectual), a *kshatriya* (ruler or manager), *vaisya* (a merchant, banker, or farmer), and *sudra* (common laborer).

Varnashrama--the system of four divisions of society and four orders of spiritual life.

Varuna--demigod of the oceans, guardian of the west.

Vasudeva--Krishna.

Vayu--demigod of the air.

Vedanta-sutras--the philosophical conclusion of the four *Vedas*.

Vedas--generally means the four primary *samhitas; Rig, Yajur, Sama, Atharva*.

Vidya--knowledge.

Vikarma--sinful activities performed without scriptural authority and which produce sinful reactions.

Vishalakshi--Parvati, consort of Vishvanatha or Vishalaksha, Shiva.

Vishnu--the expansion of Lord Krishna who enters into the material energy to create and maintain the cosmic world.

Vishvarupa--universal form of Lord Vishnu.

Vrindavana--the place where Lord Krishna displayed His village pastimes 5,000 years ago, and is considered to be part of the spiritual abode.

Vyasadeva--the incarnation of God who appeared as the greatest philosopher who compiled the main portions of the Vedic literature into written form.

Yajna--a ritual or austerity that is done as a sacrifice for spiritual merit, or ritual worship of a demigod for good *karmic* reactions.

Yamaraja--the demigod and lord of death who directs the living entities to various punishments according to their activities.

Yamuna--goddess personification of the Yamuna River.

Yantra--a machine, instrument, or mystical diagram used in ritual worship.

Yashoda--foster mother of Krishna.

Yoga--linking up with the Absolute.

Yoga-siddhi--mystic perfection.

Yuga-avataras--the incarnations of God who appear in each of the four *yugas* to explain the authorized system of self-realization in that age.

REFERENCES

Agni Purana, translated by N. Gangadharan, Motilal Banarsidass, Delhi, 1984

Art of Chanting Hare Krishna, Mahanidhia Swami, 2002.

Atharva-veda, translated by Devi Chand, Munshiram Manoharlal, Delhi, 1980

Autobiography of Srila Bhaktivinode Thakur,

Bhagavad-gita As It Is, translated by A. C. Bhaktivedanta Swami, Bhaktivedanta Book Trust, New York/Los Angeles, 1972

Bhagavad-gita, translated by Swami Chidbhavananda, Sri Ramakrishna Tapovanam, Tiruchirappalli, India, 1991

Brahma Purana, edited by J.L.Shastri, Motilal Banarsidass, Delhi 1985

Brahma-samhita, translated by Bhaktisiddhanta Sarasvati Gosvami Thakur, Bhaktivedanta Book Trust, New York/Los Angeles,

Brahma-Sutras, translated by Swami Vireswarananda and Adidevananda, Advaita Ashram, Calcutta, 1978

Brahma-vaivarta Purana, translated by Shanti Lal Nagar, edited by Acharya Ramesh Chaturvedi, Parimal Publications, Delhi, 2005.

Brihad-vishnu Purana

Brihan-naradiya Purana

Brihadaranyaka Upanishad

Caitanya-caritamrta, translated by A. C. Bhaktivedanta Swami, Bhaktivedanta Book Trust, Los Angeles, 1974

Caitanya Upanisad, translated by Kusakratha dasa, Bala Books, New York, 1970

Chaitanya-chandramrita,

Chandogya Upanishad,

Garga Samhita, Sri Garga Muni, translated by Kusakratha dasa, edited by Purnaprajna Dasa, Rasbihari Lal & Sons, Vrindavana, India, 2006.

Garuda Purana, edited by J. L. Shastri, Motilal Barnasidass, Delhi, 1985

Gautamiya Tantra,

Gayatri Mahima Madhuri, compiled and published by Mahanidhi Swami, Vrindavana, 1998

Gitagovinda of Jayadeva, Barbara Stoller Miller, Motilal Banarsidass, Delhi, 1977

Gita Mahatmya of the Padma Purana and Srimad Bhagavata Mahatmya of the Skanda Purana, by Krishna Dvaipayana Vyasa, Touchstone Media, Vrindavana, India, 2001

Gopal-tapani Upanishad, by Krsna Dvaipayana Vedavyasa, commentary by Visvanatha Cakravarti Thakura, translated by Bhumipati dasa, Ras Bihari Lal & Sons, Loi Bazaar, Vrindaban, UP, 281121, India, 2004

Hari-bhakti-vilasa,

Hymns of the Rig-veda, tr. by Griffith, Motilal Banarsidass, Delhi, 1973

Jaiva Dharma, Srila Thakur Bhakti Vinod, trans. By Bhakti Sadhaka Nishkinchana, Sree Gaudiya Math

Jaiva Dharma, The Essential Function of the Soul, Srila Bhaktivinoda Thakura,
    translated by Sarvabhavana dasa, Brihat Mrdanga Press, Vrindavana,
    India, 2004
Kali-santarana Upanishad,
Kalki Purana, by Sri Vyasadeva, translated by Bhumipati das, Jai Nitai Press,
    Mathura, India, 2006
Katha Upanishad
Kaushitaki Upanishad
Krsna-karnamrta, Sri Bilvamangala Thakura, translated by Kusakratha dasa,
    edited by Purnaprajna Dasa, Rasbihari Lal & Sons, Vrindavana, India,
    2006.
Krsnahnika Kaumudi, by Srila Kavi-karnapura, Editor & Publisher, Mahanidhi
    Swami, Vrindavana, 2002
Kurma Purana, edited by J. L. Shastri, Motilal Banarsidass, Delhi, 1981
Laghu Bhagavatamrta, Srila Rupa Gosvami, translated by Bhanu Swami, Sri
    Vaikuntha Enterprises, 2006.
Laghu-bhagavatamrta, Srila Rupa Gosvami, translated by Kusakratha dasa, Ras
    Bihari Lal & Sons, Loi Bazaar, Vrindaban, UP, 281121, India, 2007
Mahabharata, Kesari Mohan Ganguli, Munshiram Manoharlal Publisher Pvt.,
    Ltd., New Delhi, 1970
Mahabharata, Sanskrit Text With English Translations, by M. N. Dutt, Parimal
    Publications, Delhi, 2001
Matsya Purana,
Minor Upanishads, translated by Swami Madhavananda, Advaita Ashram,
    Calcutta, 1980; contains Paramahamsopanishad, Atmopanishad,
    Amritabindupanishad, Tejabindupanishad, Sarvopanishad,
    Brahmopanisad, Aruneyi Upanishad, Kaivalyopanishad.
Mukunda-mala-stotra
Mundaka Upanishad,
Narada-pancaratra,
Narada Pancharatram, Swami Vynananand, Parimal Publications, Delhi, 1993
Narada Purana, tr. by Ganesh Vasudeo Tagare, Banarsidass, Delhi, 1980
Narada Sutras, translated by Hari Prasad Shastri, Shanti Sadan, London, 1963
Narada-Bhakti-Sutra, A. C. Bhaktivedanta Swami, Bhaktivedanta Book Trust,
    Los Angeles, 1991
Narasimha Purana,
Narottam-Vilas, by Sri Narahari Cakravarti Thakur, translator unknown.
New Discoveries About Vedic Sarasvati, by Dr. Ravi Prakash Arya, Published
    by Dilip and Dipika Doctor of International Vedic Vision, in
    association with India Foundation for Vedic Science, Haryana, India,
    2002.
Padma Purana, tr. by S. Venkitasubramonia Iyer, Banarsidass, Delhi, 1988
Prameya-ratnavali, Srila Baladeva Vidyabhusana,
Prema-Vilas, by Nityananda Das
Prema Vivarta--Divine Transformations of Spiritual Love, Srila Jagadananda

Pandita, trans. by Sarvabhavana dasa, Harmonist Publications, Mumbai, 1991

Purana-vakya,

Puranic Encyclopaedia, Vettam Mani, Motilal Banarsidass, Delhi, 1964

Raga Vartma Candrika, A Moonbeam on the Path of Raganuga Bhakti, Srila Visvanatha Cakravarti Thakura, Sri Krsna Caitanya Sastra Mandira, 1994

Ramayana of Valmiki, tr. by Makhan Lal Sen, Oriental Publishing Co., Calcutta

Ramayana of Valmiki, tr. by Makhan Lal Sen, Munshiram Manoharlal Publishers, New Delhi, 1976.

Hymns of the Rig-veda, tr. by Griffith, Motilal Banarsidass, Delhi, 1973

Rig Veda, Krishna Upanishad,

Samnyasa Upanisads, translated by Prof. A. A. Ramanathan, Adyar Library, Madras, India, 1978; contains Avadhutopanisad, Arunyupanisad, Katharudropanisad, Kundikopanisad, Jabalopanisad, Turiyatitopanisad, Narada-parivrajakopanisad, Nirvanopanisad, Parabrahmopanisad, Paramahamsa-parivrajakopanisad, Paramahamsopanisad, Brahmopanisad, Bhiksukopanisad, Maitreyopanisad, Yajnavalkyopanisad, Satyayaniyopanisad, and Samnyasopanisad.

Sammohana Tantra,

Sarartha Darsini, Srila Visvanatha Cakravarti Thakura, translated by Bhanu Swami, Editor & Publisher Mahanidhi Swami, 2004.

Shri Chaitanya Mahaprabhu, His Life and Precepts, Thakur Bhakti Vinode, Sree Gaudiya Math, Madras, 1991

The Sikhs in History, Sangat Singh, Singh Brothers, Amritsar, 2005

Siksastaka, of Sri Caitanya Mahaprabhu.

Sixty Upanisads of the Vedas, by Paul Deussen, translated from German by V. M. Bedekar and G. B. Palsule, Motilal Banarsidass, Delhi, 1980; contains Upanisads of the Rigveda: Aitareya and Kausitaki. Upanisads of the Samaveda: Chandogya and Kena. Upanisads of the Black Yajurveda: Taittiriya, Mahanarayan, Kathaka, Svetasvatara, and Maitrayana. Upanisads of the White Yajurveda: Brihadaranyaka and Isa. Upanisads of the Atharvaveda: Mundaka, Prasna, Mandukya, Garbha, Pranagnihotra, Pinda, Atma, Sarva, Garuda; (Yoga Upanisads): Brahmavidya, Ksurika, Culik, Nadabindu, Brahma-bindu, Amrtabindu, Dhyanabindu, Tejobindu, Yoga-sikha, Yogatattva, Hamsa; (Samnyasa Upanisads): Brahma, Samnyasa, Aruneya, Kantha-sruti, Paramahamsa, Jabala, Asrama; (Shiva Upanisads): Atharvasira, Atharva-sikha, Nilarudra, Kalagnirudra, Kaivalya; (Vishnu Upanisads): Maha, Narayana, Atmabodha, Nrisimhapurvatapaniya, Nrisimhottara-tapaniya, Ramapurvatapaniya, Ramottaratapaniya. (Supplemental Upanisads): Purusasuktam, Tadeva, Shiva-samkalpa, Baskala, Chagaleya, Paingala, Mrtyu-langala, Arseya, Pranava, and Saunaka Upanisad.

Skanda Purana, by Srila Vyasadeva, Purnaprajna Dasa, Rasbihari Lal & Sons, Vrindavana, India, 2005.

Sri Bhajana-rahasya, Srila Bhaktivinoda Thakura, Published by Pundarika
    Vidyanidhi dasa, Vrindavana,

Sri Bhakti-ratnakara, by Sri Narahari Cakravarti Thakura.

Sri Bhakti Sandarbha, Srila Jiva Gosvami, translated by Dr. Satya Narayana
    Dasa, Edited by Bhrgu Natha Dasa, Jiva Institute, Vrindavana, India,
    2005.

Sri Brihat Bhagavatamritam, by Sri Srila Sanatana Gosvami, Sree Gaudiya
    Math, Madras, India, 1987

Sri Caitanya Bhagavat, by Sri Vrindavan dasa Thakura, 1538 AD.

Sri Caitanya-Bhagavat, by Sri Vrindavan dasa Thakura, trans. By Kusakratha
    dasa, Krsna Institute, Alachua, FL, 1994

Sri Caitanya-carita-maha-kavya, Srila Murari Gupta, translated by Swami
    Bhakti Vedanta Bhagavata Maharaja, edited by Purnaprajna Dasa,
    Rasbihari Lal & Sons, Vrindavana, India, 2006.

Sri Caitanya Mangala, Locana Dasa Thakura, trans., by Subhag Swami,
    published by Mahanidhi Swami, Vrindavana, 1994

Sri Caitanya Shikshamritam, Thakura Bhakti Vinode, Sree Gaudiya Math,
    Madras, 1983

Sri Caitanya-siksamrta, The Nectarean Teachings of Sri Caitanya, Srila
    Bhaktivinoda Thakura, translated by H. H. Bhanu Swami, Brihat
    Mrdanga Press, Vrindavana, India, 2004

Sri Caitanya Upanishad, from the Atharva-veda

*Sri Gayatri Mantrartha Dipika, Illuminations on the Essential Meaning of Sri
    Gayatri*, Gosai Publishers, Sri Rangapatna, Karnataka, India, 1999.

Sri Gaura-ganoddesha dipika, by Kavi Karnapura, translated by Bhumipati
    dasa, Ras Bihari Lal & Sons, Loi Bazaar, Vrindaban, UP, 281121,
    India, 2004

Sri Gauranga-Mahima, Sri Advaita Acarya & Sri Sarvabhauma Bhattacarya,
    trans. By Jaya Balarama dasa, Nectar Books, Culver City, CA, 1992

Sri Gopal Sahasra Nama, One thousand names of Lord Gopala Krsna, Spoken
    by Lord Shiva to Sri Parvati devi, translated by Bhumipati dasa, Ras
    Bihari Lal & Sons, Loi Bazaar, Vrindaban, UP, 281121, India, 2004

Sri Gopala-Tapani Upanishad, from the Atharva-Veda,

Sri Hari-bhakti-vilasa, Srila Sanatana Gosvami, translated by Bhumipati dasa,
    edited by Purnaprajna Dasa, Rasbihari Lal & Sons, Vrindavana, India,
    2006.

Sri Hari-bhakti-vilasa, Vilasas I & II, Srila Sanatana Gosvami, and *Panca-
    samskara*, by Saccidananda Thakura Bhaktivinoda, Brihat Mrdanga
    Press, Vrindavana, India, 2005

Sri Harinam Cintamani, Srila Bhaktivinoda Thakura, trans. Sarvabhavana dasa,
    Bhaktivedanta Books, Mumbai, 1990

Sri Isopanisad, translated by A. C. Bhaktivedanta Swami, Bhaktivedanta Book
    Trust, New York/Los Angeles, 1969

*Sri Krishna Caitanya divya sahasra-nama, One thousand transcendental names
    of Sri Krsna Caitanya*, by Srila Rupa Gosvami, Translated by

Bhumipati dasa, Ras Bihari Lal & Sons, Loi Bazaar, Vrindaban, UP, 281121, India, 2004

Sri Krishna Karnamritam & Chaitanya-chandramritam, Lilasuka & Prabhodhananda, trans. Bhakti Sadhaka Nishkinchana, Sree Gaudiya Math, Madras

Sri Krsna-samhita, Srila Bhaktivinoda Thakur, trans. Bhumipati dasa, Vajraj Press, Vrindavana, 1998

Sri Krsna Sandarbha, Srila Jiva Gosvami, edited by Purnaprajna Dasa, Rasbihari Lal & Sons, Vrindavana, India, 2006.

Srimad-Bhagavatam, translated by A. C. Bhaktivedanta Swami, Bhaktivedanta Book trust, New York/Los Angeles, 1972

Srimad Valmiki-Ramayana, Gita Press, Gorakhpur, India, 1969

Sri Manah-Siksa, Raghunatha dasa Gosvami, purports by Srila Bhaktivinoda Thakur, trans. Sarvabhavana dasa, Bhaktivedanta Books, Mumbai, 1989

Sri Narada Pancharatram,

Sri Nrsimha Sahasra-nama & Sri Nrsimha-Kavaca, translated by Bhumipati dasa, Ras Bihari Lal & Sons, Loi Bazaar, Vrindaban, UP, 281121, India, 2006

Sri Prema Bhakti-candrika, Narottama Dasa Thakur, commentary by Visvanatha Cakravarti Thakur, trans. Bhumipati dasa, Touchstone Media, Vrindavana, 1999

Sri Sanatkumara-samhita, from the Skanda Purana,

Sri Sri Krishna Bhavanamrta Mahakavya, Srila Visvanatha Chakravarti Thakura, completed in 1686

Sri Sri Premadhama Deva Stotram, Srila B. R. Sridhar Deva Gosvami, Sri Chaitanya Sarasvat Math, Nabavipa, 1983

Sri Ujjvala-Nilamani, Srila Rupa Gosvami, translated by Kusakratha dasa, edited by Purnaprajna Dasa, Rasbihari Lal & Sons, Vrindavana, India, 2006.

Sri Vishnu Sahasra Naamam, translated and Commentary by M. S. Parthasarathi, Bharatiya Vidya Bhavan, Mumbai, 1999

Sri Visnu-sahasra-nama-stotra, translated by Kusakratha dasa, edited by Purnaprajna Dasa, Rasbihari Lal & Sons, Vrindavana, India, 2006.

Stava-mala, Srila Rupa Gosvami, translated by Kusakratha dasa, Ras Bihari Lal & Sons, Loi Bazaar, Vrindaban, UP, 281121, India, 2007

Svetasvatara Upanishad,

Taittiriya Upanishad

Twelve Essential Upanishads, Tridandi Sri Bhakti Prajnan Yati, Sree Gaudiya Math, Madras, 1982. Includes the *Isha, Kena, Katha, Prashna, Mundaka, Mandukya, Taittiriya, Aitareya, Chandogya, Brihadaranyaka, Svetasvatara,* and *Gopalatapani Upanishad* of the Pippalada section of the *Atharva-veda*.

Ujjal Nilmani, by Srila Rupa Gosvami, translated and published by Puri
        Maharaja, Goudiya Vaishnava Association, Mayapur, Nadia, India,
        Feb. 24, 2000

Upadesamrta (Nectar of Instruction), translated by A. C. Bhaktivedanta Swami,
        Bhaktivedanta Book Trust, New York/Los Angeles, 1975

The Upanisads, translated by F. Max Muller, Dover Publications; contains
        Chandogya, Kena, Aitareya, Kausitaki, Vajasaneyi (Isa), Katha,
        Mundaka, Taittiriya, Brihadaranyaka, Svetasvatara, Prasna, and
        Maitrayani Upanisads.

The Upanishads, translated by Swami Prabhavananda and Frederick Manchester,
        New American Library, New York, 1957; contains Katha, Isha, Kena,
        Prasna, Mundaka, Mandukya, Taittiriya, Aitareya, Chandogya,
        Brihadaranyaka, Kaivalya, and Svetasvatara Upanishads.

Urdhvamnaya Tantra,

Varaha Purana, tr. by S.Venkitasubramonia Iyer, Banarsidass, Delhi, 1985

Vayu Purana, translated by G. V. Tagare, Banarsidass, Delhi, India, 1987

Veda of the Black Yajus School: Taitiriya Sanhita, translated by Arthur Keith,
        Motilal Banarsidass, Delhi, 1914

Vishnu Purana, translated by H. H. Wilson, Nag Publishers, Delhi

Vishnu-smriti,

Vishnu Yamala Samhita,

White Yajurveda, translated by Griffith, The Chowkhamba Sanskrit Series
        Office, Varanasi, 1976

Yajurveda, translated by Devi Chand, Munshiram Manoharlal, Delhi, 1980

INDEX

ABOUT THE AUTHOR

Stephen Knapp grew up in a Christian family, during which time he seriously studied the Bible to understand its teachings. In his late teenage years, however, he sought answers to questions not easily explained in Christian theology. So he began to search through other religions and philosophies from around the world and started to find the answers for which he was looking. He also studied a variety of occult sciences, ancient mythology, mysticism, yoga, and the spiritual teachings of the East. After his first reading of the *Bhagavad-gita*, he felt he had found the last piece of the puzzle he had been putting together through all of his research. Therefore, he continued to study all of the major Vedic texts of India to gain a better understanding of the Vedic science.

It is known amongst all Eastern mystics that anyone, regardless of qualifications, academic or otherwise, who does not engage in the spiritual practices described in the Vedic texts cannot actually enter into understanding the depths of the Vedic spiritual science, nor acquire the realizations that should accompany it. So, rather than pursuing his research in an academic atmosphere at a university, Stephen directly engaged in the spiritual disciplines that have been recommended for hundreds of years. He continued his study of Vedic knowledge and spiritual practice under the guidance of a spiritual master. Through this process, and with the sanction of His Divine Grace A. C. Bhaktivedanta Swami Prabhupada, he became initiated into the genuine and authorized spiritual line of the Brahma-Madhava-Gaudiya *sampradaya*, which is a disciplic succession that descends back through Sri Caitanya Mahaprabhu and Sri Vyasadeva, the compiler of Vedic literature, and further back to Sri Krishna. Through this initiation he has taken the spiritual name of Sri Nandanandana dasa. Besides being *brahminically* initiated, Stephen has also been to India numerous times and traveled extensively throughout the country, visiting all but three small states and most of the major holy places, thus gaining a wide variety of spiritual experiences that only such places can give.

Stephen has written numerous articles, as well as books such as *The Eastern Answers to the Mysteries of Life* series, which includes *The Secret Teachings of the Vedas*, *The Universal Path to Enlightenment*, *The Vedic Prophecies*, and *How the Universe was Created and Our Purpose In It*. He has also written *Toward World Peace: Seeing the Unity Between Us All*, *Facing Death: Welcoming the Afterlife*, *The Key to Real Happiness*, and *Proof of Vedic Culture's Global Existence.*, as well as *Reincarnation and Karma: How They Really Affect Us*, *The Heart of Hinduism*, *Vedic Culture:*

The Difference it can Make in Your Life, *The Power of the Dharma: A Short Introduction to Hinduism and Vedic Culture*, and *Seeing Spiritual India: A Guidebook to Temple, Holy sites, Festivals and Traditions*, as well as *Crimes Against India: 1000 Years of Attacks Against Hinduism and What to do About It*, and *Yoga and Meditation: Their Real Purpose and How to Get Started*. Furthermore, he has authored a novel, *Destined for Infinity*, for those who prefer lighter reading, or learning spiritual knowledge in the context of an exciting, spiritual adventure. Stephen has put the culmination of over forty years of continuous research and travel experience into his books in an effort to share it with those who are also looking for spiritual understanding.

Stephen now works full time to help preserve, protect and promote a genuine understand of Vedic culture and Sanatana-dharma. To find out more about Stephen's books, articles, and projects, along with numerous resources, you can see his website at: http://www.stephen-knapp.com, or his blog at: http://stephenknapp.wordpress.com.

If you have enjoyed this book, or if you are serious about finding higher levels of real spiritual Truth, and learning more about the mysteries of India's Vedic culture, then you will also want to get other books written by Stephen Knapp, which include:

The Secret Teachings of the Vedas

This book presents the essence of the ancient Eastern philosophy and summarizes some of the most elevated and important of all spiritual knowledge. This enlightening information is explained in a clear and concise way and is essential for all who want to increase their spiritual understanding, regardless of what their religious background may be. If you are looking for a book to give you an in-depth introduction to the Vedic spiritual knowledge, and to get you started in real spiritual understanding, this is the book!

The topics include: What is your real spiritual identity; the Vedic explanation of the soul; scientific evidence that consciousness is separate from but interacts with the body; the real unity between us all; how to attain the highest happiness and freedom from the cause of suffering; the law of karma and reincarnation; the karma of a nation; where you are really going in life; the real process of progressive evolution; life after death—heaven, hell, or beyond; a description of the spiritual realm; the nature of the Absolute Truth—personal God or impersonal force; recognizing the existence of the Supreme; the reason why we exist at all; and much more. This book provides the answers to questions not found in other religions or philosophies, and condenses information from a wide variety of sources that would take a person years to assemble. It also contains many quotations from the Vedic texts to let the texts speak for themselves, and to show the knowledge the Vedas have held for thousands of years. It also explains the history and origins of the Vedic literature. This book has been called one of the best reviews of Eastern philosophy available.

The Vedic Prophecies:
A New Look into the Future

The Vedic prophecies take you to the end of time! This is the first book ever to present the unique predictions found in the ancient Vedic texts of India. These prophecies are like no others and will provide you with a very different view of the future and how things fit together in the plan for the universe.

Now you can discover the amazing secrets that are hidden in the oldest spiritual writings on the planet. Find out what they say about the distant future, and what the seers of long ago saw in their visions of the destiny of the world.

This book will reveal predictions of deteriorating social changes and how to avoid them; future droughts and famines; low-class rulers and evil governments; whether there will be another appearance (second coming) of God; and predictions of a new spiritual awareness and how it will spread around the world. You will also learn the answers to such questions as:

- Does the future get worse or better?
- Will there be future world wars or global disasters?
- What lies beyond the predictions of Nostradamus, the Mayan prophecies, or the Biblical apocalypse?
- Are we in the end times? How to recognize them if we are.
- Does the world come to an end? If so, when and how?

Now you can find out what the future holds. The Vedic Prophecies carry an important message and warning for all humanity, which needs to be understood now!

Proof of Vedic Culture's Global Existence

This book provides evidence which makes it clear that the ancient Vedic culture was once a global society. Even today we can see its influence in any part of the world. Thus, it becomes obvious that before the world became full of distinct and separate cultures, religions and countries, it was once united in a common brotherhood of Vedic culture, with common standards, principles, and representations of God.

No matter what we may consider our present religion, society or country, we are all descendants of this ancient global civilization. Thus, the Vedic culture is the parent of all humanity and the original ancestor of all religions. In this way, we all share a common heritage.

This book is an attempt to allow humanity to see more clearly its universal roots. This book provides a look into:

- How Vedic knowledge was given to humanity by the Supreme.
- The history and traditional source of the Vedas and Vedic Aryan society.
- Who were the original Vedic Aryans. How Vedic society was a global influence and what shattered this world-wide society. How Sanskrit faded from being a global language.
- Many scientific discoveries over the past several centuries are only rediscoveries of what the Vedic literature already knew.
- How the origins of world literature are found in India and Sanskrit.
- The links between the Vedic and other ancient cultures, such as the Sumerians, Persians, Egyptians, Romans, Greeks, and others.
- Links between the Vedic tradition and Judaism, Christianity, Islam, and Buddhism.
- How many of the western holy sites, churches, and mosques were once the sites of Vedic holy places and sacred shrines.
- The Vedic influence presently found in such countries as Britain, France, Russia, Greece, Israel, Arabia, China, Japan, and in areas of Scandinavia, the Middle East, Africa, the South Pacific, and the Americas.
- Uncovering the truth of India's history: Powerful evidence that shows how many mosques and Muslim buildings were once opulent Vedic temples, including the Taj Mahal, Delhi's Jama Masjid, Kutab Minar, as well as buildings in many other cities, such as Agra, Ahmedabad, Bijapur, etc.
- How there is presently a need to plan for the survival of Vedic culture.

This book is sure to provide some amazing facts and evidence about the truth of world history and the ancient, global Vedic Culture. This book has enough startling information and historical evidence to cause a major shift in the way we view religious history and the basis of world traditions.

Available for $20.99, 431 pages, ISBN: 978-1-4392-4648-1.

Toward World Peace: Seeing the Unity Between Us All

This book points out the essential reasons why peace in the world and cooperation amongst people, communities, and nations have been so difficult to establish. It also advises the only way real peace and harmony amongst humanity can be achieved.

In order for peace and unity to exist we must first realize what barriers and divisions keep us apart. Only then can we break through those barriers to see the unity that naturally exists between us all. Then, rather than focus on our differences, it is easier to recognize our similarities and common goals. With a common goal established, all of humanity can work together to help each other reach that destiny.

This book is short and to the point. It is a thought provoking book and will provide inspiration for anyone. It is especially useful for those working in politics, religion, interfaith, race relations, the media, the United Nations, teaching, or who have a position of leadership in any capacity. It is also for those of us who simply want to spread the insights needed for bringing greater levels of peace, acceptance, unity, and equality between friends, neighbours, and communities. Such insights include:

- The factors that keep us apart.
- Breaking down cultural distinctions.
- Breaking down the religious differences.
- Seeing through bodily distinctions.
- We are all working to attain the same things.
- Our real identity: The basis for common ground.
- Seeing the Divinity within each of us.
- What we can do to bring unity between everyone we meet.

This book carries an important message and plan of action that we must incorporate into our lives and plans for the future if we intend to ever bring peace and unity between us.

$6.95, 84 pages, ISBN: 1452813744

Facing Death
Welcoming the Afterlife

Many people are afraid of death, or do not know how to prepare for it nor what to expect. So this book is provided to relieve anyone of the fear that often accompanies the thought of death, and to supply a means to more clearly understand the purpose of it and how we can use it to our advantage. It will also help the survivors of the departed souls to better understand what has happened and how to cope with it. Furthermore, it shows that death is not a tragedy, but a natural course of events meant to help us reach our destiny.

This book is easy to read, with soothing and comforting wisdom, along with stories of people who have been with departing souls and what they have experienced. It is written especially for those who have given death little thought beforehand, but now would like to have some preparedness for what may need to be done regarding the many levels of the experience and what might take place during this transition.

To assist you in preparing for your own death, or that of a loved one, you will find guidelines for making one's final days as peaceful and as smooth as possible, both physically and spiritually. Preparing for death can transform your whole outlook in a positive way, if understood properly. Some of the topics in the book include:

- The fear of death and learning to let go.
- The opportunity of death: The portal into the next life.
- This earth and this body are no one's real home, so death is natural.
- Being practical and dealing with the final responsibilities.
- Forgiving yourself and others before you go.
- Being the assistant of one leaving this life.
- Connecting with the person inside the disease.
- Surviving the death of a loved one.
- Stories of being with dying, and an amazing near-death-experience.
- Connecting to the spiritual side of death.
- What happens while leaving the body.
- What difference the consciousness makes during death, and how to attain the best level of awareness to carry you through it.

Published by iUniverse.com, $13.95, 135 pages, ISBN: 978-1-4401-1344-4

Destined for Infinity

Deep within the mystical and spiritual practices of India are doors that lead to various levels of both higher and lower planes of existence. Few people from the outside are ever able to enter into the depths of these practices to experience such levels of reality.

This is the story of the mystical adventure of a man, Roman West, who entered deep into the secrets of India where few other Westerners have been able to penetrate. While living with a master in the Himalayan foothills and traveling the mystical path that leads to the Infinite, he witnesses the amazing powers the mystics can achieve and undergoes some of the most unusual experiences of his life. Under the guidance of a master that he meets in the mountains, he gradually develops mystic abilities of his own and attains the sacred vision of the enlightened sages and enters the unfathomable realm of Infinity. However, his peaceful life in the hills comes to an abrupt end when he is unexpectedly forced to confront the powerful forces of darkness that have been unleashed by an evil Tantric priest to kill both Roman and his master. His only chance to defeat the intense forces of darkness depends on whatever spiritual strength he has been able to develop.

This story includes traditions and legends that have existed for hundreds and thousands of years. All of the philosophy, rituals, mystic powers, forms of meditation, and descriptions of the Absolute are authentic and taken from narrations found in many of the sacred books of the East, or gathered by the author from his own experiences in India and information from various sages themselves.

This book will will prepare you to perceive the multi-dimensional realities that exist all around us, outside our sense perception. This is a book that will give you many insights into the broad possibilities of our life and purpose in this world.

Published by iUniverse.com, 255 pages, $16.95.

Reincarnation and Karma: How They Really Affect Us

Everyone may know a little about reincarnation, but few understand the complexities and how it actually works. Now you can find out how reincarnation and karma really affect us. Herein all of the details are provided on how a person is implicated for better or worse by their own actions. You will understand why particular situations in life happen, and how to make improvements for one's future. You will see why it appears that bad things happen to good people, or even why good things happen to bad people, and what can be done about it.

Other topics include:
- Reincarnation recognized throughout the world
- The most ancient teachings on reincarnation
- Reincarnation in Christianity
- How we transmigrate from one body to another
- Life between lives
- Going to heaven or hell
- The reason for reincarnation
- Free will and choice
- Karma of the nation
- How we determine our own destiny
- What our next life may be like
- Becoming free from all karma and how to prepare to make our next life the best possible.

Combine this with modern research into past life memories and experiences and you will have a complete view of how reincarnation and karma really operate.

Published by iUniverse.com, 135 pages, $13.95.

Vedic Culture
The Difference It Can Make In Your Life

The Vedic culture of India is rooted in Sanatana-dharma, the eternal and universal truths that are beneficial to everyone. It includes many avenues of self-development that an increasing number of people from the West are starting to investigate and use, including:

- Yoga
- Meditation and spiritual practice
- Vedic astrology
- Ayurveda
- Vedic gemology
- Vastu or home arrangement
- Environmental awareness
- Vegetarianism
- Social cooperation and arrangement
- The means for global peace
- And much more

Vedic Culture: The Difference It Can Make In Your Life shows the advantages of the Vedic paths of improvement and self-discovery that you can use in your life to attain higher personal awareness, happiness, and fulfillment. It also provides a new view of what these avenues have to offer from some of the most prominent writers on Vedic culture in the West, who discovered how it has affected and benefited their own lives. They write about what it has done for them and then explain how their particular area of interest can assist others. The noted authors include, David Frawley, Subhash Kak, Chakrapani Ullal, Michael Cremo, Jeffrey Armstrong, Robert Talyor, Howard Beckman, Andy Fraenkel, George Vutetakis, Pratichi Mathur, Dhan Rousse, Arun Naik, Parama Karuna Devi, and Stephen Knapp, all of whom have numerous authored books or articles of their own.

For the benefit of individuals and social progress, the Vedic system is as relevant today as it was in ancient times. Discover why there is a growing renaissance in what the Vedic tradition has to offer in *Vedic Culture*.

Published by iUniverse.com, 300 pages, $22.95.

The Heart of Hinduism:
The Eastern Path to Freedom, Empowerment and Illumination

This is a definitive and easy to understand guide to the essential as well as devotional heart of the Vedic/Hindu philosophy. You will see the depths of wisdom and insights that are contained within this profound spiritual knowledge. It is especially good for anyone who lacks the time to research the many topics that are contained within the numerous Vedic manuscripts and to see the advantages of knowing them. This also provides you with a complete process for progressing on the spiritual path, making way for individual empowerment, freedom, and spiritual illumination. All the information is now at your fingertips. Topics:

- A complete review of all the Vedic texts and the wide range of topics they contain. This also presents the traditional origins of the Vedic philosophy and how it was developed, and their philosophical conclusion.
- The uniqueness and freedom of the Vedic system.
- A description of the main yoga processes and their effectiveness.
- A review of the Vedic Gods, such as Krishna, Shiva, Durga, Ganesh, and others. You will learn the identity and purpose of each.
- You will have the essential teachings of Lord Krishna who has given some of the most direct and insightful of all spiritual messages known to humanity, and the key to direct spiritual perception.
- The real purpose of yoga and the religious systems.
- What is the most effective spiritual path for this modern age and what it can do for you, with practical instructions for deep realizations.
- The universal path of devotion, the one world religion.
- How Vedic culture is the last bastion of deep spiritual truth.
- Plus many more topics and information for your enlightenment.

So to dive deep into what is Hinduism and the Vedic path to freedom and spiritual perception, this book will give you a jump start. Knowledge is the process of personal empowerment, and no knowledge will give you more power than deep spiritual understanding. And those realizations described in the Vedic culture are the oldest and some of the most profound that humanity has ever known.

Published by iUniverse.com, 650 pages, $35.95.

The Power of the Dharma
An Introduction to Hinduism and Vedic Culture

The Power of the Dharma offers you a concise and easy-to-understand overview of the essential principles and customs of Hinduism and the reasons for them. It provides many insights into the depth and value of the timeless wisdom of Vedic spirituality and why the Dharmic path has survived for so many hundreds of years. It reveals why the Dharma is presently enjoying a renaissance of an increasing number of interested people who are exploring its teachings and seeing what its many techniques of Self-discovery have to offer.

Herein you will find:

- Quotes by noteworthy people on the unique qualities of Hinduism
- Essential principles of the Vedic spiritual path
- Particular traits and customs of Hindu worship and explanations of them
- Descriptions of the main Yoga systems
- The significance and legends of the colorful Hindu festivals
- Benefits of Ayurveda, Vastu, Vedic astrology and gemology,
- Important insights of Dharmic life and how to begin.

The Dharmic path can provide you the means for attaining your own spiritual realizations and experiences. In this way it is as relevant today as it was thousands of years ago. This is the power of the Dharma since its universal teachings have something to offer anyone.

Published by iUniverse.com, 170 pages, $16.95.

Seeing Spiritual India
A Guide to Temples, Holy Sites, Festivals and Traditions

This book is for anyone who wants to know of the many holy sites that you can visit while traveling within India, how to reach them, and what is the history and significance of these most spiritual of sacred sites, temples, and festivals. It also provides a deeper understanding of the mysteries and spiritual traditions of India.

This book includes:

- Descriptions of the temples and their architecture, and what you will see at each place.
- Explanations of holy places of Hindus, Buddhists, Sikhs, Jains, Parsis, and Muslims.
- The spiritual benefits a person acquires by visiting them.
- Convenient itineraries to take to see the most of each area of India, which is divided into East, Central, South, North, West, the Far Northeast, and Nepal.
- Packing list suggestions and how to prepare for your trip, and problems to avoid.
- How to get the best experience you can from your visit to India.
- How the spiritual side of India can positively change you forever.

This book goes beyond the usual descriptions of the typical tourist attractions and opens up the spiritual venue waiting to be revealed for a far deeper experience on every level.

Published by iUniverse.com, 592 pages, $33.95, ISBN: 978-0-595-50291-2.

Crimes Against India:
And the Need to Protect its Ancient Vedic Traditions

1000 Years of Attacks Against Hinduism and What to Do about It

India has one of the oldest and most dynamic cultures of the world. Yet, many people do not know of the many attacks, wars, atrocities and sacrifices that Indian people have had to undergo to protect and preserve their country and spiritual tradition over the centuries. Many people also do not know of the many ways in which this profound heritage is being attacked and threatened today, and what we can do about it.
Therefore, some of the topics included are:

- How there is a war against Hinduism and its yoga culture.
- The weaknesses of India that allowed invaders to conquer her.
- Lessons from India's real history that should not be forgotten.
- The atrocities committed by the Muslim invaders, and how they tried to destroy Vedic culture and its many temples, and slaughtered thousands of Indian Hindus.
- How the British viciously exploited India and its people for its resources.
- How the cruelest of all Christian Inquisitions in Goa tortured and killed thousands of Hindus.
- Action plans for preserving and strengthening Vedic India.
- How all Hindus must stand up and be strong for Sanatana-dharma, and promote the cooperation and unity for a Global Vedic Community.

Few people seem to understand the many trials and difficulties that India has faced, or the present problems India is still forced to deal with in preserving the culture of the majority Hindus who live in the country. This is described in the real history of the country, which a decreasing number of people seem to recall.

Therefore, this book is to honor the efforts that have been shown by those in the past who fought and worked to protect India and its culture, and to help preserve India as the homeland of a living and dynamic Vedic tradition of Sanatana-dharma (the eternal path of duty and wisdom).

Available from iUniverse.com. 370 pages, $24.95, ISBN: 978-1-4401-1158-7.

Yoga and Meditation Their Real Purpose and How to Get Started

Yoga is a nonsectarian spiritual science that has been practiced and developed over thousands of years. The benefits of yoga are numerous. On the mental level it strengthens concentration, determination, and builds a stronger character that can more easily sustain various tensions in our lives for peace of mind. The assortment of *asanas* or postures also provide stronger health and keeps various diseases in check. They improve physical strength, endurance and flexibility. These are some of the goals of yoga.

Its ultimate purpose is to raise our consciousness to directly perceive the spiritual dimension. Then we can have our own spiritual experiences. The point is that the more spiritual we become, the more we can perceive that which is spiritual. As we develop and grow in this way through yoga, the questions about spiritual life are no longer a mystery to solve, but become a reality to experience. It becomes a practical part of our lives. This book will show you how to do that. Some of the topics include:

- Benefits of yoga
- The real purpose of yoga
- The types of yoga, such as Hatha yoga, Karma yoga, Raja and Astanga yogas, Kundalini yoga, Bhakti yoga, Mudra yoga, Mantra yoga, and others.
- The Chakras and Koshas
- Asanas and postures, and the Surya Namaskar
- Pranayama and breathing techniques for inner changes
- Deep meditation and how to proceed
- The methods for using mantras
- Attaining spiritual enlightenment, and much more

$17.95, 240 pages, 32 illustration, ISBN: 1451553269

The Soul
Understanding Our Real Identity
The Key to Spiritual Awakening

This book provides a summarization of the most essential spiritual knowledge that will give you the key to spiritual awakening. The descriptions will give you greater insights and a new look at who and what you really are as a spiritual being.

The idea that we are more than merely these material bodies is pervasive. It is established in every religion and spiritual path in this world. However, many religions only hint at the details of this knowledge, but if we look around we will find that practically the deepest and clearest descriptions of the soul and its characteristics are found in the ancient Vedic texts of India.

Herein you will find some of the most insightful spiritual knowledge and wisdom known to mankind. Some of the topics include:

- How you are more than your body
- The purpose of life
- Spiritual ignorance of the soul is the basis of illusion and suffering
- The path of spiritual realization
- How the soul is eternal
- The unbounded nature of the soul
- What is the Supersoul
- Attaining direct spiritual perception and experience of our real identity

This book will give you a deeper look into the ancient wisdom of India's Vedic, spiritual culture, and the means to recognize your real identity.

$7.95, 130 pages, ISBN: 1453733833

www.Stephen-Knapp.com

Be sure to visit Stephen's web site. It provides lots of information on many spiritual aspects of Vedic and spiritual philosophy, and Indian culture for both beginners and the scholarly. You will find:

- All the descriptions and contents of Stephen's books, how to order them, and keep up with any new books or articles that he has written.
- Reviews and unsolicited letters from readers who have expressed their appreciation for his books, as well as his website.
- Free online booklets are also available for your use or distribution on meditation, why be a Hindu, how to start yoga, meditation, etc.
- Helpful prayers, mantras, gayatris, and devotional songs.
- Over a hundred enlightening articles that can help answer many questions about life, the process of spiritual development, the basics of the Vedic path, or how to broaden our spiritual awareness. Many of these are emailed among friends or posted on other web sites.
- Over 150 color photos taken by Stephen during his travels through India. There are also descriptions and 40 photos of the huge and amazing Kumbha Mela festival.
- Directories of many Krishna and Hindu temples around the world to help you locate one near you, where you can continue your experience along the Eastern path.
- Postings of the recent archeological discoveries that confirm the Vedic version of history.
- Photographic exhibit of the Vedic influence in the Taj Mahal, questioning whether it was built by Shah Jahan or a pre-existing Vedic building.
- A large list of links to additional websites to help you continue your exploration of Eastern philosophy, or provide more information and news about India, Hinduism, ancient Vedic culture, Vaishnavism, Hare Krishna sites, travel, visas, catalogs for books and paraphernalia, holy places, etc.
- A large resource for vegetarian recipes, information on its benefits, how to get started, ethnic stores, or non-meat ingredients and supplies.
- A large "Krishna Darshan Art Gallery" of photos and prints of Krishna and Vedic divinities. You can also find a large collection of previously unpublished photos of His Divine Grace A. C. Bhaktivedanta Swami.

This site is made as a practical resource for your use and is continually being updated and expanded with more articles, resources, and information. Be sure to check it out.

Made in United States
Orlando, FL
02 June 2025

61784025R00420